*The Bloomsbury Handbook of
Rural Education in the United States*

ALSO AVAILABLE FROM BLOOMSBURY

Issues and Challenges of Immigration in Early Childhood in the USA, Wilma Robles-Melendez and Wayne Driscoll

Leadership of Place: Stories from Schools in the US, UK and South Africa, Kathryn Riley

The Bloomsbury Handbook of Culture and Identity from Early Childhood to Early Adulthood: Perceptions and Implications, edited by Ruth Wills, Marian de Souza, Jennifer Mata-McMahon, Mukhlis Abu Bakar, and Cornelia Roux

The Bloomsbury Handbook of Global Education and Learning, edited by Douglas Bourn

The Bloomsbury Handbook of Popular Music Education: Perspectives and Practices, edited by Zack Moir, Bryan Powell, and Gareth Dylan Smith

The Bloomsbury Handbook of Theory in Comparative and International Education, edited by Tavis D. Jules, Robin Shields, and Matthew A.M. Thomas

The Bloomsbury Handbook of Rural Education in the United States

Edited by
Amy Price Azano, Karen Eppley, and
Catharine Biddle

BLOOMSBURY ACADEMIC
LONDON • NEW YORK • OXFORD • NEW DELHI • SYDNEY

BLOOMSBURY ACADEMIC
Bloomsbury Publishing Plc
50 Bedford Square, London, WC1B 3DP, UK
1385 Broadway, New York, NY 10018, USA
29 Earlsfort Terrace, Dublin 2, Ireland

BLOOMSBURY, BLOOMSBURY ACADEMIC and the Diana logo
are trademarks of Bloomsbury Publishing Plc

First published in Great Britain 2022
This paperback edition published in 2023

Copyright © Amy Price Azano, Karen Eppley, Catharine Biddle, and Bloomsbury, 2022
Amy Price Azano, Karen Eppley, Catharine Biddle and Bloomsbury have asserted their right under the
Copyright, Designs and Patents Act, 1988, to be identified as Author of this work.

Cover image © Philip Nealey / Getty Images

All rights reserved. No part of this publication may be reproduced or transmitted in any form or
by any means, electronic or mechanical, including photocopying, recording, or any information
storage or retrieval system, without prior permission in writing from the publishers.

Bloomsbury Publishing Plc does not have any control over, or responsibility for, any third-party
websites referred to or in this book. All internet addresses given in this book were correct at the time
of going to press. The author and publisher regret any inconvenience caused if addresses have changed
or sites have ceased to exist, but can accept no responsibility for any such changes.

A catalogue record for this book is available from the British Library.

Library of Congress Cataloging-in-Publication Data
Names: Azano, Amy Price, editor. | Eppley, Karen, editor. | Biddle, Catharine, editor.
Title: The Bloomsbury handbook of rural education in the USA / edited by
Amy Price Azano, Karen Eppley and Catharine Biddle.
Other titles: Handbook of rural education in the USA
Description: London; New York: Bloomsbury Academic, 2021. |
Includes bibliographical references and index. |
Identifiers: LCCN 2021011475 (print) | LCCN 2021011476 (ebook) |
ISBN 9781350172005 (hardback) | ISBN 9781350172012 (ebook) |
ISBN 9781350172029 (epub)
Subjects: LCSH: Education, Rural–United States. | Rural schools–United States.
Classification: LCC LC5146.5.B56 2021 (print) |
LCC LC5146.5 (ebook) | DDC 370.91734–dc23
LC record available at https://lccn.loc.gov/2021011475
LC ebook record available at https://lccn.loc.gov/2021011476

ISBN: HB: 978-1-3501-7200-5
PB: 978-1-3502-4429-0
ePDF: 978-1-3501-7201-2
eBook: 978-1-3501-7202-9

Series: Bloomsbury Handbooks

Typeset by Deanta Global Publishing Services, Chennai, India

To find out more about our authors and books visit
www.bloomsbury.com and sign up for our newsletters.

Contents

List of Illustrations		vii
Foreword *Craig Howley and Aimee Howley*		viii
Notes on Contributors		xiv

Introduction
Unsettling Rurality: Mapping a Third Space
    Amy Price Azano, Karen Eppley, and Catharine Biddle   1

Part I Introduction: Foundations in Rural Education   5

1 Developing, Utilizing, and Critiquing Definitions of "Rural" in Rural Education
   Research *Jesse Moon Longhurst*   9

2 History and the Shape of Rural Educational Policy in the United States *Paul Theobald*   19

3 Toward a Rural Critical Policy Analysis *Devon Brenner*   30

4 Corporate Influences on Rural Schools *Jason A. Cervone*   43

5 Shifting Population Dynamics and Implications for Rural Schools *Kai A. Schafft*
   and Annie Maselli   52

6 Rural Poverty and Rural Schools *Mara Casey Tieken*   62

7 The Why and How of Enhancing Data Use in Rural Education Research
   and Practice *John W. Sipple, Peter Cody Fiduccia, and Kristie LeBeau*   72

International Response
Responding Rurally: Perspectives and Insights from One Rural Place
   to Another *Simone White*   84

Part II Introduction: Rural Schools and Communities   91

8 Educational Governance and Contemporary Policy in Rural America
   Daniella Hall Sutherland and Jennifer Seelig   95

9 Consolidation, Closure, and Charter Schools *Karen Eppley*   108

10 Rural School Leadership *Catharine Biddle*   117

11 Rural Teacher Labor Issues *Erin McHenry-Sorber*   127

12 Rural School–Community Partnerships: Creating Community-Aware Educational
   Practices *Hope G. Casto and John W. Sipple*   137

13 Collective Impact in Rural Places *Sarah J. Zuckerman*   145

Contents

14 Postsecondary Transitions and Attainment *Sarah Schmitt-Wilson and Soo-yong Byun* 157

International Response
Rural Schools and Communities: We Can Bridge, but Can We Bond? *Michael Corbett* 165

Part III Introduction: Curriculum Studies in Rural Schools 173

15 Early Childhood Education in Rural Communities *Lisa L. Knoche,*
    Hannah M. Kerby, and Susan M. Sheridan 177

16 Rural Literacies and Rural Identities *Kim Donehower* 187

17 Trauma-Informed Approaches in Rural Education *Catharine Biddle and*
    Lyn Mikel Brown 196

18 Rural School-Based Mental Health: Models of Prevention, Intervention, and
    Preparation *Jayne Downey, Anna Elliott, Rebecca Koltz, and Kirsten Murray* 204

19 Student Achievement in Rural America *Douglas J. Gagnon* 215

International Response
What Counts as Curriculum? *Philip Roberts* 225

Part IV Introduction: Identity and Equity in Rural Schools 231

20 Critical Indigenous Perspectives in Rural Education *Alex RedCorn,*
    Jerry D. Johnson, Larry Bergeron, and Jann Hayman 235

21 English Learners in Rural Schools *Maria Coady* 247

22 African American Education in the Rural South: Then and Now
    Sheneka Williams, Sarah McCollum, and Kimberly Clarida 256

23 Latinx Students in Rural Schools *Darris R. Means and Vanessa A. Sansone* 268

24 Whiteness in Rural Education *Kathleen E. Gillon* 276

25 Rural Tiered Systems of Adaptive Supports: A Person-in-Context, Place-Based
    Perspective *Thomas W. Farmer, Ann B. Berry, Jill V. Hamm, and David L. Lee* 286

26 Challenges and Innovative Responses in Rural Gifted Education *Amy Price Azano,*
    Carolyn M. Callahan, and Rachelle Kuehl 294

International Response
A Peripheral Perspective: A View from Rural Europe *Cath Gristy* 304

Notes 309
References 312
Index 384

Illustrations

Figures

12.1	Financial trends in district affected by wind farm development, 1996–2016	142
18.1	Rural Mental Health Preparation Practice Pathway (RMHP3)	213
19.1	NAEP fourth-grade reading scores, overall and by region, 2009–19	218
19.2	NAEP eighth-grade math scores, overall and by region, 2009–19	219
19.3	Fourth-grade NAEP reading scores by region, for rural and nonrural students, 2019	220
19.4	Eighth-grade NAEP mathematics scores by region, for rural and nonrural students, 2019	220
19.5	Fourth-grade NAEP reading scores by income, for rural and nonrural students, 2019	221
19.6	Eighth-grade NAEP mathematics scores by income, for rural and nonrural students, 2019	221
19.7	Fourth-grade NAEP reading scores by race/ethnicity, for rural and nonrural students, 2019	222
19.8	Eighth-grade NAEP mathematics scores by race/ethnicity, for rural and nonrural students, 2019	222

Tables

1.1	National Center for Education Statistics Locale Classifications	11
1.2	Guiding Questions for Researchers and Consumers of Rural Research	16
1.3	Guiding Questions for Researchers	17
3.1	National Center for Education Statistics Locale Classifications	36
5.1	School-Aged Child Population Living in Rural School Districts, 2000 and 2018	54
5.2	Change in Rural Minoritized Student Population, 2005–15/16	56
5.3	School-Aged Child Population Self-Identifying as "White Alone," Not Including Hispanic	57
8.1	Overview of LEA Organization Structures in the United States	97
10.1	Overview of Themes from Studies on Lived Experiences of Rural Principals	121
20.1	Frequencies for Indigenous Education Articles in Rural Journals, 1980–2020	237
25.1	A Rural Tiered Systems of Adaptive Support (TSAS) Model	289

Foreword

When we first encountered what passed for rural education research, we didn't like it. The key finding of the time? Rural schools should be more like what the profession had defined as best everywhere else. This position still dominates policy, curriculum, and pedagogy; that is, practice. Everyone should get America's best, everywhere. The position still holds considerable, if weaker, sway over education research, too.

So, this handbook astonishes us. Few education leaders harbor any interest at all in the work that concerns it most: interrogating "the best" as it deforms rural places via the schooling conducted there. At least, that's our view of the common work, including our own. Nearing the end of our own research journey, we're pleased that our work facilitates and even encourages the work of others—less for vaunted findings and more for the ideas it engages. And we hope this book and our own work helps still others later on. We encourage readers and researchers to look at the big picture, however, and not to get lost in the weeds.

We've now lived long lives in the countryside; our kids attended rural schools. But they were bad students, refusing to take the message to get out and stay out. They're all still here in the countryside with us. We'll find out about the grandkids soon enough. At any rate, by the time we arrived in the countryside in 1973, the early twentieth century struggle to keep kids *down* on the farm had been lost. The growing metropolitan massing enabled a cultural narrative in which the countryside—rural America—effectively figured as irrelevant. If you live in the countryside and have "ambition," you'd better get out. Want a chance at wealth? Come to the city.

Schooling, absolutely futile to resist, reflects that narrative. Public schooling, private schooling, corporately managed schooling may nuance the single cultural narrative, but none of the variants changes plot, characters, or meanings. Education is different from schooling because it's not an institution like schooling (even though the profession and the public confound the two). Education is an idea and a practice that exists largely apart from (mere) schooling. RedCorn and colleagues (Chapter 20) say so, and—much to the educative point—they thankfully also reiterate that place is inherently rural (and notably Indigenous). It's inherently rural because place is centered on the land, and the countryside is where you can usually *see* the land and *live* on it and with it. The "inherent" quality of land is overturned by the big business of buying and selling it (Edelman, 2019).

Seeing the land and living on it well depend on education that takes place outside the schoolhouse because a metropolitian sort of schooling doesn't care about such things. The issues of importance to the handbook explore the actual and possible connections between rural place (and land and life) and education (and culture and identity). And it explores the connection between all of those things and the organization of schooling under neoliberal capitalist dominion. The issues of importance to the *Handbook*, and to us personally, moreover, are going to persist. It is up to us to supply some of what gets voiced and to enrich the narrative as best we might.

Foreword

The issues of particular concern right now could all benefit from the empirical scrutiny of the scholars in this handbook, their colleagues, their students, and generations beyond. Four issues that we hope will draw sharp attention are: (1) rural places as global sacrifice zones, (2) the land supporting a good way to live, (3) the *grounded* imaginary, and (4) the rural legacy of genocide and enslavement.

What are Schools for When Rural Places are Sacrifice Zones?

Much of our focus over the years has been on how economic dynamics drive schooling arrangements, educational possibilities, and life chances. The term "sacrifice zone" seems to capture the story of the land in most rural places, illustrated by closed storefronts and other signs of economic loss (Edelman, 2019), or desecrations such as strip mines and hazardous waste dumps (Hedges & Sacco, 2012; Sassen, 2014). We argue, as does Cervone (2017), that closed and consolidated schools also serve as hallmarks of sacrifice. Understanding what's being stolen, degraded, and overrun, as experienced by families and communities, is essential for understanding rural places.

Choosing Appalachia as our place for "going back" to the land made it easy for us to see rural place as a sacrifice zone. West Virginia was a mining colony when we arrived almost half a century ago. It was harder to know at that time that the agricultural heartland was also being colonized: subjected to enclosure, depopulation, environmental degradation, and economic exploitation. And the intersection of race and economics seemed, in that era, like an emerging insight about the *urban* context. There's a lot we didn't see.

The elaboration of critical theories refined our analysis and offered depth to our understanding of the political economy of rural places. Our work, in league with the work of *Handbook* authors, draws on that critical legacy. At the same time, the authors in this volume provide novel interpretations. Theobald (Chapter 2) points out how the intellectual superstructure—Social Darwinist ideas in particular—justified the degradation of rural places and ways of life. Cervone (Chapter 4) offers the poignant contrast between "abstract" spaces and "lived spaces," an idea that simultaneously evokes Marx's view of alienation and the phenomenologists' attentiveness to lived experience. Schafft and Maselli (Chapter 5) provide data to illustrate the complex patterns of boom and bust, depopulation and occasional repopulation, aging, and increasing diversity—all in some ways woven into a broader global fabric of plunder and cynicism. Rural meanings get lost.

Just when we are searching for the right word, Tieken (Chapter 6) brings the term, "locally unwanted land uses" to bear on the issue. The mechanics of LULU (what an acronym!) activate the dynamics of domination—starve the population so they will eat anything. But before we are lulled into mere and straightforward indignation, RedCorn and associates (Chapter 20) and Gillon (Chapter 24) remind us that current thievery is built upon a continental lineage of historical land thievery. It feels at once Karmic and hopeless. With Corbett (Section Two, international response), we worry that what lurks in "the precarious and unpredictable politics of the present moment" is not going to be good for rural places or people, neither for the communities that try to sustain tradition *nor* for those that embrace new diversity (see RedCorn et al., Chapter 20; Coady, Chapter 21). Sure, we get it: Where domination is not complete, there's a kind of Foucauldian hope.

Foreword

The Land Supports Good Ways to Live

There isn't one best way out here, nor any other one way. After all, the countryside is a vast realm of dispossession and repossession, sordid perpetual exchange of land ownership: grabbing, exploiting, despoiling, and abandoning, over and over (often with vast sums of money). The land itself persists heedless, at least until it seems to vanish under innumerable cities and much of their obliterated environs: sites in which, as we are encouraged to believe, all humanity should and *will* live in the future.

And yet, out here in rural places there are some alternatives to the ugly American template of greed and willful ignorance. Yes, the metropole seemingly believes, as Kim Donehower suggests of these perceptions, "that rural people are inferior most particularly in their *literacy*" (Chapter 16). Indeed, this is, as she insists, the long-held supposition of national schooling itself. In fact, this ignorance of local rural meanings is observable wherever a national cultural center exerts dominion (see, e.g., Weber, 1976, for a French example; and Williams, 2014, for an international one). The ignorance proceeds naturally from alienation from the land, via its usurpation by the center: *peasants into Frenchmen.*

Absent the twittering crowds, the money, the cultural and economic power, what good can remain to life in the countryside? The pandemic of 2020 brought some transient insights to sufficiently endowed city residents (Barry, 2020, September 26): rural places offer less risk with their low population density—naturally occurring "social distance." The affluent pandemic refugee is not typically in it for work on and with the land, the development of community, or the cultivation of a true education.

The capacity to do such generative work comes from doing it with those who do it. Doing that work in schools that are overwhelmed and hobbled by neoliberal narratives and agendas is unlikely. As noted in his autobiography about the worth of a rural *education,* Rebanks (2015) notes:

> History lessons at school didn't really go like I hoped they would. We never did any kind of history of us or our landscape. I think the teachers might have been surprised at the idea that people like us had a history of any interest… When I remember the 1980s, I think of how shit that school was. (p. 93)

Rebanks's plain truth ought to provoke interest from rural education researchers. It offers a "funds of knowledge" possibility, certainly, but the educational work is also (and importantly) about literacy. For instance, Rebanks got to speak for his bit of countryside because, through a series of ordinary misfortunes, he started to read widely on his own. That he then went to Oxford is not the mark of his success, though. Continuing to read and write and farm—to make a meaningful rural life—that's what is noteworthy.

Even if schooling as an institution fails to sponsor that sort of literacy, some rural schools and some teachers might. So might other rural organizations. And if one believes Rebanks, the education he chanced upon takes just a few adults with relevant books and the encouragement of example.

The Grounded Rural Imaginary

The grounded imaginary already exists robustly in essays, novels, histories and sociological studies that anybody can read; and it also exists in films and music about rural places. This large body of work seldom makes it into school curricula because those courses of study are busy with the metropolitan narrative and the neoliberal agenda. Rebanks had to discover the rural imaginary without the help of anyone in his rural school. He discovered more of it when he—like Raymond Williams before him (see the introduction to *The Country and the City*, 1973)—got to the seat of English elitism. But access to the rural imaginary doesn't actually require reading and writing if one is part of a family that engages the relevant practices organically: it's just what the family is doing. Exploring the imaginary through reading and writing is something else. For that literate piece, one would think schools might help. There has to be an explanation for why, in general, they don't.

The fact of the land and everything it harbored—from firewood to food to raising babies—is what drew us. When we arrived, we found neighbors engaged in *living to work* in just that way (firewood, food, babies). They had seemingly always done so and were thrilled to have industrious young people return to the holler to take up the same work. All of this was tremendously educative for us, though not for them. We had a lot to learn.

Organic practice isn't enough, however. The hope of those controlling the countryside from the metropolitan centers of finance and politics is that people in the countryside won't *ever* discover reading and writing with sufficient frequency for it to matter *to them*. But literacy is obviously more than ever critical to the survival of the land itself. Travelling through west Texas in the environs of Eunice and in eastern New Mexico might be the best proof. Google Earth will show the big picture, but the on-the-ground awfulness is memorable: Jack-pumps everywhere; soil deformed as if by the shelling around Verdun.

Somehow the two sorts of knowledge (literacy and organic practice) ought to combine for the benefit of the young, certainly, but more broadly for the benefit of the countryside: both the land itself and the people. And, logically, schools would be the places to sponsor the combination. Rural education research might scaffold the grounding—articulating the understandings with empirical work and taking part in the invention of educative practices. The only reasons against it are lack of supporters, money, and power—*exactly* the right reasons for moving the work forward.

Genocide and Enslavement: A Rural Legacy

Doing good work in rural places (including schools), to which many authors in this handbook are clearly committed, has a long legacy of evil to push against. RedCorn and colleagues (Chapter 20) call it "settler-colonialism"; Williams and colleagues refer to "discriminatory policies, structural racism, and a history of government-sanctioned segregation" (Chapter 22); Means and Sansone (Chapter 23) use "marginalization." These authors name and describe historical and ongoing horrors, expressing deep concern about what these evil legacies bode for a decent education across the countryside.

At this late date we might argue, and many of the chapter authors might agree, that they actually bode ill for the prospect of decent education *anywhere* (or to be more precise, anywhere neoliberal capitalism tramples). The cultural oobleck of neoliberalism repels critique, resistance, and the progressive impulse—however compelling the counternarratives of critical theory, critical race theory, critical whiteness pedagogy, or, for that matter, place-based pedagogy might sound to us.

By framing America as a paragon of "goodness" and capitalism as the embodiment of freedom, the neoliberal version of exceptionalism supports the fiction that genocide and enslavement

Foreword

are relics from a past we've all worked through: The White ancestors didn't know any better, and current generations need not assume responsibility for (or, for that matter, even spend time pondering) the legacy of systematic oppression (Jansson, 2018).

Of course, exceptionalism does not completely dominate the narrative. Graduate students encounter the critical theories, read the first-person accounts, and glimpse the horrors. Some high school history lessons and chapters in some textbooks now acknowledge the historical truths. As of 2018, it's permissible even in Texas to teach students that slavery was a major cause of the Civil War (Fortin, 2018).

Overall, however, American exceptionalism is sufficiently widespread to act as an effective cover for racism and other forms of capitalist oppression and exploitation. In a move that Jansson (2018, p. 88) calls "southering," neoliberals regionalize racism as a way to distance themselves from it. Replacing "rural" for "Southern" in the quote below fits with what we've been hearing from the legacy news media (and even some of our researcher colleagues) since at least 2016.

> I call this discourse that creates a moral landscape of uneven racism "southering"—racism is understood as being an inherent part of the social fabric in "the South" in a way that does not apply for the rest of the country. Southering makes an important contribution to the reproduction of U.S. exceptionalism, in part through the way it understands the region as a stage for the (internal) practice of the state's exceptionalism—the cure for the region's problems is to make "the South" more like "America." (Jansson, 2018, p. 88)

Missteps Too Often Taken

Becoming both theoretical and morose, we have stopped waiting for the contradictions of (globalized, neoliberal) capitalism to lead it elsewhere. Its DNA is built of sturdy stuff. We don't imagine, however, that the foundation of our current predicament is human nature. More likely, the foundation is the greed and selfishness of the elite and the schooling for silence and obedience that so constrains our care and attention.

Watching rural life and rural people for all of our adult lives, we believe that kindness, generosity, honesty, curiosity, and reason will persist. These virtues also have a long (if checkered) history in the realm of scholarship, including especially scholarship about education and, particularly, about rural education. It is a field that often debates the common good and tries to address it.

Authors of the chapters in this handbook look to rural places, in fact, for tufts of optimism and we enumerate them in order of appearance: (1) ensuring the specificity and utility of careful research; (2) returning to a communitarian vision; (3) raising critical questions about various policies that may cause harm in rural places; (4) thinking critically to challenge injustices; (5) enlisting rural schools as critical agents of community health and well-being; (6) mobilizing rural schools to support economic and political development and reduce racial inequity; (7) using rich data to study and lead rural schools and to enhance community vitality; (8) recognizing the significance of place to policy and governance; (9) investing in traditional community schools in rural communities; (10) researching rural school leadership from an assets-based perspective; (11) studying rural teacher labor; (12) fostering school-community partnerships grounded in a community-aware perspective; (13) addressing persistent and complex community problems through a process to maximize collective impact; (14) learning more about how rural students can benefit from malleable college experiences and pathways; (15) building partnerships among parents and rural educators who work with young children; (16) ensuring that rural literacy experiences help students appreciate beauty; (17) engaging rural schools and communities in designing trauma-informed systems that are responsive to rural needs; (18) developing context-specific school mental health programs; (19) monitoring academic opportunity and outcome gaps across rural places and between rural and non-rural places; (20) working in alliance with Native nations to "to decenter colonial and assimilationist approaches to education" (Chapter 20); (21) supporting rural schools' efforts to provide dual-language programs; (22) staffing rural schools with high-quality teachers; (23) establishing and sustaining culturally relevant, anti-oppressive climates in rural schools; (24) disrupting Whiteness in rural schools and communities; (25) infusing adaptive formats and supports into rural schools to increase their responsiveness to the "lives, values, and proclivities" (Chapter 25) of all students; and (26) cultivating the gifts and talents of rural students on behalf of community development.

With this much disparate hope, one might long for a unified field. But that misstep is too often taken. In fact, good intellectual work must cross all sorts of intellectual boundaries. In this light, *individual researchers* (and not just discipline-hobbled teams) need perspectives and tools from a variety of disciplines. Multi-disciplinary teams lack intellectual depth otherwise.

So instead of a unified field, we think solidarity around a set of commitments offers firmer purchase for rural education research. After all, education research is an applied field. We're in this work to accomplish something, even if it's just helping others think better or differently.

In what would such solidarity consist? It would consist of commitments rather clearly on view in the foregoing list: (1) rural schools should foster equity instead of greed because the progress of democracy is the progress of equity; (2) rural schools must foster facility with numbers and words, including second languages, and these practices should engage students and educators in local realities; (3) schooling should serve the common good, and rural schools should struggle to enact such good much more visibly for local purposes; (4) education is childrearing into adulthood, and thus rural adulthoods should be clearly in view in rural schools and postsecondary institutions; and (5) education is authentic but schooling is too often phony: rural schools should sponsor more projects, expeditions, inquiries, productions, and performances with students and communities.

Such commitments are durable, but they need to be firmly held and upheld by a widening group of educators and community members. Solidarity is required because the worldwide grip of capital on schooling steadily subverts the particulars that educators confront.

Working with a rural community's children is wonderful work. Studying that work is an extraordinary privilege. The center of both is the struggle between education and schooling, particularly between the kind of *education* that cares for the countryside and the kind of *schooling* that abets theft (of land, of life, of community, of culture, of education, of identity). This handbook may help more education researchers affirm important rural commitments and join the struggle into the much-to-be-contested future.

Craig Howley and Aimee Howley

Contributors

Amy Price Azano is Associate Professor of Rural Education and Adolescent Literacy at Virginia Tech, USA. Her research focuses on educational equity in rural schools and communities. She is the coprincipal investigator of Promoting PLACE in Rural Schools, principal investigator of the Appalachian Rural Talent Initiative, and director of the Summer Enrichment Experience at Virginia Tech. Azano is coeditor of *The Rural Educator,* journal of the National Rural Education Association, and chair of AERA's Rural Education Special Interest Group. She is also a coauthor of *Teaching in Rural Places: Thriving in Classrooms, Schools, and Communities.*

Larry Bergeron is the Lydia E. Skeen Graduate Research Assistant and a doctoral student in Counseling and Student Development at Kansas State University, USA. His research focuses broadly on educational leadership and supporting underrepresented students in transition to postsecondary institutions.

Ann B. Berry is Associate Professor at Plymouth State University, USA, and program coordinator for the graduate programs in special education. She has a strong passion for finding innovative ways to support the professional development needs of rural teachers who serve students with disabilities. Through funding from the Center for Rural Partnerships, Berry has been researching the needs of rural teachers in northern New England so that the training and support they need to feel effective in their positions can be part of the university's outreach efforts. Berry is currently chair of the board for the American Council on Rural Special Education (ACRES) and is a member of the editorial board for *Rural Special Education Quarterly.*

Catharine Biddle is Associate Professor of Educational Leadership at the University of Maine, USA. Her research focuses on ways in which rural schools and communities respond to social and economic change in the twenty-first century. She is particularly interested in how schools can more effectively leverage partnerships with external organizations or groups to address issues of social inequality and how nontraditional leaders—such as youth, parents, and other community members—may lead or serve as partners in these efforts. Her work has been published in the *Review of Research in Education*, the *American Journal of Education*, and the *Journal of Research in Rural Education* and has been recognized by the National Rural Education Association. She is also a coauthor of the forthcoming volume, *Voice, Vitality and Healing: Centering Students in Trauma-Responsive Education.*

Devon Brenner is Professor of Teacher Education and serves in the Office of Research and Economic Development at Mississippi State University, USA. Her scholarship focuses on rural education policy and practice and the preparation of teachers for rural schools. Brenner is coeditor of *The Rural Educator,* journal of the National Rural Education Association, and is co-coordinator of the Mississippi Education Policy Fellowship, a state chapter of a national program hosted by the Institute for Education Leadership that prepares educators to engage in policy and advocacy to advance equity in education.

Lyn Mikel Brown is Professor of Education at Colby College, USA. Her research and praxis focus on positive youth development; student voice and activism; and qualitative, voice-centered research methods. She is cofounder of three girl-fueled social change organizations and six books, including her most recent *Powered by Girl: A Field Guide for Supporting Youth Activists*. She is currently working with the Rural Vitality Lab to explore healthy developmental ecologies for rural children and youth.

Soo-yong Byun is Associate Professor of Education and Demography at the Pennsylvania State University, USA. His research investigates variations in mechanisms and processes of social stratification across different countries and geographic contexts using large-scale national and international data. His work also focuses on the rigorous assessment and evaluation of educational policies and school interventions especially relating to unique populations and contexts. His articles have been published in leading peer-reviewed journals, including *American Educational Research Journal*, *American Journal of Education*, *Comparative Education Review*, and *Sociology of Education*.

Carolyn M. Callahan is Commonwealth Professor of Education Emerita at the University of Virginia, USA, and has been principal investigator on projects of the National Center for Research on Gifted Education and on five Javits grants, including Promoting PLACE, focusing on the identification and provision of services to rural gifted students. She has been recognized as Outstanding Professor of the Commonwealth of Virginia and Distinguished Scholar of the National Association for Gifted Children and has served as president of the National Association for Gifted Children and the Association for the Gifted and as editor of *Gifted Child Quarterly*.

Hope Casto is Associate Professor of Education Studies at Skidmore College, USA. Her research interests include school-community connections in rural places and the impact of education policy in different types of communities.

Kimberly Clarida is a first-year doctoral student in the Educational Leadership and Policy department at the University of Texas at Austin, USA. Her research interests revolve around educational equity and policy, school partnerships, and the historical and sociocultural contexts of education as it relates to the achievement of Black and brown students.

Jason A. Cervone is the author of *Corporatizing Rural Education: Neoliberal Globalization and Reaction in the United States*. He received his PhD in Educational Leadership and Policy Studies from University of Massachusetts at Dartmouth, USA.

Maria Coady is Professor of English to Speakers of Other Languages (ESOL) and Bilingual Education at the University of Florida, USA. She works with rural bilingual students and families and prepares teachers and leaders for rural English learner education. Dr. Coady is Director and

PI of Project STELLAR, a federally funded grant that provides rural teacher-leader professional development. She is author of several books, including *Connecting School and the Multilingual Home: Theory and Practice for Rural Educators*, *The Coral Way Bilingual Program*, *Early Language Learning Policies in the 21st Century* (Ed. with S. Zein), and *Teaching, Learning, and Leading for Rural Multilingual Students* (Ed. with P. Golombek and N. Marichal, forthcoming).

Michael Corbett has studied rural youth educational decision-making, mobilities, and education in rural contexts. While his work is principally focused in Canada, he has also worked internationally.

Kim Donehower is Professor of English at the University of North Dakota, USA, where she researches the relationship between literacy and the sustainability of rural communities. With Charlotte Hogg and Eileen E. Schell, she coauthored *Rural Literacies* and coedited *Reclaiming the Rural: Essays on Literacy, Rhetoric, and Pedagogy*. Her essays have appeared in *Literacy, Economy, and Power*, *Rethinking Rural Literacies*, and *The Routledge International Handbook of Rural Studies*. Her latest edited collection, *Rereading Appalachia: Literacy, Place, and Cultural Resistance*, was coedited with Sara Webb-Sunderhaus.

Jayne Downey is Professor and Director of the Center for Research on Rural Education at Montana State University, USA. Her academic background is in the domain of Counseling Psychology and Educational Psychology with a specific focus on contextual factors that influence the teaching and learning process. She has worked in the field of educator preparation for twenty years and her research agenda is focused on strengthening the preparation of prospective teachers and counselors and improving outcomes of P-20 education across rural contexts.

Anna Elliott is a counselor educator and Associate Professor in the Department of Health and Human Development at Montana State University, USA. Her academic areas of interest include equity, access, and social justice in mental health and counselor identity development. She is a licensed counselor in Montana, USA, with specializations in trauma recovery, adolescents, and cultural identity issues.

Karen Eppley is a former fifth-grade teacher and Associate Professor of Curriculum and Instruction at Pennsylvania State University, USA, where she teaches in the reading specialist certification program. Her research interest is at the intersection of literacy education and rural education. She writes about rurality as a contested social space within economic globalization, rural literacies, textual representations of rurality, rural education as a matter of social justice, and critical policy analysis. She edits the *Journal of Research in Rural Education.*

Tom Farmer is Professor in the Applied Developmental Psychology Program and chair of the Department of Health and Human Development in the School of Education at the University of Pittsburgh, USA. Much of his research has been conducted in rural schools in the South, the Deep South, and the Appalachian regions of the United States. His research focuses on the social inclusion of students with disabilities, bullying, classroom management, and professional development supports for teachers with diverse learners.

Contributors

Peter C. Fiduccia is a PhD candidate in the Department of Development Sociology with a Minor in Demography at Cornell University, USA. His research areas include spatial demography, human-computer interaction, and organizational institutions. He has published in areas of education policy and geographic analysis and served as editorial assistant for *Community Development.*

Douglas J. Gagnon is Senior Education Researcher at SRI International, USA, where he leads and supports technical assistance and applied research projects with a rural focus. Previously Gagnon was with Marzano Research, where he led the Rural Education Research Alliance, a research partnership across seven states in the central region of the country. He has considerable experience supporting evaluations of programs aimed at improving the recruitment and retention of educators in rural schools and also spent many years as a researcher at the Carsey School of Public Policy at the University of New Hampshire, USA, where his work largely focused on education policy related to equity, rural schooling, teacher quality, and trends in student discipline.

Kathleen E. Gillon is an assistant professor of Higher Education at the University of Maine, USA. Her research is broadly focused on understanding and disrupting systems of oppression within the postsecondary context. She has a specific emphasis on postsecondary educational opportunities and college-going practices within the rural context.

Cath Gristy is Lecturer in the Plymouth Institute of Education at the University of Plymouth, UK. Her research interests and collaborations with schools and teachers include engagement with social justice, inclusion, and exclusion. A common thread that runs through her research is a sense of rural place and space. Gristy's research with young people in isolated, rural communities in the UK has led to a sustained engagement with research methods and ethics in these places "on the edge." She is an active member of a pan-European network of researchers working and writing about education and schooling in rural places; she is an editor of *Educational Research and Schooling in Rural Europe* (2020).

Jill V. Hamm is William C. Friday Distinguished Professor of Education and Associate Dean of Research and Faculty Development in the School of Education at the University of North Carolina at Chapel Hill, USA. Her research focuses on early adolescents' social, behavioral, and academic adjustment and the role of peer relations in successful school adaptation. She has applied her research findings to the development and testing of professional development programs designed to help middle school teachers create supportive learning environments for their students. She has conducted multiple large-scale randomized trials in rural schools.

Jann Hayman is the director of the Osage Nation Department of Natural Resources and is a doctoral candidate in Educational Leadership at Kansas State University, USA. Her research interests include the intersection of extension programs, agriculture, and land stewardship viewed through critical Indigenous perspectives.

Aimee Howley is President of WordFarmers Associates and has a broad background in educational research, evaluation, and policy studies, authoring or coauthoring more than sixty refereed journal articles as well as books and book chapters. Her research has explored the intersection between

Contributors

social context and education to study a wide range of questions about rural education, educational reform, school leadership, and education for diverse learners. She is Professor Emerita at Ohio University, USA, where she served as a faculty member in the Educational Studies Department and Senior Associate Dean of the Patton College of Education.

Craig Howley has published rurally focused empirical studies about school size, school consolidation, place-based education, mathematics education, talent development (gifted education), teaching and teachers, technology, principal preparation, and education policy. His work also includes many articles, policy briefs, and books for teachers, principals, and community members. He retired from Ohio University, USA, in 2013 and participates in a busy consulting business with Aimee Howley.

Jerry Johnson is Lydia E. Skeen Endowed Professor in Education at Kansas State University, USA, where he serves as chair of the Department of Educational Leadership. A former high school English teacher and principal, Johnson also served as policy research director for the Rural School and Community Trust and was the 2017 recipient of the Stanley A. Brzezinski Memorial Rural Education Research Award from the National Rural Education Association.

Hannah Kerby is a doctoral student in the School Psychology at the University of Nebraska-Lincoln, USA. Her research interests include early childhood development and education, the influence of place and context on early development, and the protective effects of relationships within school settings.

Lisa L. Knoche is a Research Associate Professor and Director of the Nebraska Academy for Early Childhood Research in the Nebraska Center for Research on Children, Youth, Families and Schools at the University of Nebraska-Lincoln, USA. Knoche is an applied developmental psychologist with expertise in the design, development, and evaluation of early childhood intervention and prevention programs to promote healthy development in young children and support family engagement in early learning.

Rebecca Koltz is Professor in the Department of Health and Human Development at Montana State University, USA, and serves as the department head. Her academic background is in the domain of Counselor Education & Supervision. She is a licensed counselor in the state of Montana and has worked in this field for over fifteen years. Her research agenda includes topics related to wellness, prevention, and counselor development with specific focus on training counselors to work in rural settings.

Rachelle Kuehl is Postdoctoral Associate in the School of Education at Virginia Tech, USA, and project manager of the Appalachian Rural Talent Initiative. She is a reading specialist and former elementary teacher whose articles about writing instruction, children's literature, and teacher education have been published in journals such as the *English Journal,* the *Journal of Children's Literature, Theory & Practice in Rural Education, Collection Management,* and the *Teacher Educators' Journal.*

Kristie LeBeau is a PhD student in Development Sociology with a Minor in Education at Cornell University, USA. Her research focuses on the multiple, complex roles schools play in rural communities.

David Lee is Professor in the Special Education Program at Pennsylvania State University, USA. The main focus of his research is to develop, evaluate, and disseminate programs to support students with or at risk for emotional/behavior disorders across academic, behavioral, and social domains. He draws upon a behavior analytic framework to create positive, function-based interventions for students, primarily in middle/high school settings.

Jesse Moon Longhurst is Assistant Professor of Education in the School of Education at Southern Oregon University in Ashland, Oregon, USA. Her scholarship focuses on rural, remote, and island schools; rural teacher preparation and retention; rural place attachment; and the intersections of rural cultures and rural schooling. She is an advocate for faculty and students at small, regional, teaching institutions to engage in rural education research.

Annie Maselli is a doctoral candidate in the Department of Education Policy Studies at Pennsylvania State University, USA. Her research interests include the relationship between place, equity, and education and issues of educational access and spatial justice. Serving as a research affiliate with the Center on Rural Education and Communities, she is particularly interested in how rural schools can address issues of social inequity and community development.

Sarah McCollum is a PhD student in the Education Policy and Administration program at the University of Georgia, USA. Prior to graduate school, Sarah was an English Language Arts teacher in the Mississippi Delta and Nashville, Tennessee, before becoming a middle school dean of students. Her research interests include educational equity and issues of civil rights as it pertains to segregation and exclusionary discipline policies.

Erin McHenry-Sorber is Associate Professor of Higher Education at West Virginia University, USA, and coeditor of *The Rural Educator.* Her research focuses on rural schools and communities.

Darris R. Means is Associate Professor of Higher Education at the University of Pittsburgh, USA. Using critical and qualitative methodologies, his research examines college access and college success for rural Black and Latinx students. Means' research appears in *The Review of Higher Education* and the *Journal of Research in Rural Education*. He also authored a research-to-practice brief on enhancing college enrollment for rural students for the National Association for College Admission Counseling. His recent research on rural Black students and postsecondary education access has been supported by funding from the Spencer Foundation and National Academy of Education and the American College Personnel Association.

Kirsten Murray is Professor and Chair of the Department of Counseling at the University of Montana, USA. Her academic background is also in Counselor Education and Supervision. She is a licensed counselor and her clinical and academic interests align in the areas of couple

Contributors

and family counseling, foundational counseling skills, and fostering access and equity in the counseling profession.

Alex RedCorn is Assistant Professor of Educational Leadership at Kansas State University, USA, where he also serves as the executive director of the Kansas Association for Native American Education and program coordinator for the Qualitative Research Graduate Certificate. His scholarship and service is focused on building capacities for Native nations to take on a more prominent role in the education of their citizens and advocating for a stronger and more well-informed community of practice for Indigenous education across the Osage community, the State of Kansas, and the Southern Plains in the USA.

Philip Roberts is Associate Professor in Curriculum Inquiry and Rural Education in the Faculty of Education at the University of Canberra, Australia. He is the research leader of the Rural Education and Communities Research Group in the Centre for Sustainable Communities at the University of Canberra, Australia.

Vanessa A. Sansone is Assistant Professor of Higher Education in the Department of Educational Leadership and Policy Studies at the University of Texas at San Antonio (UTSA), USA. Her scholarly interests focus on understanding rural college access and the interplay between race, class, and geography. In particular, she focuses on rural Latinx youth. She uses critical lenses in her work drawn from the fields of demography, geography, and sociology to explore how rural context shapes college access and success outcomes for Latinx youth living in these areas. Sansone's empirical work has been presented at national conferences and published in such outlets as *The Review of Higher Education*, *Review of Educational Research*, and *New Directions for Student Development Services*. She recently authored a forthcoming policy brief on spatial (in)equities and postsecondary attainment for rural Latinx youth in Texas.

Kai A. Schafft is Professor of Education and Rural Sociology in the Department of Education Policy Studies at Pennsylvania State University, USA. His work broadly concerns the relationship between spatial and social inequalities and the role of rural schools for the communities they serve. He is the coauthor of *Rural People and Communities in the Twenty-First Century* (2019) and has published over ninety peer-reviewed articles, book chapters, reviews, reports, and monographs.

Sarah Schmitt-Wilson is Assistant Teaching Professor at Montana State University, USA. Her research explores the educational aspirations of adolescents and educational attainment of young adults from rural communities with a focus on factors influencing educational decision-making. Her research also examines young adults choosing to move to rural communities, specifically addressing the interplay between education and occupation. Her work has been published in the *Journal of Research in Rural Education*, *The Social Science Journal*, *Social Science Quarterly*, and *Career Development Quarterly*.

Jennifer Seelig is an associate program officer with the Spencer Foundation, Chicago, USA. Using a critical lens, she studies the political economy of rural education, school-community relationships, and teacher recruitment and retention. Seelig's work has been published in the *Australian and International Journal of Rural Education, Theory & Practice in Rural Education*, and *Educational Policy*, among others.

Susan M. Sheridan is a George Holmes University Professor of Educational Psychology at the University of Nebraska-Lincoln, USA, and founding director of the Nebraska Center for Research on Children, Youth, Families, and Schools. She has been conducting research on ecological theory, K-3 social-behavioral assessment and intervention, early intervention, and family-school partnerships for more than twenty-five years.

John W. Sipple is Professor in the Department of Global Development at Cornell University, USA. He is the director of Graduate Studies for the Field of Development Sociology, directs the *NY State Center for Rural Schools*, and is the former coeditor in chief for *Community Development*. He has published widely in areas of education policy with a focus on rural community development.

Daniella Hall Sutherland is Assistant Professor of Educational and Organizational Leadership Development at Clemson University, USA. Her work examines educational leadership and policy in rural communities. Sutherland's work has been published in the *Journal for Research on Rural Education, Educational Policy,* and *Rural Sociology*, among other journals.

Paul Theobald is Visiting Professor at the University of Southern Indiana, USA, and taught in Minnesota public schools for seven years before pursuing and receiving his PhD in educational policy studies from the University of Illinois at Champaign, USA. He is an accomplished educational historian whose work frequently crosses disciplinary boundaries. He has published more than fifty articles and chapters, plus three books. Theobald has served as an expert witness in school consolidation cases and in cases dealing with the intentions of state constitution authors with respect to providing a system of free public schools.

Mara Casey Tieken is Associate Professor of Education at Bates College in Lewiston, Maine, USA. Her research focuses on racial and educational equity in rural schools and communities. Her book *Why Rural Schools Matter* (2014) examines how rural schools define and sustain their surrounding communities, and her research has also appeared in many journals, including *American Educational Research Journal, Harvard Educational Review*, and *Peabody Journal of Education*. Before earning her doctorate from the Harvard Graduate School of Education, USA, she taught elementary school in rural Tennessee in the USA.

Simone White is Professor of Education in the School of Teacher Education and Leadership in the Faculty of Creative Industries, Education and Social Justice at Queensland University of Technology in Brisbane, Australia. She is a leading expert in teacher professional learning and the best ways to prepare teachers for diverse contexts—in particular rural, remote, and Indigenous. Her research focuses on the areas of teacher education policy, teacher learning, professional experience, and building and maintaining university-school/community partnerships. White recently led an Australian government grant focused on improving the preparation of future

Contributors

teachers to work in partnership with Aboriginal and Torres Strait Islander parents and caregivers. Through her collective work, she aims to connect research, policy, and practice in ways that bring teachers and school- and university-based teacher educators together and break down traditional borders between academics, policymakers, communities, and practitioners.

Sheneka Williams is Professor and Chair of the Department of Educational Administration at Michigan State University, USA. Williams's research focuses on two main areas: rural education and school desegregation. Her research specifically examines educational opportunity for African American students in rural contexts and the resulting effects of (de)segregated schools on students of color. Her research has been published in journals such as *Educational Policy, Teachers College Record, Urban Education,* and the *Peabody Journal of Education.* Aspects of her research have been presented at the National Press Club, American Enterprise Institute, and on CNN and NPR.

Sarah J. Zuckerman is Assistant Professor of Educational Administration at the University of Nebraska-Lincoln. She is a former special education teacher, serving in rural and urban schools. Her research uses qualitative methods to investigate state-level educational policy implementation and school-community partnerships, particularly in the context of rural communities. Her research combines organizational change theory with concepts from political science to understand how individuals, groups, and organizations mobilize and develop shared understandings that shape action at the school, community, and state policy levels. Her research has been published in journals such as *Journal of Research in Rural Education*, *The Rural Educator*, and *Community Development.*

Introduction

Unsettling Rurality: Mapping a Third Space

Amy Price Azano, Karen Eppley, and Catharine Biddle

A handbook, by definition, is about making clear the assumptions, commitments, and current preoccupations of a research community. While early rural education research could be seen as a small and insular field that sometimes fell short of appropriately representing the heterogeneity of rural people and their spaces and places, this book's reflection of the field signals a transition to a thriving scholarly community working from increasingly diverse identities, research paradigms, and questions. Corbett characterizes rural education as an "activist sub-discipline" (2016a, p. 149). The book is also a tool for activism, in that the collection is a resource and springboard to advance understandings of the diversity of rural communities in terms of histories, demography, geographies, and cultures, and also how rural communities are inextricably connected not only to other rural places but also to "less rural" spaces and places across states, regions, and nations. This handbook is an authoritative representation of current trends and emerging work, signaling a transition from subdisciplinary status to a field in its own right.

The chapters take both the wide and the close-up view. All engage the particularities of rural places. They are also useful tools for thinking about how rural communities are not only tricky to define across contexts but are also more productively understood as existing in relation to, not separate from, less rural places. The chapters include examples of current work and dominant themes; however, ample contextualization also results in historical contextualization across the volume. The chapters provide opportunities for readers to reflect on the ongoing and pressing evolution of educational research. If earlier rural education research engaged the rural-urban binary, this collection is a firm rejection of that position. Collectively, the chapters "unsettle" rurality (Corbett, 2016a, p. 141).

The careful reader will note as well that within the project of unsettling, chapters do not position rural schools and communities as places of deficiency. Amplified by post–2016 media coverage, commonsense understandings of rural places turn on discourses of deficiency (though a deficit view can be readily identified in educational research as well). To reject a deficit view is to see rural communities as sites of possibilities situated within complex webs of histories, systems, and people. Chapter authors in this collection contextualize challenges within and across rural schools and communities with care, insight, and, most importantly, hope. Their examples of analysis and critique reject a deficit view in favor of positioning issues, challenges, and problems as relational outcomes of larger governmental, economic, political, and other systemic inequities.

Rather than challenges signaling an individual's or collection of individuals' personal failings, the personal is understood as political.

Neither do chapter authors engage a rural pastoral imaginary, where rural life is agrarian and simple, and rural people are hardworking and virtuous (M. Howley et al., 2013). Research oriented to this point of view takes a celebratory approach that is ill-equipped to interrogate systemic and micropolitical challenges in rural schools and communities. Deficit and idyllic lenses are poorly positioned to enable insights that contribute to the advancement of scholarly understandings of rural education. Instead, like the rural-urban binary, the deficit-idyll binary has the potential to reinforce political and cultural tendencies to otherize, or make invisible, rural people and their communities. The authors in this collection work skillfully in the tensions with and around the third space between idyll and deficit to explore the complexities of rural education.

A Word About Our Process

After the presidential election of 2016, rural education found itself squarely in Trump country. Irrespective of the complexities of residents' personal politics, the media and popular press positioned rural communities within the shadow of racist and bigoted rhetoric associated with the former president's campaign and the four-year administration that followed. Much has been written about this topic (see, e.g., C. B. Howley & A. Howley, 2018), and we mean here not to belabor the point but, rather, to share our earliest impetus for this project. As the media and others woke up to the fact that rural communities have political *power*, journalists (and even some from within the academy) revived dated, narrow, stereotypical, and deficit narratives of rural communities reminiscent of the "War on Poverty" portrayals from Johnson's administration in the 1960s. As months turned into years, as editors, we wished we had in hand a collection of more nuanced commentary both for our own use and to recommend to colleagues and graduate students. With this vision in mind, we reached out to our rural education colleagues, some newer, some well established, and asked them to contribute to this collection. Our goal was to create a collection useful to a wide audience: scholars with a long publication history in rural education (our trailblazers!), those new to the field, and those with emerging interest in this space. The voices of the authors whose work makes up this collection inspire more complete understandings of how complex webs of historical, cultural, sociopolitical, and socioeconomic influences in rural communities intersect with education.

Early in the editorial process, we used questions about possible foundational aspects of rural education to design the sections of this handbook. What does "rural" even mean, how is it defined, and what are the implications of those definitions? How do histories and policies influence education in rural America, and what do we need to do differently to better serve rural schools and communities? How do rural populations and demographics, poverty, and corporate influences affect rural communities and schools, and how might researchers consider these varied issues to better understand needs in rural schools? For the reader, this foundation offers insight into the sections that follow, making transparent what we as editors considered to be an authoritative (though not complete) treatment of the field of rural education. We considered "rural education" writ large, seeking chapters that highlighted the relationship between rural schools and communities, as well as what might go on within the walls of a rural school building. Importantly, the final section is devoted to issues of identity and equity in rural schools. This final section serves as a particularly notable example of where this text is incomplete. For example, despite our efforts, we were not able to include work on gender and sexuality. We hope readers will note these omissions as invitations for what is needed—*not what is excluded*—from the field of rural education.

As with any text, the editorial team and chapter authors made particular decisions that shaped the final product in particular ways: some invisible, some clearly apparent. While we sought to present a diverse range of topics from scholars who could contribute to a representation of rural education in the United States, it was clear from the outset (and is even more so now) that no one text can adequately capture a field of study. Simply put, more chapters need to be written.

Readers may wonder as well why the focus of the handbook is limited to the United States. After beginning the questioning process we describe above, it quickly became apparent that our ideas about what this book could be could not be contained in one volume. We decided that limiting the book to a US focus would result in a different text than one that tried to account for rural education the world over. The breadth of the field is such that twenty-six chapters can only work as a good beginning to understand what rural education is in the United States and how that is operationalized in scholarly publications. Yet we were bothered by a US-centric representation of rural education, particularly given the recent important work being done by colleagues in Australia, Canada, and Europe (see Gristy et al., 2020). We also were wary that limiting the scope of the book to the US could inadvertently contribute to the idea that rural education in the United States is parochial and insular, seemingly unaware or perhaps uninterested in its global intersections. In the end, however, we opted for depth rather than breadth. We decided that for the handbook to be of most use, contributing authors should have ample space to discuss their topics. The international responses (by White, Corbett, Roberts, and Gristy) quite effectively invite readers to consider each section with an international lens and we wish there was more space for further international thinking. The editors are deeply grateful for their commentary.

As we note, our work is incomplete and also runs the risk of circumscribing ideas, methodologies, people, and research settings. For example, we took a topical approach. While this decision enabled a robust collection of current research questions and general areas of inquiry, it allowed only for incidental treatment of theoretical frames and research methodologies, such as can be found in White and Corbett (2014). Across the chapters, however, we note common themes. Chapter authors make clear that the affordances and challenges of life in rural places and institutions are interconnected to demographic and economic structures. They caution against zooming in on one discrete area without considering the complex web of influences and outcomes. Authors discuss, for example, the relationship between rural education and economic hardship, the ways that poverty continues to marginalize rural communities and especially people of color in rural spaces. A historical and structural understanding of poverty sheds light on the organization of rural schooling, including needed funding changes, support structures, and pedagogical opportunities. Chapter authors also discuss at length the reciprocal nature between rural schools and communities, moving away from the mythically harmonious relationship to a nuanced discussion of governance, community partnerships, labor, and leadership. And, finally, as authors reject deficit ideologies, they embrace a call for dismantling White supremacy in rural spaces and in the context of rural education research. We want to acknowledge here the extraordinary community of scholars represented in this text. Chapters were solicited prior to the

The Bloomsbury Handbook of Rural Education in the United States

Covid-19 pandemic, and we are humbled by our colleagues' commitment to this project during such challenging times.

An Invitation

Throughout our editorial process and especially where we struggled to solicit voices on certain topics, we questioned how we and our colleagues have come to think of themselves as *rural* education scholars. Identity formation of this kind is, at its core, about boundary work—iteratively coming to understand both who and what we are and are not (Biddle et al., 2019). While we hope this introduction makes clear the reasoning behind our construction of these boundaries as editors, we want to emphasize that the placement of these markers is meant to aid in the identification of intersections and bridges, rather than the building of walls. It is our sincere hope that this volume serves as a jumping-off point for robust engagement with rural education in the United States and, most importantly, the critique and growth of this research community.

This volume is an invitation. We hope that those who don't necessarily consider themselves rural researchers consider, or *re*consider, how their work is applicable to rural contexts. We are convinced that there are many urban and suburban education scholars from whom we could learn. The same is true of sociologists, geographers, economists, and so on. The best outcome we could imagine from the publication of this volume would be the explosion, reconstruction, and evolution (or whatever metaphor you wish to choose) of research on rural education. We hope the book is a resource that promotes scholarship that poses questions reflecting the complexity of rural schools and communities and their place in the world.

On the other hand, we also hope this handbook serves to solidify and affirm rural education as a field, a discipline of scholars engaged with supporting rural schools and communities. We are grateful to the overwhelmingly supportive and energetic response from our colleagues to bring about this work, to Dr. Rachelle Kuehl for her careful editing and formative feedback, and to our editor at Bloomsbury, Ally Baker, for believing in this project and in our ability to bring it to light.

Part I

Introduction

Foundations in Rural Education

The chapters in Part I provide a foundational overview of rural education, examining the various ways in which definitions, histories, and policies have shaped conceptions of rurality and how these topics continue to influence rural education. This foundational approach explores how corporatization, population changes, poverty, and the role of data affect everyday learning in rural schools, and how our subjectivities and positionalities affect our relationships with rural spaces and places.

These subjectivities, particularly as they relate to defining rural, have consequences for research and practice. Longhurst explores nuanced meanings of rurality in Chapter 1, Developing, Utilizing, and Critiquing Definitions of "Rural" in Rural Education Research. Longhurst asks what is meant by *rural* and discusses how we articulate, interrogate, and operationalize definitions of rurality in rural educational research. Longhurst provides a geographic and theoretical overview of rural definitions in the research literature, noting how and why definitions have been challenged and, also, how these definitions influence what constitutes a rural warrant or rural salience. Definitions have implications, particularly if they are simplified, exclusionary, or used as proxies for race, socioeconomic status, cultural identification, social class, or political preference. The chapter ends with a set of questions designed to enable researchers and consumers of rural research to interrogate *rural*, so they can better understand a study's relevance to a particular rural context.

In Chapter 2, History and the Shape of Rural Educational Policy in the United States, Theobald explores cultural perceptions of what rural has meant and what it means to live in the rural United States, a country deeply impacted by its rural histories. Perceptions of rurality influence all manner of public policy, including education policy. As a case in point, the chapter documents the

The Bloomsbury Handbook of Rural Education in the United States

policy developments orchestrated by Ellwood Cubberley, one of the most impactful educational spokespersons at the turn of the twentieth century. Cubberley, who was the first to create a graduate curriculum for school administrators, argued for the modernization of rural schools through consolidation to solve the "rural school problem." Theobald explores how Cubberley's contributions informed cultural assumptions about rural life and provides a theoretical and historical grounding and discusses the interconnections between cultural perceptions and subsequent policy developments, concluding with some analysis of the relatively recent work on rural policy shortcomings.

To that end, Theobald's chapter is followed by Brenner's critique of federal policies claiming place neutrality in Chapter 3, Toward a Rural Critical Policy Analysis. This chapter builds from an historical framing and presents the utility of critical policy analysis to examine and critique key aspects of federal policies and their implications for rural contexts. Brenner explains that a framework for rural policy analysis must examine assumptions of place neutrality, distributive analysis, rural salience, and the policy's proposed definition of rural. Moreover, Brenner discusses the critical work of recognizing how metrocentric policies position rural places as valuable only because of the resources they provide to urban centers and how this metrocentricity perpetuates rurality as deficient and peripheral. Her chapter concludes by discussing how a rural critical policy analysis can be a tool for asking: How is place significant in the moral implications for a particular policy or set of policies?

In yet another foundational influence in the social, political, and economic construction of rural education, Cervone examines the effects of corporate school reform in Chapter 4, Corporate Influences on Rural Schools. Cervone explains how the business sector of the United States has long attempted to transform public education into a private industry, under the guise that private industry is more innovative, efficient, and cost-effective than the overly bureaucratic and stifling public sector. Many of the promises of corporate reform have not been achieved, even by the arguably flawed measure of standardized test scores, as students in privately operated charter schools tend to score no better (or worse) than students in traditional public school districts. Cervone argues that privatization has not reduced bureaucracy as promised but that bureaucracy has transformed into an entirely new *corporate* bureaucracy—one no longer subject to public oversight and accountability. This chapter offers a discussion of how rural communities are ideally positioned to strengthen public education by making it more democratic, in part by developing and acting upon an understanding of the ways corporate logic and language have infiltrated education.

While these first several chapters provide a theoretical landscape for rural education, Schafft and Maselli explore the geographic and demographic landscape of rural places in Chapter 5, Shifting Population Dynamics and Implications for Rural Schools. Demographic shifts explored in this chapter include rural out-migration and depopulation, immigration, rural retirement migration, and rural gentrification. Out-migration has been a long-term existential issue for communities across the rural United States, having resulted in rural depopulation and, by extension, increased pressure for school closures and consolidations. Other rural places, especially high-amenity areas with full access to medical care, recreation, and shopping with close (enough) proximity to metropolitan areas, have become rural retirement destinations or have otherwise attracted in-migrants to rural communities. While this is often seen as a hopeful sign of rural development, it can come with its own unanticipated costs (e.g., rural gentrification), including new types of social exclusions and inequalities, which schools can abet or lessen, depending on their policies and practices.

Introduction

At the same time, as Schafft and Maselli explain, the rural United States has become increasingly diverse with the in-migration of historically minoritized racial and ethnic populations accounting for over 80 percent of rural population growth between 2000 and 2010. These population changes can offer new opportunities for rural communities, and they also can challenge long-ingrained community identities. Schafft and Maselli's discussion illuminates how all of these population shifts have significant and varied consequences for rural schools and communities as populations shrink, grow, or compositionally change, resulting in shifting academic and school staffing needs. They conclude with a brief discussion of implications for policy and practice, as well as the ways in which rural schools can play an integral role in rural development and the overall well-being of rural people and places.

While demographic and population shifts influence rural schools, so does rural poverty, as Tieken parses out in Chapter 6, Rural Poverty and Rural Schools. Using a spatial injustice framework, Tieken's chapter provides an overview of statistics describing rural poverty, its causes, and its effects on individuals, communities, and rural schools. Tieken explores historical and contemporary factors of racial oppression and exclusion in rural places that have resulted in entrenched high-poverty rates for many rural communities of color. The chapter discusses how these issues are intertwined with rural economies, physical isolation, and weak infrastructures. Moreover, Tieken describes how poverty is associated with a variety of negative health, civic, and employment outcomes, particularly for children and adolescents. Given the influence of poverty in rural communities, the reliance on local property taxes for education funding is a profound challenge.

In light of the many complexities facing rural communities in terms of how definitions are operationalized, the persistent influence of history and corporatization on policy and practice, shifting populations, and the effects of poverty, it is important to consider the value and challenge of looking at data across domains to develop a more complete understanding of how schools function within rural communities. Sipple, Fiduccia, and LeBeau take up this topic as they explore in Chapter 7, The Why and How of Enhancing Data Use in Rural Education Research and Practice. They discuss the utility of linking student, school, and district data with other sources of data from health care, childcare, economic and community development, and other community-based data. The authors present a conceptual model of local school-community interactions and demonstrate how linking decisions about schooling to other systems in the local community can provide a broader and deeper understanding of the implications of policy implementation, especially with respect to community vitality.

The authors offer insights into the range of possible relevant sources of data to consider in rural education research, both to assist local education and community practice. Beyond identifying various sources of data and exploring the types of research and practice questions that it enables, they also offer advice on the mechanics and challenges of joining education data with noneducation data, providing several pertinent examples highlighting research questions, practice implications, and lessons learned. In conclusion, they share their experience in trying to democratize data to help local school and community leaders, emphasizing the importance of communicating directly with stakeholders from noneducation sectors.

Part I ends with Australian scholar White's Responding Rurally: Perspectives and Insights from One Rural Place to Another. Like Longhurst, White begins her response to the chapters in Part I asking what "rural" means *to* and *for* the field of education. White examines

The Bloomsbury Handbook of Rural Education in the United States

Brenner's discussion of place neutrality as it relates to policy and practice in an Australian context, arguing that places are indeed not neutral and that policy neutrality disadvantages rural students in the United States and students in Australia via processes of "policy borrowing." Writing from her perspective in the Global South, White discusses implications for placeless education policy reforms, reflects on the role of data, and contemplates how this handbook serves as a signifier that rural educational scholarship has become increasingly relevant to the broader education research community. She explains that the United States and Australia are, in many ways, rural *cousins* and provides examples of the ways we are similar and unique. Importantly, she discusses the subjectivity of rural as a geographic and also an imagined space, drawing on Mackella's iconic poem "My Country" as an example of that subjectivity. White also shares how rurality and place in Australia are shaped in terms of colonization and describes how, as it was for her cousins in North America (an issue explored in Part IV of this volume), colonization was cataclysmic for Australian First Peoples. White concludes by noting that this volume presents an opportunity to reflect on these foundational nuances in ways that will benefit the rural education research community, but also so that we, as readers, may better understand our own places.

1

Developing, Utilizing, and Critiquing Definitions of "Rural" in Rural Education Research

Jesse Moon Longhurst

Researchers in rural education face a set of questions that have long bedeviled the field. What do we mean by rural? How do we articulate, interrogate, and operationalize definitions of rurality, and how do we proceed when definitions conflict or contradict one another?

Most studies concerning rural education provide no definition of what makes their study settings rural (Thier & Beach, 2019; Thier et al., 2021), and those that do provide a definition rarely give context or justification for their choice. While no single definition could ever be appropriate for all endeavors, engaging with these important questions of *rural context* (Azano et al., 2019) is essential for rural researchers. Failure to do so could compromise both the quality and the utility of research. This chapter attempts to assist early-career scholars and those new to the rural education research space by untangling, clarifying, and describing some of the ways *rural* has been defined in rural education literature.

This chapter presents an overview of the most commonly used *external quantitative* (Bosak & Perlman, 1982) definitions that have been developed by governmental bodies in the United States. It also describes some ways in which those definitions have been problematized and provides some advice for researchers interested in employing such definition and categorization schemas. The chapter also includes an introduction to various approaches that some scholars have taken as they theorize, define, and qualitatively describe rurality, giving particular attention to Coladarci's (2007) influential call to the field to make the "rural argument" (p. 3) and to Biddle et al.'s (2019) revisiting and reframing of that call. It provides emerging researchers with an overview of complexities and pitfalls that they may encounter as they employ or construct definitions of rurality. The chapter concludes with two sets of questions. The first set is designed to guide research consumers as they navigate scholarship about rural education. The second set of questions presents a thinking guide for researchers as they plan and conduct their own rural research projects.

The Bloomsbury Handbook of Rural Education in the United States

External Quantitative Definitions

At first glance, rurality may appear to be purely a matter of geography and population density, with formal definitions and designations designed by governmental bodies. It is true that many of the most commonly used definitions of rurality appearing in rural education research literature (as well as in policy documents) are what Bosak and Perlman (1982) called *external quantitative* definitions. Most of these were developed by federal agencies and departments, though some regional or state definitions are also in use and some researchers have developed additional external quantitative definitions based on multiple, intersecting factors (Elder, 1992). Rural education research consumers may be challenged by the different designations and definitions that appear in research literature and in policy. In an effort to provide some clarity, the following is a description of the most commonly employed external quantitative definitions developed by US federal agencies and departments.

US Federal Government Definitions and Designations

The US federal government uses two primary sets of definitions to classify the status of rural communities and schools. The first is the US Census Bureau definition; the second comes from the Office of Management and Budget (OMB). While some governmental agencies also use measurements more tailored to their missions, they have largely based their more than two dozen definitions (Cromartie & Bucholtz, 2008) on either the Census or the OMB definitions.

Census Definitions. The US Census Bureau "defines rural as any population, housing, or territory NOT in an urban area" (US Census Bureau, n.d.). In this framework, rural places are identified as "residual" or where urban places are not. The Census Bureau employs two types of urban area classifications: "Urbanized Areas (UAs) of 50,000 or more people" and "Urban Clusters (UCs) of at least 2,500 and less than 50,000 people" (US Census Bureau, n.d.). Communities and regions that do not meet either definition are considered rural. The designation of a population of 2,500 as *urban* dates to 1910. The Census Bureau has, in intervening years, divided *urban* into UAs and UCs. However, the population threshold of 2,500 as marking the end of *rural* and the beginning of *urban* has stood for over a century.

Office of Management and Budget Definitions. The second primary set of federal categorizations was developed by the OMB. The OMB divides counties into three categories: *metropolitan, micropolitan,* or *neither*. In this framework, if a county is designated as *micropolitan* or *neither*, it is considered nonmetro and therefore rural.

The threshold for a population to be considered metropolitan or micropolitan is considerably higher in the OMB definition than in the Census Bureau definition of Urban Cluster. In the OMB framework, metropolitan counties contain an urban area with more than fifty thousand people, and micropolitan counties contain an urban area of at least ten thousand (Office of Management and Budget, 2000).

National Center for Education Statistics Locale Classifications. The most frequently used classifications in rural education research (Thier et al., 2021) come from the National Center for

Education Statistics (NCES). The NCES classification system (see Table 1.1) utilizes the US Department of Education's Common Core of Data to identify each public school in the United States as belonging to one of four major locale classifications: *City, Suburb, Town,* and *Rural*. This system is referred to as the *urban-centric* classification system and has been in use since 2006. Each of those classifications is subdivided into three further subclassifications.

The NCES locale classifications are dependent upon the Census Bureau designations. For example, the Census designation *Urban Cluster* is included in the definitions of NCES *town* statuses (*fringe, distance,* and *remote*) and Urban Cluster designation is also used to distinguish between the three NCES subclassifications of *rural*. In each case, the distance from an urban cluster is what separates *rural fringe* from *rural distant* from *rural remote*. Again, we find that the Census

Table 1.1 National Center for Education Statistics Locale Classifications

City, Large	Territory inside an urbanized area and inside a principal city with population of 250,000 or more
City, Midsize	Territory inside an urbanized area and inside a principal city with population less than 250,000 and greater than or equal to 100,000
City, Small	Territory inside an urbanized area and inside a principal city with population less than 100,000
Suburb, Large	Territory outside a principal city and inside an urbanized area with population of 250,000 or more
Suburb, Midsize	Territory outside a principal city and inside an urbanized area with population less than 250,000 and greater than or equal to 100,000
Suburb, Small	Territory outside a principal city and inside an urbanized area with population less than 100,000
Town, Fringe	Territory inside an urban cluster that is less than or equal to 10 miles from an urbanized area
Town, Distant	Territory inside an urban cluster that is more than 10 miles and less than or equal to 35 miles from an urbanized area
Town, Remote	Territory inside an urban cluster that is more than 35 miles from an urbanized area
Rural, Fringe	Census-defined rural territory that is less than or equal to 5 miles from an urbanized area, as well as rural territory that is less than or equal to 2.5 miles from an urban cluster
Rural, Distant	Census-defined rural territory that is more than 5 miles but less than or equal to 25 miles from an urbanized area, as well as rural territory that is more than 2.5 miles but less than or equal to 10 miles from an urban cluster
Rural, Remote	Census-defined rural territory that is more than 25 miles from an urbanized area and is also more than 10 miles from an urban cluster

Source: National Center for Education Statistics (n.d.).

The Bloomsbury Handbook of Rural Education in the United States

designation of Urban Cluster (upon which all of the NCES classifications of rurality are based) is predicated on the urban threshold of 2,500 residents (National Center for Education Statistics, n.d.).

Prior Classification Systems. Between 1986 and 2006, the NCES used two different urban/rural classification systems for schools and school districts and it is useful to understand their frameworks.

Metro Status Codes were based on the location of the office of the district superintendent and there were only three codes available in this system:

1. Central City of a Core Based Statistical Area (CBSA)
2. Located in a CBSA but not in the central city
3. Not located in a CBSA (National Center for Education Statistics, n.d.)

Metro-Centric Locale Codes, on the other hand (sometimes called Johnson Codes; Johnson, 1990), were based on both distance from a metropolitan area and on population density. This system offered more nuance than the Metro Status codes, providing eight locale codes to describe school settings.

Additionally, in the 1970s, the Department of Agriculture's Economic Research Service (ERS) developed a coding system officially called the *ERS Rural-Urban Continuum Codes*, commonly referred to as the Beale Codes (after Calvin Beale, who developed the system). The Beale codes system categorized school districts into *metro* and *nonmetro* counties and subdivided those into nine codes (National Center for Education Statistics, n.d.).

One weakness of the Beale Codes system was that the school district location was determined at the county level and (as with Metro Status codes) was based on the address of the superintendent's office. This designation posed problems when the district office location was not representative of the district as a whole, when school districts crossed county lines, or when the mailing address of the superintendent's office was not within the district.

Scholars will also likely encounter other external quantitative definitions, most of which are based in some way on the Census or OMB codes, but that may use them in tandem or contextualize them with additional information. For example, the ERS uses the following: Rural-Urban Continuum Codes, Urban-Influence Codes, Natural Amenities Scales, ERS Typology Codes, Rural-Urban Commuting Areas, and Frontier and Remote Area Codes (US Department of Agriculture Economic Research Service, 2019). Each of these has a different set of parameters for designating degrees of rurality, and each is tailored to specific types of data collection and analysis.

One critique of all of these definitional schemas and categorization systems is that they inevitably create thresholds. If a community's population rises above an identified number, or if the community exists within an identified distance of an urban place, the community has crossed the threshold from rural to something else. Waldorf (2006) called this the "threshold trap" and suggested "a continuous multidimensional measure of rurality, the Index of Relative Rurality" (p. 2), which was designed to place rural counties on a spectrum of rurality rather than identify them as definitively rural or not rural.

Choosing, Justifying, and Contextualizing Definitions and Designations

Both consumers of research and researchers themselves are faced with a profusion of definitions and classifications developed by governmental organizations. Many of these definitions and classifications have spawned generations of increasingly complex categorizations and schemas. It is easy to make the case for employing commonly used and clearly codified definitions of rurality in rural education research, particularly in quantitative research. If, for example, a researcher uses the NCES classification system to identify a study site as *rural remote*, it is more easily compared to other sites that are similarly coded. The potential for transferability or replication seems greater when operating under shared definitions of rurality. As Koziol et al. (2015) cautioned, because of these various theoretical perspectives and the ways rural is operationalized in the research, rural researchers must ensure that their work is informative and, when appropriate, replicable. If such definitions are overly broad or applied without considering their fit for the study at hand, then the utility of a common definitional schema begins to break down. Instead, researchers should choose a definition that "meets the goals of the endeavor" (Cromartie & Bucholtz, 2008, p. 29).

One potentially sticky issue is that different classification schemas can produce drastically different statistics about rural communities or even wildly differing tallies of rural people (Cromartie & Bucholtz, 2008). Boundary choices and population thresholds in three different classification schemas, for example, counted the rural percentage of the American population quite differently during the 2010 Census: 19.3 percent (by the Census Bureau definition), 18 percent (by the Federal Office of Rural Health Policy definition), or 15 percent (by the OMB definition; Health Resources & Services Administration, 2018). These percentages may not seem drastically different on the surface. However, the difference between the 15 percent of the 2010 population designated as rural by the OMB definition and the 19.3 percent designated by the Census Bureau equates to a difference of over 13 million people. To select and utilize a definition or categorization without considering its underlying assumptions (as well as whether there might be a definition or classification that better describes the research setting) risks misrepresenting both one's research findings and the people and places concerned. When such misrepresentations or misapplications of data are taken up by policymakers, then real harm can be done to rural communities.

Quantitative researchers should also consider whether to describe their research setting using more than one definitional schema or categorization structure, understanding that different schemas provide different kinds of context. They should also clearly describe their rationale for choosing the classification schema(s) upon which they ultimately decide. Alternatively, they can modify existing frameworks and definitions or develop their own (Greenough & Nelson, 2015) in order to best answer their research questions. Koziol et al. (2015) cautioned, "Inappropriate selection, analysis and/or communication of the rural definition may result in misinformed conclusions about rural phenomena, which in turn may result in misinformed policy and program eligibility decisions" (p. 11).

Similarly, researchers engaged in qualitative research who choose to use an external quantitative definition of rurality in situating their studies should have a strong rationale for that choice and select a definition that is a good fit for their theoretical framework. When researchers or policymakers find that existing definitions and measures do not "adequately preserve and measure the unique contexts of rural places" (Hawley et al., 2016, p. 9), a more narrative, descriptive approach may be preferable. Rurality is not, of course, simply a matter of intersecting coding schemas based on population density and distance. Regardless of research tradition, it is incumbent on researchers to examine and justify the designations and descriptors that they choose.

Theorizing Rurality and Qualitative Definitions

The myriad ways in which scholars define, describe, and theorize rurality all inform the study of rural education and are the source of ongoing conversation and debate in the field (Arnold et al., 2005; Corbett, 2015a; C. B. Howley et al., 2005; Stephens, 1992). Donehower (2014) wrote, "'Rural' is typically a felt term in the USA, rather than a technical one" (p. 168). Nearly every text about rural education begins with the claim that it is nearly impossible to satisfactorily define rurality but then poses the authors' own attempts to do just that (e.g., Hargreaves, 2020; and Rios, 1988). As illustrated by the *Journal of Research in Rural Education*'s 1992 special issue on classifying rural school districts (Stern, 1992)—and many scholarly conversations since—these are deep waters. I will not attempt to resolve any controversies over those theorizations and conceptualizations here. However, it may be helpful to provide an introduction as to how some scholars in rural education research have conceptualized rurality.

Rural scholars commonly advocate for an approach to qualitative rural research that provides thick, rich descriptions in order to immerse the reader in the specifics of a rural place (Coladarci, 2007). If each place is unique in its rurality, then the specific rural setting should be described thoroughly and lucidly. In addition to advocating for robust descriptions of rural places, C. B. Howley (1997) has stressed the distinction between local and cosmopolitan as a way of understanding the difference between rural and urban spaces.

Another often-cited definition comes from Donehower et al. (2012), who conceptualized rural as quantitative, geographic, and cultural and stressed that rural "functions for many as a marker of identity, regardless of demographic criteria or current location" (p. 7). Reid et al. (2010) employed this definition of rurality in their framework of "rural social space," which they described as combining "quantitative measurement and definitions of rural space based on demographic and other social data with constructions of rurality in both geographic and cultural terms" (Reid et al., 2010, p. 263).

Some scholars, however, also question the positioning of rural in contrast to urban. John and Ford (2017) critiqued the concept of the urban/rural binary from an Indigenous and Marxist perspective arguing that the "urban/rural divide is a colonial concept" (p. 9) that positions rural places as existing in the service of metropolitan consumers: consumers of agricultural products and consumers of the rural idyll (Cloke et al., 2006). Rural places are also often positioned as inherently deficient. Deficit-based definitions of rurality have been critiqued extensively by rural education scholars (e.g., see Azano, 2015; Corbett, 2007; Corbett & White, 2014; C. B. Howley & A. Howley, 2010; Schafft & Jackson, 2010; Surface & Theobald, 2014b; Theobald & Wood, 2010).

Some authors have worked to disaggregate rurality into conceptual categories in order to provide more nuance with which to describe communities. For example, Gjelten (1982) categorized rural communities as falling into one of five types: *stable rural, depressed rural, high growth rural, reborn rural*, and *isolated rural*. In some cases, these categories of rural communities are metaphorical, as in Lawson et al.'s (2008) division of Pacific Northwest rural communities into the rhetorical categories of *playgrounds, dumping grounds*, and *unseen grounds*. Lichter and Brown (2011) cautioned against simplistic binaries or even continuums of rurality and emphasized the complex interfaces and interdependence between rural and urban places and people. They outlined ten common conceptions of rural American that include rural America as:

Cultural Deposit Box, Backwater, Engine of Urbanization, Exurbia, Place of Consumption, New Immigrant Destination, Ghetto, Food Basket, Repository of Natural Resources, and *Dumping Ground*. They argued that geographic and social boundaries between rural and urban spaces are becoming less distinct and that scholars should attend to interdependence in their descriptions of communities.

Authors also sometimes describe rurality based on their own interpretation or impressions and then frame a specific community as either fitting that interpretation or being in opposition to it. Bushnell (1999) wrote that "'rural' designates an isolated region, often the now-fragmented remnants of a once flourishing farming community . . . low socio-economic status (SES), disconnected from metropolitan areas and low in population" (p. 80). However, in describing her study site, she qualified that description, stating, "Rural in this case involves previously urban families migrating to homes surrounded by land undeveloped with buildings and industry other than farming" (p. 80).

A Sociological Lens

Corbett (2015a) wrote that a rural education research agenda should be informed by sociological questions and perspectives. To understand those sociological perspectives, it is useful to know how rural has been defined in rural sociology. In the first half of the twentieth century, rural sociologists tended to use definitions of rurality that focused on social relationships and interactions. Nelson (1955), for example, wrote that while a precise definition of rural was impossible, "the primary difference between life in a large and in a small community is *the relative extent of one's personal acquaintance with other members of the community*" (p. 9, emphasis in original).

As rural sociology began to take a more critical turn, attention grew around questions of power and discourse in rural spaces. As these conversations evolved and expanded, scholars conceived of the boundaries of rurality through different lenses (Cloke & Little, 1997; Cloke et al., 2006; Halfacree, 2006). Thomas et al. (2011) described three "competing scholarly conceptions of rural": *rural as demography and space, rural as political and economic*, and *rural as social and cultural* (pp. 28–32).

One particularly helpful conceptualization of rurality comes from the work of Bell. Bell (2007) described the different ways that rural is conceptualized in rural sociology as *first rural, second rural*, and *rural plural*. This structure can be a useful framework for examining how the field of rural education research defines and describes rurality. Bell's *first rural* encompasses the qualities of rurality typically described in terms of population density, geographic remoteness, and other material identifiers such as the external quantitative measures discussed earlier in this chapter.

In Bell's framework, *second rural* is

> The rural of associations . . . between rural life and food, cultivation, community, nature, wild freedom, and masculine patriarchal power, and the many contradictions we have also so long associated with the rural, such as desolation, isolation, dirt and disease, wild danger and the straw-hatted rube. (p. 409)

Bell's *rural plural*, however, asks us to see the interplay between first rural and second rural and to consider "a conception of rural that equally embraces the epistemology and ontology of both first rural and second rural, and as well sees them both as moments in a plural dialogue"

The Bloomsbury Handbook of Rural Education in the United States

(p. 413). The *rural plural* is a generative concept to consider as researchers develop research questions, design studies, and interpret results. How we define and conceptualize what makes a place or person rural will influence how we understand our findings. For example, a study that employs solely a *first rural* definition of rurality (i.e., NCES codes) may stymie *second rural* or *rural plural* interpretation of results. A study employing solely a *first rural* or *second rural* definition may also run the risk of overstating generalizability or transferability of its results. Rural education research exists at complex intersections of human development, space and place, culture, pedagogy, demography, and geography. Our definitions of rural must be responsive to those intersections and appropriate to the questions at hand.

Complexities and Pitfalls for Rural Researchers

When a setting is described as rural, but rural is left underdefined or undertheorized, it leaves the reader to rely on their own conceptions of rurality. Underdefinition can take the form of entirely failing to define rurality, but it can also take the form of an overly broad and unexamined definition. For example, labeling an entire state rural or setting up a rural place as a foil for an urban one without contextualizing either (Thier et al., 2021). Avoiding these pitfalls requires attending to Thomson's (2000) "thisness" of a place (p. 159) rather than leaving interpretations entirely up to the reader.

Table 1.2 Guiding Questions for Researchers and Consumers of Rural Research

Research Question	Does the research question address a uniquely rural phenomenon? Does the research question compare rural and nonrural examples of the same phenomenon? To what extent is the research question tied to a specific rural locale or context?
Theoretical Framework	Is rural defined by the researchers? If so, how is it defined? Is the definition of rural consistent with the theoretical framework?
Study Design	Why was a rural setting chosen for the research? If a classification schema is used, is it appropriate to the research question, and is a rationale provided for that choice? If an external quantitative definition of rural is used, what rationale is provided for that choice? Who is included or excluded by the definition of rural in the study? What perspectives and populations may be missing?
Data Analysis	Is rural used as an unexamined proxy for some other attribute, subgroup, cultural phenomenon, or geography? Are collected data and data analysis consistent with the author's definition of rural?
Data Reporting	How does the conceptualization of rurality in the piece help the reader understand the results of the study? How does the definition of rurality serve to contextualize the setting for the reader?

Definitions in Rural Education Research

Such oversimplification can also lead to rural stereotyping (Bryant, 2010; Donehower, 2007). If rural settings are not contextualized, then we allow those stereotypical assumptions to go unchallenged, encouraging exclusionary or romanticized assumptions about who lives in rural places (and who does not), what kinds of work that rural people do, and who belongs in rural spaces. Underdefined conceptualizations of rurality as a proxy for race, socioeconomic status, culture, class, or political orientation are problematic and can reinforce harmful misconceptions

Table 1.3 Guiding Questions for Researchers

Research Question	To what extent is your research question rural? To what extent is it tied to a specific rural locale or context?
Theoretical Framework	What kind of engagement with the definition and descriptions of rurality does your research question demand? How will you make a case for your chosen or constructed definition? What literature (theoretical and empirical) supports that case? How does the theoretical framework of your study guide your understanding of rural?
Study Design	Will your study compare rural and nonrural examples of the same phenomenon? If so, how will that influence your study design? Is there a preexisting definition of rurality that will sufficiently contextualize your study? Is there a preexisting categorization schema that would be appropriate for your study? What might be missing from such definitions or categorizations that you could supplement? Is your research question best served by a qualitative approach to defining rurality that makes its case for rurality through thick, rich description? Will you employ an externally developed definition or definitional schema, or is there benefit in developing a definition with input from participants?
Data Collection	Who is and is not represented in the rural space that you have delineated via your definitional boundaries? Who is included and who is excluded by your definition? Should you refine your definitional boundaries in light of those inclusions or exclusions? Does the definition hold during data collection?
Data Analysis	How will you check your chosen or constructed definition of rurality with participants, stakeholders, or against data sources? To what extent does your definition of rural facilitate your data analysis? Has your definition and categorization of rural created artificial thresholds that could skew your results?
Data Reporting and Dissemination	If using qualitative description to contextualize your study, how will you balance the competing imperatives of thick, rich description and participant/community privacy? Will your research be useful to the rural community that you are studying?

about rural people and places. One particularly pernicious form this can take is the conflation of rurality with whiteness. Studies that do not engage with the racial, ethnic, and cultural diversity of rural places contribute to the marginalization and erasure of rural communities of color.

Uniquely Rural or Relevant to the Rural?

Ultimately, what all of these intertwined conceptualizations of rural have in common is a desire for specificity and utility. When Coladarci's (2007) influential call to the field was published in his final editorial for the *Journal of Research in Rural Education*, he called on rural education researchers to fully describe the rural context of any research and to make the "rural argument" (p. 3) for their work by situating it theoretically as well as in design. As Biddle et al. (2019) observed, this piece has become very influential, particularly for early-career researchers or for those new to rural education research. However, Biddle et al. also cautioned us not to enshrine Coladarci's advice as a strict litmus test for quality rural education research, because to do so risks turning it into a gatekeeping mechanism for new rural education researchers. It also risks siloing rural education research and setting up unnecessary barriers between our field and other relevant scholarship. Rather, Biddle et al. (2019) encouraged rural researchers to concern themselves less with the purity of the rural warrant and more with demonstrating "the importance of their research in rural contexts" (p. 10).

In that spirit, consider the questions posed in Tables 1.2 and 1.3. The first list of questions is designed to help research consumers parse and interpret rural education research, and the second list is designed to guide researchers as they plan their own research projects—both with attention to the importance of thoroughly interrogating what is meant by *rural*.

2

History and the Shape of Rural Educational Policy in the United States

Paul Theobald

America's political identity, if such a thing can be said to exist, oscillates between contrary worldviews. At our founding, the understanding of what constitutes a state tended to fall into two camps. For many, a nation-state was thought to be a collection of self-interested individuals agreeing to rules and laws made by a centralized authority, be that a monarch, a legislative body, or both. For many others, a nation-state was thought to be a collection of mutually interested communities, or "ward republics" as Thomas Jefferson referred to them, where rules and laws would be made closest to those affected by them (Jefferson, 2013, p. 227). While these worldviews were quite different from one another, they shared a commonality that would allow them to coexist. Neither was consistent with a state defined by a monarch flanked by a title-holding aristocracy. The two worldviews that competed with one another at our nation's founding both rejected feudalism for something profoundly more democratic. With that common ground, the United States was born.[1]

Still, a pronounced difference in conceptions of statehood condemned early Americans to near-constant struggle in the policy arena. For instance, if a state is a collection of free-acting individuals, its government must be a vehicle for ensuring the economic freedom of those individuals. According to James Madison and Alexander Hamilton, that was best done by alleviating "faction," that is, controlling for the potential disruption of "aroused communities" (Madison et al., 1961, p. 130). According to the primary architects of the Constitution, that meant "keeping people apart," an expression the French philosopher, Jean-Jacque Rousseau, called the "first maxim of modern politics" (Kemmis, 1992, p. 18). The idea was to keep citizens focused on their economic role, on making a living, by limiting their political role. For Madison and Hamilton, a strong centralized authority elected by a subset of the population once every two, four, or six years was the way to accomplish that goal. But, on the other hand, if a state is a collection of mutually interested communities, the government must be a vehicle for ensuring that decisions are made at the lowest possible level (e.g., the ward or township). Initially, this latter view won the day. America's leaders, victorious in the overthrow of feudalism, set up a government called the Articles of Confederation and Perpetual Union. States would govern themselves, and they would only act as one in the interest of defense and certain trade matters. All other decision-making was supposed to occur at the local level.

Community-centered vision of statehood was anything but perpetual, as it only lasted for six years. Scholars agree that a development called "Shays's Rebellion" provided the largest catalyst to reject the community-oriented version of statehood in favor of a state defined as a multitude of free-acting individuals. Shays Rebellion was the example used by Madison and Hamilton of an "aroused community," and it demonstrated the necessity of "keeping people apart." Daniel Shays was a west Massachusetts farmer who had served as a captain in the American Revolution. After a Boston-dominated legislature passed a law stipulating that all debts must be repaid in gold or silver coin, as opposed to payment made in the form of farm produce, farmers revolted. They descended on courthouses to break up bankruptcy proceedings the law quickly created. Boston bankers and merchants were furious. They appealed to Congress under the Articles to put an army in the field and crush the farmer rebellion. Congress actually complied, sending out emissaries to the various states asking for specified sums of money from each, as well as men to serve in what would be a hastily constructed army. But that's where it ended. States located far from Massachusetts were not concerned with the troubles of Boston merchants, and they refused to send either money or men.

Their hopes dashed, the Boston merchants pooled their resources, created their own army, and sent them to the west end of the state to defeat the farmers. The merchant-paid army clashed with farmers near Springfield, but it was not much of a fight. Six farmers died, the rest were dispersed. Shays's Rebellion was over, but the move to replace the Articles was just getting started. Commercial interests across all states seized on the Rebellion as an opportunity to create a new form of government. A convention was called, and each state sent representatives to Philadelphia during the summer of 1787, charged with "amending the Articles." But that didn't happen. Instead they threw them out and created a blueprint for a brand new type of government premised on a conception of a state as a multitude of free-acting individuals. That blueprint became known as the Constitution. When a complete draft was available at summer's end, widespread debate ensued. In the end, supporters of a community-oriented government acquiesced when the Constitution authors agreed to ten amendments that became known as the "Bill of Rights."

A European Prelude

Embedded in that political drama at the end of the eighteenth century was a rural-urban schism that had roots back in England, a schism that came across the Atlantic with the earliest colonists. It was there when Daniel Shays and other farmers challenged the merchants and bankers of Boston. The schism is largely understood to be a clash of economic interests between a new mechanized, finance-dependent industrialism and an old community-dependent agrarianism. A combination of dramatic advances in science, metallurgy, and navigation gave rise to industrial factory production, banking and insurance houses, and highly skilled craftsmanship—all urban developments. Fortunes were made, although those who made them remained outside of the age-old feudal power structure. They had money, but they had no hereditary titles that would enable them to significantly participate in the creation of legislation or policy. The feudal structure was profoundly rural, not just in England but throughout western Europe. And that was a problem.

A brief example highlights the difficulty. England became the world's leading textile producer on the strength of innovative industrialized looms. This increased the demand for wool. To accommodate, Parliament passed countless "enclosure" bills that made it easy for landowners to enclose common neighborhood areas and thereafter intensify wool production. "Commons," as these areas were called, had been used by all in the immediate community. Most serfs in feudal England (and elsewhere in Europe) were not able to survive without the commons, where for generations their families had grazed their livestock and grown their food, and thus many drifted to the new industrial cities in search of work. Enclosure, then, was the first of many urban blows to rural community vitality (a process that inspired Oliver Goldsmith's famous poem, "The Deserted Village"). But if it were just a matter of dispossessing peasants and eroding their small hamlets, the circumstances might have been deemed insignificant. It went farther.

Industrialists, naturally, looked to maximize their profits. Keeping the cost of labor low was and always has been a part of the industrial worldview. During the eighteenth and nineteenth centuries, factory owners only paid workers enough to keep them returning to work each day. That meant they needed to be paid enough to feed themselves and their families and keep some kind of roof over their heads. Recognizing this, the rural title-holding aristocracy who made their living via agriculture raised the price of grain and foodstuffs, a move that forced factory owners to raise wages for their workers. This infuriated urban bankers and factory owners who responded by negotiating trade agreements with the United States to bring cheaper grain into England, so they could keep labor costs low. This, in turn, infuriated the rural aristocracy who, controlling Parliament, passed what became known as the "corn laws," forbidding the importation of food from the United States.

It was an intense struggle. Urban industrial interests had the support of city newspapers, who lauded the industrial classes as "captains of industry" while simultaneously chastising rural interests for "living in the past," for being "backward," for holding on to the foolish trappings of a waning feudal era. One of a very few agrarian journalists, William Cobbett, remarked that he had witnessed that transition in the status of rural dwellers during his own lifetime. Writing in 1830 Cobbett remarked,

> By degrees, beginning about 50 years ago the industrious part of the community, particularly those who create every useful thing by their labour, have been spoken of by everyone possessing the power to oppress them in any degree in just the same manner in which we speak of the animals which compose the stock upon a farm. This is not the manner in which the forefathers of us, the common people, were treated.

Identifying the switch from the use of the reference "the commons of England" to such phrases as "the lower orders," frequently used by David Hume and countless other urban elites, Cobbett blamed "tax-devourers, bankers, brewers, and monopolists of every sort." He noted further that one could hear these sorts of insults not only from the wealthy in English cities but also from "their clerks, from shopkeepers and waiters, and from the fribbles stuck up behind the counter" (Hammond & Hammond, 1912, p. 211). In other words, it quickly became culturally acceptable to admonish rural dwellers as substandard.

Rural Versus Urban in the Early United States

It is worth another look at the competing worldviews that defined the early history of the United States. If the state is perceived to be a multitude of free-acting individuals, and the primary political concern is the establishment and protection of economic freedom, the question of education for the nation's youth is easily settled. Each free-acting individual should decide whether or not to send their child to school. On the other hand, if the state is perceived to be a collection of mutually interested communities, and the primary political concern is widely distributing a voice in the decisions that affect citizens, the question of educating the nation's youth is not so easily settled. As Thomas Jefferson argued, if the people were not prepared to participate wisely in political matters, the answer was to educate them, not keep them out of the political arena (Lipscomb & Bergh, 1903).

The question of education further illuminates a fundamental difference between the nation's first nonfeudal government, the Articles of Confederation, and the second attempt, the Constitution. Although its duration was short, the most significant contribution of the Articles government was the passage of what came to be called the "Northwest Ordinance," a legislative blueprint for adding western territory to the United States. In that legislation, provision was made for one section of land out of each plotted township to become a revenue source for schools, since, as the ordinance stated, "schools and the means of education shall forever be encouraged" (Mattingly & Stevens, 1987, p. 1).

By contrast, the word "education" does not appear in the Constitution. That was deemed to be a private matter, although advocates for free school systems were numerous in the founding generation, including the likes of Noah Webster, Thomas Jefferson, Benjamin Rush, and Robert Coram. Obviously, they did not get their way. It would be fifty years after the Constitution was ratified before states, one by one, began to create free school systems, and then only in the north.

Education, of course, is just one example of the kinds of difficulties created by a nation divided over what should constitute its primary political objective. Throughout our first fifty years, Alexander Hamilton's national bank was a lightning rod of sorts between the two camps. Merchants hated the fact that each state coordinated its own monetary system, a circumstance that made doing business across state borders difficult. To ease that burden, Hamilton, the nation's first secretary of the treasury, created the national bank patterned after the national bank of England. As the nation's fledgling industrial interests applauded, rural residents fumed. The bank was viewed as a tool for industrial interests to maximize their profit at the expense of the nation's farmers, who believed a national bank would undermine the state banks they depended on to finance their farm operations.

On two occasions during the first half of the nineteenth century, rural voters were able to elect presidents who vowed to put rural interests first, and that meant immediately closing the national bank. The first occasion was the election of Thomas Jefferson in 1800, and the second was the election of Andrew Jackson in 1828. Both men closed the bank, only to have it reopened by their successors. Less so in 1800, but certainly by 1828, the kinds of derogatory references to rural residents that Cobbett noted in England were alive and well in the United States. Dignified urban elites were mortified by the rural dwellers who tipped the scales for Jackson, some of whom showed up for the inaugural ball in coon-skin hats. Playing off Jackson's nickname, "Old Hickory," his supporters came to be known as "hicks."[2] It was an insult with enormous staying power, as it is used routinely in the United States to this day.

The Free School Era

Jackson's ascendancy demonstrated that the built-in tension between competing visions of what constitutes a state would never be resolved in perpetuity. Given the right circumstances, the contrary vision can enjoy a renaissance. The pendulum, in other words, can swing from the perception that drove the creation of the Constitution to the perception that drove the creation of the Articles. The evidence suggests that this is indeed what took place during the antebellum period, the years between 1830 and 1860.

As Jackson closed the bank, a new generation of free school advocates enjoyed success utilizing the Tenth Amendment, which stipulates that any issue not specified in the Constitution is a matter for the various states. Horace Mann, in Massachusetts, led the way in 1836 with the creation of a free school system, and other states quickly followed suit. But it didn't end there. This was Alexis de Tocqueville's America, put on display for the world in his famous study of democracy. This was the era of universal male suffrage and as early as 1848, in Seneca Falls, women organized to demand a political voice as well. People across the country came together asking for common schools, prison reform, parks, and, in the north, the abolition of slavery. This was the era of rural, "log cabin" presidents. One historian, Christopher Clark, refers to this free school era as America's "communitarian moment," when the vision that drove the creation of the Articles was once again dominant (Clark, 1995).

The catalysts to the creation of free schools have been analyzed in great detail. The enculturation of immigrants was deemed to be a major factor (Catholic immigrants in particular), and there was also a profound and pronounced inter-Protestant struggle for denominational hegemony, a circumstance that led to a marked overrepresentation of Presbyterian and Congregationalist ministers heading state departments of education. But with all of that came a common curricular thrust: prepare Americans for the burden of self-government. Carl Kaestle used an often-heard nineteenth-century description of schools as "pillars of the republic" for the title of his award-winning history of the free school era (Kaestle, 1983). Noticeably absent in the discourse surrounding schools during the period 1830–60 was whether they should function to advance the economic interests of the nation or the economic interests of individuals. In other words, the common school era was not created so that the nation's youth could acquire employable skills to be used as adults, but so the nation's youth could responsibly shoulder a political role as adults. Common schools in the United States were created to advance the political vision of a nation composed of mutually beneficial communities, where decisions are made as close to those affected by them as possible.

The Pendulum Swings Again

It did not last. One of the world's most influential books was published at the very end of the communitarian era. Charles Darwin published *The Origin of Species* in 1859. Darwin, of course, was a biologist. He made no attempt to apply his theory of evolution to differing "races" within humankind, although there were plenty of others ready to do just that. Herbert Spencer in England and William Graham Sumner in the United States became prophets announcing the gospel of Social Darwinism, defining life as a struggle for survival, a struggle inevitably won by the "fittest." Said Spencer, "I am simply carrying out the views of Mr. Darwin in their application to the human race" (1882, p. 418). To this day, most Americans familiar with the phrase believe that "survival of the fittest" came from the pen of Charles Darwin. Not so.

It is difficult to overemphasize the popularity of Social Darwinism, coming as it did on the heels of the emancipation of millions of former slaves and amid a concerted attempt to sequester

The Bloomsbury Handbook of Rural Education in the United States

Native Americans on ever-smaller reservations. Spencer gave lectures across the United States and became something equivalent to a rock star, as huge crowds cheered loudly at the conclusion of his lectures. There was an obvious self-congratulatory feel to the gospel of Social Darwinism, and it played well with White Americans. It doesn't take much critical inquiry into these circumstances to see the way this new intellectual development—evolutionary theory applied to the races of humankind—meshed with the vision of statehood as a multitude of free-acting individuals. Life was an economic struggle, and thus a legitimate government focuses on maintaining and protecting the economic freedom of individuals. Over the last quarter of the nineteenth century, the pendulum had moved away from a rural agrarian worldview and was back on the side of urban industrialism. Still, there was heavy resistance.

Bankers jumped on the opportunity in the postbellum period to demand a return to the gold standard, looking to cash in on loans made in dollars worth 50 cents during the war years, when inflation was rampant, and taking repayment with dollars worth 100 cents after the war. Monetary policy dominated postwar politics as a result, and it intensified an already indisputable urban versus rural split. This was America's "populist" moment, where farmers came together with small-town merchants to challenge the power of huge national corporations like railroads, implement manufacturers, and grain trusts—and, as always, the loan practices of the nation's banking industry. Most historians agree that the contest came to a head with the presidential election of 1896. The candidates personified the larger worldview split. Republicans nominated an Ohio industrialist by the name of William McKinley, while Democrats (and the smaller Populist Party) nominated the attorney and agrarian spokesperson from Nebraska, William Jennings Bryan. Bryan campaigned on expanding the supply of money by coining silver, arguing that the nation's farmers must not be hung upon a "cross of gold."

McKinley won comfortably. Historians frequently point to this election as the first introduction of corporate money into the nation's electoral process. McKinley's campaign manager, businessman Marcus Hanna, secured almost seven million dollars to advance McKinley's candidacy, opposed to a mere $340,000 collected for Bryan. There were many reports of workers being told that they would be fired if Bryan won the presidency—including at McKinley's own factory. The Populist Party never recovered from the 1896 defeat. Historian Lawrence Goodwin claimed that after that point, the nation's farmers would never again constitute a significant political bloc (Goodwin, 1976). In short, the vision of a state as a multitude of free-acting individuals, fueled by the popularity of Social Darwinism, won a large victory. The community-oriented vision of a state receded significantly in the wake of Bryan's defeat.

Shifting the Goals for Public Education

Born amid America's communitarian moment, the nation's public schools sought to provide a basic education to outfit citizens for the burden of self-government. That end goal was consistent with the popular conception of a state as a collection of mutually interested communities, where ordinary Americans could exercise a voice in the decisions that affect them. But that end goal for public education did not last. It receded with the larger vision of what constitutes a state. In its place, an end goal that meshed with life as an individual economic struggle started to take hold. By the 1890s, "manual training" began to appear in education journals, with the argument that free-acting individuals required school preparation for their economic struggle.

History of Rural Educational Policy

Curiously, an ex-slave would play a major role in the shift of the nation's primary educational goal. Booker T. Washington created a manual training and normal institute in Alabama where former male slaves could learn basic trades, and females could learn to be teachers for Black schools across the South. Arguing in 1895 that Blacks and Whites should be "one as the hand" in terms of economic struggle, but as "separate as fingers" in all things social, Washington became a hit overnight (Harlan, 1974, p. 220). Northern philanthropists showered Tuskegee with money, and Washington became an honored guest of presidents. The idea that schools should outfit the nation's youth for economic struggle, for the economic roles they would play as adults, spread by leaps and bounds. In 1902 William Torrey Harris, the US Commissioner of Education, remarked that "the Booker T. Washington solution applies to the downtrodden of all races without reference to color" (Curti, 1935, p. 209).

By 1917 Congress stepped squarely into the realm of educational policy by passing the Smith-Hughes Act, a law that generated funds for the construction of "shops" and "home economics" classrooms in high schools all across the country. According to longtime Harvard president Charles Eliot, such classrooms were needed to identify "evident and probable destinies" of children and give them each an education appropriate to that destiny (Preskill, 1989, pp. 333–54). The idea that schools should provide a common curricular experience, or one common to the citizens of a republic, was rejected as out of date. In fact, what was needed was not common schools but "comprehensive" schools capable of delivering instruction in differentiated curricular tracks that were in step with the evolutionary gradations of humankind. It was a given, for instance, that minorities, be they Black, Hispanic, or Native, would require a strictly vocational curriculum. This led to the construction of "tech high schools" in the larger cities of the nation—many of which still exist, although the worst excesses of a strictly vocational curriculum, such as courses in shoe shining, have been eliminated. The "one best system," identified and described by historian David Tyack (1972), was coming into being. What would be the role of rural schools within that system? They were not forgotten.

Rural Schools in the Era of "Scientific Management"

The biological theory ostensibly supporting Social Darwinism gave rise to the view of society as something alive, like an organism, with people equating to the cells of the organism. In hindsight, of course, such a proposition sounds incredibly naïve, but at the turn of the twentieth century, this view came with all the backing of scientific consensus. If humans were analogous to the cells of an organism, then people had a particular function to perform. If the cells of an organism are not fulfilling their function, the organism becomes sick and eventually dies. Leading intellectuals at the nation's universities therefore began to look to the nation's schools to play a critical role. Schools were needed to identify the role youth would play as adults, and then tailor an education conducive to that role. Curiously, an engineer became a kind of intellectual resource for the task facing the nation's schools.

Frederick Winslow Taylor became internationally famous for his contribution to industrial efficiency, *Principles of Scientific Management*, published in 1911. Taylor argued that work needed to be broken into a series of tasks, as with an assembly line, where workers had only one or two tasks to perform, over and over. In a manner of just a year, 1912, Joseph Mayer Rice published *Scientific Management in Education*, applying Taylor's principles to the educational endeavor. To be efficient, schools would move students through school as if on an assembly line, from grade to grade. Even the construction of schools began to emulate the look of industrial factories, with factory bells moving students from one room to the next. As Stanford's Ellwood Cubberley put it,

> Our schools are, in a sense, factories, in which the raw products (children) are to be shaped and fashioned into products to meet the various demands of life. The specifications for manufacturing come from the demands of twentieth-century civilization, and it is the business of the school to build its pupils according to the specifications laid down. (Cubberley, 1916, pp. 337–8)

Rural schools looked nothing like factories. They did not operate like factories. They were not efficient. Rural schools became a part of the "rural problem," a phrase that gained surprising currency during the first decade of the new century (Fiske, 1913). But what was the problem? On one hand, there was the continuing cultural legacy of rural being equated to something substandard: hicks, country bumpkins, rednecks, and so forth. But new intellectual developments added another layer of concern regarding the countryside and those who lived there. It was connected to the incredible wave of immigration that defined the first decade of the twentieth century. Each year of that decade, millions of immigrants, most from southern and eastern Europe, came to the United States. Coupled with this development was an already identifiable demographic trend of rural youth leaving the countryside for life and careers in the city. Fully steeped in the tenets of Social Darwinism, the nation's first generation of rural sociologists believed that it was the "fittest" who were leaving the countryside, thereby creating a legacy of mediocrity in rural society. A Social Darwinian analysis, Wilbert Anderson's *The Country Town: A Study of Rural Evolution* (1906), clearly spoke of the dangers of the new urban industrial order. Said Anderson, rural communities were "vital parts of the economic organism of the world." Their health was in jeopardy, however, if, as he predicted, the "first effect" of new farm machinery was "the departure of the farmer's boy from the home." This was particularly harmful, he argued, because it is "the cream being skimmed off" (Anderson, 1906, p. 30). In other words, the "most fit" were leaving for the city.

Sociologist Warren Wilson argued that rural America was "predominantly older colonial stock" that needed to be preserved for the good of the country (Wilson, 1995, p. 18). University of Wisconsin sociologist Edward Allsworth Ross (1916) argued that the "folk depletion" caused by talented rural youth leaving the countryside left the farming areas of the Midwest "fished-out ponds populated chiefly by bullheads and suckers." According to Ross, this folk depletion meant that America was committing "race suicide" because the superior intelligence of Anglo-Saxon farm kids was corrupted when mixed in the city with the less intelligent peoples of southern and eastern Europe (Ross, 1916). Cornell University's highly lauded rural sociologist Liberty Hyde Bailey (1911) argued that the rural problem was how to keep "on our farms a civilization in full harmony with the best American ideals" (p. 24). Many educators embraced the verdict of the sociologists. According to Mabel Carney (1912), a leading rural education specialist at Teachers College, Columbia University, "the rural problem is how to keep a standard people" in the countryside (p. 230). Stanford University's education dean Ellwood Cubberley complained of the "non-Anglo-Teutonics" immigrating with the intention to farm in the United States (Tyack, 1972, p. 13). Anne Gibson Winfield (2007) cited Cubberley's claim that "east European immigrants were 'of a very different sort' and were 'wholly without Anglo-Saxon conceptions of righteousness, liberty, law, order, public decency, and government.'" Cubberley argued that these types of immigrants would corrupt American politics and "dilute" the population as a whole (Winfield, 2007, p. 42).

The imminent threat of immigrants to the overall health of American society, theorized as the "organism" that was American society, meant keeping a "standard people" on the farms doing what the cells of the organism are supposed to do. President Theodore Roosevelt was said to have been an avid follower of Edward Allsworth Ross and fully believed in his concepts of "folk depletion" and "race suicide." As a consequence, Roosevelt created the Commission on Country Life in 1907, headed by Liberty Hyde Bailey, to solve the "rural problem." Most of the individuals who served on the commission were urban dwellers, a fact that created some consternation among rural people who felt stung by the suggestion that they were substandard. The commission made many recommendations for improving rural life, but the greatest number focused on the rural school. Some were curricular, for example, advocating nature studies and pledging allegiance to rural life and living. Others aimed at structural change in keeping with the growing popularity of efficiency-minded scientific management. First on that list was rural school consolidation.

The Triumph of the Urban Industrial Worldview

Describing the first couple of decades of public education in the twentieth century, historian Raymond Callahan (1962) claimed that it devolved into a "cult of efficiency," where educational goals were routinely sacrificed to the demands of business procedures emanating from the legacy of Frederick Winslow Taylor. Much of this was directed at urban schools dealing with ever larger numbers of students. But rural schools were not forgotten. Looming large in this regard was Ellwood Cubberley.

Born in rural Indiana, Ellwood Cubberley was one of the talented rural youth who left the countryside for the city. He became a teacher and then administrator in San Diego, California, schools before joining a tiny two-person teacher education department at Stanford University. Recognizing the need for an advanced degree, Cubberley left Stanford for Teachers College at Columbia University in 1905, where he picked up a doctoral degree. Cubberley then returned to Stanford and in 1917 became dean of their growing School of Education. He remained in that position until 1933.

Cubberley was enamored with the implications of Social Darwinism and Taylor's scientific management. He was convinced that Ross was right about the cityward drain of talented rural youth and, further, the damage this might do to the health of the organism that was American society. In Cubberley's mind, in order to ameliorate those circumstances, a socially efficient school system was needed, and to create it, well-prepared school administrators, in particular, were required. Accomplishing this goal became his mission in life. He created the nation's first curriculum for the professional preparation of school administrators at Stanford, and it was quickly replicated all across the country.

In 1914, convinced that the rural population needed saving to ensure the overall health of American society, Cubberley wrote his rural education treatise: *Rural Life and Education: A Study of the Rural-School Problem as a Phase of the Rural Life Problem*. The great task facing the nation was to "urbanize our rural schools." Said Cubberley:

The rural-school problem has become so complex that the average teacher scarcely knows what to do, or how to deal with the situation which confronts her; while the absolute inadequacy of the rural school of to-day to meet the new educational and social needs of to-morrow is evident to any one who has studied the problem. The situation calls for educational insight and leadership of a high order, and for a reorganization of rural education under some authority of larger jurisdiction and knowledge than that of the district–school trustee. (Cubberley, 1914, p. 95)

Further, rural schools needed professional expertise. "The whole rural-life problem, has now become too complex to be solved by local effort alone, and nothing short of a reorganization of rural education, along good educational and administrative lines, will meet the needs of the present and of the future" (Cubberley, 1914, p. 103). For Cubberley, professionally trained administrators who understood that consolidation was the key to rural school improvement were the solution to the rural problem:

There is no business or educational reason for the continuance of so many small, poorly equipped, inefficiently managed, and relatively expensive rural schools. The needs of rural people could be much better served, much better schools for their children could be provided, and not infrequently a financial economy could be effected as well, if the long-outgrown district system of organization and maintenance were in large part superseded by a more rational and more business-like system of school organization and maintenance . . . a reorganization must be effected before material, general, or rapid progress can be made in redirecting and revitalizing rural education. (Cubberley, 1914, pp. 224–5)

School consolidation was weaved into a scientific argument legitimated by Social Darwinism and scientific management. The self-evident wisdom of consolidation became a part of Cubberley's curriculum for school administrators, and it was replicated quickly in universities all across the country.

Conclusion

Casual observers are aware of the fact that the history of twentieth-century public education was largely defined by widespread rural school consolidation. Starting here and there as early as the 1890s, it continued to be a piece of self-evident wisdom taught as part of the curriculum studied by future public school administrators. A close reading of the many books published in the wake of the Country Life Commission reveals that the perceived inadequacies regarding curriculum and instruction were always anecdotal. Empirical studies, the few that were undertaken, mainly focused on the schoolhouse itself, and which amenities it had or did not have.

It would not be overstating the case to suggest that the proposition that consolidating rural schools was one and the same as improving them could aptly be labeled "Cubberley's law." It was accepted, seemingly, without question, if the sheer number of consolidations that took place in the United States is any measure. And so it seemed to two policy researchers who, during the first decade of the twenty-first century, began to ask why so much consolidation took place during the last century without any substantial research base to suggest it was a good idea. To find out, Christopher Berry and David West conducted their own study of rural school consolidation (Berry & West,

History of Rural Educational Policy

2010). They went back to the middle years of the twentieth century and traced the lives of male students (during those years females frequently never entered the paid workforce) from high school on, looking at college attendance, college completion, test scores, and lifetime earnings. What they discovered surprised almost everyone. While students from larger consolidated schools had slightly higher test scores, students from smaller unconsolidated schools did better in terms of college attendance, college completion, and lifetime earnings.

The Berry and West study marked the first substantive empirical challenge to Cubberley's law. More followed. Other scholars began to ask whether arguments about financial savings through consolidation were, in fact, accurate. Several studies revealed that these claims, too, were most often unfulfilled. An Indiana study grabbed the headlines in *Newsweek*, in 2010. With respect to the claims of improving student outcomes and revenue savings, in Indiana, "school consolidation fails on both counts" (Dokoupil, 2010, p. 58).[3]

Rural educational history has been bound together with larger perceptions about the worth of rural people, whether they be hicks, "bullheads and suckers," or, on the other end of the spectrum, "Anglo-Teutonic" or "old colonial stock." The treatment of rural Americans has been tied to the larger contest of worldviews regarding what constitutes a state and the way that contest has oscillated between the support of urban industrial and rural communitarian interests. Those interests gave birth to intellectual movements like scientific management and Social Darwinism, both of which played a large role in the history of rural education in the United States. In the context of large historical forces, of long-term struggles between competing economic interests, it is easier to understand how rural school consolidation might be viewed as synonymous with school improvement. But it does not change the fact that rural communities have suffered as a result. A better future for rural schools likely awaits America's re-embrace of a communitarian vision—a conception of a state as a collection of mutually interested communities. The pendulum always swings back.

3

Toward a Rural Critical Policy Analysis

Devon Brenner

In the spring of 2020, schools across the United States closed their doors due to the threat of the Covid-19 virus. Classrooms sat empty, and teachers began offering, or trying to offer, remote learning options for students staying at home. The US Department Education waived assessment and accountability requirements and states adapted existing policies regarding assessment, graduation requirements, remote learning options, and teacher certification in different ways in response to the crisis.

Media coverage attempted to document the immediate impact of stay-at-home orders. School closures quickly highlighted the importance of schools in rural communities. Families and communities struggled with the lack of childcare that schools normally provide. Child advocates raised concerns about rural hunger and poverty and pointed out the importance of schools as sources of meals and social supports. Some rural districts figured out how to deliver meals to hungry children in their districts, but others could not afford the transportation costs and abandoned the programs shortly after beginning.

School closures also had an economic impact on rural communities. Without traffic to and from the school, small restaurants and gas stations faced lost revenue and threats of closure. Many districts continued to pay teachers and administrators, but hourly employees (e.g., bus drivers and custodians) experienced fewer hours or a total loss of employment, causing further economic impact for rural communities. Shelter-in-place and remote learning policies also exposed the already well-documented disparities in access to high-speed broadband internet in rural communities and inequalities in access to resources.

A Coming Era of Educational Change and New Policy

Covid-19 is an unprecedented challenge that raises questions about the ways that schools are organized, operated, and funded (Mukhopadhyay, 2020; Superville, 2020b). Scholars frame these events as the *new normal* (Anderson, 2020; Mills, 2020) likely to change K-12 education permanently (Hickey, 2020; Hopper, 2020). School closures, competency-based education, school/family relationships, and assessment practices are all predicted to change (Hargreaves, 2020; Harris, 2020).

It is likely that many state and federal policies are likely to be drafted and enacted in response to the crisis. As is typical with new policies, some will stick, and some will be revised or abandoned. It is likely that the next five years will be a time of profound experimentation and variation. Schools will return to a post–pandemic new normal. Moving forward, local, state, and federal governments may find that learning from home is advantageous and more affordable, or that the appeal of technology-based solutions is compelling, or that experiments with new school schedules, smaller class sizes, or the cancellation of high-stakes testing are practices worth continuing.

There is some precedent for rapid change in education policy that lasts even after the precipitating crisis is over. The devastation of Hurricane Katrina, for example, changed policies in New Orleans that upended the entire city school system (Harris, 2020; Osborne, 2020). Because so many children and families were displaced and so many schools impacted, the city could no longer sustain the neighborhood-based school system in place prior to the crisis. This paved the way for new policies that separated school attendance from student addresses and opened up the door for a citywide implementation of charter schools. Fifteen years later, these citywide policy changes are still in place, in spite of the fact that the city has returned to pre–Katrina population levels and in spite of ongoing concerns about demonstrated negative consequences of a market-driven school model for all but the White minority (Dixson et al., 2015).

J. D. Johnson and C. B. Howley (2015) suggest that the unique characteristics of rural places, including geography, transportation, funding, teacher shortages, local knowledge, access to resources, and the diversity of rural places, are salient issues when considering education policies. The rest of the chapters in this handbook explore the contexts and circumstances of rural education, demonstrating the unique strengths, affordances, and concerns of rural schools. It is because of these characteristics that enactment of a particular policy proposal may or may not benefit rural schools and their communities. The characteristics of rural places that J. D. Johnson and C. B. Howley (2015) identify are a useful starting point for scholars and advocates' work to analyze rural educational policy. Four key questions can frame policy inquiries:

- Does the policy assume all places are the same?
- What is revealed by a careful examination of the geographic distribution of the policy?
- Does the policy explicitly address a rurality?
- How does the policy, or the policy analysis, define rural?

Rural Policy Analysis

In this chapter, I outline a framework for rural policy analysis—guided by the questions above that education scholars and advocates can ask about policies specific to rural schools' needs and concerns. This framework builds on the work of others who have raised questions about the impact of state and federal policies for rural schools and communities (e.g., Arnold et al., 2007; Eppley, 2009; Koziol et al., 2015; Showalter et al., 2019; Tieken, 2017). For each question, I provide examples from this previous work to highlight the potential of each question to assess the impact of policy proposals for rural contexts during and after the pandemic era of education policymaking.

The Bloomsbury Handbook of Rural Education in the United States

Assumption of Place Neutrality

The first question we need to ask when examining an education policy is: *Does the policy assume all places are the same?* Most education policy presumes to be "place neutral" in that place or geography is not explicitly addressed and the policy is intended to be applied the same across locations. One-size-fits-all policies presume that a program will work equally well no matter where it is applied, that a regulation can and will be followed in the same way regardless of the location, or that a formula for distribution of funds will be equitable across all types of places.

An assumption of place neutrality often disadvantages rural schools. When policymakers assume that all places have the same resources, needs, interests, and capacity, policies can and will fail. Take, for example, critiques of the Highly Qualified Teacher provisions of the No Child Left Behind Act of 2001 (NCLB). A major component of NCLB was the requirement that classrooms be staffed with teachers who were "highly qualified" to teach. NCLB defined teaching qualifications as having full licensure and a degree or a certain number of credits and/or passing a test in the content area(s) to be taught. The Highly Qualified Teachers provision seemed, on the surface, to make sense—teachers *should* know the content that they teach and it might make sense that rural schools should be encouraged (or required) to make an effort to ensure that teachers are prepared and knowledgeable in their content areas. In practice, however, this place-neutral policy was detrimental for rural schools (Eppley, 2009). When NCLB was proposed and passed, it was challenging (often impossible) for rural districts to identify and hire teachers with content-specific training—particularly for smaller and more remote districts. More importantly, what makes a rural teacher highly qualified or effective is often difficult to quantify and likely to be context- or place-specific (Eppley, 2009). NCLB prioritized content area coursework as the definition of teacher effectiveness. However, teachers' expectations for students, knowledge of local contexts or languages, ability to build relationships, and other affective characteristics may be especially important in rural schools, and certainly make for effective teaching. As Eppley (2009) argued,

> the "neutrality" of the provision's assumptions are especially problematic in rural schools. The unique challenges facing rural schools—including staffing and retention, funding, curriculum, and enrollment—make a legislated, uniform determination of what constitutes a highly qualified teacher more complicated than the language of the provision suggests. (p. 2)

As these and other critiques (e.g., Gagnon, 2016; J. D. Johnson & C. B. Howley, 2015) point out, policy is not place neutral, and policies that assume that all places have the same needs, affordances, challenges, and resources are likely to miss the mark in rural contexts.

Distributive Analysis

A second question to ask about a policy proposal is: *What is revealed by a careful examination of the geographic distribution of the policy?* An analysis of geographic distribution evaluates policies based on geospatial criteria with a focus on whether resources, benefits, or burdens of a particular policy are equitably distributed across places or types of places. Mapping is often a cornerstone of distributive analysis, connecting geospatial data to other data sets to draw conclusions about policies and their impact (Butler & Sinclair, 2020; Morrison et al., 2017; Tate, 2008). For example, the Center on Rural Innovation has linked over 400 public data sets through its Rural Opportunity Map[1] with a focus on economic opportunity. Users can access or build maps to visualize the location of schools, distance from higher education institutions, access to public transportation, and a variety of health indicators. Every few years, the Rural School and Community Trust aggregates data and compares states on a number of social and education indicators, ranking states in order of the greatest need (i.e., for better policies and practices to address rural challenges; Showalter et al., 2019). The *Why Rural Matters* report (Showalter et al., 2019) is a widely cited source for documenting the challenges of rural education and inequitable distribution of educational resources and social and academic outcomes both within and across rural places.

Distributive analysis often serves to highlight the inequitable distribution of resources baked into policy decisions. For example, critiques of the federal Title I funding formula have shown that the way the formula is written disadvantages rural schools. The federal Title I program provides funding to schools that serve children from low-income families. The formula heavily weights the overall number (rather than the percentage) of students from low-income families and has been critiqued for disproportionally directing funds to large, urban school districts that serve many students overall (Formula Fairness Campaign, 2015; Tieken, 2017). In their critique of the Title I funding formula, Strange and colleagues (2009) compared Title I funding for rural and nonrural schools in Pennsylvania and found that urban schools received more money per student than rural schools with the same and, in some cases, even higher poverty rates. They concluded that the formula's method of counting and weighting students led to "systemic discrimination against smaller districts at all poverty levels" (Strange et al., 2009, p. 6).

These and many other examples demonstrate that metrocentric policymaking has led to inequitable access to high-speed broadband internet (Public Knowledge, 2019), teacher shortages (Latterman & Steffes, 2017), and overidentification of rural schools as low performing (Beck & Shoffstall, 2005; Jimerson, 2005b). Distributive analysis not only points out that in many cases, policy implementation does not just fail to address rural contexts, but that metrocentric policymaking "unfairly targets poor rural schools" (Beck & Schoffstall, 2005, p. 1).

Distributive analysis that connects geospatial data to proposed changes can be a powerful tool for policy analysis and, if conducted before policies are enacted, can help rural advocates provide policymakers with a concrete picture of the places that will benefit from, or be negatively impacted by, a proposed change.

Rural Salience
The third question asks, "Does the policy explicitly address rurality?" The vast majority of state and federal policies do not explicitly address and often disadvantage rural schools and districts. However, some policies are intended to address a concern or alleviate a need that is specific to rural education settings.

Shortened school weeks are an example of a rural-focused policy. An increasing number of states have changed school calendar requirements in order to allow districts to implement a shortened school week. It was presumed that a move from five days per week to four slightly longer days would result in significant savings in costs for transportation, heating and cooling, and other operational expenses. However, in states where the four day school week has been implemented, cost savings have often not been realized (Griffith, 2011). Despite this, the four-day school week continues to expand in rural places across the United States. Every state west of the Mississippi River (except Arkansas) allows and has at least one school district utilizing the four-day school week (Heyward, 2018). According to Turner et al. (2017), a state policy that allows districts to choose whether and how to implement a shortened school week can be beneficial for rural schools beyond any cost savings by helping to address critical challenges in teacher recruitment and retention and additional three-day weekends appeal to some rural teachers and offer other benefits including increased time for professional learning and increased teacher morale. In this way, a policy to allow districts to choose whether to adopt four-day school week recognizes the expertise of local administrators and needs of rural places.

However, a stated rural focus is not always meaningful or sufficient to address the needs of rural schools. For example, at the federal level, the Every Student Succeeds Act of 2015 (ESSA), the current iteration of the Elementary and Secondary Act of 1965 (ESEA), seemingly addresses the needs of rural schools more than previous versions of ESEA, including NCLB. Brenner (2016) described the many ways that ESSA, on its surface, expands attention to rural education contexts. For example, ESSA explicitly specifies that most competitive grant programs authorized under the law must ensure some portion of funded grants are awarded to rural schools or districts—with different criteria and requirements for each program. Including language about the geographic distribution of awards was intended to address critiques of education grant programs that disproportionately awarded grants to larger and more urban districts (AASA, The School Superintendents Association, 2017; Yettick et al., 2014). However, school leaders in rural districts, with smaller administrative staff and limited grant-writing capacity, often do not attempt to write, let alone win, competitive grants. Mandating geographic representation in grant-making represents a legislative attempt to ensure equitable distribution across geographic contexts into the design of competitive grant programs. However, while the legislation may have language intended to ensure geographic diversity within the range of recipients of grant programs, in the end, this language does little to address the needs of rural schools. ESSA increases the federal government's reliance on competitive grant funding to distribute federal funding to schools—directing more funds to schools that have the capacity and infrastructure to participate in grant competitions. According to AASA (2017), the schools that might most benefit from research on field-initiated interventions, school leader recruitment and support, or history and civics education programs are unlikely to apply and win. AASA argues that "competitive allocations exacerbate the resources gap between rural school districts and urban systems" (p. 8) and that the language of ESSA that attempted to address the problem of equitable distribution of funds within particular grant programs did little to address the overall needs of schools (urban, rural, and suburban) for adequate resources to teach all students.

Defining Rural

The fourth question of rural policy analysis is: *How does the policy, or the policy analysis, define rural?* How rural is defined and operationalized is an important aspect of rural policy analysis. As has been well documented, rural is hard to define (see Longhurst, Chapter 1, this volume). As a theoretical construct rurality, and what makes a place, district, or school rural, is difficult to quantify and codify. Geography and population density cannot be separated from sociocultural, political, economic, and historical characteristics of places (Coladarci, 2007; Hawley et al., 2016; Koziol et al., 2015).

And yet, that is what policymakers and policy analysts must do—explicitly define what does and does not count as "rural." Rural-focused policies, like those described above, set criteria to determine if and where resources can be distributed or who is eligible to participate in a particular program. Similarly, the policy analyst must determine which schools, districts, or communities count as rural in order to understand and evaluate a policy's impact on rural places or to evaluate geographic distribution and whether a policy is fair to or benefits rural schools.

Multiple, often contradictory, definitions of rural exist in policy, particularly at the federal level (Arnold et al., 2007; Miller, 2010; Hawley et al., 2016). According to Tieken (2017), the proportion of the US population that is rural ranges from 7 percent to 49 percent depending on the classification system being used. The geographic unit of analysis varies across classification systems. Some classification systems determine whether a location is rural based on countywide data, US Census Tracts data, or ZIP code classifications. The unit of analysis can have a profound impact (Arnold et al., 2007; Koziol et al., 2015; Waller & Gotway, 2004). Countywide classification systems may be more stable because county boundaries do not change very often (Hart et al., 2005); however, a countywide classification system tends to underrepresent rural places because of the statistical influence of metropolitan areas in otherwise rural counties (Miller, 2010) and differences between state and federal definitions can cause confusion (Yettick et al., 2014). Even the decision whether to determine rurality at the level of the school district or the individual school can have a major impact. It may make sense to determine eligibility for a policy or program at the level of the school district, because districts are the responsible administrative unit. However, many larger urban districts also include more rural schools and districts may not receive resources intended to support their rural schools if a districtwide definition is being used. J. D. Johnson and Strange (2009) found that defining rural at the district level, rather than the school level, undercounted over 750,000 rural students attending rural schools in larger, more urban districts.

Policymakers and analysis commonly turn to the National Center for Education Statistics (NCES) Urban-Centric Locale Codes system, which classifies both individual schools and school districts according to the physical location of school buildings and their relative distance from an urbanized area and population size within a defined area (Geverdt & Phan, 2006; Rural School and Community Trust, 2013). Under this classification system, rural towns have 2,500–50,000 people and rural areas have fewer than 2,500 people (Table 3.1).

Every classification system has pros and cons. Some definitions of rural are problematic because they are too narrow or too broad. For example, the federal Small Rural Schools Program provides a small amount of funding to schools if they are both small and rural. To qualify, schools must serve fewer than 600 students. This program, then, does not apply to the majority of schools located in rural areas, which, in part due to consolidation practices, tend to serve more than 600 students (J. D. Johnson & C. B. Howley, 2015; Yettick et al., 2014). On the other hand, the US Department of Agriculture has economic programs that provide funding for economic development to communities with populations under 50,000. This classification system has been criticized for directing funding to relatively larger communities and rural community hubs that may have economic infrastructure already in place (Rural School and Community Trust, 2013). In this case, a broader definition of rural may not direct funds to those communities that might most benefit from economic development.

Any attempt to define place in terms of geography or population neglects the reality that rurality is more than a location or a function of population density. What defines a place, and defines a place as rural, is identity based and connected to culture, history, and politics as much

The Bloomsbury Handbook of Rural Education in the United States

Table 3.1 National Center for Education Statistics Locale Classifications

Locale	Definition
City	
Large	Territory inside an urbanized area and inside a principal city with population of 250,000 or more
Midsize	Territory inside an urbanized area and inside a principal city with population less than 250,000 and greater than or equal to 100,000
Small	Territory inside an urbanized area and inside a principal city with population less than 100,000
Suburb	
Large	Territory outside a principal city and inside an urbanized area with population of 250,000 or more
Midsize	Territory outside a principal city and inside an urbanized area with population less than 250,000 and greater than or equal to 100,000
Small	Territory outside a principal city and inside an urbanized area with population less than 100,000
Town	
Fringe	Territory inside an urban cluster that is less than or equal to 10 miles from an urbanized area
Distant	Territory inside an urban cluster that is more than 10 miles and less than or equal to 35 miles from an urbanized area
Remote	Territory inside an urban cluster that is more than 35 miles from an urbanized area
Rural	
Fringe	Census-defined rural territory that is less than or equal to 5 miles from an urbanized area, as well as rural territory that is less than or equal to 2.5 miles from an urban cluster
Distant	Census-defined rural territory that is more than 5 miles but less than or equal to 25 miles from an urbanized area, as well as rural territory that is more than 2.5 miles but less than or equal to 10 miles from an urban cluster
Remote	Census-defined rural territory that is more than 25 miles from an urbanized area and is also more than 10 miles from an urban cluster

Source: National Center for Education Statistics (n.d.).

as it is an expression of the physical and natural characteristics of that place (Butler & Sinclair, 2020). What is important to remember with any definition is that sense of place is impacted by positionality within that place and the interplay of race, class, history, and status (Butler & Sinclair, 2020; Tuck & McKenzie, 2015) making policy, and policy analysis, a nuanced and complicated endeavor.

Beyond Rural: Rural Critical Policy Analysis

Assumption of neutrality, distributive analysis, rural salience, and definition of rural represent essential areas for a rural policy analysis framework; however, while these focus areas drive at the heart of what makes policy a complicated endeavor in rural places, they do not in and of themselves directly address equity and justice in rural places. A rural critical policy analysis builds from the framework of critical policy analysis (Butler & Sinclair, 2020; Prunty, 1985; Taylor, 1997). Critical policy analysis moves beyond a functionalist focus (i.e., does the policy work?) toward a critical frame by interrogating the power structures and moral stances from within which educational policy is conceived and enacted. Prunty's "signposts" for critical policy analysis operationalize critical theory in the tradition of the Frankfurt school and Habermas (1975, 1979). Through the lens of critical policy analysis, *policy* is an authoritative allocation of values, a version of the authors' social ideals. *Schools* are manifestations of policies and are sites of cultural transmission that cannot be understood separately from society. Critical policy analysis works from an overtly political vision of moral order and seeks to advocate for disenfranchised groups, including rural people.

A rural critical policy analysis framework must recognize two things. First, it must recognize the long history of rural places as being seen as important because of their service to more urban areas (see, e.g., Cervone, 2018; C. B. Howley et al., 2005; Theobald, Chapter 2, this volume; Wuthnow, 2019). In other words, metrocentric policies and practices assume that rural places have value because of the resources they provide to urban centers/people (the food that is grown, the materials to be mined from the land, the recreation opportunities to be visited, the labor needed for urban centers to continue to grow, etc.). Second, rural critical policy analysis must recognize that the metrocentric advantage has been leveraged by the consistent framing of rurality as invisible and/or deficient. A deficit framing of rural places as backwards, lacking, foolish, and anachronistic enables and justifies metrocentric policies for places and people who cannot take care of themselves (J. D. Johnson & C. B. Howley, 2015). It becomes the job of (mostly) urban policymakers to do for rural people what they cannot do for themselves. Therefore, rural critical policy analysis asks: *How is place significant in the moral implications for a particular policy or set of policies?*

While there are several examples of rural-focused policy analysis (e.g., AASA, 2017; Brenner, 2016; Rude & Miller, 2018; Yettick et al., 2014) and a small but increasing number of policy analyses that are both rural and critical (e.g., Butler & Sinclair, 2020; Eppley & Shannon, 2015; J. D. Johnson & C. B. Howley, 2015; Tieken, 2017; Williams, 2013), there is a need for much more work that is both critical and place-focused. Butler and Sinclair (2020) write, "the role of place and its relationship to power, pedagogy, and the social context of schooling is largely undertheorized" (p. 65). In order to advance social justice for rural students and schools, each of the rural-focused questions above should be posed with a focus not just on geography but also on power, race, class, and gender.

Rural Critical Policy Analysis and the Assumption of Neutrality
Rural policy analysis challenges the assumption of neutrality and is a useful tool with which to evaluate whether a policy that purports to treat all places the same is fair to or will be effective in rural places (i.e., Do the rural places in question have the resources, capacity, or need for a particular program?). A critical analysis of the underlying assumption of place neutrality asks not just "Does the policy treat all places the same to the detriment of rural places?" but also examines which rural places and which students and communities within rural contexts may be disadvantaged by the façade of place neutrality. Rural critical policy analysis is essential

not just because one-size-fits-all approaches might not work in rural places but also because one-size-fits-all solutions tend to represent neoliberal approaches to teaching and learning that commodify and corporatize students and their education, placing profit and efficiency above the needs of students and communities in ways that are particularly detrimental for rural communities whose residents have been marginalized or disenfranchised (Cervone, 2018; Shahjahan, 2011).

The evidence-based practice provisions of the ESSA have been critiqued based on the underlying assumption that place does not matter in education policy. Under ESSA, states, districts, and schools must spend federal funds on programs for which there is research evidence, as determined by the "quality" of research studies supporting the program or practice. The language of ESSA, and subsequent guidance provided by the US Department of Education (USDOE, 2016), requires schools to select and implement programs/interventions with the strongest evidence possible, where "strong" evidence is defined as randomly controlled trials (RCTs) that examine an intervention's efficacy as brokered by the federal What Works Clearinghouse. (Programs with "moderate" or quasi-experimental, "promising," or correlational and in some cases "ongoing" or active evaluation may also be purchased in a pinch.)

The evidence-based practice provisions of ESSA are problematic for rural schools (Eppley et al., 2018). Large-scale RCTs are rarely conducted in rural places—issues of geography, distance, cost, and confidentiality, among others, mean that most studies are conducted in places with denser populations. More importantly, local contexts, needs, resources, and capacity all impact whether an evidence-based practice can successfully be translated in a rural context. The evidence-based practice provisions of ESSA assume a place neutrality that may hamper rural schools' ability to provide appropriate instructional programs for students that "work" in their particular context for their particular students. The blanket provisions of ESSA that assume all places have the same needs and the same access to curriculum resources are unlikely to be effective in many rural contexts.

The impact of this "assumption of neutrality" represents a faith in a certain type of standardized, urbanized "evidence" about educational programs. Taking a critical perspective, several have critiqued the evidence-based practice provisions as problematic not just for rural schools but for all schools, as manifestations of neoliberal policies that place standardization and efficiency before families and communities (e.g., Cervone, 2018; Shahjahan, 2011). ESSA requires schools to consider evidence of the success of interventions, as brokered by the federal What Works Clearinghouse when spending federal funds (e.g., for Title 1). The narrow focus on measurable outcomes, standardized assessments, replicable programs, and teaching as "intervention" neglects the importance of local knowledge and teacher expertise (Bryk et al., 2010; McDonald & Klein, 2003). Local designs for instruction that leverage rural ways of knowing are more engaging and empowering than canned curriculum focusing on test preparation (Corbett & Donehower, 2017; Eppley & Shannon, 2015) that create tensions between rural educators' commitments to their students and the needs of the rural communities they serve (Budge, 2010).

Rural Critical Policy Analysis and Distributive Analysis

Distributive analysis of policy leads one to consider the role of place and to compare the distribution of outcomes or resources across places (Beck & Schoffstall, 2005). Distributive analysis falls short, however, unless it recognizes that just as inequities and histories of injustice exist across rural and nonrural places, so too are there long-standing histories of inequity and injustice within rural places.

Butler and Sinclair (2020) build from the work of others (e.g., Morrison et al., 2017; Tuck & Mckenzie, 2015) to call for a blending of geospatial analysis with critical race theory (CRT). CRT acknowledges (a) the prevalence of racism in society, (b) that racism has been normalized and is endemic in American systems, (c) that it is rarely acknowledged by Whites, and (d) that people of color must tell their stories in order to advance racial equality (Taylor, 2009). The intersection of geospatial analysis with CRT has the power to "generate insights about education policy, practice, and social contexts" (p. 70) that reveal both the locations and the mechanisms of systems of racial inequality.

Similarly, Tieken (2017) challenges rural education scholars to understand and investigate "the reproduction of educational inequity through geography" (p. 387). In the history of American education, including and especially rural education, space and place have intersected with race to contribute to systems that maintain power and wealth for the few through a funding system based on the value of property (which has historically been affected by racist practices, e.g., redlining), school boundaries that maintain and exacerbate segregation, and myriad other mechanisms. Rural critical policy analysis focuses on distributive analysis as a lens through which to investigate spatial inequality in education.

School consolidations are a manifestation of spatial inequality. Schools have been closed and combined in rural places for over a century, purportedly as a cost-savings measure based on the assumption that it might be cheaper or more efficient to operate fewer, larger schools (C. B. Howley et al., 2011). When decisions are made to close and combine schools, or to bus rural students to larger and more urban schools, they are often made in spite of evidence that school closure has a devastating economic and social impact on rural communities (C. B. Howley et al., 2011; Tieken, 2014) and in spite of evidence that smaller, community-based schools are better for children (C. B. Howley, 1996; Jimerson, 2006).

Studies of rural school consolidation decisions have demonstrated the ways that race and poverty underpin community decisions around rural school consolidation and exacerbate segregation and inequality (e.g. Jimerson, 2005a; Tieken & Auldridge-Reveles, 2019; Williams, 2013). For example, England and Hamann (2013) examined school closure and consolidation in the rural Great Plains, linking geospatial data to data about racial isolation and other school outcomes. They found that, in spite of rhetoric that consolidation would advance equality in the community, schools in Great Plains communities became more segregated after consolidation. For example, over a twenty-year period from 1990 to 2010, three trends co-occurred in Dawson County, Nebraska. Latinx families moved to the area to work in the new meatpacking plant in Lexington, an urban area in Dawson County. Statewide consolidation efforts led to the closure of eighteen of twenty-three Nebraska school districts and almost all rural schools in Dawson County, concentrating Latinx students in Lexington schools. And, finally, per-pupil funding in Lexington declined relative to per-pupil funding in other districts in the county. Using critical distributive analysis, England and Hamaan documented the ways these policies and practices led to "a geographic framework for inequality" (p. 175), and demonstrated the importance of geospatial analysis that takes a critical perspective, and concluded, "If it is our goal to challenge policies that segregate and stratify educational outcomes, it behooves us to examine all geographies (rural, urban, and suburban) where this occurs and to figure out ways to communicate such information" (p. 181).

Critical distributive analysis is complicated by the multiple definitions of rural used to collect and categorize rural data in that it can be difficult to link data from multiple sources (Koziol et al., 2015). Counties, census tracts, and school districts have different but overlapping boundaries and variations in how data is collected, aggregated, and presented. Nonetheless, this work is essential for understanding the impact, or potential impact, of policies on the diverse and changing communities in rural places.

Rural Critical Policy Analysis and Rural-Focused Policy

In order to evaluate a policy that has a stated rural focus of some sort, rural critical policy analysis recognizes that metrocentric perspectives and deficit narratives of rural places have led to policies that aim to "fix" rural "problems" to the detriment of rural people. Framing rural education as a "problem" is nothing new (Cubberley, 1914). For over 100 years reports about the reforms needed to address backwards and backwoods schools have laid the groundwork for policies built on a deficit perspective of rural places (Biddle & Azano, 2016; Kannapel & DeYoung, 1999; Tieken & San Antonio, 2016). Theobald, in this volume, traces the historic roots of rural education policymaking, showing that models of efficiency and metrocentric policymaking have had a detrimental effect on rural schools and communities throughout the history of public education in the United States.

A policy to address a rural problem should be based on an understanding of the richness, nuances, and affordances of rural places. Cuervo (2012), building from Young (1990), argues for the importance of recognitional and associational as well as distributive justice. Associational justice refers to the involvement of the people who will be impacted by decisions that are made. Recognitional justice is achieved when there is an absence of cultural domination and nonrecognition, that is, when the cultures, values, and perspectives of the individuals affected are respected (Cuervo, 2012). Often, however, this is not the case, and policies are developed and promulgated without the input of rural voices and by policymakers far removed from the circumstances through the lens of deficit framing.

The problem of teacher shortages in rural areas and the policy solutions that have been advanced are one site for investigating recognitional and associative as well as distributive justice for any policy whose stated aims are to "help" rural places. Concerns about the distribution of teachers for rural schools are numerous (e.g., Darling-Hammond, 2010; Gagnon & Mattingly, 2015; Miller, 2012) with reports that characterize rural schools as "hard to staff" (Monk, 2007) and teacher staffing as "a struggle" (Cohen & Hernandez, 2019) pointing to inequitable salaries and other deterrents to rural teaching (e.g., Jimerson, 2003)

Teacher retention—teachers staying in the profession and at the schools where they are hired—could contribute a great deal to increasing the workforce in rural areas. Retention studies show that teachers value, and continue to teach, where they find competent school leadership, supportive colleagues and school communities, and salaries that recognize their work as professionals (Amrein-Beardsley, 2007; Eckert, 2017). Yet policy proposals to address rural teacher shortages often focus on the recruitment and the pipeline of teachers, such as grow-your-own-programs and campaigns to elevate the profession (Gagnon, 2016; Rude & Miller, 2018), rather than making appropriate fiscal investment to achieve more equity in teacher salaries and working conditions.

Within a state, one-size-fits-all policies may continue to disadvantage marginalized schools. Anthony and colleagues (2017), for example, analyzed teacher shortages in Mississippi and found that race, and not rural status or socio-economic status, was the strongest predictor of shortages in a given district. In Mississippi, majority-Black schools had significantly higher rates of teacher shortages than majority-White districts in the very same county, a stark state-level example of a national trend (Darling-Hammond, 2010). Teacher shortage solutions that fail to acknowledge and address race and racial bias are unlikely to impact teacher shortages in that state.

It is also likely that local strategies that leverage the benefits of teaching in particular rural places will be more effective for addressing teacher shortages (Beesley et al., 2010; Maranto & Shuls, 2013). Each state, each region, and each district have unique challenges and affordances. The four-day school week, described above, is an example of an attempt to turn control of working conditions over to local school leaders. Programs that help new teachers meet their neighbors, become members of their community, and put down roots such as community engagement strategies and housing developments just for teachers (Gagnon, 2016; Superville, 2018) may hold promise. What is clear is that teacher staffing policies that focus only on ameliorating deficits without listening to rural teachers' and leaders' voices or knowledge of rural histories and contexts have not yet been successful.

Policy in an Era of Rapid Change

The post–Covid-19 era is likely to be a period of great change in education—but, it is important to remember that the decades leading up to the pandemic were also times of change, with changing demographics, increasing technology use, high-stakes testing, and accountability, among the profound changes in education. But amid the change, the fundamental nature of schooling has not changed. In spite of rhetoric to the contrary, schools have always served to provide educational advantage to some, and disadvantage to others—and issues of space and place have been at the center of the perpetuation of inequity (Tieken, 2017). It is possible that the coming period of change sparked by the pandemic and fueled by calls for anti-racist and abolitionist teaching raised by the Black Lives Matter Movement will advance equity across race, economics, and place. However, it is also possible that coming changes will not substantially disrupt the deliberate patterns of power and access that have already been established. Cuervo (2012) encourages us to center social justice in a critical analysis of education policy. He writes:

> Critical questions within a social justice in education framework are whose voice is heard? and who gets a chance to participate in the decision making of state educational and school policy design? A social justice framework focuses on meaningful participation by stakeholders in education, including teachers, parents and students, and the critique of dominant discourses that enables the recognition of diversity. (p. 92)

It is this type of analysis that will be essential to recognizing and resisting policies and proposals that would decenter students and families and lead to domination and detriment for rural schools and communities.

Many policy analyses focus at the level of the federal government, in part in response to the increasing role of the federal government in education through the first decades of this century. At this moment in time, however, advocates need to monitor and engage in state and local policymaking more than ever. Under ESSA, and particularly under federal waivers that were in place during the Covid-19 pandemic, states and communities increasingly have the authority to set policies that regulate K–12 education (Dulgerian, 2016; Gagnon, 2016.) It will be at the state and local level where decisions are made about issues that matter to local schools—including the design of testing and accountability systems, teacher licensure requirements, the school calendar, the role of technology in teaching and learning, and the role of schools in communities.

Rural critical policy analysis can challenge and change the systems and structures that have served to reify social, racial, economic, and geographic inequality. Rural critical policy analysis can serve to evaluate and identify problems and concerns and advance distributive, recognitional, and associative justice by providing a frame for working jointly with others (including teachers, students, and families) to engaging simply and clearly with policymakers around policy ideas to be proactive and to raise critical questions about policies that may perpetuate harm in rural places.

4

Corporate Influences on Rural Schools

Jason A. Cervone

Over the past several decades, public education in the United States has withstood a sustained push toward corporatization, coinciding with the rise of neoliberalism as a dominant ideology. Neoliberalism, briefly, is the economic belief that society is best served by entrepreneurial freedom through strong private property rights, free market, and free trade. The role of government is merely to preserve these economic freedoms in order for the markets to do their work, and where markets do not exist, such as formerly in public education, create them (Harvey, 2005). The danger of neoliberalism, writes Harvey, is in its distrust of democracy (2005). Neoliberal theorists prefer a governance by elites that will protect capitalism from democratic pressures that would impose regulations, such as trade unions or collective bargaining (Harvey, 2005). The corporatization of public schools is the neoliberal attempt to create a capitalist marketplace within education, wherein schools become economic commodities that operate under the corporate notion that economic competition creates the best outcomes. Neoliberalism also pushes the belief that public schools, like the public sector in general, are overburdened with rules and regulations, and privately operated schools would be far more efficient and, therefore, better. The purpose of schooling under corporate ideology is also bound to economic outcomes, as students are prepared to become workers in the global economy (Silva, 2013). Funding for anything deemed extraneous, such as arts and humanities, is often discontinued as they are not seen to provide any direct economic benefits (Au & Ferrare, 2015; Giroux, 2008). Neoliberal ideology is promoted by think tanks such as the Heritage Foundation, the American Enterprise Institute, the Hoover Institution, and the Fordham Institute—as well as philanthropies like the Walton Foundation, Broad Foundation, and Gates Foundation (Saltman, 2012). The danger of corporate incursion into public schooling is that it undermines democratic control of education, creates economic and cultural inequality, redistributes already limited funding to private and for-profit companies whose interest in education is exclusively economic, and requires that school's primary purpose is to rank and sort children according to their potential contribution to the economy. Corporate influence can be seen in the form of for-profit charters, school vouchers, for-profit online education, and the privatization of school services such as food and transportation (Saltman, 2012). Schools, teachers, and students are put into competition with each other and ranked according to high-stakes, standardized test scores (Au & Ferrare, 2015), and schools determined to be "failing" can be shut down or transferred to private hands (Apple, 2006; Hursh, 2015). Under the guise of private/public "partnerships," schools also can become vendees for technology companies. Rural schools previously held a unique position in that in the early years of the expansion of corporatization, the monetary potential of rural schools was not immediately apparent. Smaller and isolated rural populations meant fewer consumers to make charters profitable, and a lack of technological infrastructure meant online education has only fairly recently become a profitable option. However, given the difficulties associated with privatization in urban areas, including a disproportionately outsized urban political influence, rural communities have become more attractive. Lipman (2011) explains that under market ideology, decisions made regarding the public sector are no longer based on the general welfare of the population, but rather under a business rationale. Governance is no longer accountable to the public and instead works to keep the markets—in this case the education market—free from outside influence (Macrine, 2016).

Consequences of Public School Corporatization

One of the main concerns in regard to corporate influence on education is that it relies on a number of myths and unquestioned ideas. Saltman (2012) wrote:

> Behind corporate reforms are some myths that need to be named and challenged. One is that public education has "failed" and that it is now time to "give the market a chance." The reality is that gross inequalities in public education are the result of the linkage of real estate markets to school funding and the long-standing influence of business in thoroughly shaping the select school failures of today. The current state of schools owes much to the long-standing mistake of having given the market a chance. (p. 31)

The idea of failure is also racially and class coded, as the schools deemed to be failures under the corporate model are generally urban schools in working-class communities with high percentages of historically minoritized people, as well as small rural schools in working-class communities. It should be telling that privatizers have had little success in introducing charters to mostly White, suburban, affluent communities where students generally perform well on standardized testing and other measures of success in the corporate model (Saltman, 2012). Au and Hollar (2016) noted that the idea any school can be failing simply due to a test score ignores "social and historical conditions, complex issues of power and culture, even the life and spirit of people (and) scores become the means and ends of education" (p. 36). Failure and success, therefore, become simple numerical details, ignoring community needs and feelings toward their schools and education.

In describing the neoliberal view of public education, Apple (2006) noted that neoliberals view public schools as places that take money without providing tangible, measurable, or monetary outcomes. The only determinant of success under this line of thought is economic efficiency, and there must be tangible—and of course monetary—benefits to justify the costs of education. For this to occur, students must be viewed as human capital, economic actors who can become workers for those who are funding their education. Therefore, any money spent that cannot objectively be seen to support corporate profitability is viewed as wasteful and unnecessary. These ends are rarely specified outright, as corporate influence on schools often occurs via "philanthropy."

Corporate philanthropies claim to be strengthening education by providing needed funding while, incidentally, promoting neoliberal policies that further defund public schools (Goodman & Saltman, 2002). Students and teachers both become adherents to market logic and must deal with policies aimed at efficiency and measurability, such as standardized testing and curricula, as well as an overall de-skilling of teachers, who are often reshaped as facilitators delivering standardized and sometimes even completely scripted lessons (Eppley, 2011; Saltman, 2012). This business model of education treats schooling as an assembly line, and the pressure toward efficiency decontextualizes education, disconnecting what is being learned from broader social and cultural struggles (Goodman & Saltman, 2002). Standardization also creates a geographic disconnect as rural students often do not see themselves and their communities represented in the curriculum (Haas & Nachtigal, 1998) nor connected to the larger world, creating a sense that being rural is a deficit or an obstacle to overcome. Eppley (2011) uses the term "pedagogy of erasure" to describe this kind of standardized education, noting that it neglects, often intentionally, the culture, backgrounds, and lived experiences of students. Theobald and Wood (2010) explain that "progress" in the United States is often synonymous with urbanization and globalization, leaving rural students with the belief that they must become urban in order to be considered successful. Rural schools struggle to overcome this belief as resources such as textbooks often ignore the rural experience. In an effort to support students, rural parents and educators can often reify this belief as well, benevolently pushing students out of rural areas to help them succeed (Carr & Kefalas, 2009).

Corporate ideology in public education has allowed neoliberalism to become public pedagogy. Neoliberal pedagogy eliminates gendered, racial, and class views and analyses of society in favor of analyzing all relations through an economic lens (Giroux, 2008). This narrow economic thinking pushes young people to create market identities for themselves and view themselves as economic actors whose worth is determined by the extent to which they can accumulate wealth and their consumption practices. Students themselves, therefore, no longer see themselves as critical agents and participants in a functioning democratic society (Berliner, 2013; Giroux, 2008).

The end result of corporate privatization is a stratified society as wealthy communities maintain elite public schools while poor communities grapple with the consequences of neoliberal education (Means, 2013). It should be noted that this is not very different from the current setup of public education, where those in wealthy schools are prepared to work as managers, leaders, and professionals, while poor and working-class students are prepared for low-wage work, if any at all. The result of this is decreased class mobility, increased unemployment, and rising inequality (Bowles & Gintis, 1976; De Lissovoy et al., 2015).

Rural Corporatization

Though the focus of this chapter is on the most recent trend of corporatization, it is important to note that using economic measures for supposed rural problems is a long-standing tradition in the United States. That is, rural communities have only been as valuable as what they can produce, or what workforce they can provide to serve capitalist expansion, necessitating a change in the geography of the United States to allow for continual capitalist growth (Smith, 2008). In the late nineteenth and early twentieth centuries, rural communities were shaped to serve cities economically by providing food, raw materials, labor, and, of course, consumers to buy finished products (Soja, 1989). Henri Lefebvre (2003) describes this process as the spread of the urban fabric, that is, the transformation of local and regional features (natural resources) into a form of industrial production. The spread of the urban fabric does not refer specifically to the growth of cities but the industrial domination of the country. The result of industrialization is the growth of abstract spaces, spaces created to serve economic growth rather than lived spaces, spaces created through everyday life of the people who live there. Theobald and Campbell (2014) describe a number of activities and policies that led to the decline of rural communities and populations in the United States, such as, the damming of rivers for industrial purposes that hurt fishing communities and flood farmland. During the Civil War, policies were also enacted to provide monetary loans to farmers that would later not be honored. These policies that harmed and indebted rural citizens in favor of urban and industrial expansion resulted in an "uneven development," a concept intended to counter the notion that capitalism would create economic equilibrium. Smith (2008) noted that capitalism would never be able to create equilibrium, and to the contrary, it needed disequilibrium to promote economic growth because it allows for the capital to be constantly moved to new spaces with higher profit rates. With certain areas being intentionally underdeveloped, capitalism can ensure its mobility and keep spaces available where costs, such as rent and wages, can be artificially low. Uneven development, then, is required for growth as urban areas would need to maintain economic superiority to rural areas to ensure primary production and labor could be kept as cheap as possible in order to continue increasing profits for corporations.

Theobald (1997) chronicles the beginning of the twentieth century, detailing how President Theodore Roosevelt created the Country Life Commission (CLC) in an effort to combat the "rural problem" (p. 103)—a problem loosely defined as poverty, mostly caused by the increase in industrialization, which led to mass migrations to urban areas as agricultural jobs became increasingly scarce. This led to the reshaping of rural schools to keep pace with their urban counterparts. This required standardization and consolidation and a heavy focus on job training, specifically preparing students to work in agricultural fields (Theobald, 1997).

By the 1990s, after neoliberalism had become the dominant political ideology, federal policy with direct relevance to rural areas, specifically the Right to Farm laws, ushered in a downward spiral of poverty (Edmondson, 2003). In the Right to Farm laws, financial support was funneled from individually owned small- and mid-sized farms to large, corporate agribusinesses (Edmondson, 2003). This allowed for the most powerful corporations to consolidate land and power and to advance policies that allow for increased profits by removing labor and environmental regulations. In turn, this created increased poverty levels for rural residents, many of whom were soon forced out of jobs and homes (Cervone, 2018).

Rural corporatization can be best understood through the concept of enclosure of the commons. Historically, this was the process through which lands that were used for farming or hunting and previously held in common by communities were declared to be private property, often resulting in a literal enclosure as it was fenced or walled off (Theobald, 1997). Communal access was therefore restricted, and access was generally granted only on a monetary basis (Bowers, 2006). Enclosure was proposed as an effort to increase individual freedom, as it heralded the end of feudalism. It had the opposite effect, however, as the wealthy were able to consolidate land and resources (Theobald, 1997). This parallels contemporary neoliberal thought in its calls for removal of regulations and barriers and the privatization of public goods. For rural communities, the so-called Right to Farm laws provided financial incentives based on acreage, enabling the largest agribusinesses to acquire as much land as possible. Individually and family-owned farms were given no support and were therefore left unable to compete economically with subsidized agribusinesses. Herein lies the major contradiction to the professed values of neoliberalism and privatization. Efforts to increase economic freedom via the free-market consolidate power among the wealthiest citizens, creating a perpetual economic underclass willing to work for low wages.

Once shaped to serve economic purposes, rural areas can also become capitalist sacrifice zones. Sacrifice zones are places that are a source of resources extraction and/or sites needed to receive waste created by industrial production and consumption (Klein, 2014). These sites sacrifice clean air and water, forests, mountains, and the health of community members. Under capitalism, all space must be commodified and reappropriated for wealth accumulation and the health of the people and land is considered a necessary cost (Klein, 2014). Within economic globalization, a rural place is only as valuable as what can be taken from it, and that generally leads to its inevitable destruction. This destruction can be tangible, as seen in the Appalachians, where more than 500 mountains and one million acres of forest have been destroyed due to mountaintop removal coal mining (Ross et al., 2016) and where large-scale industrial pig farms cause bacteria levels to greatly exceed federal and state guidelines for water quality (Burkholder et al., 2007). Corporate agriculture has detrimental effects on human health as well, with large, concentrated animal farms producing antibiotic-resistant strains of disease and new forms of influenza (Cervone, 2018). Hydraulic fracturing, or fracking, has been shown to have disastrous effects on the environment, including leaking gas and oil into the groundwater and releasing toxic chemicals into the air.

Corporatization of Rural Schools

Despite federal attention paid to rural schools because of the CLC in the early part of the twentieth century, by mid-century the focus on rural was largely gone, as school closure and consolidation largely became the dominant manner of thinking as a solution to the "rural school problem" (Cubberly, 1914). However, by the 1980s neoliberalism fostered the economic shift that brought a new focus on rural education. Biddle and Azano (2016) explain that an emphasis on mobility and preparation for a skills-based economy led to an increase in programs focused on recruiting and retaining rural teachers who could prepare students for careers in the global economy. Along with this focus on rural came a focus on accountability, mainly in the form of standardized testing and curricula and quantitative evaluation. The push for standardization further increased rural school closures and consolidation (C. B. Howley et al., 2011) as this neoliberal model only continued the previous solutions to rural problems—that is, the push to make rural education more "efficient" like urban and suburban schools.

A prime example of the corporatization of rural schools began in 2013 and 2014 with a partnership between Bellwether Education Partners, a think tank advocating privatization, and the Albertson Foundation, a corporate philanthropy based in Idaho. This new group, the Rural Opportunities Consortium of Idaho (ROCI), put out a series of policy recommendations and reports from members of various privatization advocacy groups such as the Fordham Institute and American Enterprise Institute. The first of these reports, aptly titled *A New Frontier* (Smarick, 2014), suggested numerous strategies to open rural communities to privatization efforts, specifically through an increase in privately operated charter schools. C. B. Howley (2014) described *A New Frontier* document as "propaganda" (p. 2), noting that it, like much of the work of ROCI, does not attempt to engage with existing research in rural education and instead relies mostly on demographic data to assert its claims, in the process missing important research and information regarding school-community relationships, perspectives and aspirations of students, and lived experiences of rural students and educators. In short, the very things that make rural *rural*.

With advocates of privatization finding difficulty in fully advancing charters in urban and suburban areas due to caps on charter schools, reluctance from public districts, and grassroots opposition (Buras, 2014), several conservative organizations and think tanks have turned to rural areas as a way to get a foothold. Privatizers have proposed policies that would eliminate caps on charters and would reward or favor opening charters in rural areas through economic incentives and relaxing certain standards on teacher certification and school accreditation (Smarick, 2014). Proposed alternative teacher licensing policies are another major point of contention as alternative licensing is associated with the deregulation of teacher education as it places teaching under the same high-stakes testing and standardization logic as schools and students (Saltman, 2010). Weiner (2007) explains that the deregulation of teaching allows for teachers to be framed as a problem when schools are not meeting the standards of achievement, and the blame can be further placed on schools of education, wherein teacher preparation can be turned into a corporate market as well.

The logic behind privatization is that the quality of education would be increased by allowing free-market competition through profit-making ventures. However, privatization advocates have not been able to make the case that privately operated charters would actually be able to outperform public schools, even by their own metrics as evidence of effectiveness for privately operated charters does not necessarily indicate they are inherently superior to public schools (Lubienski & Lubienski, 2014). In attempting to make the case for rural charters, Bellwether partner and charter advocate Squire (2018) wrote that rural charters "cannot and will not solve the challenges in rural education" (p. 139). Instead, suggesting that charters should be given a chance as they can be successful "in the right place at the right time" (p. 135), a rather vague argument and one that could realistically be made about any school at all. The arguments for the potential of rural charters are that they can increase competition, increase local control, increase autonomy, and specialize in ways the public district cannot, while allowing parents and students to act as consumers, choosing the best option for themselves (Squire, 2018). These claims are dubious at best. Even if one adopts the assumption that competition is beneficial for schools (see Hursh, 2015, for critique), many rural districts do not have a large enough population to support multiple schools, whether charter or traditional public charter schools. Further, it seems dubious that professionally managed charters would be well-positioned to enable local control and autonomy would produce better student achievement than existing traditional community public schools.

The Effects on Rural Schools

One of the most noticeable effects of neoliberalism toward rural education is consolidation (see Eppley, Chapter 9, this volume). Under the guise of improvement—that is improving the cost-effectiveness, economic efficiency, and accountability—many rural schools have been "improved out of existence" by state- and federal-level policymakers seeking to create a one-size-fits-all, urban-inspired school system (DeYoung & C. B. Howley, 1990). This push stems from a narrowed view of education as necessarily cost-efficient without recognizing the potential of small schools or local contexts. However, closing rural schools has been shown to have negative effects on both students and communities (Lyson, 2002). Rural communities with local schools are often better off socially and economically than those without (Lyson, 2002; Sipple, Francis et al., 2019). They also tend to have better infrastructure and higher civic employment, as the school itself can often be the largest employer in the community (Lyson, 2002; Tieken, 2014). Research has also shown that deconsolidation can actually provide some of the benefits supposedly offered by consolidation, with smaller schools often proving to be more economically efficient than large, centralized schools (C. B. Howley et al., 2011). As for the potential educational benefits, there have not been conclusive results from any standardized testing indicating students at small schools perform less successfully than peers in larger schools (Egalite & Kisida, 2016; C. B. Howley et al., 2011).

Lefebvre's (1970) discussion of the spread of the urban fabric provides some insight into the limitations of the corporate model of schooling. He notes that industrialization in rural areas has become a self-legitimating process, and as a result rural spaces have been transformed into economic spaces that serve the needs of capitalist accumulation. Essentially, economic growth is the reason for continued economic growth, and whether or not it succeeds in modernizing rural areas either in terms of agricultural production or education has never been the actual purpose—it only matters that a profit can be made. Spaces, therefore, become abstract as they are defined through quantitative measures of economic productivity rather than everyday life and the humanity of the people who live there. A consolidated school meets the requirements of an abstract space, as it stems purely from the positivistic viewpoint of standardization and economic efficiency that stands in direct contrast to the needs of everyday life (Cervone, 2017). Consolidation creates abstract space, as consolidated schools are usually created for purely economic purposes, namely to decrease the cost of numerous small schools. These schools are then both figuratively and literally removed from the community.

The Effects on Rural Students

It is not just places that are abstracted under corporate ideology but people as well. With education being reduced to measurable outcomes, teachers are left to present a curriculum to their students that is often completely irrelevant to their lived, everyday realities. Corbett (2013) calls for a "space to improvise" (p. 4) within the curriculum, noting that scripted, standardized schooling cannot address the complexities that students will face (and are facing) in the world. The emphasis on test scores also places students in direct competition with each other. Competition can have damaging effects on students regardless of location (Hursh, 2015), but it can be especially harmful to rural communities, as the competition rarely takes into account rural lives, experiences, and backgrounds, so winning the competition (e.g., doing well on the tests, taking high-level courses, gaining the skills to work in the global economy) is usually connected with the ability—or necessity—to leave (Corbett, 2007; Edmondson & Butler 2010). Bauman (1998) described this process of mobility due to economic and educational need as spatial segregation, noting that both mobility (those with the means and education) and immobility (those without means and education) are necessary for the neoliberal global economy. Bauman (1998) breaks down mobility into those who are tourists and those who are vagabonds, noting there is nothing inherently good or bad about the ability to stay or leave, but rather how much agency the individual has when making the choice. However, Bauman also notes that it is the "globals," the wealthy neoliberal class (p. 2), who currently set the rules and control the choices.

The stratifying effect of neoliberal education has created the serious concern of rural out-migration (Carr & Kefalas, 2009; Corbett, 2007). Students who do well in the corporate education system are ushered out to participate in the global economy, while the rest are encouraged to join the deskilled, demobilized workforce necessary for neoliberalism to thrive. In rural schools, corporate ideology is enacted when rural schools and communities are represented to students as obstacles to be overcome. The term "success" is itself problematic. It is a corporate term that is never fully defined but tacitly suggests the accumulation of wealth. The dichotomy wherein students can leave and be successful or stay behind and be failures is problematic, as the effects on students and communities are far more complex and young people are often conflicted about whether or not they want to leave rural communities (Hektner, 1995; C. B. Howley & Hambrick, 2014; Ley et al., 1996; Schafft et al., 2011). These studies suggest that rural students do value education but do not necessarily feel a desire to move to urban or suburban places. Many rural students closely value their familial ties and living close to home, as well as rural life in general, and if they do choose to leave, it is often due to necessity and not desire (C. B. Howley & Hambrick, 2014). Parents and school staff can also be influenced by the idea that students must leave in order to be successful and will therefore push students toward out-migration, believing it to be in their best interests (Carr & Kefalas, 2009; Corbett, 2007).

For young people who do not have the desire to go to college or to pursue professional or managerial work, there is often little motivation to continue their education. In fact, many can become resistant to the very idea of it (Carr & Kefalas, 2009; Corbett, 2007; Flora & Flora, 2013). For those who remain, some develop feelings of resentment toward education and those who pursue it (Flora & Flora, 2013) while those who leave may develop a similar resentment to those who stay behind (Carr & Kefalas, 2009). The tragedy of this splitting of rural communities is an outcome of neoliberal thinking. The choice to stay or leave as a determinant of who is successful and who is not is framed by corporate ideology within which a person's worth is based on their wealth and ability to consume (Cervone, 2018).

The Need for Critical Rural Education

Giroux (2011) wrote:

> The greatest threat to our children does not come from lowered standards, the absence of privatized choice schemes, or the lack of rigid testing measures. On the contrary, it comes from a society that refuses to view children as a social investment and instead consigns 15.5 million children to live in poverty, reduces critical learning to massive testing programs, (and) promotes policies that eliminate most crucial health and public services. (p. 83)

Corporate education is a distinctly political project that claims neutrality because it bases decisions upon quantitative measures under the guise of impartiality and the related assumption that numbers are not ideological. However, there is nothing apolitical about a system that seeks to remove pedagogy from democratic discourse and civic culture. Giroux describes corporate education as stripping education of its civic functions, reducing it to nothing more than job training rather than a mode of public engagement wherein students learn to be active citizens who can question the dominant narrative and foster imagination for a better society (Giroux, 2011). Additionally, corporatized education limits the ability of the state to protect public interest and promote education as a public good, not a private commodity. When the singular goal of education is to serve the economy, students are expected to internalize the view of themselves as servants of the economy, as they are not provided with the space to create alternative ways of thinking. The system continues reproducing because a norm of critical thought is absent. When educational institutions only invest in those students they see as able to serve a profit (Edmondson, 2003), the decline of rural communities is hastened, with fewer opportunities available to imagine another kind of education or way of life.

Thomas et al. (2011) proposed a critical rural theory—that is, a study of rural space from economic, cultural, and political perspectives that questions the dominant urban-centric ideology and seeks to emancipate and define rural as something other than sites of resource-extraction and consumer markets for urban products. While capitalism does tend to increase urbanization and holds urban areas as the model of modernization, a critical rural knowledge needs to proceed from the idea that both metro and nonmetro areas are under corporate influence.

Donehower et al. (2007) proposed the notion of rural literacies, "particular kinds of literate skills needed to achieve the goals of sustaining life in rural areas" (p. 4). A destandardized education, within which rural literacies is positioned, values rural ways of life and can better prepare students to be active participants in their communities and can better prepare students to imagine a future wherein rural is not subservient to the needs of capital. As Giroux (2011) described, losing public schools to corporate control creates corporate knowledge production, which increases an antidemocratic pedagogy. A reclamation and strengthening of public schools is a democratic effort and thus cannot be politically neutral. Students and teachers must understand the forces that are both for and against public education, and the curriculum cannot be disconnected from those struggles. It is important to note this is not a call for utopic thinking, and it would not be useful to predetermine the perfect rural school for an imaginary rural community. Critical education in rural communities does not call for imagining a perfect future but for identifying, understanding, and struggling against barriers that impede it. The focus must be on creating the conditions for increasing possibilities. This requires an education that does not serve capitalism but fosters critical thought and challenges injustices. In order to achieve this kind of education, schools must serve the common *good* rather than the needs of the economy. Education of this nature can create what Berardi (2017) refers to as *potency*, the condition to enable transformation and achieve possibilities. Potency is a challenge to power; therefore, education has to challenge power and question the economic ideology that limits possibilities.

5

Shifting Population Dynamics and Implications for Rural Schools

Kai A. Schafft and Annie Maselli

The United States, like the rest of the world, is urbanizing. In 1940, 75 million people (57 percent of US residents) lived in nonmetropolitan America—more than at any time previously or since (K. M. Johnson & Lichter, 2019a). By 2018, populations had grown in metropolitan and larger, more urbanized nonmetropolitan counties but had declined in smaller and more remote nonmetropolitan counties, with only 14.1 percent, or a total of about 46.1 million Americans, residing within nonmetropolitan America (K. M. Johnson & Lichter, 2019a; Pender et al., 2019). Despite several relatively short-lived "counter-urbanization" trends between the 1970s and 1990s in which rural in-migration exceeded rural out-migration (K. M. Johnson & Cromartie, 2006), out-migration has represented a long-term issue for many rural communities across the United States (Brown & Schafft, 2019; Jacquet et al., 2017) and beyond.[1]

Population decline in nonmetropolitan areas has been shaped by economic and technological shifts, increased population mobility, the globalization of production, limited rural labor market demand, selective rural out-migration, and aging rural populations (Brown & Schafft, 2019). These demographic changes have had serious consequences for the survival of rural schools, as enrollments decline and schools face pressure to close or consolidate (Tieken & Auldridge-Reveles, 2019). In 1939, there were nearly 120,000 rural schools in the United States. This number shrank to less than 29,000 by the 2017–18 school year. The shrinking number of schools was both a consequence of public policies, such as school consolidation initiatives, driven by the pursuit of educational and fiscal efficiencies, but also by rural depopulation, ironically only exacerbated by disappearing schools (Brown & Schafft, 2019; Tieken & Auldridge-Reveles, 2019; US Department of Education, 2020c). Although the proportion of the US population living in nonmetropolitan areas has been declining since the mid-twentieth century, this proportional change hasn't necessarily meant that rural populations were declining in aggregate—they simply weren't growing as quickly as in metropolitan areas. However, between 2010 and 2016, nonmetropolitan counties experienced net population loss for the first time in US history, totaling

Shifting Populations and Rural Schools

a loss of 260,000 people (K. M. Johnson & Lichter, 2019b), a worrisome demographic trend for rural America.

While out-migration and shrinking communities have been a dominant story for many rural places, other rural places have become migration destinations for retirees and others, especially high-amenity areas with relative proximity to larger metropolitan areas (Brown & Glasgow, 2010; Scharf et al., 2016; Sherman, 2018). At the same time, as the United States overall has become increasingly racially and ethnically diverse, so has rural America (Lichter, 2012; R. L. Winkler & K. M. Johnson, 2016), and Black, Indigenous, and Latinx communities have represented increasingly sizable proportions of the rural population. However, these changes in rural diversity have in turn raised new questions about the relationship between social and spatial inequalities and the implications for educational equity (Tieken, 2017; Tieken & Auldridge-Reveles, 2019).

In this chapter, we examine various forms of rural population shifts, including the aging and diversification of rural America, but also demographic shifts resulting from largely unanticipated factors such as rural "boomtown" growth associated with the development of natural resources and cite, more recently, the potential short- and long-term impacts of the Covid-19 pandemic. In doing so, we suggest how population shifts have both overt and subtle consequences for rural schools as populations shrink, grow, or compositionally change.

Selective Out-migration and Aging in Rural Places

Rural out-migration has historically been heavily selective. That is, migration (and also staying in place) tends to be "selective" of particular kinds of people based on attributes such as age, education, socioeconomic status, skill, and so on. Hence, migration can have dramatic effects on the demographic profile of an area not simply because of the net movement in and out but also because of how selectivity of migration streams alone can make places become poorer or wealthier, older or younger (Brown & Schafft, 2019).

Overall, 19 percent of the US nonmetropolitan population is sixty-five or older, as compared to 15 percent in metropolitan counties (US Department of Agriculture, 2018). In fact, 85 percent of "older-aged" counties (those with 20 percent or more of the population made up of residents aged sixty-five and older) are rural[2] (US Department of Agriculture, 2018). There are several reasons for this. Rural economic contraction has disproportionately impacted younger and working-age populations who are disproportionately likely to leave nonmetropolitan areas in comparison to older residents and those with disabilities. This, in turn, has resulted in shrinking and aging populations, and as mentioned, increased pressure for school closures and school consolidation, as well as placing further pressure on other vulnerable critical infrastructure such as hospitals and health clinics (Brown & Schafft, 2019; Scharf et al., 2016; Thiede et al., 2017). These dynamics help explain why one-third of US "older-aged" counties are persistent population loss counties, mostly located in the Midwestern US Corn Belt and the Northern Great Plains where economies have experienced downward economic trends (US Department of Agriculture, 2018).

These demographic processes are not especially new, although, as K. M. Johnson and Lichter (2019a) note, the recent absolute population decline in rural America marks a significant and concerning demographic shift, raising questions about the further political and economic marginalization of places on the spatial margins of urbanity. This is especially the case for remote nonmetropolitan counties where shifts away from agriculture, manufacturing, and some extractive industries have left places in conditions of increasing economic insecurity (Case & Deaton, 2020). This insecurity is arguably both a cause and consequence of rural depopulation, itself characterized by selective migration streams in which rural out-migration exceeds in-migration, where out-migrants tend to be younger and more highly educated than both rural residents who remain ("stayers") *and* rural in-migrants (Lichter & Schafft, 2016; McGranahan et al., 2010; von Reichert et al., 2014). K. M. Johnson and Lichter (2019b) note that, of the 24 percent of US counties experiencing depopulation, 91 percent are rural counties. Examining these "depopulating" rural counties, K. M. Johnson and Lichter (2019b) found that in each decade between 1950 and 2010, these counties had an average loss of 43 percent of residents aged twenty to twenty-four. Many of these counties also have negative birth rates; between 2000 and 2010, the number of deaths exceeded the number of births in 60 percent of depopulating rural counties.

In examining depopulating rural counties, we note that rural remote areas (see Longhurst, Chapter 1, this volume, for defining criteria) experience greater loss of school-aged populations. In Table 5.1, we use US Census data from the National Center for Education Statistics (NCES) to examine changes in the school-aged population in rural areas between 2000 and 2018.[3] The table shows that over the eighteen-year period, distant and fringe rural areas experienced net population losses in school-aged residents, while fringe rural areas experienced a slightly more than 5 percent increase in the school-aged population. The biggest proportional losses were experienced by remote rural areas, which, during the time period, lost over 250,000 school-aged residents for a loss of nearly 20 percent of that population group. The school-aged population in rural districts overall declined by 3.95 percent, while the school-aged population in nonrural districts grew by 3.57 percent overall (data not shown here), and the population of school-aged children in all US districts has increased by 2.38 percent.

Changes within the age structure of rural places may not necessarily be tied to selective out-migration (including the out-migration of residents of an age in which they would be most likely to start families) but rather to selective *in*-migration in the form of rural retirement migration—especially within high-amenity areas, such as the Great Lakes region and the Rocky

Table 5.1 School-Aged Child Population Living in Rural School Districts, 2000 and 2018

	2000		2018		% Change
	N	**% of Rural**	**N**	**% of Rural**	
US, Total	58,628,610		60,025,240		2.38
US, Rural Total	9,256,320		8,890,735		−3.95
Fringe	4,463,140	48.22	4,702,200	52.89	5.36
Distant	3,436,300	37.12	3,097,000	34.83	−9.87
Remote	1,356,880	14.66	1,091,535	12.28	−19.56

Source: US Decennial Census 2000 and American Community Survey 2018 estimate (NCES, 2000, 2018b).

Mountain West (Brown & Glasgow, 2010; K. M. Johnson & Lichter, 2013; Ulrich-Schad, 2015). One-third of "older-aged" counties, those classified as rural retirement destinations and/or that have economies based on outdoor recreation, have seen increases in population growth since 2012 (US Department of Agriculture, 2018).

While rural county growth associated with natural amenities and rural retirement is often seen as a hopeful sign of economic development and revitalization, it can come with its own unanticipated costs, including new types of social exclusions and inequities. Of concern within high-amenity and rural retirement counties is the potential for rural gentrification and, along with it, tightened housing markets and rising living costs that risk displacing lower-income families and youth, creating increases in inequity and social division (Golding, 2016; Sherman, 2018, 2021). The "grey peril" hypothesis has also raised concerns about the willingness of newcomer seniors to support public education through local tax dollars if they don't have a stake in the system (either as alumni or through their children; Lambert et al., 2009). However, scholars have found limited support for this hypothesis, concluding that while older rural retirees constitute a significant voting bloc, attitudes about and support for school funding don't consistently align with the "grey peril" hypothesis (Schlaffer, 2018).

Rural America's Growing Diversity

As America is urbanizing, it is at the same time becoming more racially and ethnically diverse. For the first time in the country's history, historically minoritized populations comprise the majority of people under the age of ten, with Nevada, Hawaii, California, New Mexico, and Texas being states where Black, Indigenous, and People of Color (BIPOC) comprise a greater share of the population than Whites (Frey, 2017). The nation as a whole is on track to become minority-majority by 2042 (Lichter, 2012). This diversity is mostly accounted for by demographic changes in urban America. Between 2000 and 2016, the percentage of the White population in metropolitan areas dropped from 67 percent to 58 percent. However, during the same time span, nonmetropolitan America also became more racially and ethnically diverse, although its percentage of White residents only dropped from 82 percent to 78 percent (Frey, 2017).

As of the 2015–16 academic year, four states had BIPOC student majorities within their rural school districts, and a fifth, South Carolina, had a 49.5 percent BIPOC rural student population. New Mexico had the greatest proportion of BIPOC rural students at 85.6 percent, up from 70.6 percent in 2005. All five states had experienced between a 7.4 percent and 15 percent increase in the proportion of rural BIPOC students during the period (see Table 5.2).

As Table 5.2 suggests, national-level data can obscure regional patterns in demographic composition and change along racial and ethnic lines. For example, over 92 percent of the Black population living in nonmetropolitan America live in the South, in particular in five states: South Carolina, Georgia, Alabama, Mississippi, and Louisiana. Rural Latinx populations tend to cluster in the Southwest and in a few states including Washington, Florida, and Kansas. Rural American Indian populations are similarly centered in the West and Southwest (Brown & Schafft, 2019). The rise in rural diversity is reflected in school enrollments and increases in the numbers and percentages of students who identify as BIPOC and English learners (ELs). J. D. Johnson and colleagues (2018) noted that between the 1999–2000 and 2014–15 academic years nationwide, the percentage of rural BIPOC students rose from 17 percent to 25.7 percent, and the percentage of rural EL students rose

The Bloomsbury Handbook of Rural Education in the United States

Table 5.2 Change in Rural Minoritized Student Population, 2005–15/16

	Percent Rural BIPOC Students			**Change 2005–15/16**	**Percent Rural Students 2015–16**	**Total Rural Students 2015–16**
	2005	**2011–12**	**2015–16**			
New Mexico	70.6	82.6	85.6	+15.0	18.4	60,012
Alaska	52.2	71.7	63.9	+11.7	25.2	32,889
Arizona	49.9	55.3	58.5	+8.6	5.3	49,859
California	44.0	55.3	57.5	+13.5	3.1	187,176
South Carolina	42.1	40.5	49.5	+7.4	15.9	115,889

Source: Data taken from *Why Rural Matters* reports, 2005, 2011/12, and 2015/16 (J. D. Johnson & Strange, 2005; Showalter et al., 2017; Strange et al., 2012).

from 2 percent to 3.5 percent. These increases were not uniformly distributed. The rural BIPOC student populations increased by 32.1 percent in the West, 33.6 percent in the South, 104.8 percent in the Midwest, and by 128 percent in the Northeast United States.

In Table 5.3, we again use US Census data to examine changes in White school-aged populations in rural America between 2000 and 2018. The data reflect what demographers have noted as a decline in the population of White youth occurring in tandem with increasing BIPOC youth populations (Frey, 2019). While the magnitude of the decline increases along the rural-urban continuum with urban places seeing the greatest declines, between 2000 and 2018, the population of White children in rural areas still declined by over 12 percent, as compared with a nearly 15 percent decline nationwide and an over 19 percent decline in urban areas.

Increases in rural racial and ethnic diversity are more likely in places that are economically expanding and already have concentrations of immigrant populations, and they are less likely in rural areas with higher percentages of retirement-aged residents (Sharp & Lee, 2017). Lichter and colleagues (2018) noted similar findings and also demonstrated that despite the growth of rural racial and ethnic diversity, increases in diversity tend to be clustered, reproducing patterns of spatial segregation. That is, despite data showing dramatic increases in rural diversity, "White population growth is occurring disproportionately in the least racially-diverse rural communities. For Blacks and other minoritized groups, growth is taking place disproportionately in the most racially-diverse places" (p. 702; cf., Logan & Burdick-Will, 2017).

Such demographic shifts can create conditions for rural gentrification, place stratification, segregation, inequity, and exclusion, creating new implications for rural education and community well-being (Corbett & Forsey, 2017; Lichter et al., 2018; Sherman, 2021). These data suggest that the social imagination of rurality as a "White" space (Brown & Schafft, 2019) has increasingly less bearing on reality. These trends also call attention to the ways in which racial segregation and inequalities may be (re)produced in rural places as populations change (Tieken, 2017).

Shifting Populations and Rural Schools

Table 5.3 School-Aged Child Population Self-Identifying as "White Alone," Not Including Hispanic

	2000		2018		
	%, Total Sum	N	%, Total Sum	N	% Change
US Total, White	61.44	36,021,109	51.25	30,763,417	−14.60
Urban	23.06	8,306,655	21.81	6,709,275	−19.23
Suburban	42.44	15,286,363	43.02	13,235,332	−13.42
Town	13.84	4,984,808	13.90	4,276,927	−14.20
Rural	20.66	7,443,283	21.27	6,541,883	−12.11

Source: US Decennial Census 2000 and American Community Survey 2018 estimate.

Rural Boomtown Development and Effects on Education and Schooling

The late 2000s and early 2010s saw an enormous expansion in unconventional oil and gas development across many parts of the rural United States, notably associated with major oil- and gas-producing shale plays. Examples include the gas-bearing Marcellus shale formation underlying about two-thirds of Pennsylvania as well as parts of New York, Ohio, and West Virginia; North Dakota's Bakken formation; and Texas's Barnett[4] and Eagle Ford formations, among others. Unconventional oil and gas development is a highly industrialized activity used to extract energy resources from underground geologic formations like shale and sandstone. It involves a combination of vertical drilling to the oil- or gas-bearing geologic layer, horizontal drilling along the layer, and then the use of water, sand, and other additives pumped at high pressure into the well to fracture the geology and release the energy resource that then flows to the wellhead. The development and use of these technologies led to a massive increase in natural gas production in the United States, as well as sudden build-outs of infrastructure and wells in areas with unconventional resources—a natural resource boom. While we are now several years beyond most of the initial drilling and development activity associated with this boom,[5] the rapid expansion of unconventional oil and gas development in rural America remains an instructive case study in a specific instance of rapid rural population change and the implications for schools (Biddle & Schafft, 2016; Schafft, 2017; Schafft & Biddle, 2015; Schafft et al., 2014).

Unconventional gas development held the promise for new economic development in rural areas that had long struggled with rural out-migration, high unemployment, and limited opportunity—a potential that was promoted by both government and industry advocates (Kennedy et al., 2017; Matz & Renfrew, 2015). As build-out began in Pennsylvania, school administrators and educators saw the potential not only for local economic development with increases in school revenues through property taxation but also for reversing long-term trends of enrollment decline and the subsequent threat of school consolidation or closure. This anticipation was tempered by questions about changes in school demographics, such as what gas development might mean for new students and instructional needs and for EL populations (Kelsey et al., 2012).

In the case of Pennsylvania, enrollment decline trends were largely unaffected (Kelsey et al., 2012) as most of the population influx consisted of single men from out of state following jobs in a highly mobile labor market (Filteau, 2014). The few workers who brought families with them had little effect on school enrollments. The population influx *did* affect the availability of housing, however. In the early years of the Pennsylvania boom, rental prices jumped three or fourfold in some places, causing new conditions of housing insecurity for low-income residents and new incidence of rural homelessness (Schafft et al., 2018).

Kelly and Schafft (2020) examined school district resources using statistical matching techniques that mimic a randomized control trial study design and found that, in comparison to school districts that had not experienced unconventional drilling, those districts with unconventional gas drilling activity had experienced *worse* economic outcomes, including lower per-pupil revenues and school funding, lower per-pupil income, and lower property wealth. Mayer and colleagues (2018) similarly looked at the effects of the oil and gas boom on human capital within rural US counties. They found that oil and gas development was associated with modest increases in the percentage of county residents with a high school education or less and modest decreases in the percentage of county residents with a college education. In sum, they conclude, "broadly, we expect that oil and gas development will do little to address long-run, structural demographic challenges facing rural America" (p. 219).

The impacts of unconventional energy development can vary significantly by region, as well as by proximity to development activity (Schafft et al., 2019). Zachary and Ratledge (2017), in a review of research focused on educational impacts associated with unconventional energy development, found that while the trends noted in Pennsylvania (above) tended to hold for Ohio and West Virginia as well, oil and gas booms *were* associated with school enrollment increases in places like Texas, Montana, and North Dakota as well as increases in student transiency, creating additional educational and administrative burdens for schools (Ratledge & Zachary, 2017). Enrollment increases were also not evenly distributed across grade levels. Local school officials related how most of the mobile workers new to the area were too young to have children in upper grades (or if they did, they were left behind at the place of origin), and some schools reported new enrollments in the lower, elementary school grades with those students moving as a "bubble" through the upper grades over time (Ratledge & Zachary, 2017).

School finances also showed differences across regions. Ratledge and Zachary (2017) suggested that one difference accounting for divergent outcomes is the nature of settlement structures. Sites of rural unconventional development in the eastern states tend to be characterized by many small towns and school districts, whereas many of the areas in the West experiencing rapid development are far more isolated, and new populations tend to be more concentrated in fewer settlements. Districts in all regions studied, however, felt the effects of fiscal volatility associated with the rapid change in industrial development and global energy markets. In total, scholarship suggests that local and regional context matters (including taxation and school funding policies, as well as the structure of rural populations) and that effects on schools from rapid and unexpected population change, such as is associated with boomtown energy development, may vary considerably depending on local and regional context (Schafft et al., 2019).

Rural Communities and Population Change in a Post-Pandemic World

The writing of this chapter coincided with the onset of the 2020 coronavirus pandemic and the rapid economic contraction of the United States and indeed the global economy. While a global pandemic has represented a serious concern among health experts for decades (Garrett, 1994), most countries were unprepared for the exponential growth of disease incidence, and in the case of both the United States and China, leaders spent weeks ignoring or downplaying the potential severity of the threat until it was clear that more concerted measures needed to be adopted, including shelter-in-place orders, the temporary closure of schools, and the shutdown of all but the most essential businesses and services (Garrett, 2020).

Initially it appeared as though rural places were to some extent shielded from Covid-19, especially as initial "hot spots" appeared in densely populated US metropolitan areas. Rural areas, less densely populated and with less population movement in and out, posed fewer opportunities for the external introduction and spread of infection—almost certainly accounting for the disparities in Covid-19 spread across urban and rural areas early in 2020. On the other hand, rural places have significant vulnerabilities. As Covid-19 began to appear in rural America, with concentrations in rural counties with meatpacking plants, American Indian reservations, and other areas with high percentages of BIPOC residents (Marema & Bishop, 2020), existing inequities in health-care access and outcomes for communities of color were exacerbated. Employees falling ill at a Tyson meatpacking facility in Iowa, for example, accounted for a 68 percent increase in local infections in a two-week period, and outbreaks in rural prisons and penitentiaries have occurred in New Mexico, Texas, and elsewhere (Peters, 2020).

While low population density helps to limit the spread of disease, other variables—sparse infrastructure, concentrations of poverty, disproportionate rates of older residents, higher incidence of chronic health problems, lower health insurance coverage, and decreased access to health care—increase health risks once Covid-19 is introduced to rural areas (Monnat, 2020; Peters, 2020). Orgera and colleagues (2020) noted that nonmetropolitan counties have only 1.7 ICU beds per 10,000 persons as compared to 2.8 in metropolitan counties, and rural hospitals have faced long-term fiscal challenges and threat of closure (Holmes et al., 2017).

It is far too early to determine the long-term effects of the pandemic within rural America and what it will mean for schooling and population change, and the effects will almost certainly be uneven across rural America. However, the pandemic has already raised difficult questions about educational equity, access to remote or distant education across low-income and rural communities, and provision of school meals to low-income students (Dunn et al., 2020; Tinubu Ali & Herrera, 2020). The pandemic will almost certainly have longer-term demographic outcomes and implications for many rural schools and communities, though the incidence and depth of these outcomes will depend on the longevity and severity of the pandemic.

What is more immediately evident are the severe economic impacts caused by the pandemic. By mid-June 2020, forty-three states had experienced worse job losses than during the Great Recession, with 14.7 million jobs lost and record numbers of unemployment claims (Ettlinger & Hensley, 2020). These impacts will almost certainly be more severe in places already struggling economically, with relatively undiversified economies, and already disadvantaged populations. A news release by the Bureau of Labor Statistics shows that while in June 2019, the unemployment rate for working-aged adults with less than a high school diploma was 5.3 percent, and for those with a high school diploma but no college, the unemployment rate was 43.9. By June 2020, those figures had jumped to 16.6 percent and 12.1 percent, respectively, with heavy job losses in rural economic sectors such as manufacturing and services (US Bureau of Labor Statistics, 2020). Since rural residents, in aggregate, have lower educational attainment than their urban peers, these unemployment statistics point to the likelihood of disproportionately negative outcomes for rural communities (Brown & Schafft, 2019).

While at this point we may only speculate, the pandemic will likely have at least two primary outcomes for rural places, each with potential consequences for amplifying demographic processes already in play. The first is that the pandemic will likely have disproportionately negative effects on places that are already struggling economically, including many rural areas. On the face of it, this is likely to only intensify processes of selective out-migration, aging, and economic contraction already occurring, especially in more remote rural counties. This, in turn, will place further pressure on school enrollments, community resources, and local infrastructure.

The second likely outcome by contrast may be that rural areas, and especially high-amenity areas already experiencing rural in-migration, will face increased demand for housing by metropolitan residents with financial (or other) resources who are seeking safer, rural, shelter during the pandemic and into the future (see Sherman, 2021). A Harris Poll with a nationally representative sample of over 2,000 US adults found that nearly 30 percent of respondents overall and nearly 40 percent of urban residents stated that the pandemic had caused them to consider moving to a less densely populated area (2020). This calculus may be especially attractive to professional-class telecommuters. As with the first outcome, this would simply reinforce already existing demographic processes with the likelihood of creating increased strains on housing markets and health-care systems, displacement of low-income residents (and school-aged children), gentrification, and social class-based exclusions (Sherman, 2018, 2021). The Covid-19 pandemic, among many other things, serves as yet another reminder of the vulnerability of rural communities as they struggle to absorb and respond to these demographic changes (Monnat, 2020; Peters, 2020) and the need, especially during times of national economic crises, for reasoned rural development policy (see Brenner's discussion of policy, Chapter 2, this volume).

Conclusion

As this chapter suggests, there is no one grand narrative of rural change. Rural communities have experienced a wide range of demographic shifts related to migration, aging, diversity, economic changes, and—presently—a pandemic. Rural population decline creates a number of consequences for local schools, such as a diminished local property tax base presenting additional challenges for rural schools to recruit and retain teachers. New populations and in-migrants can also create new social, institutional, and academic needs, which can prove difficult to finance when rural school district funding streams are disproportionately lower than school districts in metropolitan areas—even greater for poor, BIPOC communities in rural areas, as they are further disadvantaged when it comes to school funding (EdBuild, 2016). Changing demographics have unique implications for rural schools, and policies developed to support people in urban and suburban areas may not work in rural places. Since rural schools are often the cornerstone of their communities, an enormous amount of pressure is placed on local school leaders and educators to develop strategies for adapting and responding to demographic shifts and the contexts out of which they emerge.

School districts reasonably approximate locality-based communities, and rural schools are meaningful community-level social spaces. Rural schools can be a critical agent for not only education but also rural community vitality, well-being, and sustainability. Research into the relationship between community attachment and migration intentions suggests that rural youth who build stronger social ties and report a stronger sense of identification with the community show greater commitment to their rural homes (Petrin et al., 2014). Thus, the rural school should be considered not only a particularly valuable part of the rural development equation (Schafft, 2016) but also a critical component in the rural demographic equation as well.

6

Rural Poverty and Rural Schools

Mara Casey Tieken

"Where we live influences our life chances," writes legal scholar powell (2008). Place shapes our jobs, our neighborhoods, our health care, and our schools. We also see this influence in poverty rates and their strong correlation with place. Rural places, though, have often been overlooked in research on poverty and efforts to reduce poverty.

The concept of spatial inequality—or, as some urban geographers describe it, spatial injustice—is a useful framework for understanding and addressing rural poverty. Spatial injustice is the geographic disparity in access to necessary resources and opportunities (Soja, 2010), with some places enjoying fewer economic, social, and political resources—such as good jobs or quality housing or adequate political representation (Massey & Denton, 1993; Petti, 2017; Shen, 1998)—than other, more advantaged places. Spatial injustice typically reinforces racial and class inequality, with poor communities of color experiencing the greatest disadvantages and most segregation (Massey & Denton, 1993; powell, 2008, 2010).

One manifestation of spatial injustice is the high-poverty rates experienced by many rural communities. Rural poverty intersects with other geographic inequalities such as racial and economic segregation, limited access to social services, and few options for public transportation. These intersections mean that rural poverty, while it shares some important characteristics with urban poverty, also manifests uniquely. Understanding rural poverty and its relationship to education, therefore, requires special attention to rural space and its role in shaping poverty.

This chapter provides a general overview of rural poverty, including a working definition and descriptive statistics to contextualize the causes and effects of poverty on rural people and places. It also examines rural schools and their complicated relationships with rural poverty, including their efforts to address poverty and its community effects.

Background on Rural Poverty

The US Census Bureau determines the poverty threshold annually (Lee, 2018; US Census Bureau, 2017a, 2020). First developed in the mid-1960s, this threshold is set at three times the current cost of a minimum food diet, and it is adjusted for the age of household members and

Rural Poverty and Rural Schools

family size. An individual or household is considered to be living in poverty if their household income level falls below this threshold. In 2019, the official poverty threshold for a family of two parents and two children was $25,926. Though the federal government does employ other measures of poverty, poverty thresholds are typically used to document poverty trends over time and across demographic groups.

Poverty Trends in Rural America

Both historically and today, rural America has faced high rates of poverty. Since the late 1950s, nonmetropolitan poverty has outpaced metropolitan poverty rates, though this gap narrowed dramatically during the 1960s (Jensen et al., 2003). In 2017, 16.4 percent of nonmetropolitan residents were living in poverty, compared to 12.9 percent of metropolitan residents[1] (Economic Research Service, 2018). That nonmetropolitan rate was down from a thirty-year peak of 18.4 percent in 2013.

The overall nonmetropolitan poverty rate obscures vast racial disparities. In 2017, the rural Black poverty rate was 32 percent, the rural Native American poverty rate was 31 percent, and the rural Hispanic poverty rate was 24.5 percent—while only 13.5 percent of rural White residents lived below the poverty line (Economic Research Service, 2018). These racial and ethnic differences also correlate with different regions in the United States, as many rural African American residents are concentrated in the Black Belt and Delta regions of the Southeast; many rural Latinx families live in lower Rio Grande Valley; and many rural Indigenous communities are located in the Great Plains, throughout the Southwest, and in Alaska (Lichter et al., 2012). There are some rural, majority-White locales, like Appalachia, that also face high rates of poverty. Despite significant proportions of rural Black, Latinx, and Indigenous residents living in poverty, White individuals account for nearly two-thirds of the rural population below the poverty line (Economic Research Service, 2018).

Some important features characterize rural poverty. Income inequality is growing in the United States (Telford, 2019) and, as the wealthy continue to segregate themselves in neighborhoods and gated communities, concentrated poverty has increased during the 2000s (Lichter et al., 2012). Rural America also reflects trends of rising economic segregation. From 1990 to 2009, the percentage of poor rural residents living in high-poverty rural places—that is, places where poverty rates exceed 20 percent—increased from 30.2 percent to 35.2 percent (Lichter et al., 2012). Economic segregation is starkest for rural Black residents. In fact, poor rural Black residents are more segregated than poor Black residents living in metropolitan places: in 2009, 57.6 percent of poor nonmetropolitan Black residents lived in high-poverty communities compared to 47.7 percent of poor metropolitan Black residents (Lichter et al., 2012). While not as extreme as rural Black segregation, rates of rural Latinx economic segregation also surpass White rates; however, this segregation decreased during the early 2000s due to some Latinx residents moving to wealthier, more urban areas (Lichter et al., 2012).

Persistent poverty—that is, areas with poverty rates that remain high over generations—is another challenge in many rural locales. More than 85 percent of counties with poverty rates exceeding 20 percent for at least thirty years are nonmetropolitan counties (Lavelley, 2018). For rural residents, high rates of concentrated and persistent poverty mean that "getting ahead" often requires moving out of one's rural community (Lichter & Parisi, 2008).

Finally, rural children are especially likely to grow up in poverty (Schaefer et al., 2016). Nonmetropolitan child poverty rates also surpass metropolitan rates. In 2018, 22.4 percent of nonmetropolitan children lived in poverty, compared to 17.3 percent of metropolitan children (Economic Research Service, 2020). Trends in concentrated child poverty mirror overall patterns. For example, in 2010, 64 percent of nonmetropolitan counties had high rates of child poverty, compared to 47 percent of metropolitan counties, and these rates are increasing (Schaefer et al., 2016). Poverty rates are also much higher for rural children of color than for rural White children (Schaefer et al., 2016).

Causes of Rural Poverty

These patterns of poverty—that is, elevated nonmetropolitan rates and pockets of concentrated and persistent rural poverty—reflect spatial injustice. Spatial injustice is not just an outcome, though: it's also a process. Soja argues that the processes of spatial injustice manifest across three dimensions (Soja, 2010). The first dimension is *the political organization of space*, with exogenous boundaries serving as tools of oppression and control, as with apartheid or gerrymandering. *Distributional inequality* is the second, when the policies and actions of states, corporations, or individuals produce more endogenous patterns of opportunity and disadvantage (e.g., food deserts). The third is *uneven development* due to unequal flows of capital, resources, and people across place and space.

Racial Oppression

One of the major causes of rural poverty—and its racialized manifestations—is racial oppression. Historically, rural places across the United States have been sites of racial oppression and exclusion, with White settlers and government officials displacing and killing Indigenous peoples, enslaving African peoples, and seizing Mexican land (Lyson & Falk, 1993). White control over rural enslaved and displaced people was supported through a variety of policies and state-enforced boundaries—from plantation lines to treaties granting White ownership of Native land. The effects of these policies lasted for centuries and continue to impact rural communities today. As social and political change overturned some policies, they were often replaced by new legislation and practices such as Jim Crow laws or federal land policies that ensured formerly enslaved and displaced peoples had access to fewer social and political opportunities, to schools with less funding and fewer resources, and to land with little potential for economic development (US Federal Reserve & Brookings Institute, 2008). Cumulatively, these exclusions prevented rural communities of color from accessing education, the vote, and economic opportunities and from accumulating wealth. We see these patterns still today in the form of high rural Native, Black, and Latinx poverty levels. Contemporary political and distributional factors such as gerrymandering, segregation, and unequal employment opportunities sustain these racially disparate rates, too (Duncan, 1999; Lichter & Parisi, 2008; Lichter et al., 2012).

Rural Economies

Factors specific to rural economies also contribute to uneven development, fueling rural poverty. The rural employment structure can impoverish rural places. Some rural areas—like many Native reservations—have seen very little economic growth or development (US Federal Reserve & Brookings Institute, 2008), which results in few opportunities for employment or for acquiring land

Rural Poverty and Rural Schools

and assets. Researchers have also argued that rural areas might be intentionally and systematically underdeveloped in order to keep the cost of labor and raw materials low (Jensen et al., 2003). Indeed, rural workers earn less than urban workers (Economic Research Service, 2016), even when they have the same education, job skills, and experience (Jensen et al., 2003). In addition, local paternalism and impermeable power structures can limit who accesses employment and leadership opportunities, perpetuating landlessness, limiting political power, and restricting wealth (Duncan, 1999; Tickamyer & Duncan, 1990; US Federal Reserve & Brookings Institute, 2008). And the kinds of economies long associated with rural places, like resource-based extraction economies, are shifting, bringing economic uncertainty and, in many places, rising poverty rates (Lichter & Graefe, 2011). Finally, rural economies are less diversified, tending to rely on fewer industries than urban economies, making individual communities relatively dependent upon one or two industries for economic growth and stability (Economic Research Service, 2016; Jensen et al., 2003). When those industries collapse—when coal mines or timber mills start closing—the surrounding communities have few alternatives or paths to recovery.

Currently, a variety of rural industries are facing significant economic decline (K. M. Johnson & Lichter, 2019a), due, in part, to economic globalization (Smith & Tickamyer, 2011). Automation and increasing safety and environmental regulations have decreased employment across traditional rural industries, including agriculture, mining, timber, and fishing. In many cases, new industries are not emerging to fill those employment gaps (US Federal Reserve & Brookings Institute, 2008). Recent manufacturing declines have also had disproportionate effects in rural places, and rural employment still trails pre–2007 recession growth rates (Economic Research Service, 2019).

However, some rural industries, such as recreation, retirement, or energy, are experiencing widespread growth (Reeder & Brown, 2005; Weber & Brown, 2013). Some of this growth has led to an expansion of service sector work, which is associated with lower wages and higher poverty (Lichter & Graefe, 2011). When economic shifts do bring higher-paying work, these jobs often are filled by individuals hired from outside the rural community (Kelly & Schafft, 2020; Tickamyer & Duncan, 1990). This might be due, in part, to the lower educational attainment of rural workers; only 19 percent of rural adults have bachelor's degrees or higher, compared to 33 percent of metropolitan adults (Economic Research Service, 2017). Perhaps it is unsurprising, then, that some rural economic growth, such as the expansion associated with hydraulic fracking, has a negligible impact on poverty rates (Weber, 2012). In addition, in the case of hydraulic fracking, local economic opportunity has been offset by subsidies and tax breaks to the benefit of multinational corporations, but at high costs to local infrastructure (Tickamyer & Duncan, 1990; Weber & Brown, 2013), including schools (Kelly & Schafft, 2020).

Population Changes

Uneven development can also cause population change. Many rural areas are losing population, which undermines economic growth and fuels concentrated poverty. In fact, from 2010 to 2016, nonmetropolitan America saw its first period of overall population decline (Economic Research Service, 2019). Though rural locales, on the whole, are again experiencing population growth, this growth varies dramatically from place to place. Nonmetropolitan counties adjacent to metropolitan ones have seen the largest gains, while the most isolated rural counties have experienced the largest losses.

Immigration has been an important factor in contributing to recent rural population growth—or, in some places, mitigating decline (Mathema et al., 2018). The population of rural people of color grew by about 20 percent from 2000 to 2010, from 8.6 million residents to 10.3 million, while White population growth was nearly flat during the same time (Lichter, 2012). Much of this growth was due to increases in the rural Latinx population, which grew by nearly 50 percent during this period. This Latinx growth has been highly concentrated in particular rural areas, especially those experiencing economic restructuring tied to the corporatization of the agricultural industry. However, while this growth has been an important demographic and economic stimulus in many rural places, it has also been associated with rising rural poverty, as recent immigrants tend to experience higher rates of poverty than nonimmigrants (Schaefer & Mattingly, 2016).

Isolation, Weak Infrastructure, and Environmental Destruction

Finally, the geographic isolation, environmental destruction, and weak infrastructures of many rural communities can further exacerbate spatial inequalities. Long distances, mountainous terrain, or bodies of water can impede economic diversification (US Federal Reserve & Brookings Institute, 2008). In 2017, poverty rates were indeed higher in more remote counties (Economic Research Service, 2019). Rural places have also long been sites for "locally unwanted land uses" (LULUs)—that is, power plants, factories, prisons, or landfills (Lichter & Brown, 2011; Rhubart & Engle, 2017). The presence of LULUs in rural communities is often the result of economic and political actors exploiting the limited economic and political power of rural communities, especially communities of color (Rhubart & Engle, 2017). While these projects can bring jobs, not all offer a living wage, and LULUs often have negative environmental and health impacts that depress human capital and dissuade other businesses from investing (Lichter & Brown, 2011). Finally, rural communities also tend to have fewer social services such as job training and skill development programs, and geographic remoteness can make it difficult to access employment or social services elsewhere (Jensen et al., 2003). Relying on public assistance can also bring moral censure in rural communities (Sherman, 2006), and research shows that rural residents are less likely to use public assistance than urban residents (Jensen et al., 2003). These spatial inequities in resources and access can concentrate rural poverty and intensify its effects.

The Effects of Rural Poverty

The effects of poverty on rural residents and communities are profound. These consequences can also be complex and enduring, as many of poverty's impacts—for example, poor health or environmental degradation—are also its causes. Poverty, therefore, can present as a complicated web of effects that stretches across generations.

For adults, poverty is associated with a variety of negative health and employment outcomes (Nilson, 2007). Adults living in poverty tend to suffer higher rates of chronic illness, disability, and disease. Poverty appears to lower life expectancy and compromise mental health. These health outcomes are due, at least in part, to limited access to good nutrition and health care—both acute and preventative care—and also ongoing exposure to damaging environmental conditions such as poor air, contaminated water, or substandard housing. These conditions also reduce residents' capacity to develop the skills necessary to participate in the workforce or enroll in higher education, further entrenching poverty. In addition, research shows a link between rural poverty and increased mobility, caused, in part, by a lack of quality and affordable housing (Schafft, 2006). Poverty can also compromise adults' abilities to fully provide the safe housing, adequate nutrition, and high-quality educational materials their children need. Due to inflexible or irregular work schedules or long hours, parents living in poverty often lack the time to which they are positioned to navigate the demands of the school system to advocate for their children.

The impacts of poverty on children are also multifaceted and long lasting. As with adults, poverty undermines health: poor children are twice as likely to be in fair or poor health than nonpoor children (Brooks-Gunn & Duncan, 1997). Poverty is also linked to hunger, and poor nutrition can impede cognitive and physical development. Child poverty, therefore, is related to lower verbal skills and IQ scores; children growing up in poverty are 1.3 times more likely to suffer developmental delays and learning disabilities, and they tend to have lower achievement test scores (Brooks-Gunn & Duncan, 1997; Guo, 1998). Poor children also complete fewer years of schooling than nonpoor children—two years less than children from families with incomes more than twice the poverty line (Duncan et al., 2010). Children living in poverty are less likely to enroll in institutions of postsecondary education, less likely to attend four-year colleges, and less likely to complete postsecondary training (Cabrera & La Nasa, 2000; NCES, 2019b). In addition, child poverty is associated with higher rates of aggressive behavior, anxiety, and depression (Brooks-Gunn & Duncan, 1997). These effects all have long-term consequences on health and economic welfare (Nilson, 2007), reinforcing the strong relationship between childhood income and income later in life (Berger et al., 2018).

At the community level, higher poverty rates are associated with lower economic growth due to reduced human capital, poorer health, and lower education levels (Nilson, 2007). Impoverished rural communities tend to have little private investment, and residents often face high debt (US Federal Reserve & Brookings Institute, 2008). Housing options can be limited, frequently coming with high levels of environmental toxins such as contaminated water and lead paint. Communities struggling with poverty also have little funding available to develop community capacity. Many have economies dominated by absentee corporations or, especially on Native lands, long histories of exploitative relationships with the federal government; these dynamics reduce the possibility for growth. The strong stigma attached to living in poor rural communities can also fuel stereotypes, reduce trust, and thwart economic development. In addition to all of these effects, poverty matters for education, in ways both complex and important.

The Relationship Between Rural Education and Poverty

High-poverty rates create unique educational challenges. Eligibility for free or reduced-price lunch is a typical proxy for poverty in education research, though it tends to overestimate poverty levels (Snyder & Musu-Gillette, 2015), and across the United States, nearly half of rural students are eligible for free or reduced-price lunch[2] (Showalter et al., 2017). Poverty can be understood as both a cause and an effect of inadequate education. Poverty can reduce the local funding available for education, compromising educational quality. At the same time, low-quality schools can diminish human capital. Inequitable schooling, therefore, is one of the primary processes and outcomes of spatial injustice for rural communities struggling with poverty.

Poverty, Resources, and Achievement

Perhaps the most impactful poverty-related challenge facing rural schools is the reliance on local property taxes for education funds. Nationally, nearly half of education revenue comes from local funds (Baker et al., 2018). This local dependence means that property-poor districts—even those that tax themselves at high rates—struggle to build a strong tax base to support their schools, while property-rich districts are flush with local resources to use for education. This resource inequality fuels large funding gaps between poor rural areas, especially those with high rates of concentrated or generational poverty, and wealthier locales. Though some states attempt to compensate for weak local tax bases, fourteen have flat funding formulas, with no significant additional state funding directed toward high-poverty districts, and twenty have regressive formulas, which actually provide less funding to districts with higher poverty rates.[3]

Low-income rural schools, therefore, face unique and profound resource inequities. Their lower per-pupil expenditures are associated with poorer-quality facilities, for example, and compromised systems of support for teachers (Condron & Roscigno, 2003). A lack of resources in high-poverty rural schools exacerbates the challenge of hiring and retaining talented staff and supporting important academic, extracurricular, and social programs (Strange, 2011), including rigorous courses (US Governmental Accountability Office, 2018) and gifted programming (Azano, 2014).

Resource inequalities also impact academic achievement. Lower per-pupil expenditures are linked to lower student achievement and attainment (Condron & Roscigno, 2003). Across the United States, rural areas with high rates of concentrated poverty are correlated with weaker standardized test scores (Logan & Burdick-Will, 2017; Roscigno et al., 2006), though some research suggests that the academic achievement of rural students living in poverty might be better than that of their urban counterparts (Khattri et al., 1997). Dropout rates also tend to be higher for lower-income students and communities (Smink & Reimer, 2015; South et al., 2003).

It is important to note that the effect of community socioeconomic status on educational outcomes is separate from the influence of a student's individual socioeconomic status on these outcomes (Pittman et al., 2014). Without adequate resources, schools cannot provide students with a competitive education. In addition, given the adverse effects of poverty on children's health and well-being, students living in poverty often face academic and social challenges such as lower verbal skills (Brooks-Gunn & Duncan, 1997) or increased transience (Schafft, 2006) that poorly resourced schools may be unable to adequately address.

While insufficient resources are certainly a major cause—or even the primary cause—of inadequate education for poor rural students, it is likely not the only cause. Students living in poverty—particularly, students of color—can face classism and other forms of discrimination in schools (Anyon, 1981; C. B. Howley et al., 2014). This discrimination can take the form of lower expectations from teachers, "othering" from staff and peers, and limited outreach to parents. These prejudices then translate into inequitable educational opportunities for students.

The effects of poverty at school also contribute to poverty's cyclical nature. Impoverished communities with underresourced schools often find it hard to draw businesses or middle-income residents, making it difficult to shore up the local tax base and, therefore, difficult to improve the schools (US Federal Reserve & Brookings Institute, 2008). The lower educational attainment of many rural communities facing poverty may also deter new or relocating businesses, thereby

Rural Poverty and Rural Schools

further entrenching the distributional inequalities that cause rural poverty and contribute to spatial injustice.

Efforts to Address Poverty Through Rural Schools

There are many community, government, and philanthropic strategies to alleviate rural poverty and its effects: recruiting new industries to rural communities, extending welfare and other social supports, improving rural infrastructures, and building rural political power to influence policy. Education is a critical area of focus, and, over the past century, a variety of initiatives and programs have evolved to address rural poverty through schools.

Historic efforts by the federal government to target poverty through schooling began with Roosevelt's New Deal (Fass, 1982). As the Great Depression caused poverty levels to soar, President Roosevelt responded with a comprehensive set of school construction projects, work training programs, and supplementary social service initiatives that allowed for the opening of nursery schools, employment of teachers, repair of school facilities, and expansion of courses in literacy and citizenship. While less a coordinated effort to address poverty's causes than an assortment of programs aimed at providing immediate relief, these programs marked "a broader, more welfare-oriented view of education" (Fass, 1982, p. 46).

Mid-century, efforts to ameliorate poverty's effects on children through schools increased. In 1946, the National School Lunch Act was passed, providing funding for school lunches for children living in poverty (Yarrow, 2011). President Johnson's War on Poverty further expanded school-based anti-poverty initiatives in the 1960s. One of its key initiatives was the Head Start Program, offering educational, health, and social services to low-income children in communities across the United States (Yarrow, 2011). President Johnson also passed the Elementary and Secondary Education Act (ESEA) of 1965, which authorized federal Title I funds for the education of economically disadvantaged students (Black, 2017).

Poverty levels dropped considerably in the 1950s and 1960s but have plateaued since 1970. This fifty-year plateau has resulted in political disillusionment with the potential of governmental anti-poverty efforts and, over time, has led to more limited social service programming (Yarrow, 2011). However, many of these mid-century programs still exist, including the National School Lunch Program, Head Start, and Title I. On an average day in the 2017–18 school year, for example, nearly 22 million children received free or reduced-price lunch at school, and the National School Breakfast Program, which was added in 1975, served 12.5 million children (Food Research and Action Center, 2020). Head Start now offers programming for infants, toddlers, and pregnant women, and, from 2017 to 2018, a million women and children received services (Early Childhood Learning & Knowledge Center, 2018). Title I continues to provide federal funding to low-income students, with an average allocation of $1,227 per eligible child in 2015 (NCES, 2019a).

In addition to their expansion, these programs have experienced some other key changes. For example, the No Child Left Behind Act (NCLB), the 2001 reauthorization of ESEA, introduced a variety of accountability measures that mandated annual student assessment and created sanctions for low-performing schools (Black, 2017); it also required greater attention to the academic performance of student subgroups, including low-income students. Although the 2015 reauthorization of ESEA, the Every Student Succeeds Act (ESSA), loosened some of these regulations and sanctions, state and federal governments continue to monitor academic achievement for economically disadvantaged students and pressure districts to improve student performance, often couching these policies in arguments of building human capital and expanding economic opportunity.

Programs and policies have also manifested uniquely across rural populations. For instance, because more than half of rural children live in childcare deserts, poor rural families are more dependent on Head Start for early childhood education than their urban and suburban counterparts (Malik et al., 2016). Additionally, programs' requirements sometimes pose challenges for rural students and schools. One example is the method of calculating Title I funds. This funding formula relies on either the number of poor students or the proportion of poor students, whichever is higher for a district (Strange, 2011). Urban districts with large numbers of poor students can use that metric to qualify for funding from the limited Title I pool, even if that population is only a small proportion of their overall student body, which leaves less funding available for sparsely populated, high-poverty rural districts. Similarly, some of the accountability measures tied to Title I make little sense for rural areas. Several provisions of NCLB are instructive, such as its Highly Qualified Teacher provision, which specified that every teacher must have full teaching licensure, a bachelor's degree, and proof of content knowledge in their areas of teaching (Eppley, 2009), or determinations of schools' ability to meet "adequate yearly progress," which were based on students' test scores (Jimerson, 2004). These mandates made districts with high-poverty levels—often with small or variable numbers of students and limited staff sizes—particularly subject to sanction, and they also have contributed to a contextless understanding of "quality education," one with little regard for a child's or school's location or class background (Eppley, 2009; Jimerson, 2005b). While ESSA's increased flexibility may reduce the challenges NCLB presented for rural districts (Gagnon, 2016), some worry that the relaxed regulations undermine the law's core commitment to educational equity for all students, including poor students (e.g., Black, 2017).

Other current school-centered efforts to address rural poverty are more localized. Some districts provide teachers with training to be more responsive to their low-income students. One particularly influential model, especially in rural schools, is the work of Ruby Payne, which purports to educate teachers about the "culture of poverty" and its manifestations. However, this model has been widely critiqued as relying on weak evidence and stereotype, failing to include a structural analysis of poverty, and preventing more significant change efforts (e.g., Bomer et al., 2008). Efforts that meaningfully engage local communities, such as school-community partnerships, offer a more promising avenue toward spatial justice. With these partnerships, schools and community stakeholders collaborate to provide services and initiate reforms to address local issues, including rural poverty (Schafft, 2016). Some rural schools serve as sites for career training programs that develop employable skills, build technical knowledge, and connect workers to local jobs for both youth and adults (Schafft & Harmon, 2011). Full-service schools are another model (Dryfoos, 1996; Warren et al., 2009). Full-service schools provide a range of after-school programming, evening classes, and health and dental services for students and their families. This holistic model of schooling, which requires the support of a wide array of community partners, can address many poverty-related needs, including health care, childcare, and job training. Other efforts focus more squarely on improving school quality, whether through increasing school funding, offering a more rigorous curriculum, or improving college access. Education organizing—that is, community organizing for education reform—has been a key vehicle for many rural residents to strengthen schools in their communities and push for more responsive education policies (Warren & Mapp, 2011).

Conclusion

Unjust geographies are not accidental but are instead created through inequalities, oppression, and neglect, both historic and current. And we see this injustice reflected in the poverty facing many rural places—poverty that has devastating and long-lasting consequences, for individuals and for communities.

Rural schools are implicated in both the production and the manifestation of rural poverty. But they are also essential to addressing it. They are the primary public institutions entrusted with the academic, social, and civic development of rural children, and they can support rural economies, build rural political power, and reduce rural racial inequality (Tieken, 2014).

To do this work, though, rural schools need policies and practices specifically tailored to the rural context. These policies and practices must ensure that schools are fairly resourced, explicitly anti-racist and anti-classist, and deeply responsive to their local communities. Then, rural schools can serve to dismantle the structures and address the effects of poverty, ensuring rural sustainability and promoting spatial justice.

7

The Why and How of Enhancing Data Use in Rural Education Research and Practice

John W. Sipple, Peter Cody Fiduccia, and Kristie LeBeau

Gaining a deeper and more complete understanding of how schools function within rural communities is the goal for many researchers and educational leaders alike. Studying and leading rural schools, implementing policy, responding to state demands, and enhancing community vitality all require rich data to capture the complexities and integration of schools embedded within the rural communities they serve. This chapter aims to explore the value of linking student, school, and district data with other sources of data from health care, childcare, economic and community development, and other community-based data. Such cross-sector data linking can offer important insights, but it is not done without challenges. We will discuss the values and challenges of this work.

In doing this, we first offer a conceptual model of local school-community interactions and a review of relevant literature. This will help to conceptualize the role of the school in rural communities and how linking to other systems in the local community provides a much broader and deeper understanding of the implications of the local decisions, policy implementation, and community vitality. Using only education data limits our understanding of how children, families, schools, and other local institutions interact and limits our vision for policy design and implementation (Casto, McGrath et al., 2016).

Following this conceptualization, we will offer insights into relevant sources of data to possibly include in rural education research, which may also assist in local education and community practice. Beyond identifying various sources of data and exploring the types of research and practice questions possible with such data, we will also offer advice on the mechanics and challenges of combining education with noneducation data. This includes a careful discussion of relevant units of analysis, issues of causality, time series and spatial analyses, and the challenges of merging data. We will describe several examples of successful linking of educational and other data from different community systems, highlighting research questions, practice implications, and lessons learned.

This chapter discusses the utility of linking student, school, and district data with other data sources that represent the nuance and complexity of rural communities. These additional data may originate from systems of health care, childcare, economic and community development, and other systems that impact the livelihood, opportunity, and resources for children, families, and communities. We argue that such a multifaceted data strategy is an important step in capturing the integration and influence of systems in rural communities that ultimately provide (or do not provide) valuable opportunities, support, and resources.

Conceptualizing the Need for Linking Data

It is the aim of many scholars, outreach specialists, and community leaders to better understand the opportunities and constraints in local communities. One can do this through careful ethnographic, anthropological, or qualitative sociological research, through embedding oneself within a community to understand how it supports its youth and provides opportunities both in and out of school. A community-based approach is without a doubt the best way to understand a single community, its schools, and the interaction between the two. However, when researchers, outreach specialists, and community leaders want to understand common practices across multiple communities or to explore the range of differences in opportunity, success, and practice across dozens, hundreds, or thousands of communities, the aforementioned qualitative methods are impractical if not impossible.

It is not our intent to downplay such rich and local efforts as we have learned and will continue to learn much from this work (see Carr & Kefalas, 2009; Fitchen, 1981; Tieken, 2014). Truth be told, we stand on their shoulders. We have gained so much insight into the complexity and nuance of individual rural communities that it motivates us to conduct better, richer quantitative work. However, and in contrast to the common phrase, "Once you understand one rural community, you understand one rural community," we suggest that there is much to learn about patterns of organization, resource, and opportunity across regions, states, and nations.

It is this motivation to learn across a broad context that motivates this chapter. Conceptually, we think of rural schools and their communities as interactive systems that also include central aspects of people's lives, including health, work, opportunity, and care. We root this perspective in a conceptualization of "need" advanced by Dean (2010) and Casto, McGrath and colleagues (2016). In short, children in all communities have needs, and we, as a society—through families, local programs, schools, and policy—respond to meet such needs. However, as a society, we tend to focus on a thin conception of need, ignoring root causes of need (Casto, McGrath et al., 2016). A thin conception is acute, instrumental, individual, and disconnected from family and community sources of such need. For example, in educational terms, students in need are provided with meals while we fail to understand why so many children come to school hungry.

Deeply rooted in a different conception of a vital rural community that drives our work is an understanding and related action toward alleviating deeper causes/sources of the child's need. This utilizes a "thick" conception of need that is more chronic, fundamental, and relational. In addition to the provision of providing a sandwich to temporarily solve a child's hunger, we must understand the need is considered symbolic of the inability of a family and community to provide basic necessities for the child. Clearly, a family within the community is not sustained or supported without employment or wage opportunities, but there are also other considerations.

The Bloomsbury Handbook of Rural Education in the United States

There may be a health impairment in the family or a transportation challenge limiting access beyond a food desert. Or, the community may lack childcare options, limiting parents' ability to earn sufficient wages outside the home to adequately support their children.

Examining rural schools and communities through a lens of thick need brings an entirely different set of policy, community, school, and family decisions into focus, particularly when compared to a thin conception of need. In our work, we encourage others to use a thick conception of need when studying student "performance" and outcomes, school closures, lack of school resources, or student "dysfunction."

We suggest schools interact with the communities they serve in distinct ways and work together toward achieving distinct goals. We view these sets of distinct approaches and goals through an array of four lenses that interconnect and interrelate to paint a more complete portrait of the role that schools play within rural communities (paper forthcoming). We posit that schools may serve as an economic and social force as well as a preparer of workers and citizens. Here we briefly describe our four lenses to motivate a more comprehensive search for data outside the realm of typical education research. These frames help to stimulate thoughts and ideas for how to engage in data collection and use for a richer set of research studies to advance the field of rural education.

Schools as an Economic Force

Schools contribute to the economic vitality of a community directly and indirectly. Perhaps most obviously, schools serve as a direct economic force according to their role as a large employer in rural areas (e.g., the proportion of jobs in rural communities provided by the local school system versus private sector or other public sector jobs). From bus drivers and classroom aides to licensed teachers and administrators, public schools offer steady employment with middle-class wages. This role of the school as an employer varies widely across communities, from communities in which the school is a predominant employer to a relatively minor player in the local labor market. Less overtly, schools also serve as an economic force through their potential to attract businesses and families to the community. For businesses looking to locate in a rural community, the quality of a school may serve as an important factor in determining whether a location will be appealing to potential employees. For potential home buyers, the quality of schools can be an influential factor in home purchasing decisions (Carnoske et al., 2010).

Schools as a Social Force

Schools can also act as a source of community information, norms, and entertainment. Some of the information and social connectivity is generated by the school (i.e., school plays, concerts, athletic contests), and other connectivity is generated by the community using school spaces (e.g., municipal voting, adult education, and other adult uses for the school building space). In these spaces, schools can bring community members across generations together and create social networks. Similarly, it is well documented that parents gain social capital (networks) via their children's friendships (Coleman, 1988). Referring to its practical uses, researchers have documented the potential benefits of utilizing school facilities for community development (Cleveland, 2016; MacKinnon, 2001). In small communities with limited resources, a school can serve as a shared space, not only for community events such as municipal voting and recreational activities, but it can also be used to deliver family and health services. As such, schools can offer childcare and pre-K to families in the community in addition to health services through school-based health clinics.

Schools as Preparers of Democratic Citizens

In addition to the popular view of schools as a place for cognitive skill development is the role that schools play in preparing students for community and societal democratic involvement. Becoming a citizen and active member of a community or broader society takes on many forms, including voting, engagement with local and nonlocal institutions, governments, and social groups. A place-based curriculum that connects students to their local environment has the potential to instill a sense of belonging and ownership in students, leading them to recognize that they are part of something bigger as actively engaged citizens. However, schools cannot do this adequately by themselves. In collaboration with community and civic groups, schools can offer their students exposure, motivation, connectivity, and experience in the value and impact of democratic citizenship. These skills, though developed in the local community, are transferable across places, locally and globally.

Schools as Preparers of Workers

Of course, the most common view of how schools and communities interact is around the provision of human capital development, including preparation for higher education and direct preparation for the workplace. Schools teach students to read, compute, and analyze in addition to using other higher-order skills to assist the individual to find gainful employment, but to also serve the state's economic interests through this form of *public* investment and expected *public* good of *public* education. In an increasingly global economy, schools are pressured to prepare students for a nonlocal workforce while also recognizing the out-migration taking place in rural communities—creating a need to retain rural youth in a local workforce. Ideally, schools prepare students to participate in a workforce, whether that be local or nonlocal, giving them the tools and opportunities to make the choice for themselves. As we mentioned earlier, these roles of a school interact and overlap, and in this case, the preparation of students as citizens and workers can be strengthened if the two are taught as complements of each other.

It is with this conceptualization that we seek to identify and link sources of data with data from schools and school districts to more broadly document and inform the field. While all parts of the framework have the potential to link to data sources, in this chapter, we limit our examples to the first two lenses of the conceptualization (school as an economic force and a social force) to provide more in-depth, robust examples of how data collection can be utilized. Linking data across sectors, administrative units, and state or federal agencies allows an exploration of rural communities not possible with education data alone.

Building a Multifaceted Data Strategy for Research and Projects

Thus far, we have discussed the lenses through which we believe schools interact with their surrounding communities. This not only helps to enrich the conceptual underpinning of schools' importance to rural locales but also works toward a more defined typology of the relationship between educational institutions and broader factors of community. To further operationalize our conception of "thin" and "thick" needs, we propose and support the exploration and utilization of data outside the realm of purely education-oriented sources. Schools do not operate as islands independent of outside influence and, as exemplified in our four lenses, they are in fact integral parts of rural communities. We offer support to that supposition through examples of projects utilizing our proposed multifaceted data strategy.

Case 1—Linking Schools to Community Economic Vitality

Considering schools as an economic force and advancing beyond the surface level of serving as employers in rural areas recalls research questions concerning a school's influence beyond its walls. One such consideration was illuminated in our article, "Exploring the gradient: The economic benefits of 'nearby' schools on rural communities" (Sipple, Francis et al. 2019). Stated simply, the query presented in this paper was an exploration of the relationship between how far a school building(s) was located from a village center and the economic vitality of that village. Economic vitality was measured using three individually tested dependent variables: median housing value of each village, median household income, and median per capita income. One of the original works on schools' economic relationships to their communities (see Lyson, 2002) was a motivator for this project. Findings showed the closer a school or schools are to a rural village center (the higher the School Proximity Indicator or SPI), the greater the values of all three of the dependent variables.

To simultaneously analyze the relationship between location, economic factors, and population information, data were sourced from multiple stakeholders at both the state and federal levels. Federal-sourced data included the shapefiles for village boundaries, population estimates, and American Community Survey (ACS) response data. State-level data included school locations and financial, demographic, enrollment, and performance information. To construct and then evaluate distance relationships between villages and schools, we utilized spatial data by means of Geographic Information Systems (GIS). The use of spatial data is becoming more commonplace in social science analysis (Carlson & Cowen, 2015; Hogrebe & Tate, 2012; Sipple, Francis et al., 2019), though it has been a default tool for climate and urban planning fields for decades. GIS techniques allow for the visual representation and subsequent analysis of a wide variety of place-based data from polygon shapes (such as the village boundaries in our 2019 paper), to point data (school or other institution building locations), to transportation elements (road networks used to calculate distance or driving time). In this project, spatial data was critical to enabling the identification of the village boundaries, the location of schools within or outside of those boundaries, and the establishment of the five-mile buffer analysis zones, which eventually allowed for the creation of the SPI.

Data Challenges

One of the consistent challenges in working with data of any kind is management, merging, and joining. Downloading information from the Census or ACS repositories is not always foolproof. Data collection is, at one point in the process or another, as much a human enterprise as the responses themselves. At the highest level, there are challenges in comparing data across varying units of analysis. As much as feasibility is of critical importance to analysis, so too is readability to dissemination. Ensuring units are either normalized when possible, or at least clearly identified, is of utmost concern. In this project, we observed data in per capita, household, and school districts units. These data were not contained within any packaged shapefile (such as

Leveraging Data in Rural Education

a village boundary polygon) and are considered nonspatial. Nonspatial data were then merged to spatial files, some by matching the name of the district in one source to another, some by matching school district identifier codes, and some by matching village name. The *Gradient* project also required the merging of data between federal and state sources. As we discovered, working between different levels of administrative frameworks can run the gamut from seamless to nerve-wracking. Something as small as a variance between "Anytown" and "anytown" can cause a data merge to fail.

Data Tips

As we discovered during the *Gradient* paper processes, combining data from various administrative sources can be challenging. Before attempting any merging, it is good practice to examine the single files. Our workflow usually involves the observation of case, unit, and type for each individual dataset. These checkpoints are useful for any kind of multisource data operations but are especially crucial for spatial to nonspatial merging.

The unification of case across datasets is one of the simplest—yet most powerful—pre-merge data cleaning procedures. Whether making string variables into all upper, lower, or proper cases or ensuring multiformat variables have the same length, case mismatch will cause merging errors in nearly every instance. In Excel, case mismatch can be easily rectified using formatting commands. In STATA or other statistical processing software, mismatch can also be solved by generating a new variable using the preferred case. In the case of the *Gradient* paper, we utilized STATA's reformatting capabilities to reformat the string variables of village name (e.g., "MORAVIA" in one file would not merge with "moravia" in the other, so we adjusted accordingly).

Units, as represented within a dataset to be merged, are also another critical consideration, though an easily identifiable discrepancy. In our work with data from the ACS and the New York State Education files, there were some instances of unit mismatch within data files. In the New York files, percentages (such as graduation rate) were represented as whole numbers, while percentages in the ACS files (such as population who commute less than fifteen minutes to work) were represented as decimals. This kind of mismatch would not cause issues with merging but could pose a concern for representation of data via visualization or comparison within multivariate analysis.

Ensuring a unified type of variable across datasets is the final tip we can offer for best practice in cases of multiple data sources. Type, in this instance, refers to how your data management program identifies and subsequently codifies individual variables. The most common types include string, text, integer, long, and float. In most cases where merging between various sources of data is employed, type mismatch is of the least concern. It is usually quickly rectified by either manually switching the type via a dropdown menu in programs such as Excel or by generating a new variable with the desired type in programs such as STATA. In our *Gradient* analyses, we ran into mismatch errors within datasets. Within the New York files, the village name was classified as a string type, which is preferable. The school district ID number, which we treat as an identifier like village name, was classified as a float variable. To treat the school ID as a unique identifier, we ended up creating a new variable—essentially a duplicate—in the new, preferred type while keeping the original. In our work, we found it to be good practice to avoid deleting previous iterations of variables, if only because they serve as useful references as well as 'save points' for data cleaning and preparation exercises.

Takeaways

By combining federal-level data from the ACS and spatial data in the form of village boundaries, road networks, and school building locations to state-level school district data, we were able to examine previous conceptual and empirical work while bringing to bear a novel methodological approach. As noted in the *Gradient* paper, however, the advantages of combining multiple sources of data, including spatial information, should never occlude the difficulties of assigning—or importance of acknowledging—causal direction. We state the causal direction is unclear and that it is likely a two-way effect: school proximity may promote higher economic vitality in some cases, and vibrant village economies may support the development of schools in others.

Case 2—Linking Education and Health Care

We also define schools as social forces within the rural communities in which they are located, and beyond. We began this exploration with a set of data tools to help define and illustrate the differences between schools in rural and nonrural communities (Sipple, Fiduccia et al., 2019). Most specifically, we note literature that supports school facilities serving as hubs of shared community space, particularly in rural locales with limited resources. A burgeoning example of such community-school partnerships deals with healthcare provision. School-based health clinics (SBHCs) are being piloted and evaluated with increasing frequency to increase equitable access to health care, a direct influence within the child's microsystem (Bronfenbrenner, 1975), particularly in rural communities.

A large regional healthcare provider in New York has been piloting, opening, and operating SBHCs in rural school districts across a particularly rural region of Upstate New York. As part of an ongoing project, a research question that has emanated from the work attempts to ascertain if an SBHC within a rural school district can effectively "improve the culture of health" for both students and the community at large. Though the notion of a "culture of health" is admittedly nebulous, the project group broadly identifies the research goals of increasing the frequency with which patients present for general checkups/wellness visits and decreasing the frequency with which patients present for more acute manifestations of chronic illnesses.

The SBHC project, like the *Gradient* paper, utilizes spatial data—but in a much more pivotal manner. One primary data source for all health-related information is the privacy-protected, individual health records for all patients in the system (close to 600,000 observations per year for seven years). The records are separated by year and contain demographic, diagnosis, and facility visited data. Most importantly, these records include the registered patient addresses. What is not available from the provider's database, however, is the school district in which the patient lives. This is where the utilization of a multifaceted data strategy comes into play yet again in that we can determine the school district of residence by joining other forms of data.

Data Challenges

In our ideal scenario, prior to engaging with data observation, cleaning, or analysis, we identified an iterative goal trajectory. Most pertinent to our research question was the ability to analyze health outcomes over time. This would be possible using only the healthcare provider data. It would be of limited impact, however, if we were unable to link said outcomes to the communities in which the patients lived. This next iteration would be possible, again, using the healthcare provider data + utilization of GIS techniques to geolocate patients within New York state. It

Leveraging Data in Rural Education

would be of limited use, however, to the examination of SBHC impact within rural communities of varying demographic makeup, racial composition, and the educational environment if we were unable to link the patients to a school district. This would only be possible with the combination of healthcare provider data + GIS geolocation + spatial joining to established school district boundaries. This final iteration would also help to directly inform our hypothesized function of schools as social forces, particularly in rural communities with relation to healthcare provision.

Challenges in operationalizing all three elements of the final iteration of research goals were numerous. The first step was to geolocate all patients within the provider's database for each year. Given the total number of observations over the seven study years (average of 600,000 per year), the data needed to be collapsed to a more manageable dataset of means. By utilizing the new, streamlined versions of the yearly datasets, we reduced the load on the geolocation algorithm by an estimated 80 percent. After geolocating, we needed to combine our New York education and healthcare provider data. Researchers analyzing education datasets will occasionally have to deal with privacy issues because of legislation such as FERPA. In this SBHC project, the addition of healthcare data adds an entirely new set of stringent privacy limitations. Such limitations can be expected not only on the level of data acquisition but also on the level of data storage/access. Due to detailed HIPAA regulations, as well as the stringent security procedures being undertaken as a matter of best practice by the university, the analyses of high-privacy, sensitive files take place on a secure, remote server sequestered from the internet. While this adds a layer of necessary privacy protection, it also adds time, complexity, and logistical barriers to quick data access or analysis.

Once geolocated, the patient records were then "assigned" a school district by executing a GIS technique known as a spatial join. This process takes a point layer (the address of each patient, per year) and assigns it the attribute(s) of an underlying polygon layer (school districts). To maximize efficiency, the only attribute we joined to the patient information file was the name of the school district in which they were deemed to reside, for a given year. After performing the spatial join, administrative information from specific districts could be appended as well. This merge would then create a per-patient setup of demographic, health, address, and district-specific data. Recall the previous data tip to always be mindful of case, unit, and type. We learned about the case the hard way in the SBHC project. The spatial join process created an appended district name field that was all uppercase while the district file contained proper and lowercase formats. We had to modify the stand-alone district file, re-upload it, and then redo the spatial join for all years.

Data Tips
Data preparation is often the most time-consuming task on a project, but it is arguably the most important. If using software such as STATA in which you can create syntax/code and then run it on a file, always remember the golden rule of responsible data processing. If possible, don't save iterations of datasets; simply keep a meticulously iterative syntax sheet with notes. This serves multiple purposes. First, you will be able to identify and isolate various points in your cleaning procedures in case something is either formatted incorrectly or needs to be changed later. Second, in theory, any one of your teammates can easily identify and reproduce the procedures by which you prepared the data. Finally, you reduce the clutter that inevitably can damage forward progress on a large-scale project. By only keeping the original, raw data and making changes via the syntax, you eliminate dozens of saved, altered datasets.

Data reduction as a separate technique can be useful in a variety of ways but must be undertaken with care. A primary method of data reduction used in the SBHC project was to create a dataset of means by way of the "collapse" function in STATA. Instead of observing each patient's height, weight, BMI, and so on, at each visit per year, reducing the data to an average of those variables allowed us to observe yearly trends quickly and efficiently. The "count" function within the "collapse" command also allowed us to observe the number of visits by each patient per year over time, essentially creating a previously unavailable analytic variable by means of the reduction. In the original data per year, patients are assigned a visit ID number, unique to each patient and visit. The number of unique instances of this variable, by patient, were then identified and reported as part of the reduction operation and compared across years (e.g., patient X had four visits in 2014, eight visits in 2015, and two visits in 2016).

Takeaways

The answers to complex research questions are often illuminated through a similarly robust mix of frameworks and data sources. The original research question that asked whether the presence of SBHCs helped or hindered a community's culture of health may have been answered by an analysis of the health outcomes alone. We would argue, though, that this might fall under a "thin" conceptualization of healthcare and community need. By enabling the geolocation of patients within communities, we can understand the utilization of SBHCs in a spatial context. Adding school district information such as district enrollment, demographics, and so on, we can further present a nuanced understanding of the SBHCs' influence on rural communities. Finally, through the utilization of spatial data we can ask questions unanswerable by the provider data alone by identifying any changes in address or district of residence across years.

Case 3—Linking Two State Agencies in Communities

Like many states across the United States, New York initiated a noncompetitive grant program to promote Universal Pre-Kindergarten (UPK) in 2007, building on the momentum and research that found that each dollar invested in pre-K results in a return to society of $8 (Heckman, 2012). Despite the availability of state grant money to start up a pre-K program, many rural districts were not taking advantage of this program. All urban districts were quick to participate, and suburban districts typically took the grant if they served a low-income population but did not if they served a wealthier community. Puzzled at the nonresponse of hundreds of rural districts, officials at the state education department called Professor Sipple and asked if we could study the situation and offer suggestions for what the state should do to increase adoption.

We quickly began to explore how we would study the take-up rates of districts by the number of four-year-olds served in each type of district and by the range of community characteristics (e.g., small/large, poor/wealthy, racial heterogeneity, tax rates) in districts that initiated UPK and in districts that did not. In conducting such research that would certainly shape state policy and implementation practices, we wanted to make sure we gained a complete understanding of why districts were not accepting the grant and why most of these happened to be rural. To do this, we conducted both statewide quantitative analyses of administrative data as well as six rich case studies grounded in the complexities of the communities in which these decisions were made. Through these multimethod analyses, we were able to answer the state's questions.

First, we found that rural districts did not trust that the funding would be sustainable beyond the life of the grant. Second, rural districts were concerned with significant costs the UPK program would create, such as added transportation services and the need to hire new teachers—expenses insufficiently funded by the grant. This last item included not just the addition of local dollars but a belief among the decision makers (namely, school board members) as to whether UPK was worth providing. Despite the research evidence of its effectiveness, some remained suspicious of spending local money to pay teachers to "play" with children and watch them take naps.

In doing the above work, we developed a rich knowledge of the interactions between schools, the communities they serve, and the other service agencies involved in assisting families, including early care providers. This illustrates the rich roles of the school in a community as a preparer of citizens and a social force. This led us to our research on the capacity of local communities to serve their families and children. What we uncovered, almost by accident, was a very interesting interaction effect between community capacity to serve infants and toddlers and the local school district's decision to operate a UPK program. Districts that operate UPK have less infant and toddler capacity in their communities. In this analysis, we define "capacity" as the number of slots available within a community's registered childcare facilities: the proportion of age-eligible children in the population divided by the total available openings reported by each facility. Conversely, in communities (e.g., school district boundaries) without UPK programming we found greater community capacity to serve infants and toddlers (Sipple et al., 2020). When we began to share our results, people looked puzzled because UPK was a program run out of the New York State (NYS) Education department through school districts, and early care was funded by state and federal money funneled through county childcare coordinating agencies. And yet we found that the two were somehow linked?

To conduct this research, we linked demographic, financial, and performance data from the state education department with administrative data from the NYS Office of Children and Family Services (OCFS). Only by bringing these two datasets together were we able to cross boundaries of PK-12 education with the early care and education world of OCFS.

Data Challenges
The challenges of this work lie in linking data from two different state agencies (e.g., difficulties resulting from the constant changing of variable names) as well as conflicting interpretations of what the data mean. The Education department releases data extracts of school district enrollments, demographics, finances, and performance measures annually, though at different times of the year (i.e., finances in November and performance in June). Fortunately, each data file includes a district ID, so merging these files annually into a longitudinal dataset with variables from these three categories was straightforward.

But the data for UPK enrollment was not in the main data extracts mentioned above. Rather, the UPK data started to be released in an Excel file attached to a press release. As this office of UPK matured in its collection of data, it would commonly change the variables collected—and change the names of the variables—they collected each year. Trying to create a longitudinal data set of UPK enrollments was surprisingly hard. Among the variables that have been most in flux were the locations of where the UPK students were taught (e.g., in the school, in a non-school childcare center, or in a Head Start program). These variables, when present, allow us to create

The Bloomsbury Handbook of Rural Education in the United States

a binary variable for whether the school is partnering with a community-based organization to facilitate the UPK programming.

OCFS maintains a wonderfully helpful database of all currently registered childcare providers, which includes phone numbers, addresses, and the number of slots for which they are registered to provide. For instance, a provider might be center-based and registered to serve a maximum of five infants, nine toddlers, and sixteen four-year-olds. OCFS even goes so far as to operate a publicly facing web tool where parents can search for registered providers in their town or zip code.

The trick was that the OCFS data points did not include the school district in which they were located. The town and county were listed, but in NYS the county boundaries do not align with school district boundaries (some districts are in two, three, or four counties). Our prior work in New York revealed that conversations and networks surrounding the provisions of UPK and early care seemed to coalesce around school district boundaries (McCabe & Sipple, 2011). The long tradition of home rule and small districts signals that the school district boundary is a logical boundary for the networks of early care and UPK providers. This being the case, we geolocated all 18,000 providers and then located them inside a school district. We then summed the infant and toddler capacities for each provider within each district and did this for each year of data we had available to us.

This brings us to the last major data challenge we faced using this OCFS data source. While OCFS goes to great lengths to provide an up-to-date data source for currently licensed local providers, they maintain no historical archives of this database. It is always "live" and up to date, but that means that as soon as a provider closes or has its license revoked, it disappears from the database. In 2014, the OCFS database was for the first time downloadable; prior to this, we had to send a request to OCFS for a data extract. We began doing this in May and tried to remember to secure an extract each subsequent May, but this complication was eliminated once the database became publicly downloadable.

Data Tips

In previous cases, we have illustrated data tips that reinforce the importance of technical tasks, including merging and cleaning. In this case, we struggled to understand the attributes of certain variables, the logic behind their presence in the data, and why some variables might be present in one year of data and absent in the next. Some state or federal repositories may have extensive metadata and/or dictionary files associated with each dataset, but these files rarely describe the institutional logic behind the organization of the file(s). This served as a reminder of the human component of datasets and data systems. After making an in-person visit to, and having an enlightening discussion with, our colleagues at the NYS Education department and the OFCS, our questions were quickly answered. We were able to secure copies of school district UPK forms, understand limitations of the live data systems, and provide researcher-oriented feedback to the stewards of data; this, hopefully, leads to a more efficient and productive relationship in the future.

Takeaways

The use and merging of data from multiple government agencies can provide a rich window into the variety of relationships that exist between schools and other community supports and may even lead to stumbling upon important relationships that had not been previously considered.

Leveraging Data in Rural Education

Our discovery of childcare deserts and their relationship to the presence of UPK programming was indeed unexpected and would have been impossible without the joining of data from multiple agencies and units of analysis. This value, however, comes at the expense of time and care in making sure researchers fully understand all variables and the newfound relationships among variables. Proceeding with haste can be misleading and potentially dangerous. Meeting personally with the keepers of the data to explain your goals and your interpretations of their data is therefore strongly suggested.

Conclusion

Motivated by our quest to attain a greater understanding of the many ways in which schools function within rural communities, we have developed a rich set of experiences in the novel practice of linking data from different state and federal agencies together. Much like Zanoni and A. D. Johnson (2019), we find value in linking two seemingly disparate data sets together to answer new and novel questions about the interactions between schools and the communities they serve. However, it is important to note that we do not condone "dustbowl empiricism," or the massaging of data until you find something interesting. Our work is built on a conceptual model of the various ways in which schools and communities interact, and we strongly encourage others to proceed similarly. Rural communities, and the schools embedded within them, are complex and multifaceted. To efficiently and effectively lead rural schools, we hope researchers and stakeholders recognize the benefits in using rich, diverse data to enhance community vitality.

International Response

Responding Rurally

Perspectives and Insights from One Rural Place to Another

Simone White

The notion of rurality and the importance of place continues to be subject to much debate by many education researchers and scholars who write about "the rural" and what "adding the rural" (Green, 2013, p. 17) might mean *to* and *for* the field of education. They do so, often in contrast to policy reforms that appear *placeless* and, by default, metrocentric. This volume continues the important work through a deep dive into a scholarly collection by North American education researchers exploring rurality in relation to *their* place and context. In writing a response to this collection, I have done so as a fellow rural researcher and colleague to this group. For the purposes of this chapter, however, I have taken my vantage point from a distance, from an international position, located in Australia. I discuss some of the themes that emerge across the studies and use these to reflexively explore further the contested notions of rurality and place from *my* context in Australia and the global implications.

Rurality and Place Neutrality?

A key theme across the chapters is a discussion about the importance of shining a light on rural matters in the backdrop of policy that does not *see* place. As Brenner, in this volume, notes:

> Most education policy funding presumes to be "place neutral" in that place or geography are not explicitly addressed and the policy is intended to be applied the same in every location. One-size-fits-all policies presume that a program will work equally well no matter where it is applied, that a regulation can and will be followed in the same way regardless of the location, or that a formula for distribution of funds will be equitable across all types of places. (Chapter 3)

Brenner poses a key question asking: "Does policy assume all places are the same?" The response from both the US and Australian context is yes, unfortunately, it does. To date policy is often rolled out regardless of the distinctive and culturally rich aspects of any given (rural) place. As a consequence, many rural researchers have continued to caution against such "placeless" policy reforms with several Australian rural researchers writing about this issue and the negative impact of doing so on rural student outcomes (see, e.g., Cuervo, 2012; Green & Letts, 2007; Reid, 2017; Roberts, 2014; Roberts & Green, 2013). Places are not neutral, and policy that assumes so continues to disadvantage our rural students, their families, and our schools.

Responding Rurally

For us in Australia, this issue is further magnified by a phenomenon coined as "policy borrowing" (Lingard, 2010) within the "global education reform movement" (Sahlberg, 2016). Globalization and the neoliberal agenda have resulted in many countries looking to other places for their policy reform as they compete against global performance metrics such as the Programme for International Student Assessment (PISA). Australia has historically followed both the United States and England (Mayer, 2014) in terms of education policy reforms, even though to date Australia has performed above both countries in terms of PISA results (White, 2016). As a result of following education policy reforms as set out in the United States and England, the past two decades have witnessed a rapid rise in a high-stakes testing and accountability regime rolled out for students, teachers, and schools.

Such reforms have also occurred in teacher education with the introduction of a Literacy and Numeracy Test for Initial Teacher Education (LANTITE) as a prerequisite for graduation; a national approach to the accreditation of preservice teacher education programs; new entry requirements for entry into initial teacher education programs that take into account nonacademic credentials; the replacement of the one-year postgraduate diploma in education with a two-year master of teaching qualification; new stages of career progression with attached standards; and the introduction of a teacher performance assessment (TPA) for all graduates.

As these policy reforms swirl around the globe, they lose their historical and geographical context and often their rationale for being implemented in the first place. Such "placeless" policies continue to have a negative impact on our rural students, their families, and communities (Corbett, 2017) while further marginalizing rural voices. Such practices are in line with what Cervone highlights in this volume, cautioning:

> Standardization also creates a geographic disconnect as rural students often do not see themselves and their communities represented in the curriculum (Haas & Nachtigal, 1998) nor connected to the larger world, creating a sense that being rural is a deficit, or an obstacle to overcome. (Chapter 4)

In reading the chapters in this volume from the standpoint of what has been coined as the "global South" (Dados & Connell, 2012), it is concerning to see the increasing neoliberal agenda and datafication of education occurring in the United States that Cervone describes (Chapter 4), drawing from the work of Giroux (2011), cautioning:

> The greatest threat to our children does not come from lowered standards, the absence of privatized choice schemes, or the lack of rigid testing measures. On the contrary, it comes from a society that refuses to view children as a social investment and instead consigns 15.5 million children to live in poverty, reduces critical learning to massive testing programs, (and) promotes policies that eliminate most crucial health and public services. (p. 83)

It appears for us in Australia, that if we are not careful, the stories from this volume's past could become our future too.

Rural Place Matters

To address the consequences of such "placeless education policy reforms," many rural education researchers are keen to tease out further notions of rurality and have been exploring the socio-spatial tools to do so. As Australian authors Somerville and Rennie (2012) note, despite the spatial turn that has influenced social policy, research, and scholarship, the new conceptual framework for understanding place has been relatively absent until recently in research in education. This lack of socio-spatial awareness in relation to education has been steadily changing, however, with rural education research now often including terms to describe/define/interpret "rurality" such as space, place, boundaries, edges, crossing, borders, mapping, and positionality. These words reflect a growing research focus that is inherently "spatial" in nature (Halfacree, 1993) and are reflected in the ways in which rural researchers in this volume discuss notions of rurality. Understandings of place and spatiality sit alongside this work. As Gruenewald (2003a) explains:

> A theory of place that is concerned with the quality of human–world relationships must first acknowledge that places themselves have something to say. (p. 624)

By the very nature of researching "beyond the metropolis" and to *hear place*, it is also necessary to work against homogenizing or blurring of *all* rural places, and the people who live and work there, *as one*. As such, a necessary caution has been called out to the global rural community to be mindful that "once you understand one rural community, you understand one rural community." As a way to theorize and better understand the nuances of any one place, a socio-spatial methodological tool known as "rural social space" (Reid et al., 2010) has been offered as one way to explore *a* rural place and to help researchers and educators to consider what makes a place unique. This theoretical tool encourages understanding a rural place through the intersection of its economy, geography, and demography overlaid with its history and Indigeneity.

As Sipple, Fiduccia, and LeBeau note in this volume (Chapter 7), this privileging of *a* rural place does not preclude rural researchers "learning about patterns of organization, resource, and opportunity across regions, states, and nations." This is, in essence, what this handbook and the international perspectives are seeking to do: to value and understand the uniqueness of a rural place and to look for patterns and themes across places to learn from and about both. Such a scholarly endeavor builds on the international work by other education research collections (see, e.g., Green & Corbett, 2013; White & Corbett, 2014; White & Downey, 2021) keen to inquire into what impact "adding the rural" has to aspects such as teaching, schooling, policy, and research. As Jesse Longhurst in this volume (Chapter 1) notes:

> The myriad ways in which scholars define, describe, and theorize rurality all inform the study of rural education and are the source of ongoing conversation and debate in the field. (Arnold et al., 2005; Corbett, 2015a; C. B. Howley et al., 2005; Stephens, 1992)

The emergence of a rural education dedicated handbook to the field is further evidence of a maturing research community. It will help address the challenge we face as rural education researchers and the perceived relevance of the research we do within the wider research community itself. Rural research is often marginalized due to studies that appear smaller in nature, scale, and design. Historically, becoming a rural education researcher has been a rather solitary endeavor. In attending large international education research conferences, the Rural Education Special Interest Group (SIG), in contrast with those of many other fields of inquiry, hardly filled a small room. As such, many scholars have found great synergies and strengths in connecting our research endeavors internationally. As a global rural research community, we have thus naturally and strategically gravitated together across diverse countries in order to strengthen our research and better understand global forces as they play out in our local (rural) contexts.

The field, however, has been widening and maturing, and since the turn of the millennium there has been a growing cluster of rural researchers theorizing, connecting with each other, and finding research connections in turn in their own countries. For example, there has been a greater Australian research focus on the nuances and affordances of place in relation to understanding education and teacher education (see, e.g., Brennan, 2005; Cuervo, 2012; Green, 2015; Halsey, 2006; Kline & Walker-Gibbs, 2015; Reid et al., 2010; Roberts & Green, 2013; Somerville & Rennie, 2012; White & Reid, 2008). These studies have sought to examine rural education issues alongside the significance of understanding differences in place and space for beginning teachers and experienced teachers alike, and they have shone a light on the evidence that adding the rural makes a difference to education outcomes and staffing. This series of chapters is evidence of such a group of rurally minded and place-attentive education researchers writing in and from the perspective of rural education in the United States. In writing this response, it is important to understand more about the "rural social space" (Reid et al., 2010) from where I stand.

Responding from Where? Rural Standpoint

I write this chapter from Brisbane, Queensland, Australia. In reading the various chapters, I noted that Australia and the United States share so many similar rural challenges and trends. We are in many ways (rural) cousins. For example, both our countries share similar migration trends with many younger people moving from some rural areas to the cities while increasing numbers of refugee and migrant families move to rural communities. Other rural communities have seen "tree changers" and semi-retirees moving away from the suburbs. These trends are reflected in the backdrop of many of the US studies and as Schafft and Maselli note in this volume (Chapter 5):

> While out-migration and shrinking communities have been a dominant story for many rural places, other rural places have become migration destinations for retirees and others, especially high-amenity areas with relative proximity to larger metropolitan areas. (Brown & Glasgow, 2010; Scharf et al., 2016; Sherman, 2018)

Like our US cousins, population decline in nonmetropolitan areas has occurred in Australia—a decline shaped by global economic and technological shifts, increased population mobility, the globalization of production, limited rural labor market demand, selective rural out-migration, and aging rural populations. These demographic changes have had serious consequences for the survival of rural schools, as enrollments decline and schools face pressure to close or consolidate (Tieken & Auldridge-Reveles, 2019). Like so many other rural communities across the world, we too share challenges in staffing our rural schools (both in recruiting and retaining teachers) and our rural students experience generally fewer opportunities for further education, subject choice, and as such career opportunities.

While we do share many similarities, we are also unique and different in so many ways as well. I write this response at an unprecedented time during the 2020 global pandemic in a country that is (depending on state and territory borders) at various stages of "lockdown." The pandemic has heralded drastic shifts in moving schooling and teachers' work practices to online and remote learning. Some Australian authors (Roberts & Downes, 2020) have wryly noted that metropolitan-based students are now experiencing the type of learning and teaching that many remote Australian students have embraced for some time. As they explain:

> Amid all the concerns about closing schools and setting up online learning, in Australia it is important to note that Australia is actually a world leader in school distance education. Indeed, distance learning is not only achievable for Australian students, but very normal for many students around our large island continent. In rural and remote regions of Australia, students have been learning "by distance" since the inception of "school of the air" in Alice Springs over 100 years ago. (AARE EduMatters blog)

Some international readers who have not yet visited Australia may consider all of Australia "rural" or even "remote" if they consider the amount of time it takes to travel to destinations as their measure. Australians on the whole like to travel, and we seem to accept the perception by our scholarly colleagues that it is always further for visitors to come to our shores than it is for us to travel to theirs. For us in Australia, being labeled "rural" is all a matter of perspective. What one person views as rural is viewed as outer-urban or even remote by another, and culturally such terms are viewed very differently within and across each state and territory (White, 2019). For example, each state and territory has its own definitions of rural in terms of staffing policy. In Victoria, a southern, relatively small land-size state, the challenges of staffing schools within a two-hour radius of Melbourne (the capital city) have meant that the state government is currently incentivizing teachers to relocate and awarding $50,000 to do so. This notion that a school that is positioned within two hours from a capital city could be labeled as rural and hard to staff is quite literally incomprehensible from my now home State of Queensland. How we define rural in the end is subjective, depending upon what standpoint you take.

While from a policy perspective, the term "rural" is often viewed as a geographic term denoting a space and/or place that is beyond the metropolis and often defined as inland. Subjectively, the use of the term is often dependent on one's own lived experiences of places and spaces that look or feel rural. As an "imagined" space, it can be viewed as either idealistic and romantic or barren and hellish (Sharplin, 2002). Such perceptions can dictate our views and expectations. As Donehower (2014) likewise writes, "'Rural' is typically a felt term in the USA, rather than a technical one" (p. 168). In many ways this is true, as illustrated below for the Australian psyche, with popular culture myths of the bush, mateship, and comradery in the face of hardship serving to feed idealistic, romantic, or exotic notions of the rural as "other" in the way we view our individual and collective selves.

Australians outwardly can tend to portray themselves in "rural" terms to the world. Dorothea Mackella's iconic poem "My Country," for example, paints a vivid picture of the Australian landscape. There are many poems, books, and films that portray Australia as largely "rural" and for some, speak to the ways in which we imagine and portray ourselves and our identity. Just like the critique of "placeless" policy, framing ourselves as essentially "rural" or homogenous in any way, however, can have the same negative impacts we in rural education seek to change. As Jo-Anne Reid (2021) reminds us:

> (As) residents of settler nations where land was appropriated, and its meaning altered, through invasion, migration, and globalisation, we live on land that has *become* "rural," not because of its inherent genesis, but in relation to colonial centers of power and commerce. (viii)

Thinking through "rurality and place" in relation to postcolonial centers of power and recognizing the stories and people of the lands from which we write is more important than ever. Being based in Brisbane, I write on the Country of the Turrbal and Yugara peoples, the first peoples of this land—land that was never ceded. Prior to colonization, Brisbane was called Meanjin and was home to a vibrant and active Aboriginal community with well-defined living, ceremonial, burial, and public spaces. In Brisbane, as in all places, colonization was cataclysmic for the Australian First Peoples, exactly as it was for Indigenous peoples in North America and in so many other countries that share similar colonial histories. The recent Black Lives Matter protests in the United States have sparked similar protests here in Australia, both as a sign of solidarity in what constitutes basic human rights and also, for us in Australia, as a way to bring about much-needed change to the unacceptable high level of incarceration of Indigenous peoples and systemic racism that exists. The movement has also presented an opportunity for truth telling about our history and a way to collectively move toward reconciliation while celebrating and acknowledging our First Nations peoples and rich and diverse cultures.

Conclusion

In conclusion, this volume heralds a maturing of the rural education research community. The chapters explore the distinctive affordances of a range of rural places, and they explore strategies and approaches to work against placeless policies. This volume will do much to strengthen the field overall and will assist many rural researchers from across the globe in further exploring the notions and nuances of rurality and place from their vantage points, just as these chapters have done for me. It is in the opportunity to reflect on the nuances of rurality and places afar that I have come to better understand my own place and the richness and affordances of *this* place.

Part II

Introduction

Rural Schools and Communities

Extending from the foundational overview of rural education in Part I, the chapters in Part II consider schools in their communities. Specifically, the chapters consider how school closures, charter schools, and district governance are outcomes of sometimes contested local and state decision making in K-12 rural school settings. The chapters also consider higher education attainment, rural school partnerships, and school leadership in rural places. Collectively, the chapters illustrate the ways in which schools and communities are not only connected but are also mutually co-constructed while existing in webs of local, state, national, and global ideologies and political environments. In Chapter 8, Sutherland and Seelig lay the foundation for understanding K-12 school district governance. This chapter, Educational Governance and Contemporary Policy in Rural America, begins with a historical overview of the intersection of rural public school governance and federal education policies. The authors then explain common governance structures of school districts and the leadership roles that are common to those structures. They further discuss regional governance structures for rural districts, identifying how districts are organized and governed, and the underlying political issues that influence that governance. Within the chapter, the authors invite readers to consider how school funding levels as an outcome of property taxes exacerbate educational inequities and has, in part, led to a governance shift toward scientific management in the form of centralized, consolidated school districts overseen by trained educational administrators. Consolidation is a particularly widespread perennial reform, as it is based on the belief that centralized governance promotes economic efficiencies and academic opportunities.

Chapter 9, Consolidation, Closure, and Charter Schools, focuses on the impact of consolidation, closures, and charter schools as an example of the intersection of rural public school governance and education policy discussed in Sutherland and Seelig's Chapter 8. Eppley's chapter provides an updated synthesis that traces the phenomenon of school closure and consolidation from its 1930s roots to the present day, including the relatively recent phenomenon of charter schools in rural communities. While initiated and operated under the same state-level policies as suburban and urban charter schools, charters initiated in response to closure and consolidation are typically operated by community groups with deep generational and social commitments to the previous traditional school. While discourses of efficiency, competition, and achievement typically dominate charter school initiations, Eppley describes how rural charter organizers in these specific situations privilege continuity, personalization, and community. Yet the same charter policy that provides communities the opportunity to maintain a public school in the community presents important obstacles that challenge efforts to reproduce the traditional school.

In Chapter 10, Biddle turns readers' attention to the social context of school leadership, emphasizing new frameworks for understanding rural school leadership focusing on the unique role of school leaders in placemaking and community vitality. The chapter provides a review of research literature on rural school leadership over the past two decades, focusing on the lived experiences of leaders in small, rural, and remote communities and looks broadly at the state of the rural principalship. Topics include managing the diverse responsibilities of rural school leadership, facilitating organizational change in schools with limited human and fiscal resources, navigating the high visibility of working in a small community, building and repairing relationships with local families in communities with a high degree of intergenerational closure, cross-sector collaboration, and pursuing mentoring and professional development within a context of geographic isolation. The chapter concludes with a review of the ways in which the broader field of educational leadership has and has not intersected with research on rural educational leadership, and with recommendations for future directions for research on rural school leaders.

Rural Teacher Labor Issues is the topic of Chapter 11 in Part II. McHenry-Sorber gives a historical treatment of teacher activism in West Virginia, the birthplace of a wave of teacher labor activism that took place in 2018 and 2019. The chapter highlights the rich tradition of rural labor and activism in West Virginia, particularly in the rural southern coalfields where the statewide strike began. While underscoring the need for more scholarship, the chapter examines the existing scholarship on teacher labor and rural labor issues in order to construct a research agenda for rural teacher labor, including international scholarship on rural teacher activism; broad US teacher labor research as published in historical waves of activity; US urban teacher activism and strike scholarship; research on relevant rural labor contexts; and existing literature on rural teacher labor issues. The need for an established rural teacher labor research agenda is further nuanced by a consideration of a critical point of divergence in the field: rural labor protest in the state arena versus the local district arena. The chapter also includes discussion of the potential for divergent rural community responses to teacher labor protest in local-level versus statewide movements, using West Virginia and Mountainville, Pennsylvania, as examples.

The next two chapters in Part II focus on school-community partnerships. Chapter 12, Rural School-Community Partnerships: Creating Community-Aware Educational Practices, by Casto and Sipple, positions rural school-community partnerships as having the potential to create "community-aware" educational practices that resist policy design and enactment concerned solely with students inside the four walls of the school without attention to the needs and impacts of the communities in which children and families live. The authors argue that truly understanding and meeting thicker needs such as lack of economic opportunity, nutrition, health, family stress, and obstacles to family stability is different from the more common practice of ameliorating student deficiencies in school. The chapter offers a review of the literature on school-community partnerships through the community-aware lens to better understand the

Introduction

extent to which current practice adheres to this conceptual framework. Following the literature review and a conceptualization of an ideal community-aware partnership, Casto and Sipple offer well-selected examples that enable the reader to visualize the role of researchers and school leaders in promoting community-aware partnerships.

The second chapter interrogating school-community partnerships is Chapter 13, Zuckerman's Collective Impact in Rural Places. Place-based partnerships have been viewed as a means to counter the detrimental effects of urban-centric education policy, to reverse out-migration, and to support community development, vitality, and resilience. In recent years, collective impact has emerged as a strategy for bringing together diverse partners around a common agenda to create community-level change. Collective impact provides spaces for communities to consolidate resources and develop relationships to facilitate change, but models for collective impact create both opportunities and challenges for rural areas. In this chapter, Zuckerman proposes collective impact as a strategy for rural communities to tackle complex social problems. Drawing from the general research on collective impact and two case studies conducted in rural communities, the chapter describes the collective impact process with a particular focus on the preconditions that facilitate these partnerships. Further, the chapter highlights the importance of social relationships and cautions that conscious efforts must be made to bring individuals to the table who may have experienced social isolation and exclusion based on their socioeconomic status, race, or linguistic diversity.

Chapter 14, the last chapter in Part II, examines the challenges and opportunities for rural students who transition to postsecondary education. Postsecondary Transitions and Attainment by Schmitt-Wilson and Byun examines the context of rural students' postsecondary educational decisions. The chapter focuses on two important social institutions—families and schools—that play key roles in shaping rural students' postsecondary educational decision making. The chapter addresses additional challenges that rural students face when making postsecondary educational decisions, then turns to an examination of rural students' persistence in and completion of college as compared with that of their urban and suburban peers. The authors identify factors that promote or constrain college persistence and completion among rural students from various ethnic and socioeconomic backgrounds and discuss how these factors differ from those of their nonrural peers. The chapter concludes with an explication of college experiences among rural students, describing such factors as the pathways by which they pursue postsecondary education, the selectivity of the institutions to which they apply, and the timing of their eventual enrollments. Choice of majors among rural students is also relevant to the discussion in that it contributes to graduates' decisions about whether to return to rural communities.

Part II concludes with Corbett's international response, Rural Schools and Communities: We Can Bridge, but Can We Bond? In his response, Corbett first discusses the impact of centralized and decentralized educational governance structures on the affordances and challenges of rural education, pointing to the ways in which the United States differs from other international contexts in its highly decentralized structure for educational governance. He points specifically to the ways in which privatization has forced decentralization of educational governance across national contexts, and the ways in which this change has shifted how education is understood globally. Corbett also points out that the broader global project of rural modernization has been

The Bloomsbury Handbook of Rural Education in the United States

to disrupt the closeness of personal bonds in favor of shifting those feelings onto other structures, such as the state, employers, or private interests. He reflects on the way in which school-community relationships are conditioned by the need for rural schools and their communities to continue to respond to external mandates and challenges, making do without organizing for broader political action. Corbett calls into question the role of scholarship in serving as a witness to the resilience and adaptability of rural communities and schools in these circumstances and the reification of rural community "bootstrapping" in the face of these challenges. He concludes by urging scholarship in this area to examine both resilience and inclusion as well as exclusion and marginalization, pointing to increased engagement with the implications of settler colonialism as one powerful line of inquiry that could be undertaken.

8

Educational Governance and Contemporary Policy in Rural America

Daniella Hall Sutherland and Jennifer Seelig

The decentralized nature of US public education is based on a long history of locally controlled education, where schools, as primary public institutions, are governed by their communities (Scribner, 2016). This tradition of local control dates back to colonial America when New England towns implemented common schools and participatory town meetings (Kirst, 2008). In tandem with the Industrial Revolution, educational leaders implemented a series of reforms to make educational governance more scientific, including centralizing and consolidating districts and implementing training and certification for educational administrators (Callahan, 1962). Rural communities were specifically targeted during these reforms due to perceptions that small, locally controlled rural schools were deficient (Theobald & Wood, 2010) and that centralized educational governance would improve economic efficiencies and academic opportunities (C. B. Howley et al., 2011). Over the ensuing century, state educational reforms continued to target rural communities, prompting more school consolidations.

Today, public school districts across rural America encompass a variable patchwork of organizational and governance systems. To make sense of the national variability of rural educational governance and the implications for rural policy implementation, we divide this chapter into several sections. In the first section, we introduce the organization of state and local educational governance structures. Across the roles and organizations, we highlight rural-specific research for these dimensions of educational governance. Collectively, this section provides a foundational understanding of rural US public school district governance.

In the second section, we discuss various contemporary education policies that influence rural school governance and local education practices. Given the large number of policies at the federal and state levels, we select two significant themes to summarize (a) federal mandates for specialized services and (b) standards and accountability. This overview illustrates the layered nature of intergovernmental education policy that must be navigated by rural districts.

In the final section, we present two rural-focused vignettes to articulate the tension that exists between rural school governance and federal and state education policies. The first example, from Vermont, illustrates the complexities of implementing urban-centered federal accountability policy at the state and local level in a rural state. The second example, from Wisconsin, illuminates the multilevel challenges of school funding and the choices rural school districts must consider when facing declining student enrollment. Taken together, these examples provide deeper insight into the governance and politics of rural education.

Section 1: Overview of State Educational Governance Organization in the United States

Chief State School Officer (CSSO)

Public education on the state level is led by a CSSO, designated as a commissioner, secretary, or state superintendent of education. The CSSO is the primary educational leader for the state. The position may be elected by the general population of a state, appointed by the governor, or appointed by the State Board of Education (SBOE). The CSSO typically works closely with state leadership, including the SBOE and the governor, to ensure the state is responding to federal directives, aligning educational policy with state objectives, and providing oversight and support for local districts. The CSSO usually oversees the State's Department of Education.

State Board of Education

All states have a State Board or Commission of Education that is composed of multiple elected and/or appointed members. In some states, the SBOE is overseen by the CSSO; in others, SBOE oversees the CSSO. The role of the SBOE is to create educational codes and policies and to translate laws created by the state legislature into guidelines for local districts to implement. Nationally, SBOEs have varying degrees of authority; some states use the role as a largely ceremonial position, whereas in others, SBOEs exert significant power over educational systems (Young et al., 2019).

State Department of Education (SDOE)

Each state has a department, agency, or office of Education that is responsible for oversight and implementation of state education programs, policies, and funding. SDOE staff are typically nonpartisan career employees, but some states also have politically appointed positions. SDOEs oversee assessment and accountability, federal programs, special education, funding, interventions for underperforming schools, certification, and other statewide programs. Rural states tend to have smaller SDOEs due to lower population density and smaller resource allocations (Shelly, 2012). In comparison, SDOEs in states with higher population density have not historically been responsive to their rural regions (Jimerson, 2005b), tending to construct and reproduce urban-centric educational policy and programs as a default.

Overview of Local-Level Educational Governance Organization in the United States

Within each state, educational governance is further divided to the local level. Local educational agencies (LEAs), a broad term that includes school districts and unions, oversee all public education in a given geopolitical region. LEAs can range in size from a single town to a county to an entire state, as is the case of Hawaii (see Table 8.1). Despite major variability, the governance structures for most LEAs include the same core organizational elements: superintendent, local BOE, and a district office.

Rural Educational Governance and Policy

Table 8.1 Overview of LEA Organization Structures in the United States

LEA Structures	Overview
County District	The district encompasses an entire county. These types of districts are most common in the southern US, including South Carolina, Georgia, and Kentucky, where the educational system historically was centered on plantations (Mitra, 2018).
Town or City District	The district is bounded by the geopolitical boundaries for a single city or town. This is one of the most common forms of LEA organization.
Consolidated District or Union	The district includes multiple towns that have been centralized into an LEA. Consolidated districts may include significant geographic territory. One example is Regional Supervisory Union 50 in Maine, which encompasses seven towns across 460 square miles.
Multidistrict Union	A multidistrict union is a variation of a consolidated school district. The primary difference is that local communities retain community-based school boards for oversight of budgeting, as well as some managerial and educational oversight. In contrast to consolidated districts, communities in multidistrict unions retain some local control and autonomy. They are common in Maine, Massachusetts, New Hampshire, and Vermont (Hall & McHenry-Sorber, 2017).
Native American and Tribal Education	The federal Bureau of Indian Affairs (BIA) and the Bureau of Indian Education (BIE) organize and oversee schooling for Native American and Indigenous peoples living on tribal lands or reservations. BIA/E schools are funded by the federal government; many include both boarding and day school options. The majority of Indigenous students are served by public school districts, however (see RedCorn et al., Chapter 20, this volume), such as the Gallup-McKinley County School District in New Mexico, which operates on the border of the Navajo Reservation. BIA/E schools have an ugly legacy of suppressing Native culture and language, while providing inadequate education to these students. Today, BIA/E schools must meet Title III requirements for Indigenous language instruction. Despite some improvements such as Title III, however, tribal and reservation schools remain among the most underserved rural districts in the country (Executive Office of the President, 2014).

Superintendents

Superintendents oversee LEAs. They are hired and evaluated by LEA school boards, except in atypical cases such as state takeovers for underperforming school districts or mayoral control. Broadly speaking, superintendents are responsible for oversight of educational practices, managerial governance, and political engagement and communication. However, the leadership practices of superintendents are influenced by LEA contextual factors such as geographic locale, size, governance structures, and community demographics (Hall & McHenry-Sorber, 2017; Masumoto & Brown-Welty, 2009). For example, rural superintendents are more likely to have small administrative teams in comparison to nonrural district leaders (Bredeson et al., 2011). As a result, a rural superintendent may be responsible for multiple roles in the LEA central office, a term colloquially referred to as "wearing many hats."

Rural school districts are also described by scholars as essential sites of community engagement (Schafft, 2016). Accordingly, rural superintendents are community leaders as well as educational leaders, and are more likely to operate in a "fishbowl" of community scrutiny (Budge, 2006). This highly visible leadership position can produce increased informal political engagement within the community (McHenry-Sorber & Sutherland, 2020). McHenry-Sorber and Sutherland (2020) note that "such political negotiation, particularly around social justice issues, can prove challenging for leaders facing divergent school and community values about the purpose of schooling, the work of educators, or the future of their communities" (p. 108). Additionally, rural superintendents face unique challenges implementing external policies, addressing systemic inequity, and creating community-driven change (McHenry-Sorber & Budge, 2018).

Local School Boards

School boards, also called boards of trustees or boards of directors, are collective boards that oversee their respective LEAs and superintendents. School board members are usually democratically elected community members who represent geopolitical areas, such as a town or neighborhood. For rural communities that are situated in larger, nonrural districts, it may be difficult to gain political representation through school board elections. This lack of representation can further compound urban-centric educational policies. School board members serve for a set term, although term limits are not widespread. Most boards have between five and fifteen members; however, multi-union rural districts may have over thirty members, while single community districts may have as few as three (Hall, 2016).

School boards primarily oversee local educational budgets and policies in their work with superintendents. Board members are not required to have professional educational experience, certification, or licensure. Although states require school board training, board members are notorious for avoiding such professional development (Mountford, 2004). In rural areas, board members may have to travel long distances and/or miss work to attend training, potentially limiting their inclusion in such events.

While there is limited research on rural school boards, the significance of local control of education as enacted by these boards is well established. Major questions persist, however, about the benefit of local control in rural communities: Do local school boards play a crucial, positive role in connecting rural communities with their schools (Hall, 2016), or do they exacerbate tensions and conflict within those communities (McHenry-Sorber & Schafft, 2015)? Furthermore, rural communities are not demographically monolithic, and they encompass an array of sociopolitical values (Corbett, 2014). Minority voices, particularly from historically marginalized communities, may be excluded from democratic participation in rural educational governance (C. B. Howley & A. Howley, 2010). Thus, even in cases where rural school boards have the ongoing support of their communities, the values they represent may still only reflect those of the dominant majority.

Central Office

For each LEA, the superintendent oversees a central or district office where administrators and staff oversee and implement districtwide policies and services as well as disburse federal and state funding to local schools. Central office leaders may be required to hold advanced degrees or specialized certification or licensure. While the organization of central office staff varies significantly, most LEAs include a chief financial officer, chief academic officer, and an array of assistant superintendents or directors (including, e.g., directors of human resources, grounds and facilities, technology, assessment and evaluation, and special education, among others). The organizational control of central offices varies from generating significant flexibility and autonomy on the local level to tight, centralized, and aligned oversight of school practices districtwide (Peurach et al., 2019). While research is limited, rural districts appear to be more likely to engender local-level autonomy, possibly due to smaller central offices and decreased funding in comparison to nonrural districts (Kamrath & Brunner, 2014).

Building Administrators

Public schools are overseen by building-level administrators, such as principals, assistant principals, and administrative specialists. For most states, school administrators are required to hold building-level certification and licensure, as well as have some K-12 teaching experience. Principals oversee and implement the managerial, educational, and political dimensions of their schools. The extent to which building-level leaders coordinate with central office directives and goals varies depending on LEA organizational structures (Peurach et al., 2019). In some rural areas, building-level leaders may have significant autonomy over their schools; or, they may work most closely with the school board, instead of the superintendent, due to the engagement of the board in the school community (Hall & McHenry-Sorber, 2017). Like rural superintendents, rural principals may work with smaller administrative teams, operate under greater scrutiny from community members, and wear "multiple hats" in their work (Preston et al., 2013). Less is known about other building-level administrators in rural schools, but emerging scholarship suggests they also have integral roles in engaging with the surrounding community (Bailey, 2020).

Collectively, these organizations and positions for both state and local levels must collaborate to ensure all communities have access to academically strong, economically viable schooling per federal mandates. In practice, however, the intersection of federal, state, and LEA governance can create confusion and conflict, particularly when educational perspectives do not align. In rural communities, the misalignment of urban-centric educational policies can create significant difficulties in implementing and adapting policies on the local level.

Section Two: Contemporary Education Policies

Contemporary education policy emerges from over a century of deficit-based policies, programs, and practices emanating from urban-centric educational research (Biddle & Azano, 2016; DeYoung, 1987; Theobald & Wood, 2010). As a field, education policy pays limited attention to the context in which schooling is provided, therefore defaulting to universalizing policies that take urban environments as the model for developing frameworks for pedagogical practice, provision of equitable services, enrollment options, and school funding formulas (J. D. Johnson & C. B. Howley, 2015). In the rare policies where the geographic difference comes into focus, rural education is often treated as a monolithic, homogeneous entity despite the substantial variation among rural school districts and communities across the nation. This one-size-fits-all approach to designing policy-oriented solutions to complex, context-specific educational problems obscures both the ways local rural school districts (or LEAs) respond to federal and state mandates and the assets of rural communities. In fact, rural school district strengths often become weaknesses in policies that are inattentive to rural contexts (J. D. Johnson & Zoellner, 2016), displaying the disconnect between policymakers and the realities of rural community life (Tieken, 2014). In this section, we discuss two policy categories that have significantly shaped US educational practices: (a) compensatory educational services and (b) standards and accountability.

Compensatory Educational Services

The Federal Department of Education was created in 1979 with the purpose of ensuring access to equal educational opportunity for every individual and to increase public accountability of educational practices (Hochschild & Scovronick, 2003). SDOEs and LEAs are responsible for enacting federal mandates for equitable provision of educational services, often with little guidance and less financial support. For rural LEAs, even federal policies with allocated funding cause difficulties in the provision and implementation with fidelity due to limited administrative staff, less access to licensed bilingual or special education teachers, and financial distribution formulas based on student enrollment numbers.

At the height of the Civil Rights Movement in the United States, the federal government passed monumental legislation entitled the Elementary and Secondary Education Act (ESEA) of 1965. This policy called for the federal government to invest directly in education through subsidizing the education of the neediest of students, enforcing civil rights, conducting research, gathering information, and subsidizing college costs (Ravitch, 2010). ESEA has been reauthorized eight times since 1965—most notably in 2002 when it was renamed No Child Left Behind (NCLB) and most recently in 2015 when it was again renamed the Every Student Succeeds Act (ESSA). This legislation includes the provision of educational services to low-income students through programs such as Head Start (for early childhood education and preschool), Title I (for school-aged children), and the Pell Grant program (grants for students attending institutes of higher education). For LEAs, the number of low-income students and the poverty level of the district is used to develop a metric for compensatory funding and additional support services. Unfortunately, this formula allows for "number weighting," which typically favors large *numbers* over large *proportions* of low-income students, "disproportionately benefiting urban districts with lower poverty rates over small rural districts with higher poverty rates" (Tieken, 2017, p. 385). Significantly, in twenty-three states, more than half of the rural student population come from low-income families (Lavalley, 2018).

Poverty is not the only lever by which equitable educational provisions are judged, however. In 1975, the federal government passed the Individuals with Disabilities Education Act (IDEA). IDEA established the right to a free and appropriate education for students with disabilities in the least restrictive environment as defined for each student according to their Individualized Education Plan (IEP; Hochschild & Scovronick, 2003). According to the most recent statistics from the Rural School and Community Trust, forty-eight states (excluding Alabama and Texas) provide IEPs for at least one in ten rural students (Showalter et al., 2019). IDEA was reauthorized in 2004 with updated methods for identifying students with special needs, early intervention services, and accountability measures to ensure adequate provision of services. IDEA also specifies the requirements for fully certified special education teachers (Sindelar et al., 2018). While IDEA serves as a federal mandate to ensure equity for students with special needs, SDOEs determine how to enact the policy while LEAs make decisions regarding staff and programming. Given the specific knowledge, skills, and pedagogy needed by special education teachers, rural LEAs may struggle to recruit qualified individuals (Hammer et al., 2005) and thus turn to alternative certification pathways or to teachers without standard prerequisites (i.e., training, licensure) to fill required positions (Berry et al., 2011).

A third category of educational equity addressed by the federal government is for students with limited English proficiency. In 1968, the Bilingual Education Act was passed by Congress mandating LEAs to establish educational programming for language minority students, yet the legislation did not dictate specific programs or approaches (Hochschild & Scovronick, 2003). Funding allocated to support this legislation was accessible in the form of competitive grants by which states offered specific plans to meet the policy's goals; however, political motivations have influenced the instructional methods for English acquisition with swings between support for bilingual education and dual immersion programs to English-only approaches (Nieto, 2009). SDOEs are responsible for creating both the instructional programs to meet the academic needs of their English learners (ELs) and the tools used to assess English language proficiency. LEAs not only implement these assessments and programs but are also encouraged to support academic achievement through family engagement and staff professional development. Even though the number of ELs in rural schools vary greatly, 3.8 percent of rural students are classified as ELs, compared to 9.6 percent of public school students nationally (McFarland et al., 2019). As with other specialty subject teachers, rural LEAs may have difficulties attracting and retaining highly qualified teachers for their EL students (Coady et al., 2019; Hammer et al., 2005) and providing access to professional networks of support in more isolated rural regions.

Finally, despite decades of federal desegregation policy, school districts have largely failed to integrate students of color within classrooms and within schools. Often presented as an urban challenge, segregated schools are also prevalent in rural areas due to historic patterns of housing and community discrimination (Tieken, 2017). For example, according to the Rural Schools and Community Trust, 172 rural districts are monoracial; however, this also indicates that the vast majority of rural schools have some level of school integration. In fact, "if you were to randomly choose two students from a school in a random rural district, there is a 31.9% chance that the students would identify as different races" (Showalter et al., 2019, p. 18). Again, SDOEs are required to establish mechanisms for desegregation, and LEAs must comply. Variations of desegregation policies include busing students of color in urban areas to predominantly White schools in suburbs, establishing magnet schools or racial quotas in districts with school choice models, and rezoning of school catchment areas (Hochschild & Scovronick, 2003). These integration strategies rely on the availability of more than one LEA in a geographic area, thus limiting their applicability to rural districts; however, this integration of geography, race, and class creates an embedded system of inequality that reverberates both within and between LEAs.

Standards and Accountability
Another significant educational policy arena is the standardization of multiple aspects of the schooling enterprise—from teacher certification to subject-level content and pedagogical approaches—in an attempt to codify educational processes across the country. Standardization is often coupled with the development and implementation of accountability mechanisms to measure the effectiveness of standard practices and to provide transparency of outcomes. Since the goal of standardization is to develop and maintain common educational practices across disparate school systems, rural LEAs are strongly encouraged and often mandated to closely

resemble the organizational structures and production of student learning in nonrural LEAs (J. D. Johnson & Zoellner, 2016).

Through joint efforts by education researchers and policymakers, standards and accountability took center stage in the 2001 legislation, NCLB. NCLB established national accountability mandates, including annual standardized assessments and disaggregated reporting of student performance for subpopulations (i.e., by race/ethnicity, gender, EL, economic status, and disability). Schools were required to meet specific benchmarks in order to be designated as meeting Adequate Yearly Progress (AYP), with the lauded yet unattainable goal of 100 percent of students passing state assessments by 2014 (Ravitch, 2010). NCLB delineated punitive measures for LEAs that failed to meet AYP and were therefore labeled as "failing." For example, NCLB mandated "failing" schools to provide supplemental educational services (e.g., tutoring, after-school programming) as well as permitted students to transfer and enroll in another school.

Even though student tests served as the primary measure of school quality and were established by the federal government as an accountability requirement, individual SDOEs were responsible for writing their own standards, picking their own tests, and defining student proficiency levels. LEAs responded to these high-stakes policies by narrowing their programming to tested subjects, reallocating financial and human resources to math and reading, and supporting scripted curriculums that encouraged teaching "to the test." Of significance to rural LEAs in particular was the manner in which individual SDOEs enforced the NCLB "highly qualified" teacher requirement. Specific qualifications and certifications impact the availability of "highly qualified" teachers who can (and want to) work in rural schools (J. D. Johnson & C. B. Howley, 2015). These standards of teaching quality omit any recognition of locally generated knowledge of rural lifeways or place-based pedagogy (Azano & Biddle, 2019). While alternative pathways and emergency licensure policies have emerged as options at the state level to help address the staffing challenges of rural (and often, urban) schools, they have done little to limit the challenges of recruiting and retaining high-quality teachers equitably across geographic contexts (Eppley, 2009).

In 2015, ESEA was renamed the ESSA and shifted policy from a top-down, one-size-fits-all school improvement strategy to a more flexible, state-led approach to setting and meeting accountability measures (Sutherland, 2020). Included in this adjustment is the removal of highly qualified teacher requirements in favor of state standards for certification (Sindelar et al., 2018). ESSA also continues special opportunities for rural LEAs seeking further resources to support their educational goals, particularly for districts enrolling less than 600 students or with fewer than 10 people per square mile, as well as rural LEAs serving at least 20 percent of students living below the poverty line (Brenner, 2016; J. D. Johnson & C. B. Howley, 2015).

Section Three: Rural-Focused Vignettes

The first two sections of this chapter have delineated the contours of school governance and educational policies and their broad implications for rural LEAs. These intersecting lines of governance and policy paint a complex educational landscape marked by political values and community characteristics—among these are federal mandates, subject-level standards, uniform assessments, and teacher qualifications. Similarities and differences across all fifty states form the basis of public education in the United States, and this patchwork of policies and governance dictates the provision of schooling for the next generation of students.

The Politics of Rural School Governance

Federal and state policymakers debate educational priorities and create legislation while local practitioners are responsible for on-the-ground implementation of school-based reforms. However, the in-between space of local school governance is where the politics of public education emerge. The following rural-focused vignettes serve to illustrate this important dynamic in two distinct rural contexts.

Intergovernmental Conflict: The Case of Accountability Mandates in Vermont

The majority of residents in Vermont live in rural communities (US Census Bureau, 2012), and over 75 percent of Vermont schools are classified as rural (NCES, 2015).[1] Like other predominantly rural states, Vermont retains a decentralized educational governance system largely unchanged from the common school model of the 1800s (Rogers et al., 2014). The state's educational system is led by a CSSO (superintendent of education) as well as a SBOE that includes community leaders, educational experts, and current public school students. The superintendent of education, appointed by the governor, manages a small Agency of Education (AOE).

The state-level educational leaders oversee a highly decentralized network of LEAs, which are loosely organized by region into supervisory unions, supervisory districts, multidistrict unions, and one interstate district with New Hampshire (Vermont AOE, 2017). LEAs are led by superintendents and centralized school boards. Many of the multidistrict unions also retain local school boards that oversee the educational governance for their respective communities, including tasks such as developing an annual education budget, managing local school facilities, and working with the superintendent to set policies and procedures for community schools (Hall, 2016). Centuries of local control in this decentralized state have fostered significant variability and autonomy in educational governance.

Vermont's educational leaders have been nationally recognized for setting quality standards, prioritizing educational equity, and demonstrating consistently high student outcomes on national and international assessments (Holcombe, 2014; McDermott & Jensen, 2005). The state's legal and legislative branches have initiated most of the reforms; notably, in 1997, the state implemented a comprehensive equity-based school funding reform following a lawsuit (VT SBOE, 2001). The law, revised in 2001 as Act 68, introduced state learning standards, a progressive school funding system, and a hybrid accountability system integrating local assessments, student portfolios, and national tests (VT SBOE, 2001).

However, the accountability measures introduced through Act 68 were superseded by the 2001 federal passage of NCLB, which replaced the state's progressive educational system with a federally mandated, high-stakes accountability system. State leaders opposed many of NCLB's mandates and, in some cases, circumvented the design and intent of the mandates with state accountability plans (Shelly, 2008, 2012). For example, Vermont's AOE did not implement high-stakes interventions for schools, such as state takeovers (McDermott, 2003); instead, the AOE employed technical supports to intervene in chronically underperforming schools. At the local level, multiple LEA leaders opposed the implementation of NCLB. Several LEAs joined a lawsuit led by the National Education Association on the grounds that NCLB was an unfunded mandate and therefore prohibited (Vergari, 2012). State and local resistance were overwhelmingly based on the perceived overreach of the federal government and the misalignment of the urban-centric NCLB with rural Vermont.

The Bloomsbury Handbook of Rural Education in the United States

In one notable case, a small, rural community school board in a multidistrict union refused to implement NCLB policies. At the time, the school did not receive federal funding through Title I; therefore, local leaders asserted they could opt out of NCLB mandates without incurring financial penalties. The local school board passed a formal resolution refusing to implement the assessment component of NCLB, stating:

> We believe that the No Child Left Behind Act is an inherently flawed piece of legislation that fails students and fails schools. The administrative and testing requirements are time consuming and expensive and do not serve the needs of students. The tests are not designed to challenge or engage students and they do not aid in their learning. NCLB is a vehicle to remove control of our children's education from local communities and school districts and place that control with the Federal Government.

By refusing to implement NCLB, the rural Vermont school became a national symbol of local resistance to federal mandates. Yet, it also illustrated the complexities of intergovernmental policy implementation, as Vermont's CSSO, despite not being a strong supporter of NCLB, was pressured to tamp down the resistance out of concern that other communities would follow suit. The CSSO considered the removal of the superintendent or principal related to potential licensure infractions. While the loss of the superintendent was seen as a possible benefit to the community, the principal had strong community support. Thus, the school board capitulated and developed a plan with the principal for NCLB implementation that met the letter of the law but significantly undermined its efficacy. While this community was an exceptional example, LEAs across Vermont varied significantly in their adoption of NCLB accountability measures. Some supervisory and multidistrict unions promptly approved implementation of the new policies, whereas other local boards initially resisted implementation.

The misalignment of federal education policies with Vermont's decentralized, rural educational system again surfaced conflict in 2010, when the federal government offered ESEA waivers for onerous NCLB accountability requirements. The waivers were contingent on acceptance of other accountability requirements, however. Almost all states accepted the waiver, with the exception of several predominantly rural states, including Montana, Iowa, North Dakota, and Vermont. Vermont's AOE withdrew their ESEA waiver application because the new requirements were not appropriate for the many small rural schools in the state (Vergari, 2012), particularly the requirements to use student accountability data to evaluate teachers and principals. This decision was based on research indicating that evaluating teachers of very small classes, specifically under fifteen students, did not yield reliable data (Holcombe, 2014). The CSSO wrote in a public memo: "This represents about 40–50% of our classes. It would be unfair to our students to automatically fire their educators based on technically inadequate tools" (Holcombe, 2014, p. 2).

Consequently, Vermont LEAs were never granted flexibility from NCLB's accountability and requirements. In 2014, all of Vermont's schools were identified as failing to meet AYP per NCLB requirements. The CSSO publicly opposed the punitive classification of schools, releasing a statement that read, in part:

> The Vermont Agency of Education does not agree with this federal policy, nor do we agree that all of our schools are low performing . . . . This policy does not serve the interest of Vermont schools, nor does it advance our economic or social well-being. Further, it takes

our focus away from other measures that give us more meaningful and useful data on school effectiveness. (Holcombe, 2014, pp. 1–2, emphasis in original)

This state-level opposition to NCLB accountability measures, while intended to protect small, rural schools, generated further confusion on the local level. In 2014, LEAs were also transitioning to new standards-aligned assessment, the S-Bac or Smarter Balanced tests. Local educational leaders, particularly school board members, received conflicting messaging from federal and state agencies over the use and purpose of the accountability measures. As a result, LEA boards adapted the use of accountability measures for their own designs—mainly to protect their schools from state and federal oversight (Sutherland, 2020).

The conflict over accountability mandates in Vermont reflects the complexity of intergovernmental policy implementation for rural states. Vermont's AOE never fully supported NCLB, yet when presented with the opportunity to remove the most onerous elements, the state refused because the new measures were ill-suited for small, rural community schools. NCLB was designed for nonrural communities (Jimerson, 2005b), producing resistance and necessitating significant adaptation for rural state educational leaders. In turn, rural LEA leaders had to make sense of these adaptations while receiving divergent messaging from federal and state agencies. It is not surprising that some concluded the best use of accountability data was to further preserve local control.

Declining Enrollment and School District Funding in Rural Wisconsin
Declining student enrollment is a common challenge for many rural LEAs across the United States. Due to the interplay between federal, state, and local funding mechanisms and per-pupil funding formulas, maintaining adequate levels of school funding can be challenging. While each state has its own specific school funding formula, the federal government typically provides less than 10 percent of a district's budget, with funds specifically allocated to support the equitable provision of educational services through compensatory policies such as Title I. The distribution of remaining school funding is provided by the state government and local taxpayers. State-level school funding consists in a "per-pupil" funding model and specific categorical aid programs (e.g., transportation, special education services), whereas local funding is dependent upon property taxes within the LEA's boundaries. Importantly, the per-pupil basis of state funding creates difficulties for LEAs with declining student enrollments due to the fact that costs per pupil are higher, yet state funding per pupil remains the same (J. D. Johnson & Zoellner, 2016). In order to explore this further, we share an example from Wisconsin, where approximately 44 percent of public school students attend schools in rural communities (Wisconsin Department of Public Instruction, 2016) and 77 percent of school districts across the state are considered town or rural districts (Kemp, 2016).

In Wisconsin, 47 percent of school district funding is based on local revenue consisting of real estate and property taxes, which means that the local funds are generated based on property value. State funding provides 45 percent of school district funds to ensure per-pupil expenditures remain equal across all districts (Ford, 2013) while also offering categorical aid to districts with fewer than 700 students and more remote rural districts (to offset high transportation costs). The remaining 8 percent of funds are supplied by the federal government. Yet, if two LEAs have the exact same number of enrolled students, but differing property values, the state aid allocated to each will be different—with property-rich communities receiving less state aid and property-poor communities receiving more state aid so that both LEAs receive an equal combined value of per-pupil funding. The assumption reflected in this formula is that property wealth reflects community wealth; however, in property-rich yet income-poor communities, this creates a disadvantage where taxpayers are required to carry more of the financial burden of school district funding than the state, despite having less ability to do so. Additionally, in Wisconsin, there are revenue caps placed on each LEA by the state; when the LEA needs money over the revenue cap, their only option is to ask their local voters to pass a referendum (Wisconsin Policy Forum, 2018).

The Rural School and Community Trust report, "Why Rural Matters" (Showalter et al., 2019), reveals that Wisconsin is one of twelve states that provides less funding for rural LEAs per student than for nonrural LEAs, even though it often costs rural districts more to serve each student. Meanwhile, over the last twelve years, rural school districts have seen a combined 8 percent decline in student enrollment, with a significant number of rural districts experiencing a loss of 33–50 percent of their student population (Kemp, 2019). In these dire circumstances, many rural school boards decided to seek property tax increases through referendum in order to maintain organizational solvency. In 2016, Wisconsin voters passed about $1.7 billion in referendums across all public school districts, and $1.3 billion in 2018 (Fox, 2020). Importantly, the vast majority of districts seeking taxpayer approval for funding through referendums were rural districts (Wisconsin Policy Forum, 2018) and many have sought referendums every ballot cycle—so much so that the Wisconsin legislature attempted to limit how often LEAs can place a referendum on the ballot (Beck, 2017).

At the heart of the funding challenges in rural Wisconsin is the fact that residents and taxpayers in small communities prop up the operations of their LEAs to such an extent that economic disruption—a factory downsizing, a mill closure, the selling of local farms to big agricultural conglomerates—dictate the ability of rural schools to provide quality educational services for their students and families. This financial distress impacts the ability of rural schools to offer competitive salary packages to recruit or retain staff, offer innovative programming and technology, and maintain adequate and updated school facilities. Rural school boards are thus challenged with cutting programs and services, keeping specialized positions vacant (e.g., art, music, and foreign language teachers), and sometimes even closing schools altogether (Seelig, 2017b).

For example, the small yet comprehensive Forest Lake school district in the remote interior of Northern Wisconsin serves 750 students over 600 square miles and has experienced student enrollment decline of nearly 40 percent over the last fifteen years. While a minimal number of students withdraw to virtual private schools or homeschooling, enrollment decline arose from a local manufacturing crisis resulting in massive layoffs and the relocation of families away from the community. A few years later, as this economic crisis echoed through the schools, the LEA was caught up in their own budgetary crisis, ultimately choosing to consolidate their outlying elementary and middle schools (Seelig, 2017b). This consolidation created further enrollment decline as many families who had attended those schools for generations opted to open enroll their children in the neighboring rural LEA. This was not all: the school board also made difficult decisions around special programs, reduced school administrators from five to two, and limited the number of extracurricular activities in order to balance the budget.

Five years later, in the aftermath of the Great Recession, the school district placed a referendum on the ballot to subsidize the loss of state funding fueled by the enrollment decline, only to fail by a mere seven votes (Seelig, 2017a). In 2018, the school board once again elected to seek voter approval for increased property taxes. In light of an historic number of school referendums on the ballot in 2018, in which residents across the state were asked to approve 157 referendums—the highest number since 2001—the school board and district staff were hopeful for a positive vote from their community. Despite a statewide passage rate of 90 percent (A. Johnson, 2018), the Forest Lake referendum was again turned down, placing renovations of the elementary school building on indefinite hold and continuing the tightening of local educational spending.

This example in Wisconsin illustrates how state funding formulas and school choice policies intersect with the realities of rural community life. As student enrollment declines and local economic enterprises falter, the dependence upon local property taxes destabilizes school district operations. It is within this context that rural school boards and district administrators are negotiating with each other and with taxpayers to prioritize the educational future of their children.

Conclusion

Taken together, these examples provide a deeper perspective into the governance and politics of rural education. In sum, educational organization and policy uptake in rural America encompass significant variability across the levels of government. While educational policies are often crafted universally—that is, they are intended for universal application across diverse geographies— the importance of place in policy and governance is evident when viewed through a critical lens. Importantly, the practices of policymaking and policy implementation do not happen in social vacuums but rather are crafted from and influenced by cultural values, local identities, and economic necessity.

In recent decades, rural education scholars have moved the needle on theorizing the centrality of place in classroom pedagogy; teacher recruitment and retention; community–school partnerships; and educational leadership, and they have clearly articulated the historical trajectory of the "rural school problem." However, the politics of *rural* education remains an area of need for empirical research. As the Wisconsin and Vermont vignettes illustrate, the lack of uniformity in educational organization across rural LEAs offers intriguing opportunities for further research that would both explore the ways in which urbanicity is rhetorically mobilized to promote universal policymaking and conceptualize rurality in policy implementation. Empirically, further research is needed as well where rural geographies, racial inequality, and White privilege intersect with policymaking and educational governance. Thus, following the suggestion of Biddle and colleagues (2019), we present this chapter as a starting point for "operationalizing the ways in which power manifests across space" (p. 11) in the often taken-for-granted organization of educational systems and in educational policymaking.

9

Consolidation, Closure, and Charter Schools

Karen Eppley

The rural school problem (Cubberley, 1922) provides important historical contextualization for the long-standing trend toward closing and consolidating rural schools. When school consolidation, the merging of two or more formerly separate school districts or schools within a district, began in earnest in the 1930s, there were 259,000 public schools in the United States. Today there are about 98,000 (NCES, 2019e). Rural schools serving children living in poverty have experienced closures disproportionality (Tieken, 2014; Tieken & Auldridge-Reveles, 2019), making rural school closure and consolidation an enduring issue of social justice in rural education. Although school consolidation existed in the late nineteenth century, consolidation became far more common in the 1930s. Historical arguments made for closing or consolidating schools persist today. For example, financial, academic, and demographic changes (i.e., declining populations) are often cited as objective and verifiable reasons; yet, school consolidations and closures happen far more frequently in low-income communities and in rural communities serving people of color (Tieken & Auldridge-Reveles, 2019), exemplifying underlying inequities related to educational policy and practice. Quantitative claims are frequently at the core of arguments made in favor of closure or consolidation, even though evidence that closing or consolidating rural schools saves money (Bifuloc & Bulkley, 2008) or that it leads to better academic outcomes (Center for Research on Education Outcomes [CREDO], 2013; Mann et al., 2016) is far from conclusive. Qualitative studies suggest that closures and consolidations are complex and socially situated events that trigger a myriad of anticipated and unanticipated experiences and outcomes for individuals and communities (Autti & Hyry-Beihammer, 2014; Eppley et al., 2021; McDonald, 2018; Oncescu, 2014; Peshkin, 1982). Rural communities tend to deeply value their schools (DeYoung, 1991; A. Howley et al., 2011; C. B. Howley et al., 2011; Peshkin, 1982; Post & Stambach, 1999) and, as a result, closures and consolidations have historically been met with organized and sustained community resistance as has remained the case in contemporary times (Deeb-Sossa & Moreno, 2016; Hall et al., 2004; Haller & Monk, 1988; Peshkin, 1982; Roberts, 2001; Sher, 1995; Tieken & Auldridge-Reveles, 2019). In many cases, community members' organized resistance to closing local schools persists for decades (see, e.g., Eppley et al., 2021;

Post & Stambach, 1999). Despite these efforts, when schools are eventually closed, as is most often the case, some rural communities elect to open charter schools. They do so not to compete with an existing school or to improve upon the closed school but to keep a school operating in the community after the closure of the traditional community public school (Eppley et al., 2021).

This chapter first presents a research review tracing the phenomenon of rural school closure and consolidation from its early history to the present. It then extends the conversation into the more contemporary phenomenon of rural charter schools opening in the wake of closed or consolidated schools, illustrating how some rural communities employ charter policies more commonly used in urban communities. The chapter concludes by situating the phenomenon of rural charter schools as an outcome of context-blind state and federal educational policy.

School Closure and Consolidation

There is a well-developed research base in rural education about school closure and consolidation. Rural school consolidation dates back to the beginning of the end of one-room schoolhouses as the country began to move to more "modern" town schools made accessible by newly paved roads and public school transportation. Schools are consolidated today for the same reasons they were consolidated in the 1900s. With few exceptions (see Williams, 2013), school boards vote to close community schools because they believe bigger schools provide a better education than small rural schools and, importantly, that economies of scale will produce budgetary savings. Across urban and rural contexts, school closures disproportionately affect children living in poverty and children of color (Tieken & Auldridge-Reveles, 2019).

Rural school consolidations can lead to increased segregation and inequities (England & Hamann, 2013). For example, when Black-majority schools are combined with White-majority schools, fewer Black school board members have positions on the newly consolidated school board (Jimerson, 2005a). Consolidation can also be undertaken with the goal of ameliorating segregation and inequitable access to resources (Williams, 2013) or have a secondary effect of increased racial diversity and more equitable access to resources (Nitta et al., 2010). Specific to Indigenous children, potential losses associated with consolidation include higher student-to-teacher ratios, loss of connection to the school community, and loss of autonomy in issues of school governance, while potential advantages include expanded curriculum and specialized staff, as well as resources for special needs and mental health services (Miller, 2013).

Much of the research on school closure and consolidation is about the merger of two or more school *districts*, not within-district consolidation (see, e.g., C. B. Howley et al., 2011). Within-district consolidation is the closure of one or more schools, often elementary school buildings, all belonging to the same district. After the closure, students of the formerly closed school begin attending another existing school in the same school district, or a new school is constructed to house students from multiple closing schools. The 1950s and 1960s marked the heyday of modern school consolidations, and these were followed by a final wave of consolidations in the 1970s (Peshkin, 1982; Post & Stambach, 1999). Following the surge of district consolidations in the 1950s and 1960s, consolidation more often took the form of within-district consolidation. As early as 1938, the number of school districts had declined by 90 percent (Duncombe & Yinger, 2007). Therefore, close reading of school consolidation research is required to separate findings about school district consolidation from findings about within-district consolidation. For example, some research has found increased opportunities for teacher professional development after multidistrict consolidation. This positive outcome would not be relevant to understanding within-district consolidation because professional development is generally offered districtwide rather than for individual schools within a district. Findings associated with district consolidation can sometimes appear as "false-positive" factors when misapplied to within-district closures. Not all closures and consolidations are the same.

Research on school closure and consolidation generally falls into three categories: finances, academic outcomes, and community and family impact.

Financial Implications

While early reform leading to rural district consolidation was focused on school improvement, these goals have been replaced by a desire on the parts of boards of education to seek cost savings via economies of scale, which ostensibly would provide the best possible return on taxpayer dollars (Strange, 2013). School consolidation has, therefore, "lost its innocence" (Strange, 2013, p. 107) and is now almost always a financial issue, not an academic one. As Haller and Monk observed over twenty years ago, after *A Nation at Risk* (National Commission on Excellence in Education, 1983), schools were charged with doing *more*—offer more courses and achieve better test scores—at less cost to taxpayers (1998). While finances are still the most critical factor in decisions about school consolidation, research on cost savings lacks consensus about the effects of school closures on district budgets (for a detailed analysis, see Karakaplan & Kutlu, 2019). In the decision-making process, the possibility of potential negative economic impacts of school closure on a community is often overshadowed by promises of fiscal returns to the district (Karakaplan & Kutlu, 2019). The "bigger is better" rationale is not only associated with high schools, where access to world languages and advanced courses is relevant, but it is also used as an argument to close and consolidate elementary schools, particularly in order to seek potential cost savings associated with the provision of special education for a relatively few number of children. Historically, during district consolidation, high schools were more frequently consolidated than elementary schools (Nitta et al., 2010). Contemporary evidence of this can be seen in many rural communities where former high school buildings, often in need of major repairs, are used as elementary schools.

There is evidence, however, that demonstrates the negative economic impact of a closure on a number of isolated metrics. For example, quality schools are positively associated with home value (Nguyen-Hoang & Yinger, 2011), and when a community loses its school, housing prices drop (Brasington, 2004; Lyson, 2002). Good schools, as defined by graduation rates and test scores, motivate former residents to return to their rural communities (Cromartie et al., 2015) and also demonstrate a positive pull effect for in-migration (Lawrence et al., 2002; Marré & Rupasingha, 2020). The relationship between schools and economic well-being is particularly strong for small communities (Lyson, 2002) and for communities situated farthest from urban centers (Barkeley et al., 1996). Schools contribute significantly to the vitality of local economies and are essential to a community's long-term development potential (Lawrence et al., 2002). High-quality rural schools are often among a community's most important economic assets.

Economies of scale is a long-standing assumption often garnered as a primary justification for school consolidation (Karakaplan & Kutlu, 2019; Lyson, 2002; Tholkes & Sederberg, 1990). Arguments based on "more education for the dollar" are economy of scale arguments. However, realized savings are uncertain when applied to complex school and community environments because transportation costs, capital expenditures, student dispersion, educational quality, community SES, and qualitative differences between smaller and larger schools (see Strange, 2013) must also be considered.

The increased cost of salaries, workspace, and other internal operational expenses can offset expected savings from consolidating small schools (Cotton, 2001; Karakaplan & Kutlu, 2019). An Indiana study found that increasing the size of schools lowered student achievement significantly, at a cost that far outweighed the marginal fiscal savings of closing smaller schools (Kuziemko, 2006). A recent economics study (Karakaplan & Kutlu, 2019) found that expected cost savings from school consolidation failed to be realized due to an increase in per-pupil expenditures (e.g., higher transportation costs due to increased distance between students' homes and the school). The authors concluded: "These results indicate that the actual effects of consolidation on school district expenditure may be much different than what simple cost analyses would suggest, and hence, policy implications and recommendations based on simple analyses may not be reliable" (p. 1730).

Academic Outcomes

Concern for academics, often couched in accountability language, is a financially related (though secondary) reason rural schools are slated for consolidation or closure. Whether the new school or the current school represents a "better" education is not self-evident. Community members often argue that "better" is multifaceted and cannot be adequately captured in test scores, updated facilities, or access to advanced courses (Eppley, 2015). In addition to achievement levels, what constitutes a better student educational *experience* is mired in the complexity of the interactions among the relative size of a rural school or district; the community's history and social norms; and the socioeconomic status (SES) of students. Research on the academic impacts of rural school closure and consolidation is thin and inconclusive (Tieken & Auldridge-Reveles, 2019).

The results from research on rural school size and poverty can be applied, cautiously, to understanding the academic effects of rural school closure and consolidation. In the event of a school closure, in nearly all cases, students are reassigned to a larger consolidated school outside of their community. While not all rural communities are economically disadvantaged, rural school closure and consolidation tends to occur more frequently in communities with lower per family average incomes. Research on the ideal school size is mixed, but smaller school sizes are linked to increased achievement for students living in high-poverty areas (Gershenson & Langbein, 2015). Studies that expressly consider the rural context (such as Bickel & C. B. Howley, 2000; C. B. Howley & A. Howley, 2004; J. Johnson et al., 2002; J. Johnson, 2007; Klein & J. Johnson, 2010) find positive associations for the power of small school size to mitigate the effects of poverty (for critique see Coladarci, 2006). Further, student achievement in smaller schools is generally equal to or better than that of students in large schools (Center for the Study of Education Policy, 2009). Small schools have fewer incidents of violence (Cuellar, 2018; Wasley et al., 2000) and provide opportunities for students to work with adults they know and trust (Seaton, 2007; Wasley et al., 2000).

Community and Family Impact

Research is conclusive about the negative effects of the loss of a community school. Data on community and family outcomes is persuasive against school consolidation. Community schools are associated with increased civic participation among residents as compared to communities

The Bloomsbury Handbook of Rural Education in the United States

without community schools (Lawrence et al., 2002). When rural communities lose their school districts to consolidation, residents also lose their local school boards and the opportunity for local decision making (DeYoung & C. B. Howley, 1990; Haller & Monk, 1998). Importantly, citizens who lost their community schools rated their quality of life significantly lower than did residents of communities that had retained their local schools (Sell et al., 1996). Close school-community connections are beneficial to students in that they help build a sense of community togetherness and provide more opportunities for students and families to engage fully with the school (Beaumont & Pianca, 2000; Deeb-Sossa & Moreno, 2016; C. B. Howley & A. Howley, 2001). Lengthy bus rides out of the community to consolidated school buildings burden children and families by extending the school day and reducing the time available for downtime and recreation (C. B. Howley et al., 2001) and negatively affect participation in after-school activities (Jimerson, 2006). For some, rural schools foster a sense of community and collective identity through a shared experience and intergenerational connections (Eppley, 2015) though this is by no means a universal truth as communities can be exclusionary in ways that counter simplistic (and often nostalgic) imaginaries.

Economically, data suggesting potential monetary benefits to plans for school closure and consolidation ought to be interpreted with the utmost caution. Any potential budgetary gain should be cautiously interpreted in light of other less predictable, more complex factors. Loss of a community school has documented socioeconomic impacts on communities, families, and children (Schafft & Harmon, 2011). Research on the effects of contemporary consolidations, after the last wave in the 1970s, suggests that new closures and consolidations are unlikely to result in either greater efficiency or better instructional outcomes (C. B. Howley et al., 2011).

Charter Schools

Beginning in the mid-1990s against a backdrop of nearly 100 years of school closures and consolidations (see Biddle & Azano, 2016), charter schools emerged as a school reform option in urban communities (Wolf et al., 2016). While initiated and operated under the same state-level policies as suburban and urban charter schools, rural charters are often initiated in response to school closures and consolidations, not in response to school underperformance. Charter organizers may be community groups, for example, with deep generational and social commitments to the previous traditional school. Accordingly, rural charters opened under these circumstances seek to maintain traditional ways and structures of the traditional public school that preceded it. While discourses of efficiency, competition, and achievement typically dominate charter schools (Giroux, 2012), rural charter organizers do not necessarily have these goals in mind. Instead, charter initiators seek continuity, personalization, and community. While charter law provides communities the opportunity to maintain a public school in the community, it also challenges efforts on behalf of community members to meet their goals.

What Are Charter Schools?

The US Department of Education (n.d.) defines charter schools as the following:

A charter school is a public school that operates as a school of choice. Charter schools commit to obtaining specific educational objectives in return for a charter to operate a school. Charter schools are exempt from significant state or local regulations related to operation and management but otherwise adhere to regulations of public schools—for example, charter schools cannot charge tuition or be affiliated with a religious institution.

Whether urban or rural, charter schools are initiated and operated by a group or organization that has successfully made an application to an authorizing body to open a school. The approved "charter" is essentially a performance contract between the charter school and the authorizing body (Adamson & Galloway, 2019; Wolf et al., 2016). Charter authorizers differ from state to state and can include local school districts, statewide authorizing bodies (e.g., State Departments of Education), universities, or state boards of education. Charter schools are public schools financed by tax dollars but operate under market principles of "consumer" choice and competition (Ravitch, 2010; Riel et al., 2018). Once authorized, charter schools operate with fewer restrictions related to their governance (board members are appointed, not elected) and teacher qualifications (most, but not all, states require teacher certification). If schools do not meet performance indicators and other terms of the charter agreement, the charter can be revoked by the authorizing body.

Charter school teachers are twice as likely to be new to teaching than traditional public school teachers (Ni, 2017) and are rarely unionized (Superfine & Woo, 2018). In an un-unionized charter school, teachers are paid less, have less job security, and are subject to the at-will or routine assignment of uncompensated work such as evening responsibilities, summer work, coaching and advising, longer hours, and tutoring. As a cumulative effect of a variety of factors, students at charter schools experience much higher rates of teacher turnover compared to traditional public schools (Gulosino et al., 2019).

Unlike private schools, charter schools are legally required to take any student who applies, though with important caveats. Potential students must apply to a school and students are accepted by the school via a lottery system if the number of applications exceeds the number of spaces. Once accepted, charter school students are at an increased risk of expulsion than traditional public school students (Wolf et al., 2016). Students who transfer from a traditional public school to a charter school tend to enter a more racially segregated school than the one they left (Garcia, 2008). The evidence is persuasive that charters are segregated spaces (Adamson & Galloway, 2019; Fiel, 2013; Frankenberg & Siegel-Hawley, 2013; Seamster & Henricks, 2015). Charter schools are required to serve children with special needs, and like traditional public schools, they receive increased per-pupil state allotments to implement individualized education plans (IEPs). Using free-market principles to introduce competition to public schooling (Choades, 2018), charter schools are advanced as a means of enhancing educational innovation and opportunities via consumer choice (Beck et al., 2016; Fabricant & Fine, 2012; Smarick, 2014).

Research on charter school achievement is mixed but generally suggests that students in traditional schools outperform students in charters (Center for Research on Education Outcomes [CREDO], 2013; Mann et al., 2016). Performance data is conclusively weak for online charter schools both when compared to traditional public schools and to brick-and-mortar charter schools (Ahn & McEachin, 2017; CREDO, 2015; Fitzpatrick et al., 2020; Woodworth et al., 2015). Some studies find that students who attend brick-and-mortar charter schools perform about the same as traditional public schools (Raymond et al., 2013) or outperform traditional schools (Choades, 2018; Rose et al., 2017), but others find mixed results (Berends, 2015; Ladd et al., 2017; Logan & Burdick-Will, 2016) or evidence of comparatively poor charter school performance (Chingos & West, 2015; Lubienski, 2014; Schafft et al., 2014).

Economically, charter schools negatively impact traditional school district budgets (Choades, 2018; Rose et al., 2017; Schafft et al., 2014). For example, one Pennsylvania district pays $23,000 in charter tuition for each child receiving special education services at a charter school, but

The Bloomsbury Handbook of Rural Education in the United States

the charter school receiving payment reports spending less than $9,000 to educate each child (Satullo, 2019). This scenario echoes findings that charter schools accept more money to educate special education students than they report spending to educate special education students (Schafft, Frankenberg et al., 2014). When a student enrolls in a charter, the tuition dollars follow the child to the charter school, but the sending school district's cost to educate the children who remain in the traditional public school does not decrease at the same per-pupil share. While most charter schools are located in large urban districts (NCES, 2020a), smaller rural districts with smaller budgets are disproportionately affected by charter school payments (Schafft, Frankenberg et al., 2014). Charter schools are closely associated with the neoliberal agenda of privatization, suppression of the commons, and eroding of social systems in favor of for-profit professional management corporations (Christianakis & Mora, 2011; Harvey, 2006).

Rural Charter Schools

In the 2018–19 school year in the United States, only 12 percent of all charter schools were located in rural areas, while 56 percent of all public charter schools were located in cities (NCES, 2020a). That charter schools are largely an urban phenomenon maps well onto what we know about both rural communities and market-based ideology. In most rural communities, the rural "market" is often weak, with declining populations resulting in too few children to fully enroll in any type of brick-and-mortar school and too many families committed to their community school. The idea of consumer choice, a central theme and key marketing approach for charter school proponents, is complicated by rural geography, population density, as well as social characteristics of rural communities. For example, charter schools are required to have a multidistrict student catchment area, which translates to even longer bus rides on rural roads for students who live outside the traditional school district in which the charter school is located. The potential losses of the roles that rural schools can play in rural community life—the source of social services, a community hub, a source of personal identity, economic anchor to the community—are also potent disincentives to brick-and-mortar charter school initiation (Eppley et al., 2021; Schafft, 2016; Schafft & Youngblood Jackson, 2010; Tieken, 2014). These same characteristics are vulnerabilities for communities that lose schools.

Charter schools exist in some communities as a mechanism of Native language and culture preservation. Charter schools on tribal lands enable the preservation of Indigenous knowledge and language and offer a degree of tribal autonomy. A report prepared for the National Indian Education Association describes three charter schools that serve Native children in language immersion schools in Wisconsin, Florida, and California. The schools, chosen for their higher than average local test scores, serve children from the Lac Courte Oreilles (LCO) reservation in northwestern Wisconsin, the Seminole Brighton Reservation on the northwest shore of Lake Okeechobee, Florida, and the Yurok tribe in northern California. Each charter school was established to fulfill the identified need for language and cultural preservation that was previously unmet in either traditional public schools or Bureau of Indian Affairs schools. School leaders reported that charter schools enabled local control over the mission, design, and influence of the education received (Ewing & Ferrick, n.d.). While the schools have enabled significant tribal sovereignty, study participants report that charter law is limiting in terms of resource allocation and the negotiation of tensions between state accountability and tribal jurisdiction (Brayboy & Castagno, 2009).

Rural Charter Schools as Resistance to School Closure and Consolidation

Although few rural schools are charter schools, more than a quarter-million children attend rural charter schools (Stuit & Doan, 2012). While there is a well-developed research base on all facets of charter schools in urban communities, rural charter schools have received inadequate research attention in peer-reviewed journals.[1]

In 2018–19, 80 percent of rural charter schools were independently operated, meaning they were *not* managed professionally, but operated instead by community groups (NCES, 2020b). With the exception of KIPP Delta (Maranto & Shuls, 2011), charter management organizations have demonstrated little interest in rural communities.

While neither state databases nor the National Alliance for Public Charter Schools (NAPCS) track reasons why rural community groups open brick-and-mortar charter schools, there are six rural charter schools operating in one state in the United States that opened in response to a community school closure. These six schools demonstrate a novel use of charter school law. "Novel," not because community members initiated (and continue to operate) charter schools in rural communities where charter schools are uncommon, but novel in the sense of how charter law, quintessential neoliberal policy, was used as means of resistance to the loss of the community school. Neoliberalism is the belief that free-market economic competition is the optimal solution to social problems (Giroux, 2005). Within neoliberal ideology, schools are most effectively managed by the application of economic principles such as efficiency and competition. These six charter schools aim for neither efficiency nor competition. After fighting for decades to keep the traditional community schools open, the community groups' goal in opening the charter schools wasn't to make do with less, though budgets require just that, or to compete with another school. There is none nearby. Instead, their only aim in opening the school was to replicate the traditional community school and keep their children in the community for school.

A neoliberal vision for schools, of which both rural school closures and the charter schools are a part, does not map neatly onto rural schools and communities. The neoliberal project to make schools more efficient and competitive via closures, consolidations, and charters (Hankins & Martin, 2006) is challenged by the role that rural schools play in the maintenance of the social fabric of rural communities (Oncescu & Giles, 2014; Schafft, 2016; Tieken, 2014) and the central role that rural schools play in the maintenance of a community's social safety net (DeYoung, 1995; Lyson, 2002; Peshkin, 1982).

Rural charter schools are opened within a complex web of educational policy, economic disparities, and a long history of disdain toward rural people and communities (Hatt, 2007; Wray, 2006) . Education cannot be understood separately from its local, state, and national sociopolitical and socioeconomic contexts. Like urban and suburban communities, rural communities have particular challenges and affordances that make place-blind policies problematic. Four characteristics, in particular, challenge the suitability of existing state per-pupil funding formulas that fund rural schools: lower property values, smaller overall budgets, declining enrollment, and increased transportation cost (J. D. Johnson & C. B. Howley, 2015). Context-blind federal and state policies that fail to take these characteristics into account result in harmful defunding of rural schools and their communities (J. D. Johnson & C. B. Howley, 2015). Rural people are at a disadvantage in terms of their access to policymaking processes that determine resource distribution (see Fraser, 2009) and just representation (L. Johnson et al., 2014).

Rural charter schools are an outcome of unjust historical, social, and political contexts. They are a "best worst" stop-gap solution for a community after a school closure. Charter schools are not traditional public schools and cannot function as the same. No matter how dedicated charter school founders are to the project of replicating community schools lost to budget cuts, charter law prevents residents from doing so, while further straining the budgets of the traditional school districts that divert per pupil allocations to the charter. While charter school law may allow a locally controlled community school to exist, the closed school cannot be replaced.

In fighting to keep the traditional community school open, then opening the charter school, the rural residents who opt to initiate a charter work within the neoliberal system as it exists to attempt to break down barriers for more socially just rural schools and communities. But the neoliberal intentions of charter law and characteristics of rural communities make charter schools a particularly poor fit for rural areas. The prevalence of community members' sustained resistance to rural school closures should signal the value of a rural school to its community. Sustained and meaningful investments in traditional community schools in rural communities ought to be the first and only choice. This will require a meaningful repositioning of public education in both urban and rural places as a democratic project of social justice rather than an exercise in neoliberal efficiency (Cervone, 2018; Cordova & Reynolds, 2020; Cuervo, 2012).

10

Rural School Leadership

Catharine Biddle

School leaders shoulder diverse responsibilities within their schools and districts to fulfill the promise and purpose of public education. Behind any successful school change initiative, there is often a building- or district-level leader thoughtfully preparing for change and coaching teachers, staff, and families toward a new approach to student learning (Fullan, 2007). According to the Professional Standards for Educational Leaders (PSEL; National Policy Board for Educational Administration, 2015), effective school leaders simultaneously craft and champion a mission and vision for the organization and ensure equity and cultural responsiveness for faculty, families, and students. They do this while fostering a climate of care, providing instructional supervision and encouraging professional growth for their educators, meaningfully engaging the community and families, ensuring the smooth operation and management of buildings and facilities, and engaging the organization in data-driven improvement and change. All of these responsibilities must be carried out in accordance with professional standards of ethics and within the state legal framework for educational institutions.

The breadth of these professional expectations reflects an increase in the role complexity and intensity of school leaders in the past several decades, as the work of principals and superintendents has been linked to, and increasingly focused on, increasing student achievement (Leithwood et al., 2010; Seashore-Louis et al., 2010). Given the diversity of these expectations and implied work intensification (Wang, 2020), it is perhaps no wonder that on average, principals stay in their positions for four years or less, with 35 percent turning over after only two years (Levin & Bradley, 2019). Superintendents fare slightly better, with an average turnover rate of five to six years (Kowalski et al., 2011), although the national rate masks significant variation by district type (Grissom & Mitani, 2016).

Both principals and superintendents in rural settings face unique affordances and challenges to realizing these professional responsibilities. All school leaders must navigate the expectations of their roles that are institutionally and locally defined (Foster, 2004); however, rural leaders have often faced additional complexity in reconciling these expectations because of the poor alignment between institutionally defined educational outcomes and rural realities (Budge, 2010; Schafft & Biddle, 2013; Tieken, 2014). Some of this mismatch derives from the historical and

The Bloomsbury Handbook of Rural Education in the United States

contemporary metrocentricity of the field of both education and educational administration (Theobald, 1995; Theobald & Wood, 2010). For example, prominent education reformer Ellwood Cubberley (1916) wrote of rural school administration,

> To provide properly for the administration of rural and village education and to furnish the kind of instruction and supervision children in such schools ought to enjoy, demands that the lessons learned from the study of city school-district administrative experience be applied to the organization and administration of rural and village education. (p. 447)

While Cubberley's comments were directed toward the work that had been done to reorganize city districts and professionalize school supervision, the implication that what is good for the city is also good for the country was reflected across the field of educational research at that time (Biddle & Azano, 2016). This trend continues with the relatively placeless translation of the insights of organizational theory deriving from other fields (sociology and business, primarily) into the field of educational leadership in the 1960s and 1970s (Modeste et al., 2020). Despite the evolution of the field of educational leadership and its engagement with contingency theory, feminism, postmodernism and, more recently, its critical turn (Modeste et al., 2020), the dearth of theory that concerns space along with community meaningfully leads to one of this chapter's primary insights about scholarship on rural educational leadership; namely, that while there are many pieces of published work that seek to illuminate the lives and experiences of rural leaders in ways that make their challenges legible to policymakers, there is not enough theoretically coherent scholarship on these issues to constitute a robust body of work. While we know a great deal about fragmented aspects of the lives of rural school leaders, leadership theory and rurality remain disconnected and the connections between them remain underdeveloped.

This observation is not, in and of itself, new (see Arnold et al., 2005; McHenry-Sorber & Budge, 2018; Preston et al., 2013); however, in this chapter, I seek to map some of this incoherence in order to point to the directions that will produce the most useful future scholarship on these topics and to highlight some of the best contributions toward rural leadership theory. This chapter summarizes some of the empirical and theoretical insights of the literature on rural school leadership, broadly defined, combined with findings from the 2017–18 National Teacher and Principal Survey (Taie & Goldring, 2020), in order to provide a picture of the contemporary rural school leader and to highlight the sites of intersection between organizationally and institutionally focused work with scholarship on school leadership that is framed in place-conscious ways.

Rural School Leadership in the Twenty-First Century

School leadership in the twenty-first century resembles that of the twentieth century, in that school leaders across contexts continue to grapple with the professional isolation of the building administrator, the myriad challenges of managing teachers and staff, issues around site and building management, as well as time management and juggling multiple priorities at once (Jentz, 2009). This section provides an overview of the state of rural educational leadership by outlining the working conditions of rural principals and the political changes influencing those conditions, and how rural school principals navigate these shifts professionally and ethically.

Rural School Leadership

Who Leads Rural Schools?

The question of who leads schools has become more important as the field's attention to the effects of representative bureaucracy (the presence of people in positions of authority who reflect the broader population demographics) on institutional processes and outcomes has increased (Grissom et al., 2009). There is a small body of evidence that suggests that student achievement, hiring and retention, and community or family engagement are all influenced by who is hired into school leadership roles and the ways in which their personal characteristics match those of the population that they serve (Grissom & Keiser, 2011). Demographically, rural school leaders identify as White and male at greater rates than their urban and suburban counterparts. Ninety percent of principals in rural schools identify as White, as compared to 60 percent in cities and 78 percent in suburban areas, and 53 percent identify as male, as compared to 39.3 percent of urban principals and 45.6 percent of suburban principals (Taie & Goldring, 2020).

While this trend is not unexpected given that 77.8 percent of rural America identifies as White (as compared to 63.7 percent nationally; US Department of Agriculture, 2018), it does suggest that the principal population does not proportionally reflect the racial and ethnic diversity of rural America. This discrepancy may be in part because of selection bias by local hiring committees and who controls local power structures (Ballou, 1996), although more research is needed to determine the extent to which this is the case. Evidence from a statewide study of Texas administrators reported that women and teachers of color were more likely to be hired at the assistant level (rather than as principal) when compared to White male teachers and that, overall, rural schools were less likely to hire women into any leadership position (Fuller et al., 2018; Pendola & Fuller, 2018); however, there are no national studies that examine the intersection of teacher career trajectory, identity, and geographic locale.

In other ways, the principal population in rural America does not differ demographically from other geographic locales. Despite the fact that the population of rural America trends older than suburban and urban areas, principal median age (forty-seven years) in rural communities is the same as in other geographic locales (Taie & Goldring, 2020). Furthermore, rates of master's degree attainment are also relatively consistent across geographic locales, with 59–61 percent of all principals holding a master's degree; however, while 12 percent of urban and suburban principals hold doctoral degrees, only 8.4 percent of rural principals do (Taie & Goldring, 2020). Some of these differences may be explained by the fact that rural school principals do not see the return on investment of their educational attainment and experience that urban and suburban school principals see. Rural principals consistently earned the lowest salaries, regardless of their years of experience. While a first-year urban principal earned an average of $95,000, a rural principal with over ten years of experience earned on average $90,600 (Taie & Goldring, 2020).

Overall, principal recruitment and mobility rates remain high for all principals and vary by state (Snodgrass-Rangel, 2018); however, rural schools face some specific challenges in recruitment and retention. For example, rural schools typically receive fewer applications for open leadership positions (Pijanowski et al., 2009). Interestingly, duration of service is slightly higher for rural principals than for other locale types, with an average of 4.5 years for rural principals (as compared to 3.9 for urban principals; Taie & Goldring, 2020). It is possible that their duration of service may be related to school size; principals serving schools with less than 100 or 100–499 students across locales had a longer duration of service (13.3 and 15.9 years, respectively) than principals in schools with 500 or more students (9–10 years; Taie & Goldring, 2020).

The Bloomsbury Handbook of Rural Education in the United States

Leadership Practices in Rural Schools and School Districts

One initial observation about the rural school principalship as it is currently enacted is that, despite geographic and cultural differences, there are many similarities in the role across locales due to the isomorphic nature of school management needs (Arum, 2000; DiMaggio & Powell, 1983). For example, when it comes to building-level decision-making affecting day-to-day operations and student learning, data from the most recent National Teacher and Principal Survey (Taie & Goldring, 2020) suggests that rural school administrators did not differ from their urban and suburban peers with respect to the areas of school life over which they felt they had a major influence. Rural, suburban, and urban principals showed similar perceptions of having a high degree of influence over determining the content of in-service professional development (65–71 percent), evaluating teachers (94–97 percent), setting standards of performance for students (69–74 percent), and hiring new teachers (85–91 percent). This finding concurs with the most recent cross-locale study of principal time use, which found that rural, suburban, and urban principals spend, on average, similar amounts of time across diverse job tasks, including internal administrative tasks, curriculum- and teaching-related tasks, student interactions, and parent interactions (Hoyer et al., 2017).

Despite these similarities, the scholarship on rural school leadership suggests that rural schools as organizations are different, including nonstandard grade patterns, class sizes, and support staff arrangements, weaker local labor markets, smaller central offices, and reduced access to local community partners changes. These differences, along with the changing economic, social, and demographic conditions that constitute the many different kinds of "rural" that exist in the United States (Brown & Schafft, 2011), create the context out of which adaptations of institutionally informed roles of rural principal and superintendent emerge (Forner et al., 2012). These adaptations, while they may differ across locales in their specifics, do demonstrate some consistent patterns (Table 10.1).

Role Complexity, Instructional Leadership, and Opportunities for Leadership Growth
The first of these adaptations is that rural leaders must learn to manage diverse and, at times, unpredictable responsibilities (commonly referred to in the literature as wearing "many hats," Copeland, 2013, p. 1). These responsibilities may vary from driving the local school bus, to performing janitorial responsibilities, to negotiating with multinational corporations for the use of local roads (Augustine-Shaw, 2016; Schafft & Biddle, 2014). In qualitative studies of the rural principalship, for example, school leaders often cite the diversity of tasks that are both routinely expected and informally arise as surprising and a source of job stress (Hansen, 2018). In this respect, rural school leadership may reflect the realities of rural life more strongly than the institutional life of schools. Broader studies of rural life suggest that overlapping roles is a common feature of rural civic life (Smart & Russell, 2018).

These overlapping roles result in major time constraints for rural school leaders. While time-use studies suggest that lack of time is a feature of most school leaders' experiences (Hoyer et al., 2017), the effects of limited time may differ for rural principals because of geographic location. Although it remains to be seen how the Covid-19 global pandemic will affect society's relationship to distance learning in the long term, rural principals have traditionally faced difficulties in accessing professional development, support networks, role-alike professional groups, and other ways of nurturing their own growth as leaders in their districts (Fusarelli & Militello, 2012; Klar

Rural School Leadership

Table 10.1 Overview of Themes from Studies on Lived Experiences of Rural Principals

Leadership Practice in Rural Places	Selected Studies
Managing diverse responsibilities (both contracted and noncontracted), sometimes including part-time teaching	Augustine-Shaw (2016); Copeland (2013); Hansen (2018)
Managing instructional leadership in the context of the dynamics of small faculties	Egley & Jones (2004)
Coping with public scrutiny and limited privacy	Budge (2006); Copeland (2013); Forner et al. (2012); Hansen (2018); Masumoto & Browne-Welty (2009)
Building a positive school climate and productive community relationships within local power structures	Bishop & McClellan (2016); Casto, McGrath et al. (2016); Maxwell et al. (2014); Preston et al. (2013)
Understanding and navigating community values	Budge (2006); Harris-Smedberg (2019)
Managing the implementation of external mandates that may or may not align with organizational capacity, community values, or local resources	Budge (2010); Eppley et al. (2018)
Access to and balancing time for professional development and growth of leadership practice with needs of school	Augustine-Shaw (2016); Doyen (2020); Duncan & Stock (2010); Mendiola & Sun (2018); Stewart & Matthews (2015); Tonsmeire et al. (2012); Wood et al. (2013)

et al., 2019). Doyen (2020), for example, found that rural principals struggle with time needed to be spent in their buildings versus time needed to become aware of current mandates, policies, initiatives, and other state-level issues that will affect their schools. The National Teacher and Principal Survey (Taie & Goldring, 2020) similarly suggests that while rural principals engage in professional development at similar rates (approximately 85 percent) as their peers in other locales, they engage in some kinds of professional development at lower rates. For example, while 77 percent of urban principals engaged in visits to other similar schools to observe, only 58 percent of rural principals have engaged in these visits over the last year (Taie & Goldring, 2020). Similarly, rural principals presented at conferences at lower rates and engaged in mentoring and peer coaching at lower rates (Taie & Goldring, 2020).

One encouraging finding, however, is that rural principals attended conferences, participated in university coursework, and participated in principal networks at rates similar to their peers in other locales (Taie & Goldring, 2020). There are several examples in the literature of rural school leader preparation programs, often supported by external partners, such as universities, that assist school leaders in acquiring induction or on-the-job support and mentorship (Cowan & Hensley, 2012; Fusarelli & Militello, 2012; Klar et al., 2019; Mendiola & Sun, 2018; Versland, 2013). These networks frequently feature targeted recruitment from specific geographic areas, cohort-based supports, and online networking technologies that can allow rural leaders to match with distant supports or mentors that are best suited to their unique circumstances and leadership dispositions, allowing for more effective and individualized supports (Augustine-Shaw, 2016; Fusarelli & Militello, 2012; Tonsmeire et al., 2012; Wood et al., 2013). Additionally, rural-focused preparation programs often include a rural internship experience with careful attention to how context influences leadership practice, allowing leaders to engage in rural praxis as they build connections between leadership theory and practice in a rural context organically (Fusarelli & Militello, 2012; Klar et al., 2019).

Given the research on rural school leadership preparation programs in the last decade, it would be good for the field to see more replication of these programs' strategies in other rural-facing educational leadership programs to understand how these strategies translate to diverse rural contexts. Likewise, it would be useful for university faculty, state agencies of education, and other organizations to consider later career supports for rural school leaders to combat isolation and burnout while in the field. The development of networked improvement communities may point to a way forward in providing leaders with role-alike support (Hargreaves et al., 2015), such as the Rural Innovative School Leaders Network (Superville, 2020a), which brings together rural school leaders in partnership with university faculty to discuss innovative approaches to problems of practice in rural school leadership.

Community Relationships, Public Scrutiny, and the Micropolitics of Rural School Leadership
Another common issue rural school leaders face is the need to successfully manage intense public scrutiny, sometimes called the fishbowl effect, of being in their public-facing, and often highly political, roles (Hall & McHenry-Sorber, 2017; Hansen, 2018; Harris-Smedberg, 2019). The reality of small communities is that relationships are not confined to a single context, and therefore principals and superintendents are likely to be observed at the grocery store, in their front yards, in religious settings, and when they are out for a meal (Hansen, 2018). Some school leaders choose to adapt by living outside of the communities in which they serve, an adaptation that may trade community connection for longer-term happiness in their role (Budge, 2006). Regardless of where they choose to live, some rural leaders are able to leverage their accessibility across these contexts into political goodwill for the school and strong community relationships. Cultivating successful community relationships requires a deep understanding of the values of the community and the relationship of the school to those values (Budge, 2006, 2010; Harmon & Schafft, 2009; Preston et al., 2013). While community values are as diverse as types of rural places, rural community values with regard to education are often shaped by the ways in which local opportunity, and particularly work, is structured, as well as local political culture (Hall, 2016; Sutherland, 2020). Depending on the coherence of these values, they may play a significant role in shaping the acceptance of school reform or place parameters on local leadership practice. For example, Hall (2016) found that a local school board's vision for their community's long-term growth played an important role in shaping what three rural superintendents were able to accomplish in three rural Vermont school districts.

The dynamics of how rural community values shape educational purpose are especially important for rural school leaders to understand in the context of two decades of high-stakes accountability policy that has focused on connecting effective leadership practices with student performance on standardized assessments (Seashore-Louis et al., 2010; Starr & White, 2008).

Rural districts and building leaders often must find a third way through relatively placeless or urbanormative educational policy to best meet the needs of their communities with regard to achievement, college going, and local well-being (Azano & Biddle, 2019; Casto, McGrath et al., 2016; Schafft, 2016; Tieken, 2014). The requirement, for example, under the Every Student Succeeds Act (2015) that schools choose evidence-based programs ignores the lack of rural representation within the studies that establish the evidence base for approved programs (Eppley et al., 2018). Rural leaders are left to figure out how to make programs whose evidence of success was culled from communities elsewhere work for their communities. One area of scholarship that deserves more study is the ability of school leaders not only to act in ways that reflect community values but also to work in ways that exert influence over those values. As more scholarship in the broader educational leadership literature is informed by an acknowledgment of the role race, class, gender, ability, immigration status, and other social identities mediate who has voice in our public school system and whose needs are best served by it (Modeste et al., 2020), there has been a broader examination of the role of educational leaders in holding space for marginalized voices, prioritizing the needs of minoritized groups, and buffering or even transforming pressure from dominant groups to use the school system to consolidate their own status.

Rural leaders have been surprisingly absent from this turn, with a few exceptions. Albritton and colleagues (2017) examine the ways in which rural leaders used their Christian faith and commitment to eliminating achievement disparities as a lens for performing socially just leadership, with mixed results for students from marginalized groups. Similarly, Bishop and McLellan (2016) discuss how normatively conservative values within a community affected the ways in which school leaders excluded LGBTQ+ identities in the creation of inclusive school climates. Maxwell and colleagues (2014) consider the role of resilience in the performance of socially just leadership by superintendents in rural communities, emphasizing the ways in which they used faith and other supports to sustain themselves in difficult work. More work in this area is urgently needed to understand how school leaders navigate community values, the imperative to teach deliberative democracy in our schools, and an increasingly politically polarized nation.

Rurality and Leadership Theory

Stronger frameworks for rural leadership practice that focus on the interaction between the rural context and institutional priorities of schools could help rural school leaders better leverage the strengths of rural schools and communities to define and meet institutional and community goals for rural young people in ways that foreground equity and social justice. One of the challenges to theoretically coherent guidance for rural school leadership practice is teasing out the ways in which unique features of rural contexts intersect with the expectations for leaders that derive from the institutional logic and normative grammar of schooling, as well as the individualistic focus on what constitutes educational outcomes of the last several decades (Casto, McGrath et al., 2016).

One area of rural scholarship that has helped to lay the theoretical groundwork for what constitutes rural school leadership practice has come from a reimagining of rural educational policy that places more emphasis on local vitality. For example, Casto, McGrath and colleagues (2016) and Schafft (2016) both argue for a stronger connection between educational policy and community development in rural education. While these arguments do not only focus on rural school leadership practice, they have important implications for the enactment of such leadership and suggest a paradigmatic shift in the priorities of rural school leaders. Schafft (2016) centers his argument around the "cultural, civic, economic and symbolic" (Schafft, 2016, p. 139) role that schools play in rural communities, and the ways in which broader educational policy does not leverage this critical linkage in ways that are locally beneficial for rural communities. Broadly, as Schafft (2016) and others have argued (Carr & Kefalas, 2009; Corbett, 2007) out-migration and a focus on transferrable human capital underpins this disconnection, coupled with the focus on high-stakes accountability that directs the attention of school leaders and teachers to a narrow set of metrics for student and institutional success (Schafft et al., 2010). Schafft (2016) proposes a third way for rural schools and districts through this dichotomy by fostering more explicit acknowledgment of the community development role that rural schools play for rural communities, as well as the cultivation of community partnerships that create economic and social value for both the school and the community.

Similarly, Casto, McGrath and colleagues (2016) seek to build the connection between community development and educational policy broadly, not only within rural contexts. Rather than making the case for social and economic importance of the school, they focus their argument on moving toward a "thick" conceptualization of children's needs (Casto, McGrath et al., 2016, p. 4) and the changes such a reconceptualization would imply for educational policy and educator professional practice. Like Schafft (2016), they ground their characterization of the current "thin" understanding of individual needs in broader neoliberal approaches to education; however, their argument for educational policy that is more community-aware hinges on the recognition of education as both an individual and collective good, and that embedding these collective aspects in educational policy requires an understanding of children's needs as relational and embedded across many social institutions, including the family.

Both of these arguments situate the work of the educational leader within a local ecology that positions the school not as an entity unto itself but as one with both obligations and opportunities to better serve its local community. The contours of this debate in educational leadership are not new (see Foster, 2004; Furman, 2004; Green, 2018); however, they do provide a detailed backdrop against which to understand the constraints and opportunities that rural school leaders specifically are working around and through. In this volume, both Casto and Sipple (Chapter 12) and Zuckerman (Chapter 13) highlight the importance of school leaders acting in a fashion that is both community-aware and in collaboration with efforts in other sectors, echoing earlier calls such as that of Harmon and Schafft (2009) in their ruralizing of the Interstate School Leader Licensing Consortium standards (an earlier version of the PSEL standards; 2015). The school leader plays an important role in both setting the direction and tone of the work of a school district or building, as well as serving as a connector and connection point for the broader community (Harmon & Schafft, 2009).

In a review of the literature on the rural superintendency, McHenry-Sorber and Budge (2018) advance an argument for the importance of critical, place-conscious leadership. Building on empirical work from the previous twenty years, they trace the evolution of the theoretical salience of insider/outsider status of leaders vis-à-vis their communities and the ways in which this status affects hiring, defining school purpose, initiating change, and working with the community—all critical aspects of rural leadership practice. They then argue that scholarly concern around insider/outsider status has morphed into a multidimensional appreciation of place and positioning of rural leaders in the context of high-stakes accountability policy introduced by No Child Left

Rural School Leadership

Behind in 2001; however, they point out that the foundations of this turn toward place-conscious leadership have been reductive of rural community diversity and intracommunity conflict, as well as overly prescriptive. In their conceptual review, McHenry-Sorber and Budge (2018) build a potential connection point to the broader field of educational leadership, which has grappled in the last two decades with what critically conscious, contextually responsive leadership looks and feels like (see Foster, 2004; Furman, 2004; Green, 2018).

Conclusion

Rural school leadership constitutes something of a paradox for rural education scholarship. We know a great deal about many fragmented aspects of the lives of rural leaders. However, the conceptual models for how rurality and school leadership are related remain thin. This discussion of the literature will conclude with encouragement for promising directions that could help to build that theoretical coherence in a more robust way.

First, more scholarly work is needed on rural school leadership that comes from an asset-based perspective and focuses on assessing the unique affordances of leading a small school organization in communities with relatively dense social networks. While some of these assets are teased out in the scholarship on rural school-community relationships, they are rarely considered within the context of the broad range of responsibilities that principals and superintendents shoulder. It seems likely that the pervasive deficit orientation in the rural school leadership literature represents a holdover of the rural school problem—namely, the focus on the ways in which fulfilling an institutionally defined role within a context for which the position was not designed.

Second, more research attention to the micropolitics of rural leadership through scholarship similar to McHenry-Sorber's (2014) study of the complexities of rural teacher strike or Harris-Smedberg's (2019) study of school leader responses to economic shock would help to develop more robust leadership theory that is sensitive to the dynamics of working in small communities in which a single person who wears many hats may be the barrier to or champion of a particular initiative. This direction of research should also include a focus on the interactions between rural school leaders and rural school boards, such as Sutherland's (2020) work on how rural school boards make sense of federal accountability policy. Better understanding the dynamics of power and decision-making in rural places will give depth to theories of rural leadership and the intense scrutiny that accompanies it will help to move the field beyond simply enumerating the factors that contribute to the job satisfaction and longevity of rural principals.

Finally, there is a clear necessity for scholarship on rural school leaders to engage meaningfully with issues of diversity and difference within these micropolitical relationships, most notably at the intersection of race and rurality. A critical question raised by the data from the National Principal and Teacher Survey (Taie & Goldring, 2020) is why White men are being hired in far greater numbers than women and people of color into the rural school principalship. This inquiry serves as an opportunity for bridging topics between the broader educational administration literature (which reflects this trend generally but in less extreme numbers) and the unique sociospatial considerations posed by its occurrence in rural school districts. It is here that work such as McHenry-Sorber and Budge's (2018) argument for the elevation of critical place-conscious approaches to both leadership practice and scholarship or Roberts and Green's (2013) argument for a spatial component to social justice could help to provide theoretical coherence to future work in this area, in collaboration with frameworks that have helped move this work forward in the broader field, such as critical race theory, critical policy analysis, and community equity literacy (Green, 2018; Modeste et al., 2020).

Finally, one of the lost opportunities for the field of rural education is the number of rural principals and superintendents who participate in graduate programs in educational leadership across the country and produce scholarship on their experiences that remains undisseminated. These scholar-practitioners have an opportunity to contribute meaningfully to the field through their theses or dissertation work if more of that work does not remain relegated to the pages of their unread dissertations. It is incumbent on faculty in educational leadership EdD and PhD programs to work with their students to disseminate their work in ways that can impact both practice and the scholarship more broadly and on academic journals to work with practitioner authors to make space for their contributions to the broader field.

11

Rural Teacher Labor Issues

Erin McHenry-Sorber

The two largest US teachers' unions are the National Education Association (NEA), which represents approximately 2.3 million members, and the American Federation of Teachers (AFT), which includes another 1.7 million members (Will, 2019b). Generally, states in the northeast, across the Rust Belt, and on the west coast, including Alaska and Hawaii, have the highest rates of public sector unions, a statistic that includes teacher union membership (Antonucci, 2018). While Rust Belt states and states in the northeast have large urban centers, they are also home to large numbers of rural schools and school systems. Rural teacher labor activism, like teacher activism situated in nonrural places, encompasses a range of teachers' union activity in the local, state, and national arenas, all with the goal of influencing government action. The AFT and NEA advocate for government reforms related, but not limited, to salary and healthcare benefits, student inequities, gun violence, high-stakes testing policies, immigration issues, nutrition, education funding, and a host of other issues they perceive as negatively affecting students, teachers, and paraprofessionals (AFT, 2020; NEA, 2020).

In addition to political advocacy, teacher labor actions can range from collective bargaining (the collective negotiation by teachers around issues like wages and working conditions) to strikes (mass work stoppages in response to labor grievances). Such actions might occur at the district or state level, depending on each state's education funding structure and policy mechanisms. These actions can be constrained by diverse state laws and statutes that specifically govern the rights of public sector teachers. For example, teachers legally have the right to collectively bargain in all but five states: Georgia, North Carolina, South Carolina, Texas, and Virginia.[1] In contrast, the right to strike is only legal in twelve states.[2] However, the rights of teachers to engage in myriad labor actions are ambiguous in many state contexts, and these rights can shift depending on the party in power. Further, the legality of particular labor actions does not necessarily translate into lack of labor activism, as exemplified by the wave of teacher strikes across the United States beginning in 2018.

In the predominately rural state of West Virginia, a state in which it is illegal for teachers to strike, a teacher labor activism movement launched in the form of mass protests and strikes, with Oklahoma, Arizona, Kentucky, and others following its lead. While these large-scale labor

The Bloomsbury Handbook of Rural Education in the United States

protests seemingly began over typical union issues like pay, health care, and respect for the profession, the roots of the campaign were more complex, and the movement publicly morphed into one focused on educational policy reform. The large urban strikes that followed, including those in Los Angeles, Oakland, and Denver, served as a backlash to neoliberal policies and aimed to redirect public funds and political commitments to support public education systems (McHenry-Sorber, 2019; Vyse, 2019; Will, 2019a). The wave appeared to come full circle in 2019 when West Virginia teachers staged a second mass strike, this time in response to the state's privatization efforts. The nationwide movement continued into 2020.

This heightened period of national teacher activism followed the US Supreme Court's 5–4 ruling in *Janus v. AFSCME*, which prohibits public sector unions from collecting fair share fees from nonunion workers even when they represent nonmember interests (*Janus v. American Federation of State, County, and Municipal Employees*, 2018).[3] At the time, the decision was characterized as a "huge blow to public-sector unions and the labor movement in general" (Applewhite, 2018, para. 1), but as the strike wave of 2018 suggests, the *Janus* decision did not hamper teacher union organizing or protest, even in predominantly rural states with conservative legislatures. As *USA Today* reported, "At a time when organized labor seems in terminal decline, a national public school teachers' movement emerged from the coalfields of southern West Virginia, one of the most isolated and conservative corners of America" (Hampson, 2019). National media outlets expressed surprise at the movement's origins: geographically isolated rural districts in a central Appalachian state that voted overwhelmingly for Donald Trump. Any shock over rural West Virginia serving as the epicenter of national teacher activism is due, in part, to a dearth of scholarship about rural teacher labor issues. Attention to this phenomenon would, for example, highlight the rich tradition of rural labor and activism in West Virginia, particularly in the rural southern coalfields where the statewide strike began.

In a review of key phrases including "rural teacher strike," "rural teacher unionism," "teacher strike," and "teacher activism" in Google Scholar, three empirical articles were devoted to investigation of US rural teacher labor action (McHenry-Sorber, 2014; McHenry-Sorber & Schafft, 2015; Schirmer, 2017). A handful of recent articles and books devoted to the 2018 statewide teacher strikes, situated in predominantly rural states (e.g., Webber, 2018), do not examine the strikes from a rural standpoint or make rurality a central construct in understanding the labor movement.

Given the paucity of scholarship on rural teacher labor issues, it is necessary to turn to related labor research to consider what we already know about rural teacher labor and what future research might inform us about this topic. This chapter examines multiple threads of scholarship on teacher labor and strikes, including international scholarship on teacher activism; broad US teacher labor research as published in historical waves of activity; US urban teacher activism and strike scholarship; and existing literature on rural teacher labor issues. Utilizing salient existing scholarship, the chapter establishes a research agenda focused on rural teacher labor activism.

Historically Situated Scholarship

Teacher labor activism has enjoyed historical waves of scholarly consideration, dependent, in part, on surges of urban activity, with scant research attention over the past three decades. Most often, scholarly attention has been given when labor activity reaches the level of a strike. Further, the literature that does exist is rarely neutral, largely characterized by advocates either in favor of or in opposition to teacher unionism. Even within union-supportive research, there is discord about what form teachers' unions should take: industrial unionism aimed at bread and butter issues like pay and health care, professional or reform unionism aimed at collaborative education reform, or social movement unionism aimed at equity issues (McCollow, 2017). McCollow (2017) notes, "despite analyses drawing on various research paradigms . . . theorization of the nature and role of teacher unions remains very much a work in progress" (p. 3).

Early scholarship on US teacher unionism and labor protest followed a peak of teacher labor unrest in the late 1960s and 1970s when the NEA used strikes as a tool to increase teacher unionism, and the AFT engaged in strikes in response to a host of problematic teaching conditions in urban centers (Parker, 1968; Zeluck, 1969). This early literature takes three major forms: survey research on teacher militancy, first-person strike accounts, and advice for educational leaders and board members in managing strikes and their aftermath.

Survey Research on Teacher Militancy

While there were multiple attempts to understand teacher militancy, or teacher labor protest, during and following the heightened period of teacher labor activity in the 1960s and 1970s, two studies included a discussion of rural teachers. Bacharach and colleagues (1990) found rural teachers to be more inclined to militant behavior than nonrural, a leaning they attributed to rural teachers enjoying less involvement in schoolwide decision-making than their urban counterparts. Alutto and Belasco (1974) similarly found rural teachers to be more militant than nonrural teachers. However, their study only included two school sites—one rural and one urban—making it difficult to attribute increased proclivity toward teacher militancy to something specific or unique to rural settings as opposed to institutional characteristics. Other militancy scholarship either did not account for rural/nonrural differences or focused exclusively on urban strikes and labor action. Some of these "city" problems that led to teacher militancy included consequences of White flight and failed desegregation schemes (Parker, 1968) in addition to broader issues, including low pay compared to other professions, lack of control over working conditions, lack of professional autonomy, and limited participation in decision-making (Martin, 1980; Ward, 1980).

First-Person Strike Accounts

First-person accounts of strikes by teachers expanded on these prestrike contextual factors and fell into two broad categories: explanations for failed strikes and reasons for striking. Ward (1980), for example, described a failed strike in New Orleans precipitated by a host of issues around increasing pressures on teachers to ease racial tensions, increase math and reading achievement, and engage in "fair discipline" practices while facing disparaging media commentary. In short, strike action was the consequence of increased responsibility and decreased respect for the profession. According to Ward, the strike failed, in large part due to problematic state union leadership and state-level competition for union members between the NEA and AFT. Ward's account suggests that in this case, local issues precipitated the strike while state-level issues derailed it. Another first-person account (Martin, 1980) attributed a union's strike as "inevitable" but successful in order to address a host of problems beyond substandard pay such as problematic district policies regarding due process, reduction in force procedures, sick and personal leave disputes, overcrowded class sizes, lack of school counselors, and conflict over pay for

The Bloomsbury Handbook of Rural Education in the United States

extracurriculars. A focus on issues beyond pay was a common theme across first-person accounts during this period (Kubiak, 1985; Martin, 1980; Parker, 1968; Ward, 1980).

Other first-person accounts concentrated in the 1990s were written by those who chose to cross picket lines. These narratives focused on violent or intimidating behavior by picketing teachers and the lasting discord between striking teachers and those who crossed the picket line (Righi, 1993; Wilson, 1995). While first-person accounts highlighted some similarities across cases (e.g., contributing factors), they also suggest the highly contextual nature of teacher labor protest and the role of outside interests in exacerbating or improving failed negotiations.

Practical Advice for Educational Leaders

Beyond first-person teacher accounts, a number of pieces written during this period targeted school and district leaders, providing practical advice for how to manage a strike effectively, including suggestions for launching an effective public relations strategy to win negotiations (James, 1987; Namit, 1986), tips on staying neutral during a strike in order to maintain a positive school climate, or recommendations for reestablishing working relationships in the aftermath of a strike (Hahn, 1981; Keough, 1974; Schwerdtfeger, 1984; Vyskocil & Goens, 1979).

None of these first-person accounts or advice columns focused on rural labor action. This is perhaps not surprising as numerous high-profile, large urban strikes occurred during this period. Some of these accounts failed to describe school, district, or community context at all. These research gaps were left unfilled over the course of the twentieth century, during which time little scholarly attention was paid to teacher activism broadly, despite some large-scale labor protests during this time period. However, a surge in teacher activism in the twenty-first century resulted in increased, though limited, research attention in the United States and internationally.

Contemporary Scholarship: American and International

McCollow (2017) argues the twenty-first century has been marked by significant challenges to teacher unions internationally:

> Over thirty years of neoliberal social, economic, and educational polity have increased the stakes of debates about the nature and role of teacher unions. Neoliberal reforms have reduced the capacity of teacher unions to organize, significantly changed the conditions under which teachers are employed and work, and altered the nature of the schooling received by students. (p. 16)

The research on teacher strikes across the globe encompasses a range of methodological strategies and purposes. Focused research over the past two decades includes teacher labor activity as a response to neoliberal educational reforms (Bravo et al., 2014; Compton & Weiner, 2008; Hromadžić, 2015; Synott, 2017) and, consequently, issues of teacher pay (Arenal, 2007; Barnetson, 2010; Hromadžić, 2015), job security (Gill, 1998), and classroom conditions (Arenal, 2007; Gill, 1998), among other industrial and professional concerns. Limited scholarship focuses on the effects of teacher strikes on student academic performance (Wills, 2014), with mixed results. Many international studies have described labor protests marked by violence, initiated by unions in some cases (Fleisch, 2010), but more often initiated by governments in response to strikes, rallies, and public demonstrations (Arenal, 2007; Bravo et al., 2014; Gill, 1998). Fleisch's (2010) study of a South African regional

130

strike suggests labor unrest is inherently local, though it can inform and be informed by broader educational debates and dissatisfaction. While most of these works highlight urban teacher labor activity, a few studies include a discussion of rural teacher participation in urban protests (Gill, 1998) or rural parent perceptions of teacher strikes (Bravo et al., 2014).

Common across much of this research is an emphasis on neoliberalism, class (Arenal, 2007; Hromadžić, 2015), the use of competing narratives by striking unions and governments to direct the course of public debate (Barnetson, 2010; Shenkar & Shenkar, 2011), and the use of war terminology to describe teacher labor. Compton and Weiner (2008), for example, argue, "Teachers are in a war being fought over the future of education, and . . . we have a potentially powerful weapon in our hands—our solidarity and organization into powerful teachers' unions" (p. 6). The use of such rhetoric, particularly across international studies, is not surprising, given the actual use of military force in many instances to quash teacher labor unrest (e.g., Arenal, 2007).

While the violence associated with many international cases of teacher strikes is jarring, this scholarship offers a number of potential frameworks for understanding rural teacher labor action in the United States. Drawing on lessons from international and nonrural focused American scholarship is critical in creating an agenda for rural teacher labor scholarship, as the field suffers from an urban-centric or place-neutral emphasis. Beyond these scholarship failings, in general, there is a dearth of US scholarship published on collective bargaining and teacher unionism since the mid-1980s (Cowen, 2009), leaving major gaps in our knowledge of broader teacher labor issues and rural teacher labor, specifically.

Recent US teacher union activism scholarship has explored a variety of salient topics. These range from a quantitative investigation of the likelihood of strikes as potential causes for increased mischievous youth crime in urban locales (Luallen, 2006), to historical studies of urban teacher activism amid shifting labor laws and public perceptions of teachers' right to strike (Shelton, 2013), to specific strike case studies. Of note, there were several studies published in response to the 2012 Chicago teachers' strike (Gutierrez, 2013; Rodriguez, 2016), including a case study investigation of the breakdown of reform unionism in favor of industrial-style bargaining in a large urban district (Jacoby & Nitta, 2012). These US studies, like international studies had done in the past, turned scholarly attention to teacher activism as a form of resistance to neoliberal reforms (e.g., Weiner, 2012).

A few quantitative studies published since 2009 have investigated the effects of collective bargaining on issues like teacher pay with discrepant results (Lovenheim, 2009; A. M. Winkler et al., 2012), while others have looked at the importance of union power in shaping collective bargaining agreements (Strunk & Grissom, 2010; Strunk & Marianno, 2019). The latter focus included district type (rural, urban, or suburban) as an analysis consideration. Collectively, this research suggests (a) rural district unions are less likely to collectively bargain than nonrural unions (A. M. Winkler et al., 2012); and (b) smaller, rural districts have unions with less power over teachers' working conditions than larger urban and suburban districts (Strunk & Grissom, 2010). These findings implicate the need for research aimed at understanding the causes for relatively weak rural teachers' unions and the consequences of this disempowered status in determining positive working conditions. The nationwide strike wave beginning in 2018, sparked by union action in a predominately rural state, can provide the opportunity to investigate salient phenomena, including resistance to neoliberal reforms, strike effects on students, and union power across diverse rural and nonrural districts within and across state policy contexts.

Existing Rural Teacher Labor Literature and the Nationwide Strike Movement of 2018

The nationwide strike wave that began in 2018 in West Virginia and moved across multiple predominately rural states and large urban centers was too recent at the time of this writing to have resulted in peer-reviewed research. However, Webber (2018) published a forum discussion with several renowned teacher labor scholars responsive to the 2018–19 strike movement. Akin to first-person accounts and strike research in the 1960s and 1970s, Webber's (2018) forum participants point to many of the same issues that had confronted teachers fifty years earlier, including problematic class sizes, school building infrastructure, substandard pay, reduction in programming, and lack of respect for the profession. In this forum, contributors offered analysis across a host of issues related to the 2018–19 strike wave, but one piece missing from the article was a question of rurality. Instead, labels such as "Right-to-Work" and "Red State" were used to describe the movement's origins. This framing of statewide strikes as a conservative or Red State revolt limits our ability to interrogate the role of place as a critical construct in understanding teacher activism. Further, it ignores the rich history of rural labor activism across rural places.

A Statewide Case: West Virginia

For example, West Virginia's labor history includes violent and persistent labor unrest involving coal miners in rural regions of the state (Boissoneault, 2017). In 1921, during the Battle of Blair Mountain, 10,000 mine workers clashed with government agents in what is considered the "largest armed uprising in American history since the Civil War" (Keeney, 2018, para. 2). The state has also experienced a more recent history of ecojustice activism, particularly by rural women as a response to environmental injustices such as unclean drinking water and mountaintop removal (e.g., Barry, 2012). The state experienced a nearly statewide teachers' strike in 1990, through which teachers won increased pay, a commitment to state funding of their public health insurance plan, and incentives for graduate coursework (Mochaidean, 2018). The 2018 strike also centered on issues like pay and health care, but it included other issues of importance to teachers: unsatisfactory working conditions, including a statewide teacher shortage and overcrowded classrooms; a legislative privatization agenda; and the defunding of the state's public education system, among others.

The 2018 strike was largely led by rank-and-file teachers, those teachers not elected to state union leadership positions, and was aided by a network of support that traversed the political spectrum, different community types, and multiple teachers' and service personnel unions (McHenry-Sorber, 2018). Teachers worked with community groups to establish food sites for youth who relied on the school system for daily meals, staged rallies at the state capital, and garnered mass media attention in which they successfully controlled the protest narrative. Teachers won a pay increase for all state employees and a commitment to establish a task force devoted to improving the West Virginia public employee health insurance system. Many of these strike themes are related to previous scholarship on teacher activism, including precipitating strike factors, resistance to neoliberalism, and the power of public narratives in garnering third-party support across West Virginia. Striking teachers gained widespread support beyond state borders, and their movement was widely deemed a victory for the profession, as evidenced by the number of states who followed suit.

District-Level Cases

In addition to a lack of research on statewide movements, scant research has been published on district-level cases of rural teacher union activity. Two in-depth cases are highlighted in this section: (a) Schirmer's (2017) historical exploration of a 1974 rural teacher strike in Wisconsin and (b) McHenry-Sorber (2014) and McHenry-Sorber and Schafft's (2015) research in the rural strike case of Mountainville, Pennsylvania.

The 1974 Wisconsin Strike

In a rare example of rural-focused teacher labor scholarship, Schirmer (2017) explored the dynamics of a 1974 rural teacher strike in Wisconsin, a state that had enjoyed widespread support for unionism and bargaining at the time. The community in which the strike occurred had failed to pass levies on three separate occasions to build new schools. The strike responded to a variety of related issues, including overcrowding, lack of professional autonomy, low relative pay, and the absence of a contract for the previous three years. These concerns were exacerbated by a school board proposal to increase the school day by two hours and put teachers on flexible shifts in order to manage overcrowded facilities. After failed negotiations, teachers staged a two-week strike. At the end of the strike, the school board fired all eighty-eight teachers and replaced them with substitutes, many of whom were uncertified. The school board was supported in its efforts by a local anti-strike group comprised largely of conservative farmers who called themselves the Vigilante Association. As the union brought in statewide support, the Vigilante Association also called on more farmers to support its cause. As Schirmer notes, "retired farmers came into town armed with canes, broomsticks, and even firearms" (p. 7). The president of the statewide teachers' union, an African American woman from Milwaukee, became the group's special target. "In addition to hurling racial slurs at her, Vigilantes struck her with a car and dragged her behind the vehicle for nearly an entire city block" (p. 7). The statewide union called for a one-day sympathy strike, but none of the major cities agreed to participate. Without the cover of these large, powerful, urban unions, smaller rural unions feared the same fate as the striking teachers, and the strike ultimately failed. Schirmer explains that the inability to change the fate of the district through militancy led to a shift in union tactics with a new focus on legislative action.

The Mountainville Case

The case of Mountainville (McHenry-Sorber, 2014; McHenry-Sorber & Schafft, 2015) occurred over forty years after the subject of Shirmer's research. In Mountainville, school buildings had fallen into disrepair; teachers had been working without a contract for three years; and they were at an impasse with the school board around two issues: salary and contribution to health care. In this rural district, school board members won elections with promises to cut property taxes and teachers' salaries, and the board had effectively defunded the local school system for decades. After continued failed negotiations and then a refusal from the school board to negotiate, teachers initiated the first strike in the district's history. Even though over half of the teachers were local to the community, the school board was able to socially exclude teachers from Mountainville through the propagation of a winning hegemonic narrative of community. At the height of the controversy, a sign appearing in a storefront read, "Make my day, shoot a teacher" (McHenry-Sorber & Schafft, 2015). Once teachers were successfully portrayed as enemies of Mountainville—and so consumed by greed they would destroy the economically distressed community—the teachers'

The Bloomsbury Handbook of Rural Education in the United States

union was unable to influence the final contract agreement. The school board revoked striking teachers' health insurance, and both sides were forced into court-ordered bargaining. The final contract included an increase in teachers' contributions to health care and a much smaller raise than teachers had initially sought. Unlike the Wisconsin case (Schirmer, 2017), the Mountainville teachers were not fired, though many voluntarily left the district following the strike. Those who stayed suggested the strike taught them that they were "second-class citizens" in the community hierarchy. The Mountainville case highlights the power of narratives in affecting the outcome of rural teacher labor, akin to Shenkar and Shenkar's (2011) nationally focused research in Israel. In addition, McHenry-Sorber and Schafft's (2015) research illuminates that factionalization and class divides of rural communities are exacerbated in times of labor conflict.

Striking similarities exist between the 1974 Wisconsin case and the case described by McHenry-Sorber (2014, despite the multiple decades that passed between the two events). Both cases included deep community factionalization and the influence of outside forces on the strike's outcome, whether those outside influences included the presence of union leadership or the judicial system. Both cases highlight the potentially acrimonious nature of local-level teacher strikes, with attention to widespread community opposition to rural teachers. Shirmer's and McHenry-Sorber's findings lie in contrast to the West Virginia statewide teacher strike, which appeared through media accounts to garner widespread community support and resulted in a big victory, particularly in terms of salary increases. If the West Virginia case suggests militancy can result in big wins for teacher labor, Schirmer's (2017) and McHenry-Sorber (2014) and McHenry-Sorber and Schafft's (2015) research serves as a reminder that rural teacher labor protest is a risky endeavor for unions. These markedly different outcomes suggest a critical point of divergence for future scholarship: rural labor protest in the state arena versus the local district arena.

Toward a Rural Teacher Labor Research Agenda

Multiple scholarship veins on teacher labor, whether international or domestic, historical or contemporary, implicate the need for increased scholarly attention to rural teacher labor in the United States. This rural teacher labor research agenda, informed by historical and contemporary scholarship, includes foci on union militancy, strike narratives across diverse teachers and places, and new leadership studies, given recent theoretical development of rural leadership constructs. It also includes research on rural teacher labor and neoliberal reforms, power inequities, the propagation of dominant public strike narratives, and the influence of macro and micro contexts on rural labor action.

Historical US research, largely published over fifty years ago, remains relevant to contemporary studies of teacher labor activism and can serve as a starting point for a rural education research agenda with attention to teacher militancy, strike narratives, and school and district leadership. First, studies of teacher militancy with attention to place following the 2018–19 strike movement and the US Supreme Court *Janus* decision might illuminate the new ways in which teacher militancy has resurfaced across rural and nonrural districts and states. More nuanced militancy scholarship might deepen our understanding of the phenomenon across a diversity of rural places, taking into account macro and micro factors, including institutional and community contexts, in shaping union militancy. Second, qualitative ethnographic or narrative research can expand on early first-person strike accounts with attention to context. Such inquiry, inclusive of institutional, community, and regional attributes, has the potential to illustrate the ways in which teacher labor activity is influenced by place and how teachers' unions use contextual knowledge to craft their labor activity and activist narratives in order to garner public support. Researcher attention to diverse narratives can create a robust portrait of teacher labor activity across rural and nonrural places while allowing for divergent pictures of activity to emerge within a given place. Third, understandings of rural educational leadership have shifted in recent years (Hall, 2016; Hall & McHenry-Sorber, 2017; McHenry-Sorber & Budge, 2018; McHenry-Sorber & Sutherland, 2020). Thus, scholarship focused on leadership responses to rural teacher labor might be grounded in extant literature related to critical place-conscious leadership and other contemporary theorizing on rural leadership, given new understandings about the multiple contexts that influence rural leadership practice.

More recent research, both internationally and domestically focused, contributes further avenues for a rural teacher labor research agenda, including considerations of resistance to neoliberalism in rural districts, the relative power of rural to nonrural unions, and the relationship between rural unions and state leadership. First, international teacher labor activity as a response to neoliberal reforms resembles many of the arguments propagated by teachers' unions in the United States, particularly with respect to privatization movements. Given widespread (and predominantly rural) state teachers' strike issues (and large urban strike issues) publicized in 2018 and 2019—large class sizes, poor working conditions, high-stakes testing, charter school legislation, and other privatization schemes (see Campbell, 2019; Weiner, 2019; Wong, 2018)— the study of rural teachers' responses to neoliberal reforms is warranted. Relatedly, recent critical scholarship trends in rural education research (e.g., Biddle et al., 2019; Corbett, 2016b; Tieken, 2017) coupled with this teacher labor activity suggest the need for critical research related to rural teacher pay and classroom conditions, with an eye toward equity issues within and across rural school systems. Second, research interrogating the relative power of rural teachers' unions to that of their urban counterparts might illuminate nuanced understandings of the power of community context in shaping the broad perceptions of unions by teachers and more specific beliefs regarding the union as a viable tool for influencing work conditions. Such research might benefit from theoretical conceptions of critical place-conscious pedagogy and leadership (Azano, 2011; McHenry-Sorber & Budge, 2018; Rey, 2014) as well as spatial inequality (Biddle et al., 2019; Tieken, 2017) in framing rural teacher union sensemaking and agency. Finally, studies of discourse and dominant narratives of rural teacher strikes can illuminate tensions between teachers and other community factions and highlight avenues by which they garner widespread public support, deepening our understanding of the ways in which rural teacher strikes are perceived by parents and other community members and how rural teachers might successfully (or unsuccessfully) frame labor activities (e.g., McHenry-Sorber & Schafft, 2015). Such research might investigate microcontextual influences on strike narratives and outcomes, including the role of dominant community interests regarding schooling and the worth of teachers, the effect of rural district membership size on bargaining power, and the political platforms of rural school board candidates as related to collective bargaining. From a macro perspective, related investigations might include local and state policy environments in influencing rural labor activity; the relative ability of rural union leaders to engage with broader state organization platforms; the influence of rural teacher political affiliations on labor action and organizing; and areas of convergence and divergence between state union leadership and rural teachers' union membership interests and values.

The Bloomsbury Handbook of Rural Education in the United States

This line of macro-situated scholarship would benefit from scholarly attention to labor action in West Virginia and other predominantly rural states, particularly during 2018 and 2019. Rural-focused research of these statewide cases across rural and nonrural districts and communities might explore the ways in which labor movement leaders respond to interests and values regarding teaching and schooling across community types, union strategies to increase public support across and within communities, union responses to equity issues within communities, union leadership networks, the utility of virtual activism given the potential for inequitable broadband access in rural places, and the role of media outlets in focusing public attention on labor activity in predominantly rural states.

Finally, as evidenced by divergent outcomes of recent statewide labor protests in rural states and local-level rural teacher strikes, it is essential that future rural teacher labor research investigate both large-scale and district-level rural teacher labor action. How do rural communities respond to teacher labor protest, for example, when the teachers' union is protesting the actions of the state versus the actions of locally elected school board members? How is local support influenced by the source of funding required to settle rural teacher strikes? That is, are rural community groups more likely to support striking teachers if they see the source of funding as coming from the state versus local revenue sources? What narratives are likely to resonate with rural community members, particularly in economically distressed rural communities? What are the differential roles of outside union leaders in community- and state-level strikes, and how do community members respond to these bureaucratized union structures and outside voices?

The 2016 presidential election elevated national attention to rural people and places. The wave of teacher labor activity beginning in 2018 further raised the public's consciousness about teacher labor protest and conditions that may precipitate such activity. Despite this interest in rural places and people and a widespread labor protest movement originating in predominately rural states, there is still a paucity of scholarly attention to rural teacher labor issues. A focus on rural teacher labor, particularly in relation to nonrural teacher labor, has the potential to promote new understandings of rural school–community relationships, rural teacher and leader experience and practice, micro and macro contexts for rural teacher labor perceptions and activity, and spaces of convergence and divergence between rural and nonrural teacher labor. This moment in time serves as an opportunity for the emergence of a rural teacher labor research agenda.

12

Rural School–Community Partnerships
Creating Community-Aware Educational Practices

Hope G. Casto and John W. Sipple

Rural school–community partnerships have the potential to create "community-aware" educational practices (Casto, Sipple et al., 2016). By this we mean that for schools to truly serve children, their families, and the broader community, a deeper and thicker conception of need must be addressed and measured before and after new policies, programs, and partnerships are enacted. Too often, education policies are designed and implemented with concern solely focused on students inside the four walls of the school (e.g., math scores, overrepresentation in special education, free lunch counts, homework help). Policies are designed and implemented without attention to the needs and impacts of the community in which children and families live. Understanding and meeting the thicker needs such as lack of economic opportunity, poor nutrition, poor health, family stress, and obstacles to family stability requires a different policy approach from the more instrumental practice of meeting the immediate challenges faced by students in school. In the midst of understanding these thicker needs, it is still essential to attend to the very real needs of children in day-to-day school practices. It is our contention that educational policy, as well as school partnerships and practice, can help to better understand thicker needs of children and communities including racial and economic equity, social exclusion, and historical wedges that divide communities and schools.

Rural School-Community Partnerships

School-community partnerships can be understood as any formalized arrangement between organizations or individuals in a community and the school or individuals within the school. Partnering can be seen in a variety of efforts, including coordinated services (Crowson & Boyd, 1993), full-service schools (Cummings et al., 2011; Dryfoos, 1994), community schools (Dryfoos & Maguire, 2002; Ferrara & Jacobson, 2019), in addition to partnerships with local businesses, nonprofit entities, community groups, churches, and individuals (Casto, 2016; Furco, 2013; Sanders, 2001, 2003; Shirley, 2001). Understanding and assessing the role of the community within these relationships requires defining community in the context of partnerships. The most local geographic community (i.e., village, neighborhood) may be most salient for parents or families, while an institutional definition of community (i.e., school district) may be more influential for educators and school leaders (Casto, 2019). However, geographical definitions (such as villages or neighborhoods) of community have been critiqued as colorblind leading to a need to attend to sociocultural definitions of community (LeChasseur, 2014). School and community leaders should work together, in collaboration with appropriate stakeholders, to ensure a meaningful definition of community is employed in partnering efforts.

Historically, rural schools have been understood on one hand as central to rural places (Hanifan, 1920; Peshkin, 1978) and on the other as inefficient institutions that limit progress (often as measured by an urban standard) in rural places (Schafft & Jackson, 2010a; Tyack, 1974). Nonetheless, rural schools are central and crucial to rural communities in a variety of ways (Lyson, 2002; Schafft & Jackson, 2010a; Sipple, Francis et al., 2019; Tieken, 2014). Rural school–community partnering is unique, given potential challenges of geographic isolation (Casto, 2016), population sparsity, and the associated "diffusion of human capacity" (Minner & Hiles, 2005, p. 85) due to the physical distance between people, settlements, schools, and potential partners. Successful rural schools engage families and communities in their work (Barley & Beesley, 2007), and partnering in rural places requires leaders focused on family and community involvement (Bauch, 2001; Casto, 2016; Krumm & Curry, 2017; Schafft et al., 2006).

Partnering takes a variety of forms and serves a range of purposes and goals. Some school–community partnerships focus less on the academic achievement of students and more on school reform, the support of families, community development efforts, and developing a sense of place (Casto, 2016). With this attention beyond the walls of the schools, partnering activities of schools serve as an excellent place to begin to draw attention to a community-aware perspective for school and community leaders. Complementing this understanding of partnering and drawing attention beyond the walls of the school, Bauch (2001) identifies six types of family-school-community connections: social capital, sense of place, parent involvement, church ties, school-business-agency relationships, and the community as a curricular resource. Types, forms, and goals of partnerships vary from place to place and are dependent on context; regardless, they provide an opportunity for schools and communities to work in collaboration and for mutual benefit.

While all forms of rural school–community partnering can be approached with a community-aware perspective, it is arguably the partnerships aligned with community development efforts that are most easily viewed from this perspective. School and community leaders in partnerships work together for benefits mutually experienced by the school and its community. For example, Schafft and colleagues (2006) describe a school and community working together to develop the technology infrastructure necessary for teaching and learning but also accessible to members of the whole community. Harmon and Schafft (2009) identify how school leaders can best align community development efforts with their professional educational administrative role, with an understanding that student achievement and community vitality are "inextricably connected" (p. 8). This view of community and school as intertwined and interdependent is foundational for school leaders intending to adopt a community-aware perspective in their leadership.

Partnering must take into account access and inclusion through both historical and current understandings of who has been present in a community and how power has been distributed among community members. Given the symbiotic nature of the school and community relationship, "if social injustice and inequity plague the social fabric of a community, these social issues will affect student learning within neighborhood schools" (O'Connor & Daniello, 2019, p. 312). Models of family engagement as important components of partnerships ought to account for parents' prior educational experiences, as well as differing cultural practices and understandings of schooling. Additionally, the role of educators requires listening to varied voices in the community and interventions in the school to ensure and enhance cultural competencies (Yull et al., 2014). This challenge to develop inclusive partnering practices is an echo of Dewey's insistence that "only by being true to the full growth of all the individuals who make it up, can society by any chance be true to itself" (Boydston, 1976, p. 5). The interdependence of schools and their communities creates the need for a community-aware perspective for educational policy and practice.

Community-Aware Perspective

Within a community-aware orientation, education policy and practice are connected to community vitality and development (Casto, Sipple et al., 2016). This perspective is rooted in an understanding of human need as thick rather than thin (Dean, 2010). In other words, human needs are relational and holistic rather than individualistic and narrow. While providing free lunch to children from families living near the poverty line is essential and works toward meeting some of the immediate needs of the family, it would be exponentially more beneficial to that child, their family, and the entire community to attend to the roots of poverty and hunger. The immediate and the systemic need to be addressed simultaneously. Food insecurity still exists even as broader and systemic efforts are undertaken.

This community-aware perspective is a broad orientation encompassing cross-sector policies and practices, including school-community partnering. When a community-aware perspective is adopted by policymakers, the resultant policies have the power to reduce unintended deleterious effects on communities due to the avoidance of narrowly defined or siloed polices focusing only on a single sector, such as education. As illustrated in the next section of this chapter, Universal Pre-kindergarten (UPK) in New York State (NYS) offers an example of a narrowly defined education policy with an unintended consequence that created potential deleterious effects on communities. This particular policy requires schools to partner with a community-based organization (CBO) to provide some or all of the prekindergarten programming for children in the district. On the surface one could view this as a community-aware policy that appeared to be taking into account the existing early care and education sector; however, without guidance for school and community leaders these partnerships (or waivers offered to schools to avoid the required partnering) were often taken on without careful planning and without a community-aware orientation. In this case, some communities that implemented UPK actually experienced decreased availability of infant and toddler care (Sipple et al., 2020). The type of community-aware policy implementation required to ensure UPK did not negatively impact the rest of the early childcare and education sector is unfamiliar to many school leaders. Lacking guidance to support careful planning by school and community leaders, childcare providers were negatively impacted by the implementation of UPK, especially in rural areas. The narrow goal of providing schooling for four-year-olds did not take into account a more interdependent view of the care options needed by families who have infants and toddlers in addition to four-year-olds.

The Bloomsbury Handbook of Rural Education in the United States

A community-aware perspective is focused on the full realization of individuals' needs for the good of the community with a thick view of individual and community need. This perspective unites the need for inclusive partnering as well as community development-oriented partnering. Local practice is influenced by local priorities and relationships but also shaped and constrained by nonlocal policy (Arum, 2000; Casto & Sipple, 2011). Arum (2000) argues that the modernization and professionalization of education has led to school leaders being increasingly beholden to the broader state and national influences, to the exclusion of the influences of the local, ecological community. Rural leaders are motivated by local influences (Casto & Sipple, 2011) and for isolated rural schools in particular, there may be a mediating layer that is both local and institutional: the school district (Casto, 2019). Policy design and implementation are equally critical as local practice in the application and use of the community-aware perspective. Here, we share three examples of community-aware practice, in order to engage the reader in questions of how state or federal policy might inhibit or promote such practice.

Illustrations of Community-Aware Partnering

Illustrations from schools and communities will help to provide both examples of how this perspective can be practiced as well as inspiration to understand its need. In the rural communities in which we have worked, there are often few, if any, community organizations with which a school could partner. As was the case in the New York example, small and isolated rural places are often fragile ecosystems that can easily be disturbed by missteps that can occur with even the best intentions.

The Early Childcare and Education Ecosystem

As UPK was rolled out in NYS, rural school districts were slow to accept the state grant and implement the program. Asked by the state to better understand this slow take-up rate, we engaged in a series of case studies in various rural regions of the state. In one community, we found a deep commitment to early education shared across the school board, teachers, and administrators. This district had been an early adopter of Targeted Pre-kindergarten (a prekindergarten program in NYS prior to UPK that was targeted at children from low-income families) and had what we referred to as an institutionalized PK-12 vision of schooling, rather than only K-12 (Casto & Sipple, 2011). And yet, we heard dire stories from the one local childcare center. They were suffering financially and feared having to close their doors. This would have left the community with no options for a licensed care provider for infants and toddlers. We were left with numerous questions about what had happened (or not happened, as we would come to find out) in this district during the UPK implementation process.

When NYS initiated the UPK grant opportunity, districts were required to partner with a local CBO. Per the policy, at least 10 percent of the grant funding must be subcontracted with a local organization to provide early childhood education. This community sought to embark on the implementation without consulting with the single local CBO with whom they could have partnered. According to the director of the CBO, the childcare center experienced significant financial stress as a result of families' new access to free UPK for their four-year-olds. Financially, four-year-olds were vital to the budgetary health of the center. We came to understand later that childcare centers often balance their budget on the tuition dollars from older children who require less intensive

Rural School–Community Partnerships

supervision and care, as evidenced in the ratios of teachers to children required, than infants and toddlers. Meanwhile, the elementary principal believed the school would take on the four-year-olds and the CBO could focus on the infants to three-year-olds and the county would be "rocking" early childhood education. In fact, when the school took on the four-year-olds, the CBO lost tuition-paying families and struggled to recoup these costs from families with younger children. In retrospect, the principal reflected: "I should have talked to people." And it is with this example that we can describe the state's UPK policy's requirement for partnering as suggestive of a community-aware perspective; however, without the technical assistance of how community and school leaders could engage in the planning and implementation process a truly community-aware outcome cannot be realized.

Windmills and Budget Restoration

A distinctly rural community faced typical challenges of loss of local employment, population loss, and heightened property taxes for those left behind. In the early 2000s, the school district began laying off staff in an effort to balance its very slow growth in local tax revenues with increasing retirement, energy, and healthcare costs. Embedded in this community is the K-12 school building that educated generations of students—some of whom returned to become teachers and administrators. A favorite local saying was that the community grew cows, trees, and children and exported cheese, paper, and graduates. As the superintendent and school board laid off staff, the superintendent got school board approval to collaborate with leaders from four towns in the area along with their county officials, on an ill-defined and poorly understood idea of building an industrial wind farm.

A wind farm of this magnitude was a first in the state. The infrastructure, laws, tax policy, and land use were all unknowns for these municipal leaders and one school superintendent. Over the next three years, the superintendent engaged in countless meetings with scientists, politicians, business leaders, tax attorneys, and citizens. Eventually, a set of agreements were signed between the international firm building the wind farm, the municipal governments, the local energy utility, and, importantly, the school district. Individual landowners, who agreed to allow a 400-foot-tall wind turbine on their property, would eventually receive annual checks and municipalities and the school district would enter into payment-in-lieu-of taxes (PILOT) agreements in which they would receive payments rather than subjecting the wind farm to property taxes.

Fast forward to 2005, the school district received its first PILOT check and then 2006, the wind farm first came online. After four years of near-level funding of teacher salaries (2001–4), which had resulted in the cutting of nearly twenty teaching positions, we see an increase in annual expenditures on teacher salaries of $2 million–from 2005–6 ($5.29 million) to 2010–11 ($7.28 million). This resulted in the rehiring of all teachers previously laid off. Additionally, after relatively stagnant property tax values per pupil from 1996 ($116,374) to 2004 ($135,123), the property values per pupil jumped in 2005 (to $155,112) and then nearly doubled to over $280,000 per pupil by 2011 and later. This increase was due to the combination of new annual PILOT receipts, enhanced property values across the community, and at least some homeowners receiving $10,000 checks each year to allow a turbine on their property.

This example illustrates that the involvement of a superintendent in nonschool economic development activity can pay great dividends. Had the board insisted the superintendent spend all his time on school-related issues, it is likely the district would have continued to lay off teachers, lose enrollment, and spiral into economic and educational decline (Figure 12.1).

The Bloomsbury Handbook of Rural Education in the United States

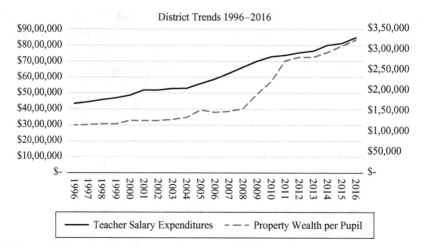

Figure 12.1 Financial trends in district affected by wind farm development, 1996–2016.

Healthy Kids Have Better Opportunities

We now offer an example of an outreach and research program that aims to better understand and assist one rural community facing economic downturns through a unique partnership. Additionally, we share research on a broader set of partnerships across a five-county region that includes twenty-one school-based health centers (SBHC) run by a single hospital. The case links a highly energetic and visionary superintendent, a dedicated and idealistic pediatrician, and a database of 3.5 million patient records across five counties. Together, we have embarked on a comprehensive effort to enhance the health and well-being of children to allow the school and healthcare providers to better serve their communities. To do this work, we initially responded to an invitation from the pediatrician. He explained that while his SBHCs are successful in caring for the acute and developmental health needs of children, the communities from which the children come are increasingly impacted by economic challenges and by the effects of drug addiction, in particular opioids, which can lead to particularly stressful environments for children. Our prior work with the superintendent allowed us insight into one of the eighteen partnerships. Here we use a community-aware perspective to enable our understanding of the data we collected.

Our example begins with a single rural PK-12 school building that is located equidistant from two small villages. Responding to the various pressures to modernize, gain efficiency, enhance academic and extracurricular programs, as well as to benefit from state incentives to consolidate school districts, the communities merged twenty years ago to build a modern K-12 school in an isolated location between the two villages. However, the consolidation of two small schools into one larger school did not stem the loss of population or employment decline in the area. Accordingly, the needs of families in this rural area are great.

This school district is one of eighteen in the region that benefits from a distinct and formal relationship with a large, rural hospital system. This hospital system "sponsors" SBHCs in twenty-one school buildings across eighteen school districts. The key to this network is the organization and financial support of the hospital along with the expertise and leadership of a pediatrician and a nurse who make it work. Each SBHC is staffed by a range of healthcare professionals who provide administration, health insurance accounting, and direct provision of health care, including somatic, dental, mental, and reproductive health care. The coordination of care and administration across the twenty-one clinics is carried out by the nurse and two pediatricians.

However, to truly have an impact on the whole child and family, the relationship and cooperation between the school and SBHC is critical. The school leaders and healthcare providers have a common goal of reducing the impact of poverty and to elevate well-being and opportunity in their respective communities and the broader region. In one of the eighteen districts with which we are most familiar, the superintendent and his staff do this through enhanced family supports and education and the pediatrician provides quality primary and holistic care in the school setting. While these relationships vary across their twenty-one sites, the relationship between this particular superintendent and pediatrician is particularly good and fruitful. Capitalizing on this strong dynamic between educational and healthcare leadership, we secured a small grant to hire a local person to act as a liaison between parents, educators, and the healthcare officials. Our hypothesis was that families that struggled to have a productive relationship with the educators were similar if not the same as those who faced communication and follow-up issues with the healthcare providers in the school-based clinic. This liaison worked to break down barriers, enhance understanding and connectivity, and generally work to enhance the positive impacts of schooling and health care for families. This particular set of relationships is emblematic of the power of a community-aware perspective in action. With this thick understanding of need, students' academic and health needs are simultaneously met.

We have now initiated an engaged research program to measure the impact of SBHCs on children and communities. The data with which we can understand the impact of SBHCs on communities includes 3.5 million cases over seven years. We link the health data (individuals ages 0–100+) with school district data (community measures) to allow for measurement of the relationships between demographics, fiscal well-being, and the presence or absence of a SBHC. Exploring the mathematical estimates of relationships would fail to provide the kind of robust analysis we seek, but with the enhanced understandings of the nuance and complexities of school-community relationships we can offer enhanced understanding.

Linking health care with educational organizations can be useful and allow for enhanced healthcare access. However, linking healthcare and educational leaders who are both focused on moving beyond student attendance, traditional forms of student achievement, and acute health to broader indicators and practices of family and community well-being is critical. This community-aware scope and perspective create an opportunity for studying and understanding the multitude of ways in which schools and hospitals can partner to enhance community well-being.

Conclusion

Rural communities can be especially fragile communities in the sense that a network of educational organizations and CBOs may be quite limited and unable to fully meet the needs of the community. In addition, rural residents are more likely to face unemployment. Recovery from the 2008 recession has been slower in some places (USDA, 2018). Children and families in rural areas face health disparities making them more likely to suffer from a range of illnesses, as well as injuries, due not only to lifestyle differences but also isolation and reduced access to health care (CDC, 2017). Rural communities also face higher rates of opioid addiction and overdose than other geographic regions (USDA, n.d.). In addition, as highlighted in this chapter, rural communities

The Bloomsbury Handbook of Rural Education in the United States

also have particular relationships with their local schools. School-community partnering stands to have a compounded impact in small, isolated, and fragile rural ecologies. This impact can be deleterious if not approached carefully. It is communities with school and community leaders who utilize community-aware perspectives that this impact can be compounded in positive ways. Community-aware policies and partnerships can enhance the resources and opportunities made available to rural schools, communities, as well as families and children. Rural school leaders not only need the time and space to pursue community-aware projects, as seen in the wind farm example, but school boards can seek to hire rural superintendents with these competencies in mind. And in order to create a pipeline of these community-aware leaders, educational leadership programs can prepare leaders who know and understand the ecology of communities. With a community-aware perspective all sectors in rural communities are enhanced and rural families and communities are able to thrive in mutually beneficial ways.

In this chapter we have focused on rural school–community partnering that is largely focused on community development (windfarm) or the support of children and families (UPK and SBHCs). The three illustrations speak to these types of partnerships; however, the community-aware perspective can also be brought to partnerships with a curricular focus, as well, through place-based pedagogies. Place-based pedagogy can be a more palatable form of partnership for some educators because the goal is aligned with the core purpose of schooling: the education of students (Casto, 2016). Place-based pedagogies, however, would be enhanced by a community-aware perspective. The inherent community development and inclusive components of community-aware perspectives would call on place-based pedagogies to reckon with past and present exclusion or differential impact in the community. For example, place-based educational experiences would not only explore the local environment or politics but also environmental racism, political exclusion, and other historical inequities endemic to a particular place. Rural school–community partnering can be especially meaningful for children and families in small and isolated places and a community-aware perspective has the potential to enhance all forms of partnering.

13

Collective Impact in Rural Places

Sarah J. Zuckerman

Complex social problems such as teen pregnancy, youth suicide, student achievement, and foster care placement result from the interplay of problems in both the public and private sectors. Isolated approaches by single organizations in individual sectors, in general, have failed to "move the needle" on many of these problems. Such "wicked" problems are defined by complexity, interrelatedness, unpredictability, open-ended, intractable, and often subjected to competing values (Head & Alford, 2015). As such, wicked problems do not respond to technical, ready-made solutions. Instead, they require adaptive and iterative approaches to learning about the causes of complex challenges, generating solutions, measuring the impact, and using knowledge generated to revise solutions (Edmondson & Zimpher, 2014; Kania & Kramer, 2011). Rural communities are not immune from such problems. For example, research suggests rural youth are more likely to die by suicide than their urban peers (Fontanella et al., 2015; Singh et al., 2013) and young women aged fifteen to twenty-four in rural places are more likely than their urban peers to experience unplanned pregnancies (Sutton et al., 2019).

Place-based, cross-sector partnerships have increasingly been seen as a strategy for tackling these types of complex social problems by bringing together local assets and drawing on strengths such as local knowledge, local leadership, and social networks to support children and families (Boyd et al., 2008; Henig et al., 2016; Kerr et al., 2014). By identifying local challenges and focusing on local assets, these partnerships seek to avoid the short-termism of shifting national priorities and policy churn, as well as policy solutions crafted by "distant experts" (Jennings, 1999; Kerr et al., 2014; Stone et al., 2001). For place-based cross-sector partnerships to be effective, they must be *"fit for purpose, in this place, at this time"* (Lawson, 2013, p. 614, emphasis original). They must also be "locally developed interventions that engage with an ecological understanding of place" (Kerr et al., 2014, p. 131). This ecological understanding of place includes local demographics, organizational environments, and social geography (Lawson et al., 2014). When partnerships fulfill these recommendations, they have the potential to be asset- and place-based interventions for complex social challenges.

The Bloomsbury Handbook of Rural Education in the United States

Collective Impact

Collective impact, a set of conditions for effective partnerships (Kania & Kramer, 2011), has risen in prominence as a guide for communities seeking to address wicked problems through partnership efforts. Collective impact efforts join other place-based community partnership models such as the Harlem Children's Zone in New York City and the federal Promise Neighborhood grant program designed to replicate the success of wrap-around services for children and families in addressing the complexities of youth development (Horsford & Sampson, 2014; Miller et al., 2017). Simply defined, collective impact is "the long term commitments of a group of important actors from different sectors to a common agenda to solve a specific social problem" (Kania & Kramer, 2011, p. 39). Collective impact provides processes to collaboratively develop flexible and adaptive cross-sector approaches to solving wicked problems (Kania & Kramer, 2011; 2013). This work requires new ways of collaboration among partner organizations to accelerate learning about approaches that do and do not work. Collective impact offers a means to braid public and private funding in order to leverage scarce resources, and it shifts the task of problem-solving to those closest to the problems by putting into place five conditions that set it apart from other cross-sector partnerships:

- *A common agenda*: Stakeholders develop a shared understanding of the problem, a common vision for the future, and an agreed-upon approach to change. This requires stakeholders to engage in dialogue, often under the guidance and facilitation of a trained convener.
- *Shared measurement systems*: In order to measure progress toward a collective vision, shared metrics and common data are needed, along with transparent discussions of data both within the collective impact effort and with the public.
- *Mutually reinforcing activities*: Collective impact efforts depend on organizations coordinating their activities with each stakeholder understanding their role in advancing the common agenda.
- *Continuous communication*: Dialogue among stakeholders over time supports the development of trust and a common language, and is supplemented by regular written communications.
- *Backbone organization*: A designated organization provides staff and resources to coordinate the work. (Kania & Kramer, 2011)

Of these conditions, the backbone organization most differentiates collective impact efforts from other types of collaborations. Existing entities such as the United Way or a local philanthropic foundation can serve as a backbone organization (Hanleybrown et al., 2012; Zuckerman, 2016a). Communities may opt to form a nonprofit organization to serve as the backbone. Backbone organization staff provide strategic leadership, facilitate conversation among members, manage and analyze data, engage in communication, direct community outreach, and bring together funding streams. Providing these functions allows partners to focus on problem-solving (Hanleybrown et al., 2012; Kania & Kramer, 2011). This work requires funding, one

Collective Impact in Rural Places

of the most challenging aspects of creating collective impact, as funders are often reluctant to support infrastructure in favor of grants for narrowly defined issues and specific outcomes (Mann, 2014). However, even a modest budget for a backbone organization can amplify the funds of partner organizations by increasing their impact. Backbone funding supports full-time staff, typically called *conveners*, whose job it is to bring together stakeholders, maintain their engagement, and facilitate dialogue. Conveners need special skills and capacities, particularly the social skills to bring stakeholders to the table and keep them there. Conveners should be skilled in focusing people's attention, using structured discussion processes, framing issues, and mediating conflict.

Although collective impact holds potential for rural communities as a place-based intervention for complex social challenges, many collective impact efforts and organizations touting their success are found in urban areas (Henig et al., 2016). The result is a set of codified design elements successful in one context and considered applicable in a variety of settings, including rural areas. Yet, rural communities have different strengths and needs that must be considered to create partnerships fit for purpose and place that are capable of supporting community development (Lawson, 2013; Zuckerman, 2016a). This requires attention to the relational and identity needs of human development, rather than serving only individual needs, further contributing to the disembedding of rural youth for the global economy (Casto, McGrath et al., 2016; Corbett, 2007).

To better understand the potential of collective impact for rural communities, this chapter draws from the general research on collective impact as well as two case studies conducted in rural communities to describe the development of partnerships in communities with low population density. These two case studies describe two rural collective impact efforts that include schools and focus on outcomes for children and youth: the Grand Isle Network and the Northeast Prairie Coalition. Each of these partnerships is located in a small community between 10,000–25,000 residents that serve as employment, service, and leisure hubs for larger rural regions dependent on traditionally rural industries, including agriculture, mining, and forestry, as well as newer industries of tourism and manufacturing. Both partnerships sought to tackle alarming social problems in their rural communities and in the surrounding areas. In Grand Isle, the Network initially sought to tackle low academic performance, but a rash of youth suicides shifted the focus of the group to strengthening relationships with youth and increasing their connections to the community. In Northeast Prairie, the initial problem identified was keeping children out of the child protective services system by reducing incidence of abuse and neglect. To do this, the Coalition works to meet the basic needs of families, to support youth as they transition to adulthood, and to increase quality and quantity of early childhood care and education in the community. Additional information about each case follows.

Cases

Grand Isle Network
The Grand Isle Network[1] is centered in a micropolitan[2] area of approximately 10,000 residents in a nonmetropolitan county[3] located in a primarily rural region of a Midwest State. It serves eight

constituent school districts in three counties generally understood by residents as the "greater Grand Isle area." These districts included are classified as town remote, rural fringe, rural distant, and rural remote by the US Census Bureau.[4] Industry in the area has historically been mining, agriculture, and paper milling, all of which have been in decline. Service and tourism jobs have been on the rise, leaving community members worried about low wages and the lack of steady, year-round work. The Network was formed in 2009, with the support of the Grand Isle Foundation, a private philanthropic foundation that served as the initial backbone organization.

The Foundation employed two full-time conveners at the time of the study, and additional staff provided support with tasks such as communication strategies. The backbone organization planned and facilitated meetings and events for the Network, took on logistical tasks, and was responsible for moving the group forward. For example, one of the two conveners of the Grand Isle Network described her role as "a cat-herder, someone who is going to make sure this moves forward every day, somebody who wakes up worrying about this and next steps." Throughout, members of the Network talked about the importance of the two conveners in pushing the work forward through ongoing communication and outreach, as well as by using specific strategies to facilitate dialogue,[5] regroup and reframe ideas, and develop consensus. The Foundation supported this work through resources and capacity building in terms of training the conveners. With over fifty years of philanthropy serving the region and rural communities across the state, the Grand Isle Foundation has developed a high level of capacity, leadership, resources, and legitimacy in the local community and across the state (Zuckerman, 2016a), making it a unique asset unavailable to many rural communities.

In addition to the unique asset of the Foundation, the Network built on previous long-term collaborative efforts, including one in the area of early childhood begun in the 1990s and a partnership between the K-12 schools and the local community college that has lasted twenty-five years. The Network initially sought to improve educational outcomes but has evolved to focus on social-emotional development in the wake of a rash of youth deaths by suicide and attempts. In 2015, the Network released baseline data, developed a smaller leadership table, and began engaging in efforts aligned to their vision at the school level. These efforts primarily focused on the engagement of youths inside and outside of school and notably were cocreated with youths at a number of schools (Zuckerman, 2016a; Zuckerman & McAtee, 2018).

Northeast Prairie Coalition

The Northeast Prairie Coalition is located in a Midwest State in a micropolitan community of approximately 25,000 people that is defined as town remote by the US Census and serves as a retail and employment hub for the surrounding agricultural communities. While the Coalition started in Northeast Prairie, it has grown to serve other communities in the county and region, including those identified as town distant and rural remote. The county where the Coalition is located has a low median income, despite low unemployment numbers, and has the highest level of income inequality in the state.

The group began with conversations among a core group of community leaders around 2011. The development of the Coalition has been supported by a statewide nonprofit organization that has provided startup funds, including the salaries for a convener and a part-time consultant, and backbone functions such as data collection. This nonprofit organization supports a number of rural and urban collective impact efforts across the state that focus on reducing child welfare system contact. According to the consultant, this organization's interest in supporting collective impact efforts across the state was due to challenges in obtaining federal and other grant funding for child abuse and neglect prevention due to the small-sized rural communities. By bringing together partners in these communities in collective impact efforts, the nonprofit hoped to increase funding and create more sustainable programs. An executive at this organization described their role as "the backbone to the backbone organizations," and the convener and consultant described their efforts to create a community of practice of collective impact leaders across the state.

The local United Way of Northeast Prairie served as the fiscal agent, conducting all of the accounting and grant management for the Coalition; it also donated office space for the convener and other staff. In 2017, the Coalition applied for 501(C)3 status to create a new backbone organization, and in 2018, the Coalition hired additional staff to provide support. Coalition members reported that hiring the current convener was a key ingredient in their success. Growing up in a nearby rural community as a bilingual daughter of an immigrant and professional experience in health care and early childhood care and education provided her with a unique background for her role as convener. Additionally, members praised her for her people skills, her ability to "dream big" and as a "facilitative" leader who empowered others to take on leadership (Zuckerman, 2020a). The Coalition has three focus areas: helping families meet basic needs of housing, food, and clothing to prevent entry into the child welfare system; increasing the quantity and quality of early childhood care and education; and supporting healthy transitions to adulthood, including preventing homelessness among youth and entry into the juvenile justice system.

Preconditions for Successful Collaboration

In addition to the five conditions listed above, three preconditions till the soil for the seeds of collective impact to grow into successful collaboration. The first precondition is an influential champion, or champions, with the credibility to bring together community leaders. Such champions must be passionate about the issue but recognize the need to let stakeholders develop the solution, rather than bringing a preconceived agenda to the table (Hanleybrown et al., 2012). These champions may be inside the schools or in other organizations. In Grand Isle, the Network had champions at multiple levels and across multiple organizations, including school leaders. One superintendent, in particular, served as a champion through his public outreach, which included publishing blog posts and speaking at public events. As a member of previous collaborative efforts, he provided confidence in the process. In addition to his public-facing role as champion across the region, he also pursued the Network's goals in his own district, including early childhood programs and creating an afterschool program (Zuckerman, 2016a, 2020b). Other school-based champions included an afterschool program director who likewise served as a public face of the collective impact effort, issuing an impassioned call to arms at a public event. Champions outside of the schools included backbone organization staff who shared the original collective impact article with colleagues, which was described by one as "putting language to what we had already been doing." Backbone organization members also championed collective impact in their work with community members. Their history of positive work in the community, bolstered by recent efforts to increase transparency, provided legitimacy to their collective impact effort.

In the Northeast Prairie Coalition, members of the initial steering committee served as champions. Although the local superintendent was described as being on board, these champions

The Bloomsbury Handbook of Rural Education in the United States

served in social service agencies outside of the education system. One was a member of the regional Department of Health and Human Services office who saw the need to reduce child protective cases and brought the idea of collective impact to a group of healthcare and mental healthcare professionals. They also put the initial steering committee in contact with another collective impact effort in the region to facilitate learning. Identifying community members who are seen as trustworthy and are passionate for the work to serve as champions is an important step in creating community buy-in.

The second precondition for successful collaboration is early financial support from an anchor funder. In Grand Isle, the Foundation dedicated resources to holding community meetings, paying salaries to the conveners, and contributing the time of their communications and policy specialists. In the case of the Northeast Prairie Coalition, early financial support came from a nonprofit organization that sought to scale up collective impact as a model for reducing negative childhood outcomes across the state (Zuckerman, 2020a). Early funding is particularly important as collective impact efforts may take several years to enact.

The third precondition for successful collaboration is a sense of urgency that mobilizes potential members, which may materialize in the form of a crisis that has reached a breaking point (Hanleybrown et al., 2012). In Grand Isle, low student achievement initially provided a sense of urgency. As the group learned about collective impact and the needs of their own community, the number of youth dying by suicide became a much more urgent concern, and the focus shifted to supporting the well-being of youth through relationship-building. The conveners and others reported that this urgent need kept members engaged and focused. In Northeast Prairie, preventing children from entering child protective services served as the initial focal point, with a community assessment further identifying needs in reducing redundancy of service providers, streamlining services, and increasing the provision of early childhood care and education.

In addition to these preconditions, previous research on rural collective impact efforts suggests that when core members have a history of working together, it provides a foundational social network from which to grow (Zuckerman, 2016a, 2020a). Research on rural cross-sector collaboration suggests building from existing collaborations and engaging active organizations is more effective than starting from scratch (Miller et al., 2017). For example, this was particularly evident in the Grand Isle Network, which built on two long-standing partnerships in K-12 and early childhood education that brought together school leaders, community college administrators, and Foundation staff to work together to improve programs. Network members commented on the strong relationships, despite the low population density. A core team member described this strength:

> When I go to meetings in [the capital city] they're like, how do you get the person, the Head Start person to work with you, and part of it is because I know who she is and I can call her up. Do you know what I mean? So, there are a lot of strengths here in that . . . it is a strength that you KNOW who needs to be at the table and so when you call a meeting, you expect that who can make the decision and can do that is there. Or else you call them again.

In Northeast Prairie, the initial steering committee had existing relationships, and the early childhood workgroup had largely been meeting previously in another form. The chair of the early childhood committee reported that previous efforts "were kind of overlapping, so many members [felt] that it made sense to blend [the two groups] . . . . Some of us are tried and true for a long time." Several members had been working on early childhood issues in the community for "around a good eight years." This committee continued previous efforts, such as growing their school supply drive, as well as starting new efforts including plans to create a new childcare center.

Developmental Phases of Collective Impact Work

Once these preconditions have been established, Hanleybrown and colleagues (2012) identified three phases of collective impact development: *Initiate Action*, *Organize for Impact*, and *Sustain Action and Impact*. Their previous work as consultants informed the development of the phases, particularly their work with primarily urban collective impact efforts spanning education, housing, employment, health, and environmental concerns.

Initiating for action includes mapping the landscape of stakeholders—identifying work already underway (e.g., existing partnerships or initiatives, collecting baseline data, and identifying a leadership table of credible champions). In Northeast Prairie, several community leaders championed the idea of collective impact and became the first steering committee. The initiating stage in Northeast Prairie also included a community needs assessment and asset mapping conducted with approximately 100 individuals. This work was undertaken by the nonprofit organization that provided backbone support during their launch. In Grand Isle, foundation staff and school leaders initially engaged in conversation about academic achievement. Building on this shared concern, they organized a trip for staff and school leaders to hear Geoffrey Canada speak about the Harlem Children's Zone. This experience shifted the conversation from "failing schools" to the need to bring the community together to support children and youth. Foundation staff then intentionally brought together a cross-sector of community members from the eight component school districts to engage in visioning activities. Over 100 individuals attended these meetings. At the third meeting, the conveners presented a strategic plan and asked volunteers to form the core team of leaders. Over forty individuals took up this challenge.

The second phase, organizing for impact, brings stakeholders together to develop a common agenda, identify shared measures, and identify a backbone organization. At this stage, partners engage in initial efforts to align the work of partner organizations to the common agenda. Part of this work includes developing a "roadmap" or a document that brings the common agenda to life and gathers members together on the same page (Hanleybrown et al., 2012). For the Grand Isle Network, the initial strategic plan failed to gain traction, and a study trip to visit the Strive Partnership in Cincinnati[6] jump-started a revision process. It took a year of conversation among members and required efforts to reframe and repackage ideas brought forth by the conveners. The aspirational goals and promises to youth in the community were revised and revisited until the group gained consensus through a "fist to five" process, which allowed members to express varying levels of agreement.[7]

Roadmaps for collective impact efforts should provide an evidence-based description of the problem, a clear goal or goals, a variety of strategies for effecting change, guiding principles, and a plan for course correction and evaluation (Hanleybrown et al., 2012). Institutionalized ways of thinking among stakeholders in different sectors can complicate this process, and developing a common agenda requires deliberate dialogue in civic spaces to reach a shared understanding of the problem (Stone et al., 2001). Once a roadmap has been developed, data systems can then be

The Bloomsbury Handbook of Rural Education in the United States

aligned to the metrics identified in the roadmap to support course corrections and evaluation. However, developing the data systems can be challenging due to the costs and risks involved in sharing data. The Grand Isle Foundation provided significant funds for a shared data dashboard that would bring together youth survey data with data from the education and public health systems (Zuckerman, 2016a). Conversely, the Northeast Prairie Coalition experienced challenges in convincing members to use a common data system, with members reporting resistance to sharing data and learning new systems. This reportedly created challenges for tracking individuals served by the Coalition and reporting to funders.

The second phase requires stakeholders to determine geographic boundaries of the project, with the knowledge they may change in time as needs evolve. In Grand Isle, the Network landed on the same geographic boundary served by the Grand Isle Foundation. Members reported this area is widely understood as the "Greater Grand Isle Area" and includes the towns and villages that rely on the economic hub of Big River. In the Northeast Prairie Coalition, members initially identified the county seat as the service area but have since expanded to include smaller neighboring communities. The convener reports they will work to connect individuals in their region with service providers regardless of where they live.

In the third phase of sustained action and impact, stakeholders prioritize actions, systematically connect data, and put processes in place to sustain active learning (Hanleybrown et al., 2012). They do so through cascading levels of collaboration, with a steering committee of community leaders providing leadership and oversight for working groups, each of which addresses a particular area of the roadmap. In Northeast Prairie, these groups include people concerned with early childhood, basic needs, and positive youth development as well as a rapid response taskforce that connects families in crisis with services. Each of these groups meets independently once a month and comes together to share every other month at the Coalition meetings. In Grand Isle, the challenges of working within such a large geographic area with diverse constituent communities prompted conveners to develop a different model of cascading collaboration, with groups of youth and community members creating action plans based on survey data in their own school (Zuckerman & McAtee, 2018). These groups were linked together to share progress across communities by the backbone organization. Both collective impact efforts have a leadership table of between eight to twelve individuals, strategically selected to represent various sectors, such as K-12 education, early childhood, mental health, health, social services, and the faith-based community.

While these phases have been presented as linear, frequently there is a need to regroup in a previous phase. For example, in the Grand Isle Network, the original Core Team of leaders mobilized around a strategic plan, yet it did not lead to action. External learning opportunities reinvigorated the group, which led to a revision of goals over the period of a year to create a roadmap document they described as the "community's promise to young people." The resulting document clearly outlined promises and aspirations for youth and provided direction for members. Following the development of the roadmap, the Foundation contracted with an educational consulting firm to develop a survey aligned to the vision. This baseline data was then released to the public, and a new, smaller, more accountable leadership team was developed to act on the baseline data. New structures were put in place to support community-level groups in developing strategies based on this data and to connect the work of these groups to accelerate learning (Zuckerman, 2016a).

Attending to the Softer Side of Collective Impact

Hanleybrown and colleagues (2012) identify the importance of social relationships, and specifically breaking bread, as the glue and lubricant of collective impact. The conveners and other backbone staff members in Grand Isle reported the importance of providing food along with a warm and welcoming environment. Another member reported the importance of conversations in such relaxed settings, "If you're just having a conversation in your backyard over a hotdish, how can you get upset? You can't! You can talk about things." Similarly, meetings of the Northeast Prairie Coalition featured lunch and candy in the middle of the tables. The strength of social relationships was observed throughout the meetings, which frequently featured good-natured teasing and laughter. The convener reported, "[Northeast Prairie] is big enough that you don't run into the same people every day . . . but small enough that somehow everyone knows [everyone]." The importance of these social relationships to collective impact suggests rural communities have an advantage in that the small size of communities provides opportunities for members to interact across multiple settings.

However, according to one of the conveners of the Grand Isle Foundation, the high level of interdependence of individuals makes it challenging to have difficult conversations that rock the boat. The isolation of rural communities can also create challenges in creating bridging relationships that bring in new ideas (Miller et al., 2017). Similarly, social and cultural divides in rural communities can limit the participation of those outside of middle-class professional networks. In Grand Isle, one member reported the need for intentional strategies to engage parents with lower incomes "because it is not going to happen by invitation or natural interactions" (Zuckerman, 2016b). Balancing the strength and unity of the leadership table with the need to attend to bridging relationships within and beyond the community is an important consideration for collective impact development.

Mindset Shifts for Collective Impact

Enacting the conditions of collective impact in place is necessary but insufficient to generate change. In order to work as intended, collective impact needs to be accompanied by mindset shifts on the part of partners and their organizations. These mindset shifts break down into three categories: *who is involved*, *how people work together*, and *how progress happens*. The first mindset shift includes getting the right mix of stakeholders' eyes on the problem. Complex problems require complex solutions. Bringing together multiple perspectives can improve the understanding of the problem while building a sense of mutual accountability through the recognition of interdependency (Kania et al., 2014; Lawson, 2004). However, this work is complicated by institutionalized ways of knowing in the helping professions (Hooper-Briar & Lawson, 1996) and requires strong facilitation from backbone staff. Additionally, bringing the perspectives of those experiencing the problem supports the development of effective strategies. This requires a further shift by human service professionals to rethink power relationships, accountability, authority, and responsibility to empower clients as keepers of invaluable knowledge (Lawson, 2004).

The Grand Isle Network primarily engaged in this mindset shift through their efforts to engage youth in problem-solving and action planning at school. Network members worked to recruit students who were not typically considered for such projects because they might, as one member described, "have a different perception of what it means to be connected because they're not involved in sports and stuff." He highlighted the importance of "reach[ing] out to kids who might not be the natural ones to go to . . . kids from a broad section who aren't used to having their voice actually being heard as much." With the facilitation of adults, these youth groups examined their school's youth survey data and planned actions and events to address them, most frequently focusing on building relationships between youth and community members. However, implementing this type of mindset shift comes with challenges. Members of the Northeast Prairie Coalition, for example, expressed a similar desire to bring family members to the table but have likewise struggled to do so, in part because their meetings are held during the workday. However, like Grand Isle, they have worked to engage youth through the schools to plan a youth forum.

The second mindset relates to how members work together. Part of this includes structuring cascading levels of collaboration to provide space for problem-solving. In Northeast Prairie, this structure consists of working groups that meet monthly and are connected to the steering committee by each group's chair. The steering committee provides vision and direction to the Coalition as a whole. Additionally, members of all of the workgroups meet every two months to share their work and engage in learning about specific programs and opportunities. In Grand Isle, these groups were place-based rather than issue-based, and structures were developed to allow members to learn across these groups. The long-term plan included multiple opportunities to bring these groups together to learn from one another, and Foundation members envisioned doing so would create a more widespread understanding of the need for regional solutions for shared challenges.

This mindset shift also includes a recognition of the importance of relationships. Diffusion of innovation, or how new ideas spread, is a social process facilitated by trust and dialogue (Kania et al., 2014, Weick, 1995; Zuckerman, 2019). Members of the Grand Isle Foundation, which served as the Grand Isle Network's backbone organization, described the focus on building trusting relationships as part of their organizational "DNA" and as the "special sauce" that allows them to bring the community together to engage in work. As noted previously, the conveners' use of facilitation strategies contributed to the development of relationships that limits contention in conversation. Additionally, members noted that previous collaborative efforts laid the groundwork for organizations to understand that the process works and to develop trust in the give and take of collaboration. According to one Grand Isle Network member, this required developing a shared understanding that partners are at the table for the same reason, but that at times, one group may receive more resources to support the greater good (Zuckerman, 2016a).

Finally, this mindset shift includes sharing credit for the work. In Grand Isle, the foundation staff spoke specifically about not wanting to be credited for the work; rather, they wanted to disappear into the background. This included creating norms that would allow members autonomy to do the work and talk about it without approval from the Foundation. Foundation members viewed this as creating wider ownership of the collective impact effort by allowing people to see themselves in the work and to "amplify" the work already happening in different communities and organizations. However, others mentioned challenges in letting go of credit. A member of a local nonprofit, for example, stated the challenges of funding the same organizations as the Foundation and that, "I don't want to take credit, but the community needs to know we're behind it."

The third mindset shift addresses the types of solutions collective impact efforts might apply. Kania and colleagues (2014) suggested the need to maintain an adaptive approach rather than

Collective Impact in Rural Places

rely on technical approaches. Similarly, they suggested looking for a variety of interventions aimed at multiple causes of complex problems rather than seeking a single solution. Complex problems require multiple approaches, executed simultaneously and in a coordinated manner across multiple organizations and sectors (Kania et al., 2014). In Northeast Prairie, Coalition members engaged in a variety of efforts within each of the working areas. For example, the early childhood group worked to improve access to professional development opportunities for childcare providers while simultaneously working on a plan to create a new childcare center. However, due to contracts and grants, they were sometimes locked into technical solutions such as the use of an evidence-based parenting workshop. While members were enthusiastic about the workshop, the chair of the committee reported challenges in getting parents to attend the free six-week program, regardless of when and where they offered it. Flexible, adaptive approaches and real-time data use would suggest that despite having a strong evidentiary base of effectiveness, it might not be the right intervention in the community at the current time. In Grand Isle, the scattershot approach took a geographically dispersed form, with groups working on issues in their school community.

Conclusion

This chapter described the process of collective impact, focusing on examples from two rural communities that used it to address wicked, complex, social problems. While collective impact has been codified into a series of preconditions, conditions, and stages, research in rural communities suggests the process is not linear (Zuckerman, 2016a). More importantly, there is no cookbook for collective impact, as the process itself is the strategy. Each collective impact effort is as unique as the community that embraces it, because successful cross-sector partnerships require adaptation to place (Lawson, 2013; Zuckerman, 2019). This work requires learning not only about how collective impact works but also about the local community (Zuckerman, 2019). As one of the conveners of the Grand Isle Network put it, models for collective impact must be *adapted* in a rural community; they cannot simply be adopted. Such adaptation requires mapping assets and social networks, collecting data on needs, and engaging in ongoing dialogue among members to create the shared understandings of local needs and potential solutions that support collective action (Zuckerman, 2019).

Collective impact requires an initial investment in a convener, through both salary and capacity building, who can mobilize community members, identify champions, and facilitate learning and dialogue. Initial funding should support a backbone organization to serve as a container for the work by providing the space for collective impact to emerge. This funding may come from within the community or from external sources but is vital to the success of collective impact efforts as they require significant time to build trusting relationships, identify and describe challenges, develop a shared vision, identify metrics, create data systems, and engage in mutually reinforcing activities. In Grand Isle, the work of collective impact emerged through cycles of visioning and revisioning over the course of five years, at which point the Network was able to support action in individual school-communities. In 2015, the Network transitioned to a smaller, more accountable leadership council, which has taken on more backbone functions. Since then, the Network has continued to work with these groups, and at the time of the writing of this chapter, they were collecting a second round of survey data aligned to their roadmap to measure progress. Similarly, the Northeast Prairie Coalition continues to evolve, growing in its geographic scope and working toward creating a new 501(c)3 to serve as a backbone organization, all while the working groups engage in mutually reinforcing activities.

Across both sites, and in alignment with findings on collective impact more generally, one of the major lessons is that collective impact takes time to develop and even more time to see results (Stachowiak & Gase, 2018). This suggests that collective impact is not for every issue a community faces but for those wicked problems with multiple causes that have proven truly intractable to isolated efforts and technical solutions. However, this long game approach holds potential for rural community development, particularly when it focuses on building the capacity of adults and youth (Zuckerman & McAtee, 2018).

14

Postsecondary Transitions and Attainment

Sarah Schmitt-Wilson and Soo-yong Byun

In 2009, President Barack Obama issued the challenge to increase college completion rates from 39 percent to 60 percent by the year 2020 (Obama, 2009). Higher levels of education are associated with various positive outcomes, including increased occupational opportunities, better health and well-being, and greater political participation. However, research consistently documents that rural high school students have lower educational aspirations (Haller & Virkler, 1993; C. W. Howley, 2006; Hu, 2003) and are less likely than their suburban and/or urban peers to attend college (Adelman, 2002; Gibbs, 1998; Irvin et al., 2017; Provasnik et al., 2007; Smith et al., 1995; Wells et al., 2019). Differences in college enrollment are notably evident at four-year institutions in the United States (Byun et al., 2012; Snyder et al., 2016).

In an important study, Byun, Meece, and Irvin (2012) used data from the National Education Longitudinal Study of 1988 (NELS:88), which followed a nationally representative sample of students who were eighth graders in 1988 until 2000, to explore whether there were differences among urban, suburban, and rural students' likelihood of attending college and earning a bachelor's degree. The authors found that rural students were significantly less likely than urban and suburban students to enroll in postsecondary education due largely to their lower socioeconomic background. Snyder et al. (2016) further found that rural students enroll in four-year institutions at lower rates than suburban students but at higher rates than individuals from urban communities and towns. Furthermore, rural students are more likely to attend a public college and less likely to attend a selective (based on the average composite SAT score of the entering class) institution (Byun, Irvin, & Meece, 2012, 2015; Byun, Meece, & Irvin, 2012).

Using data from the Educational Longitudinal Study of 2002 (ELS:2002) that followed a nationally representative sample of students who were tenth graders in 2002, Koricich et al. (2018) also found that rural students were significantly less likely to attend "any form of postsecondary education" (p. 293) and were less likely to attend selective four-year intuitions. This supports information provided by the National Center for Educational Statistics (2015), which noted that rural students were less likely than students from other locations (city, suburban, and town) to be enrolled in any postsecondary program. A recent examination of changes in rural students' postsecondary attendance rates between the NELS:88 and ELS:02 cohorts concluded that although rural students were less likely to enroll in postsecondary education, the gap between their enrollment and the enrollment of urban and suburban students was narrower in the recent cohort (Wells et al., 2019), suggesting that rural students are increasing their college attendance at higher rates than urban and suburban students.

Research also documents rural–nonrural differences in the way by which students attend college. For example, using data from the National Longitudinal Survey of Youth 1979 (NLSY79) that followed approximately 13,000 men and women who were 14–22 years old in 1979, Gibbs (1998) found that rural youth are more likely than urban youth to attend rural, public, and nonselective colleges. According to Gibbs (1998), these rural–nonrural differences in college enrollment patterns could be attributable to the following four factors: (a) public colleges in rural areas are more numerous and have larger enrollments than private colleges; (b) rural students are less able to afford the higher tuition at private colleges; (c) public colleges are less likely to require advanced coursework for admission, which is often lacking in rural schools; and (d) selective colleges are mostly located in urban areas.

Prior studies drawing other national data confirmed some of Gibbs's findings: that is, rural youth are less likely than their nonrural counterparts to attend a selective institution. Using NELS:88 data, Byun, Irvin, and Meece (2012, 2015; Byun, Meece, & Irvin, 2012) additionally found that rural youth were more likely to delay entry to college but less likely to be continuously enrolled in college compared to their urban counterparts. Furthermore, Byun et al. (2015) found that much of these rural–nonrural disparities in college enrollment patterns were explained by rural–nonrural differences in socioeconomic status (SES) and high school preparation. Recent national data, however, suggest that rural students attend college at lower rates than their suburban peers but at rates similar to their urban peers. Specifically, according to data from the National Student Clearinghouse (2018), 67 percent of students from suburban schools immediately enrolled in postsecondary education, compared to 63 percent of students from urban or rural schools.

In addition to examining rural students' prevalence of attending bachelor's degree-granting institutions, it is important to investigate whether rural students attend two-year institutions at the same rate as their urban and suburban peers. Two-year institutions are important for rural youth with over 60 percent attending a two-year institution at some point during their college career (Byun et al., 2017). Moreover, almost one in four rural students starts at a two-year college before transferring to a four-year institution (Byun et al., 2017). Among students attending postsecondary education, the percentage of rural students attending two-year colleges is higher than nonrural students (Koricich et al., 2018; Wells et al., 2019), suggesting indeed the "critical role" played by "rural community colleges . . . in providing educational opportunities for isolated communities" (Koricich et al., 2018, p. 296).

For adolescents coming of age in the "college for all era" the expectations for attending postsecondary education are high. As a result, an increasing number of rural students leave their communities for college campuses (Snyder & Dillow, 2010). However, for rural students the road to college is complicated by many factors influencing the decision to attend postsecondary education. In this chapter, we explore challenges and opportunities for rural students as they transition into postsecondary education. In the following section, we examine the importance of individual, family, school, and community factors in understanding postsecondary attendance and attainment of rural students (Hughes et al., 2019).

Individual Factors

Rural students are increasingly aspiring to attend postsecondary education (C. W. Howley, 2006; C. W. Howley & Hambrick, 2014; Meece et al., 2013). Educational aspirations are important for rural youth because increased aspirations are related to an increase in the likelihood of enrolling in postsecondary education (Adelman, 2002). Beyond educational aspirations, research suggests that academic achievement predicts rural youths' decisions to attend college (Byun, Irvin, & Meece, 2012; Chenoweth & Galliher, 2004; Demi et al., 2010; Gibbs, 1998; Wells et al., 2019).

In terms of demographic factors, gender and ethnicity have been found to influence young adults' educational aspirations (Meece et al., 2013). Nationally, females enroll in postsecondary education at higher rates than males (Aud et al., 2013; NCES, 2015a). Similarly, females in rural areas enroll in postsecondary education at higher rates than rural males (Provasnik et al., 2007) among individuals attending both two-and four-year institutions (Agger et al., 2018). While there are a number of reasons why women now outnumber men in postsecondary education at the national level, several rural scholars have highlighted that the gender difference in college enrollment among young adults in rural areas might be attributable to the fact that rural areas offer more opportunities for jobs that have been traditionally held by men (Agger et al., 2018). In other words, rural men tend to have positive perceptions of economic opportunities in their home communities and a higher desire to live in the same communities (Meece et al., 2013, 2014). By contrast, rural women have a greater desire to leave their home communities because fewer economic opportunities are available to them (Agger et al., 2018; Conger & Elder, 1994; Meece et al., 2013, 2014). These gendered patterns of rural identity and perceptions of job opportunities may shape postsecondary aspirations and enrollment (Agger et al., 2018; Meece et al., 2014).

Although peer-reviewed research on racial/ethnic differences in the college experiences of rural students is limited, differences have been found in perceived barriers to attending college in that Black and Latinx rural students perceive increased barriers to continuing education beyond high school (Irvin et al., 2012). Further, Means and colleagues (2016) found that the educational and occupational aspirations of rural Black students considering postsecondary education were bound by limited options in their rural communities; the tension between staying and leaving for postsecondary education; inadequate support and the lack of a roadmap for college enrollment; and concerns about financing college, including a limited knowledge of costs and financial aid opportunities. In contrast to previous research by Provasnik et al. (2007) and Agger et al. (2018), Byun et al. (2017) found that gender and race were not significant predictors of enrollment patterns after controlling for factors such as parental and teacher expectations.

Families

Beyond individual factors, families have direct and indirect influences on their children's decisions to attend postsecondary education. Rural parents themselves often have lower levels of education (Prins & Kassab, 2017; Roscigno et al., 2006; Sage & Sherman, 2014), a factor that is predictive of whether or not students enroll in postsecondary education (Byun, Irvin, & Meece, 2012; Byun et al., 2017; Chenoweth & Galliher, 2004; Demi et al., 2010; Gibbs, 1998). Parental education is a potential obstacle for rural youth from both a modeling and a pragmatic perspective. From a modeling perspective, it is a challenge for rural youth to see the benefit of postsecondary education if their parents have provided a good life for them without postsecondary credentials. From a practical perspective, applying for postsecondary education and filling out scholarship forms (including but not limited to the Free Application for Student Aid [FAFSA]) is a complicated process. This coupled with fewer school resources to provide support could make the process daunting.

Along with parental educational attainment, parental educational expectations are imperative for rural youth and their decision to attend postsecondary education. Parent-child discussions and parental educational expectations are significant predictors of postsecondary education enrollment (Byun, Irvin, & Meece, 2012; Wells et al., 2019). As parental expectations increase, so do the educational expectations of their child (Schmitt-Wilson, 2013). Furthermore, students' perceptions of their parents' disapproval of them not attending postsecondary education predicted college enrollment (Demi et al., 2010). Parental expectations may differ by gender. For example, Agger et al. (2018) found that females had higher perceived parental educational expectations, which were correlated with higher educational aspirations and increased college enrollment.

In the exploration of rural students' educational decision making, few factors have garnered more attention than the importance of SES. The cost of postsecondary education is a potential barrier for rural students. As noted by Morton et al. (2018), "the cost of college had the potential to dissuade participants from pursuing specific colleges of their choice due to the perceived financial obligations" (p. 164). As compared with nonrural families, rural families possess fewer financial resources, coupled with decreased educational attainment (Byun, Meece, & Irvin, 2012; Roscigno & Crowley, 2001); the notable SES differences between rural and nonrural students often influence their respective educational expectations and attainment (Byun, Irvin, & Meece, 2012; Haller & Virkler, 1993). Much of the previous research suggests that rural/urban differences in educational aspirations, the decision to attend postsecondary education, and the subsequent educational attainment are due to SES (Adelman, 2002; Gibbs, 1998; Haller & Virkler, 1993; C. B. Howley et al., 2014), with students' higher SES increasing the likelihood they will attend a four-year university (Byun, Irvin, & Meece, 2012; Byun, Meece, & Irvin 2012, 2015; Koricich et al., 2018). As such, much empirical evidence supports the rural disadvantage perspective. Yet, as discussed below, we argue that research should take into account a holistic picture of factors influencing rural students' decisions to attend college.

Rural Schools

Rural schools play a critical role in preparing adolescents for postsecondary education. Among others, college preparatory track experiences (Adelman, 2002; Byun et al., 2017) and taking advanced math courses (Irvin et al., 2017) are strong predictors of rural students' college enrollment (both two- and four-year programs). Furthermore, high school curriculum intensity (Byun, Irvin, & Meece, 2012, 2015) significantly predicts rural students' enrollment in four-year programs. In addition, teachers' expectations play an important role in shaping rural students' educational aspirations beyond family factors (Byun et al., 2012).

Unfortunately, as rural students progress through school, they may have reduced access to career counseling and college preparation programs compared to urban and suburban students (Griffin et al., 2011). Furthermore, rural students take fewer math courses and have access to a limited number of mathematics advanced placement courses when compared to students in other communities (Anderson & Chang, 2011; Irvin et al., 2017). Many rural schools are underfunded

Postsecondary Transitions and Attainment

and underresourced (Showalter et al., 2017) with lower per-pupil expenditures (Roscigno & Crowley, 2001). Therefore, increasing these services may be a difficult task for rural districts. Rural schools are being asked to do more with less as they look for ways to increase college preparatory classes and offer more postsecondary information to students.

Rural Communities and Geography

For students growing up in rural communities, the decision about attending postsecondary education is a complicated one, with rural communities providing both supports and challenges for students wanting to take that path. On the one hand, rural communities have increased social capital (Byun, Meece, & Irvin, 2012; Crockett et al., 2000; Meece et al., 2013; Petrin et al., 2014), which is defined as "social relationships that serve as resources for individuals to draw upon in implementing their goals" (Furstenberg & Hughes, 1994, p. 84). Furthermore, there is a strong sense of interconnectedness among individuals living in rural communities (Morton et al., 2018). Rural communities are characterized as being tightly knit with strong family connections (Hughes et al., 2019). Therefore, the decision to attend postsecondary education is not an easy one for rural students, notably when the "institutions emphasize values and norms different from those in their home community" (Morton et al., 2018, p. 157).

There is a relationship between educational and occupational decision making, hence local economies can influence rural residents' educational decisions. Rural students are more likely to be interested in the jobs with which they are familiar (Crockett et al., 2000; Haller & Virkler, 1993) and which are available in their communities. Unfortunately, there are fewer economic opportunities available in rural communities, notably those that require postsecondary education (Morton et al., 2018). Meece et al. (2013) asserted that rural high school students, who have access to what they consider to be good jobs in their local communities (i.e., jobs that pay fairly well but require only a high school diploma), are less likely to be interested in careers that require postsecondary education and are therefore less likely to enroll in college. However, as the percentage of jobs requiring postsecondary education has increased in recent decades, so has the likelihood that rural students will attend college.

Geography plays a role in rural students' decisions about college attendance. Rural students generally choose to attend postsecondary education close to where they live and work (Hillman, 2016), and having a two- or four-year college in their home county increases the likelihood of rural students attending postsecondary education (Gibbs, 1998). In other words, proximity to postsecondary institutions increases the likelihood that students will apply to and attend college (Turley, 2009). Urban communities are more likely to have postsecondary education options in the area (Gibbs, 1998; C. W. Howley & Hambrick, 2014). Rural counties and those with a large manufacturing labor force have a relatively large number of two-year institutions close by but fewer four-year institutions (Hillman, 2016). Similarly, Prins and Kassab (2017) analyzed the location of postsecondary institutions in Pennsylvania and found that for-profit two-year institutions were the most common type of institutions in rural counties, and 29 percent of rural counties had no postsecondary options. Rural communities are more likely to be educational desserts (Rosenboom & Blagg, 2018), which are defined as places where "zero colleges or universities are nearby" or where "one community college is the only public broad-access institution nearby" (Hillman & Weichman, 2016, p. 4).

The Bloomsbury Handbook of Rural Education in the United States

Finally, and perhaps most importantly, rural students may feel that they have to choose between pursuing occupational prosperity through education and leaving behind the rural communities in which they grew up, thus diminishing either their educational expectations or their ties to the home communities they strongly value (C. W. Howley, 2006; C. W. Howley & Hambrick, 2014; Sage & Sherman, 2014). Leaving their rural community to attend postsecondary education presents a conflict not required for suburban and urban students who may select to attend colleges closer to home. Relocation is required far more often for rural residents seeking the choices in postsecondary education options (McDonough et al., 2010), "therefore, equal choice for rural students is predicated upon equal mobility, which cannot be rightly assumed" (Hughes et al., 2019, p. 442).

Postsecondary Experiences of Rural Youth

In this section, we examine rural students' experiences once they arrive on college campuses. Rural students are sometimes referred to as the "invisible minority" (Morton et al., 2018; Rubisch, 1995) in that they are often not considered in conversations centered on minority (or otherwise disadvantaged and/or marginalized) students. While research that examines the postsecondary experiences of rural youth is very limited, the few qualitative studies that exist suggest that rural youth face a unique set of challenges when transitioning to college and while attending college (Guiffrida, 2008; Maltzan, 2006). Challenges included acclimating to the size of the university and the large class sizes (often much larger than were offered in their rural schools); attuning to campuses that may be more racially and culturally heterogeneous than their home communities (Pearson & Sutton, 1999); and negotiating the number and type of extracurricular options, which often included fewer outdoor and more cultural activities (Guiffrida, 2008). These challenges may be amplified for rural students attending college in metropolitan locations as they navigate to a new environment very different from their home communities (Guiffrida, 2008; Swift, 1988).

Compared with their urban and suburban counterparts, rural students are more likely to be the first in their families to attend a four-year college (Byun, Meece, & Irvin, 2012). This means that rural students have less cultural and social capital that can help them navigate college and attain college success (Sikes, 2018), which compounds their concerns about social integration into the campus community (Morton et al., 2018). Hence, rural students reported higher levels of stress due to feelings of alienation than their urban counterparts (Dunstan, 2013; Guyton, 2011; Sikes, 2018) because, in part, their experiences in the new urban settings were so different from their previous experiences in their home communities (Maltzan, 2006)

Some literature documents rural–nonrural differences in college major choice. For example, using data from ELS:02, Byun and Kryst (2015) found that rural students are less likely than their urban counterparts to choose social science majors relative to humanities, even after controlling for other variables. In Pennsylvania, rural students selected majors at similar rates as urban and suburban students, except that rural students were more likely to major in education and less likely to major in business (Yan, 2002).

Postsecondary Persistence and Completion

Research examining the persistence of rural students in college is inconclusive, with some results indicating rural students persist at lower levels (Pierson & Hanson, 2015) and other results suggesting that students persist at similar levels to their urban and suburban counterparts (Byun, Meece, & Irvin, 2012; C. B. Howley et al., 2014; Luo & Williams, 2013; Williams & Luo, 2010). Moreover, students living closer to their hometowns were more likely to persist in college among a sample of students attending a micropolitan[1] university (Luo & Williams, 2013), indicating the existence of a relationship between the institution's proximity to students' home communities and retention. Although the sample consisted of urban, suburban, and rural students, these findings have implications for rural students considering that there are fewer colleges—especially four-year institutions—in rural areas.

In terms of bachelor's degree attainment, Wells and colleagues found that rural students continued to earn degrees at lower rates than their urban and suburban counterparts but rural–nonrural gaps in bachelor's degree attainment were smaller. In contrast, Marré (2017) suggests that the gap between rural and urban students earning bachelor's degrees is growing (with urban students earning bachelor's degrees at increasingly higher rates), whereas rural students hold a slight advantage in the percentage of individuals completing associate degrees (Marré, 2017).

On the other hand, some empirical research suggests that rural adolescents enrolled in four-year institutions do not necessarily suffer disadvantages in their degree completion merely as the result of having attended rural high schools, despite the set of challenges in transitioning to college and attending college we articulated above. For example, using NELS:88 data, Byun, Irvin, and Meece (2012) found that about seven out of ten rural high school students who attended four-year institutions had earned bachelor's degrees as of 2000, which is similar to the completion rate of urban students. Byun et al. (2012) speculated that these nonsignificant rural/urban differences in college persistence and degree completion at four-year institutions might be due to the fact that impoverished but academically talented rural youth would especially value college education as a pathway toward economic prosperity due to declining employment opportunities in rural communities. In other words, rural students seeing college education "as a pathway to a different future from their parents may be especially dedicated to college education" (Byun et al., 2012, p. 480). On the other hand, Gibbs (1998) suggested that seemingly successful college persistence and completion of students from rural areas might be attributed to their disproportionate enrollment in public, nonselective colleges that are less demanding.

Rural students' postsecondary attainment is influenced by many factors. For example, there is a relationship between education needed for students' expected future occupation and bachelor's degree attainment in a national sample of rural students (i.e., students who believe they can earn a good living by working in a field that does not require higher education are less likely to earn bachelor's degrees; Schmitt-Wilson et al., 2018). Among predictors of bachelor's degree attainment, family income and academic preparation were the strongest predictors among rural students (Wells et al., 2019), whereas Byun and colleagues (Byun, Irvin, & Meece, 2012; Byun, Meece, & Irvin 2012) found that most of the variation was explained by lower SES. Although gender was not a significant predictor of graduating from a four-year institution, students who came from families with higher incomes, students who took rigorous high school courses, students who participated in social clubs and/or fraternities/sororities, and students with higher first-year cumulative GPAs were more likely to graduate from four-year institutions (Byun, Irvin, & Meece, 2012). In contrast, rural students who were Latinx delayed entry into postsecondary education, and those who attended college part time were less likely to graduate (Byun, Irvin, & Meece, 2012).

Conclusion

As disparities in postsecondary attainment persist among individuals living in rural, suburban, and urban communities, it is essential to understand the complexity of the postsecondary pathways of students from rural communities. Although an increasing number of rural high school students desire postsecondary credentials, research consistently documents that they are less likely than their suburban and urban peers to aspire to, attend, and graduate from college. Much of these distinctions can be explained by rural–nonrural differences in individual, family, school, and community factors. Furthermore, rural students are more likely to delay entry into postsecondary education and less likely to attend selective intuitions.

Students, families, educators, and policymakers could benefit from additional research on identifying malleable college experiences and pathways of rural students that promote their persistence and completion. Much remains unknown about how rural students attend college. For example, given that rural students attend college campuses that are largely located in urban areas, are there aspects of this transition easier or more difficult for them than for students from larger communities? Are there differences in ease of transition based on closeness to home and institution type? Are there disparities in school and work experiences, selection and consistency of major, transfer patterns, and financial aid among rural students and their nonrural counterparts? This information would be beneficial for colleges as they look to support this underrepresented group of students. Furthermore, it is important to examine the consequences of postsecondary attainment for labor market outcomes (e.g., rates of employment, income levels) among people from rural and nonrural places.

International Response

Rural Schools and Communities

We Can Bridge, but Can We Bond?

Michael Corbett

This section takes up a number of themes and issues relating to community and schooling in rural contexts in the United States. This work is generally focused on assets rather than the deficit perspectives that have marked how rural education and rural communities have been understood. How the problems raised in these accounts might speak to related issues in other national contexts and, indeed, in transnational space is what I will consider in this afterword.

Sutherland and Seelig open with an analysis of decentralization and school governance. The United States is, of course, often cited as a textbook case of decentralized educational governance, which flows from a separation of powers that provide the states with most of the control over education. However, other more or less decentralized systems operate around the world, such as Brazil, Canada, Chile, Zimbabwe, New Zealand, El Salvador, Nicaragua, Germany, and Australia. It is really quite interesting to explore the way that centralized or decentralized education systems support rural communities and schools in different ways. On the one hand, it is possible that a centralized system might provide better standards of instruction, curriculum, and assessment. However, on the other hand, the responsiveness and flexibility of strong local or regionally focused governance, curriculum, and assessment might be more sensitive to local needs. This is a line of international inquiry that could be quite productive.

I am also intrigued by how the term "community" and the idea of a school jurisdiction interrelate. Historically, a school board or board of trustees was established in a place by those who built and largely maintained a school building. The process of shifting control of governance from community members to other levels of authority has been a long historical tendency. Indeed, it might well be said that this historical drift has been the central problem in rural education scholarship from its inception. This delocalization, bureaucratization, and professionalization of education has not, however, led to direct decentralization in many parts of the world. On the contrary, what we have witnessed globally in recent decades has been: (a) de facto decentralization through privatization and quasi-privatization initiatives and (b) the emergence of loose-tight systems of centralized control with devolution of responsibility to local sites. With a combination of a decentralized state education system and further fragmentation though charter, voucher, and other quasi-privatization initiatives, it seems problematic to even speak of a national system of education in the United States.

The piece by Eppley illustrates the force of this movement toward disaggregation and decentralization, which has played out in urban educational "markets" through the expansion of neoliberal choice politics into rural areas. What indeed does school choice look like in rural places with low population and low density? How has an urban phenomenon like charter schools played into the kinds of centralization moves represented by the unrelenting force of rural school consolidation? It could be argued that England and a number of other national jurisdictions have developed decentralized governance structures as well through privatization and quasi-privatization initiatives such as the British "academy" system.

In rural communities, this trend has perhaps been felt more keenly than in larger centers where governance structures have long been complex and professionalized. Eppley in particular illustrates how property assessment-driven funding formulas are designed to work for large urban administrative units with large enrollments concentrated in relatively densely populated geographies. What happens in rural contexts is that different forms of "adjustment" need to be made for things to work at all and in such loose-tight systems. Adjustments, in the US context often come in the form of neoliberal choice initiatives that more or less independently fill the gaps left by the retreat of universal public services. Federal initiatives to provide educational inclusion and compensatory programming increase pressure that is exacerbated by standardized testing initiatives, which add to the complexity that rural schools face in neoliberal times.

There is a certain irony that arises in the way that each of the pieces in this section tend to laud the independent work of communities forced to "bootstrap" and recognize the pressures brought to bear by the need to respond to centralized mandates and neoliberal governance pressures. For instance, Sutherland and Seelig's call for "theorizing the centrality of place in classroom pedagogy, teacher recruitment and retention, community-school partnerships and educational leadership" would probably not be challenged by those who promote educational privatization and quasi-privatization.

In Chapter 11, McHenry-Sorber shows how issues of teacher unionism are rife with difficulty. In terms of this section, the community in focus here is the collective of teachers as a unionized workforce. The general erosion of union power in West Virginia is one part of a larger international picture, highlighting the ambivalent position of professional unions generally. The significance of "right to work" legislation, the Janus decision, and the irony of the emergence of teacher labor activism in West Virginia, a rural, conservative, and relatively impoverished state, is taken up in this chapter. It is not common in the United States for rural professionals to emerge as nationally significant labor activists, yet a very limited literature on the topic of teacher labor activism suggests that this is consistent with rural teacher activism historically. This resonates with McHenry-Sorber's union work as well as my own teacher union activism in the 1990s in which nonurban historically resource extraction areas (mining, logging) tended to greater levels of union militancy.

This illustrates how educational governance and politics do not always go in predicted or predictable directions. And perhaps this is just one instance of a larger phenomenon that represents the precarious and unpredictable politics of the present moment. The chapter also focuses on the influence of neoliberal reforms on teacher unionism. This is an important part of the picture and we do need, as the author notes, more and better research into the structural and systemic forces that have eroded teacher unionism and professionalism simultaneously, particularly in female-dominated areas such as teaching and nursing.

The relationship between teacher unionism, current social justice struggles, and a broader sense of what constitutes the locus of solidarity illustrates contemporary labor movement tensions. Teachers are a relatively poorly paid professional group on the whole (although in a radically decentralized system, this is not always the case), and so, they are, in one sense, a disadvantaged labor force. But the relationship between teachers and other social justice struggles, including struggles over the inclusion of women, disabled people, racialized minorities, and other equity-seeking groups into the mainstream of educational, economic, and social opportunity, is one that requires new sensibilities and theory as well as robust and courageous research. But it is also an ongoing activist mission relating to pedagogy, organizing, activism, and solidarity in relation to contemporary social movements such as Black Lives Matter and increasingly polarized and charged electoral politics. This dimension of the issue is taken up in the middle section of McHenry-Sorber's chapter and illustrated by two moving accounts of historical teachers' strikes. We need more of this!

In keeping with this historical and political critique, Eppley's chapter documents and analyzes the effects of small rural school closure. After generations of consolidations and closures there are no clear conclusions regarding whether or not closing schools saves money or whether keeping them open saves communities as many small school activists claim. What is most interesting for me in Eppley's discussion of the closure phenomenon is the way that it articulates with the charter agenda and the general shift toward neoliberal policy orientations. Here we see the tensions emerge as the neoliberal pull toward local autonomy and small government is met by the centralizing tendencies of regulatory, testing and oversight regimes that demand local operations be scrutinized and subject to marketized comparisons that require standardized metrics.

Both economic globalization and the move toward standardized testing instruments generate interesting tensions between local control and what Eppley calls free-market ideologies. Charter schools and vouchers work in the space opened up in these tensions in a way that is particular to the United States under the broad umbrella of choice politics. In rural areas, Eppley argues, charter schools reflect rural resistance to school consolidations and closure, but in ways that deepen existing disparities and download responsibility for school governance onto already stressed local citizens. In the emerging world of social media, and the new surveillance, marketing, and manipulation capabilities of contemporary capitalism, it should come as no surprise that the communal, deregulation ideologies associated with charter schools end up advancing and increasing inequality.

Internationally, choice politics, privatization, and quasi-privatization of schools have taken on a different character in different national contexts, which in turn has different effects in rural areas. Chile is probably the most radical, and yet perhaps the most pertinent exemplar for the United States at the current moment where vouchers and privatization in the context of a dictatorial government created a core shift in how education itself is understood (Carnoy, 1998; Carrasco & Gunter, 2019). School choice in rural areas has been an issue in rural Australia where about 35 percent of all schools are some form of private institution, and in parts of Canada where denominational schools have operated in some provinces for generations. In both of these countries, though, Catholic education has significantly driven school choice, and because of the infrastructure established in these systems, it seems virtually impossible to imagine education without them. In the Canadian provinces of Ontario and Alberta, for example, and in all of the Australian states, Catholic education is principally government-funded. But the charter movement breaks new ground in the United States by offering a model of education

The Bloomsbury Handbook of Rural Education in the United States

that in many ways fits better with the Norwegian folk school model (initially designed for rural schools) offering curricular flexibility and autonomy along with state funding.

As Casto and Sipple demonstrate, the image of the rural school is a support to community. Still, the argument that this support tends to preserve anti-modern values and practices is one that goes back a very long way. Almost as soon as rural schools are established, they are subject to the criticism of conservatism and insularity in settler societies (Cubberley, 1922; Theobald, 1995, 1997). Partnerships are challenging enough but set against the troubled history of rural school–community relations and the modernizing imperative that has marked these relations, the work can be additionally tricky. There is tremendous potential for unworkable and insensitive "metrocentric" (Roberts and Green, 2013) or deficit-based initiatives (Gorski, 2011) and the history of rural education is dotted with them. Casto and Sipple write, "(S)mall and isolated rural places are often fragile ecosystems that can easily be disturbed by missteps that can occur with even the best intentions." But their chapter is essentially about how carefully thought-out partnerships can work very well.

The mission of modernization is the disruption of communal bonds and the creation of new solidarities (with the nation-state, to industrial employers, to corporate interests, to non-local teachers who are what the Australians call "blow-ins" who bring alternative values). There are inevitable tensions and challenges that emerge, not the least of which is the problematic nature of partnerships between schools and the communities they serve, or at least operate within. Like the idea of community itself, it is very difficult to problematize or critique the idea of school-community partnerships. As Raymond Williams (1985) put it, there tend to be no negative associations for the idea of community, but of course, subsequent work has raised plenty of questions (Barrett, 2015; Corbett, 2014; Nancy, 1991, 2016). The question then becomes who represents community in these collaborations, or whose community is given status or invited/ allowed to connect to the school?

In addition to Casto and Sipple's chapter, Zuckerman's raises questions about a broad sense of the common good, critiquing, at least implicitly, band-aid partnerships, poorly designed change initiatives, and missionary projects that seek to improve the lives of rural citizens— often developed and implemented without ever consulting those whose lives are deemed to require improvement. Community awareness is crucial to partnerships and the unanticipated consequences of partnerships related by Casto and Sipple raise interesting questions. For instance, a prekindergarten program that might be expected to support community and school simultaneously turned out to be largely problematic due to poor planning and a lack of consultation. Yet, a wind farm project initiated by a school administrator, which on the face of it might seem to have little to do with educational improvement, made excellent sense in the context of school and community. If we know one thing from rural education research, it is that schools need functioning communities with economic infrastructure in order to provide children to teach. Zuckerman's account of collective impact as a model for rural community and school development provides a structural framework that might serve to at least diminish the probability of unproductive community-school partnerships that fail for all-too-predictable reasons.

Schmitt-Wilson and Byun's chapter plays on the established theme of rural social capital and how it relates to youth and family aspirations and postsecondary participation. This is a complex subject and their analysis nuances some key issues. Rural youth are less likely to attend higher education, but the gap is decreasing. It also appears that rural youth are more likely to attend two-year programs and bridge into four-year degrees through that portal. They are also more likely to attend public, nonselective colleges. These findings, many of which draw from large national data sets, should by now be well understood.

This analysis relates to international evidence from Australia and Canada that also links geographic distance from a rural home place to the nearest postsecondary institution as a factor in higher education choice. Here we encounter the complexity of educational decision-making for rural youth who tend to have more circuitous paths to completion, well-known rural race and gender gaps in participation, and attempts to explain further their propensity to choose initial two-year programs. In particular, they illustrate how well-funded rural schools that offer advanced courses address structural impediments to youth participation such as parental education levels. Challenges associated with what they call rural social capital are consistent with work in Australia by Kilpatrick and Abbott-Chapman (see Abbott-Chapman, 2011; Falk & Kilpatrick, 2000; Kilpatrick & Abbott-Chapman, 2002) as well as my own work in Canada and Australia (Corbett, 2016b; Corbett & Ackerson, 2019; Corbett & Forsey, 2017) that indicate a tension between nonacademic skill sets, opportunity structures and networks, and postsecondary educational decision-making. The research Schmitt-Wilson and Byun survey tells the story of narrowing rural-suburban-urban gaps in participation and completion and, more interestingly, a looser coupling between parental education and family structure and degree completion. This illustrates, if anything, a stronger aspirational influence in terms of completion amid increased challenges that rural youth face to survive and thrive in higher education.

The importance of the school itself and its leadership is well known in the rural education literature, and Biddle's chapter reinforces the sense in which rurality can become an advantage rather than a problem for education, which is the default. Biddle, Casto and Sipple, Zuckerman, and Schmitt and Byun, in different ways, address this potential rural education advantage that is situated within the general social capital network of smaller communities. Chapter 10, in particular, illustrates both the well-known challenges associated with the many hats a rural education leader must play in day-to-day work but more importantly the lesser-known inclusions and exclusions of identifiable populations within rural school communities (i.e., race, gender, social class, disability, etc.) as well as theoretically attuned understandings of how rural school leaders imagine their work in relation to place and space.

Nevertheless, this positive framing of community, which tends to harken back to Williams's (1985) idea that community has no negative connotation, can tend put a happy face on different reactive responses and approaches to neoliberal governmentality in rural contexts. These range from the changing state of teacher union politics through local efforts to deal with change and challenge in rural locations using the different community-building tools made available under neoliberalism. Here we see charter schools and a variety of school-community partnerships designed to respond to a range of structural changes that put pressure on rural communities. Rather than a unified response to the protection of universal public education, the more common default is to try and make the best of a bad situation by mobilizing local resources strategically under the circumstances.

But how have these pressures and the problems that they represent come into being? Without raising such questions, existing conditions seem fixed and largely immutable. The solutions that emerge are localized and individualized and themselves illustrate the extent to which the privatization and quasi-privatization choice-oriented agendas have infiltrated how we think about rural schools and the communities they serve. These days we hear a great deal about grit

(Duckworth, 2016) and the importance of developing a "growth mindset" rather than one that is fixed (Dweck, 2007). I also think what is required is political grit and a sociological growth perspective that confronts and challenges what might be called a fixed structural sociology. One of the things that rural communities have perhaps learned to do best is to respond tactically to externally imposed policy and governance that do not fit well with their own local situations. This section reports this kind of work. But the question of influencing and developing rurally sensitive social and educational policy that operates through what has been called a "rural lens" is perhaps more important. To achieve this perspective, theoretical tools are necessary and, indeed, concepts that allow for a rurally attuned systemic and structural point of sight.

But at the same time, the power of many rural communities is in their resilience and ability to organize in the face of overwhelming odds and in the face of change forces that seem to foreshadow ubiquitous urbanization. Rural America and indeed rural places generally somehow manage to survive, typically through some combination of bootstrapping, imagination, ingenuity, and gritty refusal to either disappear or assimilate. But, is it possible to argue that the world is simultaneously urbanizing and ruralizing (Krause, 2013), which suggests the importance of understanding global change forces using a rural lens as well as the default metrocentric perspective? Change is inevitable and in the context of the global pandemic rural places take on a new meaning, and indeed, a new attractiveness. One of the reasons I have seen proposed for the relatively slow spread of Covid-19 in Africa is the cultural pattern of retired people returning to their rural places of origin, which means that large cities have relatively few aged people living in them. In the less densely populated and architecturally packed countryside the virus has been easier to contain (Soy, 2020). Just this morning as I was sitting down to write this chapter (October 9, 2020), the morning news was reporting a spike in U-Haul truck rentals and real estate agencies doing a brisk business as urban Canadians move back to the "Atlantic Bubble," a name given to the eastern Canadian provinces that are much more predominantly rural than others and virtually disease-free.

Each of the pieces in this section, in different ways, speaks to the importance of face-to-face community and the parallel need for community projects to be sensitive to the nuances of local rural perspectives as well as the affordances that these communities provide. For instance, Casto and Sipple's account of a rural school superintendent who chose to look beyond the school ground and into the community to a wind-generation project demonstrates a community-sensitive productive approach that created the conditions for sustainable economic growth in emerging industries. This is also reinforced by Zuckerman's analysis of the multisectoral collective impact approach and its applicability in rural settings.

What we need to understand better is how rurality and community have evolved in tandem both as sources of inclusion, resilience, and strength and at the same time as spaces of exclusion, violence, and insularity (Corbett, 2020; Holloway, 2007; Jackson, 2010). We are beginning to learn how new vulnerabilities are emerging in the confluence of the climate crisis, a global pandemic, and geographies of risk in which racialized, Indigenous, and migrant rural people face increased risk. This, in combination with the myriad ways social media contribute to a highly effective, exclusive, and possibly incendiary form of community building, raises the stakes of the neoliberal experiment to create new and emerging social and political "dilemmas" as a recent Netflix blockbuster has illustrated (Orlowski, 2020).

Rural Schools and Communities

These chapters illustrate that bonding is possible and productive in rural communities—but can we learn to bridge as Putnam framed it in his classic analysis of social capital? In part, this is the lingering, yet vibrant, resonance of colonialism that involves the nature of (rural) land, property, and justice (Tuck & Yang, 2012). As I write, the part of Atlantic Canada where I lived for close to two decades and where I did much of my own foundational educational research is quite literally in flames over a dispute between non-Indigenous settler fishing families and Indigenous groups who are prosecuting a moderate livelihood fishery guaranteed by treaty, the Canadian constitution, and a 1999 Supreme Court decision. When our work engages critical and messy intersections of settler colonialism and the constitution and maintenance of real and imagined rural space, new, yet long overdue questions emerge. For me, the questions that face us today relate to the emerging solidarities and antinomies playing out on the streets in global cities and in the global countryside (Woods, 2007). This raises critical questions about what community might be and what a socially just rural education might look like in the face of these challenges.

Part III

Introduction

Curriculum Studies in Rural Schools

Parts I and II provide a foundational overview of rural education and how schools function within rural communities. Part III further narrows this focus to address structural components of rural schooling as they relate to curriculum studies, including early childhood education, rural literacies and identities, trauma-informed approaches to rural schooling, school-based mental health considerations, and rural achievement.

In Chapter 15, Early Childhood Education in Rural Communities, Knoche, Kerby, and Sheridan discuss early childhood as a critical developmental period for children's lifelong success and well-being. They review brain development and the ways experiences can impact the trajectories of children's learning and growth. Moreover, they review multiple types of early childhood education experiences available to children and identify key dimensions of high-quality early childhood experiences while keeping in mind the variability that exists in programming. Within this frame, they then consider early childhood education against the geographic and economic constraints in rural communities and how it can intersect with inequities in children's school readiness and early development. Importantly, in addition to exploring the limitations facing rural early childhood programs and services, the authors identify existing strengths and capacities within rural communities that may bolster early childhood education efforts. Additionally, they address the intersection of rurality and race/ethnicity, and the implications of this intersection on the future directions of early childhood education programs and policies in rural communities.

Donehower further explores the connection between childhood experiences and rural identities. Chapter 16, Rural Literacies and Rural Identities, offers a framework for considering curricular rural literacy projects that are either rhetorical, aesthetic, or performative in nature. Using well-curated examples of each, the chapter emphasizes the potential of the projects to offer opportunities for rural students to question and critically reconsider the typical ways rural places and people are represented in terms of, and through, reading and writing. The concluding analysis emphasizes a common thread: the need to push back against typical constructions of rural people and places in relation to literacy. Effective literacy projects in rural schools interrogate and

The Bloomsbury Handbook of Rural Education in the United States

remediate some of these stereotypes, but they also provide space for rural students to challenge some of their rural communities' own assumptions about literacy, schooling, and local identity. Ultimately, this chapter captures and categorizes common emphases in research on rural literacies in US schools and suggests parameters for future work on rural literacy curricular projects.

The next chapter offers an analysis of the role that trauma plays in mediating young people's school experiences and personal development. In their chapter, Trauma-Informed Approaches in Rural Education (Chapter 17), Biddle and Brown make clear that schools have an important role to play in both preventing retraumatization for children who have experienced adversity and in promoting healing during the time that children spend at school. Rural schools, in particular, have unique opportunities to support this work by leveraging small classroom environments, when they exist, and dense rural social networks to support healthy, caring relationships between students and teachers that promote the production of the hormone oxytocin, which controls feelings of belonging and love, and decreasing the production of the stress hormone cortisol. This chapter reviews the fundamental principles of this work and approaches that have been used in rural schools. The chapter closes with considerations for trauma-informed work in rural school settings framed by a case study of one school deeply engaged in creating a healing-centered environment for elementary-age children.

Following the review of trauma-informed approaches, Chapter 18 furthers the discussion about responding to the emotional needs of rural students. In their chapter, Rural School-Based Mental Health: Models of Prevention, Intervention, and Preparation, authors Downey, Elliott, Koltz, and Murray argue persuasively that mental health issues are becoming a growing critical concern for rural and tribal students, their families, and their communities all over the United States. One approach to rural mental health service delivery with the potential to mitigate these barriers is school-based mental health (SBMH) services and programs, where mental health services are provided to rural students, and in some cases their families, in the context of the school day and building. This chapter reviews the rural mental health needs at national, regional, and local levels and highlights several successful programs and protocols of rural SBMH delivery that are making a difference in terms of prevention, intervention, and support. This chapter also reviews the research-based recommendations for implementing and sustaining SBMH programs in rural settings and the competencies needed by rural SBMH professionals and teachers. The chapter concludes with a review of best practices related to prevention, assessment, and intervention for rural students.

For the final chapter in Part III, Student Achievement in Rural America (Chapter 19), Gagnon examines educational outcomes, including achievement and educational attainment, for rural students in the United States. After positioning the rural context as affording unique opportunities as well as challenges that may impact the educational outcomes of rural students, the chapter provides an in-depth analysis of student achievement on the National Assessment of Educational Progress (NAEP). The chapter documents trends in educational attainment for rural students, exploring variation both within and across locale and highlights differences in educational attainment across region, student income, and student race and ethnicity. Key questions prompt the reader to consider why trends exist across poverty, race, and place in the United States—questions explored in great depth throughout the handbook.

Introduction

Part III concludes with Roberts's international response, What Counts as Curriculum? Providing an Australian perspective, Roberts reflects on the chapters in Part III and considers the territory of curriculum studies by asking what counts as knowledge in rural education. Roberts describes the role of curriculum in shaping the organization of Australian schooling and the challenges of rural inclusion/exclusion within this organization as a counterpoint and comparison to the chapters situated in the US context. He reviews the impact of a century's worth of reports on Australian rural education in terms of framing rural schools and people as deficient. He notes that these reports fail to account for the complex social and economic realities facing rural communities and the ways in which early childhood education, access to mental health resources, and the role of schools in supporting trauma-responsive environments affect these challenges. Finally, he reviews two important differences between the Australian and US contexts that provide opportunities for reflection and challenges in comparative work. First, he raises the question of what constitutes curriculum studies and how that is engaged in Part III. Last, he points to the critical role of epistemology in shaping curriculum and the ways in which failure to engage rural, Indigenous, and global South perspectives shape the ways in which deficit perspectives of rurality are constructed and reconstructed.

15

Early Childhood Education in Rural Communities

Lisa L. Knoche, Hannah M. Kerby, and Susan M. Sheridan

Remarkable physical, cognitive, and social-emotional development occurs for young children from birth to age eight. This developmental trajectory is different for children based on the communities in which they live and their available resources; accordingly, children growing up in rural communities have unique experiences that make lasting contributions to their growth and development. The social and educational services and supports available through early childhood programming contribute to a set of experiences affecting the development of many young children. Early childhood program offerings for children and families can take many forms, and the availability and quality of programs in rural communities can be quite variable. This chapter will highlight the significance of early childhood development and related programs, describe the specific issues and needs facing rural early childhood education programs, and detail family engagement as one method to positively support the development of young children growing up in rural communities.

Significance of Early Childhood and Early Childhood Programs

The experiences afforded to young children during their early years are significantly associated with developmental trajectories well beyond the early childhood period. Early childhood programming is available to children and families via varying service delivery models designed to meet the unique needs of families. The benefits of this programming, however, are highly related to the quality of services offered.

Early Childhood Development

Early childhood, or the period from birth to age eight (Copple & Bredekamp, 2009), has long been recognized as a significant developmental period in the human life cycle. Children's experiences in their youngest years have lasting implications for their lifelong learning, behavior, health, and overall well-being (Anderson et al., 2003; Shonkoff & Phillips, 2000). The significance, in part, is due to rapid brain development that occurs throughout the early childhood period.

The Bloomsbury Handbook of Rural Education in the United States

Young children's brain development is swift and complex with early experiences shaping children's developing neural circuitry. Specifically, warm, nurturing, and predictable interactions with adults support productive and healthy brain development for young children, which is essential for their academic success and emotional competence (Landry et al., 2003; Meaney, 2010). Additionally, responsiveness and encouragement by caregivers are important for fostering children's feelings of safety and security (Edwards et al., 2010), allowing them to successfully explore new environments and experiences.

Furthermore, children's early social skills and academic performance have significant and lasting implications for their future success. Evidence demonstrates that results on tests of reading abilities that emerge by third grade (approximately age eight) are linked to reading test results in ninth grade and the likelihood of both high school graduation and college attendance (Lesnick et al., 2010). Additionally, during the early childhood period, children learn and practice important social skills that contribute to immediate and long-term behavioral and academic success (Caemmerer & Keith, 2015; Durlak et al., 2011). Children who gain developmentally appropriate social and academic skills in the early childhood period are more likely to maintain positive outcomes well beyond high school graduation than children who do not develop appropriate competencies (Campbell et al., 2012).

Given the strong associations between early childhood experiences and later academic and social success, it is imperative to create and implement experiences that will foster healthy development during the early childhood period, especially for children in rural communities. The demand is great given that child poverty rates are higher than urban communities (Schaefer et al., 2016), and there is often limited access to employment and educational opportunities (Malik et al., 2018; Vernon-Feagans et al., 2008; Schmitt-Wilson & Byun, Chapter 14, this volume). Early childhood experiences can be individualized and offered via multiple service delivery models to meet the needs of children and families in rural communities.

Early Childhood Service Delivery Models

To target the needs of families served, early childhood programming is offered using multiple delivery models (e.g., home-based, center-based) via different funding structures (e.g., public sources, private pay). Early childhood programming also varies based on children's ages. One model of programming that might be offered to children and families in rural communities includes center-based services. In center-based programming, children aged birth to five years attend a setting with other children and are cared for by one or more adults. This type of programming might be housed in a childcare facility or a school building. Families generally drop off and pick up children and, in some instances, children are transported to and from the center by center staff (e.g., busing). Another model of services includes family, friend, or neighbor care, where children participate in services in another person's home. Finally, early childhood programming can take place as part of home-based early childhood services. These are generally offered for children from birth to age three years, though this format is sometimes available through age five. In home-based early childhood services, an educator meets with the parent and child at the family home or another agreed-upon location regularly (e.g., weekly, biweekly) to support child and family needs. Rural communities have variable access to the different early childhood service delivery models depending on community resources, needs, and priorities.

Early childhood programming includes publicly funded options that are supported by local, state, or federal funds; it also includes services that are privately operated and paid for directly by families. Some publicly funded programs have eligibility criteria based on child and family demographics (e.g., income, disability status) with eligibility criteria generally consistent regardless of program context (e.g., rural, urban). Finally, some programs use a combination of public and private funds. This blended funding arrangement is commonly used in rural communities where there are a smaller number of children to serve—to meet the needs of all children in a community, multiple funding sources are used to support programming.

Early Childhood Program Quality

Quality is an important consideration across the various early childhood program types and can be quite variable. Quality in early childhood programs, across rural and urban settings, can be measured in multiple ways. Structural and process features of quality are commonly measured (National Institute of Child Health and Human Development [NICHD], 2006). For center-based programs, structural features include factors such as safety, room arrangements, ratio of staff to children, educator background, and training as well as availability of educational resources/materials. Alternatively, process elements focus on the interactions that occur between adults and children, such as the responsiveness of caregivers and the language richness of the setting. Process quality also includes interactions that take place between children. For home-based early childhood services, structural features include the frequency of visits and the format/agenda of the visit; process features might include the behaviors used by the educator during the visit to engage the parent and child. Structure and process quality are interdependent; that is, the structural features of quality are related to process elements wherein high structural quality is generally a prerequisite to high levels of process quality (Cryer et al., 1999).

Empirical evidence suggests that the quality of center-based programming strongly influences children's cognitive and language development, over and above family characteristics (e.g., income level, race/ethnicity, parents' educational attainment). The association between program quality and children's development is repeatedly demonstrated in evaluations of early childhood programs (Duncan & Magnuson, 2013; Phillips et al., 2017). In center-based settings observed to be of high quality, children show improved developmental skills (NICHD Early Child Care Research Network [ECCRN], 2002) and these effects have been observed into adolescence and adulthood (Campbell et al., 2012; Vandell et al., 2010). Similar associations have also been noted for children in rural communities (Broekhuizen et al., 2016), where children attending high-quality programs demonstrated better social skills and fewer behavior problems after experiencing classrooms that offered high levels of emotional and organizational quality. Quality of programming often varies significantly by the type of program (e.g., family childcare, home- or center-based), especially in rural communities where resources are limited. A recent review of existing research concluded that rural families often rely more on family childcare than center-based care, such as Head Start or publicly funded preschool (Anderson & Mikesell, 2019). Family childcare settings are likely to be deemed by evaluators as being of lesser quality than center-based settings, which directly and negatively impacts children's early developmental outcomes (Bassok et al., 2016).

Rural Communities

Rural communities provide a unique landscape for implementing early childhood programming. There are unique strengths and challenges of the rural geographic context that contribute to children's development. The distinctive strengths and capacities of rural communities can be leveraged to foster effective early childhood programming and promote young children's healthy development.

Strengths of Rural Communities

Rural communities, families, and schools have significant strengths that contribute to the positive development of young children. Unique strengths of rural communities include strong personal connections and cultural norms of faith and community building (Hartman & Hines-Bergmeier, 2015; Vernon-Feagans et al., 2008). Although community cohesiveness is often cited as an idyllic rural norm, it should be acknowledged that rural communities are not without complexities and idiosyncrasies (Corbett, 2014). Nevertheless, faith and community building in rural communities may provide families with valuable social capital and ultimately benefit rural children. For instance, religious participation among single mothers has been found to be associated with greater involvement with children, reduced parenting stress, and a lower likelihood of engaging in corporal punishment (Petts, 2012). Further, rural residents are more likely to live near family members than urban and suburban residents, which may provide more opportunities to develop strong family ties and support (Parker et al., 2018). Additionally, children in rural communities have been found to have higher attachment to their caregivers than urban children (Bender et al., 2011). Rural teachers may also have more opportunities to develop close connections with students and their families, as they are more likely to personally know the families of the children they teach and to see their students outside of school (Eppley, 2015). Additionally, rural communities have strong school-home-community ties and an especially dedicated educational workforce (Holmes & Sheridan, in press; Iruka et al., 2019). Practices that foster or build upon existing relationships, such as those between the home and school, teacher and child, and parent and child, may be particularly promising for bolstering early childhood efforts in rural communities.

However, it is important to note that rural communities are heterogeneous. Though it is common for rural communities to be characterized as places where "everyone knows everyone," not every rural community is characterized by harmonious social relations. That is, some rural families may experience supportive networks and a sense of connection or belonging (Hegney et al., 2007; Larson & Dearmont, 2002) while other rural families may experience social disconnection. Social and geographic distance, stigma, and prejudice in some rural communities may contribute to disjointed rural community ties (Edwards & Cheers, 2007; Fennelly, 2008), particularly as diversity within rural communities increases. These differences in rural communities might have differential effects on young children's development and education.

Challenges Confronting Rural Communities and Families

Rural communities and families also face challenges in promoting the academic and social success of young children. By nature, rural communities are sparsely populated and geographically isolated from various resources and services, including medical facilities, mental health care, and social services. The geographic isolation limits access to employment and educational opportunities, and developmentally salient resources such as health care, food banks, libraries, and childcare (Malik et al., 2018; Vernon-Feagans et al., 2008). Further, though there have been recent trends in rural residents becoming more highly educated, rural children are still less likely to have parents with college degrees than their urban counterparts (USDA, 2017). Moreover, rural residents may be forced to travel long distances to get to work and are more likely to have nonstandard work schedules because of the scarcity of jobs with typical work schedules (Kotras et al., 2014). Taken together, these factors pose challenges for rural families as parents may be less able to spend time with their young children than parents in other contexts and may be more likely to rely on multiple childcare arrangements. This is of concern as multiple care arrangements have been found to be associated with lower school readiness in both social-emotional and academic domains (Bratsch-Hines et al., 2017). Further, limited resources may place severe stress on families and create familial disorganization (e.g., lack of routines or schedules, clutter, noise in the home), both of which are linked to poor short- and long-term outcomes for rural children (Bratsch-Hines et al., 2016).

Additionally, rural communities have disproportionately higher rates of child poverty than urban communities (Schaefer et al., 2016). The poverty experienced in rural communities is also more persistent, lasting for multiple generations (Schaefer et al., 2016). This is of concern for rural children's early development because poverty experienced in the first two years of life is associated with lower cognitive, language, executive functioning, and social skills by ages two to three (Burchinal et al., 2018). Furthermore, children in families with low incomes have a higher incidence of health problems that may interfere with learning, such as asthma, ADHD, and vision problems (Fiester, 2010).

Early childhood programs are largely recognized as one mechanism for mitigating the detrimental effects of poverty on early development (Magnuson & Duncan, 2016). However, rural families may have little choice in where to send their young children for early childhood programs, as only about 50 percent of rural children have access to center-based preschool programs (Smith et al., 2008) and 59 percent of rural communities are situated in areas with little or no capacity for licensed childcare (Malik et al., 2018). And even when publicly funded preschool is available, rural stakeholders have described difficulties in providing full-time programs to *all* eligible children in need due to having limited resources and being unable to provide a range of reliable and affordable services, including transportation and wraparound services (Iruka et al., 2019). Additionally, rural families may have little access to special education services for young children (e.g., support for families of children with autism) and often express a higher need for special education services than nonrural families (Azano, 2016; Murphy & Ruble, 2012).

Although it is important to acknowledge the challenges that exist in rural communities, to fully understand the implications of rurality on early childhood education stakeholders must also recognize the already existing capacities of rural communities, such as the close school-home-community ties. Only by mobilizing powerful adaptive systems will policy, practice, and intervention be sustainable for rural settings and thus be able to promote rural children's healthy development. That is, gaps in development will undoubtedly continue to persist without a *systems-focused* and *strengths-based* approach that seeks to understand how the existing strengths of rural communities, schools, and families interact to influence children's development. In the section that follows, we highlight two evidence-based interventions that leverage the strengths of rural schools and families to promote young children's success.

The Bloomsbury Handbook of Rural Education in the United States

Supporting Child Development in Rural Communities: Family Engagement

Across all geographic settings, families play a critical role in the lives of young children. As a result, family engagement is a priority for early childhood programs, including those in rural communities. Many early childhood programs have standards, regulations, and guidelines that guide their efforts toward supporting and engaging families in early learning (e.g., Head Start Performance Standards; Parent Family Community Engagement Framework). We define family engagement to mean both the interactions that parents have with their young children as well as the interactions that take place between families and other educators who share responsibility for their child's well-being and development. The impact of these interactions on children's positive development has been well established through past research; thus, family engagement is an important target for early childhood programs and is aligned with priorities of rural stakeholders (Iruka et al., 2019).

Family engagement is first defined as the interaction between parents and children. Children's early development is influenced in large part by early parental caregiving patterns (Luby et al., 2013). Specifically, when parents engage in warm and sensitive interactions with their child; support their child's emerging autonomy and self-regulation; and participate actively as partners in their child's learning in culturally comfortable and responsive ways, children's skill development is positively influenced (deRuiter & van Ijzendoorn, 1993; Weigel et al., 2006). Positive parental interactions are important for fostering children's feelings of safety and security (Edwards et al., 2010); these secure relationships enable them to interact with and benefit from early learning environments. Early interactions between parents and young children that are stimulating and nurturing promote neural connections that are foundational for young children's academic success and emotional competence (Landry et al., 2003).

Family engagement also includes the interactions that take place between families and other educators who share responsibility for their child's welfare and learning. Children enrolled in early childhood programs have the opportunity to develop and learn within multiple contexts (e.g., home, childcare, preschool, school) and are supported by caring adults across these settings. Interactions with early childhood educators, be they home visitors, childcare providers, or preschool/infant-toddler classroom teachers, are often the first opportunities for parents to formally partner with others in their children's education. Young children's development is optimized when effective connections among these multiple settings are consistent and coherent (Rimm-Kaufman et al., 2000). Establishing strong connections between children's homes and their early childhood program experiences supports children's development across domains and prepares them for later school success (Elicker et al., 2013; Forry et al., 2011).

The importance of creating connections between rural families and educators in early development is underscored by research that shows family involvement with their children's education is often lacking in rural settings as compared to reports from urban communities (e.g., Keys, 2015). Rural parents have been found to talk with their children about school programs, attend school meetings, and interact with teachers less frequently relative to their counterparts in suburban and urban schools (Prater et al., 1997). While some stakeholders report strong ties between schools and families (Iruka et al., 2019), only 54 percent of rural parents reported being satisfied in their interactions with school staff (NCES, 2007). Thus, establishing mechanisms to promote and support family engagement early in children's educational experiences is of particular importance for families and educators in rural communities.

Early Childhood Interventions to Support Family Engagement

To show how family engagement during early childhood can be supported in rural communities, two intervention programs are described below: Getting Ready (Sheridan et al., 2008) and Teachers and Parents as Partners (Sheridan, 2014). This selection is not intended to be exhaustive but rather a sampling of family engagement interventions that have been implemented successfully with families and educators in rural communities.

The Getting Ready Intervention

Getting Ready (GR) is a relationally based parent engagement intervention promoting school readiness for young children from birth to age five (Sheridan et al., 2008). GR focuses on enhancing parent-child relationships and strengthening collaborative partnerships between early childhood educators (ECEs) and parents. GR is conceptualized as an approach by which ECEs support the engagement of parents, promoting warmth, sensitivity, and active participation in their children's early learning. Rather than representing an "add-on" to current services, GR is integrated within established early childhood programs (such as Early Head Start/Head Start, other publicly funded preschool programs, and private childcare settings), thereby augmenting existing programming. Through GR, professionals in early childhood programs learn strategies for establishing and maintaining relationships with parents and supporting the parent-child relationship.

The GR intervention includes strategies to encourage parent-child interaction and promote parent-ECE partnership as well as a structured, collaborative planning process to guide goal setting. The eight GR strategies support parents' competencies to facilitate their child's learning across contexts and reinforce parents' active engagement in their child's development. Strategies used by ECEs include (a) helping to establish the parent-child interaction, (b) communicating openly, (c) affirming parent competencies, (d) focusing parents' attention, (e) sharing information and resources, (f) using observations and data to guide decisions, (g) making mutual/joint decisions, and (h) modeling/suggesting as needed (for complete definition of strategies, see Marvin et al., 2019; Sheridan et al., 2019). In addition, structured collaborative planning procedures (including observation review and the creation of partnership plans) are incorporated into family contacts to promote shared responsibility between parents and ECEs for encouraging children's school readiness. The GR strategies are based on triadic consultation (McCollum & Yates, 1994) that establish and strengthen relationships and collaborative parent–teacher partnership interventions (Sheridan & Kratochwill, 2008) that guide shared goal setting and decision-making.

The GR intervention readily accommodates the unique contexts of families in rural communities. The "curriculum of the home" (i.e., the relationships, practices, and patterns of life in the home that influence a child's development) is considered in all interactions (Redding, 1997). Thus, unique features of the child's home life that were previously unknown or underestimated by the early childhood educator (e.g., the role of extended family in promoting children's learning) are validated and utilized in instructional planning and goal setting.

Efficacy studies of the GR intervention indicate its effectiveness for children and families. These studies took place in a variety of early childhood programs, including many that were located in rural communities. In these studies, ECEs were randomly assigned to deliver either the GR intervention with families or engage in typical parent engagement program activities. Rural parents who experienced the GR intervention were observed to be significantly more warm and sensitive in interactions with their children and more supportive of their children's autonomy, and they offered more developmentally appropriate guidance, directives, and learning supports as compared to parents in the control group (Knoche et al., 2012). Additionally, preschool children involved in the GR intervention consistently showed significantly greater gains in social-emotional and behavioral functioning, including a reduction in observed overall unusual or hyperactivity level over time compared to children in comparison classrooms (Sheridan et al., 2010, 2014, 2019). Similarly, these children showed advances in language skills at faster rates than children whose parents did not experience GR (Sheridan et al., 2011).

Teachers and Parents as Partners

Teachers and Parents as Partners (TAPP; Sheridan, 2014), also known as conjoint behavioral consultation (CBC; Sheridan & Kratochwill, 2008), is "a structured, indirect form of service delivery in which parent and teachers are joined to work together to address the academic, social, or behavioral needs of an individual for whom both parties bear some responsibility" (Sheridan & Kratochwill, 1992, p. 122). It is a strengths-based, shared decision-making intervention that emphasizes both the inherent contributions of families and educators for students from preschool to grade three and the development of partnerships as parents and educators work across settings to mutually support children's development and functioning.

In practice, TAPP is delivered in a manner that provides structure to interactions between parents and teachers as they jointly address concerns they share about a child's academic, social, or behavioral functioning. Often supported by an educational specialist or consultant, its implementation is organized around four stages wherein parents and teachers share responsibility for identifying and addressing needs. The first stage, Building on Strengths, involves parents and teachers collaboratively determining a student's strengths and challenges, pinpointing specific target behaviors, and collecting behavioral data to understand the issues that may interfere with children's learning or development. The second stage is referred to as Planning for Success and involves parents and teachers reviewing and analyzing baseline data, setting a behavioral goal, determining conditions that may impede or support children's progress, and jointly establishing home–school plans aimed at promoting academic or behavioral skill development. During the third stage, Plan Implementation, parents and teachers implement codeveloped strategies in their respective settings and maintain communication about their execution and effects. The final stage is Checking and Reconnecting. In this stage, the parent, teacher, and consultant meet to review intervention data, discuss changes in the student's behaviors and progress toward goals, determine the need to continue or modify the plan, and discuss methods to maintain the student's positive growth and the collaboration between parents and teachers.

Research on TAPP has generated data substantiating its efficacy in addressing academic, behavioral, and social concerns of students across both urban and rural contexts. The efficacy of TAPP in rural communities (as defined by the National Center for Education Statistics classification system) was indicated in a randomized controlled trial with early elementary students (grades K-3) and their families. Specifically, significant reductions in school-related problems were reported by teachers of students whose family members participated in TAPP compared to students serving in a "business as usual" control condition (Sheridan, Witt, Holmes,

Coutts et al., 2017). Direct observations in classrooms revealed that compared to students in the control group, those in the TAPP condition made more rapid improvements in on-task and prosocial behaviors, and more rapid decreases in off-task behaviors and motor movements. Parents of students in the TAPP group reported significantly greater rates of improvement in their children's adaptive and social skills at home, compared to their control group counterparts (Sheridan, Witt, Holmes, Wu et al., 2017). Compared to the children receiving business as usual, there was a significant reduction in challenging behaviors (e.g., aggression, tantrums) in the TAPP group, as noted on daily reports from parents.

Rural teachers and parents reported benefits of their involvement in the TAPP process, relative to their control group counterparts. Specifically, rural teachers reported greater rates of improvement in their use of appropriate classroom behavioral strategies (e.g., prepare student for transitions, label student's feelings), competence in addressing student-focused problems (e.g., set goals for the student, gather specific information to measure student's progress), and greater use of positive attention and delivery of rewards over time (Sheridan et al., 2018). Relative to parents in the control group, those who participated in TAPP indicated greater rates of improvements in their own positive parenting practices, ability to engage in problem-solving, and feelings of efficacy in helping their child succeed in school (Sheridan, Witt, Holmes, Wu et al., 2017).

Both parents and teachers who participated as partners in the TAPP process reported significant improvements in their relationships with one another (Sheridan, Witt, Holmes, Coutts et al., 2017; Sheridan, Witt, Holmes, Wu et al., 2017). Importantly, the quality of the relationship for both parents and teachers was found to mediate the effects of TAPP on students' outcomes (Sheridan, Witt, Holmes, Coutts et al., 2017; Sheridan, Witt, Holmes, Wu et al., 2017), indicating the important contribution of the parent-teacher relationships in partnership interventions. Unpacking the relationship variable a bit more, Holmes et al. (2020) reported that rural parent–educator dyads who displayed high and moderate patterns of interactional sensemaking characterized by engaging interactions, turn taking, perspective taking, and coherent communication (Koenig Kellas & Trees, 2006) reported better-quality relationships than those demonstrating low patterns of interactional sensemaking.

Conclusion

For young children, the period from birth to age eight is a time of incredible growth and development. The foundational experiences that take place during this time contribute in lasting ways to children's health and development. Creating meaningful early experiences for young children will support their successful progression through rural educational systems and ultimately support their college and career readiness. This is vital for the livelihood and well-being of rural communities.

Families participate in a variety of early childhood programs that offer supports to young children; however, there is considerable variability in the availability of and access to these services in rural communities. Rural families experience unique challenges related to education, social services, employment, and income. The distinct characteristics of rural settings must inform early childhood education and programming policies and practices if services are to benefit young children and work toward minimizing the readiness gap between rural and nonrural children.

The Bloomsbury Handbook of Rural Education in the United States

Family engagement is one method that can be embedded within rural early childhood programs to support positive outcomes for children. Early efforts to build relationships between parents and children as well as partnerships among parents and rural ECEs are foundational for sustaining these critical connections as children transition out of early childhood programs into and through the formal K-12 educational system.

16

Rural Literacies and Rural Identities

Kim Donehower

Rural literacies research is a small (but growing) subfield of New Literacy Studies (NLS), which positions literacy as a set of social practices and relations around language, rather than focusing on the developmental aspects of encoding and decoding text (Gee, 1991; Street, 1995, 2003). NLS scholars research literacy among all ages and in a variety of contexts but always with an emphasis on the social purposes of literate behaviors.

Rural literacies, then, have come to be defined as literate behaviors with the social purpose of sustaining rural communities (Donehower et al., 2007). This sustenance can deal with psychological, ecological, educational, technological, and economic factors, among others. Corbett and Donehower (2017) documented the state of rural literacies research, reviewing 115 publications with the term "rural literacies" in the abstract. The most common themes that emerged emphasized literacy's potential connections to managing rural identity, building social capital, promoting social justice, and prioritizing rural schooling.

This chapter describes the ways in which literacy has been understood as an important factor in these four areas and the connections of these areas to rural sustainability. It then considers the role of the rural school in sponsoring (Brandt, 1998) these kinds of literate behaviors, describing curricular projects that focus on one or more of these potentialities of rural literacies.

Rural Literacies and Identity

Viewed through popular media and some academic works, rural identity in the United States can be seen as a "spoiled" identity, in Erving Goffman's terms. The title of Goffman's formative work, *Stigma: Notes on the Management of Spoiled Identity* (2009), makes clear the position rural US residents find themselves in. A long representational history of rural people as yokels, hicks, barbarians, rubes, rednecks, and other stereotypes (Batteau, 1990; Donehower, 2007) means that rural identity cannot be simply *lived* in the US context; it must be *managed*. Even positive stereotypes of rural people rooted in nostalgia must be managed since they set rural people aside as living in the past (Eppley, 2010).

The Bloomsbury Handbook of Rural Education in the United States

Literacy has long been seen as a performative means of managing identity (Ferdman, 1990)—for example, through writing to a public audience to dispel stereotypes or privately choosing reading material that runs counter to or complicates typical notions of the interests and intellect of rural people. Communal literate behaviors, such as book clubs or study groups, can also serve these purposes (Donehower, 2013a, 2013b). While it's important to note that some of these literate behaviors may attempt to shift the perceptions nonrural people have about rural communities, it's also salient that even within rural communities, people need means to sort out their particular rural identity. Rural identities are multiple and can run counter not only to urban and suburban notions of rural but also to ideas about rurality rooted in rural communities themselves (Donehower, 2003). These identities include diversities of race, gender and sexual identity, (dis)ability, religion, and language.

Rural identities centered in literacy connect to sustainability in a number of ways. One that is deeply influenced by schooling is rural out-migration. Corbett, along with Kefalas and Carr, have documented what Corbett calls "learning to leave," the tendency of some rural schools to assume, or directly influence, more "literate" rural children (by school standards) to seek opportunities in urban areas (see Carr & Kefalas, 2009; Corbett, 2007). If the literacy behaviors and abilities of these students do not match the school's notion of rural identity, the assumption is made that these students can only enhance and deploy those literacies outside of a rural space. Out-migration of young people is a major demographic threat to sustaining rural communities (Pender et al., 2019), although a smaller trend of "rural return" has been documented (Winchester, 2012).

K-12 literacy projects can assist in the management of rural identity in a number of ways. There are, of course, preservationist projects, such as conducting oral histories, which can build pride of place. But there are also endeavors that can help rural students explore the nuances of rural identity, making space for a multiplicity of rural identities.

David Jolliffe, the former Brown Chair in English Literacy at the University of Arkansas, has implemented multiple literacy projects throughout rural Arkansas; you can read about these in Goldblatt and Jolliffe (2020). Joliffe has a background in theater as well as English and education, and argues that "reading and writing dramatic texts . . . represents the quintessence of literacy experiences" because "when you're reading/writing fiction and most nonfiction, you usually have the advantage of a narrator's voice or an arguer's voice that guides your construction of the text's reality" (Goldblatt & Jolliffe, 2020). But in the creation and/or performance of dramatic texts, one uses words "to create the world," Jolliffe says (Goldblatt & Jolliffe, 2020). Different ways to play a particular character or deliver a certain line allow performers—and perhaps audiences—to play with identity.

Jolliffe describes two such projects in *Literacy as Conversation*. In the first, a rural high school student, Lori Browning, writes a play set in the Arkansas Delta and is linked with a professional playwright at the University of Arkansas who guides her in shaping the script for performance by a professional theater company based in Fayetteville, Arkansas. Jolliffe describes how forty people from Lori's hometown come to the city of Fayetteville to see the play performed, thus giving both rural and urban viewers new ways to think about what "rural" means in the specific Arkansas context.

In a second project, Jolliffe and colleagues recruit students from four rural Arkansas high schools to form "Team Shakespeare" to create a production of *The Tempest* that would be performed in both Augusta (a town of 3,000 centered in a rural region) and Fayetteville (near the campus of the University of Arkansas). The students did some of their own writing as part of learning about the process of putting on the play and created a 20-minute "curtain-raiser" called "The Tempest Tossed." Jolliffe argues that this piece

> told the stories of . . . how their travels and travails helped them come to a deep understanding, not only of how a Shakespeare play works but also of how they bonded by reading, writing, and performing drama together and how the immersive experience made them new kinds of readers and writers, different literate beings than they had ever been before. (Goldblatt & Jolliffe, 2020)

In other words, the immersive reading, writing, and performance of the theater experience, combined with reflection, gave students a new perspective on their literate identities. Instead of consumers of the kinds of "great texts" taught in school, these students were now cocreators with such texts. They could articulate not only the text's influence on them as readers but their influences on the text as performers, producers, and as writers of the "curtain-raiser."

These are only two examples of curricular projects that contribute to the management of rural identities. Any literacy project that offers opportunities for rural students to question and critically reconsider the typical ways rural places and people are represented in terms of, and through, reading and writing would serve this purpose.

Rural Literacies and Social Capital

Reading, writing, and rhetorical savvy can be a means to build social capital in a number of ways. Writers on social capital typically describe these as bonding, bridging, and linking (Putnam, 2001; Woolcock, 2001). Bonding capital provides in-group coherence and commitment; bridging capital can create alliances and relationships among dissimilar groups; and linking capital provides a group access to institutions or entities with power over them.

It is readily apparent how important all three types of social capital are to rural sustainability. Bonding capital strengthens rural groups and creates a strong sense of community; such a sense can be one of the perks of small-town life that prevent out-migration and/or encourage in-migration or cross-migration across rural communities. Bridging capital is vital to create economic and social relationships with people in urban and suburban spaces; such alliances are important both for feeling a sense of connectedness to the "outside world" and because US food, water, and recreational systems depend on connections among rural and urban populations.

Typically, social capital literacies are documented as happening outside K-12 classrooms, in book clubs, writing groups, and internet spaces. For example, a local history-writing group might create bonding capital (Amato, 2002), digital and virtual spaces can create bridging capital (Hibbert, 2013), and community grant-writing can create linking capital. Social capital theorists such as Putnam (2001) typically document the ways social capital is created in "associational groups," and compulsory schooling does not exactly fit the definition of an associational group space.

However, school literacy projects, as already described, can also assist in the exploration and management of rural identity. Similarly, they can lead to a sense of communal identity or bonding capital. An interesting case in point is described in "Rural Media Literacy: Youth Documentary Videomaking as a Rural Literacy Practice" (Pyles, 2016). Every new generation in a rural community has to find ways to "belong" to the local group in some fashion because, as Pyles notes, people in small communities are under much more scrutiny from one another than in more populous spaces. As Pyles describes it, "Rural youths' issues are not so much about standing out among many people to find a sense of who they are; instead, they are about standing within their community to find a sense of who they are" (Pyles, 2016, p. 2).

In the project Pyles documents, Appalachian youth create video documentaries as part of a summer workshop produced by Appalshop, but such projects could also take place within school curricula—especially as "digital literacies" become an expectation of many literacy standards. Pyles writes that the young people's documentaries were expository in nature; she describes these as "an ideal mode for organizations intent on telling particular truths to themselves" (Pyles, 2016, p. 5). While the documentaries can have audiences outside the young people's local communities, they also give the young documentarians a chance to retell "particular truths" to their home communities, in an act of social bonding.

Bonding capital is not the only possibility here, however. Pyles also describes the ways in which the use of video documentary tools and strategies created a sense of belonging to Appalshop. She writes that through their documentaries, "these youth are locating themselves as part of the organizations by using the organizations' past footage and by staying in keeping with themes that the organization has explored before" (Pyles, 2016, p. 7). This is a form of bridging capital on which these young people—and Appalshop—can draw.

Such acts of bonding and bridging, enacted through literacy, refine young people's sense of their connectedness to community and region. I do not want to suggest that these projects will stop the out-migration and "brain drain" that plagues many rural communities, but they can certainly ameliorate the effects of "learning to leave" that Corbett (2007) and Carr and Kefalas (2009) describe. The USDA's own research found that poverty is not the main driver of rural out-migration in the United States; instead, isolation and lack of natural amenities are the factors that distinguish "out-migration counties" (McGranahan et al., 2010). Literacy activities can be one way to strengthen relationships to place and people, reducing perceived isolation, and enhancing appreciation of geography.

Rural Literacies and Social Justice

When it comes to "linking" social capital, which links people to organizations and entities that have power over them in some way (Woolcock, 2001), we move into the realm of social justice. Social justice can take many forms and run in complex, often counter, directions in rural communities. Economic justice for rural communities can be pitted against environmental justice and can pit rural communities against one another, such as when agricultural practices that ensure a good yield in one community have negative effects on a downstream rural place that depends on nature tourism for its economy (Robinson, 1990). Rural cultural traditions can conflict along racial and ethnic lines, as in battles between ranchers and Indigenous tribes over water or mineral rights (Kmetz, 2012). In general, much of the rural literacies research on social justice focuses on economic and environmental injustices wrought by neoliberalism and globalization (e.g., Edmondson, 2003).

Whatever the type or source of injustice, literacy comes into play rhetorically, as the ability to do things with words—reading, writing, and speaking—to "speak to power" and win concessions, reparations, and, possibly, to create linking capital to get a voice at the tables where decisions are made. This involves literate practices that are not only persuasive but create what Welch (2005) calls "rhetorical space" (p. 475) in which to be heard.

In many decision-making venues, rural communities in the United States are often not accorded much rhetorical space. From educational policies that don't account for the characteristics of rural schools (Eppley, 2009; Jimerson, 2005b) to media descriptions of rural broadband access as a potential "cyberbridge to nowhere" (Herszenhorn, 2009), many decisions are made at both corporate and government levels that do not take into account the particularities of rural life and places. Even in states with a large rural base, certain communities may have difficulty getting those in power to take their circumstances into account.

In "Voices of Young Citizens: Rural Citizenship, Schools, and Public Policy," Brooke (2012) gives an example of one school-based literacy project designed to address exactly this situation. As director of the Nebraska Writing Project, a site of the National Writing Project, Brooke collaborated with Nebraska Educational Telecommunications-Television (NET-TV) and the Nebraska Humanities Council to help students from five different rural schools create video segments based on essays they had written about critical issues in their local communities. As Brooke writes, NET-TV provided the "rhetorical space," a particular one that already existed from an earlier statewide project called "Saving Small Towns" (Brooke, 2012, p. 166). In Brooke's description, some of the students' projects blended aspects of identity and social capital building to influence political conversations:

> Central to all three Albion seniors' episodes is the rhetorical strategy of identification, in the Burkean sense of creating a shared common interest through which an audience might "identify with a rhetor, even across distances, and thereby be moved to action" (Burke, 1969). . . .There is some evidence that the Albion seniors' segment did in fact help create a wider conversation about the issue . . . [one student] was invited to read her essay . . . in a public forum devoted to rethinking the historical Homestead Act. (Brooke, 2012, pp. 170–1)

Since the project Brooke describes, the "red state/blue state" discourse of American politics has created new rhetorical barriers for rural places. Rural people's votes have disproportionate influence owing to the electoral college (Kurtzleben, 2016), and social media commentary after Donald Trump's election tended to represent rural political opinion as monolithic, irrational, and racist. Within this climate, it's easy to discount the potential contribution to civil and sensible political conversation on the part of rural citizens. Perhaps new versions of projects such as Brooke's can provide entry points for the nuance of rural voices to be heard.

Rural Literacies and Rural Schooling

As Azano (2015, p. 268) notes of US educators and researchers,

> We have to address rural literacies and the inherent inequities and limited access to funding and resources. On the one hand, we have 21st-century demands telling us that literacies must be cultural, critical, digital, "multiple, dynamic, and malleable" (National Council of Teachers of English, 2013). Yet, on the other hand, we have educational policy that discriminates against rural students. (Jimerson, 2005b)

The Bloomsbury Handbook of Rural Education in the United States

Much rural literacies research has studied "the effects of metrocentrism on education policy, theory, and praxis" (Corbett & Donehower, 2017, p. 6). These effects can be quite severe on the sustainability of both rural schools and, by extension, rural communities. Lyson (2002) describes a host of social, economic, and educational repercussions when a rural community loses its school. Metrocentric education policies and funding formulas accelerate school consolidation, increasing the likelihood of the scenarios Lyson details.

Eppley (2009) documents the consequences for rural schools of the highly qualified teacher provision in the 2001 No Child Left Behind Act (NCLB). In addition to the difficulty many rural schools have in recruiting and retaining a teaching staff that meets the act's "highly qualified" guidelines, Eppley (2009) notes that the act "declar[es] consensus about the role of subject matter knowledge to the exclusion of other factors particularly salient in rural schools" (p. 7). In other words, understandings of the specificities of place—the particular conditions of rural schools—are not valued as part of the "highly qualified" equation.

One common trait among all the rural literacies school projects already described is an intimate knowledge and understanding of rural place. Whether the purpose is to explore identity, create or reinforce social capital, or to participate in conversations about social justice, all these rural literacy projects presume a general understanding of the nature of rurality and a willingness to observe and learn about the particularities of specific rural places. Decontextualized "content knowledge" does not apply; it is the ability to both contextualize content knowledge and let context redefine content that the teacher of rural literacies needs.

A policy brief on what counts as evidence in rural schools "considers the limitations of Evidence Based Practice (EBP) as the foundational philosophy of contemporary education policy in rural schools and suggests Practice Based Evidence as a socially just alternative" (Eppley et al., 2018, p. 36). Similarly to the highly qualified teacher provision of NCLB, evidence-based practice (EBP) attempts to create a standard, in this case of teaching practices, that applies across all contexts of place and community. When it comes to literacy, the success of such practices is measured, in part, by students' literacy performances according to standardized assessments. But such standards have long shown an urban bias and are inevitably affected by the long-held supposition in US education that rural people are inferior most particularly in their *literacy* (Mortensen, 1994; Theobald & Wood, 2010).

In arguing for Practice Based Evidence, the authors note that "considering how to make something work in local contexts suggests an important distinction between rurality as a factor to be overcome as opposed to rurality as a site from which to contribute to more nuanced understanding of instructional practices" (Eppley et al., 2018, p. 38). Similarly, distinctive "rural" qualities of students' literacy practices are not something to be eliminated but something to be understood. In addition to local dialects, many rural places also have distinct rural rhetorics—ways of using language to have certain effects on audiences. In "A Functional Linguistics Approach to Appalachian Literacy," Iddings and Angus (2015) describe how a Systemic Functional Linguistics (SFL) approach in one Appalachian classroom explored the rhetorical effects of Appalachian dialect and aesthetics in "speaking truth to power" effectively about the devastation coal mining can wreak on Appalachian families. Analyzing the Diane Fisher poem "Explosion at Winco No. 9" with students via SFL, Iddings and Angus describe ways in which teachers can bring rural attributes of language and rhetoric within the purview of literacy.

Mobility as a Factor in Rural Literacies Teaching and Research

This chapter has confined its description of rural literacies projects in schools to issues of identity, social capital, and social justice, but there are, of course, other ways to conceptualize how school-based literacy projects might contribute to rural sustainability. For a chapter on rural literacies, there are two important components yet to address, both of which have become preoccupations of geographers: mobility and aesthetics.

Mobility has become a dominant feature of rural places, in contrast to images of rural communities as stable, preserved, and largely unchanging. The "new mobilities paradigm" (Sheller & Urry, 2006) in the social sciences considers the increased physical mobility of people and the mobilities of ideas, information, and relationships through digital means. As Bell and Osti (2010) describe, "mobility is central to the enactment of the rural. Markets, employment, shopping, socialising, schooling, attending church, seeing a doctor, visiting parks: these all require traversing space, often great reaches of it, whether one lives in a rural place or is travelling to one" (p. 199). Increasing school consolidation has only increased the number of miles many students must travel between home and school, often from one rural location to another. But as Bell and Osti also note, rural places themselves, depending on their specific character, economy, and location, are comprised of "migrants, visitors and long-term rural residents alike. Commuters, newcomers and holiday-makers have become central to the life of many rural regions today, although this often entails considerable conflict" (p. 200).

What might this mean for our understanding of rural literacies and the role of rural schools in fostering literacies? On the one hand, increased physical mobility of people seems to warrant teaching the kind of portable, decontextualized literacy standards that rural literacies scholars have resisted. But another way to look at it is that rural communities are comprised by distinctive combinations of the literacy beliefs, practices, and values of the different peoples who inhabit, for however long, that rural space. Much as Heath (1983) found at least three separate ways of practicing and valuing literacy in a small Piedmont mill town, rural towns and schools may serve as the intersection of different types of literacy, each worth exploring and documenting, and perhaps with something to offer the others.

The increased mobility of ideas, information, and relationships that Sheller and Urry describe provides potential access to even more ways of practicing and valuing reading and writing (Donehower & Green, 2016). These are what Brandt (1998) calls "literacy sponsors": "any agents, local or distant, concrete or abstract, who enable, support, teach, model, as well as recruit, regulate, suppress, or withhold literacy—and gain advantage by it in some way" (p. 166). In the new mobility paradigm, physically distant sponsors can access (and be accessed by) rural people through technological means. Green and I assert that the "rural literacies" of a particular rural community "can only be seen and fully scrutinised when they are considered as the product of multiple, overlapping literacy sponsors, many of them geographically remote from the town itself, whose many ways of valuing and practicing literacy must be accepted, rejected, altered, and combined by residents for their own purposes" (Donehower & Green, 2016, p. 573).

This may make rural literacies seem such a complex matter as to be nearly incomprehensible, or perhaps, once again, something that would benefit from some attempt at standardizing certain literacy behaviors and values. The point for rural teachers and researchers, however, is one Eppley makes very well when she redefines the "rural highly qualified teacher":

The Bloomsbury Handbook of Rural Education in the United States

All rural teachers have a special obligation to ground curriculum and instruction in the immediate locality. They have a special obligation to awaken students to the concept of sustainability and to help them develop and nurture a sense of place. This is an urgent requirement of the rural highly qualified teacher and has little to do with test scores and certifications, and everything to do with nurturing students and sustaining communities. (Eppley, 2009, p. 9)

Grounding curriculum, instruction—and research—"in the immediate locality" means accounting for all "local" literacies, including those that flow into, and out of, rural communities within the new mobilities paradigm. It can also mean connecting rural students with new literacy sponsors, much as Brooke connected rural students with Nebraska Educational Television in his "Voices of Young Citizens" project.

Aesthetics as a Factor in Rural Literacies Teaching and Research

While the new mobilities paradigm has influenced the social sciences, what might be called a new landscape paradigm has guided an explosion of research in geography and rural and urban planning. Some examine people's aesthetic preferences for particular landscapes (P. Howley, 2011). Some consider the connection between landscape aesthetics and identity: "Rural identity is also strongly interconnected with the aesthetic quality of rural settlements and the surrounding open landscape. . . . Aesthetically valuable landscapes manifest stronger identity, as they evoke clear and precise mental images (Hagerhall, 2001). This aspect of rural identity is of considerable complexity" (Janečková Molnárová et al., 2017, p. 3).

Literacy practices can play a role in this connection between landscape and identity, configuring people's relationships with, and aesthetic experiences of, certain landscapes (Rautio, 2010b). Artistic literacy endeavors can also enrich and bring meaning to the repetitive practices of "everyday" rural life (Rautio, 2010a). Finding such aesthetic meaning in rural life can help influence attachment to place, whether that results in a choice to stay in a rural community, or to stay connected to it (Donehower, 2013a). In these ways, aesthetic literacy practices that might seem far from the types of critical and digital literacies celebrated in standards documents can have an effect on rural sustainability. Interestingly, even urban and suburban people generally show a preference for landscapes deemed more "rural" (P. Howley, 2011). Since connections and identifications among rural, urban, and suburban people are generally seen as key to rural sustainability (Schell, 2007), literacy projects exploring the aesthetics of rural landscape could be valuable in all types of schools.

The National Council of Teachers of English (2013) offers a definition of literacy in a digital age, asserting that the world demands a literate person be able to

- Participate effectively and critically in a networked world;
- Explore and engage critically, thoughtfully, and across a wide variety of inclusive texts and tools/modalities;
- Consume, curate, and create actively across contexts;
- Advocate for equitable access to and accessibility of texts, tools, and information;
- Build and sustain intentional global and cross-cultural connections and relationships with others so as to pose and solve problems collaboratively and strengthen independent thought;

- Promote culturally sustaining communication and recognize the bias and privilege present in the interactions;
- Examine the rights, responsibilities, and ethical implications of the use and creation of information;
- Determine how and to what extent texts and tools amplify one's own and others' narratives as well as counter unproductive narratives;
- Recognize and honor the multilingual literacy identities and culture experiences individuals bring to learning environments, and provide opportunities to promote, amplify, and encourage these differing variations of language.

Much of this description fits in well with the social justice, social capital, and identity issues with which this chapter has concerned itself. But aside from a brief use of the word "create," there does not seem to be much room here for beauty, for literacy practices that evoke or invoke aesthetic experiences. As rural educators and researchers continue to examine the important ways literacy links to rural sustainability, let us not forget that for many of us, our most formative experiences with texts were ones of beauty, of aesthetic resonance. Let's remember every once in a while to allow ourselves, and our students, to look up from our studies and to fully experience the aesthetic power of our rural places.

17

Trauma-Informed Approaches in Rural Education

Catharine Biddle and Lyn Mikel Brown

Adverse childhood experiences (ACEs) are an important public health issue that affect just under half (45 percent) of all the children under eighteen in the United States (Sacks & Murphey, 2018). Identified as potentially traumatic events in children's lives, ACEs include economic insecurity, institutionalized racism, abuse, neglect, exposure to substance use disorder in the home, and medical illness, among others (Felitti et al., 1998). Furthermore, one in ten children has had multiple experiences with significant adversity, increasing the possibility that these potentially traumatic experiences will overwhelm their ability to cope and result in trauma (Sacks & Murphey, 2018). In the everyday business of responding to mild episodes of stress, children draw on a combination of internal and external systems that constitute resilience, including healthy relationships with adults and family and community assets (Cantor et al., 2018; Heim & Nemeroff, 2002). However, repeated exposure, clustering of adversity (i.e., ACEs that are more likely to co-occur), or compounded disadvantage (i.e., ACEs combined with other chronic stressors such as institutional racism or economic insecurity) may overwhelm children's resilience, causing trauma and leading to maladaptive behaviors and, without intervention, detrimental short- and long-term effects that influence life chances (Hair et al., 2015; Johnson et al., 2013).

Childhood adversity that results in trauma has been associated with long-term negative outcomes. Felitti (2009) argues that there are two primary mechanisms by which these negative outcomes occur. The first is disease that is the result of the experience of chronic stress, which results in elevated levels of cortisol over long periods of time, hypercortisolemia, such as coronary disease or chronic pain. The second mechanism is disease that results from the extended use of maladaptive coping strategies, such as smoking, drug use, or overeating, among others. These maladaptive strategies, while they may meet an individual's immediate need for comfort, have long-term health effects such as type 2 diabetes, coronary disease, or other health problems (Felitti, 2009). Childhood adversity and trauma also negatively influence development through biological stress, particularly health, learning, and behavior (Burke et al., 2011; Larkin et al., 2012; Mersky et al., 2013; Shonkoff et al., 2012).

The concept of compounded stress and the resulting increased occurrence of trauma helps to explain why economically marginalized youth and youth of color may be disproportionately affected by trauma. Institutionalized racism and economic marginalization are a form of childhood adversity and can cause chronic, ongoing stress. Therefore, when other forms of adversity occur, youth already experiencing these forms of chronic stress may be more easily overwhelmed (Sacks & Murphey, 2018).

Trauma-Informed Systems Approaches to Reduce Inequality Related to ACEs

While ideally, every child would grow up safe from psychological or physical harm, it is inevitable that some children will experience adversity. Over the past two decades, trauma-informed care has gained increasing attention as a philosophy of practice in social service, medical, and school settings to address the needs of individuals who have experienced adversity (Cole et al., 2005; Elliot et al., 2005; Muskett, 2014). Trauma-informed care reframes patterns of maladaptive behavior that individuals may manifest in service settings as coping strategies formed under experiences of duress (Fallot & Harris, 2006). For practitioners in these settings, this reframing is often captured in the shift from the question "What's wrong with you?" to "What happened to you?" (Wolpow et al., 2009). Key principles of trauma-informed care include opportunities for empowerment, control, and choice by those receiving services, cultural competence, and respect from providers, as well as a shared emphasis on recovery from trauma, the establishment of safety, and the minimization of opportunities for retraumatization (Elliot et al., 2005). For many service and institutional settings, these principles represent a radical shift in both philosophy and systems of service delivery framed around individual pathology (Chafouleas et al., 2016; Muskett, 2014).

Schools are considered high-leverage institutional contexts for addressing the development of resilience and the mitigation of stress from childhood adversity (Cantor et al., 2018; Chafouleas et al., 2016; Cole et al., 2005). Although healthy, supportive relationships that mitigate trauma can be fostered across the life course, childhood and adolescence are considered particularly sensitive periods and therefore the effects of chronic or toxic stress that result from ACEs can be mitigated through school environments aware enough of its developmental implications to take appropriate action (Cantor et al., 2018). For many schools, however, trauma-informed care represents a radical departure from more typical practices and therefore requires careful planning, training, and support in order to implement (Cole et al., 2005; Dorado et al., 2016).

As more research emerges on the prevalence and implications of childhood adversity, districts and individual schools are taking on this work of shifting their institutional practices toward trauma-informed approaches, sometimes in partnership with external intermediary organizations and sometimes on their own. Studies of these efforts have focused primarily on the ways in which large, urban-based districts or suburban schools with large student enrollment have approached this work of systems change (see Bloom & Sreedhar, 2008; Cole et al., 2005; Dorado et al., 2016; Perry & Daniels, 2016; Stein et al., 2003; Wiet & Ferguson, 2017; Zakszeski et al., 2017). However, there are a handful of studies that examine promising approaches for this work within the context of rural schools and school districts (see Blitz et al., 2018; Morton & Berardi, 2018; Shamblin et al., 2016).

Childhood Adversity in Rural America

Rural America, while quite diverse, faces many common challenges to its vitality in the twenty-first century (Ulrich-Schad & Duncan, 2018). In rural communities dependent on manufacturing, the automation of industrial jobs and the shifting of labor overseas during the past several decades has taken a toll on their local economies (Bailey et al., 2014). In natural resource-dependent communities, the changing technologies of resource extraction have influenced the salary structure and mobility of labor opportunities, leading to rapid boom and bust cycles and unpredictable local opportunity (Brasier et al., 2015; Schafft & Biddle, 2015). Across the nation, fewer independent, small businesses thrive as national retail supercenters with globally integrated supply chains provide more competitively priced goods, contributing to the decline in living wage work and the growth of low-wage, low-skill job opportunities (Corbett, 2007; Goetz & Swaminathan, 2006). While these patterns vary among rural communities and are dependent on regional economies, rural places across the nation have seen falling median incomes and a corresponding rise in economic insecurity for rural families (Tickamyer et al., 2017). As family poverty increases in rural communities, the combination of economic and spatial inequality compounds the challenges of addressing other forms of childhood adversity, particularly related to mental health (Anderson-Butcher et al., 2017).

The effects of these changes have been felt across rural communities and the remaining social institutions that serve them. While networks of social service and mental health provision in rural areas have faced obstacles related to distance or remoteness, these have become increasingly challenging as rural populations experience decline or out-migration, with fewer people to justify the continuance of these services (Flora et al., 2016). Meeting the human service and mental health needs of rural populations has, at the same time, become more complex as new-destination immigrants have settled in some rural places across the United States (Gutierrez, 2016). These populations also require the development and retooling of services to meet their unique needs in culturally responsive ways. As a result, additional pressure has been put on the institutions that remain, such as schools, to broaden their institutional missions to meet these needs through wraparound and whole child services (see Zuckerman et al., 2018). Within accountability structures, schools are increasingly held responsible for student performance that is adversely affected by unmet needs. As a result of accountability and increasing awareness of the effects of childhood adversity, there has been an increasing interest within many rural schools and school districts in transforming their practices to be trauma-informed.

However, rural school systems face a unique array of opportunities and challenges when it comes to transforming their practices, particularly as they relate to implementing principles of trauma-informed care. Distance and remoteness, small faculties and small student enrollments, dense social networks, and close but sometimes ambivalent school-community relationships characterize many rural school systems across the diversity of rural settings in the United States (Biddle & Azano, 2016; Corbett, 2016b; Schafft, 2016; Schafft & Biddle, 2014; Tieken, 2014). Furthermore, educational policies emphasizing fiscal constraint, despite being rhetorically presented as opportunities to enhance organizational clarity of purpose and efficiency, have significantly diminished the capacity of schools as organizations to effectively meet the needs of their students or experiment with shifts in their practices (Zuckerman et al., 2018).

What Constitutes Trauma-Informed Care in a Systems Approach?

Trauma-informed care is a set of practices by human service professionals (including schools, social service providers, or mental or physical health providers) that recognize the effects of adversity on children and adults (Fallott & Harris, 2006; Ko et al., 2008). While trauma-informed care within the context of a therapeutic relationship with a professional mental health provider might include individual skill development through an understanding of the biological systems governing symptomatic behaviors, reliving the trauma through detailed narrative orally or in written form and practicing coping skills (Black et al., 2012; Carrion & Hull, 2010), a trauma-informed systems approach centers trauma in the way it approaches all of its service relationships, recognizing that it is not always possible to know an individual's history or life experiences.

Trauma-informed systems approaches rely on the capacity of institutional environments to embrace and translate into practice value-driven methods to client services to leverage these practices toward healing from chronic stress and adversity and minimize the risk of retraumatization (SAMHSA, 2014). Service environments characterized by these practices support the production in the brain of the hormone and neurotransmitter oxytocin for those they serve, which in turn mitigates the effects of extended exposure to increased levels of the stress hormone cortisol (Osher et al., 2018). For youth-serving institutions, this is especially important as childhood and adolescence are particularly sensitive developmental periods in which healing from adversity can occur (Cantor et al., 2018). There is an emerging literature discussing the key principles that organizations should embrace to guide these practices, informed by the concurrent growth in the literature on adversity.

Principles of Trauma-Informed Care

The primary goals of trauma-informed care are to (a) promote healing of individuals from trauma and (b) avoid retraumatization of individuals through their engagement with the institutional environment (Substance Abuse and Mental Health Services [SAMHSA], 2014). The first essential component of meeting these goals is establishing an environment of *safety* (Australian Childhood Foundation, 2010; Black et al., 2012; Elliott et al., 2005; Raja et al., 2015). Safety, within trauma-informed care, means both physical and emotional safety with no direct threats to which the individual needs to respond within the environment (SAMHSA, 2014). A component of safety is also the perception of providers as trustworthy and respectful of professional boundaries (SAMHSA, 2014). The second of these is *connection*. Healthy relationships have been shown to buffer the negative effects of adversity for children. These relationships consist of healthy attachments formed through collaboration and coregulation (Cantor et al., 2018), or the experience of adults and youth attuning their interactions in ways that sustain connection and intimacy with one another. A third and critically important component of building these healthy relationships is *cultural responsiveness*. Trauma responses may look very different across cultures and it is important for trauma-informed environments to take these differences into consideration (Beehler et al., 2012; Ko et al., 2008). Last, it is important for trauma-informed care to maximize *self-determination and empowerment*, or the ability of those affected by trauma to have choice within their environment about how their needs are met (Elliot et al., 2005) and decisions that are made about their future care (SAMHSA, 2014). In the face of adversity, particularly when that adversity overwhelms an individual's coping skills, a person may experience feelings of powerlessness and loss of control. Trauma-informed care

The Bloomsbury Handbook of Rural Education in the United States

returns control to the person seeking assistance, while also giving them support for skill-building that will help them in the future.

Practices Connected to Trauma-Informed Care

While there is growing evidence for a link between human service practices and healing from trauma, the translation of theory to practice is still being studied. However, it is clear that trauma-informed practices prioritize meeting children and adults where they are in their recovery, and do so holistically, rather than merely responding to specific behaviors or symptoms (Cantor et al., 2018). In a relationship with a professional mental health provider focused on healing from trauma, individuals might work through the identification of their triggers, develop self-relaxation techniques, practice methods for regulating and expressing emotions, identify thought patterns unhelpful to recovery, and make plans for future skill development (Muskett, 2014). Trauma-informed systems approaches, by contrast, focus on (1) equipping practitioners with the awareness sensitivity necessary to respond to symptomatic behavior in individuals in a thoughtful, responsive, and relational manner, (2) creating opportunities for some universal skill-building within the context of their service provision, and (3) helping practitioners connect individuals or families with more intensive supports as needed (Anderson et al., 2015; Blitz et al., 2018; Bloom & Sreedhar, 2008; Dorado et al., 2016; Shamblin et al., 2016).

An important first step toward cultivating a trauma-informed system is the mindset shift in the provider from viewing a person's behaviors and symptoms as ingrained pathology or character flaws to understanding them as ways of coping with a traumatizing developmental ecology (Australian Childhood Foundation, 2010; Baweja et al., 2016; SAMHSA, 2014). Cultivating trauma sensitivity also encompasses revising one's own responses to those behaviors to prioritize connection and relationality, rather than censure or correction. Enhancing practitioner toolsets for universal skill-building is one way of enriching the trauma-informed environment as well as providing opportunities for self-determination and empowerment for those being served. Typically, universal skill-building includes opportunities for mindfulness, emotional awareness activities, practice expressing emotions, role plays, or other expressive tools in the service environment (Durlak et al., 2011; Walkley & Cox, 2013). Finally, creating more connected organizations with better pathways to support families and manage individual cases is often an important part of trauma-informed systems approaches (Ko et al., 2008). Depending on the type of organization, this can include links with mental health providers and organizations, connections with educational institutions, basic needs provision, or other organizations that will help address individual recovery needs, mitigate additional adversity, and promote physical and emotional safety (Shamblin et al., 2016).

Centering Rurality in Trauma-Informed Systems Change Efforts: A Case Study

While fostering healthy relationships within the institutional context of school may seem, at first glance, self-contained, the socio-spatial context in which this occurs has a profound influence on the array of opportunities and challenges to this work. Rural communities in the United States share several common features that routinely affect school change efforts: (a) a social and institutional context defined by distance and sometimes remoteness; (b) smaller staff numbers serving smaller numbers of students; (c) dense social networks with strong bonding and weaker bridging capital, within which social exclusion has profound personal effects; and (d) close but often ambivalent relationships between the school and the local community. We explore these features and their impact on school transformation through the lens of a rural community-informed education initiative designed to create supportive learning environments for children challenged by adversity, stress, and trauma (Biddle et al., 2018; Brown & Flaumenhaft, 2019).

Our case example focuses on Seabrook, a small, racially and ethnically diverse pre-K to sixth-grade school in a high-poverty rural community in northeastern New England. The school enrolls 114 students, 68 percent of whom are eligible for free and reduced-price lunch and 30 percent of whom are children of Latinx farmworkers who chose to leave the migrant stream and settle in the community over the past few decades. The project embeds a trauma-informed instructional coach and part-time mental health professional in the school to work closely with administration, teachers, students, as well as caregivers to build on inherent strengths, expand and deepen existing relationships, and create healthier ecologies for young people.

Distance and Remoteness

Distance and remoteness are often one of the defining features of rural life (Lichter & Brown, 2011; Schafft, 2016). Policies to address challenges to youth well-being tend to downplay the difficulties posed by remoteness and distance (sometimes called spatial inequality) in their formulation of interventions or solutions. In Seabrook, as in other rural communities, lack of public transit and a reliance on family vehicles limits the mobility of rural youth and their access to doctors, food pantries, social and educational programs, mental health providers, and dentistry (Arcury et al., 2005; Bischoff et al., 2004; Hauenstein et al., 2007). For example, the closest mental health service is 35 miles away, with wait-lists of seven to eight months. There are seven dentists serving a county population of 32,000, covering 3,258 square miles. Economically insecure families in Seabrook travel nearly 40 miles to take advantage of an annual free dental clinic. For families without reliable transportation, even this is an insurmountable challenge (Braveman et al., 2010).

Smaller Staff Numbers Serving Small Numbers of Students

Rural schools are typically smaller than schools in other locations due to declining populations and out-migration (Brown & Schafft, 2011). They tend to employ fewer staff and have flatter administrative structures with little-to-no central office support (Starr, 2015; Surface & Theobald, 2014). Until this past year, Seabrook employed a teaching principal—every afternoon she taught a full slate of classes—a not uncommon reality in rural schools (Rhoda, 2017). Seabrook has a front office administrative assistant but no assistant principal, no school nurse, social worker, or other specialists. One English Learner (EL) education teacher serves all schools in the district. A guidance counselor, shared among schools in the district, visits the school one day a week (Camera, 2016). School staff and faculty take on many roles that go beyond those typically seen in a larger organizational structure in order to offer similar opportunities and services (Preston & Barnes, 2017; Starr, 2015). For example, the administrative assistant informally serves as the school nurse and case manager for families; teachers and the principal take on counselor and social work responsibilities (and without training), while teachers and ed techs work in the afterschool program and coach sports teams (Parson et al., 2016).

Teacher shortages in rural areas continue to be a national policy issue (Biddle & Azano, 2016). Because of the multiple roles rural educators and administrators play, in addition to few

The Bloomsbury Handbook of Rural Education in the United States

fiscal resources and little training and support in the face of childhood adversity, burnout is always a risk (Garwood et al., 2018). Teacher retention and mitigating burnout are critical issues for rural schools because of the challenges that weaker teacher and staff labor markets present to hiring (Fowles et al., 2014). Because of their remote rural location and comparatively low salaries, Seabrook chronically struggles to find qualified applicants for teacher positions. As a result, staff stay on beyond their planned retirement dates and substitute teachers become stand-ins for unfilled staff positions.

Dense Social Networks

Rural communities are typically characterized by dense networks of tightly clustered social ties. The closeness, familiarity, and enduring nature of these relationships is often a source of community pride and perceived as a strong asset for both rural community life and rural community development (Tieken, 2014). Typically referred to as bonding social capital (Flora et al., 2016), dense networks of social ties in Seabrook are leveraged in a variety of ways, including informal social service provision (through neighborly support or community fund-raising); finding work in this close-knit fishing and agricultural community, especially during thin labor markets (Agnitsch et al., 2006); and sustaining informal, part-time livelihood strategies that are common in rural labor markets with high rates of unemployment (Thiede et al., 2016).

However, Sherman (2009) argues that moral capital may play an important role in social relationships in rural communities, with certain behaviors stigmatizing families such that it limits their access to work and other important social resources necessary for survival. The opioid epidemic has hit Seabrook especially hard. Public perception and the threat of community sanction yields a high degree of social control and limits the ways in which economically insecure families take advantage of addiction management services and recovery programs. The possibility of social exclusion has economic as well as social consequences and therefore may be avoided even at the expense of assistance. Access to mental health services, already so difficult to manage, is stigmatized because of the precariousness of drawing attention to what is socially regarded as a family's private struggles or worries about the consequences of attention from child welfare services.

Racism plays a role in exclusion from the community as well. In Seabrook, as in other rural communities, new-destination immigrants from Mexico and Central America are met with expectations that they culturally assimilate with White residents (Lichter, 2012; Massey, 2008). White residents remain in control of local power structures, including school boards, town councils, and other administrative positions. These power dynamics contribute to additional challenges to informal and formal social service provision. While a local nonprofit provides access to essential services for immigrants and farmworkers, Latinx families and workers experience institutionalized racism in school and in the structure, administration, and disparate access to county, state, and federal services (Mader, 2018).

Close, Ambivalent School-Community Relationships

Schools, as one of the few public social institutions within rural communities, can serve as powerful allies in reducing the effects of spatial inequality on mental and physical health for youth, particularly as spatial inequality intersects with other challenges, such as economic inequality. The majority of children aged five to eighteen physically attend school and are provided transportation to and from the school building. Most schools have some mechanisms for engaging families in their work, albeit with varying effectiveness. School is therefore a powerful site for overcoming the challenges of remoteness and distance that characterize many rural places. However, as in Seabrook, schools are also often one of the largest employers in rural areas and are financed using local tax dollars. As such, their work is subject to a high degree of public scrutiny, and teachers are often the best paid workers in the area (McHenry-Sorber & Schafft, 2015). In Seabrook, support for ELs and educational programs designed to address representation and inclusion of the Latinx community receive a large share of such scrutiny. Also controversial are efforts to support students with special needs, those who experience signs of trauma, and basic need support for those who live in economically precarious households. Class differences between teachers and families in the community can lead to powerful and enduring assumptions about students' home lives and, in particular, lend themselves to explanations that favor "culture of poverty" hypotheses to explain student behavior and performance (Gorksi, 2013).

Future Directions for Research

Taken together, these four factors affect rural school systems' ability to implement existing trauma-informed systems approaches. Much of the research on trauma-informed system approaches has been conducted in urban or residential treatment settings; therefore, it is not clear which strategies may be feasibly implemented in rural settings, with the resources, social realities, and organizational capacity unique to rural schools and communities. Specialized programs designed to account for rural institutional and social differences are needed in order to reduce inequalities related to childhood adversity in rural settings. This is particularly critical given the ways in which co-occurring adversity compounds for children of color and economically marginalized youth. It is too often the case that, as new knowledge emerges that informs and changes youth-serving practices, the way in which this knowledge will translate to rural contexts is an afterthought. Studies of trauma-informed systems that center on schools is an emerging field; it is critical that rural schools and communities be a part of the formation of best practice in the field.

18

Rural School-Based Mental Health

Models of Prevention, Intervention, and Preparation

Jayne Downey, Anna Elliott, Rebecca Koltz, and Kirsten Murray

Mental Health Needs in Rural Contexts

The rural places called home by sixty million people in the United States are defined by the US Census Bureau (2017b) and the National Center for Education Statistics (n.d.) as areas both with low population density and located a significant distance from large metropolitan areas. However, "rural" is not a monolithic construct; it cannot be demarcated simply by geographical and population parameters alone. Rather, across the nation, rural communities and their schools have complex and dynamic cultures shaped by distinct social, economic, political, cultural, and historical relations. These communities, while rich with unique strengths and assets, also demonstrate wide contextual variations in important attributes such as geographic and professional distances, community size and amenities, salaries, broadband internet access, health disparities, and poverty rates.

Mental health issues are a growing critical concern for rural communities, their families, and students. Diverse rural areas report higher rates of death by suicide (Fontanella et al., 2015) and levels of substance abuse and overdose (Lambert et al., 2008). Studies suggest that for adolescents diagnosed with a mental health issue, their treatment outcomes are potentially compromised (Sanchez et al., 2018) due to geographical barriers to effective care (Hefflinger et al., 2015). Experts also indicate that the "urgent need for effective mental healthcare in rural settings . . . goes largely unmet" (Siceloff et al., 2017, p. 21). This chapter reviews some of the key barriers to the delivery of rural mental health services connected to limitations in availability, accessibility, and acceptability of services. It then describes a School-Based Mental Health (SBMH) model providing prevention and intervention services that can mitigate these barriers in rural schools and communities. The chapter concludes with a review of a promising model of a research-based, place-conscious approach for preparing and sustaining the next generation of rural SBMH professionals.

Barriers to Mental Health Services in Rural Contexts

The need for reliable mental health services in rural contexts is clear. Yet rural communities face significant barriers that prevent them from receiving adequate services (Siceloff et al., 2017). This disparity between rural mental health needs and services has been shaped by five main factors: availability, accessibility, affordability, accommodation, and acceptability (Penchansky & Thomas, 1981). Specifically, rural communities experience limited *availability* of providers/specialists, difficulties in *accessibility* due to geographic distances and costs incurred for travel time and resources, limited *accommodations* of service delivery to meet specific clients' needs, such as appointment times and hours of operation, *affordability* disparities in the clients' access to insurance and/or ability to pay for services, and the limited *acceptability* of services due to stigma attached to mental health care in the face of cultural values of independence and self-reliance (National Rural Health Association [NRHA], 2015; Penchansky & Thomas, 1981; Siceloff et al., 2017). These factors contribute to delayed initiation of services by rural community members resulting in an increase in symptom severity requiring a more intense and sometimes expensive treatment protocol (NRHA, 2015). In considering how to develop models and protocols that allow students in rural schools and communities to receive appropriate mental health services, it is valuable to consider each of these barriers, both independently and in relationship to one another.

Lack of Availability of Mental Health Providers
While the shortage of mental health providers is of concern to regions all across the country, the shortages "disproportionately affect rural areas and reduce the availability, accessibility, and acceptability of mental healthcare options for all rural community members" (Siceloff et al., 2017, p. 20). Because the specific mental health needs of rural communities have only received serious consideration and examination in recent years (Gamm et al., 2010; Siceloff et al., 2017), a complete understanding of all the intersecting factors that contribute to the disparity of services between rural and nonrural settings is still developing. The issue is complex and nuanced, and recent research is providing insight into factors that contribute to lower availability of mental health services in rural communities (e.g., Brems et al. 2006; Fontanella et al., 2015; Gamm et al., 2010, Hefflinger et al., 2015; Siceloff et al., 2017).

Rural communities often struggle to recruit and retain mental health providers (Gamm et al., 2010; NRHA, 2015; Siceloff et al., 2017). National data indicates that only 25 percent of rural counties have a practicing psychiatrist, and even fewer are able to recruit and retain a child psychiatrist (NRHA, 2015). These data also indicate a scarcity of psychologists, counselors, and social workers in rural settings. Barriers to recruitment and retention identified in one study include local or national competition (referring to alternative employment options that involve better pay and/or less isolation); difficulties in dealing with Medicaid-related issues (challenges of balancing lower reimbursement rates and greater paperwork requirements in limited caseload capacity); lack of appropriate preparation (clinical training and supervision) providing insight regarding rural contexts and resources to address specific concerns and/or barriers; lack of resources for complex cases; isolation; cultural differences; and impact on spouses' ability to find employment (Watanabe-Galloway et al., 2015).

Mental health providers in rural settings have also reported a variety of stressors and barriers to sustaining employment over time (Breen & Drew, 2012; Gamm et al., 2010; Pearson &

The Bloomsbury Handbook of Rural Education in the United States

Sutton, 1999) such as resource limitations, confidentiality limitations, overlapping roles (e.g., functioning in nonprofessional community roles alongside clients or clients seeking help in nonprofessional community settings), provider travel, service accessibility given client distances and/or ability to afford services, training constraints, and patient avoidance of care (Brems et al., 2006). Additionally, professional isolation and a lack of opportunities for collaboration negatively contribute to the retention of mental health providers in rural communities (Gamm et al., 2010; Pearson & Sutton, 1999; Siceloff et al., 2017). In examining the interaction of these factors, it is important to recognize that a scarcity of providers in rural settings leads to heavy caseloads for the few available providers, with a wide variety of client presentations that may fall outside of providers' scope of training or expertise, accompanied by a lack of consistent professional support or collaboration. A study examining the roles of rural school counselors found that the small size and limited resources of rural schools contribute to limited opportunities for collaboration, role ambiguity, or blurred boundaries between roles within the school (Pearson & Sutton, 1999). It is important to note that while advantages such as fewer layers of administrative hierarchy, direct contact with staff, ease of access to others, and greater autonomy and freedom were identified in rural contexts, they were found insufficient to fully offset the potential challenges that mental health providers may experience.

In addition to a lack of professional support and satisfaction, mental health providers' personal wellness is also a relevant factor. In order to serve rural communities, mental health providers have two options: living in the rural communities where they serve or living elsewhere and traveling to the rural community or communities. For those who live in the same community where they serve, mental health providers are likely to see their clients outside the clinical setting, increasing the challenge of maintaining professional boundaries and separation of roles (Brems et al., 2006; Gamm et al., 2010; NRHA, 2008; Pearson & Sutton, 1999). This may limit the providers' potential for their own social network and increase a sense of social isolation. Mental health providers who choose to commute to a rural setting have a greater ability to separate their professional and personal lives; however, they must deal with significant travel time that can be "burdensome" (Brems et al., 2006, p. 114). Thus, it is evident that each of these stressors can have a compounding effect and can contribute to mental health providers feeling overwhelmed and experiencing compassion fatigue (the negative impacts on a helper's well-being due to work-related burnout and secondary traumatic stress), making them less effective and less likely to retain their positions (NRHA, 2008; Sprang et al., 2011).

The increased use of telehealth for prescription and therapy services has provided some options for increasing access to mental health services in rural communities. Still, this approach has several limitations: (a) the lack of consistently available high-speed internet; (b) challenges in building a therapeutic alliance and potential discomfort experienced by clients when discussing vulnerable topics through video technology; and (c) licensure and insurance barriers that make coverage of services through telehealth difficult for clinicians and clients alike (Siceloff et al., 2017).

Difficulties in Accessibility, Accommodation, and Affordability of Mental Health Services

The scarcity of mental health providers in rural areas is directly related to the burden of accessing care. Not only does the demand exceed supply, but the challenges rural residents experience when seeking and accessing care can result in fatigue, delays, and in some cases no service at all. Rural residents often have limited options for mental health services within their community and are forced to commute large distances to access services (Gamm et al., 2010; Fontanella et al., 2015; Siceloff et al., 2017). Community members' ability to commute depends on multiple factors, including reliable transportation (either personal or public), financial means to afford travel costs, and a work schedule that allows for travel time (Fontanella et al., 2015; Hefflinger et al., 2015; Siceloff et al., 2017). Further, rural residents' ability to accommodate to rural mental health provider parameters of operation (appointment wait times, response times, clinic hours, and methods of delivery) may also be limited, ultimately decreasing the mental health care available and accessible to rural residents (Penchansky & Thomas, 1981). There simply is less of an opportunity to "shop around" to find someone that fits requirements for availability, schedule, proximity, and budget.

In addition to challenges posed by geographical distances, access can be further inhibited by finding affordable services with limited financial resources. Rural families may be more likely to have lower incomes than urban or nonrural populations because of smaller economic networks and limited job availability in rural towns. Insurance plans are also less likely to cover mental health services (Fontanella et al., 2015). For rural residents who may be reluctant about seeking out mental health services, these cost barriers may prevent them from accessing the care they need.

Limited Acceptability in Seeking Out Mental Health Services

Reticence toward seeking mental health services in rural communities is not uncommon and is related to the lack of anonymity in rural settings and the stigma associated with experiencing mental illness and seeking help (Breen & Drew, 2012; Brems et al., 2006; Fontanella et al., 2015; Siceloff et al., 2017). Client avoidance of mental health services has been found across both urban and rural settings but is reported as a more significant barrier in rural environments (Brems et al., 2006; Fontanella et al., 2015; Gamm et al., 2010; Siceloff et al., 2017). Mental health concerns can be seen as less legitimate than physical concerns and may be viewed as something that should be managed privately. Given that self-reliance and rugged individualism have been espoused as important American values, particularly among rural residents (Brems et al., 2006), some rural community members may be more likely to view help-seeking behaviors as an indication of weakness (Fontanella et al., 2015; Gamm et al., 2010). To further compound the issue, it can be difficult to seek out mental health services privately in a small community. The lack of anonymity in a rural setting can serve as an additional deterrent for residents to seek out mental health services (Brems et al., 2006; Gamm et al., 2010; NRHA, 2015).

Rural School-Based Mental Health (SBMH) Services

One approach to addressing the challenges of availability, access, and affordability associated with traditional community-based mental health service delivery in rural contexts is through the development of SBMH services and programs. This strategy incorporates coordinated comprehensive mental health services that can be provided by a team of specialists to rural students, and in some cases to their families, during the school day and in the school building (e.g., Michael et al., 2009; Owens et al., 2013).

SBMH services and programs for rural schools are developed through the collaboration of district and school professionals, including administrators, educators, and specialized instructional support personnel (e.g., school psychologists, school social workers, school counselors, school nurses and other school health professionals), in strategic collaboration with students, families, and community health and mental health partners. (Hoover et al., 2019, p.10)

SBMH services are provided during school hours by either mental health specialists employed by the district or community-based specialists employed by an outside agency such as a Comprehensive School and Community Treatment (CSCT) program. Using this design, SBMH programs have the capacity to offer an accessible, team-based approach to address rural student and family mental health concerns. Additionally, the school system allows for multiple adults in a child's life to observe potential issues and offer validation and support from a range of social roles (Lee et al., 2009). SBMH models acknowledge and highlight how each member of the school system team can play a positive role in supporting students' well-being. SBMH arrangements increase students' access to mental health and/or intensive outpatient treatment in a convenient, private manner with as little negative impact on instruction as possible through shorter sessions or alternating the class sessions from which the student is pulled (Capps et al., 2019). As more services move into the school setting (food banks, medical care, dentistry), mental health services are no exception. While providers must remain vigilant about confidentiality in school settings, there is also an opportunity for increased privacy. Rather than being seen at an office specifically designated for mental health care in a rural community (where word can travel fast), students and their families can access to mental health care in the school where their attendance cannot be singled out for a specific cause.

SBMH services are effective in addressing the unique needs of rural students and can help to overcome some of the barriers that prevent them from receiving consistent and effective mental health services (Albright et al., 2013; Belhumeur et al., 2017; Capps et al., 2019; Isaac et al., 2009; Lee et al., 2009; Owens et al., 2008; Owens et al., 2013; Sale et al., 2014). Research has shown positive mental health outcomes for the majority of students who participate in SBMH services (Albright et al., 2013) as well as improvement in academic outcomes (Michael et al., 2013; Richardson et al., 2012) and reductions in discipline and attendance problems (Michael et al., 2013). Furthermore, in a meta-analysis of the effectiveness of SBMH services for elementary-aged children, Sanchez et al. (2018) found that overall, school-based services demonstrated a small-to-medium effect in decreasing mental health problems. These effects were found for targeted intervention (i.e., services for students identified as having a mental health problem) and selective prevention (services for students identified at risk for mental health problems according to results of a referral or screening). Notably, strong effect sizes were found when addressing problems with externalized symptomology (hyperactivity, aggression, opposition) in collaboration with teachers where services were integrated into academic instruction, contingency management, and implemented multiple times per week (Sanchez et al., 2018). In light of recent data that suggest that 50 percent of psychiatric disorders present before age fourteen (Guerrero et al., 2019), there is a strong rationale for the implementation of SBMH programs and services for rural schools to provide much needed intervention and prevention for a vulnerable population.

Rural School-Based Mental Health

Successful Programs and Protocols for Rural SBMH Delivery
The SBMH model is a systemic approach that addresses rural students' mental health needs and vulnerabilities through increased access to prevention and intervention services and multiple points of contact to effectively engage with mental health issues (Fontanella et al., 2015; Gamm et al., 2010; Hefflinger et al., 2015; Hirsch, 2006; Lambert et al., 2008; NRHA, 2015). SBMH systems offer a networked approach to providing mental health interventions, as well as a set of prevention strategies through the engagement of school personnel and the students' extended support systems.

Prevention
Types of prevention approaches relevant to student mental health are classified as universal, selective, or indicated methods. *Universal prevention* is aimed at the general school population with the goal of raising awareness about mental health issues and increasing protective factors. *Selective prevention* is designed to attend to students with various risk factors that may make them vulnerable to mental health distress, and *indicated prevention* is provided for those who are displaying active signs of suicidality or acute mental distress (Robinson et al., 2013; Saeki et al., 2011; Sanchez et al., 2018).

Studies have found that universal prevention methods specifically aimed at increasing awareness and reducing stigma have shown an increase in student likelihood to seek out support when feeling suicidal (Robinson et al., 2013). However, there is also some evidence that such curricula, when presented in a large group/assembly format, have the potential to negatively affect students vulnerable to suicide risk and self-harm behaviors as they may not have an opportunity to delve further with the information and its personal impact with a trained mental health provider (Sanchez et al., 2018; Shaffer & Gould, 2000). Universal prevention methods that have been found to be most effective are those that focus on building prosocial development and emotional awareness by focusing on increasing protective factors rather than reducing vulnerability (Gibson et al., 2015). Psychoeducation that specifically targets social-emotional learning has also been found to produce positive social outcomes and reduced aggression and disruptive behavior in schools (Gibson et al., 2015). Studies have shown that in the context of elementary schools, the integration of social and emotional learning into the classroom curricula has been successful in reducing student mental health concerns (Sanchez et al., 2018).

Considering these findings, effective SBMH programs can address mental health issues through judicious use of universal prevention and carefully designed targeted approaches. For instance, small counseling groups run by mental health clinicians or school counselors that address specific mental health issues may be more appropriate than curricula delivered via a school-wide assembly. This approach allows for more individualized attention to students who are especially impacted by the information and ensures that a mental health provider, trained for focused intervention, facilitates the process.

Screening programs are another prevention strategy that may identify students who are at risk for mental health distress or suicidality who might otherwise not come forward (Robinson et al., 2013). While students with externalizing/behavioral issues are likely to be offered mental health services, students with more internal presentations of distress, such as depression or anxiety, are more likely to be overlooked (Lee et al., 2009). Screening also increases the likelihood of students accessing mental health services earlier, when an issue is less severe, and thus increasing the chances of a positive outcome (Gilbody et al., 2006). Prevention efforts not only protect children and adolescents from distress and the risk of suicide, but they also have the potential for helping them develop long-lasting coping strategies that will support them into adulthood. Over time, this has the potential to positively impact a rural community on a systemic level, increasing norms in help-seeking behavior and implementing interventions much sooner, so less severe cases accumulate. As systems move toward prevention efforts, fewer resources are necessary for crisis response, and mental health providers are able to intervene earlier. Ultimately, prevention efforts are designed to serve many rather than orienting resources to a few in crisis. Increasing prevention efforts results in more responsive networks and strategies readily available to students and their families.

The PATHS (Promoting Alternative Thinking Strategies) curriculum is an example of an evidence-based universal prevention program that has shown effectiveness in enhancing rural elementary students' social and emotional development (Gibson et al., 2015; Greenberg et al., 1995; Kam et al., 2004). The curriculum is designed to reach students at an early age to build a strong foundation of emotional competence. Studies testing the effectiveness of the curriculum have found it useful across traditional and special education classrooms and intervening with low- and high-risk students. PATHS curriculum improved students' "vocabulary and fluency in discussing emotional experiences, their efficacy beliefs regarding the management of emotions, and their developmental understanding of some aspects of emotions" (Greenberg et al., 1995, p. 117).

The program is based on the integration of affective, behavioral, and cognitive understanding as it translates into social and emotional development of children (Greenberg et al., 1995). This aspect of child development is understood as beginning with emotional processing, followed by the ability to integrate emotional awareness with cognition, and the verbalization of these emotional experiences. Children then develop the awareness of how their own emotions are distinct from others as well as the differences between needs and desires. Children who are supported in this process in a healthy way are able to begin internally regulating based on their growing capacity for noticing and naming their experience through cognition. This can facilitate children's abilities to express themselves and advocate to have their needs met in socially appropriate ways. Research indicates that children with healthy demonstrations of social skills who appear well-adjusted and perform well in school also exhibit higher levels of emotional awareness than children who display disruptive behavior, anxiety, and depression, or who are known to have been physically abused (Greenberg et al., 1995).

The PATHS model is based upon four assumptions:

- Children's ability to understand and discuss emotions is related to and influenced by their behavior. For example, when emotions are understood and discussed, they can be managed and regulated, ultimately decreasing problematic behavior; when the opposite is true, problematic behaviors can escalate and as they build the ability to discuss and regulate emotions is more challenging.
- Children's ability to manage, understand, and discuss emotions operates under developmental constraints and is also affected by socialization practices.
- Children's ability to understand their own and others' emotions is a central component of effective problem solving.

- The school environment is a fundamental ecology and one that can serve as a central locus of change. (Greenberg et al., 1995, p. 120)

Different versions of the curriculum are available based on student grade, with varying numbers of units that focus on self-control, emotions, and problem solving (Greenberg et al., 1995). Studies that test the effectiveness of the PATHS model have found that after one school year, rural elementary school students improve their range of emotional language, the ability to discern when it is appropriate to conceal, regulate, or adjust their emotional experience, and their ability to detect emotional cues from others (Gibson et al., 2015; Greenberg et al., 1995; Kam et al., 2004). Some evidence has demonstrated that students who entered the program with less problem behavior showed greater improvements in prosocial behavior (Gibson et al., 2015; Raimundo et al., 2013), suggesting that universal approaches may be best suited for students with healthier social-emotional skills in place, and that longer-term interventions are needed for children with higher levels of problematic behavior.

Intervention

Intervention in a school system is understood as a set of specific methods utilized by trained mental health clinicians and support staff in response to acute presentation of distress in a manner that is appropriate to the school context. It is important to note that SBMH interventions are directly related to the availability of trained mental health providers, their defined roles in the school, and the level of support from the administration to address student mental health needs. Given that the combination of these factors varies according to different school contexts, the delivery of interventions also varies due to the attitudes and availability of stakeholders in the system.

Mental health providers in a SBMH system may include psychologists, social workers, or counselors hired either by the school or through a contract with a local agency to provide intervention for the more acute mental health presentations within the school system. In many instances, these licensed professionals work in collaboration with one another and bill for services through Medicaid or private insurance, alleviating the school from the financial responsibility of care (Siceloff et al., 2017).

However, in rural schools with limited resources, access to a network of mental health professionals may not be an option. In these situations, the primary mental health professional may be the school counselor. According to the American School Counselor Association (n.d.), a school counselor's role includes classroom lessons focused on success and emotional education, short-term counseling, referrals for longer-term mental health support, and collaboration with students' families. School counselors are trained to manage short-term mental health issues and refer students to outside care if the mental health issues are deemed as more serious or pose a safety risk.

When the school counselor serves as the school's primary mental health professional, agreement must be reached with the school administration regarding expectations for the school counselor's level of intervention when students present with more serious mental health issues. School counselors may find themselves working to manage large caseloads of students and must constantly decide how to best spend their limited resources, often navigating pulls on their time whereby saying yes to one need is the equivalent to saying no to another. In some instances, initiating long-term therapeutic relationships with a small percentage of students leaves a majority of the students in the school without regular prevention and intervention efforts. However, when there are no practical referral sources available for students, school counselors must consider whether the services they can provide are preferable to no services at all (Owens et al., 2013).

Another type of intervention is known as postvention, referring to a system's response after a major crisis that affects many or all students (Robinson et al., 2013), such as a peer's death, a natural disaster, or a school shooting. There is limited research available that verifies the most effective practices for this type of crisis, but several practices have been anecdotally identified in the literature as being helpful. These interventions include education or therapy-oriented group sessions, individual sessions for students and families, and the use of external professionals (American Foundation for Suicide Prevention and Suicide Prevention Resource Center, 2011; Robinson et al., 2013).

The PEACE (Prevention of Escalating Adolescent Crisis Events) protocol is an example of an evidence-based program used in rural schools that provides tools for evaluation of suicidal, homicidal, and self-injury risks (Capps et al., 2019). The PEACE protocol also provides a guided decision-making process for intervention.

The PEACE protocol uses a color-coded system to identify risk severity—Green, Yellow, Orange, and Red. Green is characterized by suicidal ideation or thought with no intent or plan. Yellow denotes suicidal ideation with unclear plans or no plans. Orange indicates suicidal ideation, with plans and some access to means. Red indicates all three—suicidal ideation, with a plan, and clear access to means. The level of risk is assessed through self-report and other reports, counselor observations, and clinical history (Capps et al., 2019).

Intervention varies based upon protective and risk factors for each student. Steps range from removal of means, initiating parent/caretaker meetings, and making nonschool-related referrals if further treatment is needed to include in-patient care. The treatment program also includes scaffolded responses to care after major intervention (such as in-patient care) that include plans for safe reentry to school after in-patient services and initiating regular safety check-ins and plans for reentry. During the entire protocol, communication with the student is clear and direct. Capps et al. (2019) found that the PEACE protocol was effective in stopping rural youth death by suicide due to its direct approach with clear steps.

Rural Education for Mental Health Professionals

While widespread adoption of the SBMH model in rural schools would be ideal, implementation is limited by the scarcity of available rural mental health providers and specialists. Studies that explore the experience of counselors and mental health professionals in rural schools and communities have found that strong self-efficacy is crucial to successful practice in rural contexts, and networking, seeking support, and consultation are all key to maintaining self-efficacy in a rural SBMH setting (Breen & Drew, 2012; Morrissette, 2000; Pearson & Sutton, 1999; Sutton, 1988; Sutton & Pearson, 2002; Sutton & Southworth, 1990). Carefully structured place-conscious professional preparation is a significant contributor to the development of mental health professionals' self-efficacy. Research suggests that counselor education programs seeking to prepare mental health professionals for rural contexts consider the following place-conscious recommendations: include rural-specific content and culture in coursework; introduce students to the need to prepare for broad roles; provide rural internships; emphasize the value (and necessary investment) of peer supervision and mentorship; and demonstrate the effective use of technology as means to network and encourage continuing education (Breen & Drew, 2012). Providing specific training about rural life implications for mental health practice is a key component to building the self-efficacy necessary to engage in place-conscious mental health practice. Given the connection between professional preparation and eventual professional practice, one approach to reducing the scarcity of rural professionals is a research-based place-conscious approach to preparing and sustaining SBMH professionals for rural contexts.

The Rural Mental Health Preparation/Practice Pathway (RMHP3) is an example of a cohort-based model of rural SBMH counselor preparation and practice developed through a collaboration between Montana State University and the University of Montana. These two counselor education programs came together to design a sustainable, cohort-based model of preparation and practice for rural SBMH professionals. The RMHP3 model offers a unique pathway for graduate candidates in counseling to establish the professional and personal knowledge and skills needed to serve and thrive as rural professionals throughout their preparation and their postgraduate, prelicensure employment (Paisley et al., 2010). This model recognizes that *what* is taught and *where* students are placed during their professional preparation will significantly shape what they learn about rural cultures and contexts. This in turn will increase their effectiveness and longevity in delivering mental health intervention and prevention for rural students and their families.

The RMHP3 model of preparation addresses the factors of accessibility, acceptability, and availability that uniquely shape rural mental health professionals' work. It is composed of a set of four graduated clinical experiences (Figure 18.1) designed to equip counselors with the knowledge, skills, and self-efficacy needed to engage in rural mental health practice. The design is composed of a place-conscious curriculum accompanied by a set of embedded-in-place rural field experiences (Rural Life Orientation, Rural Professional Practicum, and Rural Internship) with time, space, and transportation support that provide opportunities for graduate counseling candidates to develop a more accurate understanding of rural life, its connections to the context of counseling, and a deeper sense of cultural humility (Tervalon & Murray-Garcia, 1998).

Specifically, this involves counselors-in-training monitoring both the nature of the power dynamic between themselves and clients as well as acknowledging cultural differences and

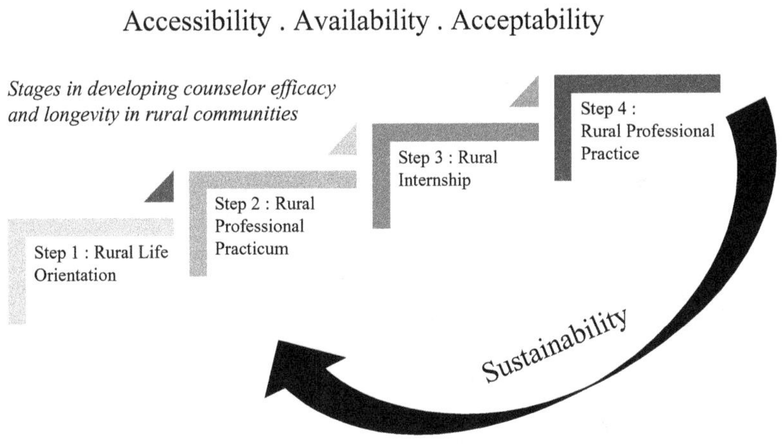

Figure 18.1 Rural Mental Health Preparation Practice Pathway (RMHP3).

The Bloomsbury Handbook of Rural Education in the United States

adapting methods of communication and connection to build relationships (Chang et al., 2012; Tervalon & Murray-Garcia; Velott & Sprow Forté, 2019). The model also addresses the issue of rural isolation and limited professional support by employing a cohort model in which graduate counseling candidates participate in a professional learning community throughout their program and postgraduate prelicensure employment.

In the Rural Life Orientation, candidates are invited to bring their preexisting assumptions about rural schools and communities to awareness and engage in structured opportunities to gather a variety of information about a specific rural or tribal community. Then through group discussion, reflection, and personal assessment, graduate counseling candidates critically examine previous knowledge, beliefs, and assumptions in light of new information about rural people and places and work to build contextually relevant understandings of place and community that will support their future ability to live and thrive as rural mental health professionals.

In the Rural Professional Practicum, candidates prepare for their year-long Rural Internship the following fall by starting to build relationships and connections with the rural school community. They also start to construct a map of the resources and assets in the community in order to build awareness regarding existing strengths and resources in a rural or tribal school setting. A unique course titled Special Issues in Working with Rural Populations serves as a bridge between the early field experiences and the 600-hour Rural Internship. In this step of preparation, interns engage in professional practice with regular in-person supervision, participate in regular webinars, and connect with other members of their cohort. The webinars provide support beyond what they experience in the university to help them process issues specific to working in rural schools and as they transition into the last step of serving as a Rural Professional. In this one-year post-master's experience, candidates remain connected to their professional learning community—something specifically noted by Breen and Drew (2012) as networking, seeking support with peers, and ongoing consultation and supervision that culminate to alleviate isolation and burnout. The outcome of the RMHP3 is not only the development of knowledge and skill in specific treatments for a variety of mental health disorders, it is also about developing a network of support for the rural practitioner so that they in turn can provide support across the school and community.

This model of place-conscious professional preparation for rural counselors is a key innovation to help reduce the barriers to mental health services experienced in many rural communities. The development of training programs that overtly prepare counselors for the place they are working can increase the availability of mental health service providers and help rural communities achieve greater access to mental health resources. The insights and networks developed during this type of training also provide the ongoing support needed for mental health professionals to invest in and sustain their positions in rural communities. Place-conscious counselor preparation can also contribute to the reduction of stigma around seeking out mental health support through greater presence and normalization of mental health services.

The presence of serious mental health issues in rural communities concurrent with a critical lack of access to services demands significant, systemic changes. The development of context-specific SBMH programs, in combination with place-conscious professional preparation attuned to the distinct and dynamic nature of rural contexts, will provide the tools needed to appropriately attend to the needs of students and families in rural environments and create meaningful opportunities for long-lasting change.

19

Student Achievement in Rural America

Douglas J. Gagnon

Our nation's public schools educate about fifty million K-12 students, roughly a fifth of whom live in rural areas (Showalter et al., 2019). The goals of education, in rural and nonrural areas, are as broad as they are deep. Even a cursory inspection of mission statements in education reveals ambitious and varied objectives: to create college-, career-, and life-ready students; to promote an informed citizenry; and to ensure equal educational opportunity. Any attempt to fully quantify the success of those served by public education is sure to fall short. However, any comprehensive look into progress toward education goals must include student achievement, especially if one seeks to understand how the state of education outcomes varies across time, place, and student characteristics. While instruments may not take into account the context in which students are assessed, the standardized assessments measuring student achievement have rigorous reliability standards, resulting in data that allow for substantial disaggregation and meaningful comparisons. Just as importantly, there is a vast body of evidence connecting student achievement to important education, health, and economic outcomes later in life (Chetty et al., 2014; Goldhaber & Özek, 2019; Heckman et al., 2006). In other words, there is good reason to care about the landscape of achievement, and it can give us important insights about rural America.

This portrait of rural student achievement is motivated by two essential questions. First we ask, how does the achievement of rural students fare compared to their nonrural peers? Second, how does the achievement of rural students vary according to student background? Consequently, this chapter entails an inspection of achievement both *between* rural America and the rest of the nation as well as *within* rural America. These complementary questions allow us to not only situate the state of rural achievement with respect to the nation as a whole but also to determine the extent to which one can speak of rural achievement in a more monolithic sense. In other words, to what extent should the *between* or *within* story warrant more scrutiny and attention, or vice versa.

A strong case exists for conducting a thorough examination of the achievement landscape across the United States. Reasons abound as to why conditions that either promote achievement or hinder it may vary in a meaningful way as one looks across the urbanicity gradient from large metropolitan centers to remote rural places. Even more straightforward is the rationale for also looking at how other characteristics of a particular place, and the students who reside there, relate to student achievement—especially given the long-standing disparities in test scores according to race and income in particular (Barton & Coley, 2010; Hanushek et al., 2020).

Considerations of Place

Meaningful historical and cultural differences exist between more and less rural places, many of which likely interact with how students connect to school and ultimately their achievement. This variation is due, in part, to the considerably different circumstances that caused many people to reside in cities versus rural areas, particularly for racial and ethnic minorities. This includes the forced relocation of Native American populations to largely rural areas, where a slight majority of the population continues to live (Dewees & Marks, 2017). The predominant migration story for African Americans in the last century is one of moving out of the Jim Crow rural South and into urban centers in the Northeast, Midwest, and West. The driving migration narrative for Latinx populations, however, is a much more recent trend of moving into rural areas in search of economic opportunity (Johnson & Lichter, 2008). Clearly the forces that bind people to place are complex, as are the ways in which historical legacy interacts with the present-day achievement of students in different locales. And, of course, meaningful cultural and historical differences exist between communities, even holding constant population density and distance from cities. Ultimately, the reasons for which people live in a place, and the expectations placed on families, communities, and local institutions there, can be quite different.

These expectations and norms—which are, of course, shaped by the geography of place—can lead to very different relationships between families and schools in rural places. Many have noted that rural schools in particular often serve as a focal point in rural communities (Tieken, 2014) and may act to bring community members together. It may be that connections to family, place, and school in rural areas act as a catalyst for achievement, as some research suggests that rural students may be afforded social capital as a result of the opportunities, structure, and experiences unique to rural places (Byun et al., 2012; C. B. Howley & A. Howley, 2014). However, at the same time, rural parents generally have lower education levels than do nonrural parents (Byun et al., 2015), which represents a relative disadvantage in the cultural capital and academic expectations for rural students compared to their nonrural peers. It is also worth noting that, like more urban places, this capital is not spread out evenly across rural communities. However, the smaller size and greater integration of rural places could have implications for how those with more and less capital interact to shape norms and expectations.

The nature of work is yet another factor worth consideration. Viewed in one sense, rural places offer fewer high-paying careers (Thiede et al., 2016), which in turn prompts many of the most talented rural youth to leave home for greater opportunities in more metropolitan locales (Carr & Kefalas, 2009). It is easy to see how such trends could depress achievement in rural places. However, viewed another way, the more limited economic opportunities in rural places could lead to a tighter and more deliberate connection between the work of schools and the economic needs of their community or region.

Overall, nonmetropolitan areas experience higher rates of joblessness and poverty than do metropolitan ones (Pender et al., 2019). Furthermore, rural places are more likely than urban ones to experience higher rates of poverty, concentrated poverty, and poverty that spans generations (Schaefer et al., 2016)—though this deep poverty is not spread out evenly across region and race. Given the powerful connection between family income and student achievement (Reardon, 2016), these socioeconomic disparities may make it more of a challenge for rural students, as a whole, to reach high levels of academic success.

However, it is not straightforward to understand the differential impacts of poverty on achievement across place. Even if the poverty profiles between rural and nonrural places were identical, there is plenty of reason to suspect that poverty could impact students and their achievement in very different ways. There are various pathways through which poverty impacts child outcomes, including health and nutrition, the home environment, parental interactions with children, parental mental health, and neighborhood conditions (Brooks-Gunn & Duncan, 1997; Bronfenbrenner & Morris, 1998). Furthermore, these pathways generally look quite different across place. For instance, people living below the poverty line in urban places are more likely to experience overcrowding, a lack of green space (Wells & Evans, 2003), and less stable housing (George & Holden, 2000), whereas people living below the poverty line in rural communities can experience greater levels of isolation and exposure to environmental toxins (Burton et al., 2013). Much like the other differences across locales discussed so far, this research gives us a strong rationale for suspecting that achievement might differ between rural and nonrural students, but it presents far too complex a mix of factors to suggest directionality. The brief account presented here serves to motivate our examination of achievement between and within locale.

The Nation's Report Card

The National Assessment of Educational Progress (NAEP), often referred to as *The Nation's Report Card*, offers the most powerful glimpse into achievement between and within place in the United States. In response to a congressional mandate, the National Center for Education Statistics (NCES) administers NAEP to a representative sample of US students to assess a variety of subjects in fourth, eighth, and twelfth grades. A full exploration by grade and subject would be too extensive for the purposes of this chapter. Rather, this chapter will document important achievement patterns in two grade–subject combinations of NAEP: fourth-grade reading and eighth-grade mathematics. There are two reasons for choosing these grade–subject combinations. The first is practical: reading and mathematics are the two NAEP subject areas most extensively administered, which permits a more nuanced analysis of achievement patterns across time and demographic factors. Additionally, fourth-grade reading and eighth-grade mathematics are both important benchmarks, serving as powerful proxies into other outcomes of interest. For instance, some claim that fourth grade roughly marks the time when children are beginning to read to learn, as opposed to learning to read (Fiester, 2010), and fourth grade corresponds to a time of marked increase in expectations of content literacy. In this way, fourth-grade reading proficiency serves as a proxy for a child's ability to develop a wealth of capacities and, therefore, represents a key educational metric for understanding overall progress. Similarly, success in eighth-grade mathematics is commonly seen as a critical gateway to accessing advanced mathematics courses in high school (Star et al., 2015), which are in turn seen as important in preparing students for higher education.

The Bloomsbury Handbook of Rural Education in the United States

Achievement Across Time and Locale

We begin by looking at achievement trends between more and less urban places between 2009 and 2019. Here we use the NCES urban-centric locale classification system's major locale codes of city, suburb, town, and rural.[1] Figures 19.1 and 19.2 show NAEP fourth-grade reading achievement and eighth-grade mathematics achievement, respectively, from 2009 through 2019 for students in each major category of urbanicity, as well as the nation as a whole. Several notable trends emerge from these results. The first is that rural students consistently outperformed their city and town peers in these subjects and were consistently outperformed by suburban students throughout the decade.[2] For example, the difference between the average 2019 NAEP eighth-grade mathematics achievement for rural students (283) and their town and city peers (277) is six scaled points. A similar gap exists between rural and suburban students as well, though with the balance favoring suburban students.

To put these findings in context, we can examine how six scaled points compare to proficiency levels. In the 2019 NAEP eighth-grade mathematics assessment, students needed to score 262 to reach the *Basic* level, 299 to be deemed *Proficient*, and 333 to be considered *Advanced*. Therefore, the six scaled point difference is about one-sixth of the range between *Basic* and *Proficient* or between *Proficient* and *Advanced*. Another way to put this difference in perspective is to consider the overall distribution: 6 scaled points equates to 0.15 standard deviations on this assessment. Thus, while these figures at first glance may seem to portend large differences across place, the largest differences amount to meaningful, but not extremely large, gaps on average between rural students and their city, suburban, and town peers.

The second trend made apparent by Figures 19.1 and 19.2 is that rural achievement in both subject-grade combinations has mirrored national trends over this decade—and in general rural achievement falls quite close to the national average. NAEP achievement does

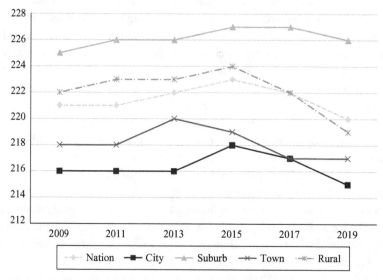

Figure 19.1 NAEP fourth-grade reading scores, overall and by region, 2009–19.
Source: NAEP Data Explorer.

Student Achievement in Rural America

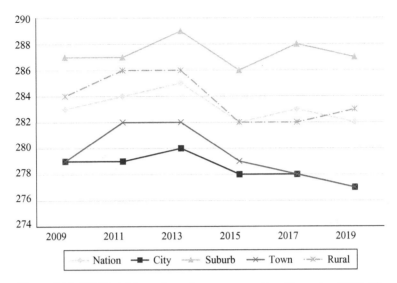

Figure 19.2 NAEP eighth-grade math scores, overall and by region, 2009–19.
Source: NAEP Data Explorer.

exhibit a statistically significant decline for rural students in fourth-grade reading between 2015 and 2019, and in eighth-grade mathematics between 2013 and 2019—trends that are less evident for suburban students. However, given the transition from paper and pencil to digital administration over this period as well as the differences in rates of transition and digital familiarity across place, strong conclusions as to the overall rural achievement trends, as well as relative differences in longitudinal trends between rural students and their suburban peers, are probably not warranted.

Achievement Differences Across Region, Income, and Race/Ethnicity

It is important to not only view how rural students compare to their more urban peers but also to inspect how achievement varies within rural communities in the United States. There is good reason to suspect that such an examination would uncover more striking results, given the tremendous variability in rural spaces and the people that inhabit them. And, in fact, it does. Here we document how rural student achievement varies with respect to region, family income, and race/ethnicity and compare these patterns to those of nonrural students. Again, we examine NAEP fourth-grade reading and eighth-grade mathematics, though here we focus only on 2019 results.

Differences by Region

Figures 19.3 and 19.4 show the average NAEP fourth-grade reading and eighth-grade mathematics scores by region (Northeast, South, Midwest, and West) for rural and nonrural students. These figures reveal considerable differences in rural math achievement, with rural students in the Northeast outscoring their rural peers from the South and West by between eleven and thirteen points in fourth-grade reading and eleven points in eighth-grade mathematics. These within-rural student achievement gaps are roughly twice the magnitude of the differences between rural students and their city, suburban, and town peers. Moreover, these same gaps are not seen within

219

The Bloomsbury Handbook of Rural Education in the United States

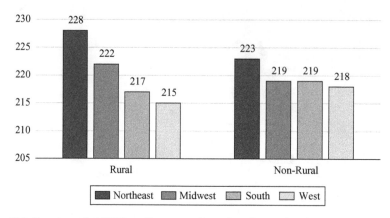

Figure 19.3 Fourth-grade NAEP reading scores by region, for rural and nonrural students, 2019. *Source*: NAEP Data Explorer.

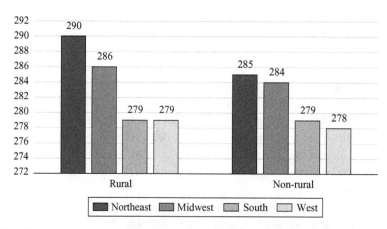

Figure 19.4 Eighth-grade NAEP mathematics scores by region, for rural and nonrural students, 2019. *Source*: NAEP Data Explorer.

nonrural students: fourth-grade reading achievement is quite similar across regions, and the gaps between in eighth-grade NAEP mathematics are smaller in magnitude for nonrural students as compared to rural students.

Differences by Income

Next we examine differences in fourth-grade reading and eighth-grade mathematics achievement between students from lower- and higher-income families, using free or reduced-price lunch (FRPL) eligibility as a proxy in both rural and nonrural locales (see Figures 19.5 and 19.6). Considerable achievement gaps by income are evident: rural students from higher- and lower-income families are separated by twenty-four scaled points in both assessments, or roughly twice the within-rural gaps across region and about four times the overall gaps between rural and nonrural students. Such achievement gaps along economic lines have been thoroughly documented by prior research (Hanushek et al., 2020; Reardon, 2016). These gaps within rural areas, however, are slightly smaller than those found in nonrural ones—a product of both slightly

Student Achievement in Rural America

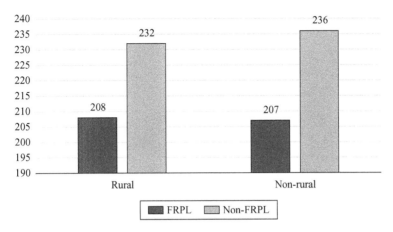

Figure 19.5 Fourth-grade NAEP reading scores by income, for rural and nonrural students, 2019. *Source*: NAEP Data Explorer.

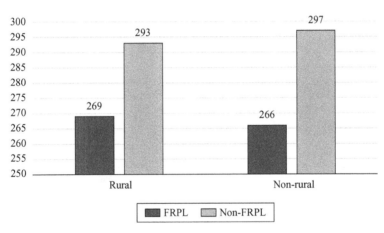

Figure 19.6 Eighth-grade NAEP mathematics scores by income, for rural and nonrural Students, 2019. *Source*: NAEP Data Explorer.

lower achievement for students from higher-income families and slightly higher achievement for students from lower-income families than their corresponding subgroups experience in nonrural locales.

Differences by Race/Ethnicity

Here we present 2019 NAEP achievement results in fourth-grade reading and eighth-grade mathematics for rural and nonrural students across four race/ethnicity categories: White, Black, Hispanic, and American Indian/Alaskan Native (AIAN) students (see Figures 19.7 and 19.8). Evident here are wide gaps between rural White students, on one hand, and their Black, Hispanic, and AIAN rural peers on the other. Fourth-grade reading gaps of 22, 17, and 23 scaled points separate rural White students from each of these subgroups, respectively. These racial/ethnic achievement gaps in rural areas are only slightly smaller than the corresponding achievement gaps by income.

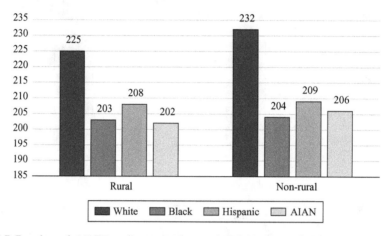

Figure 19.7 Fourth-grade NAEP reading scores by race/ethnicity, for rural and nonrural students, 2019. *Source*: NAEP Data Explorer.

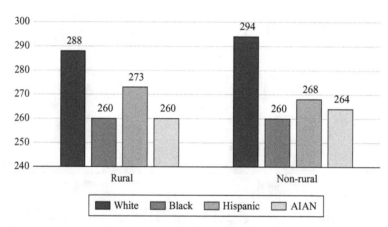

Figure 19.8 Eighth-grade NAEP mathematics scores by race/ethnicity, for rural and nonrural students, 2019. *Source:* NAEP Data Explorer.

Note that while achievement gaps across income and race/ethnicity in rural schools are large and of concern, these gaps are generally smaller than national trends for this assessment. Specifically, the White-Black and White-Hispanic achievement gaps in NAEP eighth-grade mathematics for rural students are considerably smaller than those for city and suburban students. These patterns are consistent with prior research that examined state achievement data linked and pooled across states, years, grades, and subject areas (Gagnon & Mattingly, 2018); this study found that White-Black and White-Hispanic achievement gaps in rural districts were meaningfully smaller than those found in city districts, and that these findings persist even when accounting for socioeconomic factors, levels of segregation, and other important district characteristics.

Conclusion

It is important to not overstate the insight that achievement, alone, provides into more durable education attainment. For instance, despite rural students having higher achievement and

Student Achievement in Rural America

graduation rates than city students, they are less likely to attend college (Brown & Schafft, 2011; Byun et al., 2015). Moreover, of those rural students who do continue on to higher education, they are more likely to delay entry and experience discontinuous enrollment than are students from urban and suburban schools (Byun et al., 2015). Thus, while national assessments do provide an important benchmark to understand outcome differences across place, we must remain mindful that additional barriers exist, including rural schools being located further from colleges and rural students experiencing more difficulty in transitioning to the college environment (see Chapter 14, this volume). These barriers, among others, may keep many rural students from translating success in high school into higher levels of educational attainment, which in turn unlocks additional important opportunities.

Despite the limitations of using standardized achievement as a benchmark, patterns documented here are still worthy of serious consideration. Three things emerge from this systematic, locale-focused review of student achievement. First, despite all the reasons one might suggest a net advantage—or disadvantage—for rural students: in aggregate they perform similarly to nonrural students. When we view achievement separately for each locale, we do see relatively small but noteworthy gaps, as rural students lag behind their suburban peers but outperform students in towns and cities. It will be important to continue to monitor these trends in the coming years to see if these gaps grow or shrink. Given the unequal economic recovery between more and less metropolitan places since the Great Recession, and the children born then for whom we are just starting to have assessment data, there is reason to worry what the next decade portends for rural student achievement. This is especially true in the wake of Covid-19, as the wholesale shift to remote learning with highly unequal access to high-quality internet (Center on Rural Innovation, 2020) may exacerbate achievement differences across place.

The second major finding here relates to the large achievement gaps within rural schools when cutting across region, income, and race/ethnicity. Given the substantial literature that has documented disparities in achievement (Barton & Coley, 2010; Hanushek et al., 2020; Reardon, 2016), this is unsurprising. It is important to reiterate that the magnitude of achievement gaps across race, region, and poverty dwarfs those between rural students, on one hand, and their more urban peers on the other. Ultimately, the well-documented challenges that urban schools have faced in raising the achievement of historically underserved students are present in rural places as well.

However, the third major finding is that these within-locale gaps look different in rural places than in nonrural ones: rural students exhibit larger gaps between regions but smaller gaps along the lines of income, race, and ethnicity. The large gaps across regions for rural students are predominantly due to the high achievement found in the rural Northeast—which brings to mind the very different contours of Northeast rural communities compared to the often more remote rural areas in the West and Midwest and the communities that have experienced deep and persistent poverty in the South. Conversely, rural places exhibit smaller racial/ethnic and income achievement gaps than do nonrural ones. An argument could be made that the greater levels of shared experience for students within a rural school could be partly responsible for these smaller achievement gaps. Or, viewed in a slightly different way, it might suggest that White students and students from higher-income families in urban locales experience greater levels of social capital and educational opportunity than do the relatively advantaged students of rural places. Ultimately these achievement patterns provide the reader with a general landscape of achievement between and within place, but questions of why must be left unanswered here.

What is to be made of these patterns in achievement? Clearly disparities *within* rural places are far greater than those *between* rural and nonrural ones. This suggests that we should focus particular attention on those rural subgroups that are on the wrong end of achievement gaps and work to increase opportunity for the most disadvantaged. However, we should not ignore the *between* story, either. Aggregate patterns in achievement between rural and nonrural students obscure the fact that suburban students consistently outperform both town and rural students. Additionally, more recent NAEP data show a relative dip in rural achievement, and the two major economic events of this century—the Great Recession and the Covid-19 pandemic—are likely to disproportionately impact rural achievement in a manner that will likely be revealed in the coming years. For these reasons, we must continue to monitor the achievement of students within and between places, as disparities in achievement serve as both powerful lagging indicators of compounding gaps in early opportunities as well as potent leading indicators of future outcome gaps.

International Response

What Counts as Curriculum?

Philip Roberts

When I think "Curriculum Studies," I think, *What knowledge is of most worth?* (Pinar, 2012) or *Whose knowledge is of most worth?* (Apple, 2004). In these questions, and the field as I understand it, the question of knowledge is central (Green, 2017). It immediately strikes me then that these chapters may not all fall into the curriculum studies field I know. Then again, the Latin origin of the term "curriculum"—to run the course (Pinar, 2012)—also signifies the field as related to a notion of a broadly defined "course." Is it that in these chapters "curriculum" is the course, and the topics covered relate to the fairness of that course for rural students?

As I write this, I am on extended fieldwork in remote communities in the far west of the state of New South Wales, on the Australian continent, and on the lands of First Nations peoples (whom I will not name to maintain the anonymity of the research sites). The town I am in now has about 700 residents and a K-12 school with about 65 students. It is about 180 kilometers (111 miles) to the nearest small town, itself the same distance to what may be termed a large center, and of the three nearby towns two are on dirt roads impassable after rain. Here I am immersed in the perspectives on education, and the knowledge system it is founded upon, of those positioned as falling behind in the curriculum race. Whose rules are the race run by though, what is the course, are there obstacles, and how are the winners determined?

Reviews Without Change

In Australia, the challenges associated with achieving equity in education for rural communities and their students have been an issue since European colonization in 1788. Though such a perspective belies the modernist conception of education as is in use in this volume. Education had, of course, been occurring in Aboriginal and Torres Strait Islander society on the Australian continent prior to its displacement by the European colonists, with an ongoing struggle to define what counts as education continuing ever since. Nonetheless, "the rural problem" has been the defining character of education in these contexts from the earliest records and mirroring similar concerns in the United States (Biddle & Azano, 2016; Cubberley, 1914; Green & Reid, 2012). Countless reports and inquiries into equity and rural education have been undertaken over the subsequent decades, with the most recent reporting in 2018 (Halsey, 2018).

The countless reports on rural education in Australia over the last century can be summed up quite simply as continuity upon a theme: rural students are disadvantaged by lack of access to quality education, and consequently their educational outcomes are below the national average.

The Bloomsbury Handbook of Rural Education in the United States

Considering the outcomes of rural schools, the latest review into rural, regional, and remote education (Halsey, 2018) identified senior secondary completion, post-school matriculation rates, and literacy and numeracy benchmarks as particular concerns. These were couched in terms of the ongoing challenges of attracting and retaining staff, access to services, the availability of subjects in senior secondary schools, and the generally lower socioeconomic status of rural communities, including significant proportions of Aboriginal and Torres Strait Islander students, as factors influencing these outcomes (Halsey, 2018).

This review in rural, regional, and remote education (Halsey, 2018) was itself a follow-up to major federal reviews into equity in Australian education (Australian Government, 2011, 2018). These reviews noted that the key dimensions of disadvantage that are having a significant impact on educational performance in Australia are socioeconomic status, Indigeneity, English language proficiency, disability, and school remoteness. Furthermore, when these dimensions intersect, outcomes are further impacted. To address these challenges, the reviews recommended a resource standard for schools with specific loadings for identified categories of disadvantage. I should note here that school funding was a particular focus of these reviews.

These recommendations have largely been taken up at a federal and state level in Australia. While making a positive contribution to addressing recognized causes of inequity in education, they nonetheless leave the specifics of the production of that inequality unexplained. For instance, location and socioeconomic status operate as catchalls for an array of unaddressed outside school influences on student achievement. Curriculum is not raised or addressed as an issue in and of itself. This, I suggest, is because the problem of curriculum is assumed to have been solved through the move to a form of an Australian National Curriculum. This is curious as it is *through* curriculum that inequity is measured—in terms of school completion, matriculation, results, literacy, numeracy, and so on. Put another way, curriculum is what schools are organized around, and staffed in relation to.

National Context

The structural complexities of education in Australia tend to exacerbate the challenges of achieving equity for rural schools. Australia is a federal system of seven states and two territories, each of which has its own education system. The federal (national) government has no constitutional authority over schools. However, the federal government has the greatest revenue-raising capacity and consequently exerts a degree of power over the states and territories through coercion related to funding, such as the loadings noted above (e.g., English language proficiency). Part of this coercion (Savage & O'Connor, 2019) includes the move to a national curriculum framework that requires the agreement of each jurisdiction to align their curriculum in return for education funding benefits.

Australia, the only nation and continent, occupies a vast geographic space—marginally less than the United States (without Alaska)—though Australia is home to only twenty million people (Australian Bureau of Statistics [ABS], 2018) due to the extremes of its geography. This population is highly urbanized, with over 85 percent of the population living in urban areas, within 50 kilometers (~31 miles) of the coast. Indeed, the greater Sydney and Melbourne areas comprise nearly half the population of Australia (ABS, 2018). Australia uses a geographical classification, the Australian Statistical Geography Standard (ABS, 2011), to describe areas from

What Counts as Curriculum

major cities through to remote areas, based on distance, population density, and access to services in public policy (noting here the diversity of definitions as discussed in Chapter 1 of this volume).

Context to Curriculum

This unique geography matters in considering curriculum. As a highly urbanized nation, one entwined with global cosmopolitan urban sensibilities, it is not surprising that the rural is absent within the Australian Curriculum, though this is itself an issue of spatial and epistemic justice (Roberts, 2018). Nationally, 29.3 percent of Australian students are in rural, regional, or remote contexts; however, schools in these contexts make up 47 percent of all schools (Halsey, 2017). So while Australia is largely urban, there are significant populations of rural students and rural schools spread across a vast geographic space. Yet, *rural* in this context continues to be envisioned as a monolith in Australia's curriculum history and in recent developments. In these diverse rural spaces, students learn the Australian Curriculum, a curriculum that does not acknowledge the very places from which they are learning.

From where I am writing this, distance, town size, the availability of health specialists, and access to a range of fresh food and other produce are certainly issues. In towns like this the schools are small and students who choose to stay access several subjects via internet technologies—something they have been doing for thirty years now pre-Covid-19—though they can only do this at school as otherwise internet access is limited in rural Australia. What is missing seems to be any relevance in the curriculum to the world around these classrooms or any engagement with the knowledges rural students bring to school with them. There is knowledge though; it is just a different type of knowledge produced through this place.

The lack of attention to the question of knowledge in the curriculum is curious, especially when so many rural education scholars write about the importance of knowing place. It seems knowing place is itself positioned as pedagogy—here, how one enacts the curriculum in place with the curriculum itself unchallenged. However, the place from where I write this certainly produces knowledge through its production of place. A notable example here are the local literacies and the observable tension between what Donehower (Chapter 16) describes as the functionality and innateness of rural literacies versus the benchmarks of formal literacies set by the national curriculum against which these students are positioned as behind or failing.

Rural literacies, to me, operate as an entry point to other forms of knowledge and highlight the metro-normative standards of contemporary education. They give shape to other forms of expression and in so doing ask important questions of the standards and benchmarks that are applied. Furthermore, as Donehower describes, rural literacies reflect *place* and the diverse ways that the diversity of rural peoples understand rurality—here giving rise to the diversity of definitions and meanings of the rural (see Longhurst's Chapter 1, this volume).

We might do well to turn to what has been termed southern theory (Connell, 2007) and the epistemological south as proposed by Santos (2014) and Paraskeva (2016). This epistemological south refers to peoples and cultures that have been marginalized through the imperialism of the global knowledge system. This growing body of work is becoming extremely influential in Transnational Curriculum Inquiry (Green et al., 2020) as nations across the world speak back to the dominance of knowledge of, and from, the global metropole. I include rural spaces in this notion of epistemicide, the erasure of knowledges (Santos, 2014). This applies to the knowledge of Aboriginal and Torres Strait Islander peoples in Australia who were displaced by European

The Bloomsbury Handbook of Rural Education in the United States

knowledge through the process of settler colonialism, as well as the knowledges of all peoples in the global south for whom "achievement" is through Eurocentric knowledge systems.

The questions raised through Donehower's chapter (Chapter 16) directly tie into Gagnon's examination of student achievement (Chapter 19). Here Gagnon asks researchers to focus upon student achievement. Importantly, Gagnon shows that disparities among rural are greater than between rural and urban. This draws attention to the constituent parts of student achievement, knowledge, and practices represented in school subjects, and the scale upon which these results are reported. Gagnon's critique of "blunt" reporting of differences is a concern I share and something I have been working against in the Australian context (Roberts et al., 2019). Here we see differences in subject access and achievement between the cities and the different gradations of rural in the statistics; however, reporting blunt rural-urban differences remains the norm (Halsey, 2018) and continues to paint rural spaces in monolithic terms. This, I suggest, reflects a move from curriculum as the object of academic study to curriculum as some hybrid form of policy study. The issue of knowledge is replaced by the study of who and how many study subjects and their achievement in those subjects. This move leaves knowledge untroubled and, in so doing, facilitates the ongoing marginalization of rural and Indigenous knowledges. Knowledge, and its appropriateness, is of course entwined with student aspirations to study certain subjects and their engagement in those studies. Furthermore, comparing at a rural-urban scale puts both at odds and implicitly assumes that patterns of access and achievement from the urban, often the majority population in modernity, are the norm (Roberts & Green, 2013).

Using the recent review into rural, regional, and remote education (Halsey, 2018) as a reference point, there are some notable exemptions in the Australian rural education research oeuvre, namely a focus upon early childhood education (Knoche, Kerby, and Sheridan, Chapter 15), trauma-informed approaches (Biddle and Brown, Chapter 17), and school-based mental health (Downey, Elliott, Koltz, and Murray, Chapter 18). My own reflection on the field reinforces to me that this is a significant gap. Though reading these chapters in the context of this volume, in the community where I am writing this, leads to important questions about why this is so. Each is a major concern to this and other communities I have spent time in recently.

Knoche and colleagues (Chapter 15), for example, begin their chapter with the statement that "remarkable physical, cognitive, and social-emotional development occurs for young children from birth to age eight" (p. 177). This beginning starts a child—the future student and citizen—on their course and influences the pathway they will take through schooling. Ensuring that location and the social context of some rural communities does not provide a disadvantage to equitable access to early childhood education is critical. While I agree with teachers and parents working as partners, I wonder if we need more attention to the problem of curriculum in mediating this relationship. In a recent study of parents on isolated properties who support their children's early learning, my colleague found that it was the assumptions inherent in the curriculum provided by the distance learning center that caused obstacles to learning and created tensions between teachers and parents (Downes & Roberts, 2015). The parents found the material they were sent to instruct their children, aged five to eight, made no sense to their children, so they often had to substitute examples that reflected their lives. However, when they did this, the teachers saw the parents as not following their prepared script and undermining their expertise, itself located in a particular form of curriculum and knowledge.

Trauma (Biddle and Brown, Chapter 17) and mental health (Downey et al., Chapter 18) also impact considerably on a child's ability to "run the course." While absent from the recent Australian review into rural, regional, and remote education, the access to mental health professionals is a major issue in rural Australia (Malatzky et al., 2018) that parallels the situation outlined by Downey and colleagues. Their suggestion of school-based mental health services, and even some preservice training for teachers to work in rural schools, is certainly something that would be beneficial in the Australian context. Similarly, coupling health and education services in place through this approach can only achieve positive outcomes. Entwined here, of course, is the impacts of trauma, as discussed by Biddle and Brown.

The social context of many rural places in Australia parallels that described by Biddle and Brown, though the specifics of trauma are often masked by reference to low socioeconomic status. Rural economic decline, intergenerational poverty, and the in-migration of those enduring poverty from the cities are all trends in many rural locations. For other locations close to major cities or on transport corridors, the in-migration of the well-off who can work remotely results in deep community division. Australia has its own version of the rural-urban (metropole) political fractures along race and economic lines, as has been seen in other parts of the world over the last decade. Consequently, the trauma-informed care Biddle and Brown describe also offers useful insights for rural education in Australia.

As I write in this small, remote, town, two further reflections about trauma come to mind. The first relates to the knowledge question. I wonder what role the marginalization of rural knowledges, dispossession, and the epistemicide of Indigenous knowledges in the curriculum play in trauma and mental health. When one cannot see themselves in the value system of the nation, or even the dominant global knowledge system, what impact does it have on one's sense of belonging, especially when they are forced by law to attend institutions that reinforce this each day? Logically, this would seem to play a role then in achievement as discussed by Gagnon (Chapter 19), and references that central tenet of educational sociology from the seminal reports by US economist Coleman and colleagues (1966), and Australian sociologist Connell and colleagues (1982), that the unequal distribution of educational outcomes between social backgrounds is mediated by the different relationships that each had with schooling. Implicated here are the existence or absence of preexisting relationships to school knowledge, ways of being and acting, valuing intellectual work, and the value of labor.

The second reflection on trauma-informed practice, as it is termed here, relates to the growing theme in schools that serve Aboriginal communities. In these communities, like the one I write this from, trauma runs deep (Menzies, 2019): from dispossession of lands and the severe social dislocation and health crisis that followed, racism, the denial of language, violence and massacres, and the forced removal of children through to the ongoing violence of continued social marginalization. Key here is the ongoing reproduction of dispossession through a school system that denies the knowledges, languages, and literacies of Aboriginal and Torres Strait Islander peoples. While progress has been made in the inclusion of Aboriginal and Torres Strait Islander perspectives and languages in recent years, there is still immense work to be done. This is curriculum work, both for schools and the nation. It is also intimately entwined with trauma and mental health. Taken together, these chapters, as a form of "curriculum studies" provide important perspectives on the question of knowledge and open important considerations for rural practitioners and researchers.

Just how we operationalize these insights are the challenges for the future of the field. As I finish this response, in this remote community, I can reflect that this was an unusually challenging task. Not being able to name where I write from due to research ethics and the demand for anonymity seems itself unethical, especially when as a field we write about the importance of place. Similarly, place promotes disciplinary diversity; however, internationalization, as an aim of much educational research, pushes disciplinary homogeneity—something that led to my initial thought line asking, *What is curriculum studies?* That my initial thought that the perspective used was foreign to me makes me wonder what the implications are for researching the global rural and policy transfer. It also causes me further disequilibrium as it heightens my consciousness of how the institution of schooling, as I understand it in Australia, is foreign to Aboriginal and Torres Strait Islander communities, and all communities of the global south. Much work lies ahead.

Part IV

Introduction

Identity and Equity in Rural Schools

Part IV considers issues of identity and equity in rural schools by providing a sampling of some of the work being done highlighting diverse populations in rural places. While this section includes attention to Indigenous populations, Black and Latinx communities, Whiteness, exceptional learners, and students with disabilities, the editors acknowledge that the representation of identity and issues of educational equity in this section are incomplete. We regret, for example, the absence of a discussion of rural Asian/Pacific Islander students and families, especially in light of the surge in anti-Asian violence since the onset of the Covid-19 pandemic. In particular, the editors' plans to include a chapter on gender and sexuality did not come to fruition. An estimated 2.9–3.8 million lesbian, gay, bisexual, transgender, and queer (LGBTQ+) people live in rural communities across the United States. Rural youth are just as likely as urban youth to identify as LGBTQ+. The editors encourage readers to access publications such as Pace's (2004) case study of a rural K-12 school as well as Hash and Morrow's (2019) case study about an older adult's experience with sexual orientation and aging in a rural community. Importantly, the editors note the yawning gap in rural educational research that engages people who identify as LGBTQ+.

Critical Indigenous Perspectives in the Field of Rural Education (Chapter 20), the first in Part IV, by RedCorn, Johnson, Bergeron, and Hayman, opens this collection of chapters about identity and equity. Their chapter explores the intersection of Indigenous education and rural education in order to make Indigenous perspectives more visible within the field of rural education and to cultivate understandings in a way that encourages more culturally responsive scholarship and praxis at this intersection. The authors discuss the visibility and presence of Indigenous peoples in the field of rural education, pertinent critical Indigenous perspectives, and how these perspectives relate to durable issues in rural education. They conclude with a call for mindful action, scholarship, and partnership building at the intersection of these fields.

Following RedCorn and colleagues' call for centering Indigeneity in rural education, Coady examines the growth of diverse K-12 students in previously White monolingual communities in Chapter 21, English Learners in Rural Schools. As Coady makes clear, rural communities should never be assumed to be White, English-speaking, and demographically static. Language minoritized students account for 83 percent of the nonmetropolitan growth in the United States. This chapter provides an overview of the landscape of rural English Learner (EL) education.

Although the population of EL students is itself diverse, Coady focuses on the various language and ethnic backgrounds of students and families, the preparation of teachers and educational leaders to work in the context of rural EL education, and issues of equity surrounding EL education in the United States.

Williams, McCollum, and Clarida further extend Coady's examination of language variation as a difference (not a deficit) with their chapter that emphasizes the strengths present in rural African American communities. Specifically, using narrative inquiry, the authors highlight the ways in which community cohesiveness, familial support, and motivation connect to African American college going. Chapter 22, African American Education in the Rural South: Then and Now, examines educational opportunity, rurality, and race, offering a counternarrative to deficit representations of Black rural youth and their college attainment.

Recent increased attention to rural communities in the popular media is marked by misunderstandings of rural communities as monolithic in terms of race and ethnicity. This homogenization ignores the lives of Black, Indigenous, and People of Color (BIPOC) residents living in rural and small towns. In Chapter 23, Latinx Students in Rural Schools, Means and Sansone center rural K-12 Latinx learners. They include demographics of rural Latinx people in the United States, including the diversity across Latinx people living in rural areas, literature from the past two decades on PK-12 education and achievement for rural Latinx students, and literature from the past two decades on postsecondary education access, experiences, and outcomes of rural Latinx students.

Concluding this set of chapters about racial and ethnic diversity in rural communities that are often assumed White, Gillon's Chapter 24 on Whiteness in Rural Education seeks to replace inaccurate assumptions about the homogeneity of rural communities with a more complete view appropriately centering people of color. Via an exploration of migration/globalization and colonization, the chapter explores the (re)production of Whiteness as a hegemonic narrative of rural education highlighting ways in which Whiteness can both erase learners, educators, and leaders of color and also essentialize the experience of the White rural learner. The chapter suggests practical ways in which educators and scholars can decenter Whiteness.

The final two chapters in Part IV transition to issues around inclusive pedagogy in rural schools. In Rural Tiered Systems of Adaptive Supports: A Person-in-Context, Place-Based Perspective (Chapter 25), Farmer, Hamm, Berry, and Lee consider students with disabilities as an important category of difference in addition to racial and ethnic diversity. The authors argue for place-based strategies and supports as critical to the growth and outcomes of diverse rural learners including students with disabilities. They explain that in order for rural schools to respond to the needs of diverse learners, special education, social-emotional learning, and tiered systems of adaptive supports should be linked within a place-based framework.

Learners are diverse as well in terms of ability. In Challenges and Innovative Responses in Rural Gifted Education (Chapter 26), Azano, Callahan, and Kuehl discuss the socially constructed nature of rural gifted education and how its social construction influences perceptions about gifted education in rural schools. The authors provide a review of the literature related to rural gifted education to highlight opportunity gaps between rural gifted learners and their nonrural peers, emphasizing existing challenges in providing equitable services for high achieving students in geographically remote areas. Innovative practices designed to address the known challenges in

Introduction

rural gifted education are highlighted, with examples situated in schools serving children living in high-poverty communities.

Finally, Gristy provides an international response in her chapter, A Peripheral Perspective: A View from Rural Europe. Gristy writes that marginal or peripheral perspectives are often the most important for initiating change in our educational systems. Through these perspectives, we come to better understand the ways in which the existing system creates exclusions. She argues that for rural education, these perspectives constitute important sites of reimagining how we challenge the peripheralization of rural itself. Similarly, Gristy points out the ways in which the theoretical grounding of these chapters allow for more robust connections in rural scholarship across global contexts. Finally, the chapter brings this collection full circle with a return to the question of how definitions of rurality circumscribe the ways in which work from disparate contexts can be brought meaningfully together to constitute a robust body of scholarly work.

20

Critical Indigenous Perspectives in Rural Education

Alex RedCorn, Jerry D. Johnson, Larry Bergeron, and Jann Hayman

Education in what is now called rural America existed long before Europeans ever set foot on the continent. Indigenous peoples created various forms of place-based and experiential learning systems in order to prepare individuals to take on various social roles in their communities. These learning systems predated forced land dispossessions and the removal of Indigenous peoples, which laid the groundwork for the establishment of land grant/grab universities (Lee & Ahtone, 2020; Nash, 2019) and extension offices. These historical processes of settler colonialism pushed Indigenous peoples to the rural periphery as manifest destiny and westward expansion invaded the continent, and many Native communities still remain in these rural areas today. Throughout these histories and into the present, schools have been used as a weapon of settler colonialism with sustained attempts to erase Indigenous languages, cultures, and worldviews (Lomawaima, 1999; Reyhner & Eder, 2004; Szasz, 1999), persisting to this day in rural, suburban, and urban America. As a result, there is a need to acknowledge that through these sustained efforts the perspectives of Indigenous peoples are often less visible across the subfields of education, including rural education. As Greenwood (2009) states, while challenging rural educators to think more deeply about these shared spaces and interests, "discourses around rural and Indigenous education remain distinct and overlap only infrequently, which means that coalition-building between the two groups is rare" (p. 4). Furthermore, if we are to truly embrace concepts such as place-based education, this must begin by confronting the problematic nature of place, the entangled social, cultural, and historical foundations upon which our education systems rest—that is, displacing Indigenous peoples and stealing their land in the name of conquest—and using that land as capital to develop and sustain educational systems.

This chapter explores the intersection of two subfields, Indigenous education and rural education, in an effort to make Indigenous perspectives more visible within the field of rural education and to cultivate understandings in a way that encourages more culturally responsive scholarship and praxis at this intersection. In doing so, we discuss the visibility and presence of

Indigenous peoples in the field of rural education, pertinent critical Indigenous perspectives, and how these perspectives relate to durable issues in rural education. We then conclude with a call for mindful action, scholarship, and partnership building at the intersection of these fields.

The Visibility of Indigenous Peoples in the Field of Rural Education

For context on the discussion of Indigenous perspectives and the implications for rural education, we examine the visibility of Indigenous peoples in rural education. Specifically, we provide background to highlight the scale, scope, substance, and nuance of Indigenous education in the United States (with an emphasis on the salience of rural contexts), and we present a brief analysis of the representation of Indigenous peoples within the rural education literature.

Indigenous Education in the United States: A Brief Background
With over 600 state and federally recognized Native nations (Salazar, 2016), Indigenous education in the United States operates in a unique legal and political context not found in other marginalized populations. Through removal efforts to reservation lands, the federal government made promises to Native nations through treaties in which they agreed to provide education (among other things) in exchange for land (McCoy, 2005). Additionally, the US Supreme Court determined that Native nations had a "domestic dependent" status, solidifying a unique form of sovereignty, and a responsibility carried by the US government toward those nations, known as the federal trust responsibility (see *Cherokee Nation v. Georgia, 30 U.S. 1* [1831]; *Johnson v. M'Intosh, 21 U.S. 543* [1823]; *Worcester v. Georgia, 31 U.S. 515* [1832]). As described by the National Congress of American Indians (NCAI, 2020), "The Supreme Court has defined this trust responsibility as a 'moral obligation of the highest responsibility and trust' (*Seminole Nation v. United States*, 1942)" (p. 23). This legal history is essential to understanding sovereignty for Native nations, but it is also important to acknowledge that the act of treaty-making in general is an acknowledgment of the existence of inherent rights, including the right to educate their citizens and pursue other forms of self-determination. However, despite these treaties and their intended protections, persistent governmental relocation efforts to reservations, and later to urban communities, have created a multilayered entangled network of overlapping sovereignties and jurisdictions. Regardless, the federal trust responsibility and sovereignty of Native nations remain; this is true even if it makes things complicated in our educational systems. Moreover, we must remember: *All schools* sit on land taken through these shared histories—the same lands used to fund and sustain public schools through local property taxes (RedCorn et al., 2019).

Indigenous education in the United States now stretches across multiple institutions and agencies, such as Native nations (tribal education departments and/or agencies, TEDs/TEAs); local education agencies (LEAs); state education agencies (SEAs); and various other federal entities (e.g., the Bureau of Indian Education [BIE], the Office of Indian Education [OIE], the Administration for Native Americans [ANA], among others). Collectively, these organizations share responsibility for education across Indian Country[1] (see RedCorn et al., 2019). Often, people associate Indigenous education with the federal "Indian schools," which are a network of 183 schools and dormitories affiliated with the BIE, as well as two institutions of higher education. Roughly 130 of those schools are under the control of Native nations through contracts with the BIE (P.L. 93-638 Indian Self Determination Contracts or P.L. 100-297 Tribally Controlled

Grant Schools Act; US Department of Interior, 2018). While their mission has evolved over time, these represent the contemporary version of the assimilationist boarding school systems that historically aimed to destroy the cultures and languages of Indigenous peoples (Spring, 2012). However, only 7 percent of American Indian students in the United States attend BIE institutions, while approximately 93 percent of American Indian/Alaska Native (AI/AN) students are attending general state-run public schools (National Indian Education Association, n.d.), many in rural communities. For example, in 2018–19, 38.4 percent of all AI/AN students attended a rural school, and 71.9 percent of all high-density schools (those with 25 percent or more AI/AN students) were located in rural communities (US Department of Education, 2020b).

This means that the great majority of American Indian students are attending schools that are not run by Native nations, but are run by SEAs and LEAs, creating a situation in which TEDs/TEAs, LEAs, SEAs, and the federal government share responsibility for the education of Native students, and the need for development of partnerships (see Beesly et al., 2012; National Indian Education Association, 2016, 2017; Red Owl et al., 2000). Still, through these complex and layered contexts, Indigenous educators are often working toward what Brayboy (2006) asserts as one of the key tenets of TribalCrit: "Indigenous peoples have a desire to obtain and forge tribal sovereignty, tribal autonomy, self-determination, and self-identification" (p. 429), and sovereignty is central to understanding Indigenous perspectives in education. Lomawaima and McCarty (2002) make that direct connection to education when they explain how "sovereignty is the right of a people to self-government, self-determination, and self-education" (p. 284), and this endures even when Native citizenship and sovereignty overlap with LEA, SEA, and federal education contexts. We believe navigation of these realities is possible. Toward that aim there is a need to further explore the intersection of these two fields. The next sections are intended to explore this overlap and lay the groundwork for educators to engage in synergistic collaboration in both research and praxis.

Visibility of Indigenous Peoples in the Rural Education Literature
To get a sense of the visibility of Indigenous perspectives in the rural education research literature, we conducted an ERIC search of forty years of publications in four prominent rural-focused scholarly journals (*Journal of Research in Rural Education*, *The Rural Educator*, *Rural Society*, and *Rural Sociology*). Using fairly broad search terms (Indigenous education, Indian education, Native American education), we identified a total of forty-four articles that addressed issues related to Indigenous education. Table 20.1 presents the number of articles on Indigenous education by journal from 1980 to 2020.

Table 20.1 Frequencies for Indigenous Education Articles in Rural Journals, 1980–2020

Journal	*N* Articles
Journal of Research in Rural Education	16
The Rural Educator	20
Rural Society	3
Rural Sociology	5

We saw no discernible patterns or trends when considering the number of publications by year. Most (61 percent) of the articles were published between 2001 and 2012. The most active years were 2007 and 2009 with five and seven published articles, respectively. Most years reported two or fewer publications, and no publications were reported in seventeen of the forty years. In all cases, the number of articles represents less than 1 percent of all published articles during the time frame. Additionally, we searched major rural education conferences (National Rural Education Association, Rural Sociological Society, American Educational Research Association Rural Special Interest Group, and American Council on Rural Special Education) for this same time frame and using the same search terms, and found $n = 35$ conference papers/reports (proportionally, even less representation than in published work).

Of note, there are journals in rural subfields (e.g., *Rural Special Education Quarterly*) and rural-focused special issues of others (e.g., *Phi Delta Kappan*) that have included articles related to Indigenous education, but the point remains that there is a disproportionately low number of scholarly articles examining the nexus of rural-Indigenous education. Taken as a whole, these numbers suggest that the visibility of Indigenous education issues is quite limited in the rural education research arena. That is an especially pressing concern when we consider how closely linked the two populations are and how central the rural context is to the organization and operation of schooling for Indigenous people. As noted above, the percentage of AI/AN students attending a rural school is more than double the rate for non-AI/AN students. Moreover, the proportional size of the AI/AN population in rural schools is nearly three times what it is in nonrural schools (2.2 percent of all rural students self-identify as AI/AN, while only 0.8 percent of nonrural students do so). Finally, schools designated as *high density* via the National Indian Education Study (meaning the student population is 25 percent or more AI/AN students) are predominantly rural (71.9 percent); by comparison, only 25.7 percent of *low-density* schools (schools with less than 25 percent AI/AN student populations) are rural (US Department of Education, 2020b).

Introducing Critical Indigenous Perspectives: Centering Land, Sovereignty, and Survivance

When exploring the intersections of rural and Indigenous education, land, sovereignty, and survivance are good starting points. Starting with land, on a basic level, Indian country as a landmass is substantial. According to the NCAI (2020), "the total land mass under American Indian or Alaska Native control is about 100 million acres and would make Indian Country the fourth largest state in the United States" (p. 8), with 56 million acres of trust land and 44 million acres controlled by Alaska Native corporations and villages as fee simple land (see NCAI, 2020, for explanation on trust lands, types of Indian lands, non-Indian fee lands, Alaska Native lands and corporations, etc.). The Navajo Nation alone is larger than nine states in the union. This substantial landmass provides some perspective as we consider overlap with rural education.

On a much deeper level, however, land in the context of Indigenous education and research often works as a deeper philosophical foundation for generating knowledge and understanding. In relation to the important role of sovereignty, there is a need to think beyond political and legal interpretations when talking about land. Grande (2008) channels Lyons (2000) in her framework for Red Pedagogy when she defines sovereignty broadly as "a people's right to rebuild its demand to exist and present its gifts to the world . . . an adamant refusal to dissociate culture, identity, and power from the land" (p. 250). In this context, when Indigenous educators and researchers center land and the natural world in their work, they are inherently pushing back against assimilationist systems that were aimed at removing land from Native worldviews—both physically and mentally. This assimilationist history has worked to commodify this connection to land and, over time, it has eroded its meaning and tried to replace it with stereotypical imagery of romanticized notions of the noble savage and/or the purist Native who is one-with-nature. Furthermore, a homogenization of diverse Indigenous worldviews has created oversimplified understandings of place-based relationships with Indigenous environments, and (re)instilling plural and diverse understandings of Native peoples has been an ongoing effort. These stereotypes have unfolded in media and curricular contexts in interesting ways, such as the problematic anti-pollution public service announcements in the 1970s that showed "Iron Eyes Cody" (an Italian American actor born Espera Oscar DeCorti with questionable Native ancestry) shedding a tear over pollution (Baird, 2012). There is a need to avoid this pitfall and seek a deeper and more nuanced understanding that is "neither naive naturalism nor romantic noble savage reverie" (as described by Wildcat, 2017, p. ix). To move past these stereotypes, we must look deeper than just protecting the earth (which is still an important goal) or moving backward in time to capture some romanticized past.[2] Indigenous peoples evolve, too, and it is more appropriate to look into the past in a manner that informs Indigenous futures.

Our work here is to highlight opportunities to synthesize and apply deeper cultural worldviews in ways that explore Indigenous populations and their modern complexities. In other words, we provide a brief description of dispossessed histories to situate these understandings, but this work is less about bringing attention to recycling during Earth Day and perpetuating noble savage stereotypes but rather about engaging in what Cajete (1994) describes as a "quality of thinking that embodies an ecologically-informed consciousness" (p. 46). It is a way of thinking and seeing the world through plurality and dynamic relationality, with an energy and substance moving through layers of interconnected relationships. As Deloria and Wildcat (2001) assert, "Instead of talking of an Indian 'science' or Indian 'religion,' we should focus our attention on the metaphysics possessed by most American Indian tribes and derive from this central perspective the information and beliefs that naturally flowed from it" (p. 2). Furthermore, they explain how, "being *indigenous* means 'to be of a place'" (p. 31), and there are core principles found across many Indigenous worldviews, which can be represented by a simple equation: "Power and place produce personality. This equation simply means that the universe is alive, but it also contains within it the very important suggestion that the universe is personal and, therefore, must be approached in a personal manner" (Deloria & Wildcat, 2001, p. 23). While these concepts are rooted in a worldview that sees interconnectedness with the natural world (Kawagley & Barnhardt, 1999), it is important to recognize that these ideas are applicable beyond the fields of land conservation and experiential learning environments in nature. As an example, Secatero (2015) from the Cañoncito Band of Navajo outlines a framework for Indigenous well-being in rural leadership and higher education but grounds his work in his family's history and knowledge as it relates to a specific Leadership Tree located on their reservation in northwest New Mexico. Using this local and place-based understanding rooted in connections to land, he presents a model for conceptualizing rural leadership and well-being that can be used in research and praxis. While this is a good example of deepening the concept of being connected to land, we must acknowledge that the history of assimilation, relocation, and land dispossession has made

The Bloomsbury Handbook of Rural Education in the United States

it challenging for many (Native and non-Native) to understand those deeper connections to land. Regardless, the field of Indigenous studies encourages these forms of intellectualism, with a caution against overromanticizing and oversimplifying.

American systems (i.e., economic, educational, political) rely and operate on an assimilative assumption put in motion long ago and, as some critical rural educators (e.g., C. B. Howley et al., 2014) have observed, these old power dynamics and settler-colonial trajectories originated primarily in rural agrarian contexts. As a result, there is a need to acknowledge that "governmental policies and educational policies toward Indigenous peoples are intimately linked around the problematic goal of assimilation" (Brayboy, 2006, p. 429), and this occurs at all levels. One example of this at the intersection of land dispossession, education, assimilation, and policy is looking back at the process of allotment through the General Allotment Act of 1887 (or The Dawes Act), which took 90 million acres away from reservations to be given to settlers (NCAI, 2020), creating a patchwork effect on reservation lands. This also coincided with imposing a Eurocentric sedentary lifestyle on Indigenous peoples through agriculture and education (Burns, 2004; Hurt, 1987; Lewis, 1994; Nash, 2019). Then, with the help of the Morrill Act of 1862, land for land grant and extension was accumulated in order to further dispossess Indigenous people (Stein, 2017), and money accumulated through that process was used to fund land grant/ grab institutions (Lee & Ahtone, 2020) still operating in the present. With this history in mind, educators and scholars working at the intersection of rural and Indigenous education need to further explore how these Eurocentric assimilationist aims, and other Indigenous and culturally diverse perspectives, continue through modern extension and agricultural education programs and how Native nations sponsoring such programs might engage in these critical discussions as they build programming (Hart, 2006; Hayman et al., 2018; Schauber, 2001). Furthermore, the field of rural education could benefit from incorporating important perspectives in scholarship, praxis, and advocacy work revolving around food sovereignty, which inherently overlaps with policy, health, decolonizing diets, food systems, agribusiness, and more (e.g., Echo Hawk Consulting, 2015).

As evident through food sovereignty advocacy work, Indigenous peoples have proven to be resilient and adaptable. This emphasis on adaptability brings forward the notion of survivance, a term coined by Vizenor et al. (2014) and forwarded by Sabzalian (2019) in *Indigenous Children's Survivance in Public Schools*. She writes, "Native courage, creativity, intelligence, determination, and artfulness—acts of Native survivance—are our inheritance and our legacy as Indigenous peoples" (p. 1). Using this lens of survivance shifts our mindset from the deficit-based narratives that have long shaped understanding of who Indigenous peoples are, toward an asset-based narrative that shows the agency and strengths of Indigenous peoples—people who have found ways to creatively resist, adapt, and endure through the onslaught of assimilationist settler colonialism. This asset-based approach is further supported through culturally sustaining and revitalizing pedagogies, which "attend directly to asymmetrical power relations and the goal of transforming legacies of colonization" (Lee & McCarty, 2017, p. 62).

Yet, through generations of adaptation and ongoing negotiation through entangled settler-colonial systems, creativity and ingenuity still hold space for this kind of thinking, which allows for this deeper form of (re)centering to occur. This space has been held open by Indigenous ancestors to make room for Indigenous futures, as they have passed down cultural systems of education outside of state-sponsored school systems, which still work as systems of education, although usually only viewed as "cultural ceremonies" or "traditions." As Lomawaima (1995) describes, educating Native students should be conceptualized as a "500 year old battle for power: first, the power to define what education is—the power to set its goals, define its policies, and enforce its practices—and second, the power to define who native people are and who they are not" (p. 331). This brings us back, again, to the notion of sovereignty and the need to deepen its meaning by considering the role of intellectual sovereignty, as Pewewardy (2015) does when asserting, "I believe the first step in becoming self-determined is examining the 'sovereign self'" (p. 71). Later, Pewewardy et al. (2018) generated a model to give some intellectual structure to the process of deepening our critical consciousness through what they call Transformational Indigenous Praxis (TIP), which represents the kind of intellectual work associated with moving toward a more powerful degree of self-determination—an important component of any decolonizing project (Smith, 1999). Warrior (1995) writes about intellectual sovereignty while exploring the intellectual work of Indigenous scholars Vine Deloria Jr. and John-Joseph Mathews, stating, "I contend that it is now critical for American Indian intellectuals committed to sovereignty to realize that we too must struggle for sovereignty, *intellectual sovereignty*, and allow the definition and articulation of what that means to emerge as we critically reflect on that struggle" (p. 98).

For non-Natives sharing space and communal responsibility with Indigenous peoples, this is the struggle: an ongoing fight over sovereignty in legal, political, and intellectual forms; not surprisingly, educational systems play a key role in this fight. From this positionality, non-Native educators in rural America are inherently entangled in this same struggle, as they are working with Native communities, on Native land, in schools funded by theft of Native lands.

Deepening the Concept of Place-Based Education: Interrogating Culture and Curriculum

Place is an inherently rural construct (C. B. Howley et al., 2014; Leopold, 1949) and the centrality of place to rural schooling has a long history predating what we have come to view as formalized public education (Theobald, 1997). When considering the role of place, Greenwood (2009) calls for some acknowledgment of histories with Indigenous peoples in rural contexts, and he also discusses the need for a critical pedagogy of place (Gruenewald, 2003b), which makes room for us to draw connections to Indigenous scholars for the purpose of adding depth to place-based education. First, we start by connecting back to Deloria and Wildcat's (2001) emphasis that power and place produce personality. But going deeper, one example to consider is Larsen and J. T. Johnson's (2017) work on being-together-in-place, and how they frame the world as a pluriverse and place as having agency—calling us into coexistence in a manner that acknowledges difference and diversity but is still connected to lands and the more-than-human world (cf. Theobald's, 1997, discussion of *intradependence* in rural spaces). As they put it: "Place calls us to the struggles of coexistence in this pluriverse, a world of many worlds" (Larsen & J. T. Johnson, 2017, p. 1), and as they discuss their research into various perspectives found in the literature on place, they explain:

> What we did not find, though, was an active agency for place. Repeatedly we saw place described as the platform for human agency, the locale for social interaction, or the colorful stage upon which human meaning, history, and experience are set. (p. 16)

Clearly, this discourse on place is an extension of connectedness to land and the living energy that moves through place to generate local personality; additionally, the work makes clear that understanding place as having agency helps us to better understand the notion of coexistence. In other words, it's as if Larsen and J. T. Johnson (2017) are asking us to let the call of place take the lead—front and center—when doing research on coexistence and diversity of peoples, instead of letting human philosophy and theory take that position. This is a potentially valuable concept when exploring rural-Indigenous place-based allyship.

Furthermore, when considering place-based approaches to education there is also a need to consider critical perspectives in rural-urban Indigenous geographies. John and Ford (2017), citing Goeman (2013), discuss the history of naming and mapping, which eventually led to dispossession, but they also interrogate the role of urban relocation programs in the 1950s, which created spatial separation that in turn created "cultural separation aimed at dismantling traditions, languages, and spiritual practices" (p. 10). However, rural reservations still serve a place-based role to Native folks living in cities. John and Ford (2017) describe how

> The reservation has, by necessity, always betrayed any town/country dialectic, for although reservations are never in or too close to city centers, they themselves are the centers of culture, language, spirituality, commerce, and all of those things that hold Indigenous social formations together. (p. 10)

What has happened over time, John and Ford (2017) criticize, is that this process has created false dichotomies related to rural-urban lived experience that has "fractured solidarity among Indigenous communities by designating reservation Indians as more Native than urban Indians" (p. 10). Here, the main point to consider is that while reservations are rural they still serve as a place-based hub for many educational (as well as political and economic) endeavors. In other words, relocation histories have led to a significant number of Natives living off-reservation, but the reservation often still serves as the primary hub for spiritual, cultural, and linguistic education, as well as political and economic operations that connect Indigenous communities in both on-/off-reservation contexts. Through the lens of Corbett's (2007) notion of *Learning to Leave*, Coharie Indigenous educational leadership scholar Faircloth (2009) does a wonderful job of using story to share her experiences and tensions in these Indigenous urban-rural contexts, and more of this kind of work would be valuable to the field of rural education.

Furthermore, place-based education is inherently connected to the concept of "culture," but there is a need to unpack that term further and to interrogate its foundations and commonly held understanding of the term. In doing so, it is important to explore the narrow ways in which Indigenous peoples in the United States have been seen, and taught about, through curricula and the media. First, a comprehensive review of social studies curricula by Shear et al. (2015) found that 87 percent of all standards about American Indians were situated in a pre-1900s context, meaning the vast majority of what people learn about Natives is a stuck-in-the-past stereotype. This generally gives the impression that American Indians are extinct, as Ladson-Billings (2003) explains:

> We see them as welcoming European settlers, joining them in a Thanksgiving celebration, guiding them as they explore the west, being massacred as settlers push westward, and finally being removed and subdued by Andrew Jackson. After the "Trail of Tears," American Indians disappear from the pages of our textbooks and the curriculum. For our students, American Indians are museum exhibits. (p. 3)

These stuck-in-the-past stereotypes have strong roots in the status quo and can be found easily in curricula, ancillary teaching resources, school branding, and across the media—all of which have a negative impact on the way Native students can see themselves, and their futures. Specifically,

Critical Indigenous Perspectives in Rural Education

Leavitt et al. (2015) outline the clear underrepresentation of Natives in media, and that the limited representation that does exist is very narrow in a way that both homogenizes an extremely diverse demographic as well as reinforces stereotypes mentioned above. As an example, they discuss how conducting image searches for "Native American" and "American Indian" yielded a vast majority (i.e., of the first 100 images for each term, 95.5 percent on Google [n = 191]; 99 percent of images on Bing [n = 198]) of these intransigent stereotypes. When we then explore how psychological research has shown us how American Indian mascots and branding "are harmful because they remind American Indians of the limited ways others see them and, in this way, constrain the way they can see themselves" (Fryberg et al., 2008, p. 208), the connections between all these issues start to become more clear. Furthermore, research also shows that students exposed to this imagery are actually more likely to stereotype other ethnic groups (Kim-Prieto et al., 2010). The critical point here is that there is a serious disconnect between what is learned *about* Indigenous peoples and what is experienced *by* Indigenous peoples—and this discrepancy and invisibility of the actual everyday lived realities reproduces harm for Indigenous communities.

Bringing this back to place-based education, we need to expand how we think about incorporating "culture" into culturally responsive education. For starters, there is a need to make it plural—*cultures*—as a way to show diversity across Indigenous peoples, and even within particular place-based contexts. Moving forward, the obvious answers lie in revising learning standards, teaching materials, educator training programs, incorporating local languages and place-/land-based worldviews, and creating events that allow students to experience and/or learn about American Indian customs and traditions (see State of Washington Office of Superintendent of Public Instruction, 2018; Montana Office of Public Instruction, 2018; and Wisconsin Department of Public Instruction, 2018, for examples of statewide reform). When thinking about how to create culturally relevant programming people tend to fall into a trap in which they think of incorporating culture(s) only as bringing drum and feather cultural exhibits to the school, providing opportunities to make American Indian arts or crafts, or looking only to social studies and English language arts as curricula to reform. These are all positive steps forward, and very commendable, but alone they fail to embrace the depth of place-based education and a more holistic understanding about what Indigenous cultures, and futures, are beyond their ceremonies and traditions. Indigenous cultures are not merely exotic people to be studied, they are lifeways, values, and relational interactions that should be embedded throughout the culture of educational institutions and should connect students to the appropriate communities and nations within the place-based locale. Those *connections and relationships* can be just as important, or potentially more important, than the content being taught to Native students. This place-based nuance, or disconnect, is often overlooked when working to create culturally sustaining and revitalizing programming. In other words, educators (and researchers) need to resist the temptation to only see Native cultures as topics to be moved into scope and sequence curricula or cultural fairs and explore how one might consider a deeper and more holistic place-based approach to education that embeds Indigenous cultures into the fabric of the institution and connects people through relationships.

Revisiting *Durable Issues in Rural Education*: A Call to Action, or the Call of Place?

J. D. Johnson (2014a) offers for consideration several *durable issues* for rural schools and communities. While by no means a comprehensive set of issues facing rural education practitioners and/or researchers, the list offers utility as a conceptual framing for engaging varied issues of policy and practice. The issues are not specific problems of practice and policy; rather, they represent broad patterns and dynamics that resist simple solutions and instead help to frame and articulate the scope and scale of the work to be engaged by both researchers and practitioners (hopefully, in collaboration). Attentive to the critical Indigenous perspectives presented here, we recognize the value in revisiting these issues and challenging traditional conceptualizations in order to offer enhanced opportunities for understanding rural schools and communities (and for supporting them, sustaining them, and promoting their well-being). Here, we briefly consider how our understandings of four of those durable issues are enhanced and/or problematized by the application of critical Indigenous perspectives, and we offer recommendations for how critical Indigenous perspectives might inform scholarship and praxis moving forward.

Rural Out-Migration

The life experiences of rural people vary considerably, as do the experiences of people who migrate out of rural areas (see Schafft & Maselli, this volume). Nevertheless, there are consistent findings from the extant literature investigating rural out-migration (e.g., Carr & Kefalas, 2009; Corbett, 2007; C. W. Howley & Hambrick, 2014), and these findings collectively describe an issue that continues to demand attention from researchers, policymakers, and practitioners: the pursuit of educational and economic opportunities as a motivating influence for the decision to leave one's rural place of origin; attachments to place among rural people and the resulting feelings of ambivalence about adult places of residence and life trajectories; and the role of schooling with regard to those pursuits, attachments, and ambivalence. There is a need to further explore the issue of out-migration from rural-Indigenous communities, but also how land, cultures, education, economics, and sovereignty influence those life processes. As Faircloth (2009) points out, "Education has the potential to be used as a tool for learning to leave, learning to stay and learning to return—skills that are not at odds, but are necessary in an increasingly globalized world" (p. 4), and the Indigenous contexts outlined in this chapter are inherently connected to those migration dynamics.

Rural Community Viability and Economics

Themes here include declining rural populations; the impacts of globalization on rural communities; the idea of rural spaces as political and cultural alternatives to a dominant neoliberal ideology; the idea of the school as a community center; and the relationship between curriculum and place. Collectively, work in this line of inquiry suggests that rural sensibilities and lifeways (and thus rural communities and rural people) are largely incompatible with many aspects of contemporary economic, political, and social structures—and that this incompatibility renders life more difficult for many rural people and communities. The solution is not, however, to change rural places and rural lifeways to align with their suburban and urban counterparts; on the contrary, rural sensibilities and lifeways represent an alternative to the failed and failing neoliberal agenda (Theobald, 1997). Indigenous perspectives represent a dramatic counter to contemporary neoliberal defaults and can offer insights and guideposts for developing and maintaining the kind of education that prepares children for living in ways that value land, family, and neighbors and allow them to serve and steward things of shared importance to their communities. Against a backdrop of assimilationist and survivance histories in Indigenous education, and attempted

Critical Indigenous Perspectives in Rural Education

sociocultural fracturing through relocation and migrations, it is compelling to consider how this overlaps, and is entangled with, contemporary rural education experiences. Furthermore, considering that Native nations also engage in various forms of economic development and enterprise, and therefore community employment, there is a need to explore how sovereignty and economics connected to Native nations are inherently part of conversations about rural community viability.

Social Reproduction and Interruption

These themes are prevalent in the education literature more broadly, of course (Bourdieu & Passeron, 1990; Bowles & Gintis, 1976), but the ways in which these dynamics manifest differ according to context, with rural settings presenting both unique challenges and unique opportunities (C. B. Howley et al., 2014). The role of schooling in the process of maintaining and reinforcing inequities in the distribution of challenges, opportunities, and rewards (schools as sorting mechanisms) is contrasted here with the alternative role of schooling as a vehicle for challenging and interrupting inequity (schools as equalizing mechanisms). Some key characteristics of rural schools (e.g., smaller organization scale, close attachments to community) position them well to play this equalizing role. Schools serving higher densities of Indigenous student populations (which are mostly rural) share many of these characteristics and thus offer opportunities for interrupting social reproduction—and pushing back against assimilationist status quos. Like other rural schools, their success in doing so depends largely on their ability to resist being co-opted into replicating the default setting of suburban and urban schools but instead focusing on marshaling their resident resources and community assets to provide the kind of schooling experience that honors history, place, traditions, and multiple forms of sovereignty (see RedCorn, 2020, for a relevant educational capacity building model for Native nations).

Increasing Diversity and Rural Cultural Adaptation

Recent decades have seen dramatic shifts in the demographics of rural America, with sudden change often occurring in specific communities as a result of economic opportunities and the recruitment of workers from outside the community and abroad (e.g., Davidson, 1996). The role of schooling in welcoming new and diverse residents and incorporating them into the community is a complex matter, with experiences ranging from authentic engagement and leveraging educational structures and processes to build community to organizing and operating the schooling enterprise in ways that marginalize new and diverse students and families. Indigenous people know all too well about the role schools can play in diminishing culture and forcing assimilation, and critical Indigenous perspectives have much to teach us regarding adaptation and maladaptation.

Conclusion

With these durable issues in mind, bringing critical Indigenous perspectives into rural education spaces helps deepen our understandings of how history, power, economics, governance, and cultures are connected to our shared educational systems, and places. We encourage those looking to work in alliance with Native nations and educators to decenter colonial and assimilationist approaches to education and make substantial room for intellectual labor from Indigenous scholars done near the nexus of land, sovereignty, survivance, place-based education, and more.

The Bloomsbury Handbook of Rural Education in the United States

Therefore, this is a call to action in research and praxis: a need to explore how we can build alliances across these fields while we simultaneously entangle and detangle *place* within the intersecting work of Indigenous-rural education. Furthermore, we must dive into the nuance and ask critical questions about alliance building in a manner that acknowledges separate, but shared, social, cultural, economic, and political power dynamics within *ongoing* processes of assimilation, colonization, and dispossession. From that position, a critical question worth pursuing is: How can we build alliances from a place of mutual respect that honors difference, without appropriating one another's struggles in the process? Perhaps Larsen and J. T. Johnson's (2017) notion of giving place agency to consider coexistence is a starting point for rural-Indigenous synergistic endeavors in scholarship and praxis. In a way, maybe we consider how the introduction of particular characteristics and organisms in an ecosystem can in some ways overtake other components of that shared place and create imbalance; but diversity and balance within ecosystems can also be found to increase the strength and health of those systems. In other words, how can we find balance in our entanglements for the benefit of all of our students in these shared rural-Indigenous spaces? Or, rather, how does place call us to action in our shared spaces? What are we overlooking and where might we find solutions?

21

English Learners in Rural Schools

Maria Coady

Vignette

Esdras, Edwin, Marisol, and Isabel arrived in rural Ivy County, Florida, in the fall of 2018. They came from Guatemala with their father, José (all names are pseudonyms), but their mother remained in their home country. Esdras, then 18 years old, and his younger siblings (Edwin 16, Marisol 13, and Isabel 9) were found by the local Migrant Education program staff working in fields picking peanuts. Although the Migrant Education staff suggested that Esdras enroll in high school, he decided not to, stating that he needed to work to earn money for the family. The district informed José that the other three children were required to attend school under US law.

About a year after their arrival, José abruptly returned to Guatemala, leaving Esdras in charge of his brother and sisters. Before leaving, José signed a Power of Attorney in Spanish allowing Esdras to make decisions on behalf of the children. Shortly thereafter, Edwin was pulled over while driving, and, unable to provide legal documents, was placed into a deportation holding center about 35 miles away.

At that time, Isabel's fourth-grade teacher, Mrs. Roberts, started to notice changes to Isabel's behavior at school. Isabel was disengaged in classroom learning, had a short attention span, and refused to eat. She self-isolated from other children at recess. Isabel also began to miss school, sometimes several days in a row, and told her teachers that the bus never showed up.

As a high-poverty, Title I school, students were provided backpacks with nonperishable food items each Friday so that they could eat during the weekends. Isabel refused to take the backpack home. Making matters worse, with some prompting from the Spanish–English bilingual paraprofessional who inquired what was going on, Isabel uttered that Esdras was asked to sign a document stating that their father abandoned them. This frightened the children, who feared being separated. The school teachers, guidance counselor, principal, and staff were perplexed about what they could do to advocate for the children and were also

The Bloomsbury Handbook of Rural Education in the United States

fearful that signing a letter of abandonment would force the family to be separated and the younger children placed in foster care.

Introduction

The short scenario above is based on a true story about a family living in a rural Title I school district with low-density—or a small percentage of—EL students. In the current sociopolitical context, these stories are more than just anecdotes: they are increasingly recounted by teachers and school leaders working with rural EL students in the United States. Concerns surrounding the physical, social, and emotional well-being of ELs are intertwined with schools' concerns of how best to educate students learning English as an additional language. In addition, the rural school teachers and leaders with whom I work describe the increasing range of linguistic diversity among their EL student population. Although Spanish continues to be the most widely used language of EL students in the United States (US Department of Education, 2020d), refugee and asylee students who speak lesser-used languages, as well as students from Central America who speak Indigenous languages and know little or no Spanish, seem increasingly common in rural schools. What are the characteristics of rural EL students in the United States today, and how can education for ELs be more equitable? This chapter addresses these questions by providing an overview of rural EL education and opportunities for equitable EL education in rural America.

Linguistic diversity is fact and fabric of the United States. Currently, one in three US children comes from a home in which one or both parents speak a language other than English (Park et al., 2018). In this chapter, I refer to students who speak languages other than English and who are in the process of learning English as an additional language as "ELs" because a significant amount of research, resources, and materials use this terminology. However, ELs are often referred to as English Language Learners (ELLs) and more recently as Emergent Bilinguals (EBs), a term that affirms language as a resource of bilingual and multilingual families (García et al., 2008). EL students today represent a new "superdiversity" among American youth (Park et al., 2018, p. 6). Immigrants are a significant subgroup that contributes to the linguistic landscape of the United States, but American Indian students (Carjuzaa & Ruff, 2016) and children born in the United States to non-English-speaking parents also contribute to the linguistic diversity of the country (Zong & Batalova, 2015).

Native peoples and new immigrants represent two subgroups that contribute to the social richness and economic well-being of the United States. In the case of new immigrants, families arrive for multiple reasons, including to escape war-torn countries; to flee persecution, discrimination, or gang violence; or in search of economic opportunity. Immigration trends over the past three decades indicate that the US immigrant population has doubled in number since 1990 (Pew Trusts, 2014), with an increase of nearly thirty million immigrants who live, work, and attend schools across the United States (Batalova et al., 2020). Immigrants continue to arrive, despite national narratives, poor immigration policies, and federal cuts to social services that create a negative context of reception (Stepick & Stepick, 2009). According to Massey (2020), the current sociopolitical climate and anti-immigrant sentiment has effectively become a "war on immigrants" (p. 30) that targets all newcomers, but Latino immigrants in particular. Massey describes how new federal policies that limit the ability of immigrants to traverse the southern US border have contributed to the number of undocumented persons who must remain in the United States. Moreover, as Showalter and colleagues (2019) confirm, the main barriers to accessing educational and health services for immigrant families in rural communities include fear of legal repercussions due to immigration, undocumented status, language differences, and transportation.

Although anti-immigrant policies and sentiments continue unabated, immigrant families contribute socially and financially to rural America and have effectively revitalized rural economies. In fact, scholars (J. Johnson et al., 2018; K. Johnson, 2012) reported that ethnic and racial minorities accounted for 83 percent of population growth in rural communities between 2000 and 2010. Lichter and colleagues (2016) note that immigrants from Latin America have brought a much needed lifeline to rural communities, countering trends of outward mobility and population decline, and this has been especially noteworthy in rural "new" destinations—places where immigrants did not formerly settle—in states such as South Carolina, Alabama, and Tennessee (Terrazas, 2011; US Department of Education, 2020d). Terrazas (2011) reports that more than one-third of immigrants in new destinations arrive from Mexico, and males over the age of sixteen in new destinations are employed in construction, extraction, such as mining, and transportation industries.

Rural English Learner Students

Schools are one domain experiencing national and international migration trends, economic policies, and social narratives surrounding language-minoritized students and families. Schools are where language policies and attitudes toward languages and speakers of languages are enacted (Kaplan & Baldauf, 2005). The US Department of Education reports that EL students are among the fastest-growing population in the United States. Data from the National Center for Education Statistics (NCES) indicate that during the 2000–1 school year, the percentage of identified EL students—those considered in need of English as a second language (ESL) services—was 8.1 percent nationwide, or roughly 3.8 million students. Recent data from the 2016–17 school year indicate that EL students now account for 9.6 percent of the total K-12 student population, or just under five million students across the country (NCES, 2018a). In fringe, distant, and remote rural settings, defined following US guidelines for rurality (NCES, 2006), EL students account for about 14 percent of the total EL population (NCES, 2012). It is conceivable that the number of rural EL students is well over 650,000 students in 2021.

The US Office of English Language Acquisition reports that rural locations are particularly impacted by changes in the EL student population. Over the past ten years, Arkansas, Kansas, Missouri, and North Dakota experienced an increase in ELs between 200 percent and 399 percent. Other states such as Kentucky, Mississippi, and South Carolina experienced a 400 percent or greater increase in their EL student population (US Department of Education, 2020a). These are states that were formerly not identified as having significant numbers of EL students. In other words, over the past decade there has been intense growth of EL students in rural new destination settings and states.

Despite the fact that one-third of US schools are located in rural settings, a disproportionately small amount of research on education is focused on rural students and even less on rural EL students (Williams & Grooms, 2016). In a literature review published in 2005, Arnold and colleagues reported no studies conducted on rural EL education. Calls from both the National Rural Education Association (NREA, 2016) and scholars of rural education (e.g., Cicchinelli & Beesley, 2017) have brought heightened awareness of the limited work conducted on rural EL education including how best to prepare educators for linguistic diversity. A more recent review (Coady, 2020a) identified nine studies on rural EL students that addressed how to improve education for rural ELs, six of which focused on teacher education and three that emphasized and examined the social and ecological context of rural EL education.

Several reasons account for this dearth in research on rural EL education. One is that scholars do not always identify the geographic context of rurality or might not list rurality as a descriptive keyword when publishing their work. Another reason for the limited number of studies is that rural EL students are frequently "low density"—that is, small numbers of EL students in relatively large school districts—making them a low priority for federal research funding in education. The state of Florida is a good case in point. Florida has sixty-seven large school districts, and about one-third of its districts are rural (NCES, 2014). Due to their geographic size, some districts labeled as "nonrural" contain rural, small town, suburban, and urban schools. Deeming the entire district not rural disqualifies it from supplemental funding that might otherwise be allocated under federal programs aimed to mitigate funding disparities for rural schools (Brenner, 2016). Yet despite fewer financial and human resources to support learning for EL students, rural schools face the same metrocentric norms in student learning outcomes, teacher education, and demands for family engagement, a phenomenon that Green and Letts (2007) refer to as being geographically "blind" (p. 60).

Challenges in Rural EL Education

Several challenges exist at the intersection of rural education and EL education in the United States. These include obtaining accurate demographic data on EL students' home languages and educational backgrounds; knowledge surrounding how best to prepare specialist ESL teachers, mainstream teachers, and school leaders; variations across the United States at the state level that determine EL student English and native language proficiency; different instructional models and approaches that best serve rural EL students; and funding for rural EL education. Due to the variation across the fifty states and US territories surrounding language programs, policies, and practices, scholars who examine and advocate for rural EL students and families face difficulties in aligning policies and practices (Coady, 2020a). Moreover, due to these variations, Villegas and Pompa (2020) describe the national landscape of EL policies inconsistent and "patchy." These are described below.

Home Languages and Educational Backgrounds of ELs
Although Spanish remains the most widely spoken language among EL students in the United States, this is not the case across all states, and ELs nationwide speak more than 400 languages (US Department of Education, 2020a). The US Department of Education reports that Alaska, Maine, Vermont, Hawaii, and Montana's EL populations have larger numbers of speakers of Yupik, Somali, Nepali, Iloko, and German, respectively. In addition, recent studies conducted in rural communities with low-density ELs report increasing numbers of immigrant EL students from Guatemala, Honduras, and El Salvador who speak Indigenous languages such as Mam,

Kanjobal, and K'iché (Carcamo, 2016; Holder, 2017; Tussey, 2017; Wang, 2014). Although Indigenous languages only account for a small proportion of languages spoken in US classrooms, they complexify linguistic diversity for rural educators who might have some knowledge of Spanish but no knowledge of Indigenous languages. In order to understand rural EL education and the linguistic diversity of classrooms, educators at local and state levels need to capture these shifts. What "works" with rural ELs who are Spanish speakers is not necessarily applicable to ELs from different language backgrounds.

A related issue is identifying the educational backgrounds and experiences of rural EL students from various countries who move into rural communities. A notable trend is students coming to the United States who have experienced interrupted or limited formal education due to border crossing and detention, temporary residence in refugee camps, or limited education in their home countries (DeCapua & Marshall, 2011; Massey et al., 2015). Rural educators report working with increasing numbers of EL students who have limited or interrupted education, which frequently equates to limited first language literacy development (Hansen-Thomas et al., 2016; Montero et al., 2014). Students who have limited literacy in their first language face the drawback of not being able to transfer literacy skills from their first language into English. Scholars have found that language transfer is a more effective approach to acquiring English than "time-on-task" (MacSwan et al., 2017). In other words, more English is not always better. For teachers working with ELs, knowledge of students' first language literacy development and their prior education is a critical component of teaching ELs. The need to capture the changing and nuanced backgrounds of EL students in rural schools is urgent in order to reverse misconceptions surrounding second-language acquisition. Misconceptions for rural teachers are especially acute due to limited access to ESL professional development (PD). These have important implications for how teachers and educational leaders might be prepared to work with rural EL students and families, and the instructional decisions that teachers need to make to build student learning in the context of high-stakes testing (Heffington, 2019).

Preparation of Teachers and Leaders for Rural ELs

Teacher and educational leader preparation programs have similarly experienced metrocentric bias in their approach to preparation of educators to work with EL students. Where in urbanized areas specialist EL teachers can work alongside mainstream teachers, pull students out of classrooms for targeted English language instruction, or provide dual-language (DL) bilingual education programs, rural schools often lack funding and the human resources to provide such specializations. Even in states like Florida, which requires the preparation of all teachers to work with EL students, teachers struggle to differentiate instruction (Coady et al., 2016). One reason for limited teacher specialization is that schools across the country continue to face an overall decline in teachers (Sutcher et al., 2016).

Teacher educators have noted the difficulty of preparing teacher candidates for linguistic diversity (Coady et al., 2011, 2016; Lucas, 2010; Wong-Fillmore & Snow, 2000). With current demographic changes—that is, increases in rural EL students—and the need for more highly prepared ESL teachers in rural schools, this issue is ever more pressing (Cicchinelli & Beesley, 2017). A report by the Education Commission of the States found that more than thirty states lacked guidelines for the preparation of teachers to work with EL students beyond the federal requirements (Wixom, 2014). Teacher preparation for EL students is essential in order to ensure equitable access to the curriculum under federal mandates (*Lau v. Nichols*, 1974).

Educators in rural locales appear particularly underprepared to provide the educational and language-learning supports that EL students need, including ESL instruction, and adequate teacher and leader PD that affirm the linguistic resources of students and families (Kandel et al., 2011). Ankeny and colleagues (2019) investigated twenty-one teachers, coaches, counselors, and leaders of rural EL students in a graduate-level, six-course PD program. They found that the participants preferred on-site—as opposed to virtual—coursework, where they were able to align the PD to their actual rural schools. Field trips to local farms and plant nurseries and small group discussion allowed for deeper understanding of rural EL students. In contrast, when taking online courses that lacked a place-based rural lens, the same participants stated feeling misunderstood and undervalued for their leadership skills (Coady, 2019c).

In a telling study of educational leaders, McHenry-Sorber and Provinzano (2017) reported the social challenges that resulted from expansion of the hydraulic fracturing industry in one rural community in Pennsylvania. In the local schools, educational leaders managed these social changes through a "discourse of compliance" rather than through a lens of critical place-conscious leadership or social justice (p. 614). In another study set in northern Minnesota where low numbers (where 25 percent or less of the student population is identified as ELL) of Ukrainian, Mexican, and Honduran families relocated, Christianson (2016) found that little or no systematic second-language supports existed. Some of those absent supports included adequate ESL screening, language proficiency testing, differentiated instruction, and family engagement. The authors found that the community struggled to identify timely interventions to support EL student learning. These studies underscore the work of Ringler and O'Neal (O'Neal et al., 2009; Ringler et al., 2013) who found that strong school leadership was essential to support teachers of EL students.

State-Level Variations in Definitions for ELs

The definition of ELs and the identification and exit criteria for language services vary across states. Currently, thirty-eight states in the United States use a framework for EL identification and assessment called WIDA, which provides a screener for identifying ELs and annual language proficiency tests. While most states avail of the WIDA framework (2020), which includes language proficiency levels aligned to language-learning objectives, other states with large numbers of rural ELs do not. For those states, identifying an EL depends on teacher and leader preparation and a knowledge of the process of EL identification and placement. In addition, varying definitions of English language proficiency make identifying national trends in rural EL education difficult. Individual states determine exit criteria for EL student services. Thus, a student who is identified as an EL in one state and who migrates seasonally north to a different rural community in another state might not be identified as an EL using that state's criteria.

Instructional Models and Programs for Rural ELs

Another challenge facing rural schools with EL students is access to high-quality instructional programs to support EL student learning. Only half of all rural schools reported offering ESL instruction as a scheduled class versus 89 percent of city schools. Moreover, 26 percent of rural high schools had a bilingual paraprofessional who spoke the student's home language versus 55 percent in cities, and only 32 percent of rural high schools offered Sheltered English instruction—a teaching approach that reduces language complexity for ELs—versus 81 percent in cities (Lewis & Gray, 2016).

Relatively few rural school districts offer bilingual education programs, that is, educational programs that provide some academic content instruction in the native language of students such as in Spanish. Data from 2015 to 2016 (NCES, 2016a) indicate that only 5 percent of rural high schools offered bilingual programs versus 14 percent in cities. The number of EL students in high schools in 2016 were 354,400 in cities and 42,800 in rural locales. The same report indicated that only 50 percent of rural districts offered ESL instruction versus 89 percent in cities. In a study of one DL program in rural Illinois, Paciotto and Delany-Barmann (2011) identified the challenges associated with implementing DL for rural EL students. DL is a specific type of bilingual education in which two languages are used as mediums of instruction for two different groups of students, such as native-English and native-Spanish speakers. Educators responded to top-down language policies that had a monolingual (English) orientation by implementing a DL program in "Rivertown," the pseudonym given to the town in the Paciotto and Delany-Barmann study. The absence of supports, such as teacher and leader PD, and materials and curriculum were barriers to effective implementation of the rural DL program. Thus, across rural settings, educators were less likely to use students' first language for language and literacy development (Kena et al., 2016), resulting in negative implications for the academic success of rural EL students.

Funding

Finally, related to teacher and leader preparation is the issue of funding in order to implement effective instructional models for rural ELs and build family engagement. Low-density EL schools, in particular, coupled with the low local tax base generated from agricultural land, means that funding for many ESL services is disproportionately low or sometimes nonexistent. Brenner (2016) describes how the federal Rural Education Achievement Program (REAP), which includes funding from the Small Rural School Achievement (SRSA) program and the Rural and Low Income Schools (RLIS) program, can support rural schools. However, how funding from these programs can be targeted for EL student services is less clear. Geographically large US school districts that have low-density EL students in one geographic region of the district but not in another may be disqualified for such funding. In addition, new federal funding guidelines being proposed aim to delete targeted EL student funding as a line item in favor of block funding to states (US OMB, 2020). The rationale for combining twenty-nine federal programs into a single block grant is to "empower States and districts to decide how to best use Federal funds" (p. 20). However, this potential change to the US education budget could undermine or eliminate language support for rural ELs if states and rural school districts reallocate block funding for non-EL purposes.

Strengths and Opportunities for Rural EL Students and Families

Undoubtedly, EL students and families in rural schools bring linguistic and cultural diversity, unique and specialized knowledges, and ways of knowing that enrich local communities (Coady, 2019b). Although education for ELs in rural settings has some ground to cover in terms of educator preparation, instructional programs, equitable funding, and models to enhance

EL student learning, there are opportunities for growth and change in rural communities to improve EL education. As increasing numbers of ELs relocate to rural communities, the nature of rural communities is likely to challenge persistent stereotypes and inequities. In a recent survey conducted on the context and conditions of rural communities, *Life in Rural America* (Robert Wood Johnson Foundation, 2018), respondents indicated that racially minoritized individuals in their rural communities do not face discrimination. In the same study, Latinx, African American, or transgender adults stated that they experienced discrimination in their rural communities. Moreover, economic revival in rural communities is directly associated with immigrant labor, and the reversal of student population decline is a result of EL students (Mathema et al., 2018).

Studies surrounding the knowledges, backgrounds, and contributions of rural EL families are likely to become more common, as the reach of EL families and students becomes broader. For instance, in 2015, Coady and colleagues conducted a study of rural EL families and teachers. Using survey, interview, and observation techniques, and framed by strengths and family funds of knowledge (Moll et al., 1992), they found that families optimized informal communication networks, established interdependent relationships to rotate home care for younger children, and infused linguistic and cultural diversity into community events such as soccer games, local harvest fairs, and in local restaurants. Although research on rural EL students and families is in a relatively nascent stage, demographic changes will likely increase demands among educators for more diverse approaches to communicate with non-English-speaking families through the use of technology in order to equip families to participate more fully in their child's education. Some recent studies during the 2020 global pandemic appear to be moving in that direction (e.g., Blagg et al., 2020).

Synergistic educational reports align with the need for equitable language programs for rural ELs. A 2017 report by the American Academy of Arts and Sciences (AAAS, 2017), for example, underscored the need to increase both the number of languages and proficiency levels in the United States. The report describes three ways to do so: first through domestic educational programs such as DL programs that include local communities; second through heritage and Native American language education; and third by enhancing international educational programs for students to learn abroad. The first trend is taking hold as some states have begun to provide financial incentives to grow DL programs. For example, in 2008 Utah passed the International Education Initiative that funded the establishment of DL education programs (State of Utah, 2008). Data indicate that more than 30,000 students in Utah are enrolled in DL (AAAS, 2017). In 2011, Delaware followed suit by appropriating nearly $2 million of their education budget for DL education (Boyle et al., 2015). These trends may have a positive effect on rural communities going forward. Achievement data from students who participate in DL underscores the success of DL for ELs and for students who speak English as a native language (Cervantes-Soon, 2014; Collier & Thomas, 2017).

In the context of twenty-first century rural EL education, demographic and social changes are bringing new opportunities for more equitable educational programs and improved preparation for educators. Scholars working in EL education are noting demands among rural teachers for equitable programs that demonstrate strong academic outcomes for EL students (Coady, 2019c). Teachers see the benefits of native language use and its impact on student learning outcomes. For that reason, dual-language programs are making inroads into rural communities, but successful implementation of DL will depend on leaders' and teachers' knowledge of second-language teaching and learning (Padron & Waxman, 2016; Sugarman, 2018). As teacher shortages persist and educational funding is systematically reduced, US teachers and leaders are likely to continue their demands for improved funding, support, and for equity (Jacobson, 2020). Rural EL students and families are our collective past, present, and future, and the quality of education in the United States will depend on the commitment to equitable education for all.

22

African American Education in the Rural South Then and Now

Sheneka Williams, Sarah McCollum, and Kimberly Clarida

An examination of the contemporary realities of rural education in the South generally requires going back to enslaved individuals' arrival on Southern slave plantations and progressing toward the present day. While we do not have the space to cover all aspects of that in this chapter, we do highlight a few monumental moments for the education of African Americans in the US South and bring to bear the current realities of their educational opportunities. The entire South is not rural, as there are a few urban centers: Atlanta, Charlotte, and Birmingham, namely. However, in this chapter, we will focus on African American education in the rural South, as it is rare for urban education and rural education to be examined together. Given the unique history of both, we find it important to elucidate what it means to be educated as an African American in the rural South.

During the first thirty-five years of the nineteenth century, most southern states passed legislation that made it a crime for former enslaved people to be taught how to read or write. However, as the Emancipation Proclamation gained momentum, so did the education of formerly enslaved Americans. Thus, the formal, systemized schooling of African Americans began shortly after 1863. The first attempt at education was short-lived in the South, as the early 1880s ushered in a time when African Americans were again disenfranchised by law. As such, their citizenship, voting, and schooling rights faced major resistance by Whites until the 1950s and 1960s (Anderson, 1988). However, African Americans rose above the political turbulence of the nineteenth and early twentieth centuries and began their own schools for their own children. With help from the Freedmen's Bureau, former enslaved African Americans taught themselves how to survive in a labor economy, as well as trained their minds for intellectual debate. This form of segregated education was paramount and necessary in the Deep South until the late twentieth century. More importantly, while de jure segregation was determined unconstitutional in 1954, there are places in the rural South in which de facto school segregation persists.

Perhaps no legal decision of the twentieth century had as much of an impact on the education of all children, but African American children in particular, than the *Brown v. Board of Education*

(1954) decision. That decision ended de jure segregation, resulting in a racial opportunity cost paid by students and families who bore the burden of desegregating schools (Venzant Chambers, 2019). Moreover, the loss of Black educators—Black teachers and leaders in majority Black schools—changed the schooling experiences of Black students. This is not to say that we advocate for segregated schools, but we do argue that much was lost for Black students when schools desegregated (Siddle Walker, 2000; Tillman, 2004). However, research supports that students of all races benefit both academically and socially in desegregated schools.

Some schools in the South did not fully desegregate until the early 1970s, and some schools and districts in the South and other parts of the nation remain under federal desegregation orders. One such district in Cleveland, Mississippi, gained national attention just three years ago when an all-White and all-Black high school merged into one (Amy, 2019).

This chapter focuses on contemporary African American education in the rural South. The three authors of this chapter all attended rural schools in the American South, and one of us taught in a majority African American school in the rural South. Our schooling experiences and settings differed, but our outcomes are similar. One author, a White woman, attended a predominantly White high school in the foothills of the Blue Ridge Mountains in South Carolina. The total student of color enrollment in the school was less than 10 percent, and nearly half of enrollment was classified as economically disadvantaged (McFarland et al., 2019). Another author, a Black woman, attended a predominantly White high school near the coast of North Carolina. She contributed to the 24 percent Black population within a school with a nearly 70 percent White enrollment, and over half of the students were classified as economically disadvantaged (National Center for Education Statistics, 2019a, 2019b). One other author attended a school comprised of 40 percent students of color and approximately 60 percent White students. As of today, the entire district qualifies for free and reduced-priced lunch (US Department of Agriculture, 2019).

As scholars who have both insider and outsider perspectives on African American education in the rural South, we find it important to share data concerning that context. A number of scholars have written about the differences in types of rural schools, but few have written specifically about majority African American schools in the rural South. African American students make up the highest percentage of students of color in the South (National Center for Education Statistics, 2016). The large numbers of African Americans who live in the Deep South correlate to former slave port towns in the South: Savannah, New Orleans, Mobile, and Charleston. In an effort to further expound upon the nuances of opportunity and education in the rural South in general, and rural Mississippi in particular, we lift the voices of three students who attended school in the Mississippi Delta. While we understand that their stories cannot be generalized, findings from their narratives can be transferred to similar contexts. Moreover, findings from their stories can influence practice and policy development for rural education in general, and African American education in rural contexts specifically.

Place, Race, and Educational Opportunity

According to the US Census (2016), rural spaces are those that are neither urbanized areas (consisting of 50,000 people or more) nor urbanized clusters (consisting of at least 2,500 people). Despite the effects that many researchers associate with place, Galster and Killen (1995) contend that geography is not typically included in the definition of "equal educational opportunity," and they further argue that inequalities based on geographic location can affect individual opportunities. The geographic distribution of opportunity is particularly important for families and children because it impacts children's schooling experiences. Schools in underserved communities—which are often racially and spatially isolated from opportunities—struggle to meet the needs of students from low-income neighborhoods (Cashin, 2014; Miller, 2012; Reece & Gambhir, 2008).

Researchers increasingly recognize that access to opportunity is largely a function of geographical location, which accentuates the relationship between where one resides and the opportunities afforded to him or her as a result (Green, 2015; Tate, 2008). Discriminatory policies, structural racism, and a history of government-sanctioned segregation led to the concentration of poverty in many urban cities today (Rothstein, 2017), and, by extension, rural communities as well.

Moreover, the geographic dissemination of opportunity is especially important for children because of the implication it has for their schooling opportunities and educational outcomes, which are tied to economic outcomes, health, and overall well-being (Green, 2015). Some scholars have thus advocated for more comprehensive educational reforms that consider schools' social and community-based contexts in decisions pertaining to equitable distribution of resources to high-needs schools (Green, 2015; Holme & Rangel, 2012; Horsford & Heilig, 2014; Miller et al., 2011; Milner, 2013; Noguera & Wells, 2011; Warren, 2005).

Scholars who study the geography of opportunity also pay close attention to how communities of color, in particular, are often segregated from important opportunities such as access to adequate health care, safe neighborhoods, affordable housing, and sustainable employment (Briggs, 2005; Drier et al., 2013; Powell et al., 2007). These important elements to overall well-being have perpetuated the concentration of poverty in low-income neighborhoods, as inadequate access to opportunity continues the cyclical process of poverty. Further, inequitable geographies of opportunity are often associated with children's access to out-of-school contexts that support their academic, socioemotional, and cognitive development (Milner, 2013).

Poverty and geography of opportunity discussions typically center on levels of urban poverty, particularly those in the inner city, while far less research and policy attention target the rural poor (Lichter & Parisi, 2008). Consequently, rural people living in economically disadvantaged communities are frequently left behind, forgotten, and are not the targets of reforms to improve educational and economic outcomes (Lichter & Parisi, 2008). Compared to metro areas, rural communities tend to have higher concentrations of poverty such that residents are more likely to live in neighborhoods where the proportion of people living in poverty is greater than 20 percent. Further, the overall percentage of people living in poverty tends to be significantly higher in rural areas compared to metro areas (Lichter & Parisi, 2008). As such, increased policy attention must be devoted to the geography of opportunity and educational opportunity in rural settings to better understand how and to what extent students are being marginalized in such settings. We find that the Mississippi Delta, a place rich in heritage but lacking in financial resources, is one such place in which to better understand the complexities of place, race, and educational opportunity.

The State of Education in the Mississippi Delta

While contemporary characterizations of predominantly African American schools and educators who serve them tend to focus on urban communities (Cowan et al., 2016), throughout the South, the White-rural versus racially diverse urban/suburban binary paradigm simply does not hold. It is certainly not the case in Mississippi. Mississippi shows the highest poverty rate in the nation, and it happens to be the state with the highest share of African Americans—many of whom live in the Mississippi Delta. The Mississippi Delta, with the loss of agricultural and manufacturing jobs, is marked by economic instability and unequal educational opportunity for African American families and students who reside there. During the 2017–18 academic year, the average graduation rate for all high school seniors in the United States was 85 percent. Nationally, the graduation rate for Black public high school students is 79 percent (White 89 percent, Hispanic 81 percent, Asian/Pacific Islander 92 percent, and American Indian/Alaska Native 74 percent). However, in Mississippi, the graduation rate for Black students is 81 percent, compared to 88 percent for White students.

Tallahatchie County, a county in the Mississippi Delta, for example, has a population under 15,000, and over 3,000 residents (28 percent) live below the poverty line (Data USA, 2017). The child poverty rate is 48 percent and the county ranks near the bottom of all Mississippi counties for quality of life and health (County Health Rankings, 2019). Research shows that poverty has adverse effects on student health, cognitive development, behavioral health, and educational outcomes (Brooks-Gunn & Duncan, 1997). The intersection of history and race deeply influences the manifestation of poverty in the Delta, which extends to some of the challenges that educators, families, and students face.

Methods and Data

An in-depth narrative interview approach (Pinnegar & Daynes, 2007; Polkinghorne, 1995; Squire et al., 2008) offered a glimpse into the academic and social experiences of former students who attended school in Tallahatchie County. A White researcher conducted the initial Zoom interviews with three African American participants. The interviews lasted approximately forty-five minutes. We thought the White researcher might be most suitable because she once taught the students. Upon an initial review of the data, we realized that participants were reluctant and careful with their responses. We then conducted follow-up Zoom meetings with participants to gain better clarity on their narratives, particularly with respect to race. Based on the research of Wetzel and Wright-Buckley (1988), who found that there is a reciprocity effect when interviews are led by Black interviewers and a reciprocity breakdown when led by White interviewers, we conducted follow-up interviews with cross-racial research dyads (one Black, one White) because we thought that participants might feel more comfortable with another African American person in the interview and provide more thorough responses.

In the section below, we discuss how we analyzed data from the interviews to develop narratives.

Data Analysis

Data analysis for this study began with transcriptions of the audio-recorded interviews. Each narrative, constructed from in-depth interviews with participants, was constructed to highlight participants' lived educational experiences in the Mississippi Delta and how that shapes their opportunities today. The process used to create these narratives is akin to Moustakas's (1994) process of phenomenological reduction. Moustakas (1994) explained that in phenomenological

The Bloomsbury Handbook of Rural Education in the United States

reduction the "qualities of the experience become the focus; the filling in or completion of the nature and meaning of the experience becomes the challenge" (p. 90) for the researcher to take up. In this study, each individual narrative, constructed from interview data, offers a rich look at the intersections of geography and educational opportunity. We present the participants' stories in the section that follows.

"You Have to Get Your Own at West Tally"

The three African American young people highlighted here all attended the same all-Black high school in Webb, Mississippi, a small town in Tallahatchie County in the Mississippi Delta. Surrounded by farmland with soil as rich as the community's culture and history, the school sits at the intersection of Highways 49 and 32, in between Clarksdale and Greenwood. The two highways are named for two people at different ends of the same history: Highway 49 memorializes Emmett Till, while Highway 32 honors the racist sheriff and senator H. C. Stryder, who promised no one would be convicted for Till's lynching. This kind of irony is not lost on the community; rather, the historical, socioeconomic, and cultural context serve as motivation to deny the statistics and outsider expectations for their children's futures. This is especially true for the three participants: Jay, Nathan, and Joi. Even though their postsecondary lives have diverged, they share an understanding that their relationship to their schooling and community is complex and complicated: full of appreciation and recognition of its challenges. We share their stories below.

Jay—A Cultural Curator
Growing up in Webb, there were few places for students to spend time together. Some students would congregate at the gas station on the corner or the mini mart across from the post office. Others, like Jay, could be found at the gym or field. After school and on weekends, coaches would open up the campus to give students a structured place to spend time. It was in Jay's nature to surround himself with friends and teachers, and he knew the importance of avoiding idle time. Whether he was shooting baskets in the gym or completing assignments in class, he was eager to connect with his teachers and friends, often through laughter. Beneath his exterior, though, just as he was committed to staying "out of the streets," he was equally dedicated to his writing. Even as a teenager, Jay recognized the significance of developing his craft in analyzing literature and writing narratives. To Jay, the relevance of English Language Arts was clear because "it's [a part of] everyday life." Sharing his literary insights and narrative snapshots of his life eventually transferred into his career.

After graduating high school, Jay attended two community colleges in northern Mississippi. He did not finish his degree, but once he returned home, he wanted to invest his time into his creativity and community. He added, "I'm just working on my CDL (Commercial Driver License) . . . I've been trying to get my stuff together."

Over the last eight years, Jay has worked with countless friends and producers to develop his creative writing passion through music. As a hip-hop artist, he loves a catchy trap song with hooks. While he hopes people have fun with his music, he is quick to include the realities of poverty and violence in the Delta. After losing his best friend to gun violence, he devoted several tracks to themes of loyalty and respect because he believes that these are the ties that hold the community together during tragedies and struggles.

Jay chooses to live in the community where he grew up. He spends hours driving to Memphis, Nashville, and Atlanta to connect with producers and studios. Rather than moving to one of these cities, Jay believes in staying connected to Tallahatchie County because of his strong ties to his family and friends, although he does believe it is important for young people to leave the community for at least a little while. When we asked about the pros and cons of staying close, he replied, "We're just exposed to what we know until we get out. Once you get out, you meet new people, you learn new things, you advance." Jay remains in his hometown and takes on personal responsibility for mentoring the next generation by sharing what he learns from his travels.

Nathan's Story—Coming Back to Give Back
At twenty-two, Nathan returned to the same high school hallways he once walked as a student. Not much had changed. There were some new faces, but the faded paint and broken desks still lined the classrooms. The same textbooks he once used could be found along the classroom bookshelves, collecting dust with some occasional new graffiti. He did not plan for this seven years ago when he first left, but returning to teach in his hometown school is a decision he is proud that he made.

Nathan grew up in Glendora, Mississippi, a place some consider ground zero of the Civil Rights Movement. In the sleepy town of 135 people, a railroad runs through the town and across the Black Bayou, a tributary of the Tallahatchie River. This is where Emmett Till's body was thrown into the water sixty-five years ago. While Till's lynching became a catalyst and cornerstone in the Civil Rights Movement, Glendora's place in history faded. Today, most stories about this community tend to focus on the consequences of abject poverty and dismal educational outcomes, but Nathan sees the value that cannot be captured by numbers on a page.

Before Nathan decided to become a teacher, he had plans of pursuing law. He excelled at school and developed a reputation for his work ethic and focus. His teachers also appreciated his kindness, for he never wasted an opportunity to tutor friends with their homework and assignments. Classmates would blurt out Nathan's name as soon as teachers uttered "partner work." Nathan had a knack and a passion for working with others, but during his sophomore year, he and his family felt they needed to invest in his education in ways the high school could not. At the end of that year, Nathan was accepted into the Mississippi School for Mathematics and Science (MSMS). As the only public residential high school in the state, it is designed for students gifted in math and science. Nathan spoke specifically about the differences in educational opportunities between the two schools: "Coming to a setting like MSMS, it was shockingly noticeable how much I hadn't been exposed to and it made it very hard to acknowledge that there was a purpose for my being in that space." Nathan transitioned from an all-African American high school with limited resources to a racially and economically diverse school lauded for its abundance of resources and academic opportunities. Determined to invest in his hometown, Nathan earned a full scholarship to an HBCU, Jackson State University, where he majored in mathematics and graduated in three years. He earned another full scholarship for his master's in education at the University of Mississippi so that he could earn his teaching credential while teaching at his alma mater. When he reflects on his experiences as a teacher and student, he shares,

Sadly, nothing has changed about the educational opportunities afforded to my students since I attended here. In many ways it seems as if we have reverted back. Many students

The Bloomsbury Handbook of Rural Education in the United States

have never been out of the state and lack exposure to things other than their surrounding areas. Educationally, there are more teachers who aren't here for the benefit of their students, academically or holistically.

Nathan has always valued his education, but now he sees it as imperative to close the opportunity gaps for others who grow up in communities similar to his own.

Joi's Story—An Artist in the Making

Joi lives in Tutwiler, Mississippi, a town with faded murals of Blues legends scattered throughout downtown. Few stores remain open, but the pictures serve as reminders of the storied history of artists hailing from this small town. An artist in her own right, Joi hopes to leave her mark one day, too. When Joi first arrived at school, she stood out among her peers. She and her twin sister stand nearly six feet tall, but their sharp wit and creativity is what their teachers and peers noticed. Even though Joi loved pushing boundaries within the school uniform policy by adding accessories and coloring her hair, she was kind and quiet. As she recalls, she was not quiet because she was shy; she was quiet because she was paying attention. She added,

> I occasionally just sit back and observe the adults around me, they would constantly talk of their regrets about not going to school and how it affected them . . . struggle with bills and scarcity of good-paying jobs. I didn't want to be in the same predicament they were in.

Her observations and appreciation for details would serve her well as she created a vision of what she wanted to pursue in life. Joi knew at a young age that she thrived when she could share her creativity in art, music, and writing. However, she found few creative outlets in her community and at school. She says that the teachers did the best they could to provide chorus, band, and dance, but there were no art classes or computer-based art classes. Joi lamented some of the missed opportunities at school by adding, "My K–12 experiences didn't prepare me due to a lack of creativity-provoking opportunities. Most schools in the South don't provide adequate classes that target students with creativity and vivid imaginations." With limited resources and few qualified teachers for the arts, students had to find their own ways to creatively express themselves.

Once Joi graduated high school, she enrolled in college in Memphis and finally had her chance to take classes that excited her and aligned with her passions. Majoring in graphic design, Joi feels purposeful and excited for what she can create and share through her coursework. She mentioned that her first semester was difficult, though. "I observed that most of the kids who had grown up there were far more prepared. . . . Maybe it was because their schools had classes specifically for college assimilation. In many ways it intimidated me because I felt that I was behind."

Not only was Joi adjusting to the rigor of the content, she transitioned from living in a town of 500 to a city of 1.5 million. She is not sure if she will move back to Tutwiler after she finishes college. With each trip back down the quiet highways stretching between Memphis and the Delta, she is reminded of the differences in educational opportunities compared to her friends who grew up in more suburban and urban areas. The barriers to returning home have nothing to do with the people and everything to do with the economic opportunities, and she does not want to get "stuck" at home. She wants to see her former school develop an arts program and have a downtown filled with storefronts and people, but she is also realistic about the likelihood of such dramatic changes coming. In the meantime, she plans to make the most of her time in Memphis and hopefully one day find a way to give back to her hometown.

The Triumphs and Challenges of Home

Despite different postsecondary trajectories, similar themes emerged from the three participants' narratives. At the heart of their stories lies the tension between the realities of their schools and communities and hope for better educational and economic outcomes. When reflecting on how they felt while in school, they could identify supportive relationships with educators and appreciation for the interconnectedness of school and the community. They felt known and a sense of belonging even if they considered themselves to be on the margins of most student groups. As quickly as they acknowledged the effort of educators to invest in knowing and supporting students, they also lamented that those relationships and effort could not fully negate the effects of inadequate resources and opportunities.

Each of the three participants acknowledged their hometowns and schools lacked financial resources and that limited their options. They spoke in a matter of fact sense about the struggles, and they were frustrated by the consequences of coming from schools that facilitated "gaps" or a "lack of creativity-provoking opportunities." For those who continue to visit or live in their communities, they expressed that few opportunities are present today. For example, Nathan believes that one way to address resource and opportunity gaps is to return to teach at his alma mater. Jay may not have the financial means to support his community, but he gives back by remaining a positive presence at high school sports and encouraging the youth to create opportunities for themselves. Even though each participant felt "othered" or marginalized at some point in relation to their rural education and upbringing, they believe the cohesion of their hometown provided the relationships and encouragement to pursue their passions.

What the schools and communities may have lacked in educational experiences, they did not lack in influential relationships and community cohesiveness (Bauch, 2001; Killian & Byrd, 1988; Milner, 2006). Even though questions might have been raised about the motivations or qualifications of some current educators in their former schools, each participant mentioned at least one adult, typically a parent or teacher, who communicated the importance of getting an education and supported the pursuit of their passion. The overlap and interconnectedness of the community and school provided most participants with an adult mentor invested in the academic and character development of them as students.

In general, participants did not discuss their rural education positively, but considering the funding inequities and resulting gaps in educational experiences, they show resilience to navigate college despite feelings of marginalization. Regardless of where the participants currently live, they feel a connection to their communities that has led many of them to give back to their communities or center their careers on their communities. Moreover, each participant remains connected to the community with an understanding of its influences and hope for its improvement.

Race—in the School and the Community

Race and poverty are permanent fixtures in the lives of people who live in the Mississippi Delta. While living in the middle of it, the beauty of its farmland might go unnoticed. When living outside of it, one recognizes its beauty in the midst of the ugly poverty and tense race relations in which it rests. The Mississippi Delta lies at the center of the nation's struggle for equality, with one of Dr. King's first rallies being held in Clarksdale, Mississippi. Called "The Most Southern Place on Earth" because of its unique racial, cultural, and economic history, the Delta region was named as such because it attracted many speculators who developed land along the riverfronts for cotton plantations. They became wealthy farmers dependent on the labor of enslaved people who comprised the vast majority of the population in these counties well before the Civil War. Hence, today's population is majority African American, and it also explains why de facto segregated schools persist in the area. We asked participants about the role of race in their schooling experiences, and they replied honestly, though differently. Jay replied,

> To be honest, it um, didn't play out. We had different color teachers, like White teachers, but we didn't think much of it. They act normal; we act normal. We ain't ever had no racist stuff going on, but outside of school maybe.

Nathan, on the other hand, had a more negative view of race in his educational trajectory. He replied, "I feel like kids who went to schools like mine [West Tally] are kind of being sold short, like they're not getting the same opportunities." He went on to add, "A lot of us pretty much tend to stay within that realm [county]. Everyone stays close to Tallahatchie—they don't move away." Teachers in the community are from the community, as it is difficult to recruit teachers to a town in which a big box store is many miles away. Nathan added, "A lot of the teachers in rural areas grew up there, so they teaching but they lack exposure and opportunities themselves as educators." Even though there are strengths in having teachers connected to the community, rural schools grapple with how to prepare, support, and distribute a quality teacher labor force (Clotfelter et al., 2011; Sutcher et al., 2019). As such, programs like Teach For America place alternatively trained, novice teachers in the area, but they are typically underprepared to meet the needs of the communities in which they are placed (Lapayese et al., 2014).

Nathan expressed that the local school in the Delta did not challenge him intellectually. Moreover, race was not as salient in that setting because all students were Black. He did not experience the effects of race in his education until he attended MSMS.

> Race really played a role there [MSMS] because I had never gone to school with other races. Like, I had only been in school with other African American students, so when I got there I kind of went looking for a challenge. I had to put forth more of an effort to kind of be at the level where they were.

He later completed his undergraduate degree at one of the state's Historically Black Colleges and Universities (HBCUs). Upon college graduation he went back to West Tally to teach, as he saw that as a gift to the community. He shared,

> I decided to go into education because African American students are being failed by the system. I felt like I had something to give to students like me. I want to impact education to make it better for African American students.

Now that the participants are adults and beginning to have their own children, they reflect on the Delta as a community and as a place where their children will also go to school. When we asked Jay about his thoughts on that, he added,

I don't want them [my kids] to see color. You know, I don't want them to just look at it [White teachers] like, when they learn in school, to think too much about it. I don't want my kids to have the mindset that they don't like White people.

He continues: "As far as the Black community, like this situation today, like I don't know. It's just wrong."

In many ways, education for African Americans in the rural South resembles what it did pre-*Brown*. While this chapter focuses on the Mississippi Delta, other states and towns in the rural South are plagued by fewer fiscal resources, less qualified teachers, and geographic and physical isolation from hospitals and grocery stores with fresh produce. These problematic issues that continue to negatively contribute to the well-being of rural southern communities are not a factor of happenstance. Instead the economic disadvantages are tied to delayed desegregation measures and policies and practices that are not beneficial to African American communities as the majority of African American schools in the South remain segregated and underfunded.

Race and place play a key role in identifying the type of education African American students in the rural South receive. For many students within rural southern communities, race and geography act as barriers that systematically prevent them from having access to highly qualified teachers, Advanced Placement courses, and other resources that will provide them with an academic advantage. Therefore, it is vital that education leaders and policymakers have more conversations about the impact history, geography, race, and poverty has on the quality of schooling for African American students in the rural South.

Jay, Nathan, and Joi revealed a few important findings. First, they demonstrate how rich social capital is within rural southern communities. The relationship among the former students and their teachers and community members was so strong that students rarely leave. Each participant could identify at least one person who supported or encouraged them throughout their educational journey. Unexpectedly, students displayed an appreciation for their teachers even if their teachers were not as experienced as teachers in larger, urban districts. Perhaps the biggest discovery was when students realized that their schools were inadequate after they were exposed to more integrated educational settings with students from more privileged backgrounds. For example, it was not until Nathan attended MSMS that he realized that his peers had access to better resources. The same is true for Joi when she enrolled in college. It was also in these diverse settings that the participants were privy to more resources. Thus, we understand that desegregation of schools and the ultimate integration of financial resources matter in terms of students' educational opportunity. This is not to say that a majority African American school cannot thrive, as we have examples of that in this country. It is to say, though, that a combination of African American and poverty and Southern context rooted in racial tensions continues to deny students equal educational opportunity.

Implications for Policy and Practice

Practice

As previously stated, the educational challenges rural African American students face do not differ entirely from other rural students, but there are opportunities to utilize the strengths of their community. A common theme echoed by our participants was a lack of access to a diverse curriculum with advanced course offerings and highly effective teachers trained for such courses.

While teacher labor market constraints in rural areas present struggles to recruit and retain teachers, school districts may look to community partnerships and virtual classes to fill those needs.

Given the connectedness of schools and communities in rural areas, community partnerships between local businesses and organizations and schools may offer the relationships and experiences students seek. Provided the rich cultural heritage in music and the arts across rural African American communities like the Delta, for instance, arts-based after-school clubs and field trips through community groups create an alliance that broadens student experiences, interests, and positive adult relationships (Combs & Bailey, 1992; Love, 2019). African American educators often extend their leadership beyond schools to other facets within the community (Milner, 2006); however, expanding those relational pathways to welcome community members into schools can widen access to enrichment opportunities and relationships for rural African American students who can better prepare them for postsecondary opportunities (Alleman & Holly, 2013).

Along with community partnerships, rural districts can also look to virtual classes to support the gaps in course offerings. From remedial to Advanced Placement courses, rural schools, especially rural schools with high numbers of African American students, have not been able to offer comparable course catalogs as nonrural schools (Gemin et al., 2018). Without qualified faculty to support the variety of student needs and opportunities, virtual schooling may provide access to content and activities that would otherwise never exist. It should be noted that virtual schooling is currently underperforming compared to traditional school settings (Toppin & Toppin, 2016), but provided further research on this topic, rural districts may find this to be the most logical pathway forward for offering courses to prepare students for postsecondary experiences. We offer this as a plausible solution with the full understanding that high-speed internet remains a challenge in rural areas.

Policy

As often noted by scholars and policymakers in rural education, rural perspectives and voices must be included in policy development to address their unique strengths and challenges. Participants alluded that their educational experiences were inadequate, especially compared to peers from Whiter, higher-income, and nonrural communities. In order to combat the funding and opportunity inequities, state and federal policies must implement context-appropriate strategies so that African American rural schools may be able to achieve the educational outcomes families, communities, and governments espouse (C. B. Howley et al., 2005).

While states vary in the structure of their educational funding formulas, the use of property taxes as a primary school funding mechanism is a common, yet detrimental, approach. The use of property taxes to fund schools disproportionately impacts rural Black, Indigenous, and people of color communities, thus further widening the opportunity gap. Considering an impoverished area like the Mississippi Delta, the local property value and ability of residents to pay higher taxes limit school funds and districts' ability to compete with wealthier districts and labor markets. Even when states provide greater per-pupil spending to rural schools, the funding is not enough to counteract rural challenges. Rural districts often direct funds disproportionately toward operational costs such as transportation (i.e., $100 per urban pupil versus $900 per rural pupil) as opposed to instructional costs (i.e., professional development and salaries) compared to their

African American Education in the Rural South

nonrural counterparts (Levin et al., 2011). More progressive funding formulas and strategies will help account for those nuanced challenges, but state and federal governments must also look to school composition as a means to address educational opportunities.

As court-ordered desegregation plans have been lifted and neighborhoods become more economically segregated, schools and districts are more segregated today than in the 1990s (Reardon & Owens, 2014). Changes in desegregation litigation and neighborhood composition, coupled with school funding formulas that favor wealthier neighborhoods, compromise the educational opportunities of students like our participants who live in remote, low-income communities. Additionally, our participants, like most students of color, attended a majority student of color (or segregated) school. The negative relationship between racial and economic segregation and student achievement reflects inequitable access to educational opportunities similar to that of pre-desegregation legislation (Reardon et al., 2019). Access to the resources and effective teachers associated with more economically advantaged student populations can have significantly improved short- and long-term outcomes for students (Chetty et al., 2014; Hanushek, 2011). However, it is essential that Black students do not lose access to same-race teachers, who provide additional benefits. Research finds that having same-race teachers can increase academic performance, improve graduation rates, reduce absenteeism and suspensions (Gershenson et al., 2017; Holt & Gershenson, 2015), and leave positive impressions for subsequent years for students of color (Tillman, 2004). In order to expand educational outcomes for rural Black students, districts must look to consider consolidating smaller schools to garner resources into a larger school, recruit teachers from outside the area, and offer programs to cultivate student integration, while relying on the strengths and leadership of Black educators and White allies. Regardless of school composition, the goal of rural education policy should be equitable access to high-quality teachers and educational opportunities to ensure that race and place are points of strength rather than indicators of low educational outcomes.

23

Latinx Students in Rural Schools

Darris R. Means and Vanessa A. Sansone

Latinx people represent the fastest-growing population by race and ethnicity in rural and small town areas (Housing Assistance Council, 2012). For example, between 2000 and 2010, the Latinx population in rural and small towns increased by 1.9 million people (Housing Assistance Council, 2012). While one in eight rural students in public elementary and secondary schools identify as Latinx (NCES, 2013), educators, policymakers, and researchers should be reminded there is diversity among rural Latinx students, including geographical region (e.g., Southeast, Midwest, Southwest, Northeast), race, and ethnicity (Housing Assistance Council, 2012; Wortham & Rhodes, 2015), and a diversity across rural schools and communities, including school sizes, poverty rates, and racial and ethnic diversity (Greenough & Nelson, 2015; Sierk, 2017). In addition, the local economic and social infrastructure of one's rural community, and visibility of local, political Latinx leadership varies across rural communities, uniquely shaping the challenges and opportunities facing rural Latinx people (Wortham & Rhodes, 2015). In the same way that rural itself shouldn't be understood as a monolith (Genovese, 2019; Means, 2018), educators, policymakers, and researchers cannot assume the experiences of all rural Latinx students will be the same.

In order to challenge the idea of rural Latinx homogeneity, this chapter explores the following topics: (a) demographics of rural Latinx people in the United States, including the diversity across Latinx people living in rural areas; (b) PK-12 education and achievement for rural Latinx students; and (c) postsecondary education access, experiences, and outcomes of rural Latinx students. The chapter concludes with suggested future directions for research focused on enhancing educational equity and justice for this student population.

Demographics and Rural Latinx Individuals

In this section, we introduce some key ideas about rural Latinx demographics in the United States. This is important in order to counter common misperceptions about the presence of Latinxs in rural areas. We focus on population growth and geographic context in the rural areas where Latinxs have traditionally resided and where they are new. However, we begin this section by offering a foundation for understanding the migration patterns of Latinxs in rural areas to understand the changing demographics of these areas and how these demographics intersect with and influence the education of rural students in these areas.

It is important to note rural demographers' concerns about identifying and conceptualizing the geography of rural areas: there is currently no widely agreed-upon definition of rural. It is, therefore, difficult to generalize that specific social and geographic phenomena in any one rural area are relevant to others (Murdock et al., 2012). This includes rural areas where large proportions of Latinxs reside. Despite this concern, we offer some of the more common patterns characteristic of rural Latinx populations.

History of Rural Latinxs Migration
Rural Latinxs have played an important role in the changing demographics of rural areas in the United States. Historically, many events have influenced the in- and out-migration patterns of Latinxs in rural areas across the United States, specifically immigration and economic policies (Lichter, 2012; Sáenz, 2012). For example, the 1942 Bracero guest worker program and the 1994 North American Free Trade Agreement (NAFTA) were two large-scale agrolabor policies that brought many Latinxs, particularly Mexicans, to fill rural workforce labor shortages in predominantly low-wage jobs that spanned across the entire United States (Mandeel, 2014; Sáenz & Torres, 2003). Such policies were major drivers of early US rural migration patterns for Latinxs bringing about Latinx clusters to areas in the Southwest, like Texas, California, and Arizona (Sáenz, 2012). Beginning in the 1980s, changes in the agriculture, meatpacking, and manufacturing industries shifted, moving plants from urban to rural areas and actively recruiting Latinxs from the Southwest (Sáenz, 2012; Sáenz & Torres, 2003). As a result, Latinxs began to move to where these new employment opportunities were located—in new rural settlement areas in the South and Midwest.

Demographic Characteristics of Rural Latinxs
Recent trends suggest that the rural Latinx population is very young and faces issues associated with poverty and social mobility (Kandel & Cromartie, 2004). In fact, research has found that rural Latinxs lag behind their rural White and rural racial/ethnic minoritized counterparts in the key areas of income, health, and education (Sáenz & Torres, 2003). For example, 24 percent of all Latinxs living in rural areas in the United States live in poverty (USDA, 2018). And, about 41 percent of rural Latinx households have an annual income below $25,000 (Sáenz, 2008). For comparison, 13 percent of rural White people live in poverty and 30 percent have yearly incomes below $25,000. Rural Latinxs are also the least likely rural racial/ethnic group to have access to health insurance and retirement plans (Sáenz, 2012; Sáenz & Torres, 2003). With regard to education, rural Latinxs have the lowest educational attainment levels among their rural counterparts. For example, among all rural Latinxs aged twenty-five or older, 39 percent have not completed a high school diploma and only 14 percent have an associate's degree or higher (USDA, 2017). For comparison, among all rural White people aged twenty-five or older, 13 percent have not completed a high school diploma, and 29 percent have an associate's degree or higher (USDA, 2017). At the same time, rural Latinxs are on average a much younger population who have the highest birth rates of any rural racial/ethnic group (Kandel & Cromartie, 2004; Lichter et al., 2016; Sáenz, 2012).

The Bloomsbury Handbook of Rural Education in the United States

As such, Latinxs are a key population in shifting rural demographics and are, in many rural communities, maintaining population growth in areas that were previously experiencing declines and out-migration. This also means that in new rural settlement areas, PK-12 educational leaders may be ill-equipped to effectively support Latinx families and youth, especially in consideration of rural Latinxs' diverse demographic characteristics and needs (Sáenz, 2012; Sáenz & Torres, 2003). For example, many rural Latinx youth have English language proficiency needs. Close to 70 percent of all foreign-born rural Latinxs are English Language Learners, while 45 percent of rural Latinx individuals born in the United States are English Language Learners (Sáenz, 2012). Poverty adds further complexity. Several rural areas of historic Latinx settlement experience the highest rates of historical poverty in the United States—more than the Mississippi Delta and Appalachia (Tickamyer et al., 2017). For example, high numbers of Latinx farmworkers and their families live in settlements on unincorporated land along the US-Mexico border called *colonias*. Children and their families living in *colonia*s often lack access to potable water, sewage, and other basic resources (Barton et al., 2015). With these shifting and varied demographics, histories, and experiences with poverty in mind, we shift to PK-12 and postsecondary education for Latinx students.

PK-12 and Postsecondary Education and Latinx Students

The following sections focus on (a) PK-12 education, achievement, and Latinx students and (b) postsecondary education access, experiences, and outcomes of rural Latinx students as these issues manifest in literature published in the past two decades. As we do so, we aim to be especially sensitive to deficit-oriented narratives in which Latinx students and families are viewed as lacking skills, experiences, and assets that can be employed to lead to academic success (Keis, 2006; Moll et al., 1992; Yosso, 2005). Instead, we frame our work using the concept of funds of knowledge, which acknowledges and explicitly values the strengths of minoritized communities to recognize the assets of rural Latinx students and their families (Moll et al., 1992). For example, in their work on children's literature, Keis (2006) argued that the funds of knowledge of rural Latinx communities are often overlooked in education. At the same time, we name structural barriers that perpetuate opportunity gaps for rural Latinx students.

PK-12 Education, Achievement, and Latinx Students
PK-12 education and achievement of rural Latinx students cannot be understood separately from their school environment and structural challenges that limit educational opportunities and experiences. In this section, we provide an overview of literature about rural Latinx students' schooling experiences, support from families, and school-family engagement.

Schooling Experiences
The intersection of students' race, ethnicity, racism, and rural geography shapes their educational experiences (Hondo et al., 2008; Means, 2018). Across rural schools, researchers explored how schooling experiences can hinder and/or support achievement and outcomes for rural Latinx students (e.g., Hondo et al., 2008; Peralta, 2013; Zuniga et al., 2005).

Researchers have identified multiple challenges for Latinx students in rural schools, including marginalization and racism embedded in school culture, practices, policies, and approaches (Carrillo, 2016; Hondo et al., 2008; Peralta, 2013; Zuniga et al., 2005). Notably, Hondo and colleagues (2008) found that rural Latinx students who did not graduate from high school or were pushed out of their schools began to experience "feelings of marginalization, disconnection from school, and failure" (p. 96) in middle school. The marginalization experienced by rural Latinx students is perpetuated in two ways: teacher attitudes and behaviors and formal and informal school practices and policies.

Teacher Attitudes and Behaviors. The marginalization of rural Latinx students is enacted through teachers' attitudes and behaviors (Carrillo, 2016; Hondo et al., 2008; Irvin et al., 2016). Some rural Latinx students reported feeling that their teachers did not care about them and that their teachers had lower expectations for them compared to their White rural peers (Carrillo, 2016; Hondo et al., 2008; Irvin et al., 2016). Students' perceptions of low teacher expectations may lead to lower self-efficacy and lower achievement among rural Latinx students. For example, Irvin and colleagues (2016) found that rural Latinx youth had less confidence in their ability to learn compared to rural Black and White peers, and rural Latinx students had lower self-reported grades compared to rural White peers. In a separate study by Hondo and colleagues (2008), rural Latinx students reported feeling blamed for the overall decline in school performance (e.g., adequate yearly progress). Rural Latinx students experience racism from teachers, which is internalized in beliefs about their abilities to be successful in school (Hondo et al., 2008). While researchers have identified how low teacher expectations, experiences with racism, and low self-efficacy may influence student achievement for rural Latinx students, Irvin and colleagues (2016) found that, along with rural Black youth, rural Latinx students had the highest level of belief in the value of schooling (Irvin et al., 2016). In addition, rural Latinx students' aspirations remained just as high compared to their White peers (Ali & Menke, 2014).

School Practices and Policies. The marginalization of rural Latinx youth is also perpetuated by formal and informal school policies, such as tracking and policing and surveillance related to language (Hondo et al., 2008; Peralta, 2013; Zuniga et al., 2005). Rural Latinx students are tracked into lower-proficiency courses that will not qualify them for college admissions (Hondo et al., 2008; Zuniga et al., 2005). For example, Zuniga and colleagues (2005) found that rural Latinx students were more often tracked into lower-proficient science courses compared to their White peers even when they performed well in school. In addition, rural Latinx students who did not complete high school believed they were pushed out by their high school leaders by being transferred to alternative schools for low grades and low attendance without understanding the circumstances that led to the school challenges (Hondo et al., 2008). Rural Latinx students also described how their language was policed in schools, and they were discouraged from speaking Spanish by educators (Hondo et al., 2008; Peralta, 2013). This policing and surveillance of language led some students to believe this to be a reflection of how their rural school educators and leaders did not care for them or their culture (Hondo et al., 2008).

Educator-Student Relationships, Caring Schooling Environments, and Positive Youth Development Programs. While PK-12 schools can be deeply problematic for rural Latinx students, supportive school educators and classrooms can enhance the schooling experiences of rural Latinx students (Peralta, 2013; Reese et al., 2014). Specifically, Peralta (2013) found that students "received emotional support . . . in school from caring individuals who helped them navigate degree requirements and scholarship opportunities" and "who believed in them and in their potential as future citizens, teachers, and other professionals" (p. 239). There may be patterns among teachers who are most supportive of rural Latinx students. Reese and colleagues (2014) found a correlation between teachers who identify as Latinx and their ability to create a supportive classroom atmosphere based on respectful and strong interpersonal relationships with rural Latinx students. However, the racial or ethnic identity of the teachers in the study was strongly associated with other factors (e.g., years of teaching). The authors concluded that the ethnicity of a teacher did not equate to more Latinx student success. Instead, in the study, the Latinx teachers in the study interacted with Latinx students in a way "that helped to create supportive classroom environments where children felt free to ask questions, seek clarification, approach the teacher with needs or concerns, and take a more active role in their own learning" (p. 521).

Research also suggests that positive youth development participation enhances school success (Arriero & Griffin, 2019; Goedeken et al., 2016; Riggs, 2006). For example, Goedeken and colleagues (2016) found that participation in youth development programs enhanced interpersonal and life skills for rural Latinx students. A quarter of the participants attributed youth development programs as supportive of their school success. Rural Latinx students who attend after-school programming more frequently and over a longer period of time demonstrated increased social competence compared to rural Latinx students who attended the after-school program fewer days (Riggs, 2006). Arriero and Griffin (2019) examined a college readiness program that was developed for and received design input from rural Latinx high school students; the researchers found that students increased their self-efficacy as a result of the program. The development of strong educator-student relationships, caring schooling environments, and positive youth development programs have the potential to enhance the learning, development, and achievement of rural Latinx students.

Latinx Families, Student Achievement, and School-Family Engagement in PK-12 Education
Despite the deficit-oriented perspectives about Latinx students and families, families play a critical role in the lives of rural Latinx youth in two primary ways: (a) emotional support and encouragement and (b) support with academic work (Goedeken et al., 2016; Hondo et al., 2008; Peralta, 2013; Smith et al., 2008). Contrary to deficit discourses that Latinx families do not value education, rural Latinx students do receive emotional support and encouragement from their families to pursue their education and aspirations (Hondo et al., 2008; Irvin et al., 2016; Peralta, 2013; Smith et al., 2008). For example, Peralta (2013) found that parents provided emotional support, encouraged their children to pursue aspirations, and also passed "cultural values and aspirations" (p. 240) to their children, and, in return, the students were committed to supporting their families. In addition, Smith and colleagues (2008a) found that rural Latinx families played a significant role in supporting their children with their academic work and motivated their children to do well in school.

Rural school leaders and educators have an opportunity to develop and enhance the role of schools as a site of trust and resources for Latinx families (Dewees & Valázquez, 2000). For example, Dewees and Valázquez (2000) presented a case study on how a school district in rural Texas created, developed, and implemented services (e.g., a health clinic) and instructional practices that reflected the needs of the predominantly Latinx community. However, while one study found that rural schools have stronger family-school partnerships with Latinx families than do urban schools (Burke, 2017), there is still work to be done. Rural schools have ample opportunity to enhance existing outreach and engagement with Latinx families by providing information and resources in English and Spanish (C. E. Johnson & Viramontez Anguiano, 2004; Smith et al., 2008), reaching out to families when students are experiencing academic challenges (Hondo et al., 2008), and addressing barriers related to "racism, immigrant status, and discrimination" (Burke, 2017, p. 61).

Postsecondary Education Access and Outcomes of Rural Latinx Students

Only a handful of studies have given particular attention to rural Latinx students and higher education. This is in contrast to the relatively well-developed literature on college choice, access and success for rural youth, writ large (e.g., Koricich et al., 2018; Sparks & Núñez, 2014; Wells et al., 2019). Published studies tend to focus on disparities in postsecondary enrollment or degree attainment between urban and rural students (Byun, Meece, & Irvin, 2012) but do not necessarily attend to racial/ethnic differences. When rural race/ethnicity disparities in higher education are made explicit in research, the experiences of rural Latinx students differ significantly from those of their counterparts from other racial/ethnic backgrounds and those from urban areas (Sansone, 2019).

Rural Latinx Students and Postsecondary Aspirations and Access

Researchers have found that rural Latinxs have high aspirations to attend college (Meece et al., 2013; Stone et al., 2020), but rural Latinx students' access to college resources and information about postsecondary opportunities are negatively influenced by several constraints (Byun, Irvin, & Meece, 2012). For instance, researchers have found that rural Latinx youth rely heavily on having a close proximity to college preparation resources, like counselors and school-university partnerships, to gain knowledge about the admissions process and academically prepare them for college rigor and decide where to enroll for postsecondary education (Freeman, 2017; Irvin et al., 2016; Means, 2019).

The issue of proximity makes sense when one considers that rural Latinxs report having a much harder time accessing information about college than their rural peers from different racial and ethnic groups (Griffin et al., 2011; Irvin et al., 2012). Although it is unclear whether this is related to rurality, rural Latinx youth have expressed concern about their rural high school's limited access to college resources, primary focus on state testing, and heavy use of a college information approach that minimally involves parents and families (Cabrera et al., 2012; Gildersleeve, 2010).

Rural Latinx Students and Postsecondary Education Enrollment and Graduation

Existing research is inconclusive about whether there are unique factors specific to rural Latinx students that influence their college selection as well as experiences and outcomes within higher education. One study sought to identify factors that influenced whether rural Latinx students enrolled at a two- or four-year institution (O'Connor et al., 2010). Using a national dataset, these researchers found, when compared to their rural White peers, rural Latinxs were less likely to attend a four-year university.

Once rural Latinx students begin higher education, they can find their college and university campuses lacking spaces for Latinx students (Carrillo, 2016). For example, Carrillo (2016) documented how one rural Latinx man in North Carolina found their college campus to be lacking spaces for Latinx students to develop a sense of belonging, and, thus, they found ways to advocate for change at their university. In addition to postsecondary education experiences, we know there are significant differences in the numbers of rural high school students who aspire to pursue postsecondary education, as opposed to those who do so *and* graduate (Byun, Irvin, & Meece, 2012). Byun, Irvin, and Meece (2012) measured actual degree attainment of rural Latinx students using a national dataset that sampled high school graduates. This study reports that when compared to rural White peers, Latinxs living in rural areas were less likely to graduate from college.

With regard to the role that rural high schools and rural educators play on Latinx students' postsecondary access and success, we offer a brief overview of general literature on Latinx students in higher education. Overall, this literature suggests that postsecondary Latinx students' access and success is influenced by an interplay of several factors such as a student's immigration status, gender, socioeconomic status, English language proficiency, familial support, as well as anti-Latinx policies/governance (Núñez, 2014). Research also finds that increasing cultural knowledge about college and access to social actors with college experience has a positive influence on rural Latinx students' postsecondary decisions and success (Stanton-Salazar, 1997). More specifically, when Latinx students have more exposure to (a) rigorous academic coursework; (b) supportive teachers, counselors, and administrators; (c) college campuses and on-campus resources; (d) financial resources to pay for college costs; and (e) culturally relevant college preparation programs that engage families, include Spanish-speaking resources, and encourage engagement on campus, positive experiences and outcomes in higher education are more likely to occur (Crisp et al., 2015; Nora & Crisp, 2009).

More work is needed to expand the knowledge base about rural Latinx students at all levels of higher education, including undergraduate and graduate education. Specifically, there is still much to be learned about rural Latinx students and what mechanisms contribute to their experiences and outcomes in higher education. There is also a need to better understand how and to what extent the intersection of race/ethnicity and rural place contributes to unique experiences for rural Latinx students and communities. Emerging work by rural Latinx researchers suggests that this is the case, but more work is necessary to confirm and further explain these results (Sansone et al., 2020).

Implications for Practice, Policy, and Future Research

We offer implications for practice, policy, and future research as a way to advance educational equity for rural Latinx students and their families. For PK-12 education, rural leaders and educators must address the learning environment for Latinx students. School climate could be enhanced by the intentional creation of caring, inviting educator-student and educator-family relationships and classroom atmospheres that recognize the assets of rural Latinx students (Burke, 2017; C. E. Johnson & Viramontez Anguiano, 2004; Peralta, 2013; Reese et al., 2014; Smith et al., 2008). It is imperative that school leaders and educators assess school climates, school practices and policies, and the behaviors and attitudes of school staff and students with the goal of determining ways to develop and sustain culturally relevant, anti-oppressive climates that better support student learning, development, and achievement. Researchers also demonstrated the benefit of out-of-school and after-school learning for rural Latinx students (Arriero & Griffin, 2019; Riggs, 2006); rural schools and communities should continue to invest in programs that enhance the well-being of rural youth and center the assets of racially/ethnically marginalized youth. The benefits of this work, a culture of student care and success, extends to all students but is of particular importance for individuals marginalized within current structures.

In addition to PK-12 leaders, higher education leaders should enact and collaborate on practices and policies that enhance the educational outcomes and experiences of rural Latinx students. Researchers have documented the high college aspirations of rural Latinx youth (Meece, et al., 2013; Stone et al., 2020). To help rural Latinx youth actualize aspirations, higher education leaders have an opportunity to partner with PK-12 school leaders and state policymakers to ensure resources and information are provided about postsecondary education options and processes, such as adequate number of school counselors, programs, and services focused on college access and readiness, and statewide initiatives and resources. However, information and support are not enough: higher education leaders and state policymakers must collaborate with federal policymakers to determine ways to reduce or eliminate college costs that may hinder students from pursuing postsecondary education.

Once students begin postsecondary education, higher education leaders should consider programs and services, such as offices, programs, and student organizations that support Latinx students, that could enhance postsecondary education experiences and, ultimately, graduation. While offices, programs, and organizations are an important step in enhancing postsecondary education outcomes, administrators, faculty, and staff cannot solely rely on them; college retention and graduation are the responsibility of all employees at a higher education institution and will require every department to consider policies and practices that advance educational equity for Latinx students at their intersections of identity (e.g., geographical locale, gender, race, ethnicity, sexuality, social class).

The advancement of our knowledge base about the intersection of geography, race, ethnicity, and student educational outcomes and experiences is currently inadequate. Researchers need to further document the assets of rural Latinx students and their families navigating PK-12 and postsecondary education *and* identify and address structural challenges that lead to inequitable opportunities for rural Latinx students. In addition, as policymakers, school and higher education leaders, and educators develop and implement policies and practices intended to address opportunity gaps based on the interaction of geography, race, and ethnicity, researchers must examine the efficacy of these policies and practices in order to ensure they are advancing educational equity and educational outcomes for Latinx students living in rural places.

24

Whiteness in Rural Education

Kathleen E. Gillon

During the spring of 2020, broad attention was drawn to the murders of three Black individuals—Ahmaud Arbery, Breonna Taylor, and George Floyd. These deaths follow numerous Black individuals murdered over the past decade, at the hands of both civilians and police officers.[1]

As I write this chapter, people throughout the United States are demonstrating and actively protesting against the historical legacy and present-day realities of white supremacy in the United States. While much of the national attention on these protests has focused on urban areas, rural communities are also demonstrating against white supremacy.[2] As a nation built and sustained by racism and white supremacy, whiteness can be found embedded in most social institutions, especially that of education. Central to rural communities are rural schools. With a close-knit and symbiotic relationship, interrogating whiteness in rural education means interrogating whiteness in rural communities as well.

In this chapter, I introduce four central tenets of Critical Whiteness Studies (CWS). I then use these tenets as a tool to analyze three recent events that took place within rural educational settings to demonstrate how whiteness manifests itself in rural education. I conclude by offering a multipronged approach to disrupting whiteness in rural education, focusing on the role of educators and the broader community, curriculum, and rural research.

Drawing on the work of Pérez Huber (2010) and Harris et al. (2019), I have intentionally capitalized terms that refer to minoritized communities, including "Black," "People of Color," and "Students of Color." Conversely, I intentionally do not capitalize "white" as a way to actively resist and "reject the grammatical representation of power capitalization brings to the term white" (Pérez Huber, 2010, p. 93).

Author's Positionality

I write this chapter as a scholar-teacher-practitioner committed to anti-racist education. Yet, I am acutely aware of the ways in which whiteness allows me to claim that identity. As a critical scholar, I understand that my identities and experiences influence my research and my understanding of the field of education. I come to this work as a cis-gender, white woman who grew up in a rural county in northwest Tennessee. While I lived in a working-class, mixed-race neighborhood, the majority of my small town was highly segregated—the railroad tracks serving as a physical manifestation of that segregation. The building where I attended junior high school was previously the town's Black school, yet that information was never shared with us while we attended that school. I was privileged to have multiple Black educators and school leaders throughout my elementary and secondary education. Yet, whiteness infiltrated my education. I didn't know or understand this at the time (a product of whiteness itself). However, over time, I have come to understand how whiteness operated in very specific ways that shaped my educational experiences and outcomes.

Defining Whiteness

One of the major challenges of understanding whiteness in education is that there is no single agreed-upon definition of the concept (Cabrera et al., 2016). Some argue that this ambiguity and malleability is what allows whiteness to continue to work in our society (Cabrera et al., 2016). For the purpose of this chapter, I draw on CWS to help contextualize this concept and illustrate how whiteness shows up in rural education.

An important distinction within CWS research is that whiteness does not mean white people (Cabrera et al., 2016). As Leonardo (2009) noted, "whereas the category 'white people' represents a socially constructed identity, usually based on skin color . . . Whiteness is not a culture but a social concept" (pp. 169–70). That said, white people are often the subjects of whiteness because it benefits and privileges them. Whiteness is supported by material practices and institutions and has real material impacts on people in US society (Cabrera et al., 2016).

While critical scholars often describe whiteness as a racial discourse, it can also be described as a racial perspective or a worldview (Leonardo, 2009). Leonardo further defines whiteness as "a collection of everyday strategies (p. 32)" characterized by a reluctance to name racism as well as a hesitancy to engage with the historical legacy and present-day realities of racism (Frankenberg et al., 2003).

For the purpose of this chapter, I draw on four tenets of CWS as utilized by Cabrera and colleagues (2016) in their discussion of whiteness in higher education. While the focus of this handbook is primarily on K-16 education, these tenets speak broadly to whiteness in education and are applicable to the many types of educational institutions within a US context. These tenets include (a) whiteness as colorblindness, (b) whiteness as ontological expansiveness, (c) whiteness as property, and (d) whiteness as assumed racial comfort.

Critical scholar Bonilla-Silva (2006) has theorized and written extensively on the notion of colorblindness. He defines colorblindness as an ideology in which racial inequality is acknowledged but not attributed to racism. He further contextualizes this concept by providing four frames of colorblindness: (a) abstract liberalism, (b) naturalization, (c) cultural racism, and (d) minimization of racism. With abstract liberalism, one might claim to support racial equity but at the same time oppose a race-conscious policy or program (Cabrera et al., 2016). Naturalization is an argument invoked to try and explain something as just naturally occurring. For example, in my segregated rural town, the argument might be that it is just natural that the Black community members would want to live together on one side of town rather than looking at the history of redlining in my community. Cultural racism shifts the focus from racist arguments made about biological differences between races to cultural differences (Kendi, 2019). Cabrera et al.

(2016) offer the example of how Latino families have been wrongly stereotyped as not valuing education. Finally, the minimization of racism does just that: it dismisses and/or downplays the role of racism in our society.

Perhaps most overtly connected to a discussion of whiteness in rural education is that of whiteness as ontological expansiveness. Drawing on the work of Sullivan (2006), this concept is connected to the ways in which white people understand space—typically that all spaces were created for them to move freely in and out of. Conversely, People of Color are acutely aware that not all space is open to them. This is often cited as a reason why some Black students choose to attend Historically Black Colleges and Universities or why Students of Color find multicultural centers to be such important places for them on historically and predominantly white campuses (Patton, 2010). These spaces counter the feelings and experiences Students of Color have within broader white spaces. Gusa (2010) has theorized this concept of the normalization of whiteness within postsecondary educational spaces, referring to it as White Institutional Presence (WIP).

Another important tenant is that of Cheryl Harris's (1993) concept of whiteness as property. In crafting her argument, Harris posited that the United States is built on property rights and that whiteness, itself, has evolved over time into a form of property protected by law. More so, she operationalized this argument into four specific rights: (a) the rights of disposition, (b) the right to use and enjoy, (c) reputation and status property, and (d) the absolute right to exclude.

Last, integral to an analysis of whiteness in rural education is that of whiteness as assumed racial comfort. Educators often like to frame educational spaces as safe spaces. However, CWS scholars have drawn this claim into question. Cabrera and colleagues (2016) refer to the work of Franz Fanon, stating that "within the Fanonian framework, the linguistic violence of the colonizer can serve as a form of dehumanization to the colonized" (p. 26). This is significant because without examining the role of whiteness and allowing for a critical analysis of racist language, dialogue, and discourse, educators may in effect reinscribe linguistic violence within educational spaces.

Whiteness in Rural Education

Empirical research (Love, 2019), including my own lived experiences in rural states like Tennessee, Iowa, and Maine (Gillon, 2017), supports the claim that whiteness is embedded in all of our schools and institutions of higher education, especially public schools. This is primarily due to the historical legacy of public schooling in the United States. The first schools, notably referred to as grammar schools, were created for white males. This was the same for the early colleges (Thelin, 2019). Whiteness has continued to moderate who has access to education and what that education looks like in practice. Native American children were removed from their homes and families and placed in boarding schools (Masta, 2018; Reyhner & Eder, 2017). Black children were recipients of underfunded and sometimes nonexistent education under the legal premise of "separate but equal" (Fireside, 2004; Love, 2019; Wilder, 2014). California forced English-only education upon their students. The historical legacy of whiteness in education is powerful and sustaining throughout all schools. These educational laws and practices were/are steeped in whiteness across all geographical spaces.

At the same time, there is a distinct relationship between whiteness and rurality that is intricately tied to our comprehension of how we understand and define rural, both historically and contemporarily, in a US context. Definitions of rural, especially within education, are heavily influenced by bureaucratic agencies such as the US Census Bureau and the National Center for Education Statistics (Flora & Flora, 2013; Gillon, 2017). These definitions tend to rely heavily on quantitative metrics such as population density and physical proximity to urban spaces (Flora & Flora, 2013; Gillon, 2017). While these definitions provide guidance for government agencies, their focus on geography and demography provides one-dimensional understandings of rural. As such, they do not always capture the essence of what rural is in the United States, both historically and socially.

Drawing on the work of Leopold (1949), J. D. Johnson (2014b) states that "place is inherently rural because it embodies a land ethic. Rural ways of living are strongly nuanced by a relationship with the land" (p. 5). This is further evidenced by the ways in which rural scholars have categorized rural areas. Specifically, C. B. Howley and A. Howley (2010) have categorized rural as (a) durable agrarian communities, (b) resource-extraction communities, and (c) suburbanizing rural places. These examples of the categorization of rural illustrate the centrality of land and communities' relationship to that land.

Rural areas in the United States have a long and complex relationship with land. Dunbar-Ortiz (2015) states, "The history of the United States is a history of settler colonialism—the founding of a state based on the ideology of white supremacy, the widespread practice of African slavery, and a policy of genocide and land theft" (p. 2). Today, these stolen lands, many of which are rural, are homes to meatpacking plants and farms that rely heavily on the employment of migrant workers from countries such as Mexico, Guatemala, and Honduras (Holmes, 2013; Koreishi & Donahoe, 2010). Subsequently, children of these workers are often enrolled in local rural schools (Tieken, 2014).

Centering land in our understanding of whiteness and rurality provides for an important and specific way to interrogate the tenets of whiteness, especially that of ontological expansiveness. Yet, while land is central to our understanding of rurality, so are the social relationships that are constructed within rural environments. In defining rurality, Etheridge (2017) positions place "not simply as a geographic location, but also as a socially produced space in which social inequalities are embedded, reproduced and contested through everyday practices" (p. 235). In the next section of this chapter, I explore three contemporary examples of the manifestation of whiteness in rural education, highlighting specifically how colorblindness, ontological expansiveness, property, and assumed racial comfort support the reproduction of oppression in these educational spaces. The first example explores the changing of the school mascot in Skowhegan, Maine, and the community's response to this change. The second example explores racist incidents in high school athletics in two rural communities—Perry, Iowa, and Storm Lake, Iowa—amid the 2016 presidential election. The third example explores the ways in which colleges and universities have reified the dominant narrative of "rural spaces = white people" by assigning popular texts, such as J. D. Vance's (2016) *Hillbilly Elegy: A Memoir of a Family and Culture in Crisis* and Tara Westover's (2018) *Educated: A Memoir*, as a common reading for students, faculty, and staff.

Whiteness and Native Mascots

In 2019, Maine became the first state in the nation to outlaw the use of Native American mascots. This move came just a couple months after the last school in Maine voted to change their 100-year-old mascot—the Skowhegan "Indians." While Maine has been lauded for this

The Bloomsbury Handbook of Rural Education in the United States

action, the process took several years and was deterred repeatedly by racist initiatives. In 2015, members of all the Indigenous nations of Maine met with the Skowhegan school district to request the removal of the Native mascot (McCauley, 2018). While not the first request, it is notable because of its targeted approach by the collective Native people of Maine. The request was ignored as the school board voted to retain the mascot. Dana Maurelian, tribal ambassador for the Penobscot Nation (located about 50 miles from Skowhegan), shared that in 2015, "We were told by some to mind our business and that we were 'from away'—even though we are descendants of the ancestors that were the original inhabitants of that land" (McCauley, 2018). Subsequently, Skowhegan community members in opposition of the change created a closed Facebook group called "Skowhegan Indian Pride" (McCauley, 2018). Additionally, racist mascot paraphernalia continued to be used such as athletic sweat towels that were referred to as "scalp towels."

By late 2018, Skowhegan remained the only Maine school using a Native mascot. Once again, local tribe members petitioned to remove the mascot. Opponents of the petition argued the mascot honored Native American culture and employed timeworn arguments that the 100-year-old mascot was part of the community's heritage. Despite opposition, the school board supported the change with a 14-9 vote and, in 2019, removed the mascot.

While this was a major victory and catapulted the state legislature to pass the bill that would outlaw Native mascots in the state, many members of the rural Skowhegan community continued to protest the change, most notably by creating and wearing T-shirts and other paraphernalia that said, "Indian Pride."

In this example, we see whiteness operating in multiple capacities, most explicitly as ontological expansiveness and property but also as assumed racial comfort. A key enactment of whiteness in this situation is the use of the term "from away" by the community members against the name change. "From away" is a nativist term used in Maine to distinguish those who were born in the state from those who migrate/move to the state. By referring to an Indigenous person as "from away," the local community is invoking linguistic violence, a key component of assumed racial comfort. This language quickly indicates who belongs and who does not belong in a specific space. This is closely connected to ontological expansiveness and its understanding of how whiteness mitigates space. In addition to using language to dictate who can move freely within educational spaces, we also see the use of digital/social media groups as a manifestation of ontological expansiveness. The "Skowhegan Indian Pride" closed Facebook group operated in two distinct ways. One, it served as another mechanism for demonstrating who can move freely in and out of specific spaces. Second, because of the closed nature of the group, it provided a level of anonymity for those who chose to join the group. Thus, the members could assume a sense of racial comfort within this private space.

The right to use and enjoy, a component of whiteness as property (Harris, 1993), also provides insight into this situation. In this rural community, we see local members exercising what they understand as their right to use and enjoy an Indigenous name as their mascot. This right was thoroughly established and supported throughout the 100-year history of using "Indian" as their mascot. However, we see community members continuing to exercise the right to use and enjoy even after the formal dismissal of the mascot by the school board through the creation of a social media page and the creation of "Indian Pride" T-shirts and paraphernalia. This act is extremely important to understanding the potency of whiteness as property. While legally, the school board had mandated the dismissal of the nativist mascot, members of the community continued to exercise their right to use and enjoy the mascot in other manners.

Whiteness and High School Athletics

Perry and Storm Lake are two communities located in the central and northwest parts of Iowa, respectively. They are both home to two different Tyson meatpacking plants staffed primarily by a migrant Latino/a/x worker population (Haedicke, 2013). Perry is a community of approximately 9,500 people, while Storm Lake is a community of approximately 12,000 people. Latino/a/x people constitute about one-third of the population in each community (NCES, 2020c). It is important to note that these communities were at one time predominantly white. The increase in Latino/a/x community members is directly related to employment at the meatpacking plans.

While neither community would be defined as rural by the US Census or the National Center for Education Statistics, these small towns embody many of the characteristics of rural communities—close-knit relationships, single economies, remoteness (Brown & Schafft, 2011). In this context, these meatpacking towns of the Midwest somewhat resemble the coal mining towns of parts of Appalachia (Johnson, 2014a). Additionally, my decision to include Perry and Storm Lake as part of this chapter is supported by Tieken's (2014) assertion "that which feels rural is rural" (p. 5).

Between 2016 and 2018, a time marked by the beginning of President Trump's term in office and increased policing and attention to walls along the US southern border, both Perry High School and Storm Lake High School were sites of linguistic violence. In playing a boys high school basketball game against a mostly white rural team from Central Iowa, Perry players and community members in attendance endured chants of "Trump!," presumably meant to disparage players because of the town's Latinx/Hispanic population (Bieler, 2016).

Student athletes from Storm Lake endured similar threats at a basketball game where an opposing team chanted "USA!" and during a football game where a visiting team changed, "Go back from where you came!" (Larson, 2018). School officials sought to explain or remedy the situations and, in one case, developed a cross-racial dialogue exchange program for students between the schools.

There are several points of significance to these two examples within the context of whiteness. First, education research can have a propensity to focus on what takes place within the formal classroom. However, rural schools often serve as hubs for community gatherings (Brown & Schafft, 2011). Rural schools, and subsequently rural athletic programs, can shape the identity of rural communities as they provide a source of community engagement via these gatherings. At the same time, this calls into question who is made to feel part of the community and who is not. Volk (2014) posits that "when a community has a drastic population shift in a closed demographic area, especially in the beginning years, feelings of xenophobia often arise among the established majority" (p. 270).

In these examples, we see how feelings of xenophobia manifest into actions that perpetuate ontological expansiveness as well as the right to exclude. The students from the predominantly white communities and schools used racist and nativist chants to signal to Students of Color and their broader community members that not only do they not belong in that space, but that they also have the power to decide who belongs and who does not belong. This is important because as John and Ford (2017) state, "There is no doubt that the place in which one engages in the educational relationship and process impacts the educational experience" (p. 12). Thus, while

The Bloomsbury Handbook of Rural Education in the United States

these actions may have taken place on the basketball court or the football field, they are still connected to one's education and thus can broadly and negatively impact that experience.

Last, it is important to also consider the actions of the Storm Lake school administration in their response to the situation at their school. CWS, specifically, the notion of assumed racial comfort, provides caution when creating programs grounded in activities such as cross-racial dialogue (Cabrera et al., 2016; Leonardo & Porter, 2010). Oftentimes, while the intention comes from a place of good, there is a great risk for the potential for harm, specifically for Students of Color. Without great care and training, cross-racial dialogues can reinforce feelings of assumed racial comfort for the oppressor while relegating the oppressed to additional linguistic violence through potential microaggressions.

Whiteness and Curriculum

In June 2016, author J. D. Vance released his memoir titled *Hillbilly Elegy: A Memoir of a Family and Culture in Crisis*. Two years later, Tara Westover (2018) published her own memoir titled *Educated: A Memoir*. Both books became popular texts and were soon adopted by colleges and universities as common/first-year reads (DeLozier, 2019; Roll, 2017). *Hillbilly Elegy* became an immediate top choice as a common read, selected by institutions such as the University of Denver, University of Wisconsin-Madison, and Wake Forest University. *Educated* was chosen as the common read in 2019 by institutions including Emory University, New York University, University of Delaware, and University of Virginia, and was slated as the 2020 common read for California State University-Northridge. The purpose of common reading programs, often targeted for entering first-year college students, is to provide a shared academic experience across the entering class. As such, common reads expose thousands of students to a specific topic selected by the university.

Both *Hillbilly Elegy* and *Educated* are memoirs, capturing the individual experiences of the authors who grew up in Ohio/Appalachia and Idaho, respectively. As such, these books offer insight into the lived experiences of two rural people, more specifically two rural white people. Additionally, neither text engages with systemic issues of oppression, rather blaming their challenging upbringing on their individual families and rural communities. The consequence of assigning texts such as these is harmful to both Students of Color and white students (Harkins & McCarroll, 2019; Peine & Schafft, 2018). The dominant narrative that rural = white people is reified through the selection of books that only feature white people and never fully engage in discussions of race (Gruenewald, 2014). Students who believe that only white people live in rural areas are subsequently supported in their beliefs. I posit that this form of colorblindness—specifically, naturalization—is especially harmful because it frames the analogy of rurality = white as Truth, thus disallowing for the possibility of People of Color in rural spaces. For Students of Color, this harm comes in the form of erasure. For white students, this harm manifests in assumed racial comfort.

Disrupting Whiteness in Rural Education

Rural places are often characterized by the close personal relationships that exist within these communities (Brown & Schafft, 2011; Gillon, 2017). As such, if we are to disrupt whiteness in rural education, we have to understand that it will take the entire community to do so. This is not to say that individual work is not important. However, given the systemic nature of racism, it will require more than just educational leaders in the classroom. Additionally, I posit that disrupting whiteness in rural education requires a multipronged approach. Specifically, we need to consider who is teaching in rural schools and communities, what is being taught in rural schools, and what our research about rural education looks like.

Educators and Community Members

One of the most important things we need to consider is who is teaching in and leading our rural schools and communities. Love (2019) says, "Pedagogy, regardless of its name, is useless without teachers dedicated to challenging systemic oppression with intersectional justice" (p. 19). This charge is intricately connected to curriculum and what is taught in our teacher education and educational leadership programs. It must also be reinforced during practicum experiences and supported throughout the educational career. Teachers who espouse a dedication to challenging oppression are not absolved from whiteness. If anything, they must be vigilant to the ways in which whiteness continues to permeate their personal and professional lives and seek to disrupt that whiteness.

The boundaries of personal and professional are often blurred in rural communities due to their close-knit nature (Brown & Schafft, 2011). Teachers are community members and, oftentimes, community members serve as informal teachers. Thus, if the goal is to disrupt whiteness in rural education, this must be a community endeavor. What is taught in the classroom must be reinforced in community activities.

Curriculum

One of the first places we can begin to disrupt whiteness in rural education is through curriculum. This includes the curriculum of teacher education and educational leadership programs as well as the curriculum within the K-12 classrooms facilitated by these teachers and leaders. Love (2019) posits, "Teachers need to be taught how to question Whiteness and White supremacy, how to check and deal with their White emotions of guilt and anger, and how these all impact their classrooms" (p. 75). In my own graduate education classes, we spend a great deal of time doing self-work to better understand how whiteness manifests in our daily lives and professional roles. I have found great utility in bell hooks's work specifically in introducing the relationship between rurality and whiteness. In her essay, "Kentucky is my fate," published in *belonging: a culture of place (2009)*, hooks details her life growing up in eastern Kentucky/Appalachia and the ways in which her experiences were mitigated by both racism and classism. Not only is her narrative writing engaging to the audience, her identity as a Black woman writer is important to disrupting the dominant narrative of who lives, learns, and teaches in rural spaces. Affrilachian poet, Frank X. Walker, similarly and intentionally, uses his writing to disrupt whiteness in literary spaces. His poetry, which focuses on the experiences of Black individuals in Appalachia, may also be especially helpful to educators seeking to disrupt whiteness in their classrooms and curriculums (see www.frankxwalker.com).

Similarly, it is important in our rural K-12 classrooms to think about what we are centering in our courses. In the early part of the twenty-first century, Maine legally mandated the teaching of Maine Native American History and Culture in Maine's elementary and high schools through the passage of LD 291.[3] While this one requirement is not going to eradicate whiteness in education,

The Bloomsbury Handbook of Rural Education in the United States

it is still significant in that this action is in opposition to abstract liberalism, acknowledging that racial inequality does exist and supporting measures that require students to consider how their own lives are connected to the historical legacy of Native peoples.

Research

My final implication is for those who identify as rural scholars—those who do research with and for rural education and rural communities. One of the ways in which whiteness operates in scholarly spheres is through colorblindness, and specifically the minimization of racism. Harper (2012) posited that while education scholars often discuss racial differences, they do not always discuss how racism dictates these differences. How are we interrogating whiteness and subsequently racism and white supremacy in our research? Additionally, J. D. Johnson (2014b) argued that a rural comprehension of education must engage with the understanding that rural is, in fact, the intersection of history and geography. In what ways are we acknowledging and engaging with the historical legacies of whiteness and rurality within our educational research? Since the 2016 election of Donald Trump, there has been an increased interest in rural spaces in the United States, inclusive of rural schools. However, as discussed previously, the contemporary realities of whiteness and rurality that are often discussed in popular media have historical roots that must be acknowledged and discussed within the context of present-day experiences.

Equally important to how we study rural education is who is studying rural education. In what ways has whiteness allowed for the centering of rural education scholarship published by white-identified scholars? If we consider academic journals as linguistic spaces, then we have an important opportunity to challenge both ontological expansiveness and the right to exclude by fighting against gatekeeping and dictating who is allowed to move freely in and out of those spaces. In response to the renewed public attention to the Black Lives Matter Movement, many journals, including *the Journal for Research in Rural Education* (JRRE), are curating special issues focused on racism and white supremacy within varied contexts. These issues and the knowledge distributed from them are an extremely important step forward. Yet, we must also ask, how can we ensure that scholarship that disrupts and decenters whiteness is part of every journal issue?

Conclusion

As rural educators and scholars, we have a responsibility to push against any assumed racial comfort in an effort to interrogate whiteness through the naming of white supremacy and the disruption of harmful and racist narratives that paint rural areas as racial monoliths. Whiteness is not merely present but is entrenched in all of our educational institutions, including rural education. CWS helps us to understand the varied and almost invisible ways in which whiteness might manifest in our professional practices, (in)formal curriculum, language and dialogue, and our rural educational spaces. Understanding whiteness as colorblindness, ontological expansiveness, property, and assumed racial comfort provides context for identifying whiteness in rural education and ultimately committing to its disruption in our professional and personal lives.

But what does that commitment to disruption actually look like? How might we practice this in our daily lives? Perhaps you might feel called to engage in public scholarship and write an op-ed for a newspaper. Azano (2020) provides a helpful example of this in the op-ed she published in *The Washington Post* where she discussed the tensions of whiteness in her own rural home community. Perhaps you plan to continue organizing and/or attending Black Lives Matter rallies in your own rural communities. Maybe you commit to revisiting your lesson plans and syllabi to unearth ways that you can decenter whiteness in your own curriculum and teaching. Regardless, let us not let the activism of the summer of 2020 live in that moment. Disrupting whiteness in our rural communities and schools requires an intentional and daily commitment.

25

Rural Tiered Systems of Adaptive Supports

A Person-in-Context, Place-Based Perspective

Thomas W. Farmer, Ann B. Berry, Jill V. Hamm, and David L. Lee

Rural schools vary in terms of their characteristics and resources to provide supports for students, particularly students with diverse learning and social support needs (Berry & Gravelle, 2013; Greenough & Nelson, 2015). Further, the concept of "place" and the importance of linking instruction to students' lives are fundamental to rural education (Azano & Stewart, 2016). With such diversity, special education and schoolwide prevention services, including multitiered systems of support (MTSS) and social-emotional learning (SEL), must be tailored to respond to the unique backgrounds, capacities, and circumstances of rural schools and the students they serve (Farmer, 2020). We propose that tiered systems of adaptive supports (TSAS) are particularly well suited to address this need while emphasizing place-based perspectives of instruction and learning. Building upon ecological and dynamic systems theories of child development, we discuss the need to establish infrastructures in rural communities that link prevention, SEL, and special education services to provide a seamless, comprehensive framework of supports for youth with diverse learning needs.

Diversity in Rural Schools: "There Is No Other Place Like Here"

In our work in rural areas across the United States, we find that there is considerable diversity in terms of the characteristics of students, the values and expectations of communities, the organization and resources of schools, and the experiences and backgrounds of teachers. Such diversity is well documented in the literature and reflects cultural, economic, geographic, political, and sociological factors (Greenough & Nelson, 2015; Nadel & Sagawa, 2002; Schafft, 2016; Showalter et al., 2019). Further, there is significant change in many rural areas, with some becoming more populated and developed, while others are losing industry and population or experiencing shifting demographics as work opportunities in the community transition in response to economic circumstances (Farrigan, 2020; J. D. Johnson et al., 2018; Lichter & Schafft,

2016; Williams & Grooms, 2016). In this context of diversity and change, there are three common refrains that we hear from many rural teachers and administrators. First, "we are unique. There is no other place like here." Second, "we need help in working with the diverse needs of the students in our classrooms." Third, "we tend to have one of everything, but not enough of anything, which means that we can't have specialists."

Special educators in rural communities are often expected to address issues related to diversity and change and to support teachers as they work to meet the needs of students with disabilities or who are not responsive to universal strategies (Berry, 2012; Dexter et al., 2008; Weiss et al., 2014). This means that special educators who work with rural schools often become generalized specialists. If a school or a teacher has a student that they are not sure how to serve, the special educator is likely to be called on to provide supports even if the student's characteristics and needs may be outside of her or his expertise and training (Berry et al., 2011). An important issue for many rural schools is that within a single classroom, a teacher may have a very diverse range of students in terms of their academic, behavioral, and support needs and resort to "teaching to the middle" in hopes that all students will get something that supports their success (Farmer, 2020).

Such diversity often overlaps with poverty and a lack of resources. Compared to other rural schools, rural low-income schools tend to struggle to meet the needs of low-income students, students with disabilities, and people of color (Farmer, Leung et al., 2006). Further, child poverty is often most concentrated in rural areas that have high concentrations of people of color (Nadel & Sagawa, 2002). The Economic Research Service reports that in 2018, nonmetro poverty was higher than metro poverty (16.1 percent vs. 12.6 percent). Nonmetro Black populations have the highest incidence of poverty (33 percent), while nonmetro Latinx populations also have elevated rates (25.9 percent; Farrigan, 2020). Rural special education may be strengthened by creating a framework of data use strategies and intervention supports to help special educators work as intervention specialists who are integrated into the school culture with general educators who have the resources, background, and training to adapt services to a broad range of diverse learners (Berry & Gravelle, 2013; Farmer, Hamm et al., 2018).

Developmental Systems, Rural Schools, and Tiered Systems of Adaptive Supports

A developmental systems perspective is instructive for clarifying services and supports for diverse learners, including students with exceptionalities, in rural schools. Two aspects of a developmental systems perspective are highly informative for rural special education: ecological systems theory and dynamic systems theory.

An ecological systems perspective suggests that youth are embedded in a nested arrangement of social systems. These systems include proximal social settings and relations (microsystem); the interrelations among the major proximal social settings of the student at a specific time in their development (mesosystem); other social structures, both formal and informal, that do not directly contain the students, but that influence their experiences in the setting (exosystem); and overarching institutional structures (macrosystem) composed of societal factors (e.g., economics, social, educational, legal, and political systems) including cultures and subcultures that contribute to the manifestation of the other systems (Bronfenbrenner, 1977).

From a dynamic systems perspective, youth develop as an integrated whole. This means that multiple factors both within (e.g., biophysical, cognition, psychological) and external to students (e.g., family, peer groups, school, community, culture, sociopolitical) are organized in a

The Bloomsbury Handbook of Rural Education in the United States

bidirectional manner in which each of the factors influences all the other factors and coactively contribute to their development and functioning (Magnusson & Cairns, 1996; Smith & Thelen, 2003). A critical point of a dynamic systems perspective is that features of both the individual and the ecology have the continuous capacity to change in relation to other factors (Bronfenbrenner, 1996; Cairns & Cairns, 1994). However, when efforts are made to change one factor, it is necessary to consider how other factors will respond to either foster adaptation or constrain the impact of the change on the broader system (Farmer, Gatzke-Kopp et al., 2020). This dynamic interplay means that development is not universal, and two students in the same classroom may have very different developmental experiences and associated long-term outcomes (Cairns & Cairns, 1994; Chen et al., 2019; Nasir, 2018; Rogers & Way, 2018).

The developmental systems perspective has important implications for rural special education services. Specifically, there is a need to understand how to align the characteristics, resources, and practices in rural classrooms with the characteristics, needs, opportunities, and constraints experienced by diverse learners. This should not be viewed as a situation in which evidence-based practices (EBPs) generated from large, national cluster randomized trials (CRTs) are implemented with the teacher's expectation that unique students and the classroom as a whole ought to adapt to the intervention (Farmer, 2020). On the contrary, there is a need to provide teachers with a framework and corresponding consultation support to create responsive learning environments and classroom social ecologies to foster individual students' positive engagement, adjustment, and opportunities that promote their successful developmental pathways and desired outcomes. This means carefully adapting EBPs to the developmental needs of students and the values, circumstances, resources, and needs of the community. Reflecting current views of the need for research-practice partnerships (e.g., Bryk, 2015), research in rural schools can benefit by shifting from a universal evidence-based practice perspective to a practice-based evidence perspective for diverse rural settings (Eppley et al., 2018).

A TSAS is well suited to provide such a framework for general education teachers and can serve as a foundation from which special educators can work as consultants to help general educators adapt strategies to students' needs. Like MTSS, TSAS was created from a three-tiered model that is meant to address universal (tier 1), selected (tier 2), and targeted (tier 3) levels of intervention. However, MTSS centers on response to intervention and focuses on implementing manualized EBPs with high levels of fidelity and moving from less to more intensive services until the student is responsive to the intervention (Lane et al., 2015). In contrast, the TSAS model centers on linking the practice elements of EBPs to the developmental needs of youth. Rather than waiting for the student to be responsive to intervention, the goal of TSAS is to adapt specific strategies of EBPs to the developmental needs and ecological circumstances of the student.

A critical aspect of the TSAS model is that strategies are adapted at each level, but such efforts are purposeful, driven by data, and focused on critical developmental considerations and aims. The overarching goal of the TSAS model is to create experiences and opportunities within the ecology that align with the features of the student in ways that promote the positive growth and adaptation of each. Table 25.1 outlines considerations, aims, and approaches of a rural TSAS.

Tier 1 (i.e., universal supports and adaptations) focuses on the general functioning of all children in the classroom. The aim at this tier is to create routine supports for daily activities that foster students' general success. This is not a one-size-fits-all model. Rather, this level centers on approaches that are individualized to the functional needs and capacities of each student and

Rural Tiered Systems of Adaptive Supports

Table 25.1 A Rural Tiered Systems of Adaptive Support (TSAS) Model

Tier	Considerations	Aims	Approaches
Tier 1: Universal Supports and Adaptations	Local circumstances, values, beliefs, and needs Classroom context, resources, needs, opportunities, and constraints	Recognize that all children need supports during routine daily functioning and that needs can change day-to-day and moment-to-moment Create routines and adaptable supports for commonplace aspects of daily functioning Move beyond one-size-fits-all to an adaptable model that can be individualized to functional need	Create academic, behavioral, and social supports for all students regardless of their level of risk to promote their general daily functioning and success in routine activities Adapt supports to characteristics of the student and context; have routines for all students but different students will have different routines that reflect their needs and capacities
Tier 2: Selected Supports and Adaptations	Local circumstances, values, beliefs, and needs Programs in the school or district to address needs School personnel and resources to address needs	Develop a screening process to identify youth at risk for the negative reorganization of their developmental system (DS) Establish a comprehensive multifactored intervention approach to prevent the negative reorganization of students' DS	Use person-oriented strategies to identify students who are at risk as well as potential intervention leverage points Ameliorate risk in the subsystem of difficulty; promote strengths in that subsystem as well as the student's other subsystems
Tier 3: Targeted Supports and Adaptations	Local circumstances, values, beliefs, and needs School resources and personnel to address need Formal and informal community resources	Create a screening and ongoing progress monitoring system to identify youth who manifest correlated risks across multiple subsystems in their DS Establish comprehensive multiagency, multifactored service framework to promote positive reorganization of the DS of youth with correlated risks	Identify how multiple factors/subsystems contribute to the student's adjustment problems Ameliorate risks in each domain Foster and monitor changes across multiple subsystems Promote school and community support for the reorganization of the student's DS and monitor the positive realignment of her or his developmental trajectory

involves differentiated supports to enhance students' success during routine events and procedural tasks (e.g., starting class, transitioning to a new activity, doing group work).

Tier 2 (i.e., selected supports and adaptations) centers on using programs and resources in the classroom and school to prevent the negative reorganization of the developmental system of a student who experiences risk in one of three primary domains of school functioning (i.e., academic, behavioral, social). The aims are to screen and identify students who are experiencing difficulty in one of these three domains and creating individualized multifactored supports. This involves adapting strategies from EBPs to strengthen the student's functioning and competencies in the domain of difficulty while supporting the student's strength in the other developmental domains to prevent the spread of risk into these domains (i.e., negative reorganization of the developmental system).

Tier 3 is designed to address the needs of students who have manifested difficulties in multiple domains (usually within school and in the home and/or community settings). The goal of tier 3 intervention is to promote the positive reorganization of the student's developmental system by coordinating informal and formal supports both in the school and the community. To do this, the primary aims of tier 3 are to identify how problems across multiple domains of functioning in school and the community contribute to each other and to carefully establish a comprehensive multifactored intervention approach to systematically change the functioning of the student in each of these domains in relation to her or his functioning in the other domains. This involves identifying which domains are malleable and ameliorating the student's risk in these domains while carefully monitoring and working to promote new competencies and strengths in the other domains in a coordinated fashion. The overarching goal of tier 3 is to establish natural and/ or community agency supports that help to foster and sustain the positive realignment of the student's developmental trajectory over time.

Linking Special Education and TSAS

Because of issues of distance, isolation, and low critical mass, many rural special educators tend to serve a broad range of students, take on multiple roles, and become a school resource to support the needs of diverse learners regardless as to whether they are identified for special education services (Berry & Gravelle, 2013; Weiss et al., 2014). Rural special educators often feel isolated, unsupported, and not connected with a network of colleagues (Berry, 2012). As rural schools adopt tiered systems of support there is a need to link such efforts with special education. To do this, rural school administrators and special educators, operating as intervention specialists, can work with all teachers and other personnel in the school to create a system of supports that is responsive to all students' needs while working within the resources, culture, values, and constraints of the community (Farmer, Hamm et al., 2018).

On this count, it is necessary to create TSAS programs in a way that prepares diverse learners, including students with special needs, for their futures that build toward their self-determined success within their home communities (Irvin et al., 2011; Petrin et al., 2011; Schafft, 2016). Rural students with disabilities and other students who struggle in school and who are at risk for dropout often have difficulty in one or more academic domains, experience interpersonal problems and have few close friends, have difficulties complying with adults' behavioral expectations, and feel as though they do not belong in school (Cairns & Cairns, 1994; Farmer, Hall et al., 2011; Farmer, Leung et al., 2011). Rural high school students who experience difficulties in multiple domains that place them at risk for school failure also tend to feel that they do not fit in in their home communities, have not prepared for life after high school, and want to leave their home communities but generally have no realistic plans to do so (Farmer, Dadisman et al., 2006; Hutchins et al., 2012; Petrin et al., 2011).

The purpose of TSAS is to create school contexts where all students feel as though they are valued and belong, where they can develop positive relationships with peers and adults, and where they can develop personally meaningful competencies and a pathway to success. The isolation many rural special education teachers experience likely reflects a lack of meaningful integration of the students they serve in general education settings and the possibility that rural special education teachers are either expected to be responsible for all of their students' school services or that they play a peripheral role without any clear responsibilities other than directing IEP meetings (Berry & Gravelle, 2013; Weiss et al., 2014). By utilizing special educators to work within a TSAS framework that focuses on adapting and differentiating strategies to the needs of individual students, teaming with others, and working from both a prevention and promotion perspective, it should be possible to create classroom and school ecologies where students feel supported and feel like they belong, while general and special educators develop the sense that they have a team of colleagues to help them meet the needs of all the students they serve. Such efforts must go beyond academic supports and discipline issues and include a focus on social and emotional learning.

Social and Emotional Learning Within TSAS: A Person-Centered, Place-Based Perspective

SEL focuses on "what must children learn to be socially competent students, and how might educators support the development of these skills most effectively?" (Wentzel, 2019, p. 127). Social and emotional competencies grow in supportive relationships and are dependent upon opportunities, experience, and context (Jones et al., 2019). Although many SEL programs center on manualized curricula and structured training groups that focus on explicitly teaching new skills and remediating deficits (Durlak et al., 2011), there is a need to recognize that students' daily experiences and interactions with their peers are central to SEL. These experiences are often culturally bound, depend on a variety of factors (e.g., gender, race, propinquity, socioeconomic status, physical characteristics, athletic ability) that extend beyond students' social competencies, and can be managed by classroom teachers (Farmer, Dawes et al., 2018).

In rural communities, we have found that factors such as classroom and school size, familiarity with peers, and local values and norms for interpersonal behavior can affect students' social opportunities and relationships. For example, rural early adolescents who transition to middle school experience less bullying and perceive the environment as being more supportive than students who remain with the same peers in K-8 settings (Farmer, Hamm et al., 2011). In small communities where everyone knows everyone, it is possible that students take on social roles and reputations that sustain their relationships and social behaviors.

For students with disabilities, it is important to understand how their social competencies are linked to other interpersonal features (e.g., academic ability, behavioral, athletic ability, and physical appearance) as well as ecological factors (i.e., family characteristics, where they live, access to recreational activities; Farmer, Dawes et al., 2018). From a person-centered vantage, many rural students with disabilities experience risk across multiple interpersonal domains that are associated with low social status and social isolation or affiliations with other low-status

The Bloomsbury Handbook of Rural Education in the United States

peers that contribute to a sense of not belonging in school (Farmer, Hall et al., 2011; Farmer, Leung et al., 2011). However, some youth develop positive social roles and relationships that both reflect and contribute to their ability to build upon strengths in other interpersonal domains.

As rural schools establish TSAS, it is necessary to include a focus on students' social needs without explicitly focusing on social deficits. Rather, it is beneficial to use a holistic, person-centered perspective that identifies and promotes patterns of strengths in relation to community contexts. Consistent with place-based perspectives that center on being responsive to the values, norms, and culture of local communities, there is a need for SEL programs that can be tailored to the needs of subtypes of rural students within the social ecologies in which they are embedded (Farmer, Dawes et al., 2018). Such efforts should include managing and supporting students' day-to-day and moment-to-moment social opportunities and experiences and should be integrated with academic and behavioral support strategies in a seamless approach for managing classroom and school contexts (see Farmer et al., 2019; Farmer, Hamm et al., 2020).

Responsive Professional Development, Consultation, and Research

To create the types of collaborative TSAS described above, it is necessary to have a framework for ongoing professional development support and training that is responsive to the strengths, resources, and constraints of the school and the needs and values of the community (Farmer, Hamm et al., 2018). Special educators can play a critical role in such a system by operating as intervention specialists who collaboratively support general education teachers in the use and adaptation of evidence-based programs tailored to the needs and circumstances of students, the school, and the community (Farmer et al., 2016). Such efforts can be enhanced if they are guided by complementary technical assistance and community-engaged research.

Professional development in rural schools is often constrained by distance (Barrett et al., 2015; IES, 2014). Using technology to reduce the constraints and barriers of distance has been a priority of rural special education research in recent years (e.g., Alexander et al., 2012: Hager et al., 2012; Jimenez et al., 2016). As the use of technology to support professional development continues to advance in rural schools, there is a need to link such efforts with training and technical assistance centers (T-TACs) and regional educational labs (RELs) to foster a new type of research (Farmer, 2020; IES, 2014). Rather than conducting cluster randomized control trials in rural schools, there is a need to collect local data at the school, classroom, teacher, and student level and to use these data within a research-practice partnership framework between rural schools and T-TACs and/or RELs (Farmer, Hamm et al., 2018). This means shifting the focus away from the unattainable goal of generating universal strategies that work anywhere to using practice-based evidence to guide efforts in diverse settings (Eppley et al., 2018). Such work should operate from an improvement science framework and should use local analytics and person- and process-oriented analyses along with information about practice elements of EBPs to provide consultation to guide the adaptation of interventions that are responsive to diverse rural students, schools, and communities (Farmer, 2020).

Improvement science centers on establishing interdisciplinary networks of researchers and practitioners who bring together different but complementary skills to address a problem of practice (Bryk, 2015). A critical aspect of this work is that it builds from insights of frontline professionals to yield practice-based research that is likely to resonate with practitioners while being amenable to generating data-driven, adaptive approaches to intervention that can be more responsive to individual students and contexts (Farmer, Hamm et al., 2018; Snow, 2015). CRTs are not well suited for such research (Bryk, 2015; Farmer, 2020; Snow, 2015).

Although CRTs have been viewed as the gold standard for research designs to identify whether an intervention works (see Slavin, 2020), the question of "what works?" is only part of the process and does not answer fundamental questions for rural schools. Rural schools need to know how to support the success of diverse learners with the resources and personnel they have and with strategies that are responsive to community needs, interests, values, and opportunities (Azano & Stewart, 2016; Barrett et al., 2015; Johnson et al., 2018; Schafft, 2016). CRTs utilize the general linear model and generate findings at the level of a sample or population. They tell us whether there is a difference in intervention and control group participants on specific variables of interest. They do not tell us which students the intervention works for, the processes that contribute to the impact, or how a specific outcome relates to the student's broader adjustment or her or his likely long-term outcomes. Person- and process-oriented analyses can be valuable on this count.

Research that combines person- and process-oriented approaches with local analytics can yield rigorous empirical methods that examine change in the organization of key developmental variables that are predictive of pathways to outcomes of interest (i.e., school completion, healthy adolescent/adult adjustment, successful postsecondary educational and work attainment). Person-oriented analysis (e.g., latent profile analysis, cluster analysis) involves identifying subtypes of youth who are similar to each other on key variables of school functioning including academic, behavioral, and social factors. The identification of subtypes of youth (e.g., high competence, average youth, youth with risk in one domain, youth with significant difficulties across multiple domains) makes it possible to determine which youth are likely to experience positive long-term outcomes and which youth are at risk for poor outcomes. These subtypes can be linked to process-oriented analysis (e.g., causal analysis, prodigal analysis) to identify factors that contribute to pathways to success or patterns of difficulty. When such approaches are used with local analytics to identify key developmental processes and linked to the practice elements of EBPs, it should be possible to better tailor intervention to students and the rural ecology.

Conclusion

In many respects, special education and rural education share similar issues and opportunities. In some ways they are each often perceived as different and outside of the mainstream. And, in fact, services and supports that are developed for society in general often are not responsive to the needs or circumstances of exceptional learners or rural schools and communities. But special education and rural education are each fertile ground for innovation and discovery. Rather than creating frameworks where we expect special education students and teachers or rural schools and communities to conform to practices and expectations that do not fit their worlds, we need to establish adaptive formats and supports that help them forge new pathways to success that are consonant with the interests, capacities, and resources that are central to their own lives, values, and proclivities. In so doing, we can expand the frontiers of educational science in ways that should be of great benefit to society broadly.

26

Challenges and Innovative Responses in Rural Gifted Education

Amy Price Azano, Carolyn M. Callahan, and Rachelle Kuehl

Since nearly the first mention of rural gifted education, scholars working in that subfield have identified opportunity gaps related to inequitable spending and, inevitably, less access to specialized teachers and staff. And just as challenges hold true, so too do "promising solutions" (Spicker et al., 1987, p. 156)—such as the use of broadened, equitable identification procedures and offering rural students more opportunities to engage in challenging learning activities and interactions with peers socially and academically. Naming these "solutions," however, has proven insufficient to effectively close the opportunity gap for rural gifted students. This is primarily because the barriers often are representative of inequities and systemic challenges that affect rural schooling for all learners. In other words, the barriers to quality gifted education cannot be adequately ameliorated by the rural school because their root causes lie elsewhere. This chapter means not to minimize the inequities related to school funding or the other systemic conditions that make gifted education programming challenging in rural schools. Rather, it acknowledges their persistent influence and describes innovative responses that are within the scope of rural school districts.

Here we provide a review of relevant literature on gifted education in rural settings, focusing specifically on the socially constructed nature of rural gifted education, conceptualizing the need for increased research and describing the ways in which robust gifted education services can disrupt persisting deficit notions of rural students and rural schools. In particular, we note the value gifted education can provide to rural communities, and we respond to curricular or community practices that are sometimes perceived as encouraging bright rural students to leave their home communities (Corbett, 2007)—even if they have aspirations to stay (C. B. Howley et al., 1996). We also examine the ways in which implications of gifted education manifest differently across various rural settings. After foregrounding with this review, we look specifically at the challenges and innovative responses and conclude with an example of these strategies at work.

Disrupting Deficit Notions of Rural Students

To the larger US culture, rural people are often stereotyped as "backwards" or "slow" (Dunstan & Jaeger, 2015, p. 780)—stereotypes that are perpetuated in popular media depictions such as reality shows *Buckwild* and *Call of the Wildman*, which follow in a long tradition of these representations (e.g., *The Beverly Hillbillies*) and are perpetuated still by Hollywood portrayals of rural America as crude and scary (Belden, 2018). These stereotypes were reified, in part, by the 2016 presidential election and the resulting soundbite of "Trump Country" pointing to rural America as a source of blame for the presidential outcome and for critique of a presumed political base not understanding how to vote in its own best interests (Catte, 2017, 2018; Harkins & McCarroll, 2019). Stereotype threat is the feeling that an individual's actions may be viewed as representative of a particular cultural group to which a person belongs (Aronson & Steele, 2005; Steele et al., 2002). For example, McCarroll (2019) described her move to the Northeast after college graduation, writing, "powerful stereotypes about Appalachia had arrived in places like Boston well before me and had influenced the way that even the most considerate people thought about me" (p. 250). Because people made derogatory remarks about her accent, implying that her way of speaking was a sign of low intelligence, she tried to hide it when applying to doctoral programs, but she also internalized the feeling that "I might not belong in a Boston graduate school" (p. 251). While deficit perceptions of rural people have existed for decades, the increased negative attention to rural places and people (due to the rhetoric of the 2016 election) may have exacerbated stereotype threat for rural learners.

Rural education scholars have called for a disruption of deficit notions (e.g., Azano & Biddle, 2019), and innovative responses to increase rural students' positive perceptions of their own gifts and talents have proved effective. For example, C. B. Howley and colleagues (2012), in discussing the math talent that exists among rural students, noted that efforts to make instruction more responsive to rural contexts can provide an avenue for thinking about how gifted education can address stewardship and educational purpose. Similarly, in a study examining the use of new technologies in a digital storytelling project designed to help rural high school students enhance their literacy skills beyond state standards, Chisholm and Trent (2013) found that the article's focal student "leveraged her multiple ways of knowing to expand the meaning-making potential of her extended composition about place" (p. 308). Although students in the remote school district had earned scores on standardized tests that placed the district in the lowest-achieving 5 percent in the state, the researchers showed how innovative place-based activities can propel students past deficit perceptions by delineating how the student's digital composition exceeded Common Core State Standards for her grade.

Barriers to High-Quality Gifted Programming

While costs and logistical details (e.g., long distances between schools served by a single itinerant teacher) certainly contribute to the challenges in providing gifted education services in rural schools, Delcourt and colleagues (2007) suggested that a lack of understanding of the benefits of gifted programming may intensify school leaders' unwillingness to devote resources to such programming.

Lack of local understanding of giftedness stems partially from the degree to which giftedness is a social construct (Davis et al., 2010; Heuser et al., 2017) that is conceptualized differently across different cultures and places. For example, some people may consider high achievement as a mark of giftedness, whereas others may view giftedness as the *potential for* high achievement; likewise, some might believe giftedness can exist in just one domain (e.g., musical ability), whereas others may feel a person must demonstrate high ability across multiple domains to be considered gifted (Heuser et al., 2017).

Because of the different ways in which people understand giftedness, misunderstandings and persistent myths about gifted learners—for example, that they will "be okay" without instruction or programming—prevail (National Association for Gifted Children [NAGC], n.d.-b) and thwart the ability of educators to provide appropriate instruction.

Disrupting these myths and communicating with stakeholders about small successes in gifted education can dramatically increase "buy-in" about the importance of continuing to serve gifted students (Azano et al., 2020). For example, in the case described in further detail later in the chapter, some rural principals and superintendents worried that implementation of a place-based literacy curriculum for third- and fourth-grade gifted students might prevent the students from receiving instruction geared toward preparing them for high-stakes end-of-year testing. When researchers recognized their concerns, they were able to present preliminary data from pilot study participants to reassure teachers and other school leaders that although the curriculum was framed in an unfamiliar way, it had actually helped other rural gifted students achieve higher scores on standardized tests because of its deeper, more comprehensive approach to educating students.

Resistance to Preparing Gifted Students for Nonrural Futures

When it comes to rural students who are viewed as having the highest academic potential, a concern exists among rural communities that differentiating instruction to provide extra challenge could equip the "best and brightest" students to leave their hometowns in favor of metropolitan places that could provide more opportunities. Biases associated with gifted programming (e.g., the perception of the pursuit of higher education as "elitist") can influence not only curriculum and programming but the extent to which rural students are nominated for, identified for, and encouraged to participate in gifted education services (Lawrence, 2009). Place-based instruction can help students make meaningful connections between the curriculum and their lives outside of school (Azano, 2011; McInerney et al., 2011; Smith, 2002). In fact, "Not only is it possible to make the curriculum more relevant to the students' past and present" with a place-based approach, opportunities are provided "for connections between the students' futures and their rural communities" (Rasheed, 2019, pp. 74–5).

Additionally, the real concern of the effects of out-migration on rural communities, particularly communities that have experienced economic downturns due to circumstances such as factory closures and the diminishing coal mining industry, may add to the sense that gifted programming could provide a threat to the vitality of rural places (Corbett, 2007; C. B. Howley, 1998). Lawrence (2009) argued that rather than deny gifted students needed academic challenges in school, government agencies and economic development organizations need to mobilize to address the systemic inequities and underlying public policies that make it difficult for talented young people to sustain productive employment in their home communities. In fact, C. B. Howley and colleagues (1996) argued that students' aspirations to stay in their communities are often ignored. They noted that "bright" rural students in the Appalachian communities about which they wrote might actually view staying in their hometowns as a "mark of failure" (p. 159), so they would leave, even as their sense of place made them long to return. Instead of forcing students to make a "devil's bargain"—accessing advanced academic opportunities outside the community but giving up the possibility of making a life in their hometowns—Lawrence (2009) challenged rural students "to imagine what might be possible if, as adults, they invested their abilities in rural communities" (p. 462). A. Howley and colleagues (2009) presented a similar appeal, writing that "helping talented students understand the value of contributing as leaders to their own communities would be a worthy aim for gifted programs in rural places" (p. 528).

Gifted Education in Varying Rural Contexts

In the same way that the concept of giftedness is socially constructed, rurality is also a social construct, which further complicates the ability of rural education researchers to define the landscape of the field (Rasheed, 2019). In Chapter 1 of this volume, Longhurst detailed the various ways rurality is defined by governmental agencies and how those definitions affect decisions about how to serve rural communities. Rural education research relies heavily on the definitions developed by the National Center for Education Statistics (NCES), which are based on US Census data and geographic realities. The distance from a rural school district to the nearest urbanized area or urban cluster is used to categorize the entire district as rural fringe, rural distant, or rural remote; Longhurst pointed out this can be problematic in that geographically widespread districts could be very different from one side to the other. When discussing rural gifted education, Puryear and Kettler (2017) found that rural fringe districts had more in common with nonrural districts than with districts classified as rural distant and rural remote. Importantly, this finding provides direction to the field in focusing research, funding, and other supports on the rural distant and rural remote districts whose students might be most "at risk" for having their educational needs go unmet (Azano, 2014, p. 299), thus adversely affecting students' individual opportunities and the likelihood that they will gain needed knowledge and skills to help their communities thrive.

Challenges in Providing Services to Rural Gifted Students

The challenges in providing for the education of gifted rural students are parallel in many ways to those of educating any student in rural schools (e.g., lack of adequate funding), but they take on a unique character when considering the distinct and defining characteristics of this subpopulation of students. The challenges begin with defining the students in a school district who will be considered gifted. As noted above, giftedness and rurality are both social constructs. Hence, we would expect that educators would take great care in defining the group of students whom they consider exceptional in their learning or performance capabilities *in their school district.* However, because of three intersecting factors, educators are often limited to antiquated and narrow conceptions of giftedness:

- The significant number of teachers and administrators who are not likely to have received guidance in the creation of programming and/or differentiated curriculum and instruction for gifted students as part of their preservice preparation programs (Basister & Kawai, 2018; Fraser-Seeto et al., 2013; Gindy, 2016; NAGC and Council of State Directors of Gifted Programs, 2013; Riley & Bicknell, 2013);

- Geographic isolation that inhibits the exchange of the most current ideas and practices in the field of gifted education; and
- Lack of funding for professional development for teachers, administrators, and/or counselors (e.g., attendance at state or national conferences, school visits from experts in gifted education for training sessions; Jarzabkowski, 2003; Stambaugh & Wood, 2016) and limited internet capabilities that might provide alternative access.

Constraints of Narrow Definitions of Giftedness

In quality programming for gifted students, educators align the definition of giftedness and the adopted identification processes to the curricular options for gifted students. Quality programming is also dependent on access to the most recent theory, research, and recommended practice. However, the combination of the challenging factors noted may easily lead to the adoption of narrow, dated conceptions of giftedness—usually ones reflecting only extraordinarily high performance on intelligence and/or or achievement measures compared to national samples of students. Hence, the first challenge in identifying gifted rural students is to develop a definition or conception of giftedness that is reflective of the context in which students learn and incorporates the most recent thinking about the definition of gifted students. The current federal definition (US) provides basic guidance:

> Students, children, or youth who give evidence of high achievement capability in areas such as intellectual, creative, artistic, or leadership capacity, or in specific academic fields, and who need services and activities not ordinarily provided by the school in order to fully develop those capabilities. (NAGC, n.d.-a)

The federal definition provides a conception of giftedness that is more inclusive of a range of gifts and talents than one based only on general intellectual ability. The inclusion of artistic and specific academic fields has particular value in that it allows schools to consider students gifted in a particular area such as the fine and performing arts, mathematics, or language arts in addition to those who might show intellectual aptitude more generally.[1]

The broadened NAGC definition also capitalizes on the concept of "opportunity to learn" (OTL). This construct is based on acknowledgment that local contexts and socioeconomic status, among other factors, can influence the "opportunities" students have to learn and demonstrate their talents. As Husen explained, OTL may influence test performance or "whether or not . . . students have had the opportunity to study a particular topic or learn how to solve a particular type of problem presented by the test" (Husen, 1967, pp. 162–3, cited in Burstein, 1993). Husen pointed out that without these opportunities, students' chances of responding correctly to test items on standardized aptitude or achievement tests are less than for students who have had exposure to the particular content and skills measured by those items. In current interpretations, OTL includes experiences students have had with content of the disciplines and direct instruction in critical thinking skills as well as their experiences with quality instruction, quality and scope of instructional materials and resources, and facilities such as laboratories (Elliott & Bartlett, 2016; Lohman, 2013). The degree to which students have these experiences or resources reflects the prospects for students to acquire knowledge and skills and *express* ability. As Lohman (2013) noted, "Clearly, the intellectual abilities of students who live in poverty, who have irregular or poor schooling, and who have less experience with the language of instruction (or testing) are often underestimated when their behavior is compared with that of other children who are the same age or in the same grade" (p. 119). That is, educators should evaluate students relative to the school population served by the school or school district—those who have a similar OTL—rather than relative to a national sample. The NAGC's inclusion of the need for "services and activities not ordinarily provided by the school in order to fully develop [students'] capabilities" in their definition of gifted students supports the application of OTL in consideration of giftedness.

Challenges Related to Identifying Gifted Rural Students

Despite the widespread acceptance of broader definitions of giftedness in the scholarly literature and the development of clear criteria for identification of students with gifts and talents by professional associations and government agencies (e.g., Australian Association for the Education of the Gifted and Talented (n.d.); NAGC (2010b); Northern Territory Government Department of Education, 2016), the definitions have often not translated into corresponding identification processes and procedures at the local district or school level (Brodersen, 2016; Callahan et al., 2017b; Jarvis & Henderson, 2012). Identification as gifted is often determined on the basis of "cut-off" scores derived from national norms on instruments purported to measure IQ or matrices[2] that arbitrarily assign points to test scores and/or rating scales (Callahan et al., 2017b). Application of these processes likely limits the identification of students who would not be considered part of the dominant culture—those who have not had the same OTL.

A second challenge to identifying rural gifted students that emerges from the limiting factors noted above is overreliance on teacher nomination in creating the pool of students to be considered for placement in gifted services. A lack of understanding of the severe limitations of this practice can result in the creation of a pool of students that reflects teachers' inherent beliefs about giftedness, one of which may be that students cannot be gifted if they are earning poor grades. This belief fails to recognize that one frequent outcome of a learning environment that is not challenging or engaging is underachievement resulting from boredom (Siegle, 2013). Even when the school district's definition has been revised to reflect the state of the art in gifted education (Brown et al., 2005), teachers with insufficient training on how to operationalize the definition are likely to fall back on their own fundamental, narrow beliefs about giftedness, thus disenfranchising students whose behaviors do not reflect those beliefs.

Challenges Related to Serving Gifted Rural Students

Some of the same factors inhibiting the identification of gifted students in rural areas (e.g., absence of preservice training and/or professional development in differentiating instruction for gifted students) also affect the development and implementation of gifted services. In addition, lack of funding for administrative and teaching staff often results in the assignment of one individual to oversee a rural district's gifted program while they have multiple other duties (e.g., overseeing special education programming) which have priority because of strict, complex federal guidelines. Because many states have only minimal legal requirements for gifted education, time and attention to the special education role is likely to be given priority. Lack of funds sometimes results in the assignment of one gifted resource teacher for a very large, rural district, necessitating long travel, thus limiting the amount of time the teacher can spend providing services and contributing to the sense of professional isolation felt by many rural gifted teachers (Azano et al., 2014). Further, limited funding for curricular resources (e.g., advanced-level printed sources, computer access or programs, laboratory equipment), combined with the absence of preservice training and/or professional development in gifted education, leaves teachers without the needed competencies to develop lessons and curriculum appropriate for gifted learners and contributes to placing rural gifted students at an instructional deficit as compared with their urban and suburban peers.

Other underlying factors that contribute to the difficulties in delivering appropriate programming to gifted students lies in the belief of administrators and teachers in myths about gifted students. The first persistent myth is that "gifted students will be okay" without instruction or programming (e.g., Bain et al., 2007) despite evidence that gifted students often fail to reach their potential. Other common myths that have been refuted in the research on gifted students include the idea that teachers challenge all students, so gifted students are well served in the regular classroom; gifted students contribute to the achievement of all students by elevating the level of discussion and serving as role models; and acceleration (i.e., grade skipping or having students work faster through the curriculum) is socially harmful for gifted students (NAGC, n.d.-b). These myths sometimes serve as a rationale for budgetary decisions that limit the allocation of resources for gifted programs, and the effects of these beliefs are compounded by the lack of federal and state mandates requiring specific and relevant accommodations for gifted learners. And, when only small numbers of students in any one school or school district are identified as gifted, it can be harder to justify spending.

Mitigating Challenges in Identifying and Serving Rural Gifted Students

Creating Defensible Identification of Rural Gifted Students

Underlying the specific recommendations to address the challenges noted above are the general principles for defensible identification of gifted students. Hence, the process should begin with specification of multiple data points for the identification of rural gifted students—a move away from using one arbitrary test score or relying on arbitrary matrices. Decision makers should identify and use both test and nontest data sources (Australian Association for the Education of the Gifted and Talented, n.d.; NAGC, 2010b; Northern Territory Government Department of Education, 2016). Scores from standardized measures of cognitive ability and/or standardized tests should be considered in tandem with teacher ratings and portfolio assessments and/or performance assessments to ascertain which students would benefit from advanced instruction and the opportunities provided by gifted services. The appropriateness of any instrument rests on its validity as an indicator of talent for the area of giftedness to be assessed and evidence of its effectiveness in predicting success with the services and curriculum to be offered (Callahan et al., 2018). In other words, educators would use a different set of assessments to assess talent in language arts than to assess mathematical talent, and these instruments would be distinct from those used to assess talents in the fine arts.

Recent data on the impact of universal screening, or giving a screening assessment to *all students* in a given grade, support the use of a standardized test of cognitive ability as a critical first step when assessing ability in general intellectual domains or specific academic areas (Card & Giuliano, 2015). Further, research on teacher rating scales suggests they can be another valuable source of data when teachers are provided training in the use of the instruments within the context of the schools and community in which the students live and learn (Peters & Gentry,

2010). In the case of rural schools, it is critical that the language of the instrument and the training provided to teachers include ample access to examples of the ways giftedness may manifest in students in the particular rural setting. For example, advanced ability in the language arts might manifest in a student's request for a teacher to help them read and interpret a repair manual for a piece of farm equipment.

However, none of these tools will suffice to ensure that rural students gain equitable access to gifted education opportunities. Of equal importance is the appropriate interpretation and decision-making based on the scores obtained from universal screening, teacher rating scales, and portfolio assessments. Lohman (2013) recommended using local norms, and scholars such as Peters and Gentry (2010) recommend using group-specific local norms for students from families with relatively low incomes as they will "locate those students who have demonstrated high achievement (when compared with their peers), but who also often go unnoticed" (p. 140).

Serving Rural Gifted Students

A fundamental step in creating defensible programs for rural gifted students would be to provide sustainable professional development and effective, differentiated curricula that teachers can easily access and use without the expense of considerable supplemental material. Ideally, this type of professional development would be to thoroughly orient teachers in the underlying principles of differentiating instruction for gifted students. However, it is best if curricular materials provided to teachers are structured so that teachers can successfully implement them simply by following the written guidelines (Plucker & Callahan, 2014). This ensures that teachers understand and can readily identify foundational aspects in the unit (i.e., differentiation, depth, complexity, and enrichment; Kaplan, 2013).

In addition, in rural communities where teachers of gifted students are distributed across many classrooms and schools, school personnel need to foster a sense of community for the teacher (Azano et al., 2014, 2017). To this end, school districts should consider how to facilitate support for teachers, perhaps through web-based relationships (in places where internet access is reliable) or partnerships at the regional level.

Educators should also consider the grouping arrangements that will facilitate the greatest instructional time devoted to appropriate differentiation for individual students. While pull-out arrangements provide opportunities for work with peers of equal ability, the time that can be devoted to this option is limited in rural settings. Supplementing the pull-out program with cluster grouping, or assigning most or all gifted students in a grade to one classroom (with appropriate teacher preparation as described by Gentry, 2018), and providing options for acceleration of certain students (Assouline et al., 2014), may help ensure the specific academic needs of more children are met.

Conclusion: A Case Study in Rural Gifted Education

To conclude this chapter, we offer a case study in rural gifted education that was designed to address the unique needs inherent in combining the fields of rural education and gifted education research. Promoting PLACE in Rural Schools was the product of a five-year, federally funded Jacob K. Javits grant designed by coauthors Callahan and Azano, who served as coprincipal investigators for the project. After working together on a previous grant to design and implement a language arts enrichment curriculum for gifted students in grades 3–5, the CLEAR curriculum (Callahan et al., 2017a), Azano and Callahan recognized the need to ensure curricula like CLEAR could be taught optimally in rural schools, and to do so, they revised the curriculum to center a place-based pedagogy. That is, lessons and lesson materials were modified to include stories of rural people and places as well as opportunities for students to consider the ways in which their own identities had been shaped by the particular rural context in which they lived. Notably, teachers were presented with a questionnaire asking them to describe the area in which they taught (e.g., the major industries conducting business in the area, the geographic characteristics of the area, and the educational expectations for students generally held by community members), and their answers heavily informed the curriculum adaptations.

Moreover, in recognition of the persistent challenges to rural gifted education described in this chapter, Promoting PLACE sought to provide access to gifted services to more rural elementary students by encouraging districts to consider alternative identification criteria. Rather than relying on national norms on standardized tests, the project staff screened all second-grade students in participating districts on the verbal subtests of the Cognitive Abilities Test (CogAT) and provided local norms as the first step in identifying a larger cohort of students to receive gifted services. Grant personnel also trained teachers to use specific subscales (Motivation, Creativity, and Reading) of the Scales for Rating the Behavioral Characteristics of Superior Students (SRBCSS; Renzulli et al., 2010), urging teachers to attend to ways rural students may exhibit gifted behaviors that are different from the traditionally perceived characteristics of giftedness (e.g., a student who may have intricate knowledge of the rules, regulations, and "best practices" involved in deer hunting; or a student who entertains her classmates with well-crafted stories representative of the rich storytelling traditions of her rural culture). The project staff then calculated both district and local classroom norms on the three SRBCSS scales (to avoid potential bias from leniency ratings of teachers).

In meeting with the gifted specialists, classroom teachers, principals, and superintendents across the fourteen participating rural districts in Virginia and Kentucky, grant personnel collaborated in reviewing spreadsheets developed to chart the data of students who would be considered for assignment to gifted education services. In all, over 2,000 students were screened and nearly 300 students were identified as gifted (in addition to those who would have been identified using the districts' traditional criteria). Districts were randomly assigned to treatment and control conditions, and students in the treatment condition (both those identified by the district and by the project) participated in four language arts units—Poetry and Folklore in third grade and Research and Fiction in fourth grade—using delivery models that ranged from small-group pull-out lessons with a gifted specialist to weekly full-day instruction at a gifted center to differentiation within the general elementary classroom. Teachers kept track of the lessons they taught and any adjustments they made to the lessons, and grant personnel conducted classroom observations to both ensure fidelity of implementation and to determine whether adjustments that were made added value to the curriculum (e.g., a teacher replacing a poem in the Poetry unit with one written by a local author) or, in some cases, diminished the impact of a particular lesson (e.g., shortening certain aspects of the lesson due to time constraints). Additionally, treatment group students participated in two full-day interventions geared toward reducing stereotype threat (Aronson & Steele, 2005) and encouraging a growth mindset (Dweck, 2006), one intervention taking place at the end of third grade and the other at the end of fourth grade. Control group students (project identified and district identified) participated in the gifted program offered in their schools.

Many successes were celebrated across the project. For one thing, students grew in their understanding of language arts concepts far above what is expected by state standards. Bass (2019), for example, revealed students' growth in writing skills based on assessments of their pre- and post-intervention writing samples. And, in a close examination of all 237 narrative fiction stories written by fourth graders as the culminating project of the Fiction unit, Kuehl (2020) discovered incredible talent, strong connections to place (Kuehl et al., 2020), and tender depictions of rural families (Kuehl, 2021) across the stories. In particular, Kuehl (2020) noted that of the twenty stories designated as "most rural" (i.e., characters engaged in activities connected with the local community such as hunting, fishing, farming, and gathering together at small community events), seventeen were written by boys, suggesting that a place-based focus may be especially powerful in reaching male students who often lag behind their female peers in writing (e.g., Berninger et al., 1996; McKeough & Genereux, 2003; Olinghouse, 2008; VanTassel-Baska et al., 2002).

Perhaps, though, the biggest success of the project is reflected in outcome data. First, the students who were identified as gifted through the alternative criteria established by Promoting PLACE actually *outperformed* students who were identified traditionally on post-intervention testing on the reading and writing subscales of the Iowa Assessments and scored equally as well on specific tests on the content of the units (Callahan et al., 2021). And finally, when treatment and control group outcomes were compared, the treatment group demonstrated greater gains on the Reading, Vocabulary, and Written Expression subscales of the Iowa Assessments and outperformed control group students on the Poetry and Research unit tests (all unit tests reflected grade-level standards for the content focus of the unit). Average differences on the Folklore and Fiction unit tests also favored the treatment group, though not significantly (Callahan et al., 2021).

These findings go a long way in refuting long-held beliefs that students who did not score in the highest percentiles nationally on standardized tests for giftedness would not be able to keep up with other gifted students using advanced curricula. In fact, some of the rural school leaders who had expressed doubts about Promoting PLACE's identification processes came to understand the different ways giftedness can manifest, and expanding this understanding will likely lead to many more rural students benefiting from needed gifted services.

Being designated as gifted can have a real impact on how children are seen by their families, their communities, and even themselves. If more rural students who possess gifts and talents are described as such, and if these gifts and talents are cultivated by their local schools, it would open up many possibilities for students to see themselves as having the potential to access higher education and skills that they could then bring back to their rural communities—many of which are in need of revitalization and reinvestment. Beyond naming the strategies we have described in this chapter as "promising solutions," we present readers with viable implementations to invest in rural gifted students and contend that this investment holds great promise to yield rich dividends for their communities.

International Response

A Peripheral Perspective

A View from Rural Europe

Cath Gristy

Reflecting on these chapters in the times of the Covid-19 pandemic in 2020, we are reminded anew of the interconnectedness of the world—the forces that link and join but also divide and separate groups, communities, and populations. It is in a spirit of international connection that this reflection, focusing on issues of identity and equity, is written from my position as a European. To provide contemporary contexts for juxtaposition and comparison with the US scenarios presented in this collection of chapters, I draw in part on a recently published collection of work from researchers across rural Europe, *Educational Research and Schooling in Rural Europe: An Engagement with Changing Patterns of Education, Space and Place* (Gristy et al., 2020). This collected work with contributions from authors across twelve countries has its roots in the European Education Research Association (EERA) and particularly Network 14, Communities, Families, and Schooling in Educational Research. EERA's interdisciplinary and inclusive approach and practices make it a great source of diverse, new, and innovative work.

This reflection begins with some consideration of changes taking place in rural Europe for the reader to juxtapose with those from the United States in this handbook. Europe has seen seismic changes in the last few years that have shaken and disrupted social and political as well as material fabrics, opening new opportunities and possibilities, as well as exposing new and old inequities and injustices. Geographies have changed in response to shifts in migration patterns, political directions, and a destabilizing of the idea of a united Europe (see Kučerová et al., 2020; Kvalsund, 2020; and Solstad & Karlberg-Granlund, 2020, in *Educational Research and Schooling in Rural Europe* [Gristy et al., 2020] for useful discussions). Ongoing decision-making by countries looking to leave the European Union (EU) includes that of the recent departure of the UK and the troubling, disruptive Brexit process. Very recently, the wide-ranging impacts of the Covid-19 pandemic include in some countries a challenging of the dominant assumption that city life epitomizes rich cultural opportunity and desirable lifestyle choices. Some areas of England, for example, are witnessing an increased interest from city dwellers in buying property in, and "escape" to, rural places (Rural Services Network, 2020).

With a disruption to, and questioning of, established ways of working and living, this handbook is timely; it is a good time to be focusing on education in peripheral and rural places. Across the world, researchers are looking to learn about sustainable human flourishing from practices and sites of education in rural places—learning about resilience, hope, innovation, and change (see proceedings of the annual EERA conference for examples from Europe and the World Education Research Association conference for a global view).

This collection of chapters that focus on issues of identity and equity illustrates the great potential in peripheral or marginal perspectives; a view from the periphery can be considered a good place for insights for those looking to enact change. Work at "the margins" can develop understanding of exclusionary forces operating in education systems by "repositioning" (Apple, 2001) the analytical framework. Voices from the margins (such as those heard in Chapter 22 by Williams and colleagues) can interrogate the inner workings of the system, as being on the edge offers a perspective that can challenge traditional hierarchies (Foucault, 1988) and act as a place for oppositional and transformative consciousness (Giroux, 2005). Considering education through a rural lens repositions the usual metrocentric perspective offering possibilities for different insights and the opening up of new avenues for thinking and action. The chapters on gifted students from Azano and colleagues (Chapter 26), English Learner education from Coady (Chapter 21), and Means and Sansone's consideration of Latinx students in rural contexts (Chapter 23) all illustrate how the "rurality lens" can intensify or offer new perspectives on old issues of inequity and injustice.

There are now significant bodies of published material from across all continents of the world centered on education in rural places. However, Corbett and White (2014) and Schafft (2016) have noted the low status of rural educational research and the tendency for it to lie outside the mainstream. Literature and research of and with education in rural places can become isolated in silos, entrapped by the label "rural" (Corbett, 2015b). When identified as "rural education," important work can have limited access to and exposure in other bodies of education literature and research. I do wonder, perhaps provocatively in the context of this handbook, whether the word "rural" could be left out of some publications leaving just "education" to be the key word. What would happen for example if the contents of this handbook were dispersed into other more general education handbooks? Perhaps there would be the risk of getting lost in the melee but perhaps their powerful stories would be heard among a wider readership. All the chapters here would hold their own in other collections not labeled "rural." Caught in the horns of this dilemma, a handbook of rural education perhaps both perpetuates the separation of rural education literature while also promoting and raising the status.

Coladarci (2007), Corbett (2015b), and Shucksmith (2018) have argued that to raise the status of "rural" educational research, rural education researchers should increase criticality, objectivity, and empirical study and replace rich descriptions of rural deficiency with imaginative, constructive ideas and community involvement (Hargreaves et al., 2009). In their watershed study of British and Nordic European rural educational research, Kvalsund and Hargreaves (2009, p. 147) identified four areas of research design and methodology that require attention. These are (a) the epistemological stance, of life- or system-world perspectives (Harbermas, 1968, 1981); (b) the variety of research designs employed; (c) the "voices" of rural research, notably absent were those of children and policymakers; and (d) the role of theory in a field easily dominated by policy-led and pragmatic research. Kvalsund and Hargreaves (2009) conclude by proposing a new agenda for education research in rural areas where they saw "considerable scope for better-thought-out designs with theoretical rather than policy based foundations" (p. 148). This collection of chapters from the United States can be considered to be responding to this call in many ways. For example there are a wide variety of epistemological stances in evidence including echoes of

The Bloomsbury Handbook of Rural Education in the United States

lifeworld approaches in the chapter by RedCorn and colleagues (Chapter 20) and Coady's work with multiple knowledges in English Learner education (Chapter 21).

Studies that engage deeply and explicitly with theory are less common in rural education literature, so it is good to see chapters such as Gillon's use of Critical Whiteness Theory (Chapter 24) and Means and Sansone's working with Bronfenbrenner's (1977) ecological systems (Chapter 23). Working with appropriate theory develops ideas from cases, specific sites, or incidents and makes connections with other work using the same theoretical principles. It also provides insights that could otherwise go unnoticed. Gillon's work on whiteness in this collection of chapters is a very good example; her detailed examination of classroom practices around the selection and use of key reading texts using a Critical Whiteness Studies framework connects her work based in rural education with other work using similar conceptual frames, much of which has been done in urban contexts. Studies from Europe include Bagley and Hillyard's (2018) use of Bourdieu in their studies with head teachers in rural schools, Beach and colleague's (2018) use of Soja's ideas of spatial justice and injustice in the education systems of three Nordic countries, and my work (Gristy, 2019) that puts post-qualitative assemblage ideas to work on understanding challenges with rural home–school transport. For those hoping to connect rural education research and scholarship with other bodies of "mainstream" education and social sciences work, these developments in theoretically engaged publications are very welcome.

Education research in rural areas remains dominated by policy-led, pragmatic research, and some argue that a focus needs to remain on the negative consequences for sites and practices of education in rural places. In its focus on groups including Indigenous peoples (RedCorn and colleagues, Chapter 20), English Language Learners (Coady, Chapter 21), Black students in the rural South (Williams and colleagues, Chapter 22), Latinx populations (Means and Sansone, Chapter 23), students with special needs (Farmer and colleagues, Chapter 25), and rural gifted students (Azano and colleagues, Chapter 26), this collection of chapters offers support to the view that there are general challenges of organizing and managing education systems experienced universally and globally in all places, rural and otherwise. These include insufficient funding, high-stakes testing regimes, limitations to access and provision, particularly for students with additional needs of various kinds, and the training and recruitment of well-qualified, high-quality teachers. These chapters also add weight to the notion that being located in rural, peripheral, or geographically isolated places can exacerbate these challenges and lead to inequalities and injustices.

There are attempts, in Europe as elsewhere in the world, at assessing the impact of "rurality" on education issues such as school attendance, journeys to school, access to higher education, academic success, and dropout rates. A significant problem faced by these studies is the ongoing debate and complexity of the defining of "rural." There are a wide variety of definitions of rural found within Europe. Some definitions come from international or national authorities; others are locally defined, some countries have no formal definitions at all: a wonderful expression of the plurality of Europe! This can be illustrated through drawing on examples from the countries represented in the *Educational Research and Schooling in Rural Europe* collection. Kovács (2020) defines rural schools in the Hungarian context as schools run by villages and rural towns smaller than 10,000 inhabitants, a term developed by the author and colleagues to identify rural issues from government statistics. Similarly, a "rural" area and its schools are defined by English authorities as falling outside of settlements with populations of more than 10,000 residents, although there was no national definition or designation of rural schools until the 2000s (Bagley &

Hillyard, 2018). In Czechia, Kučerová and Trnková (2020) use a local definition of rural to mean municipalities with fewer than 3,000 inhabitants. In Spain, national statistics define extremely rural places as those with fewer than 2,000 inhabitants. Finland has a comprehensive series of territorial definitions, including several pertaining to rural areas (see Tantarimäki & Törhönen, 2020). There is no official definition of rural in the Netherlands, Austria, or Serbia. In Serbia, just two kinds of territory are defined, "city" and "other" (see Pešikan et al., 2020, for a very enlightening discussion). In Italy, there are no formal definitions of rural, and in fact the word is so drenched in negative connotations associated with the abuse of rural people and places in the past, it is not used in education policy and practice.

There have been calls for standardization or definitions to make international comparisons possible, and some multinational territory classification systems such as those of the Organisation for Economic Co-Operation and Development (OECD; 2011), the United Nations Educational, Scientific and Cultural Organization (UNESCO), and Eurostat (the statistical office of the EU; 2019) are used. One example of a comparison study looking to discern the impact of locality on student achievement is a large-scale Programme for International Student Assessment (PISA) study in 2013, which used the OECD definitions of "nonurban" and urban schools to look at so-called "urban advantage." This study found the significant differences between the schools and student outcomes were primarily related to socioeconomic status, school size, organization, and governance (OECD, 2013) rather than locality per se. (See Gristy et al., 2020, Chapter 15, for a detailed discussion on definitions and use of the label "rural" in European contexts and arguments for the use of other locator labels.)

Although it is important to acknowledge the particular challenges of education provision in rural places, the chapters in this book also illustrate the importance of surfacing and communicating positive stories and developments and move away from the recalculation of the emiseration (Slee, 2001) so prevalent in rural education literature of the past. Those interested in improving the quality, equity, and access to education for all students want and need to hear about successful innovations and opportunities for positive change (Hlale, 2014). Stories of hope are heard loud and clear in Williams and colleagues work in Chapter 22, offering a platform to voices relaying positive lived experiences of being Black in rural places. Hearing stories like these, from those with lived experience of living, learning, and working in rural places, is crucial in the disruption of deficit narratives of rurality and identity. They also contribute to the important work that articulates rural education institutions as sites of innovation, at the center of change.

This collection of chapters from the United States also raises some issues that appear to be less universal and perhaps more particular to US contexts. The divisions of society and groups and the segregation that can result along identity lines based on race, ethnicity, and skin color witnessed in the United States generally seem particularly sharp. Andersson and colleagues (2018) report findings of a large-scale, multidimensional study across five countries in Northwest Europe that suggest that segregation in communities in Europe tends to be conceptualized and experienced differently from the United States. Dramatic division and segregation of groups of people is witnessed in Europe and, in some countries, has led to civil unrest and political schisms. However, the inherent plurality of Europe perhaps means lines drawn around identities on the grounds of sexuality, ethnicity, religion, and so on are generally more fluid. Acknowledgment and awareness of the inherent and historical cultural diversity in Europe blurs some of the dividing lines. The diversity of languages, histories, and cultures perhaps leads to pluralities rather than binaries: witness the diversity in definitions of the term "rural" for example! There are also many experiences and understandings

The Bloomsbury Handbook of Rural Education in the United States

of the *concept* of rurality both within and between countries—a plurality of rurality. For example, in England, Austria, and perhaps some Nordic countries, there remains an attachment to the idea of the rural idyll, and rural schools and communities may be regarded as desirable places for children (see Raggl's, 2020, work on small schools in Austria). Whereas in Italy, Spain, and countries in the former Eastern Bloc, rural areas may be seen in more negative ways—linked to more conservative ideas—and schools face more challenges regarding resourcing and regard.

The historical and cultural diversity of Europe may also explain the difference in the numbers of people who speak more than one language as compared to the United States. In the EU in 2016, more than 80 percent of the adult working-age population of the EU with a tertiary level of education knew at least one foreign language (Eurostat, 2019). There are many countries in Europe where it is the norm to speak three or four languages, and many countries have more than one language spoken by the majority in all regions, including rural ones. Rural areas may be particularly important in the conservation of linguistic diversity (Koenig & de Varennes, 2001). In Wales, for example, where the majority of regions require children to learn Welsh and English in school, rural areas are envisaged as "heartlands" of the Welsh language (Huws, 2020). One of the EU's founding principles is multilingualism, and one of its ambitions is for all citizens to learn at least two foreign languages and to begin learning foreign languages at an early age (EU, 2020). As in the United States, historical and more recent migrations of workers across Europe has led and continues to lead to increased numbers of additional language learners in rural communities that increases the need for language learning support in schools. With the majority of Europeans speaking more than one language, there is much to be learned about language teaching and support in schools, particularly those in rural and peripheral areas. For some examples, see Smit et al. (2015) for an interesting discussion of teaching in rural multigrade schools across Europe and Paulgaard's (2019) accounts of the education of migrant children by schools and communities in the Arctic regions of Norway.

An important resource for all learning, including language learning, is the community in which education is taking place. A great source of hope for the successful future for education in rural places is through increased community involvement. As in the United States, across Europe, authors highlight the importance of communities of place and space in which education institutions are located (see Tantamariki & Törhönen, 2020, from Finland) and the making of "community active" schools (Solstad & Karlberg-Granlund, 2020; see Arrazola & Bozalongo, 2020, for examples from Spain). Perhaps a more recent addition to the work on the importance of the community and locality of education institutions is the recognition of the value of migrants to the continuation and repopulation of rural communities as referenced in this collection of chapters by Coady (Chapter 21) and Means and Sansone (Chapter 23). There has been extensive reporting of the scale and detail of movement of refugees and migrants across rural Europe (see, e.g., European Commission/EACEA/Eurydice, 2019; and Jelen, 2020), and now a welcome sharing of stories and voices from lived experience is emerging, such as the collection from Dovigo and colleagues (2018).

There are moves here, in the engagement with the context and community of education institutions, toward the criteria for Corbett's (2015b) rural sociological imagination and Shucksmith's (2018) reimagining of the rural. Perhaps here, in the potential for education spaces in rural places to become "community active" and renewed and diversified by new residents, are prospects for sustainable, collective, and collaborative education systems and structures.

Notes

Chapter 2

1 The intellectual lineage for these conceptions of statehood goes back to the sixteenth century. Specifically, in England, Thomas Smith coined the phrase "a multitude of free acting individuals," and in France, Jean Bodin coined the phrase "mutually interested communities." These philosophers were the intellectual sources for the conceptions of nonfeudal statehood espoused by leading elites in Europe and colonial America. See Smith (1969, p. 17). See Bodin (1967, p. 97). The Canadian political philosopher Charles Taylor referenced the role of John Locke, on one side, and Charles de Montesquieu, on the other, giving additional strength to these conceptions, calling the urban industrial worldview the L Stream for Locke and the rural community-oriented worldview the M Stream for Montesquieu. See his *Philosophical Arguments* (Cambridge University Press, 1989, p. 157).
2 Linguists have traced the term "hicks" back into England's feudal past, although it was resurrected pejoratively in reference to Jackson's rural supporters in the United States.
3 Also see Duncombe and Yinger (2007, pp. 341–75). Craig Howley, Jerry Johnson, and John Petrie conducted a meta-analysis of research related to rural school consolidation that reveals the lack of substantive justification for the practice. See their *Consolidation of Schools and Districts: What the Research Says and What It Means* (National Education Policy Center, 2011).

Chapter 3

1 See https://ruralopportunitymap.us/data/

Chapter 5

1 Rural out-migration and depopulation and the implications for spatial and educational inequity are challenges internationally within the context of an urbanizing global society. A discussion of these issues within an international context is beyond the scope of this chapter, but these questions are taken up by multiple scholars including Bell and Osti (2010), Bock et al. (2016), Corbett and Forsey (2017), Ferrugia (2016), Østby (2015), and Schafft et al. (2021), among many others.
2 In this chapter we use "rural" and "nonmetropolitan" interchangeably, referring to county geographies unless noted otherwise.
3 The population estimates we use include all resident school-aged children ages five to seventeen inclusive, both enrolled in public or private school or not enrolled and residing within a rural school district. A rural school district is considered any district where a plurality of students attended a rural school. In the 2018–19 academic year, less than 6 percent of students living within rural school districts attended a nonrural designated school (NCES, 2018b).
4 Parts of the Barnett formation underlie the metropolitan Dallas-Fort Worth area, although most of the shale play is located in rural Texas.
5 The Covid-19 pandemic has only further depressed resource extraction activity due to decreased travel and, as a consequence, the decreased demand for energy (Kuzemko et al., 2020). However, the initial industry contraction occurred earlier as unconventional oil and gas development rolled out globally, increasing energy supplies and depressing energy prices, leading to challenges for many in the industry who had heavily financed their operations (Ji et al., 2019; McLean, 2018).

Notes

Chapter 6

1 It should be noted that metropolitan poverty rates include both central city poverty rates and suburban poverty rates—locales facing very disparate economic and social conditions (Jensen et al., 2003).
2 Students qualify for free lunch if their household income is at or below 130 percent of the federal poverty threshold; an income of up to 185 percent of the poverty threshold qualifies them for reduced-price lunch.
3 For more information on states' funding formulas and funding equity, see the report "Is school funding fair?" (Baker et al., 2018); it is published annually by the Education Law Center.

Chapter 8

1 This classification of school districts is based on the National Center for Education Statistics School Locale Codes. In Wisconsin, town and rural districts are often grouped together for funding and policy discussions. More information can be found at https://nces.ed.gov/surveys/ruraled/definitions.asp

Chapter 9

1 The National Alliance for Public Charter Schools (NAPCS), an organization with the expressed intent of expanding charter schools across the United States, provides its own nonpeer-reviewed research and quantitative information such as charter student demographics, charter school enrollment by state and locale, as well as charter management and financing statistics (see https://data.publiccharters.org/).

Chapter 11

1 Arizona has no state statute regarding the legality of collective bargaining.
2 According to Sanes and Schmitt (2014), teacher strikes are explicitly legal in the following states: Alaska, California, Colorado, Hawaii, Illinois, Minnesota, Montana, Ohio, Oregon, Pennsylvania, and Vermont.
3 The Taft-Hartley Act (1947) curbed several labor union activities, including the ability of a union to collect full dues from nonmembers as long it represented their interests. Instead, public sector unions, like teachers' unions, required nonmembers to contribute a portion of union dues to offset the costs associated with representation of that employee's interests. This is often referred to as paying a "fair share." Right-to-Work legislation, which was passed in over half of US states, further curtailed union power by eliminating this "fair share" component, thus requiring teachers' unions in these states to represent all teachers regardless of union status or payment (Ungar, 2012). The *Janus* decision effectively expanded this idea nationwide for public sector unions.

Chapter 13

1 Grand Isle Network and the Northeast Prairie Coalition are pseudonyms.
2 The US Census defines a micropolitan statistical area as having at least one urban cluster with a population of at least 10,000 but less than 50,000.
3 The USDA defines a nonmetropolitan county as those outside the boundaries of metro areas and have no cities with 50,000 residents or more.
4 The US Census Bureau/National Center for Educational Statistics defines these districts by the size and proximity of their communities to urbanized areas.
5 These strategies include ORID; Chaordic Stepping Stones (http://www.chriscorrigan.com/parkinglot/new-version-of-the-chaordic-stepping-stones/); Art of Hosting (http://www.artofhosting.org/); and Technology of Participation (https://icausa.memberclicks.net/).
6 Strive Partnership, http://www.strivepartnership.org/
7 https://agileforall.com/learning-with-fist-of-five-voting/

Chapter 14

1 As noted by Luo and Williams (2013), "the metropolitan and micropolitan statistical areas defined by the U.S. Office of Management and Budget (2000) . . . micropolitan areas must have at least one urban cluster of at least 10,000 but fewer than 50,000 inhabitants. Any core-based area with a population fewer than 10,000 is defined as a rural area" (p. 81).

Chapter 19

1 Note that other chapters in this handbook explore the various concepts and definitions of rurality in depth. Here it is simply acknowledged that "rural" is notoriously difficult to operationalize, and any attempt to categorize rural apart from nonrural in space as diverse as the United States is certain to mischaracterize to some degree. This chapter utilizes the NCES urban-centric locale classification system, as this system avails itself to the most robust statistical examination of educational outcomes across locale.
2 All differences between rural students and city, suburb, and town students are statistically significant in Figures 19.1 and 19.2, with the lone exception of eighth-grade mathematics achievement between rural and suburban students in 2011.

Chapter 20

1 As per the National Congress of American Indians (2020), the term "Indian country" (lowercase) is a legal and policy context to denote areas where Native nations and the federal government have primary jurisdiction. "Indian Country" (both capitalized) is a "broader term used to refer more generally to tribal governments, Native communities, cultures, and peoples" (p. 28) found across the country.
2 Cf. Williams (1975) for a Marxist perspective on this same kind of *backward glance* as reflected in the treatment of rural people and spaces in the canon of English literature.

Chapter 24

1 See, e.g., https://www.bbc.com/news/world-us-canada-52905408; https://www.latimes.com/opinion/story/2020-06-04/police-killings-black-victims
2 https://dailyyonder.com/in-historic-first-protests-spread-to-more-than-3000-towns/2020/06/10/
3 http://www.mainelegislature.org/legis/bills/display_ps.asp?snum=120&ld=291

Chapter 26

1 Other broadened conceptions of giftedness have been offered by scholars such as Renzulli (1977; Renzulli & Reis, 1997); Subotnik et al. (2011); and Sternberg (2011).
2 Application of matrices is sometimes criticized for the misapplication of principles of sound assessment; see Moon (2018).

References

AASA, The School Superintendents Association. (2017). *Leveling the playing field for rural students.* https://www.aasa.org/uploadedFiles/Policy_and_Advocacy/Resources/AASA_Rural_Equity_Report_FINAL.pdf

Abbott-Chapman, J. (2011). Making the most of the mosaic: Facilitating post-school transitions to higher education of disadvantaged students. *The Australian Educational Researcher, 38*(1), 57–71.

Adamson, F., & Galloway, M. (2019). Education privatization in the United States: Increasing saturation and segregation. *Education Policy Analysis Archives, 27*(129), 1–48. https://doi.org/10.14507/epaa.27.4857

Adelman, C. (2002). The relationship between urbanicity and educational outcomes. In W. G. Tierney & L. S. Hagedorn (Eds.), *Increasing access to college: Extending possibilities for all students* (pp. 35–63). State University of New York Press.

Agger, C., Meece, J., & Byun, S. (2018). The influences of family and place on rural adolescents' educational aspirations and post-secondary enrollment. *Journal of Youth and Adolescence, 47*(12), 2554–68. https://doi.org/10.1007/s10964-018-0893-7

Agnitsch, K., Flora, J., & Ryan, V. (2006). Bonding and bridging social capital: The interactive effects on community action. *Community Development, 37*(1), 36–51.

Ahn, J., & McEachin, A. (2017). Student enrollment patterns and achievement in Ohio's online charter schools. *Educational Researcher, 46*(1), 44–57. https://doi.org/10.3102/0013189X17692999

Albright, A., Michael, K. D., Massey, C., Sale, R., Kirk, A., & Egan, T. (2013). An evaluation of an interdisciplinary rural school mental health program in Appalachia. *Advances in School Mental Health Promotion, 6*, 1–14. https://doi.org/10.1080/1754730x.2013.808890

Albritton, S., Huffman, S., & McClellan, R. (2017). A study of rural high school principals' perceptions as social justice leaders. *Administrative Issues Journal, 7*(1), 3, 19–38. https://dc.swosu.edu/aij/vol7/iss1/3

Alexander, M., Williams, N. W., & Nelson, K. L. (2012). When you can't get there: Using video self-monitoring as a tool for changing the behaviors of pre-service teachers. *Rural Special Education Quarterly, 31*(4), 18–24. https://doi.org/10.1177/875687051203100404

Ali, S. R., & Menke, K. A. (2014). Rural Latino youth career development: An application of social cognitive career theory. *The Career Development Quarterly, 62*, 175–86. https://doi.org/10.1002/j.2161-0045.2014.00078.x

Alleman, N. F., & Holly, N. L. (2013). Multiple points of contact: Promoting rural postsecondary preparation through school-community partnerships. *The Rural Educator, 34*(2). https://doi.org/10.35608/ruraled.v34i2.398

Alutto, J. A., & Belasco, J. (1974). Determinants of attitudinal militancy among teachers and nurses. *ILR Review, 27*(2), 216–27. https://doi.org/10.1177/001979397402700204

Amato, J. A. (2002). *Rethinking home: A case for writing local history.* University of California Press.

American Academy of Arts and Sciences (AAAS). (2017). *America's languages: Investing in language education for the 21st century.* AAAS.

American Federation of Teachers. (2020). Take action. https://educationvotes.nea.org/take-action/

American Foundation for Suicide Prevention and Suicide Prevention Resource Center. (2011). *After a suicide: A toolkit for schools.* Education Development Center, Newton, MA. http://www.sprc.org/library/AfteraSuicide-ToolkitforSchools.pdf

American School Counselor Association. (n.d.). *The role of the school counselor.* https://www.schoolcounselor.org/asca/media/asca/Careers-Roles/RoleStatement.pdf

References

American School Counselor Association. (2012). *The ASCA national model: A framework for school counseling programs* (3rd ed.). Author.

Amrein-Beardsley, A. (2007). Recruiting expert teachers to hard-to-staff schools. *Phi Delta Kappan, 89*(1), 64–7. https://doi.org/10.1177/003172170708900111

Amy, J. (July 11, 2019). *As Dems debate busing, Southern schools slowly desegregate*. Associated Press. https://apnews.com/article/race-and-ethnicity-joe-biden-us-news-ap-top-news-mississippi-f0374c7191c94c2fb5d2a78e3c915e0d#:~:text=Two%20rival%20high%20schools%20in,were%20-illegal%20vestiges%20of%20segregation.

Anders, J., Brown, C., Ehren, M., Greany, T., & Nelson, R. (2017). Evaluation of complex, whole-school interventions: Methodological and practical considerations. *Education Endowment Foundation*, 1–65.

Anderson, E. M., Blitz, L. V., & Saastamoinen, M. (2015). Exploring a school-university model for professional development with classroom staff: Teaching Trauma-Informed Approaches. *School Community Journal, 25*(2), 113–34.

Anderson, J. (1988). *The education of blacks in the south, 1860–1935*. The University of North Carolina Press.

Anderson, J. (2020, March 26). *Adjusting to a new 'normal' in education*. Education Commission of the States. https://ednote.ecs.org/adjusting-to-a-new-normal-in-education/

Anderson, L. M., Shinn, C., Fullilove, M. T., Scrimshaw, S. C., Fielding, J. E., Normand, J., Carande-Kulis, V. G., & The Task Force on Community Preventive Services. (2003). The effectiveness of early childhood development programs: A systematic review. *American Journal of Preventive Medicine, 24*(3S), 32–46. http://doi.org/10.1016/S0749-3797(02)00655-4

Anderson, R., & Chang, B. (2011). Mathematics course-taking in rural high schools. *Journal of Research in Rural Education (Online), 26*(1), 1–10. https://jrre.psu.edu/sites/default/files/2019-08/26-1.pdf

Anderson, S., & Mikesell, M. (2019). Child care type, access, and quality in rural areas of the United States: A review. *Early Child Development and Care, 189*(11), 1812–26. https://doi.org/10.1080/03004 430.2017.1412959

Anderson, W. L. (1906). *The country town: A study in rural evolution*. Baker and Taylor.

Anderson-Butcher, D., Hoffman, J., Rochman, D. M., & Fuller, M. (2017). General and specific competencies for school mental health in rural settings. In K. Michael & J. P. Jameson (Eds.), *Handbook of Rural School Mental Health* (pp. 49–62). Springer.

Andersson, E. K., Lyngstad, T. H., & Sleutjes, B. (2018). Comparing patterns of segregation in North-Western Europe: A multiscalar approach. *European Journal of Population, 34*, 151–68. https://doi.org/10.1007/s10680-018-9477-1

Ankeny, R., Marichal, N., & Coady, M. (2019). Emerging teacher-leaders for English Learners: A professional development model in rural Florida. *School Leadership Review, 14*(2), 4. https://scholarworks.sfasu.edu/slr/vol14/iss2/4/

Anthony, K. V., Franz, D., & Brenner, D. (2017). Understanding the nature of the teacher shortage in Mississippi. *The Mississippi Economic Review, 1*, 24–31. http://www.mississippi.edu/URC/downloads/mer_volume1.pdf

Antonucci, M. (2018, January 31). As union membership drops among teachers, will weaker states survive Janus? *The 74*. https://www.the74million.org/article/as-union-membership-drops-among-teachers-will-weaker-states-survive-janus/#:~:text=Last%20year%2044.9%20percent%20of,rate%2C%20down%20from%2053.9%20percent

Anyon, J. (1981). Social class and school knowledge. *Curriculum Inquiry, 11*(1), 3–41. https://doi.org/10.2307/1179806

Apple, M. (2001). *Educating the "right" way: Markets, standards, God, and inequality*. Falmer Press.

Apple, M. (2004). *Ideology and curriculum* (3rd ed.). Routledge.

Apple, M. W. (2006). *Educating the "right" way: Markets, standards, God, and inequality* (2nd ed.). Routledge.

Applewhite, J. S. (2018, June 27). Is this the end of public-sector unions in America? *The Atlantic*. https://www.theatlantic.com/politics/archive/2018/06/janus-afscme-public-sector-unions/563879/

References

Arcury, T. A., Preisser, J. S., Gesler, W. M., & Powers, J. M. (2005). Access to transportation and health care utilization in a rural region. *The Journal of Rural Health, 21*(1), 31–8.

Arenal, E. (2007). Women in the Oaxaca teachers' strike and citizens' uprising. *Feminist Studies, 33*(1), 107–17. https://jstor.org/stable/20459123

Arnold, M. L., Biscoe, B., Farmer, T. W., Robertson, D. L., & Shapley, K. L. (2007). *How the government defines rural has implications for education policies and practices* (Issues & Answers Report, REL 2007–No. 010). U.S. Department of Education, Institute of Education Sciences, National Center for Education Evaluation and Regional Assistance, Regional Educational Laboratory Southwest, Washington, DC. https://ies.ed.gov/ncee/edlabs/regions/southwest/pdf/REL_2007010_sum.pdf

Arnold, M. L., Newman, J. H., Gaddy, B. B., & Dean, C. B. (2005). A look at the condition of rural education research: Setting a direction for future research. *Journal of Research in Rural Education, 20*(6), 1–25. https://jrre.psu.edu/sites/default/files/2019-08/20-6.pdf

Aronson, J., Fried, C. B., & Good, C. (2002). Reducing the effects of stereotype threat on African American college students by shaping theories of intelligence. *Journal of Experimental Social Psychology, 38*(2), 113–25. https://doi.org/10.1006/jesp.2001.1491

Aronson, J., & Inzlicht, M. (2004). The ups and downs of attributional ambiguity: Stereotype vulnerability and the academic self-knowledge of African American college students. *Psychological Science, 15*(12), 829–36. https://doi.org/10.1111/j.0956-7976.2004.00763.x

Aronson, J., Lustina, M. J., Good, C., Keough, K., Steele, C. M., & Brown, J. (1999). When White men can't do math: Necessary and sufficient factors in stereotype threat. *Journal of Experimental Social Psychology, 35*(1), 29–46. https://doi.org/10.1006/jesp.1998.1371

Aronson, J., & Steele, C. M. (2005). Stereotypes and the fragility of human competence, motivation, and self-concept. In C. Dweck & E. Elliot (Eds.), *Handbook of competence and motivation* (pp. 436–56). Guilford.

Aronson, J., Steele, C. M., Salinas, M. F., & Lustina, M. J. (1998). The effect of stereotype threat on the standardized test performance of college students. In E. Aronson (Ed.), *Readings about the social animal* (8th ed., pp. 415–30). Freeman.

Arrazola, B., & Bozalongo, J. (2020). Development and research of the rural school situation in Spain. In C. Gristy, L. Hargreaves, & S. R. Kučerová (Eds.), *Educational research and schooling in rural Europe: An engagement with changing patterns of education, space, and place* (pp. 175–99). Information Age Publishing.

Arriero, E., & Griffin, D. (2019). ¡Adelante! A community asset mapping approach to increase college and career readiness for rural Latinx high school students. *Professional School Counseling, 22*(1), 1–9. https://doi.org/10.1177/2156759x18800279

Arum, R. (2000). Schools and communities: Ecological and institutional dimensions. *Annual Review of Sociology, 26*(1), 395–418. https://doi.org/10.1146/annurev.soc.26.1.395

Assouline, S. G., Marron, M., & Colangelo, N. (2014). Acceleration: The fair and equitable intervention for highly able students. In J. A. Plucker & C. M. Callahan (Eds.), *Critical issues and practices in gifted education: What the research says* (pp. 15–28). Prufrock Press.

Au, W., & Ferrare, J. J. (2015). *Mapping corporate education reform: Power and policy networks in the neoliberal state.* Routledge.

Au, W., & Hollar, J. (2016). Opting out of the education reform industry. *Monthly Review, 67*(1), 29–37. https://doi.org/10.14452/mr-067-10-2016-03_3

Aud, S., Wilkinson-Flicker, S., Kristapovich, P., Rathbun, A., Wang, X., & Zhang, J. (2013). *The condition of education 2013.* Report No. 2013–037, National Center for Education Statistics, U.S. Department of Education, Washington, DC. https://nces.ed.gov/pubs2013/2013037.pdf

Augustine-Shaw, D. (2016). Developing leadership capacity in new rural school district leaders: The Kansas educational leadership institute. *The Rural Educator, 37*(1), 1–13. https://doi.org/10.35608/ruraled.v37i1.274

Australian Association for the Education of the Gifted and Talented. (n.d.). The identification of gifted and talented students. Author. http://www.aaegt.net.au/?page_id=753

Australian Bureau of Statistics. (2011). *Australian Statistical Geography Standard (ASGS): Volume 1—Main structure and greater capital city statistical areas, July 2011* (1270.0.55.001). https://www.abs.gov.au/ausstats/abs@.nsf/mf/1270.0.55.001

Australian Bureau of Statistics. (2018). *Schools: Data on students, staff, schools, rates and ratios for government and non-government schools, for all Australian states and territories, 2018*. https://www.abs.gov.au/statistics/people/education/schools/2018

Australian Childhood Foundation. (2010). *Making SPACE for learning: Trauma informed practice in schools*. http://www.theactgroup.com.au/documents/makingspaceforlearning-traumainschools.pdf

Australian Government. (2011). *Review of school funding: Final report, December 2011*. Department of Education, Employment and Workforce Relations. https://docs.education.gov.au/system/files/doc/other/review-of-funding-for-schooling-final-report-dec-2011.pdf

Australian Government. (2018). *Through growth to achievement report of the review to achieve educational excellence in Australian schools*. Commonwealth of Australia: Department of Education and Training. https://docs.education.gov.au/documents/through-growth-achievement-report-review-achieve-educational-excellence-australian-0

Autti, O., & Hyry-Beihammer, E. (2014). School closures in rural Finnish communities. *Journal of Research in Rural Education, 29*(1), 1–17.

Azano, A. P. (2011). The possibility of place: One teacher's use of place-based instruction for English students in a rural high school. *Journal of Research in Rural Education, 26*(10), 1–12. https://jrre.psu.edu/sites/default/files/2019-08/26-10.pdf

Azano, A. P. (2014). Gifted rural students. In J. A. Plucker & C. M. Callahan (Eds.), *Critical issues and practices in gifted education: What the research says* (pp. 297–304). Prufrock Press.

Azano, A. P. (2015). Addressing the rural context in literacies research: A call to action. *Journal of Adolescent & Adult Literacy, 59*(3), 267–9. https://doi.org/10.1002/jaal.480

Azano, A. P. (2016, November). *The ruralities of autism* [Video]. TED Conferences. https://www.ted.com/talks/amy_price_azano_the_ruralities_of_autism

Azano, A. P. (2020, August 6). Our mayor's racist comments don't define Luray. *The Washington Post*. https://www.washingtonpost.com/opinions/2020/08/06/our-mayors-racist-comments-dont-define-luray/

Azano, A. P., & Biddle, C. (2019). Disrupting dichotomous traps and rethinking problem formation for rural education. *The Rural Educator, 40*(2), 4–11. https://doi.org/10.35608/ruraled.v40i2.845

Azano, A. P., Callahan, C. M., Bass, E. L., & Rasheed, M. (2020). Supporting gifted education in rural schools. *The Rural Educator, 41*(2), 47–54. https://doi.org/10.35608/ruraled.v41i2.851

Azano, A. P., Callahan, C. M., Brodersen, A. V., & Caughey, M. (2017). Responding to the challenges of gifted education in rural communities. *Global Education Review, 4*(1), 62–77.

Azano, A. P., Callahan, C. M., Missett, T. C., & Brunner, M. (2014). Understanding the experiences of gifted education teachers and fidelity of implementation in rural schools. *Journal of Advanced Academics, 25*, 88–100.

Azano, A. P., Downey, J., & Brenner, D. (2019). Preparing pre-service teachers for rural schools. *Oxford Research Encyclopedia of Education*. https://doi.org/10.1093/acrefore/9780190264093.013.274

Azano, A. P., & Stewart, T. T. (2016). Confronting challenges at the intersection of rurality, place, and teacher preparation: Improving efforts in teacher education to staff rural schools with qualified teachers. *Global Education Review, 3*(1), 108–28. https://files.eric.ed.gov/fulltext/EJ1090174.pdf

Bacharach, S., Bamberger, P., & Conley, S. (1990). Professionals and workplace control: Organizational and demographic models of teacher militancy. *ILR Review, 43*(5), 570–86. https://doi.org/10.2307/2523329

Bagley, C., & Hillyard, S. (2018). In the field with two rural primary school head teachers in England. *Journal of Educational Administration and History, 51*(3), 273–89. https://doi.org/10.1080/00220620.2019.1623763

Bailey, C., Jensen, L., & Ransom, E. (2014). *Rural America in a globalizing world: Challenges and prospects for the 2010s*. West Virginia University Press.

Bailey, J. M. (2020). *"How do I shrink myself?" A veteran assistant principal's micropolitical experiences in an unfamiliar rural school* [Unpublished doctoral dissertation]. Clemson University. https://tigerprints.clemson.edu/all_dissertations/2667

References

Bailey, L. H. (1911). *The country life movement in the United States*. Macmillan.

Bain, S. K., Bliss, S. L., Choate, S. M., & Sager-Brown, K. (2007). Serving children who are gifted: Perceptions of undergraduates planning to become teachers. *Journal for the Education of the Gifted, 30*(4), 450–78. https://doi.org/10.4219/jeg-2007-506

Baird, R. (2012). Cries with Indians: "Going Indian" with the ecological Indian from Rouseseau to Avatar. In E. D. Hoffman (Ed.), *American Indians and Popular Culture: Media, Sports, and Politics* (Vol. 1, pp. 69–85). Praeger.

Baker, B. D., Farrie, D., & Sciarra, D. (2018). *Is school funding fair? A national report* (7th ed.). Education Law Center.

Baker, C. N., Brown, S. M., Wilcox, P. D., Overstreet, S., & Arora, P. (2016). Development and psychometric evaluation of the Attitudes Related to Trauma-Informed Care (ARTIC) scale. *School Mental Health, 8*(1), 61–76.

Ballou, D. (1996). Do public schools hire the best applicants? *The Quarterly Journal of Economics, 111*(1), 97–133.

Barkeley, D. L., Henry, M. S., & Bao, S. (1996). *Good schools aid rural development in South Carolina* (SRDC Series No. 195). Southern Rural Development Center.

Barley, Z. A., & Beesley, A. D. (2007). Rural school success: What can we learn? *Journal of Research in Rural Education, 22*(1). https://jrre.psu.edu/sites/default/files/2019-08/22-1.pdf

Barnetson, B. (2010). Alberta's 2002 teacher strike: The political economy of labor relations in education. *Education Policy Analysis Archives, 18*(3), 1–26. https://doi.org/10.14507/epaa.v18n3.2010

Barrett, G. (2015). Deconstructing community. *Sociologia Ruralis, 55*(2), 182–204.

Barrett, N., Cowen, J., Toma, E., & Troske, S. (2015). Working with what they have: Professional development as a reform strategy in rural schools. *Journal of Research in Rural Education, 30*(10), 1–18. https://jrre.psu.edu/sites/default/files/2019-08/30-10.pdf

Barry, J. M. (2012). *Standing our ground: Women, environmental justice, and the fight to end mountaintop removal*. Ohio University Press.

Barton, J., Perlmeter, E. R., Blum, E. S., & Maquez, R. R. (2015). *Las colonias in the 21st century: Progress along the Texas-Mexico border*. Federal Reserve Bank of Dallas.

Barton, P. E., & Coley, R. J. (2010). The Black-White achievement gap: When progress stopped. Policy Information Report. Educational Testing Service. https://www.ets.org/Media/Research/pdf/PICBWGAP.pdf

Basister, M. P., & Kawai, N. (2018). Japan's educational practices for mathematically gifted students. *International Journal of Inclusive Education, 6*(2), 1–11. https://doi.org/10.1080/13603116.2017.1420252

Bass, E. L. (2019). Examining a place-based curriculum for high-performing learners: A place-based, critical, dialogic curriculum for high-performing rural writers [Doctoral dissertation, Virginia Tech]. vtechworks.lib.vt.edu/bitstream/handle/10919/89343

Bassok, D., Fitzpatrick, M., Greenberg, E., & Loeb, S. (2016). Within- and between-sector quality differences in early childhood education and care. *Child Development, 87*(5), 1627–45. https://doi.org/10.1111/cdev.12551

Batalova, J., Blizzard, B., & Bolter, J. (2020, January). *Frequently requested statistics on immigrants and immigration in the United States*. Migration Policy Institute.

Batteau, A. W. (1990). *The Invention of Appalachia*. University of Arizona Press.

Bauch, P. A. (2001). School-community partnerships in rural schools: Leadership, renewal, and a sense of place. *Peabody Journal of Education, 76*(2), 204–21. https://doi.org/10.1207/S15327930pje7602_9

Bauman, Z. (1998). *Globalization: The human consequences*. Columbia University Press.

Baweja, S., Santiago, C. D., Vona, P., Pears, G., Langley, A., & Kataoka, S. (2016). Improving implementation of a school-based program for traumatized students: Identifying factors that promote teacher support and collaboration. *School Mental Health, 8*(1), 120–31.

BBC News. (2020, September 23). Breonna Taylor: Timeline of black deaths caused by police. https://www.bbc.com/news/world-us-canada-52905408

Beach, D., From, T., Johansson, M., & Öhrn, E. (2018). Educational and spatial justice in rural and urban areas in three Nordic countries: A meta-ethnographic analysis. *Education Inquiry*, *9*(1), 4–21. https://doi.org/10.1080/20004508.2018.1430423

Beaumont, C., & Pianca, E. (2000). *Historic neighborhoods in the age of sprawl: Why Johnny can't walk to school*. The National Trust for Historic Preservation. https://files.eric.ed.gov/fulltext/ED450557.pdf

Beck, D., Maranto, R., & Shakeel, M. D. (2016). Does rural differ? Comparing parent and student reasons for choosing cyber schooling. *The Rural Educator*, *37*(3), 1–16. https://doi.org/10.35608/ruraled.v37i3.243

Beck, F. D., & Shoffstall, G. W. (2005). How do rural schools fare under a high-stakes testing regime? *Journal of Research in Rural Education*, *20*(14), 1–12. https://jrre.psu.edu/sites/default/files/2019-08/20-14.pdf

Beck, M. (2017, March 31). Republican lawmakers seek limits on school referendums. *Wisconsin State Journal*. https://madison.com/wsj/news/local/govt-and-politics/republican-lawmakers-seek-limits-on-school-referendums/article_0240fd83-c61c-59dc-90a1-07b01c8a2e85.html

Beehler, S., Birman, D., & Campbell, R. (2012). The effective of Cultural Adjustment and Trauma-Services (CATS): Generating practice-based evidence on a comprehensive, school-based mental health intervention for immigrant youth. *American Journal of Community Psychology*, *50*, 155–68.

Beesley, A. D., Atwill, K., Blair, P., & Barley, Z. A. (2010). Strategies for recruitment and retention of secondary teachers in central U.S. rural schools. *The Rural Educator*, *31*(2), 1–9. https://doi.org/10.35608/ruraled.v31i2.937

Beesly, A. D., Mackety, D., Cicchinelli, L. F., Shebby, S., Rainey, J., & Cherasaro, T. (2012). *Profiles of partnerships between tribal education departments and local education agencies* (Rel 2012-No. 137; Issues & Answers). U.S. Department of Education, Institute of Education Sciences, National Center for Education Evaluation and Regional Assistance, Regional Education Laboratory Central. https://ies.ed.gov/ncee/edlabs/

Belden, J. (2018, September 7). Speak your piece: Hollywood's rural America is a scary place. *Daily Yonder*. https://dailyyonder.com/speak-piece-hollywoods-rural-america-scary-place/2018/09/07

Belhumeur, J., Butts, E., Michael, K., Zieglowsky, S., DeCoteau, D., Four Bear, D., Crawford, C., Gourneau, R., Bighorn, E., Ryan, K., & Farber, L. (2017). Adapting crisis intervention protocols: Rural and tribal voices from Montana. In K. Michael & J. Jameson (Eds.), *Handbook of Rural School Mental Health* (pp. 307–22). Springer International Publishing.

Bell, M. M. (2007). The two-ness of rural life and the ends of rural scholarship. *Journal of Rural Studies*, *23*(4), 402–15. https://doi.org/10.1016/j.jrurstud.2007.03.003

Bell, M. M., & Osti, G. (2010). Mobilities and ruralities: An introduction. *Sociologia Ruralis*, *50*(3), 199–204. https://doi.org/10.1111/j.1467-9523.2010.00518.x

Bender, S. L., Fedor, M. C., & Carlson, J. S. (2011). Examining protective factors and risk factors in urban and rural head start preschoolers. *Journal of Community Psychology*, *39*(8), 908–21. https://doi.org/10.1002/jcop.20477

Benson, P. L. (2003). Developmental assets and asset-building community: Conceptual and empirical foundations. In R. Lerner & P. Benson (Eds.), *Developmental assets and asset-building communities* (pp. 19–43). Springer.

Berardi, F. (2017). *Futurability: The age of impotence and the horizon of possibility*. Verso.

Berends, M. (2015). Sociology and school choice: What we know after two decades of charter schools. *Annual Review of Sociology*, *41*, 159–80. https://doi.org/10.1146/annurev-soc-073014-112340

Berger, L. M., Cancian, M., & Magnuson, K. (2018). Anti-poverty policy innovations: New proposals for addressing poverty in the United States. *The Russell Sage Foundation Journal of the Social Sciences*, *4*(3), 1–19. https://doi.org/10.7758/rsf.2018.4.2.01

Berliner, D. C. (2013). Inequality, poverty, and the socialization of America's youth for the responsibilities of citizenship. *Theory into Practice*, *52*(3), 203–9. https://doi.org/10.1080/00405841.2013.804314

Berninger, V. W., Fuller, F., & Whitaker, D. (1996). A process model of writing development across the life span. *Educational Psychology Review*, *8*, 193–218. https://doi.org/10.1007/bf01464073

References

Berry, A. (2012). The relationship of perceived support to satisfaction and commitment for special education teachers in rural areas. *Rural Special Education Quarterly*, *31*, 3–14. https://doi.org/10.1177/875687051203100102

Berry, A., & Gravelle, M. (2013). The benefits and challenges of special education positions in rural settings: Listening to the teachers. *Rural Educator*, *34*(2), 25–37. https://doi.org/10.35608/ruraled.v34i2.400

Berry, A. B., Petrin, R. A., Gravelle, M. L., & Farmer, T. W. (2011). Issues in special education teacher recruitment, retention, and professional development: Considerations in supporting rural teachers. *Rural Special Education Quarterly*, *30*(4), 3–11. https://doi.org/10.1177/875687051103000402

Berry, C. R., & West, M. R. (2010). Growing pains: The consolidation movement and student outcomes. *Journal of Law, Economics, & Organization*, *26*(1), 1–29. https://doi.org/10.1093/jleo/ewn015

Bickel, R., & Howley, C. B. (2000). The influence of scale on school performance: A multi-level extension of the Matthew Principle. *Education Policy Analysis Archives*, *8*(22), 1–32. https://doi.org/10.14507/epaa.v8n22.2000.

Biddle, C., & Azano, A. P. (2016). Constructing and reconstructing the "rural school problem": A century of rural education research. *Review of Research in Education*, *40*, 298–325. https://doi.org/10.3102/0091732X16667700

Biddle, C., Mette, I., Brown, L. Tappan, M., Ray, B., & Strickland, S. (2018). Addressing rural, wicked problems through collaboration: Critical reflections on a school-university-community design process. In R. M. Reardon & J. Leonard (Eds.), *Making a positive impact in rural places: Change agency in school-university-community collaboration in education* (pp. 145–67). Information Age Publishing.

Biddle, C., Mette, I., & Mercado, A. (2018). Partnering with schools for community development: Power imbalances in a rural community collaborative addressing childhood adversity. *Community Development*, *49*(2), 191–210.

Biddle, C., & Schafft, K. A. (2016). Educational and ethical dilemmas for STEM education in Pennsylvania's Marcellus Shale gasfield communities. In R. A. Duschl & A. S. Bismack (Eds.), *Reconceptualizing STEM education: The central role of practices* (pp. 205–14). Routledge.

Biddle, C., Sutherland, D. H., & McHenry-Sorber, E. (2019). On resisting "awayness" and being a good insider: Early career scholars revisit Coladarci's swan song a decade later. *Journal of Research in Rural Education*, *35*(7), 1–16. https://jrre.psu.edu/sites/default/files/2019-12/35-7_0.pdf

Bieler, D. (2016, February 25). In Iowa, fans chant "Trump! Trump!" at racially diverse high school basketball team. *The Washington Post*. https://www.washingtonpost.com/news/early-lead/wp/2016/02/25/in-iowa-fans-chant-trump-trump-at-racially-diverse-high-school-basketball-team/

Bifuloc, R., & Bulkley, K. (2008). Charter schools. In H. F. Ladd & E. B. Fiske (Eds.), *Handbook of Research in Education Finance and Policy* (pp. 425–46). Lawrence Erlbaum.

Bischoff, R. J., Hollist, C. S., Smith, C. W., & Flack, P. (2004). Addressing the mental health needs of the rural underserved: Findings from a multiple case study of a behavioral telehealth project. *Contemporary Family Therapy*, *26*(2), 179–98.

Bishop, H. N., & Mcclellan, R. L. (2016). Resisting social justice: Rural school principals' perceptions of LGBTQ Students. *Journal of School Leadership*, *26*(1), 124–53. https://doi.org/10.1177/105268461602600105

Black, D. W. (2017). Abandoning the federal role in education: The Every Student Succeeds Act. *California Law Review*, *105*(5), 1309–74. https://doi.org/10.15779/Z38Z31NN9K

Black, P. J., Woodworth, M., Tremblay, M., & Carpenter, T. (2012). A review of trauma-informed treatment for adolescents. *Canadian Psychology*, *53*(3), 192–203.

Blagg, K., Blom, E., Gallagher, M., & Rainer, M. (2020, April). Mapping student needs during COVID-19: An assessment of remote learning environments. Urban Institute. https://www.urban.org/sites/default/files/publication/102131/mapping-student-needs-during-covid-19-final_1.pdf

Blitz, L. V., Anderson, E. M., Mulcahy, C. A., & Bronstein, L. (2018). The heart of our community. In R. M. Reardon & J. Leonard (Eds.), *Making a positive impact in rural places: Change agency in school-university-community collaboration in education* (pp. 168–93). Information Age Publishing.

Bloom, S. L. (1997). *Creating sanctuary: Toward the evolution of sane societies*. Routledge.

Bloom, S. L., & Sreedhar, S. Y. (2008). The Sanctuary Model of trauma-informed organizational change. *Reclaiming children and youth, 17*(3), 48–53.

Bock, B., Osti, G., & Ventura, F. (2016). Rural migration and new patterns of exclusion and integration in Europe. In D. Brown & M. Shucksmith (Eds.), *International handbook of rural studies* (pp. 71–84). Routledge.

Bodin, J. (1967). *Six books of the commonwealth* (M. J. Tooley, Ed. and Trans.). Blackwell Publishers.

Boissoneault, L. (2017, April 25). The coal mining massacre America forgot. *Smithsonian Magazine.* https://www.smithsonianmag.com/history/forgotten-matewan-massacre-was-epicenter-20th-century-mine-wars-180963026/

Bomer, R., Dworin, J. E., May, L., & Semingson, P. (2008). Miseducating teachers about the poor: A critical analysis of Ruby Payne's claims about poverty. *Teachers College Record, 110*(12), 2497–531. http://sites.nd.edu/poverty-cap/files/2012/07/TCRecord_Payne_Critique.pdf

Bonilla-Silva, E. (2006). *Racism without racists: Color-blind racism and the persistence of racial inequality in the United States* (2nd ed.). Rowman & Littlefield.

Bosak, J., & Perlman, B. (1982). A review of the definition of rural. *Journal of Rural Community Psychology, 3*(1), 3–34. https://files-eric-ed-gov.ezproxy.lib.vt.edu/fulltext/ED238667.pdf

Bourdieu, P., & Passeron, J. (1990). *Reproduction in education, society, and culture* (R. Nice, Trans.). Sage. (Original work published 1970)

Bowers, C. A. (2006). *Revitalizing the commons.* Rowman & Littlefield.

Bowles, S., & Gintis, H. (1976). *Schooling in capitalist America: Educational reform and the contradictions of economic life.* Basic Books.

Boyd, C. P., Hayes, L., Wilson, R. L., & Bearsley-Smith, C. (2008). Harnessing the social capital of rural communities for youth mental health: An asset-based community development framework. *Australian Journal of Rural Health, 16*(4), 189–93. https://doi.org/10.1111/j.1440-1584.2008.00996.x

Boydston, J. A. (Ed.). (1976). *Essays on school and society 1899–1901: The middle works of John Dewey, 1899–1924, Volume 1.* Southern Illinois University Press.

Boyle, A., August, D., Tabaku, L., Cole, S., & Simpson-Baird, A. (2015). Dual language education programs: Current state policies and practices. U.S. Department of Education, Office of English Language Acquisition. https://ncela.ed.gov/files/rcd/TO20_DualLanguageRpt_508.pdf

Brandt, D. (1998). Sponsors of literacy. *College Composition and Communication, 49*(2), 165–85. https://doi.org/10.2307/358929

Brasier, K., Davis, L., Glenna, L., Kelsey, T. W., McLaughlin, D. K., Schafft, K. A., Babbie, K., Biddle, C., Delessio-Parson, A., Rhubart, D., & Suchyta, M. (2015). Communities experiencing shale gas development. In W. Hefly & Y. Wang (Eds.), *Economics of unconventional shale gas development: Cases and impacts* (pp. 149–78). Springer Publishing.

Brasington, D. (2004). House prices and the structure of local government: An application of spatial statistics. *Journal of Real Estate Finance and Economics, 29*(2), 211–31. http://dx.doi.org/10.1023/B:REAL.0000035311.59920.74

Bratsch-Hines, M. E., Baker, C., & Vernon-Feagans, L. (2016). Minority families in the rural United States: Family processes, child care, and early schooling. In L. Crockett & G. Carlo (Eds.), *Rural Ethnic Minority Youth and Families in the United States: Theory, Research and Applications* (pp. 143–164). Cham, Switzerland: Springer International Publishing.

Bratsch-Hines, M. E., Mokrova, I., & Vernon-Feagans, L. (2017). Rural families' use of multiple child care arrangements from 6 to 58 months and children's kindergarten behavioral and academic outcomes. *Early Childhood Research Quarterly, 41*, 161–73. DOI:10.1016/j.ecresq.2017.05.005

Braveman, P. A., Cubbin, C., Egerter, S., Williams, D. R., & Pamuk, E. (2010). Socioeconomic disparities in health in the United States: What the patterns tell us. *American Journal of Public Health, 100*(S1), S186–S196.

Bravo, A. A. J., Zuniga, F. L. R., & Infanzón, M. L. N. G. (2014). The teachers strike: the perspective of parents in rural and urban communities of chiapas. *Academic Papers, 41.*

Brayboy, B. M. J. (2006). Toward a tribal critical race theory in education. *Urban Review: Issues and Ideas in Public Education, 37*(5), 425–46. https://doi.org/10.1007/s11256-005-0018-y

References

Brayboy, B. M. J., & Castagno, A. E. (2009). Self-determination through self-education: Culturally responsive schooling for Indigenous students in the USA. *Teaching Education, 20*(1), 31–53.

Bredeson, P. V., Klar, H. W., & Johansson, O. (2011). Context-responsive leadership: Examining superintendent leadership in context. *Education Policy Analysis Archives, 19*(18), 1–28. https://doi.org/10.14507/epaa.v19n18.2011

Breen, D., & Drew, D. (2012). Voices of rural counselors: Implications for counselor education and supervision. Counseling VISTAS (1). https://www.counseling.org/resources/library/vistas/vistas12/article_28.pdf

Brems, C., Johnson, M. E., Warner, T. D., & Roberts, L. W. (2006). Barriers to healthcare as reported by rural and urban interprofessional providers. *Journal of Interprofessional Care, 20*(2), 105–18. https://doi.org/10.1080/13561820600622208

Brennan, M. (2005). Putting rurality on the educational agenda: Work towards a theoretical framework. *Education in Rural Australia, 15*(2), 11–20.

Brenner, D. (2016). Rural educator policy brief: Rural education and the Every Student Succeeds Act. *The Rural Educator, 37*(2), 23–7. https://doi.org/10.35608/ruraled.v37i2.271

Briggs, X. (Ed.). (2005). *The geography of opportunity: Race and housing choice in metropolitan America*. Brookings Institution Press.

Brodersen, A. V. (2016). *Exploring alignment in gifted education program policies and practices* [Doctoral dissertation]. University of Virginia. https://doi.org/10.18130/V31P3N

Broekhuizen, M. L., Mokrova, I. L., Burchinal, M. R., Garrett-Peters, P. T., & Family Life Project Key Investigators. (2016). Classroom quality at pre-kindergarten and kindergarten and children's social skills and behavior problems. *Early Childhood Research Quarterly, 36*(3), 212–22. https://doi.org/10.1016/j.ecresq.2016.01.005

Bronfenbrenner, U. (1977). Toward an experimental ecology of human development. *American Psychologist, 32*, 513–31. https://doi.org/10.1037/0003-066x.32.7.513

Bronfenbrenner, U. (1996). Foreword. In R. B. Cairns, G. H. Elder, & E. J. Costello (Eds.), *Developmental science* (pp. ix–xvii). Cambridge University Press.

Bronfenbrenner, U., & Mahoney, M. A. (Eds.). (1975). *Influences on human development* (2nd ed.). Dryden Press.

Bronfenbrenner, U., & Morris, P. A. (1998). The ecology of developmental processes. In W. Damon & R. M. Lerner (Eds.), *Handbook of child psychology: Theoretical models of human development* (5th ed., Vol. 1, pp. 993–1028). Wiley.

Brooke, R. (2012). Voices of young citizens: Rural citizenship, schools, and public policy. In K. Donehower, C. Hogg, & E. E. Schell (Eds.), *Reclaiming the Rural: Essays on Literacy, Rhetoric and Pedagogy* (pp. 161–72). Southern Illinois University Press.

Brooks-Gunn, J., & Duncan, G. J. (1997). The effects of poverty on children. *The Future of Children, 7*(2), 55–71. https://doi.org/10.2307/1602387

Brown, D. L., & Glasgow, N. (2010). *Rural retirement migration*. Springer.

Brown, D. L., & Schafft, K. A. (2011). *Rural people & communities in the 21st century: Resilience & transformation*. Polity Press.

Brown, D. L., & Schafft, K. A. (2019). *Rural people and communities in the 21st century: Resilience and transformation* (2nd ed.). Polity Press.

Brown, L. M. (2016). *Powered by girl: A field guide for supporting youth activists*. Beacon Press.

Brown, L. M., & Flaumenhaft, J. (2019). Student-empowered curricular change as trauma informed practice. *Phi Delta Kappan, 100* (6), 13–19.

Brown, S. W., Renzulli, J. S., Gubbins, E. J., Zhang, W., Siegle, D., & Chen, C. H. (2005). Assumptions underlying the identification of gifted and talented students. *Gifted Child Quarterly, 49*(1), 68–79. https://doi.org/10.1177/001698620504900107

Bryant, J. A., Jr. (2010). Dismantling rural stereotypes. *Educational Leadership, 68*(3), 54–8.

Brown v. Board of Education, Topeka, 347 U.S. 483 (1954).

Bryk, A. S. (2015). 2014 AERA Distinguished Lecture: Accelerating how we learn to improve. *Educational Researcher, 44*, 467–77. https://doi.org/10.3102/0013189x15621543

References

Bryk, A. S., Sebring, P., Allensworth, E., Luppescu, S., & Easton, J. (2010). *Organizing schools for improvement: Lessons from Chicago*. Harvard Education Press.

Budge, K. (2006). Rural leaders, rural places: Problem, privilege, and possibility. *Journal of Research in Rural Education, 21*(13), 1–10.

Budge, K. M. (2010). Why shouldn't rural kids have it all? Place-conscious leadership in an era of extralocal reform policy. *Education Policy Analysis Archives, 18*(1), 1–26. https://doi.org/10.14507/epaa.v18n1.2010

Buras, K. L. (2014). *Charter schools, race, and urban space: Where the market meets grassroots resistance*. Routledge.

Burchinal, M., Carr, R. C., Vernon-Feagans, L., Blair, C., Cox, M., & The Family Life Project Key Investigators. (2018). Depth, persistence, and timing of poverty and the development of school readiness skills in rural low-income regions: Results from the family life project. *Early Childhood Research Quarterly, 45*, 115–30. https://doi.org/10.1016/j.ecresq.2018.07.002

Burke, K. (1969). *A rhetoric of motives* (1st ed.). University of California Press.

Burke, M. M. (2017). Examining empowerment, family–school partnerships, and advocacy among rural and urban Latino families of children with disabilities. *Rural Special Education Quarterly, 36*(2), 56–63. https://doi.org/10.1177/8756870517707218

Burke, N. J., Hellman, J. L., Scott, B. G., Weems, C. F., & Carrion, V. G. (2011). The impact of adverse childhood experiences on an urban pediatric population. *Child abuse & neglect, 35*(6), 408–13.

Burkholder, J., Libra, B., Weyer, P., Heathcote, S., Kolpin, D., Thorne, P. S., & Wichman, M. (2007). Impacts of waste from concentrated animal feeding operations on water quality. *Environmental Health Perspectives, 115*(2), 308–12. https://doi.org/10.1289/ehp.8839

Burns, L. F. (2004). *A history of the Osage people*. The University of Alabama Press.

Burstein, L. (1993). Prologue: Studying learning, growth, and instruction cross-nationally: Lessons learned about why and why not engage in cross-national studies. In L. Burstein (Ed.), *The IEA Study of Mathematics III: Student growth and classroom processes* (pp. xxvii–lii). Pergamon Press.

Burton, L. M., Lichter, D. T., Baker, R. S., & Eason, J. M. (2013). Inequality, family processes, and health in the "new" rural America. *American Behavioral Scientist, 57*(8), 1128–51. https://doi.org/10.1177/0002764213487348

Bushnell, M. (1999). Imagining rural life: Schooling as a sense of place. *Journal of Research in Rural Education, 15*(2), 80–9. http://citeseerx.ist.psu.edu/viewdoc/download?doi=10.1.1.515.2927&rep=rep1&type=pdf

Butler, A., & Sinclair, K. A. (2020). Place matters: A critical review of place inquiry and spatial methods in education research. *Review of Research in Education, 44*(1), 64–96. https://doi.org/10.3102/0091732X20903303

Byun, S., Irvin, M. J., & Meece, J. L. (2012). Predictors of bachelor's degree completion among rural students at four-year institutions. *The Review of Higher Education, 35*(3), 463–84. https://doi.org/10.1353/rhe.2012.0023

Byun, S., Irvin, M. J., & Meece, J. L. (2015). Rural–nonrural differences in college attendance patterns. *Peabody Journal of Education, 90*(2), 263–79. https://doi.org/10.1080/0161956x.2015.1022384

Byun, S., & Kryst, E. L. (2015, April). *Rural-nonrural differences in college major choice* [Paper presentation]. Annual meeting of the American Educational Researchers Association, Chicago, IL.

Byun, S., Meece, J. L., & Agger, C. A. (2017). Predictors of college attendance patterns of rural youth. *Research in Higher Education, 58*(8), 817–42. https://doi.org/10.1007/s11162-017-9449-z

Byun, S, Meece, J. L., & Irvin, M. J. (2012). Rural nonrural disparities in postsecondary educational attainment revisited. *American Educational Research Journal, 49*(3), 412–37. https://doi.org/10.3102/0002831211416344

Byun, S., Meece, J. L., Irvin, M. J., & Hutchins, B. C. (2012). The role of social capital in educational aspirations of rural youth. *Rural Sociology, 77*(3), 355–79. https://doi.org/10.1111/j.1549-0831.2012.00086.x

Cabrera, A. F., & LaNasa, S. M. (2000). Overcoming the tasks on the path to college for America's disadvantaged. In A. F. Cabrera & S. M. L. Nasa (Eds.), *Understanding the college choice of disadvantaged students* (pp. 31–44). Jossey-Bass. https://doi.org/10.1002/ir.10703

References

Cabrera, N. L., Franklin, J. D., & Watson, J. S. (2016). Whiteness in higher education: The invisible missing link in diversity and racial analyses. *ASHE Higher Education Report*, *42*(6), 7–125. https://doi.org/10.1002/aehe.20116.

Cabrera, N. L., López, P. D., & Sáenz, V. B. (2012). Ganas: From the individual to the community, and the potential for improving college going in the "land that Texas forgot." *Journal of Latinos and Education*, *11*(4), 232–46. https://doi.org/10.1080/15348431.2012.715499

Caemmerer, J. M., & Keith, T. Z. (2015). Longitudinal, reciprocal effects of social skills and achievement from kindergarten to eighth grade. *Journal of School Psychology*, *53*, 265–81. https://doi.org/10.1016/j.jsp.2015.05.001

Cairns, R. B., & Cairns, B. D. (1994). *Lifelines and risks: Pathways of youth in our time*. Harvester Wheatsheaf.

Cajete, G. (1994). *Look to the mountain: An ecology of Indigenous education* (1st ed.). Kivaki Press. http://eric.ed.gov/?id=ED375993

Callahan, C. M. (2020, October). *Identification and curriculum for rural gifted learners*. Presentation at the Fall Institute of the California Association for the Gifted (virtual conference).

Callahan, C. M., Dmitrieva, S., Park, S., Hull, M. F., & Azano, A. P. (2021). Impact: Student outcomes. In A. P. Azano & C. M. Callahan (Eds.), *Gifted education in rural schools: Developing place-based interventions* (pp. 152–64). Routledge.

Callahan, C. M., Missett, T. C., Azano, A. P., Caughey, M., Brodersen, A. V., & Tackett, M. (2017a). *CLEAR curriculum units from the University of Virginia for grade 4: Fiction and Nonfiction*. Prufrock Press.

Callahan, C. M., Moon, T. R., & Oh, S. (2017b). Describing the status of programs for the gifted: A call for action. *Journal for the Education of the Gifted*, *40*, 20–49. https://doi.org/10.1177/0162353216686215

Callahan, C. M., Renzulli, J. S., Delcourt, M. A. B., & Hertberg-Davis, H. L. (2018). Considerations for the identification of gifted and talented students. In C. M. Callahan & H. L. Hertberg-Davis (Eds.), *Fundamentals of gifted education* (2nd ed., pp. 85–93). Routledge.

Callahan, R. E. (1962). *Education and the cult of efficiency*. University of Chicago Press.

Camera, L. (2016). Many school districts don't have enough school nurses. *U.S. News & World Report*. https://www.usnews.com/news/articles/2016-03-23/the-school-nurse-scourge

Campbell, A. F. (2019, February 19). West Virginia teachers are on strike again. Here's why. *Vox*. https://www.vox.com/2019/2/19/18231486/west-virginia-teacher-strike-2019

Campbell, F. A., Pungello, E. P., Burchinal, M., Kainz, K., Pan, Y., Wasik, B. H., Barbarin, O. A., Sparling, J. J., & Ramey, C. T. (2012). Adult outcomes as a function of an early childhood educational program: An Abecedarian Project follow-up. *Developmental Psychology*, *48*(4), 1033–43. https://doi.org/10.1037/a0026644

Cantor, P., Osher, D., Berg, J., Steyer, L., & Rose, T. (2018). Malleability, plasticity, and individuality: How children learn and develop in context. *Applied Developmental Science*, *23*(4), 307–37. https://doi.org/10.1080/10888691.2017.1398649

Capps, R., Michael, K., and Jameson, J. (2019). Lethal means and adolescent suicidal risk: An expansion of the PEACE Protocol. *Journal of Rural Mental Health*, *43*(1), 3–16.

Carcamo, C. (2016, August). Ancient Mayan languages are creating problems for today's immigration courts. *Los Angeles Times*. https://www.latimes.com/local/california/la-me-mayan-indigenous-languages-20160725-snap-story.html

Card, D., & Giuliano, L. (2015). *Can universal screening increase the representation of low income and minority students in gifted education?* NBER working paper No. 21519. http://www.nber.org/papers/w21519

Carello, J., & Butler, L. D. (2014). Potentially perilous pedagogies: Teaching trauma is not the same as trauma-informed teaching. *Journal of Trauma & Dissociation*, *15*(2), 153–68.

Carjuzaa, J., & Ruff, W. G. (2016). American Indian English Language Learners: Misunderstood and under-served. *Cogent Education*, *3*(1), 1–11. https://doi.org/10.1080/2331186X.2016.1229897

Carlson, D., and Cowen, J. M. (2015). Student neighborhoods, schools, and test score growth: Evidence from Milwaukee, Wisconsin. *Sociology of Education 88*(1), 38–55.

Carney, M. (1912). *Country life and the country school*. Row and Peterson.

Carnoske, C., Hoehner, C., Ruthmann, N., Frank, L., Handy, S., Hill, J., Ryan, S., Sallis, J., Glanz, K., & Brownson, R. (2010). Developer and realtor perspectives on factors that influence development, sale and perceived demand for activity-friendly communities. *Journal of Physical Activity and Health*, *7*(1) Supplement 1, 48–59. https://www.ncbi.nlm.nih.gov/pmc/articles/PMC3718394/

Carnoy, M. (1998). National voucher plans in Chile and Sweden: Did privatization reforms make for better education? *Comparative Education Review*, *42*(3), 309–37.

Carr, P. J., & Kefalas, M. J. (2009). *Hollowing out the middle: The rural brain drain and what it means for America*. Beacon Press.

Carrasco, A., & Gunter, H. M. (2019). The "private" in the privatisation of schools: The case of Chile. *Educational Review*, *71*(1), 67–80.

Carrillo, J. F. (2016). Searching for "home" in Dixie: Identity and education in the New Latin@ South. *Educational Studies*, *52*(1), 20–37.

Carrion, V. G., & Hull, K. (2010). Treatment manual for trauma-exposed youth: Case studies. *Clinical Child Psychology and Psychiatry*, *15*(1), 27–38.

Case, A., & Deaton, A. (2020). *Deaths of despair and the future of capitalism*. Princeton University Press.

Cashin, S. (2014). *Place, not race: A new vision of opportunity in America*. Beacon Press.

Casto, H. G. (2016). "Just one more thing I have to do": In search of sustainable school community partnerships. *School Community Journal*, *26*(1), 139–62.

Casto, H. G. (2019). "We're nine miles from the Board building, but the perception is that we're 100 miles away out in farm country": The case of a rural school in a non-rural district. *Journal of Rural Studies*, *72*, 164–73. https://doi.org/10.1016/j.jrurstud.2019.10.025

Casto, H. G., McGrath, B., Sipple, J. W., & Todd, L. (2016). "Community aware" education policy: Enhancing individual and community vitality. *Education Policy Analysis Archives/Archivos Analíticos de Políticas Educativas*, *24*, 1–30. https://doi.org/10.14507/epaa.24.2148

Casto, H. G., & Sipple, J. W. (2011). Who and what influences school leaders' decisions: An institutional analysis of the implementation of Universal Prekindergarten. *Educational Policy*, *25*(1), 134–66. https://doi.org/10.1177/0895904810387591

Casto, H. G., Sipple, J. W., & McCabe, L. M. (2016). A typology of school–community relationships: Partnering and Universal Pre-Kindergarten policy. *Educational Policy*, *30*(5), 659–87. https://doi.org/10.1177/0895904814557770

Catte, E. (2017, March 22). Liberal shaming of Appalachia: Inside the media elite's obsession with "the hillbilly problem." *Salon*. https://www.salon.com/2017/03/21/liberal-shaming-of-appalachia-inside-the-media-elites-obsession-with-the-hillbilly-problem/

Catte, E. (2018). *What you are getting wrong about Appalachia*. Belt Publishing.

Center for Applied Linguistics (CAL). (2020). *Two way immersion*. http://www.cal.org/twi/

Center for Research on Education Outcomes (CREDO). (2013). National charter school study. https://credo.stanford.edu/sites/g/files/sbiybj6481/f/ncss_2013_final_draft.pdf

Center for Research on Educational Outcomes (CREDO). (2015). Online charter school study. https://credo.stanford.edu/sites/g/files/sbiybj6481/f/online_charter_study_final.pdf

Center on Rural Innovation. (2020). *Broadband access map*. https://maps.ruralopportunitymap.us/broadband-access-map

Center for the Study of Education Policy. (2009). County school districts: Research and policy consolidations. Center for the Study of Education Policy. https://files.eric.ed.gov/fulltext/ED517802.pdf

Centers for Disease Control and Prevention (CDC). (2017). About rural health. https://www.cdc.gov/ruralhealth/about.html

Cervantes-Soon, C. G. (2014). A critical look at dual language immersion in the new Latin@ diaspora. *Bilingual Research Journal*, *37*(1), 64–82. https://doi.org/10.1080/15235882.2014.893267

Cervone, J. A. (2017). The reproduction of rural spaces through education. *Policy Futures in Education*, *15*(4), 427–40. https://doi.org/10.1177/1478210316688356

Cervone, J. A. (2018). *Corporatizing rural education: Neoliberal globalization and reaction in the United States*. Palgrave Macmillan.

References

Chafouleas, S. M., Johnson, A. H., Overstreet, S., & Santos, N. M. (2016). Toward a blueprint for trauma-informed service delivery in schools. *School Mental Health*, *8*(1), 144–62.

Chang, E., Simon, M., & Dong, X. (2012). Integrating cultural humility into health care professional education and training. *Advances in Health Science Education*, *17*, 269–78. https://doi.org/10.1007/s10459-010-9264-1

Chen, C. C.-C., Farmer, T. W., Hamm, J. V., Brooks, D. S., Lee, D. L., Norwalk, K., Lambert, K., Dawes, M., Sterrett, B., & Rizzo, K. (2019). Emotional and behavioral risk configurations, students with disabilities, and perceptions of the middle school ecology. *Journal of Emotional and Behavioral Disorders*, *28*(3), 180–92. https://doi.org/10.1177/1063426619866829

Chenoweth, E., & Galliher, R. V. (2004). Factors influencing college aspirations of rural West Virginia high school students. *Journal of Research in Rural Education*, *19*(2), 1–14. Retrieved from http://www.jrre.psu.edu/articles/19-2.pdf

Chetty, R., Friedman, J. N., & Rockoff, J. E. (2014). Measuring the impacts of teachers II: Teacher value-added and student outcomes in adulthood. *The American Economic Review*, *104*(9), 2633–79. https://doi.org/10.1257/aer.104.9.2633

Chingos, M. M., & West, M. R. (2015). The uneven performance of Arizona's charter schools. *Educational Evaluation and Policy Analysis*, *37*(1S), 120S–34S. https://doi.org/10.3102/0162373715576077

Chisholm, J. S., & Trent, B. (2013). Digital storytelling in a place-based composition course. *Journal of Adolescent & Adult Literacy*, *57*(4), 307–18. https://doi.org/10.1002/jaal.244

Choades, S. (2018). Charter schools and the achievement gap. *The Future of Children* (Policy Issue: Winter), 12–16.

Christianakis, M., & Mora, R. (2011). Charting a new course for public education through charter schools: Where is Obama taking us? In B. Porfilio & P. Carr (Eds.), *The phenomenon of Obama and the agenda for education: Can hope audaciously trump neoliberalism?* (pp. 97–120). Information Age Publishing.

Christianson, R. I. (2016). *Concern and difficulties in a rural district with a low ELL population* [Unpublished master's thesis]. St. Cloud State University.

Cicchinelli, L. F., & Beesley, A. (2017). Introduction: Current state of the science in rural education research. In G. C. Nugent, G. M. Kunz, S. M. Sheridan, T. A. Glover, & L. L. Knoche (Eds.), *Rural education research in the United States* (pp. 1–14). Springer.

Clark, C. (1995). *The communitarian moment: The radical challenge of the Northampton Association*. Cornell University Press.

Clark, J. K., Eno, C. A., & Guadagno, R. E. (2011). Southern discomfort: The effects of stereotype threat on the intellectual performance of US southerners. *Self and Identity*, *10*(2), 248–62. https://doi.org/10.1080/15298861003771080

Cleveland, B. (2016). *A school but not as we know it! Towards schools for networked communities* [Paper presentation]. Australian Association for Research in Education (AARE) Conference 2016, Melbourne, Australia. http://hdl.handle.net/11343/191208

Cloke, P., & Little, J. (1997). *Contested countryside cultures: Otherness, marginalization and rurality*. Routledge.

Cloke, P., Marsden, T., & Mooney, P. (Eds.). (2006). *Handbook of rural studies*. Sage.

Clotfelter, C. T., Ladd, H. F., & Vigdor, J. L. (2011). Teacher mobility, school segregation, and pay-based policies to level the playing field. *Education Finance and Policy*, *6*(3), 399–438. https://doi.org/10.1162/EDFP_a_00040

Coady, M. R. (2019a). *An overview of rural EL education* [Conference presentation]. Conference on Rural English Learner Education and Research (CREER), Gainesville, FL.

Coady, M. R. (2019b). *Connecting school and the multilingual home: Theory and practice for rural educators*. Multilingual Matters.

Coady, M. R. (2019c). "They just don't know who we are": Rural English Learner teacher education. In J. I. Liontas (Ed.), *The TESOL encyclopedia of English language teaching*. TESOL International Association & Wiley. https://doi.org/10.1002/9781118784235.eelt0979

References

Coady, M. R. (2020a). A review of rural English Learner education: Call for a focused national research agenda. *Educational Researcher*, *20*(10), 1–9. https://doi. 10.3102/0013189X20931505

Coady, M. R. (2020b, February). ¿Qué pasa with bilingual education in Alachua County? *The Gainesville Sun*. https://www.gainesville.com/opinion/20200220/maria-coady-iquestqueacute-pasa-with-bilingual-education-in-alachua-county-schools

Coady, M. R., Coady, T. J., & Nelson, A. (2015). Assessing the needs of immigrant, Latino families and teachers in rural settings: Building home-school partnerships. *NABE Journal of Research and Practice*, *6*. https://www2.nau.edu/nabej-p/ojs/index.php/njrp/article/view/42

Coady, M. R., Harper, C. A., & de Jong, E. J. (2011). Preservice to practice: Mainstream teacher beliefs of preparation and efficacy with English Language Learners in the state of Florida. *Bilingual Research Journal*, *34*(2), 223–39. https://doi.org/10.1080/15235882.2011.597823

Coady, M. R., Harper, C. A., & de Jong, E. J. (2016). Aiming for equity: Preparing mainstream teachers for inclusion or inclusive classrooms? *TESOL Quarterly*, *50*(2), 340–68. https://doi.org/10.1002/tesq.223

Coady, M. R., Lopez, M. P., Marichal, N., & Heffington, D. (2019). Preparing teacher leaders for English Language Learners in rural settings. *Theory & Practice in Rural Education*, *9*(1), 44–60. https://doi.org/10.3776/tpre.2019.v9n1p44-60

Cohen, M., & Hernandez, S. (2019, August 28). Back to school, without a teacher: Inside the struggle to keep teachers at rural schools. *USA Today*. https://www.usatoday.com/story/news/education/2019/08/28/teacher-first-day-of-school-back-teaching-jobs-salary/2018092001/

Coladarci, T. (2006). School size, student achievement, and the "power rating" of poverty: Substantive finding or statistical artifact? *Education Policy Analysis Archives*, *14*(28), 1–26. https://doi.org/10.14507/epaa.v14n28.2006.

Coladarci, T. (2007). Improving the yield of rural education research: An editor's swan song. *Journal of Research in Rural Education*, *22*(3), 1–9. https://jrre.psu.edu/sites/default/files/2019-08/22-3.pdf

Colangelo, N., Assouline, S. G., & New, J. K. (1999). *Gifted education in rural schools: A national assessment*. University of Iowa.

Cole, S., O'Brien, J., Gadd, M., Ristuccia, J., Wallace, D., & Gregory, M. (2005). Helping traumatized children learn: A report and policy agenda: Supportive school environments for children traumatized by family violence. *Massachusetts Advocates for Children*.

Coleman, J. S. (1988). Social capital in the creation of human capital. *The American Journal of Sociology*, *94*, S95–S120. https://doi.org/10.1016/b978-0-7506-7222-1.50005-2

Coleman, J. S., Campbell, E. Q., Hobson, C. J., McPartland, J., Mood, A. M., Weinfeld, F. D., & York, R. L. (1966). *Equality of educational opportunity*. Government Printing Office. https://eric.ed.gov/?id=ED012275

Collier, V., & Thomas, W. (2017). Validating the power of bilingual schooling: Thirty-two years of large-scale, longitudinal research. *Annual Review of Applied Linguistics*, *37*, 203–17. https://doi:10.1017/S0267190517000034

Combs, L., & Bailey, G. (1992). Exemplary school–community partnerships: Successful programs. *Rural Educator*, *13*, 8–13.

Compton, M., & Weiner, L. (2008). The global assault on teachers, teaching, and teachers unions. In L. Weiner & M. Compton (Eds.), *The global assault on teaching, teachers, and their unions: Stories for resistance* (pp. 3–10). Palgrave McMillan.

Condron, D. J., & Roscigno, V. J. (2003). Disparities within: Unequal spending and achievement in an urban school district. *Sociology of Education*, *76*(1), 18–36. https://doi.org/10.2307/3090259

Conger, R. D., & Elder, G. H. (1994). *Families in troubled times: Adapting to change in rural America*. Aldine Transaction.

Connell, R. (2007). *Southern theory: The global dynamics of knowledge in social science*. Polity.

Connell, R. W., Ashenden, D. J., Kessler, S., & Dowsett, G. W. (1982). *Making the difference: Schools, families and social division*. Allen & Unwin.

Cook-Sather, A. (2002). Authorizing students' perspectives: Toward trust, dialogue, and change in education. *Educational Researcher*, *31*(4), 3–14.

References

Copeland, J. (2013). One head – many hats: Expectations of a rural superintendent. *The Qualitative Report, 18*(77), 1–15.

Copple, C., & Bredekamp, S. (2009). *Developmentally appropriate practice in early childhood programs serving children from birth through age 8* (3rd ed.). National Association for the Education of Young Children.

Corbett, M. (2007). *Learning to leave: The irony of schooling in a coastal community.* Fernwood.

Corbett, M. (2013). Improvisation as a curricular metaphor: Imagining education for a rural creative class. *Journal of Research in Rural Education, 28*(10), 1–11. https://jrre.psu.edu/sites/default/files/2019-08/28-10.pdf

Corbett, M. (2014). The ambivalence of community: A critical analysis of rural education's oldest trope. *Peabody Journal of Education, 89*(5), 603–18. https://doi.org/10.1080/0161956x.2014.956532

Corbett, M. (2015a). Rural education: Some sociological provocations for the field. *Australian and International Journal of Rural Education, 25*(3), 9–25.

Corbett, M. (2015b). Towards a rural sociological imagination: Ethnography and schooling in mobile modernity. *Ethnography and Education, 10*(3), 263–77. https://doi.org/10.1080/17457823.2015.1050685

Corbett, M. (2016a). Reading Lefebvre from the periphery: Thinking globally about the rural. In A. Schulte & B. Walker-Gibbs (Eds.), *Self-studies in rural teacher preparation* (pp. 141–56). Routledge.

Corbett, M. (2016b). Rural futures: Development, aspirations, mobilities, place and education. *Peabody Journal of Education, 91*(2), 270–82.

Corbett, M. (2020). Place-based education: A critical appraisal from a rural perspective. In M. Corbett & D. Geryluk (Eds.), *Rural teacher education: Connecting land and people* (pp. 279–98). Springer.

Corbett, M., & Ackerson, Z. (2019). Vocational education and training: Discourse, systems, and practices of VET in rural Tasmania and Nova Scotia. *Canadian Journal of Education/Revue Canadienne de l'éducation, 42*(2), 464–91.

Corbett, M., & Donehower, K. (2017). Rural literacies: Toward social cartography. *Journal of Research in Rural Education, 32*(5), 1–13. https://jrre.psu.edu/sites/default/files/2019-08/32-5.pdf

Corbett, M., & Forsey, M. (2017). Rural youth out-migration and education: Challenges to aspirations discourse in mobile modernity. *Discourse: Studies in the Cultural Politics of Education, 38*(3), 429–44. https://doi.org/10.1080/01596306.2017.1308456

Corbett, M., & Helmer, L. (2017). Contested geographies: Competing constructions of community and efficiency in small school debates. *Geographical research, 55*(1), 47–57. https://doi.org/10.1111/1745-5871.12209

Corbett, M., & White, S. (2014). Introduction: Why put the "rural" in research? In S. White & M. Corbett (Eds.), *Doing educational research in rural settings: Methodological issues, international perspectives and practical solutions* (pp. 1–5). Routledge.

Cordova, R., & Reynolds, W. (2020). *Educating for social justice: Field notes from rural communities.* Brill.

Cotton, K. (2001, December). *New small learning communities: Findings from recent literature.* Northwest Regional Educational Laboratory. http://www.nwrel.org/scpd/sirs/nslc.pdf

County Health Rankings: Tallahatchie. (2019). University of Wisconsin Population Health Institute. County Health Rankings & Roadmaps 2019. https://www.countyhealthrankings.org/app/mississippi/2016/rankings/tallahatchie/county/outcomes/overall/snapshot

Cowan, J., & Hensley, J. (2012). Preparing and supporting principals in rural South Dakota schools. In K. Sanzo, S. Myran, & A. H. Normore (Eds.), *Successful school leadership preparation and development* (pp. 137–51). Emerald Publishing.

Cowan, J., Goldhaber, D., Hayes, K., & Theobald, R. (2016). Missing elements in the discussion of teacher shortages. *Educational Researcher, 45*(8), 460–2. https://doi.org/10.3102/0013189x16679145.

Cowen, J. M. (2009). Teacher unions and teacher compensation: New evidence for the impact of bargaining. *Journal of Education Finance, 35*(2), 172–93. https://doi.org/10.1353/jef.0.0010

Creswell, J. W., & Clark, V. L. P. (2017). *Designing and conducting mixed methods research.* Sage.

Crisp, G., Taggart, A., & Nora, A. (2015). Undergraduate Latina/o students: A systematic review of research identifying factors contributing to academic success outcomes. *Review of Educational Research, 85*(2), 249–74. https://doi.org/10.1080/00131946.2015.1120208

Crockett, L. J., Shanahan, M. J., & Jackson-Newsom, J. (2000). Rural youths: Ecological and life course perspectives. In R. Montemayor, G. Adams, & T. Gullotta (Eds.), *Adolescent diversity in ethnic, economic, and cultural contexts* (pp. 43–74). Sage. https://doi.org/10.4135/ 9781452225647.n3.

Cromartie, J., & Bucholtz, S. (2008, June 1). Defining the "rural" in rural America. *Amber Waves, 6*(3). https://www.ers.usda.gov/amber-waves/2008/june/defining-the-rural-in-rural-america

Cromartie, J., Von Reichert, C., & Arthun, R. (2015). *Factors affecting former residents' returning to rural communities*, ERR-185, U.S. Department of Agriculture, Economic Research Service.

Crowson, R. L., & Boyd, W. L. (1993). Coordinated services for children: Designing arks for storms and seas unknown. *American Journal of Education, 101*(2), 140–79.

Cryer, D., Tietze, W., Burchinal, M., Leal, T., & Palacios, J. (1999). Predicting process quality from structural quality in preschool programs: A cross-country comparison. *Early Childhood Research Quarterly, 14*, 339–61. https://doi.org/10.1016/S0885-2006(99)00017-4

Cubberley, E. (1914). *Rural life and education: A study of the rural-school problem as a phase of the rural-life problem.* Riverside Press.

Cubberley, E. (1916). *Public school administration: A statement of the fundamental principles underlying the organization and administration of public education.* Houghton Mifflin.

Cubberley, E. (1922). *Rural life and education: A study of the rural-school problem as a phase of the rural-life problem* (Revised edition). Houghton Mifflin.

Cuellar, M. (2018). School safety strategies and their effects on the occurrence of school-based violence in U.S. high schools: An exploratory study. *Journal of School Violence, 17*(1), 28–45. https://doi.org/10.1 080/15388220.2016.1193742

Cuervo, H. (2012). Enlarging the social justice agenda in education: An analysis of rural teachers' narratives beyond the distributive dimension. *Asia-Pacific Journal of Teacher Education, 40*, 83–95. https://doi.org/10.1080/1359866X.2012.669829

Cummings, C., Dyson, A., & Todd, L. (2011). *Beyond the school gates: Can full service and extended schools overcome disadvantage?* Routledge.

Curti, M. (1935). *Social ideas of American educators.* Charles Scribner and Sons.

Dados, N., & Connell, R. (2012). The global south. *Contexts, 11*(1), 12–13. https://doi. org/10.1177/1536504212436479

Darling-Hammond, L. (2010). *The flat world and education: How America's commitment to equity will determine our future.* Teachers College Press.

Data USA: Tallahatchie County, MS. (2017). https://datausa.io/profile/geo/tallahatchie-county-ms#economy

Davidson, O. G. (1996). *Broken heartland: The rise of America's rural ghetto.* University of Iowa Press.

Davis, G. A., Rimm, S. B., & Siegle, D. (2010). *Education of the gifted and talented* (6th ed.). Prentice Hall.

Dean, M. (2010). *Understanding human need: Social issues, policy and practice.* Policy Press.

DeCapua, A., & Marshall, H. W. (2011). Reading ELLs at risk: Instruction for students with limited or interrupted formal education. *Preventing School Failure, 55*(1), 35–41. https://doi. org/10.1080/10459880903291680

Deeb-Sossa, N., & Moreno, M. (2016). ¡No cierren nuestra escuela! Farm worker mothers as cultural citizens in an educational community mobilization effort. *Journal of Latinos & Education, 15*(1), 39–57. https://doi.org/10.1080/15348431.2015.1045145

Delcourt, M. A., Cornell, D. G., & Goldberg, M. D. (2007). Cognitive and affective learning outcomes of gifted elementary school students. *Gifted Child Quarterly, 51*, 359–81. https://doi. org/10.1177/0016986207306320

De Lissovoy, N., Means, A. J., & Saltman, K. J. (2015). *Toward a new common school movement.* Paradigm.

Deloria, V., & Wildcat, D. R. (2001). *Power and place: Indian education in America* (First Printing, Underlining edition). Fulcrum Publishing.

DeLozier, L. (2019, September 18). Emory hosts Tara Westover, best-selling author of "Educated," in lead-off event for common read. *Emory news center.* https://news.emory.edu/stories/2019/09/er_common_ read_westover/campus.html

References

Demi, M. A., Coleman-Jensen, A., & Snyder, A. R. (2010). The rural context and secondary school enrollment: An ecological systems approach. *Journal of Research in Rural Education*, *25*(7), 1–26. https://jrre.psu.edu/sites/default/files/2019-08/25-7.pdf

deRuiter, C., & van Ijzendoorn, M. H. (Eds.). (1993). Attachment and cognition: A review of the literature. *International Journal of Educational Research*, *19*(6), 521–600.

Dewees, S., & Marks, B. (2017). *Twice invisible: Understanding rural native America*. First Nations Development Institute.

Dewees, S., & Valázquez, J. A. (2000). Community development in rural Texas: A case study of Balmorhea Public Schools. *Journal of the Community Development Society*, *31*(2), 216–32. https://doi.org/10.1080/15575330009489704

Dexter, D. D., Hughes, C. A., & Farmer, T. W. (2008). Responsiveness to intervention: A review of field studies and implications for rural special education. *Rural Special Education Quarterly*, *27*(4), 3–9. https://doi.org/10.1177/875687050802700402

DeYoung, A. J. (1987). The status of American rural education research: An integrated review and commentary. *Review of Educational Research*, *57*(2), 123–48. https://doi.org/10.3102/00346543057002123

DeYoung, A. J. (1991). Economic underdevelopment and its effects on formal schooling in Southern Appalachia. *American Educational Research Journal*, *28*(2), 297–315. https://doi.org/10.2307/1162942

DeYoung, A. J. (1995). *The life and death of a rural American high school: Farewell Little Kanawha*. Garland Publishing.

DeYoung, A. J., & Howley, C. B. (1990). The political economy of rural school consolidation. *Peabody Journal of Education*, *67*(4), 63–89. https://doi.org/10.1080/01619569009538701

DiMaggio, P. J., & Powell, W. W. (1983). The iron cage revisited: Institutional isomorphism and collective rationality in organizational fields. *American Sociological Review*, *48*(2), 147–60. 10.2307/2095101

Dixson, A. D., Buras, K. L., & Jeffers, E. K. (2015). The color of reform: Race, education reform, and charter schools in post-Katrina New Orleans. *Qualitative Inquiry*, *21*(3), 288–99. https://doi.org/10.1177/1077800414557826

Dokoupil, T. (2010, October 25). New study: School consolidation gets failing grade. *Newsweek*, *156*, 58. https://www.newsweek.com/new-study-school-consolidation-gets-failing-grade-74145

Donehower, K. (2003). Literacy choices in an Appalachian community. *Journal of Appalachian Studies*, *9*(2), 341–62.

Donehower, K. (2007). Rhetorics and realities: The history and effects of stereotypes about rural literacies. In C. Hogg, E. E. Schell, & K. Donehower (Eds.), *Rural literacies* (pp. 37–76). Southern Illinois University Press.

Donehower, K. (2013a). Why not at school? Rural literacies and the continual choice to stay. In B. Green & M. Corbett (Eds.), *Rethinking rural literacies: Transnational perspectives* (pp. 35–52). Palgrave Macmillan.

Donehower, K. (2013b). Connecting literacy to sustainability: Revisiting literacy as involvement. In J. Duffy, J. N. Christoph, E. Goldblatt, N. Graff, R. S. Nowacek, & B. Trabold (Eds.), *Literacy, economy, and power: Writing and research after "Literacy in American Lives"* (1st ed., pp. 97–110). Southern Illinois University Press.

Donehower, K. (2014). Metaphors we lose by: Re-thinking how we frame rural education. In S. White & M. Corbett (Eds.), *Doing educational research in rural settings: Methodological issues, international perspectives and practical solutions* (pp. 166–80). Routledge.

Donehower, K., & Green, B. (2016). Rural literacies and rural mobilities: Textual practice, relational space, and social capital in a globalised world. In M. Shucksmith & D. L. Brown (Eds.), *Routledge International Handbook of Rural Studies* (pp. 599–609). Routledge.

Donehower, K., Hogg, C., & Schell, E. E. (Eds.). (2007). *Rural literacies*. Southern Illinois University Press.

Donehower, K., Hogg, C., & Schell, E. E. (2012). Introduction: Reclaiming the rural. In K. Donehower, C. Hogg, & E. E. Shell (Eds.), *Reclaiming the rural: Essays on literacy, rhetoric, and pedagogy* (pp. 1–16). Southern Illinois University Press.

Dorado, J. S., Martinez, M., McArthur, L. E., & Leibovitz, T. (2016). Healthy Environments and Response to Trauma in Schools (HEARTS): A whole-school, multi-level, prevention and intervention program for creating trauma-informed, safe and supportive schools. *School Mental Health*, *8*(1), 163–76.

Dovigo, F. (Ed.). (2018). *Challenges and opportunities in education for refugees in Europe: From research to good practices*. Studies in Inclusive Education (Vol. 37). Brill. https://doi.org/10.1163/9789004383227

Downes, N., & Roberts, P. (2015). Valuing rural meanings: The work of parent supervisors challenging dominant educational discourses. *Australian and International Journal of Rural Education*, *25*(3), 80–93.

Doyen, P. (2020). *A closer look at how rural principals continue to develop professionally* [Unpublished doctoral dissertation]. University of Maine.

Drier, P., Mollenkopf, J., & Swanstrom, T. (2013). *Place matters: Metropolitics for the 21st century* (3rd ed.). University of Kansas Press.

Dryfoos, J. (1994). *Full-service schools: A revolution in health and social services for children, youth and families*. Jossey-Bass.

Dryfoos, J., & Maguire, S. (2002). *Inside full-service community schools*. Corwin Press.

Dryfoos, J. G. (1996). Full-service schools. *Educational Leadership*, *53*(7), 18–23.

Duckworth, A. (2016). *Grit: The power of passion and perseverance*. Scribner.

Dulgerian, D. (2016). The impact of the Every Student Succeeds Act on rural schools. *Georgetown Journal on Poverty Law and Policy*, *24*, 111. https://heinonline.org/HOL/Page?collection=journals&handle=hein.journals/geojpovlp24&id=114&men_tab=srchresults

Dunbar-Ortiz, R. (2015). *An Indigenous peoples' history of the United States*. Random House.

Duncan, C. M. (1999). *Worlds apart: Why poverty persists in rural America*. Yale University Press.

Duncan, G. J., & Magnuson, K. (2013). Investing in preschool programs. *Journal of Economic Perspectives*, *27*(2), 109–32. https://www.aeaweb.org/articles?id=10.1257/jep.27.2.109

Duncan, G. J., Ziol-Guest, K. M., & Kalil, A. (2010). Early-childhood poverty and adult attainment, behavior, and health. *Child Development*, *81*(1), 306–25.

Duncan, H., & Stock, Mark J. (2010). Mentoring and coaching rural school leaders: What do they need? *Mentoring & Tutoring: Partnership in Learning*, *18*(3), 293–311. DOI: 10.1080/13611267.2010.492947

Duncombe, W., & Yinger, J. (2007). Does school district consolidation cut costs? *Education Finance and Policy*, *2*(4), 341–75.

Dunn, C. G., Kenney, E., Fleischhacker, J. D., & Bleich, S. N. (2020). Feeding low income children during the COVID-19 pandemic. *The New England Journal of Medicine*, *382*(18), e40(1)–(3). https://doi.org/10.1056/NEJMp2005638

Dunstan, S. (2013). The influence of speaking a dialect of Appalachian English on the college experience (Publication No. 3575619) [Doctoral dissertation, North Carolina State University]. ProQuest Dissertations and Theses.

Dunstan, S. B., & Jaeger, A. J. (2015). Dialect and influences on the academic experiences of college students. *The Journal of Higher Education*, *86*(5), 777–803. https://doi.org/10.1353/jhe.2015.0026

Durlak, J. A., Weissberg, R. P., Dymnicki, A. B., Taylor, R. D., & Schellinger, K. B. (2011). The impact of enhancing students' social and emotional learning: A meta-analysis of school-based universal interventions. *Child Development*, *82*, 405–32. https://doi.org/10.1111/j.1467-8624.2010.01564.x

Dweck, C. (2006). *Mindset: The new psychology of success*. Random House.

Dweck, C. S. (2007). *Mindset: The new psychology of success* (Reprint, Updated ed.). Ballantine Books.

Early Childhood Learning & Knowledge Center. (2018). Head Start program facts: Fiscal year 2018. https://eclkc.ohs.acf.hhs.gov/sites/default/files/pdf/no-search/hs-program-fact-sheet-2018.pdf

Echo Hawk Consulting. (2015). *Feeding ourselves: Food access, health disparities, and the pathways to healthy Native American communities*. Echo Hawk Consulting. https://nebula.wsimg.com/891e74d1afe847b92abe87b2a1df7c63?AccessKeyId=2EF8ECC329760AC5A98D&disposition=0&alloworigin=1

References

Eckert, J. (2017). *Not a mystery: How to permanently end the teacher shortage.* Center for Teaching Quality. https://www.teachingquality.org/not-a-mystery-how-to-permanently-end-the-teacher-shortage/

Economic Research Service. (2016). Rural America at a glance: 2016 edition. https://www.ers.usda.gov/publications/pub-details/?pubid=80893

Economic Research Service. (2017). Rural education at a glance: 2017 edition. https://www.ers.usda.gov/webdocs/publications/83078/eib-171.pdf?v=42830

Economic Research Service. (2018). Rural America at a glance: 2018 edition. https://www.ers.usda.gov/publications/pub-details/?pubid=90555

Economic Research Service. (2019). Rural America at a glance: 2019 edition. https://www.ers.usda.gov/webdocs/publications/95341/eib-212.pdf?v=5832

EdBuild. (2016). Fault lines: America's most segregating school district borders. https://edbuild.org/content/fault-lines

Economic Research Service. (2020). Rural poverty & well-being. https://www.ers.usda.gov/topics/rural-economy-population/rural-poverty-well-being/

Edmondson, J. (2003). *Prairie Town: Redefining rural life in the age of globalization.* Rowman & Littlefield Publishers.

Edmondson, J., & Butler, T. (2010). Teaching school in rural America: Toward an educated hope. In K. Schafft and A. Y. Jackson (Eds.). *Rural education for the 21st Century* (pp. 150–74). The Pennsylvania State University Press.

Edmondson, J., & Zimpher, N. L. (2014). *Striving together: Early lessons in achieving collective impact in education.* SUNY Press.

Edwards, C. P., Sheridan, S. M., & Knoche, L. (2010). Parent–child relationships in early learning. In E. Baker, P. Peterson, & B. McGaw (Eds.), *International encyclopedia of education* (Vol. 5, pp. 438–43). Elsevier.

Edwards, J., & Cheers, B. (2007). Is social capital good for everyone? The case of same-sex attracted women in rural South Australian communities. *Health Sociology Review, 16*(3–4), 226–36. https://doi.org/10.5172/hesr.2007.16.3-4.226

Egalite, A. J., & Kisida, B. (2016). School size and student achievement: A longitudinal analysis. *School Effectiveness and School Improvement, 27*(3), 406–17. https://doi.org/10.1080/09243453.2016.1190385

Egley, R., & Jones, B. (2004). Rural elementary administrators' views of high-stakes testing. *The Rural Educator, 26*(1), 1–10.

Elder, W. L. (1992). The use of Census geography and county typologies in the construction of classification systems for rural schools and districts. *Journal of Research in Rural Education, 8*(3), 47–68. https://jrre.psu.edu/sites/default/files/2019-08/8-3_4.pdf

Elicker, J., Wen, X., Kwon, K., & Sprague, J. B. (2013). Early Head Start relationships: Association with program outcomes. *Early Education and Dev+elopment, 24*, 491–516. https://doi.org/10.1080/10409289.2012.695519

Elliott, D. E., Bjelajac, P., Fallot, R. D., Markoff, L. S., & Reed, B. G. (2005). Trauma-informed or trauma-denied: Principles and implementation of trauma-informed services for women. *Journal of Community Psychology, 33*(4), 461–77.

Elliott, S. N., & Bartlett, B. J. (2016). Opportunity to learn. *Oxford Handbooks Online.* https://doi.org/10.1093/oxfordhb/9780199935291.013.70

England, W., & Hamann, E. T. (2013). Segregation, inequality, demographic change, and school consolidation. *Great Plains Research: A Journal of Natural and Social Sciences, 23*, 171–83. https://digitalcommons.unl.edu/greatplainsresearch/1026/

Eppley, K. (2009). Rural schools and the highly qualified teacher provision of *No Child Left Behind*: A critical policy analysis. *Journal of Research in Rural Education, 24*(4), 1–11. https://jrre.psu.edu/sites/default/files/2019-08/24-4.pdf

Eppley, K. (2010). Picturing rural America: An analysis of the representation of contemporary rural America in picture books for children. *The Rural Educator, 32*(1), 1–10.

Eppley, K. (2011). Reading Mastery as pedagogy of erasure. *Journal of Research in Rural Education, 26*(13), 1–5. https://jrre.psu.edu/sites/default/files/2019-08/26-13.pdf

Eppley, K. (2015). "Hey, I saw your grandparents at Walmart": Teacher preparation for rural schools and communities. *The Teacher Educator, 50*(1), 67–86. https://doi-org.ezaccess.libraries.psu.edu/10.1080/08878730.2014.975061

Eppley, K., Azano, A. P., Brenner, D. G., & Shannon, P. (2018). What counts as evidence in rural schools? Evidence-based practice and practice-based evidence for diverse settings. *The Rural Educator, 39*(2), 36–40. https://doi.org/10.35608/ruraled.v39i2.208

Eppley, K., Maselli, A., & Schafft, K. (2021). Charter schools and the reconfiguring of the rural school-community connection. In P. Roberts & M. Fuqua (Eds.), *Ruraling educational research: Connections between rurality and the disciplines of educational research* (pp. 91–105). Springer.

Eppley, K., & Shannon, P. (2015). Literacy education for the Lumps and Divots of smart cities and rural places. In S. Williams & A. Grooms (Eds.), *The politics of educational opportunity in rural contexts* (pp. 59–73). Information Age Press.

Etheridge, B. (2017). Rural in a different caye: Listening to early school leavers about the importance of place. In W. M. Reynolds (Ed.), *Forgotten places: Critical studies in rural education* (pp. 235–54). Peter Lang.

Ettlinger, M., & Hensley, J. (2020, July 17). *COVID-19 Economic crisis: By state*. Carsey School of public policy. https://carsey.unh.edu/COVID-19-Economic-Impact-By-State

European Commission/EACEA/Eurydice. (2019). *Integrating students from migrant backgrounds into schools in Europe: National policies and measures*. Eurydice Report. Office of the European Union. https://eacea.ec.europa.eu/national-policies/eurydice/sites/eurydice/files/integrating_students_from_migrant_backgrounds_into_schools_in_europe_national_policies_and_measures.pdf

European Union. (2020). *EU languages*. https://europa.eu/european-union/about-eu/eu-languages_en

Eurostat. (2019). *Foreign language skills statistics*. https://ec.europa.eu/eurostat/statistics-explained/index.php/Foreign_language_skills_statistics

Every Child Succeeds Act (ESSA) of 2015, Public Law No. 114–95, S.1177, 114th Cong. (2015). Retrieved from https://www.congress.gov/114/plaws/publ95/PLAW-114publ95.pdf

Ewing, E., & Ferrick, M. (n.d). For this place, for these people: An exploration of best practices among charter schools serving Native students. https://leg.mt.gov/content/Committees/Interim/2015-2016/State-Tribal-Relations/Meetings/July-2016/charter-school-case-study.pdf

Executive Office of the President. (2014). *Native Youth Report*. https://obamawhitehouse.archives.gov/sites/default/files/docs/20141129nativeyouthreport_final.pdf

Fabricant, M., & Fine, M. (2012). *Charter schools and the corporate makeover of public education: What's at stake?* Teachers College Press.

Faircloth, S. C. (2009). Re-visioning the future of education for Native youth in rural schools and communities. *Journal of Research in Rural Education, 24*(9), 1–4. https://jrre.psu.edu/sites/default/files/2019-08/24-9.pdf

Falk, I., & Kilpatrick, S. (2000). What is social capital? A study of interaction in a rural community. *Sociologia Ruralis, 40*(1), 87–110.

Fallot, R. D., & Harris, M. (2006). *Trauma-informed services: A self-assessment and planning protocol*. Community Connections.

Fanon, F. (1967). *Black skin, white masks*. Grove Press.

Farmer, T. W. (2020). Reforming research to support culturally and ecologically responsive and developmentally meaningful practice in schools. *Educational Psychologist, 55*, 32–9. https://doi.org/10.1080/00461520.2019.1698298

Farmer, T. W., Dadisman, K., Latendresse, S. J., Thompson, J., Irvin, M. J., & Zhang, L. (2006, September 15). Educating out and giving back: Adults' conceptions of successful outcomes of African American high school students from impoverished rural communities. *Journal of Research in Rural Education, 21*(10), 1–12. https://jrre.psu.edu/sites/default/files/2019-08/21-10.pdf

Farmer, T. W., Dawes, M., Hamm, J. V., Lee, D., Mehtaji, M., Hoffman, A. S., & Brooks, D. S. (2018). Classroom social dynamics management: Why the invisible hand of the teacher matters for special education. *Remedial & Special Education, 39*, 177–92. https://doi.org/10.1177/0741932517718359

References

Farmer, T. W., Gatzke-Kopp, L., Latendresse, S. J. (2020). The development, prevention, and treatment of emotional and behavioral disorders: An interdisciplinary developmental systems perspective. In T. W. Farmer, M. Conroy, E. M. Z. Farmer, & K. S. Sutherland (Eds.), *Handbook of research on emotional & behavioral disorders: Interdisciplinary developmental perspectives on children and youth* (pp. 3–22). Routledge.

Farmer, T. W., Hall, C. M., Weiss, M. P., Petrin, R. A., Meece, J. L., & Moohr, M. (2011). The school adjustment of rural adolescents with and without disabilities: Variable and person-centered approaches. *Journal of Child and Family Studies, 20,* 78–88. https://doi.org/10.1007/s10826-010-9379-2

Farmer, T. W., Hamm, J. V., Dawes, M., Barko-Alva, K., & Cross, J. R. (2019). Promoting inclusive communities in diverse classrooms: Teacher attunement and social dynamics management. *Educational Psychologist, 54,* 286–305.

Farmer, T. W., Hamm, J. V., Lee, D. L., Sterrett, B. I., Rizzo, K., & Hoffman, A. S. (2018). Directed consultation and supported professionalism: Promoting adaptive evidence-based practices in rural schools. *Rural Special Education Quarterly, 37,* 164–75. https://doi.org/10.1177/8756870518781307

Farmer, T. W., Hamm, J. V., Lee, D. L., Sterrett, B., Rizzo, K., & Norwalk, K. (2020). An adaptive, correlated constraints model of classroom management: The behavioral, academic, and social engagement (BASE) program. In T. W. Farmer, M. Conroy, E. M. Z., Farmer, & K. S. Sutherland (Eds.), *Handbook of research on emotional & behavioral disorders: Interdisciplinary developmental perspectives on children and youth* (pp. 227–42). Routledge.

Farmer, T. W., Hamm, J. V., Leung, M-C., Lambert, K., & Gravelle, M. (2011). Early adolescent peer ecologies in rural communities: Bullying in schools that do and do not have a transition during the middle grades. *Journal of Youth and Adolescence, 40,* 1106–17. https://doi.org/10.1007/s10964-011-9684-0

Farmer, T. W., Leung, M.-C., Banks, J. B., Schaefer, V., Andrews, B, & Murray, R. A. (2006). Adequate yearly progress in small rural schools and rural low-income schools. *Rural Educator, 27*(3), 1–7. https://doi.org/10.35608/ruraled.v27i3.488

Farmer, T. W., Leung, M.-C., Weiss, M. P., Irvin, M. J., Meece, J. L., & Hutchins, B. C. (2011).The social network placement of rural high school students with disabilities: Centrality and peer affiliations. *Exceptional Children, 78*(1), 24–38. https://doi.org/10.1177/001440291107800102

Farmer, T. W., Sutherland, K. S., Talbott, E., Brooks, D., Norwalk, K., & Huneke, M. (2016). Special educators as intervention specialists: Dynamic systems and the complexity of intensifying intervention for students with emotional and behavioral disorders. *Journal of Emotional and Behavioral Disorders, 24*(3), 173–86. https://doi.org/10.1177/1063426616650166

Farrigan, T. (2020). *Rural poverty & well-being.* USDA, Economic Research Service. https://www.ers.usda.gov/topics/rural-economy-population/rural-poverty-well-being/

Farrugia, D. (2016). The mobility imperative for rural youth: The structural, symbolic and non-representational dimensions of rural youth mobilities. *Journal of Youth Studies, 19*(6), 836–51. https://doi.org/10.1080/13676261.2015.1112886

Fass, P. (1982). Without design: Education policy in the New Deal. *American Journal of Education, 91*(1), 36–64. https://doi.org/10.1086/443664

Felitti, V. J. (2009). Adverse childhood experiences and adult health. *Academic Pediatrics, 9*(3), 131–2.

Felitti, V. J., Anda, R. F., Nordenberg, D., Williamson, D. F., Spitz, A. M., Edwards, V., & Marks, J. S. (1998). Relationship of childhood abuse and household dysfunction to many of the leading causes of death in adults: The Adverse Childhood Experiences (ACE) Study. *American Journal of Preventive Medicine, 14*(4), 245–58.

Fennelly, K. (2008). Prejudice toward immigrants in the Midwest. In D. S. Massey (Ed.), *New faces in new places: The changing geography of American immigration* (pp. 151–78). Russell Sage Foundation.

Ferdman, B. (1990). Literacy and cultural identity. *Harvard Educational Review, 60*(2), 181–205. https://doi.org/10.17763/haer.60.2.k10410245xxw0030

Ferrara, J., & Jacobson, R. (Eds.). (2019). *Community schools: People and places transforming education and communities.* Rowman & Littlefield.

Fiel, J. E. (2013). Decomposing school resegregation: Social closure, racial imbalance, and racial isolation. *American Sociological Review, 78*(5), 828–48. https://doi.org/10.1177/0003122413496252

Fielding, M. (2001). Students as radical agents of change. *Journal of Educational Change, 2*(2), 123–41.

Fiester, L. (2010). *Early warning! Why reading by the end of third grade matters.* KIDS COUNT Special Report. Annie E. Casey Foundation. https://files.eric.ed.gov/fulltext/ED509795.pdf

Filteau, M. (2014). Who are these guys? Constructing the oilfield's new dominant masculinity. *Men and Masculinities, 17*(4), 396–416. https://doi.org/10.1177/1097184X14544905

Finkel, M. L., & Law, A. (2011). The rush to drill for natural gas: A public cautionary tale. *American Journal of Public Health, 101*(5), 784–5.

Fireside, H. (2004). *Separate and unequal: Homer Plessy and the Supreme Court decision that legalized racism.* Carroll & Graf.

Fiske, G. W. (1913). *The challenge of the country.* Association Press.

Fitchen, J. M. (1981). *Poverty in rural America: A case study.* Westview Press.

Fitzpatrick, B. R., Berends, M., Ferrare, J. J., & Waddington, R. J. (2020). Virtual illusion: Comparing student achievement and teacher and classroom characteristics in online and brick-and-mortar charter Schools. *Educational Researcher, 49*(3), 161–75. https://doi.org/10.3102/0013189X20909814

Fleisch, B. (2010). The politics of the governed: South African democratic teachers' union Soweto Strike, June 2009. *Southern African Review of Education with Education with Production, 16*(2), 117–31.

Flora, C. B., & Flora, J. L. (2013). *Rural communities: Legacy + change* (4th ed.). Westview Press.

Flora, C. B., Flora, J. L., & Gasteyer, S. P. (2016). *Rural communities: Legacy + change* (5th ed.). Routledge.

Fontanella, C. A., Hiance-Steelesmith, D. L., Phillips, G. S., Bridge, J. A., Lester, N., Sweeney, H. A., & Campo, J. V. (2015). Widening rural-urban disparities in youth suicides, United States, 1996–2010. *JAMA pediatrics, 169*(5), 466–73. https://doi.org/10.1001/jamapediatrics.2014.3561

Food Research & Action Center. (2020). Research & Data. https://frac.org/research

Ford, M. (2013). Understanding school finance in Wisconsin: A primer. *The Wisconsin Policy Research Institute, 26*(7). https://www.badgerinstitute.org/BI-Files/Special-Reports/Reports-Documents/schoolfinanceprimerfinalpdf.pdf

Formula Fairness Campaign. (2015). *Formula fairness campaign: Ending discrimination against rural and small schools.* http://www.ruraledu.org/articles.php?id=2423

Forner, M., Bierlein-Palmer, L., & Reeves, P. (2012). Leadership practices of effective rural superintendents: Connections to Waters and Marzano's Leadership correlates. *Journal of Research in Rural Education, 27*(8), 1–13.

Forry, N. D., Moodie, S., Simkin, S., & Rothenberg, L. (2011). *Family–provider relationships: A multidisciplinary review of high quality practices and associations with family, child, and provider outcomes* (Issue Brief OPRE 2011–26a). Office of Planning, Research and Evaluation, Administration for Children and Families, U.S. Department of Health and Human Services. https://www.acf.hhs.gov/sites/default/files/opre/family_provider_multi.pdf

Foster, W. P. (2004). The decline of the local: A challenge to educational leadership. *Educational Administration Quarterly, 40*(2), 176–91. https://doi.org/10.1177/0013161X03260360

Foucault, M. (1988). *Politics, philosophy, culture: Interviews and other writings, 1974–1984* (L. D. Kritzman, Ed.). Routledge.

Fowles, J., Butler, J. S., Cowen, J. M., Streams, M. E., & Toma, E. F. (2014). Public employee quality in a geographic context: A study of rural teachers. *The American Review of Public Administration, 44*(5), 503–21.

Fox, M. (2020, April 9). *Wisconsin schools had more than $1.6B on Tuesday's ballot, but results are still a ways away.* Wisconsin Public Radio. https://www.wpr.org/wisconsin-schools-had-more-1-6b-tuesdays-ballot-results-are-still-ways-away

Frankenberg, E., Lee, C., & Orfield, G. (2003). *A multiracial society with segregated schools: Are we losing the dream?* The Civil Rights Project. https://civilrightsproject.ucla.edu/research/k-12-education/integration-and-diversity/a-multiracial-society-with-segregated-schools-are-we-losing-the-dream

References

Frankenberg, E., & Siegel-Hawley, G. (2013). A segregating choice? An overview of charter school policy, enrollment trends, and segregation. In G. Orfield & E. Frankenberg (Eds.), *Educational delusions: Why choice can deepen inequality and how to make schools fair* (pp. 129–45). University of California Press.

Fraser, N. (2009). *Scales of justice: Reimagining political space in a globalizing world*. Columbia University.

Fraser-Seeto, K., Howard, S. J., & Woodcock, S. (2013). Preparation for teaching gifted students: An updated investigation into university offerings in New South Wales. *Australasian Journal of Gifted Education, 22*(2), 45–51. https://doi.org/10.21505/ajge.2016.0006

Freeman, E. (2017). Diversion or democratization: Do rural, Hispanic, community college students show signs of academic undermatch? *Journal of Hispanic Higher Education, 16*(1), 77–97. https://doi.org/10.1177/1538192716628604

Frey, W. H. (2017, June 27). *Census shows nonmetropolitan America is Whiter, getting older and losing population. Will it retain political clout?* Brookings Institution. https://www.brookings.edu/blog/the-avenue/2017/06/27/census-shows-nonmetropolitan-america-is-whiter-getting-older-and-losing-population/

Frey, W. H. (2019, June 24). *Less than half of US children under 15 are white, census shows*. Brookings Institution. https://www.brookings.edu/research/less-than-half-of-us-children-under-15-are-white-census-shows/

Fryberg, S., Markus, H. R., Oyserman, D., & Stone, J. (2008). Of warrior chiefs and Indian princesses: The psychological consequences of American Indian mascots. *Basic and Applied Social Psychology, 30*(3), 208–18. https://doi.org/10.1080/01973530802375003

Fullan, M. (2007). *The new meaning of educational change*. Routledge.

Fuller, E. J., LeMay, M., & Pendola, A. (2018). Who should be our leader? Examining female representation in the principalship across geographic locales in Texas public schools. *Journal of Research in Rural Education, 34*(4), 1–21.

Furco, A. (2013). Legitimizing community engagement with K–12 schools. *Peabody Journal of Education, 88*(5), 622–36.

Furman, G. C. (2004). The ethic of community. *Journal of Educational Administration, 42*(2), 215–35. https://doi.org/10.1108/09578230410525612

Furstenberg, F. F., & Hughes, M. E. (1994, November). *The influence of neighborhoods on children's development: A theoretical perspective and a research agenda* [Paper presentation]. Conference Indicators of Children's Well-Being, Bethesda, MD.

Fusarelli, B. C., & Militello, M. (2012). Racing to the top with leaders in rural high poverty schools. *Planning and Changing, 43*, 46–56.

Gagnon, D. (2016). ESSA and rural teachers: New roads ahead? *The Phi Delta Kappan, 97*(8), 47–9. https://doi.org/10.1177/0031721716647019

Gagnon, D. J., & Mattingly, M. J. (2015). Rates of beginning teachers: Examining one indicator of school quality in an equity context. *The Journal of Educational Research, 108*(3), 226–35. https://doi.org/10.1080.00220671.2013.878300

Gagnon, D. J., & Mattingly, M. J. (2018). Racial/ethnic test score gaps and the urban continuum. *Journal of Research in Rural Education, 33*(2), 1–16. https://jrre.psu.edu/sites/default/files/2019-08/33-2.pdf

Gallagher, N. (2016). Special education teacher shortage worsens in Maine schools. *Portland Press Herald*. https://www.pressherald.com/2016/08/29/special-education-teacher-shortage-worsens-at-maine-schools/

Galster, G., & Killen, S. (1995). The geography of metropolitan opportunity: A reconnaissance and conceptual framework. *Housing Policy Debate, 6*(1), 7–43. https://doi.org/10.1080/10511482.1995.9521180

Gamm, L., Stone, S., & Pittman, S. (2010). Mental health and mental disorders—A rural challenge: A literature review. *Rural Healthy People, 2*, 97–113. https://www.researchgate.net/publication/255683562_Mental_health_and_mental_disorders-a_rural_challenge_A_literature_review

Garcia, D. (2008). The impact of school choice on racial segregation in charter schools. *Educational Policy, 22*(6), 805–29. https://doi.org/10.1177/0895904807310043

García, O., Kleifgen, J., & Falchi, L. (2008). From English Language Learners to emergent bilinguals. *Equity Matters*: *Research Review No. 1*. https://files.eric.ed.gov/fulltext/ED524002.pdf

Garrett, L. (1994). *The coming plague: Newly emerging diseases in a world out of balance*. Farrar Straus & Giroux.

Garrett, L. (2020, April 2). Grim reapers: How Trump and Xi set the stage for the coronavirus pandemic. The New Republic. https://newrepublic.com/article/157118/trump-xi-jinping-america-china-blame-coronavirus-pandemic

Garwood, J. D., Werts, M. G., Varghese, C., & Gosey, L. (2018). Mixed-methods analysis of rural special educators' role stressors, behavior management, and burnout. *Rural Special Education Quarterly, 37*(1), 30–43.

Gee, J. P. (1991). *Social linguistics: Ideology in discourses*. Falmer.

Gemin, B., Smith, B., Vashaw, L., Watson, J., Hattington, C., & LeBlanc, E. (2018). *Digital learning strategies for rural America: A scan of policy and practice in K–12 education*. The Foundation for Blended and Online Learning and Evergreen Education Group. https://www.blendedandonlinelearning.org/research-reports/rural-report

Genovese, H. (2019, January 16). People of color living in America's rural spaces face constant erasure. *Teen Vogue*. https://www.teenvogue.com/story/people-of-color-in-americas-rural-spaces-face-erasure

Gentry, M. (2018). Cluster grouping. In C. M. Callahan & H. L. Hertberg-Davis (Eds.), *Fundamentals of gifted education* (2nd ed., pp. 213–24). Routledge.

George, L., & Holden, C. (2000). *Why housing matters: HAC's 2000 report on the state of the nation's rural housing*. Housing Assistance Council.

Gershenson, S., Hart, C., Lindsay, C., & Papageorge, N. (2017). *The long-run impacts of same-race teachers*. IZA Discussion Paper Series. Bonn, Germany: IZA Institute of Labor Economics.

Gershenson, S., & Langbein, L. (2015). The effect of primary school size on academic achievement. *Educational Evaluation and Policy Analysis, 37*(1s), 135–55. https://doi.org/10.3102/0162373715576075

Geverdt, J., & Phan, T. (2006). *Documentation to the NCES common core of data public elementary/secondary school locale code file: School year 2003–04* (NCES 2006–332). U.S. Department of Education. National Center for Education Statistics. https://nces.ed.gov/ccd/pdf/sl031agen.pdf

Gibbs, R. M. (1998). College completion and return migration among rural youth. In R. M. Gibbs, P. L. Swaim, & R. Teixeira (Eds.), *Rural education and training in the new economy: The myth of the rural skills gap* (pp. 61–80). Iowa State University Press.

Gibson, J. E., Werner, S. S., & Sweeney, A. (2015). Evaluating an abbreviated version of the PATHS curriculum implemented by school mental health clinicians. *Psychology in the Schools, 52*(6), 549–61. https://doi.org/10.1002/pits.21844

Gilbody, S., Sheldon, T., & Wessely, S. (2006). Should we screen for depression? *British Medical Journal, 332*, 1027–30. https://doi.org/10.1136/bmj.332.7548.1027

Gildersleeve, R. E. (2010). *Fracturing opportunity: Mexican migrant students and college-going literacy*. Peter Lang.

Gill, L. (1998). Neoliberalism and public education: The relevance of the Bolivian teachers' strike of 1995. In L. Phillips (Ed.), *The third wave of modernization in Latin America: Cultural perspectives on neoliberalism* (pp. 125–41). Scholarly Resources.

Gillon, K. E. (2017). Writing rural: Critical perspectives on rural students and the college going experience. *Texas Education Review, 5*(1), 10–23.

Gindy, M. (2016). Gifted awareness week: Australia. http://www.aaegt.net.au/wp-content/uploads/Gifted-Awareness-Week-Australia-2016-Media-Release.pdf

Giroux, H. (2005a). *Border crossings: Cultural workers and the politics of education*. Routledge.

Giroux, H. (2005b). The terror of neoliberalism: Rethinking the significance of cultural politics. *College Literature, 32*(1), 1–20.

References

Giroux, H. A. (2008). *Against the terror of neoliberalism*. Paradigm.

Giroux, H. A. (2011a). *Education and the crisis of public values: Challenging the assault on teachers, students, and public education. Counterpoints: Studies in the postmodern theory of education. Volume 400*. Peter Lang.

Giroux, H. A. (2011b). *On critical pedagogy*. Continuum.

Giroux, H. A. (2012). *Education and the crisis of public values: Challenging the assault on teachers, students, and public education*. Peter Lang.

Gjelten, T. (1982). *A typology of rural school settings* [Paper presentation]. Rural Education Seminar, United States Department of Education, Washington, DC. https://eric.ed.gov/?id=ED215858

Goedeken, J. A., Xia, Y., Durden, T., & de Guzman, M. R. T. (2016). Rural Hispanic youths' perceptions of positive youth development experiences. *Journal of Extension, 54*(4), [4R1B3].

Goeman, M. (2013). *Mark my words: Native women mapping our nations*. University of Minnesota Press.

Goetz, S. J., & Swaminathan, H. (2006). Walmart and county-wide poverty. *Social Science Quarterly, 87*(2), 211–26.

Goffman, E. (2009). *Stigma: Notes on the management of spoiled identity* (Reissue edition). Touchstone.

Goldblatt, E., & Jolliffe, D. (2020). *Literacy as conversation: Learning networks in urban and rural communities*. University of Pittsburgh Press.

Goldhaber, D., & Özek, U. (2019). How much should we rely on student test achievement as a measure of success? *Educational Researcher, 48*(7), 479–83. https://doi.org/10.3102/0013189x19874061

Golding, S. A. (2016). Gentrification and segregated wealth in rural America: Home value sorting in destination counties. *Population Research Policy Review, 35*, 126–46. https://doi.org/10.1007/s11113-015-9374-9

Goodman, R. T., & Saltman, K. J. (2002). *Strange love, or how we learn to stop worrying and love the market*. Rowman & Littlefield.

Goodwin, L. (1976). *Democratic promise: The Populist moment in America*. Oxford University Press.

Gorski, P. C. (2011). Unlearning deficit ideology and the scornful gaze: Thoughts on authenticating the class discourse in education. *Counterpoints, 402*, 152–73.

Gorski, P. C. (2013). Building a pedagogy of engagement for students in poverty. *Phi Delta Kappan, 95*(1), 48–52.

Grande, S. (2008). Red pedagogy: The un-methodology. In N. K. Denzin, Y. S. Lincoln, & L. T. Smith (Eds.), *Handbook of critical and Indigenous methodologies* (pp. 233–54). Sage. https://doi.org/10.4135/9781483385686

Green, B. (2013). Literacy, rurality, education: A partial mapping. In B. Green & M. Corbett (Eds.), *Rethinking rural literacies: Transnational perspectives* (pp. 17–34). Palgrave Macmillan.

Green, B. (2015). Australian education and rural-regional sustainability. *Australian and International Journal of Rural Education, 25*(3), 36–49.

Green, B. (2017). *Engaging curriculum: Bridging the curriculum theory and English education divide*. Routledge.

Green, B., & Corbett, M. (Eds.). (2013). *Rethinking rural literacies: Transnational perspectives*. Palgrave Macmillan.

Green, B., & Letts, W. (2007). Space, equity, and rural education: A "trialectical" account. In K. V. Gulson & C. Symes, *Spatial theories of education: Policy and geography matters* (pp. 57–76). Routledge.

Green, B., & Reid, J. (2012). A new teacher for a new nation? Teacher education, "'English"', and schooling in early twentieth-century Australia. *Journal of Educational Administration and History, 44*(4), 361–79. https://doi.org/10.1080/00220620.2012.713927

Green, B., Roberts, P., & Brennan, M. (2020). *Curriculum challenges and opportunities in a changing world: Transnational perspectives in curriculum inquiry*. Palgrave Macmillan.

Green, T. L. (2015). Places of inequality, places of possibility: Mapping "opportunity in geography" across urban school–communities. *The Urban Review, 47*(4), 717–41. https://doi.org/10.1007/s11256-015-0331-z

Green, T. L. (2018). Enriching educational leadership through community equity literacy: A conceptual foundation. *Leadership and Policy in Schools, 17*(4), 487–515. https://doi.org/10.1080/15700763.2017.1326148

Greenberg, M. T., Kusche, C. A., Cook, E. T., & Quamma, J. P. (1995). Promoting emotional competence in school-aged children: The effects of the PATHS curriculum. *Development and Psychopathology, 7*, 117–36. https://doi.org/10.1017/S0954579400006374

Greenough, R., & Nelson, S. R. (2015). Recognizing the variety of rural schools. *Peabody Journal of Education, 90*(1), 322–32. https://doi.org/10.1080/0161956X.2015.1022393

Greenwood, D. A. (2009). Place, survivance, and White remembrance: A decolonizing challenge to rural education in mobile modernity. *Journal of Research in Rural Education, 24*(10), 1–6. https://jrre.psu.edu/sites/default/files/2019-08/24-10.pdf

Griffin, D., Hutchins, B. C., & Meece, J. L. (2011). Where do rural high school students go to find information about their futures? *Journal of Counseling & Development, 89*(2), 172–81. https://doi.org/10.1002/j.1556-6678.2011.tb00075.x

Griffith, M. (2011). *What savings are produced by moving to a four-day school week?* Education Commission of the States. https://www.ecs.org/clearinghouse/93/69/9369.pdf

Grissom, J. A., & Keiser, L. R. (2011). A supervisor like me: Race, representation, and the satisfaction and turnover decisions of public sector employees. *Journal of Policy Analysis and Management, 30*(3), 557–80. https://doi.org/10.1002/pam.20579

Grissom, J. A., & Mitani, H. (2016). Salary, performance, and superintendent turnover. *Educational Administration Quarterly, 52*(3), 351–91. https://doi.org/10.1177/0013161X15627677

Grissom, J. A., Nicholson-Crotty, J., & Nicholson-Crotty, S. (2009). Race, region, and representative bureaucracy. *Public Administration Review, 69*(5), 911–19. https://doi.org/10.1111/j.1540-6210.2009.02040.x

Gristy, C. (2019). Journeys to school in rural places: Engaging with the troubles through assemblages. *Journal of Rural Studies, 72*, 286–92. https://doi.org/10.1016/j.jrurstud.2019.10.016

Gristy, C., Hargreaves, L., & Kučerová, S. R. (Eds.). (2020). *Educational research and schooling in rural Europe: An engagement with changing patterns of education, space, and place.* Information Age Publishing.

Gruenewald, D. A. (2003a). Foundations of place: A multidisciplinary framework for place-conscious education. *American Educational Research Journal, 40*(3), 619–54. https://doi.org/10.3102/00028312040003619

Gruenewald, D. A. (2003b). The best of both worlds: A critical pedagogy of place. *Educational Researcher, 32*(4), 3–12. https://doi.org/10.3102/0013189X032004003

Gruenewald, D. A. (2014). Place-based education: Grounding culturally responsive teaching in geographical diversity. In D. A. Gruenewald & G. A. Smith (Eds.), *Placed-based education in the global age: Local diversity* (pp. 5–28). Routledge.

Guerrero, A. P. S., Balon, R., Beresin, E. V., Louie, A. K., Coverdale, J. H., Brenner, A., & Roberts, L. (2019). Rural mental health training: An emerging imperative to address health disparities. *Academic Psychiatry, 43*, 1–5. https://doi.org/10.1007/s40596-018-1012-5

Guiffrida, D. A. (2008). Preparing rural students for large colleges and universities. *Journal of School Counseling, 6*(14), 1–25. https://files.eric.ed.gov/fulltext/EJ894785.pdf

Gulosino, G., Yongmei, N., & Rorrer, A. (2019). Newly hired teacher mobility in charter schools and traditional public schools: An application of segmented labor market theory. *American Journal of Education, 125*(4), 547–92. https://doi.org/10.1086/704096

Guo, G. (1998). The timing of the influences of cumulative poverty on children's cognitive ability and achievement. *Social Forces, 77*(1), 257–88. https://doi.org/10.2307/3006017

Gusa, D. L. (2010). White institutional presence: The impact of Whiteness on campus climate. *Harvard Educational Review, 80*, 464–90.

Gutiérrez, D. G. (2016). A historic overview of Latino immigration and the demographic transformation of the United States. In R. A. Gutierrez & T. Almaguer (Eds.), *The new Latino studies reader: A twenty-first century perspective* (pp. 108–25). University of California Press

Gutierrez, R. R. (2013). Beating the neoliberal blame game: Teacher and parent solidarity and the 2012 Chicago teachers' strike. *Monthly Review, 65*(2), 24–32. https://doi.org/10.14452/mr-065-02-2013-06_3

References

Guyton, C. D. (2011). Exploring the lived experiences of rural African American millennials at predominantly White institutions (Publication No. 3491227) [Doctoral dissertation, Indiana State University]. ProQuest Dissertations & Theses.

Haas, T., & Nachtigal, P. (1998). *Place value: An educator's guide to good literature on rural lifeways, environments, and purposes of education*. ERIC Clearinghouse on Rural Education and Small Schools.

Habermas, J. (1968). *Technik und Wissenschaft als 'Ideologie'*. Suhrkamp.

Habermas, J. (1975). *Legitimation crisis*. Heinemann.

Habermas, J. (1979). *Communication and the evolution of society*. Beacon Press.

Habermas, J. (1981). *Theorie des kommunikativen Handelns. Band I. Handlungsrationalita¨t und gesellschaftlige Rationalisierung*. Suhrkamp.

Haedicke, M. A. (2013). From collective bargaining to social justice certification: Workers' rights in the American meatpacking industry. *Sociological Focus, 46*(2), 119–37.

Hager, K. D., Baird, C. M., & Spriggs, A. D. (2012). Remote teacher observation at the University of Kentucky. *Rural Special Education Quarterly, 31*(4), 3–8. https://doi.org/10.1177/875687051203100402

Hagerhall, C. M. (2001). Consensus in landscape preference judgments. *Journal of Environmental Psychology, 21*(1), 83–92. https://doi.org/10.1006/jevp.2000.0186

Hahn, R. A. (1981). Remaining neutral during a teacher strike. *NASSP Bulletin, 65*(445), 57–61. https://doi.org/10.1177/019263658106544509 https://doi.org/10.1177/019263658106544509

Hair, N. L., Hanson, J. L., Wolfe, B. L., & Pollak, S. D. (2015). Association of child poverty, brain development, and academic achievement. *JAMA Pediatrics, 169*(9), 822–29.

Halfacree, K. (2006). Rural space: Constructing a three-fold architecture. In P. Cloke, T. Marsden, & P. Mooney (Eds.), *Handbook of rural studies* (pp. 44–62). Sage.

Halfacree, K. H. (1993). Locality and social representation: Space, discourse and alternative definitions of the rural. *Journal of Rural Studies, 9*(1), 23–37. https://doi.org/10.1016/0743-0167(93)90003-3

Hall, D. (2016). *Local control as resistance: Policy and practice of autonomous school boards* (Publication No. 10903664) [Doctoral Dissertation, Pennsylvania State University]. ProQuest Dissertations and Theses.

Hall, D., & McHenry-Sorber, E. (2017). Politics first: Examining the practices of the multi-district superintendent. *Education Policy Analysis Archives, 25*(82), 1–26. https://doi.org/10.14507/epaa.25.2934

Hall, R. F., McCaw, D. S., Philhower, S., & Pierson, M. E. (2004). *School district reorganization in Illinois: Improving educational opportunities for students*. Illinois Institute for Rural Affairs.

Haller, E. J., & Monk, D. (1988). New reforms, old reforms, and the consolidation of small rural schools. *Educational Policy Administration, 24*(4), 470–83.

Haller, E. J., & Virkler, S. J. (1993). Another look at rural–nonrural differences in students' educational aspirations. *Journal of Research in Rural Education, 9*(3), 170–8. https://jrre.psu.edu/sites/default/files/2019-08/9-3_5.pdf

Halsey, J. (2017). *Independent review into regional, rural and remote education* [Discussion paper]. Commonwealth of Australia. https://docs.education.gov.au/node/44526

Halsey, J. (2018). *Independent review into regional, rural and remote education* [Final report]. Commonwealth of Australia. https://www.education.gov.au/independent-review-regional-rural-and-remote-education

Halsey, R. J. (2006). Towards a spatial "self-help" map for teaching living in a rural context. *International Education Journal, 7*(4), 490–6.

Hammer, P., Hughes, G., McClure, C., Reeves, C., & Salgado, D. (2005). *Rural teacher recruitment and retention practices: A review of the research literature, national survey of rural superintendents, and case studies of programs in Virginia*. Appalachian Educational Laboratory at Edvantia.

Hammond, J. L., & Hammond, B. (1912). *The village labourer, 1760–1832*. Longmans, Green, and Company.

Hampson, R. (2019, February 19). "Any talks of striking?" How a West Virginia teacher's facebook post started a national movement. *USA Today*. https://www.usatoday.com/story/news/education/2019/02/20/teacher-strike-west-virginia-school-closings-education-bill/2848476002/

Hanifan, L. J. (1920). *The community center*. Silver, Burdett and Company.

Hankins, D., & Martin, D. (2006). Charter schools and urban regimes in neoliberal context: Making workers and new spaces in metropolitan Atlanta. *International Journal of Urban and Regional Research*, *30*(3), 528–47. https://doi.org/10.1111/j.1468-2427.2006.00678.x

Hanleybrown, F., Kania, J., & Kramer, M. (2012). Channeling change: Making collective impact work. *Stanford Social Innovation Review*, 1–8. https://ssir.org/articles/entry/channeling_change_making_collective_impact_work

Hansen, C. (2018). Why rural principals leave. *The Rural Educator*, *39*(1), 41–53. https://doi.org/10.35608/ruraled.v39i1.214

Hansen-Thomas, H., Grosso Richins L., Kakkar, K., & Okeyo, C. (2016). "I do not feel I am properly trained to help them!" Rural teachers' perceptions of challenges and needs with English Language Learners. *Professional Development in Education*, *42*(2), 308–24. https://doi.org/10.1080/19415257.2014.973528

Hanushek, E. A. (2011). The economic value of higher teacher quality. *Economics of Education Review*, Elsevier*, 30*(3), 466–79.

Hanushek, E. A., Peterson, P. E., Talpey, L. M., & Woessmann, L. (2020). *Long-run trends in the U.S. SES-achievement gap*. (National Bureau of Economic Research Working Paper No. 26764). https://www.nber.org/papers/w26764.pdf

Hargreaves, A. (2020, April 16). What's next for schools after Coronavirus? Here are 5 big issues and opportunities. *The Conversation*. https://theconversation.com/whats-next-for-schools-after-coronavirus-here-are-5-big-issues-and-opportunities-135004

Hargreaves, A., Parsley, D., & Cox, E. K. (2015). Designing rural school improvement networks: aspirations and actualities. *Peabody Journal of Education*, *90*(2), 306–21. https://doi.org/10.1080/0161956X.2015.1022391

Hargreaves, L. (2020). Introduction: European rural schools and their communities: "The stone in Europe's shoe?" In C. Gristy, L. Hargreaves, & S. R. Kučerová (Eds.), *Educational research and schooling in rural Europe: An engagement with changing patterns of education, space, and place* (pp. 1–20). Information Age Publishing.

Hargreaves, L., Kvalsund, R., & Galton. M. (2009). Reviews of research on rural schools and their communities in British and Nordic countries: Analytical perspectives and cultural meaning. *International Journal of Educational Research*, *48*(2), 80–8. https://doi.org/10.1016/j.ijer.2009.02.001

Harkins, A., & McCarroll, M. (Eds.). (2019). *Appalachian reckoning: A region responds to* Hillbilly Elegy. West Virginia University Press.

Harlan, L. (1974). *Booker T. Washington: The making of a Black leader*. Oxford University Press.

Harmon, H. L., & Schafft, K. (2009). Rural school leadership for collaborative community development. *The Rural Educator*, *30*(3), 4–9. https://doi.org/10.35608/ruraled.v30i3.443

Harper, S. R. (2012). Race without racism: How higher education researchers minimize racist institutional norms. *The Review of Higher Education*, *36*(1), 9–29. https://doi.org/10.1353/rhe.2012.0047

Harris, C. I. (1993). Whiteness as property. *Harvard Law Review*, *106*, 1707–91.

Harris, D. N. (2020, April 24). *How will COVID-19 change our schools in the long run?* Brookings Institution. https://www.brookings.edu/blog/brown-center-chalkboard/2020/04/24/how-will-covid-19-change-our-schools-in-the-long-run/

Harris, J. C., Barone, R. P., & Finch, H. (2019). The property functions of Whiteness within fraternity and sorority culture and its impact on campus. *New Directions for Student Services*, *165*, 17–27.

Harris Poll. (2020). *Harris Poll COVID-19 Survey, Wave 9*. https://theharrispoll.com/wp-content/uploads/2020/04/The-Insight-Wave-9.pdf

Harris-Smedberg, K. J. (2019). *Shocks to the system: The micropolitics of communities in economic shock when determining the outcome of local education* [Unpublished Dissertation]. University of Maine. https://digitalcommons.library.umaine.edu/etd/3036

Hart, J. G. (2006). Exploring tribal leadership: Understanding and working with tribal people. *Journal of Extension*, *44*(4). https://archives.joe.org/joe/2006august/a3.php

References

Hart, L. G., Larson, E. H., & Lishner, D. M. (2005). Rural definitions for health policy and research. *American Journal of Public Health, 95*(7), 1149–55. https://doi.org/10.2105/AJPH.2004.042432

Hartman, S., & Hines-Bergmeier, J. (2015). Building connections: Strategies to address rurality and accessibility challenges. *Journal of Museum Education, 40*(3), 288–303. https://doi.org/10.1179/10598 65015Z.000000000105

Harvey, D. (2005). *A brief history of neoliberalism.* Oxford University Press.

Harvey, D. (2006). Neoliberalism as creative destruction. *Human Geography, 88*(2), 145–58.

Hash, K. M., & Morrow, D. F. (2019). Lesbian, gay, bisexual, and transgender persons aging in rural areas. *The International Journal of Aging and Human Development, 90*(2), 201–8.

Hatt, B. (2007). Growing up as poor, White trash: Stories of where I came from. In J. A. Galen & G. W. Noblit (Eds.), *Late to class: Social class and schooling in the new economy* (pp. 19–28). State University of New York Press.

Hauenstein, E. J., Petterson, S., Rovnyak, V., Merwin, E., Heise, B., & Wagner, D. (2007). Rurality and mental health treatment. *Administration and Policy in Mental Health and Mental Health Services Research, 34*(3), 255–67.

Hawley, L. R., Koziol, N. A., Bovaird, J. A., McCormick, C. M., Welch, G. W., Arthur, A. M., & Bash, K. (2016). Defining and describing rural: Implications for rural special education research and policy. *Rural Special Education Quarterly, 35*(3), 3–11. https://doi.org/10.1177%2F875687051603500302

Hayman, J., RedCorn, A., & Zacharakis, J. (2018). New horizons in the Osage Nation: Agricultural education and leadership development. *Journal of Research in Rural Education, 34*(5), 1–10. https:// jrre.psu.edu/sites/default/files/2019-06/34-5_0.pdf

Head, B. W., & Alford, J. (2015). Wicked problems: Implications for public policy and management. *Administration & society, 47*(6), 711–39.

Health Resources & Services Administration. (2018, December). *Defining rural population.* Federal Office of Rural Health Policy. https://www.hrsa.gov/rural-health/about-us/definition/index.html

Heath, S. B. (1983). *Ways with words: Language, life, and work in communities and classrooms.* Cambridge University Press.

Heckman, J. J. (2012). The case for investing in young children. In B. Falk (Ed.), *Defending Childhood: Keeping the promise of early education* (pp. 235–42). Teachers College Press.

Heckman, J. J., Stixrud, J., & Urzua, S. (2006). The effects of cognitive and noncognitive abilities on labor market outcomes and social behavior. *Journal of Labor Economics, 24*(3), 411–82. https://doi. org/10.3386/w12006

Heffington, D. (2019). *Higher order thinking skills among Latinx English Language Learners in elementary classrooms* [Unpublished doctoral dissertation]. University of Florida, Gainesville.

Hefflinger, C., Shaw, V., Higa-McMillan, C., Lunn, L., & Brannan, A. (2015). Patterns of child mental health service delivery in a public system: Rural children and the role of rural residence. *Journal of Behavioral Health Service & Research, 42*(3), 292–309. https://doi.org/10.1007/s11414-015-9464-9

Hegney, D. G., Buikstra, E., Baker, P., Rogers-Clark, C., Pearce, S., Ross, H., King, C., & Watson-Luke, A. (2007). Individual resilience in rural people: A Queensland study, Australia. *Rural and Remote Health, 7*(4), 620–33. http://www.rrh.org.au/articles/subviewnew.asp?ArticleID=620

Heim, C., & Nemeroff, C. B. (2002). Neurobiology of early life stress: Clinical studies. *Seminars in Clinical Neuropsychiatry, 7*(2), 147–59.

Hektner, J. M. (1995). When moving up implies moving out: Rural adolescent conflict in the transition to adulthood. *Journal of Research in Rural Education, 11*(1), 3–14. https://jrre.psu.edu/sites/default/ files/2019-08/11-1_3.pdf

Henig, J. R., Riehl, C. J., Houston, D. M., Rebell, M. A., & Wolff, J. R. (2016). *Collective impact and the new generation of cross-sector collaborations for education: A nationwide scan.* Department of Education Policy & Social Analysis, Teachers College. https://www.wallacefoundation.org/knowledge-center/ Documents/Collective-Impact-andthe- NewGeneration-of-Cross-Sector-Collaborationfor-Education.pdf

Herszenhorn, D. M. (2009, February 2). Internet money in fiscal plan: Wise or waste? *The New York Times.* https://www.nytimes.com/2009/02/03/us/politics/03broadband.html

Heuser, B. L., Wang, K., & Shahid, S. (2017). Global dimensions of gifted and talented education: The influence of national perceptions on policies and practices. *Global Education Review*, *4*(1), 4–21.

Heyward, G. (2018). *What do we actually know about the four-day school week?* Center on Reinventing Public Education. https://www.crpe.org/publications/what-do-we-actually-know-about-four-day-school-week

Hibbert, K. (2013). Reconfiguring the communicational landscape: Implications for rural literacy. In B. Green & M. J. Corbett (Eds.), *Rethinking rural literacies transnational perspectives* (pp. 155–75). Palgrave Macmillan. http://public.eblib.com/choice/publicfullrecord.aspx?p=1249579

Hickey, P. (2020, May 13). The future of schools after COVID-19. *Reno Gazette Journal*. https://www.rgj.com/story/opinion/voices/2020/05/13/future-schools-pat-hickey/5183369002/

Hillman, N., & Wetchman, T. (2016). Education deserts: The continued significance of "place" in the twenty-first century. *Viewpoints: Voices from the Field*. http://hdl.voced.edu.au/10707/408013

Hillman, N. W. (2016). Geography of college opportunity: The case of education deserts. *American Educational Research Journal*, *53*(4), 987–1021. https://doi.org/10.3102/0002831216653204

Hirsch, J. K. (2006). A review of the literature on rural suicide. *Crisis*, *27*(4), 189–99. [PubMed: 17219751].

Hlale, D. (2014). Creating sustainable rural learning ecologies: Realities, lessons, and prospects. *Journal of Human Ecology*, *45*(2), 101–10.

Hochschild, J., & Scovronick, N. (2003). *The American dream and the public schools*. Oxford University Press.

Hogrebe, M. C., & William F. Tate. (2012). Geospatial perspective: Toward a visual political literacy project in education, health, and human services. *Review of Research in Education*, *36*(1), 67–94.

Holcombe, R. (2014). *Vermont's commitment to continuous improvement*. Vermont Agency of Education.

Holder, A. B. (2017). A quest for equity in language: Educating Maya-American children [Unpublished doctoral dissertation]. Arizona State University. https://repository.asu.edu/attachments/194026/content/Holder_asu_0010E_17445.pdf

Holloway, S. L. (2007). Burning issues: Whiteness, rurality and the politics of difference. *Geoforum*, *38*(1), 7–20.

Holme, J., & Rangel, V. (2012). Putting school reform in its place: Social geography, organizational social capital, and school performance. *American Educational Research Journal*, *49*(2), 257–83. https://doi.org/10.3102/0002831211423316

Holmes, G. M., Kaufman, B. G., & Pink, G. H. (2017). Predicting financial distress and closure in rural hospitals. *The Journal of Rural Health*, *33*(3), 239–49. https://doi.org/10.1111/jrh.12187

Holmes, S. M. (2013). *Fresh fruit, broken bodies*. University of California Press.

Holmes, S. R., & Sheridan, S. M. (in press). Considerations for family–school partnerships in rural communities. In G. Miller, A. Arthur, & R. Banerjee (Eds.), *Advances in family-school-community partnering (FSCP): A practical guide for school mental health professionals and education stakeholders* (2nd ed.). Routledge.

Holmes, S. R., Sheridan, S. M., & Smith, T. E. (2020). Unpacking conjoint behavioral consultation: A latent profile analysis of parent–teacher interactions. *Journal of Educational and Psychological Consultation*. DOI:10.1080/10474412.2020.1759080

Holt, S., & Gershenson, S. (2015). The impact of teacher demographic representation on student attendance and suspensions. (Discussion paper No. 9554). *IZA Discussion Paper Series*. IZA Institute of Labor Economics.

Hondo, C., Gardiner, M. E., & Sapien, Y. (2008). *Latino dropouts in rural America*. State University of New York.

hooks, b. (2009). *Belonging: A culture of place*. Routledge.

Hooper-Briar, K., & Lawson, H. A. (1996). Toward interprofessional education and practice: Definitions, choices, and the challenges of accreditation, certification, and licensing. In K. Hooper-Briar & H. A. Lawson (Eds.), *Expanding partnerships for vulnerable children and families* (pp. 176–80). Council on Social Work Education.

References

Hoover, S., Lever, N., Sachdev, N., Bravo, N., Schlitt, J., Acosta Price, O., Sheriff, L., & Cashman, J. (2019). *Advancing comprehensive school mental health: Guidance from the field*. National Center for School Mental Health. University of Maryland School of Medicine.

Hopper, S. (2020, March 24). How COVID-19 will change K–12 education forever. *Medium*. https://medium.com/@thestevenpost/how-covid-19-will-change-k-12-education-forever-bf197794c596

Horsford, S. D., & Heilig, J. V. (2014). Community-based education reform in urban contexts. *Urban Education, 49*(8), 867–70. https://doi.org/10.1177/0042085914557647

Horsford, S. D., & Sampson, C. (2014). Promise neighborhoods: The promise and politics of community capacity building as urban school reform. *Urban Education, 49*(8), 955–91.

Housing Assistance Council. (2012). *Race & ethnicity in rural America*. http://www.ruralhome.org/storage/research_notes/rrn-race-and-ethnicity-web.pdf

Howley, A., & Howley, C. B. (2001, December). *Rural school busing*. ERIC Digest EDO-RC-01-7. https://files.eric.ed.gov/fulltext/ED459969.pdf

Howley, A., Howley, M., Camper, C., & Perko, H. (2011). Place-based education at Island Community School. *Journal of Environmental Education, 42*(4), 216–36. https://doi.org/10.1080/00958964.2011.556682

Howley, A., Rhodes, M., & Beall, J. (2009). Challenges facing rural students: Implications for gifted students. *Journal for the Education of the Gifted, 32*(4), 515–36. https://doi.org/10.1177/016235320903200404

Howley, C. B. (1996). Compounding disadvantage: The effects of school and district size on student achievement in West Virginia. *Journal of Research in Rural Education, 12*(1), 25–32. https://jrre.psu.edu/sites/default/files/2019-08/12-1_2.pdf

Howley, C. B. (1997). How to make rural education research *rural*: An essay at practical advice. *Journal of Research in Rural Education, 13*(2), 131–8. https://jrre.psu.edu/sites/default/files/2019-08/13-2_4.pdf

Howley, C. B. (1998). *Distortions of rural student achievement in the era of globalization*. Appalachia Educational Laboratory. https://files.eric.ed.gov/fulltext/ED419634.pdf

Howley, C. B. (2014, March 13). Review of *A new frontier: Utilizing charter schooling to strengthen rural education*. https://nepc.colorado.edu/thinktank/review-new-frontier

Howley, C. B., Hobart, H. L., & Leopold, G. D. (1996). Rural scholars or bright rednecks? Aspirations for a sense of place among rural youth in Appalachia. *Journal of Research in Rural Education, 12*(3), 150–60. https://jrre.psu.edu/sites/default/files/2019-08/12-3_5.pdf

Howley, C. B., & Howley, A. (2010). Poverty and school achievement in rural communities: A social-class interpretation. In K. A. Schafft & A. Y. Jackson (Eds.), *Rural education for the twenty-first century* (pp. 34–50). Penn State Press.

Howley, C. B., & Howley, A. (2014). Making sense of rural education research. In S. White & M. Corbett (Eds.), *Doing educational research in rural settings* (pp. 7–25). Routledge.

Howley, C. B., & Howley, A. (2018). How blue was my valley? Invited paper for the American Educational Research Association special interest group on rural education. *Journal of Research in Rural Education, 33*(4), 1–10. https://doi.org/10.18113/P8JRRE3304

Howley, C. B., Howley, A., & Johnson, J. D. (Eds.). (2014). *Dynamics of social class, race, and place in rural education*. Information Age Publishing.

Howley, C. B., Howley, A., & Shamblen, S. (2001). Riding the school bus: A comparison of the rural and suburban experience in five states. *Journal of Research in Rural Education, 17*(1), 41–63. https://jrre.psu.edu/sites/default/files/2019-08/17-1_4.pdf

Howley, C. B., & Howley, A. A. (2004). School size and the influence of socioeconomic status on student achievement: Confronting the threat of size bias in national data sets. *Education Policy Analysis Archives, 12*(52), 1–35.

Howley, C. B., Howley, A. A., Howley, C. W., & Howley, M. D. (2014). Saving the children of the poor in rural schools. In C. B. Howley, A. Howley, & J. D. Johnson (Eds.), *Dynamics of social class, race, and place in rural education* (pp. 139–64). Information Age Publishing.

References

Howley, C. B., Johnson, J., & Petrie, J. (2011, February 1). *Consolidation of schools and districts: What the research says and what it means.* National Research Policy Center. http://nepc.colorado.edu/publication/consolidation-schools-districts

Howley, C. B., Showalter, D., Klein, R., Sturgill, D. J., & Smith, M. A. (2012). Rural math talent, now and then. *Roeper Review, 35,* 102–14. https://doi.org/10.1080/02783193.2013.766963

Howley, C. B., Theobald, P., & Howley, A. (2005). What rural education research is of most worth? A reply to Arnold, Newman, Gaddy and Dean. *Journal of Research in Rural Education, 20*(18), 1–6. https://jrre.psu.edu/sites/default/files/2019-08/20-18.pdf

Howley, C. W. (2006). Remote possibilities: Rural children's educational aspirations. *Peabody Journal of Education, 81*(2), 62–80. https://doi.org/10.1207/s15327930pje8102_4

Howley, C. W., & Hambrick, K. (2014). Getting there from here: Schooling and rural abandonment. In C. B. Howley, A. Howley, & J. D. Johnson (Eds.), *Dynamics of social class, race, and place in rural education* (pp. 193–216). Information Age Press.

Howley, C. W., Johnson, J., Passa, A., & Uekawa, K. (2014). College enrollment and persistence in rural Pennsylvania schools. REL 2015–053. *Regional Educational Laboratory Mid-Atlantic.* https://ies.ed.gov/ncee/edlabs/regions/midatlantic/Docs/Events/19/AERA_2016_PA_rural_college_enrollment_and_persistence_2016-04-06_508c.pdf

Howley, M., Howley, A., & Eppley, K. (2013). How agricultural science trumps rural community in the discourse of selected U.S. history textbooks. *Theory & Research in Social Education, 41*(2), 187–218. https://doi.org/10.1080/00933104.2013.778715

Howley, P. (2011). Landscape aesthetics: Assessing the general publics' preferences towards rural landscapes. *Ecological Economics, 72,* 161–9. https://doi.org/10.1016/j.ecolecon.2011.09.026

Hoyer, K., Sparks, D., & Ralph, J. (2017). *How principals in public and private schools use their time 2011–2012.* U.S. Department of Education NCES 2018–54. https://nces.ed.gov/pubs2018/2018054.pdf

Hromadžić, A. (2015). Dissatisfied citizens: Ethnonational governance, teachers' strike and professional solidarity in Mostar, Bosnia–Herzegovina. *European Politics and Society, 16*(3), 429–46. https://doi.org/10.1080/23745118.2015.1061803

Hu, S. (2003). Educational aspirations and postsecondary access and choice. *Education Policy Analysis Archives, 11*(14), 1–13. https://doi.org/10.14507/epaa.v11n14.2003

Hughes, R. P., Kimball, E. W., & Koricich, A. (2019). The dual commodification of college-going: Individual and institutional influences on access and choice. In M. B. Paulsen & L. W. Perna (Eds.), *Higher Education: Handbook of Theory and Research* (pp. 415–77). Springer. https://doi.org/10.1007/978-3-030-03457-3_10

Hursh, D. (2015). *The end of public schools: The corporate reform agenda to privatize education.* Routledge.

Hurt, R. D. (1987). *Indian agriculture in America: Prehistory to the present.* University of Kansas Press.

Husen, T. (Ed.). (1967). *International study of achievement in mathematics: A comparison of twelve countries* (Vol. I). John Wiley & Sons.

Hutchins, B. C., Meece, J. L., Byun, S., & Farmer, T. W. (2012). Planning for the future. *The Rural Educator, 33*(2). https://doi.org/10.35608/ruraled.v33i2.414

Huws, M. (2020). *Short inquiry into the implications of Brexit on areas within the Culture, Welsh Language and Communications Committee's remit.* Comisiynydd y Gymraeg Welsh Language Commissioner. http://www.comisiynyddygymraeg.cymru/English/Publications%20List/20181008%20DG%20S%20Ymchwiliad%20Brexit.pdf

Iddings, J., & Angus, R. (2015). A functional linguistics approach to Appalachian literacy. In S. Webb-Sunderhaus & K. Donehower (Eds.), *Rereading Appalachia: Literacy, place, and cultural resistance.* University Press of Kentucky.

Institute of Education Sciences. (2014). The IES rural education technical working group summary. https://ies.ed.gov/ncer/whatsnew/tecworkingroup

Iruka, I. U., DeKraai, M., Walther, J., Sheridan, S. M., & Abdel-Monem, T. (2020). Examining how rural ecological contexts influence children's early learning opportunities. *Early Childhood Research Quarterly, 52,* 15–29. https://doi.org/10.1016/j.ecresq.2019.09.005

References

Irvin, M. J., Byun, S., Meece, J. L., Farmer, T. W., & Hutchins, B. C. (2012). Educational barriers of rural youth: Relation of individual and contextual difference variables. *Journal of Career Assessment*, *20*(1), 71–87. https://doi.org/10.1177/1069072711420105

Irvin, M. J., Byun, S., Meece, J. L., Reed, K. S., & Farmer, T. W. (2016). School characteristics and experiences of African American, Hispanic/Latino, and Native American youth in rural communities: Relation to educational aspirations. *Peabody Journal of Education*, *91*(2), 176–202. https://doi.org/10.1080/0161956x.2016.1151739

Irvin, M. J., Byun, S., Smiley, W. S., & Hutchins, B. C. (2017). Relation of opportunity to learn advanced math to the educational attainment of rural youth. *American Journal of Education*, *123*(3), 475–510. https://doi.org/10.1086/691231

Irvin, M. J., Farmer, T. W., Weiss, M. P., Meece, J. M., Byun, S., McConnell, B., & Petrin, R. (2011). Perceptions of school and postsecondary aspirations of rural high school students with learning disabilities and their nondisabled peers. *Learning Disabilities Research & Practice*, *26*, 2–14. https://doi.org/10.1111/j.1540-5826.2010.00320.x

Isaac, M., Elias, B., Katz, L. Y., Belik, S. L., Deane, F. P., Enns, M. W., & Sareen, J. (2009). Gatekeeper training as a preventive intervention for suicide: A systematic review. *Canadian Journal of Psychiatry*, *54*, 260–68. https://doi.org/10.1177/070674370905400407

Jackson, A. Y. (2010). Fields of discourse: A Foucauldian analysis of schooling in a rural, U.S. Southern town. In K. A. Schafft & A. Y. Jackson (Eds.), *Rural education for the twenty-first century: Identity, place, and community in a globalizing world* (pp. 72–94). The Pennsylvania State University Press.

Jacobson, L. (2020, March 13). Tracker: Florida teachers rally in Tallahassee. *Education Dive*. https://www.educationdive.com/news/tracker-teachers-on-strike/547339/

Jacoby, D. F., & Nitta, K. (2012). The Bellevue teachers strike and its implications for the future of postindustrial reform unionism. *Educational Policy*, *26*(4), 533–63. https://doi.org/10.1177/0895904811417585

Jacquet, J. B., Guthrie, E., & Jackson, H. (2017). Swept out: Measuring rurality and migration intentions on the upper Great Plains. *Rural Sociology*, *82*(4), 601–27. https://doi.org/10.1111/ruso.12145

James, B. (1987). If it can happen here, it can happen anywhere. *Thrust for Educational Leadership*, *16*(4), 41–2.

Janečková Molnárová, K., Skřivanová, Z., Kalivoda, O., & Sklenička, P. (2017). Rural identity and landscape aesthetics in exurbia: Some issues to resolve from a Central European perspective. *Moravian Geographical Reports*, *25*(1), 2–12. https://doi.org/10.1515/mgr-2017-0001

Janus v. American Federation of State, County, and Municipal Employees, 16 U.S. 1466 (2018). https://www.supremecourt.gov/opinions/17pdf/16-1466_2b3j.pdf

Jarvis, J. M., & Henderson, L. C. (2012). Current practices in the education of gifted and advanced learners in South Australian schools. *Australasian Journal of Gifted Education*, *24*(2), 5–22. https://doi.org/10.21505/ajge.2015.0018

Jarzabkowski, L. (2003). Teacher collegiality in a remote Australian school. *Journal of Research in Rural Education*, *18*, 139–44. https://jrre.psu.edu/sites/default/files/2019-08/18-3_3.pdf

Jefferson, T. (2013). *The papers of Thomas Jefferson: Retirement series* (Vol. 10). Princeton University Press.

Jelen, L. (2020). The European migration crisis and the status of immigrant children in education systems. In C. Gristy, L. Hargreaves, & S. R. Kučerová (Eds.), *Educational research and schooling in rural Europe: An engagement with changing patterns of education, space, and place* (pp. 357–69). Information Age Publishing.

Jennings, N. E. (1999). Reform in small places: Examining two rural schools' implementation of state reform. *Journal of Research in Rural Education*, *15*(3), 127–40. https://jrre.psu.edu/sites/default/files/2019-08/15-3_1.pdf

Jensen, L., McLaughlin, D. K., & Slack, T. (2003). Rural poverty: The persisting challenge. In D. L. Brown & L. E. Swanson (Eds.), *Challenges for rural American in the twenty-first century* (pp. 118–31). The Pennsylvania State University Press. http://doi.org/10.5325/j.ctv14gp32b.15

References

Jentz, B. (2009). First time in a position of authority. *Phi Delta Kappan*, *91*(1), 56–60. https://doi.org/10.1177/003172170909100110

Ji, Q., Li, J., & Sun, X. (2019). New challenge and research development in global energy financialization. *Emerging Markets, Finance and Trade*, *55*(2), 2669–72. https://doi.org/10.1080/1540496x.2019.1636588

Jimenez, B. A., Mims, P. J., & Baker, J. (2016). The effects of an online data-based decisions professional development for inservice teachers of students with significant disability. *Rural Special Education Quarterly*, *35*(3), 30–40. https://doi.org/10.1177/875687051603500305

Jimerson, L. (2003). *The competitive disadvantage: Teacher compensation in rural America* [Policy brief]. Rural School and Community Trust. https://www.ruraledu.org/articles.php?id=2064

Jimerson, L. (2004). *The devil is in the details: Rural-sensitive best practices for accountability under No Child Left Behind* [Policy brief]. Rural School and Community Trust. https://www.ruraledu.org/user_uploads/file/Devil_Is_in_the_Details.pdf

Jimerson, L. (2005a). *The impact of Arkansas' Act 60 consolidation on African-American school leadership and racial composition of school districts* [Policy brief]. Rural School and Community Trust. http://www.ruraledu.org/user_uploads/file/docs/Impact_of_Arkansas.pdf

Jimerson, L. (2005b). Placism in NCLB—How rural children are left behind. *Equity & Excellence in Education*, *38*(3), 211–19. https://doi.org/10.1080/10665680591002588

Jimerson, L. (2006). *The Hobbit effect: Why small works in public schools*. Rural Trust Policy Brief Series on Rural Education. Rural School and Community Trust. http://www.ruraledu.org/articles.php?id=2026

John, K. D., & Ford, D. R. (2017). The rural is nowhere: Bringing indigeneity and urbanism into educational research. In W. M. Reynolds (Ed.), *Forgotten places: Critical studies in rural education* (pp. 3–15). Peter Lang Publishing.

Johnson, A. (2018, November 8). Wisconsin School referendums break records in "landslide for public education". *Milwaukee Journal Sentinel*. https://www.jsonline.com/story/news/politics/elections/2018/11/08/wisconsin-election-school-referendums-break-records/1920426002/

Johnson, C. E., & Viramontez Anguiano, R. P. (2004). Latino parents in the rural Southeast: A study of family and school partnerships. *Journal of Family and Consumer Sciences*, *96*(4), 29–33.

Johnson, F. H. (1990). *Assigning type of locale codes to the 1987–88 CCD public school universe* [Paper presentation]. American Educational Research Association Annual Meeting. Boston, Massachusetts. https://eric.ed.gov/?id=ED312113

Johnson, J. (2007). School size, social justice, and conflicting state objectives: An investigation of achievement distributions among Kentucky public schools. *Education Leadership Review*, *8*(1), 51–64.

Johnson, J. D. (2014a). Durable issues in rural education. In C. B. Howley, A. Howley, & J. D. Johnson (Eds.), *Dynamics of social class, race, and place in rural education* (pp. 325–50). Information Age Publishing.

Johnson, J. D. (2014b). Grappling with constructs. In C. B. Howley, A. Howley, & J. D. Johnson (Eds.), *Dynamics of social class, race, and place in rural education* (pp. 1–18). Information Age Publishing.

Johnson, J. D., & Howley, C. B. (2015). Contemporary federal education policy and rural schools: A critical policy analysis. *Peabody Journal of Education*, *90*(2), 224–41. https://doi.org/10.1080/0161956X.2015.1022112

Johnson, J. D., Howley, C. B., & Howley, A. A. (2002). *Size, excellence, and equity: A report on Arkansas schools and districts*. Ohio University, Educational Studies Department. (ERIC Document Reproduction Service No. ED 459 987). https://eric.ed.gov/?id=ED459987

Johnson, J. D., Ohlson, M. A., & Shope, S. (2018). Demographic changes in rural America and the implications for special education programming: A descriptive and comparative analysis. *Rural Special Education Quarterly*, *37*(3), 140–9. https://doi.org/10.1177/8756870518771381

Johnson, J. D., & Strange, M. (2005). *Why rural matters 2005: The facts about rural education in the 50 states*. Rural School and Community Trust. http://www.ruraledu.org/articles.php?id=2092

References

Johnson, J. D., & Strange, M. (2009). *Why rural matters 2009: State and regional challenges and opportunities*. Rural School and Community Trust. http://www.ruraledu.org/articles.php?id=2312

Johnson, J. D., & Zoellner, B. P. (2016). School funding and rural districts. In S. M. Williams & A. A. Grooms (Eds.), *Educational opportunity in rural contexts: The politics of place* (pp. 3–20). Information Age Publishing.

Johnson, K. M. (2012, Winter). *Rural demographic change in the new century: Slower growth, increased diversity*. Issue Brief No. 44. Carsey Institute. University of New Hampshire. https://scholars.unh.edu/cgi/viewcontent.cgi?article=1158&context=carsey

Johnson, K. M., & Cromartie, J. (2006). The rural rebound and its aftermaths: Changing demographic dynamics and regional contrasts. In W. Kandel & D. L. Brown (Eds.), *Population change and rural society* (pp. 25–50). Springer.

Johnson, K. M., & Lichter, D. T. (2008). Natural increase: A new source of population growth in emerging Hispanic destinations in the United States. *Population and Development Review, 34*, 327–46. https://doi.org/10.1111/j.1728-4457.2008.00222.x

Johnson, K. M., & Lichter, D. T. (2013). Rural retirement destinations: Natural decrease and the shared demographic destinies of elderly and Hispanics. In N. Glasgow and E. Berry (Eds.), *Rural aging in 21st century America: Understanding population trends and processes* (pp. 275–94). Springer.

Johnson, K. M., & Lichter, D. T. (2019a). Rural depopulation: Growth and decline processes over the past century. *Rural Sociology, 84*(1), 3–27. https://doi.org/10.1111/ruso.12266

Johnson, K. M., & Lichter, D. T. (2019b). *Rural depopulation in a rapidly urbanizing America*. National Issue Brief #139. Carsey School of Public Policy. https://doi.org/10.34051/p/2020.347

Johnson, L., Mitchell, A. L., & Rotherham, A. (2014). *Federal education policy in rural America*. Rural Opportunities Consortium of Idaho. https://bellwethereducation.org/sites/default/files/ROCI_2014FedEdPolicy_Final.pdf

Johnson, S. B., Riley, A. W., Granger, D. A., & Riis, J. (2013). The science of early life toxic stress for pediatric practice and advocacy. *Pediatrics, 131*(2), 319–27.

Jones, S. M., McGarrah, M. W., & Kahn, J. (2019). Social and emotional learning: A principled science of human development in context. *Educational Psychologist, 54*, 129–43.

Kaestle, C. (1983). *Pillars of the Republic: Common schools and American society, 1780–1860*. Hill and Wang.

Kam, C. M., Greenberg, M. T., & Kusche, C. A. (2004). Sustained effects of the PATHS curriculum on the social and psychological adjustment of children in special education. *Journal of Emotional and Behavioral Disorders, 12*(2), 66–78. https://doi.org/10.1177/10634266040120020101

Kamrath, B., & Brunner, C. C. (2014). Blind spots: Small rural communities and high turnover in the superintendency. *Journal of School Leadership, 24*(3), 424–51. https://doi.org/10.1177/105268461402400302

Kandel, W., & Cromartie, J. (2004). *New patterns of Hispanic settlement in rural America* (No. 99). U.S. Department Agriculture, Economic Research Service.

Kandel, W., Henderson, J., Koball, H., & Capps, R. (2011). Moving up in rural America: Economic attainment of nonmetro Latino immigrants. *Rural Sociology, 76*(1), 101–28. https:doi.org/10.1111/j.1549-0831.2011.00047.x

Kania, J., Hanleybrown, F., & Splansky Juster, J. (2014). Essential mindset shifts for collective impact. *Stanford Social Innovation Review: Collective Insights on Collective Impact* (Sponsored supplement), 2–5. https://ssir.org/articles/entry/essential_mindset_shifts_for_collective_impact

Kania, J., & Kramer, M. (2011). Collective impact. *Stanford Social Innovation Review, 9*(1), 36–41. https://ssir.org/articles/entry/collective_impact

Kania, J., & Kramer, M. (2013). Embracing emergence: How collective impact addresses complexity. *Stanford Social Innovation Review*. https://ssir.org/articles/entry/social_progress_through_collective_impact.

Kannapel, P., & DeYoung, A. (1999). The rural school problem in 1999: A review and critique of the literature. *Journal of Research in Rural Education, 15*(2), 67–79. https://jrre.psu.edu/sites/default/files/2019-08/15-2_4.pdf

Kaplan, R. B., & Baldauf, R. B. (2005). Language-in-education policy and planning. In E. Hinkel (Ed.), *Handbook of research in second language teaching and learning* (pp. 1013–34). Lawrence Erlbaum.

Kaplan, S. N. (2013). Depth and complexity. In C. M. Callahan & H. L. Hertberg-Davis (Eds.), *Fundamentals of gifted education: Considering multiple perspectives* (pp. 277–86). Routledge.

Karakaplan, M. U., & Kutlu, L. (2019). School district consolidation policies: Endogenous cost inefficiency and saving reversals. *Empirical Economics, 56*(5), 1729–68. https://doi.org/10.1007/s00181-017-1398-z

Kawagley, A. O., & Barnhardt, R. (1999). Education indigenous to place: Western science meets Indigenous reality. In G. Smith & D. Williams (Eds.), *Ecological education in action* (pp. 117–40). SUNY Press.

Keeney, C. B. (2018, February 28). *The Battle of Blair Mountain is still being waged.* The Cultural Landscape Foundation. https://tclf.org/battle-blair-mountain-still-being-waged

Keis, R. (2006). From principle to practice: Using children's literature to promote dialogue and facilitate the "coming to voice" in a rural Latino community. *Multicultural Perspectives, 8*(1), 13–19. https://doi.org/10.1207/s15327892mcp0801_3

Kelly, M. G., & Schafft, K. A. (2020). A "resource curse" for education?: Deepening education disparities in Pennsylvania's shale gas boomtowns. *Society & Natural Resources,* 1–17. https://doi.org/10.1080/08941920.2020.1728000

Kelsey, T., Hartman, W., Schafft, K. A., Borlu, Y., & Costanzo, C. (2012). *Marcellus Shale gas development and Pennsylvania school districts: What are the implications for school expenditures and tax revenues?* Marcellus Education Fact Sheet. Penn State Cooperative Extension.

Kemmis, D. (1992). *Community and the politics of place.* University of Oklahoma Press.

Kemp, S. (2016, January/February). A perfect storm. *Wisconsin School News,* 14–17. https://wasb.org/wp-content/uploads/2017/03/perfect_storm_JanFeb_2016.pdf

Kemp, S. (2019, September 9). *Why more Wisconsin schools are enrolling fewer students. Wiscontext.* https://www.wiscontext.org/print/why-more-wisconsin-schools-are-enrolling-fewer-students

Kena, G., Hussar, W., McFarland, J., de Brey, C., Musu-Gillette, L., Wang, X., Zhang, J., Rathbun, A., Wilkinson Flicker, S., Diliberti, M., Barmer, A., Bullock Mann, F., & Dunlop Velez, E. (2016). *The Condition of Education 2016* (NCES 2016–144). U.S. Department of Education, National Center for Education Statistics. https://nces.ed.gov/pubs2016/2016144.pdf

Kendi, I. X. (2019). *How to be an antiracist.* One world.

Kennedy, A., Schafft, K. A., & Howard, T. (2017). Taking away David's sling: Environmental justice in land use conflicts over natural resource extraction in Australia's Mount Thorley-Warkworth open-cut coal mine and Pennsylvania's Marcellus Shale gas fields. *Local Environment, 22*(8), 952–68. https://doi.org/10.1080/13549839.2017.1309369

Keough, W. F., Jr. (1974, February). Fence mending after the strike (Report No. 139-080) [Paper presentation]. Annual Meeting of American Association of School Administrators.

Kerr, K., Dyson, A., & Raffo, C. (2014). *Education, disadvantage and place: Making the local matter.* Policy Press.

Keys, A. (2015). Family engagement in rural and urban Head Start families: An exploratory study. *Early Childhood Education Journal, 43,* 69–76. https://doi.org/10.1007/s10643-014-0643-8

Khattri, N., Riley, K. W., & Kane, M. B. (1997). Students at risk in poor, rural areas: A review of the research. *Journal of Research in Rural Education, 13*(2), 79–100. https://jrre.psu.edu/sites/default/files/2019-08/13-2_5.pdf

Killian, J. E., & Byrd, D. M. (1988). Tapping the strengths of rural schools: An exemplary staff development model [Paper presentation]. Annual Meeting of the National Staff Development Council. https://files.eric.ed.gov/fulltext/ED308051.pdf

Kilpatrick, S., & Abbott-Chapman, J. (2002). Rural young people's work/study priorities and aspirations: The influence of family social capital. *The Australian Educational Researcher, 29*(1), 43–67.

Kim-Prieto, C., Goldstein, L. A., Okazaki, S., & Kirschner, B. (2010). Effect of exposure to an American Indian mascot on the tendency to stereotype a different minority group. *Journal of Applied Social Psychology, 40*(3), 534–53. https://doi.org/10.1111/j.1559-1816.2010.00586.x

References

Kirst, M. W. (2008). The evolving role of school boards: Retrospect and prospect. In T. L. Alsbury (Ed.), *The future of school board governance: Relevancy and revelation* (pp. 37–59). Rowman & Littlefield.

Klar, H. W., Huggins, K. S., Andreoli, P. M., & Buskey, F. C. (2019). Developing rural school leaders through leadership coaching: A transformative approach. *Leadership and Policy in Schools*, 1–21. https://doi.org/10.1080/15700763.2019.1585553

Klein, N. (2014). *This changes everything*. Simon and Schuster.

Klein, R., & Johnson, J. (2010). On the use of locale in understanding the mathematics achievement gap. In P. Brosnan, D. B. Erchick, & L. Flevares (Eds.), *Proceedings of the 32nd annual meeting of the North American chapter of the International Group for the Psychology of Mathematics Education* (pp. 489–96). https://www.pmena.org/pmenaproceedings/PMENA%2032%202010%20Proceedings.pdf

Kline, J., & Walker-Gibbs, B. (2015). Graduate teacher preparation for rural schools in Victoria and Queensland. *Australian Journal of Teacher Education*, *40*(3), 68–88. https://doi.org/10.14221/ajte.2014v40n3.5

Kmetz, M. (2012). A river runs by it: The performance of rural civic ethos in the Wind River water disputes. In K. Donehower, C. Hogg, & E. E. Schell (Eds.), *Reclaiming the rural: Essays on literacy, rhetoric, and pedagogy* (pp. 17–33). Southern Illinois University Press.

Knoche, L. L., Edwards, C. P., Sheridan, S. M., Kupzyk, K. A., Marvin, C. A., Cline, K. D., & Clarke, B. L. (2012). Getting ready: Results of a randomized trial of a relationship-focused intervention on parent engagement in rural Early Head Start. *Infant Mental Health Journal*, *33*, 439–58. https://doi.org/10.1002/imhj.2132

Ko, S. J., Ford, J. D., Kassam-Adams, N., Berkowitz, S. J., Wilson, C., Wong, M., Brymer, M. J., & Layne, C. M. (2008). Creating trauma-informed systems: Child welfare, education, first responders, health care, juvenile justice. *Professional Psychology: Research and Practice*, *39*(4), 396–404.

Koenig, M., & de Varennes, F. (Ed.). (2001). Lesser used languages and the law in Europe [Special issue]. *International Journal on Multicultural Societies*, *3*(1). https://unesdoc.unesco.org/ark:/48223/pf0000143789

Koenig Kellas, J., & Trees, A. R. (2006). Finding meaning in difficult family experiences: Sense-making and interaction processes during joint family storytelling. *The Journal of Family Communication*, *6*(1), 49–76. https://doi.org/10.1207/s15327698jfc0601_4

Koreishi, S., & Donohoe, M. T. (2010). Historical and contemporary factors contributing to the plight of migrant farmworkers in the United States. *Social Medicine*, *5*(1), 64–73.

Koricich, A., Chen, X., & Hughes, R. P. (2018). Understanding the effects of rurality and socioeconomic status on college attendance and institutional choice in the United States. *The Review of Higher Education*, *41*(2), 281–305. https://doi.org/10.1353/rhe.2018.0004

Kotras, M. J., Sharp, E. H., Dolan, E. M., & Baron, L. A. (2014). Non-standard work and rural low-income mothers: Making it work. *Journal of Family and Economic Issues*, *36*, 84–96. https://doi.org/10.1007/s10834-018-9596-1

Kovács, K. (2020). Turbulent times and reshaped rural school network in Hungary. In C. Gristy, L. Hargreaves, & S. R. Kučerová (Eds.), *Educational research and schooling in rural Europe: An engagement with changing patterns of education, space, and place* (pp. 79–102). Information Age Publishing.

Kowalski, T. J., McCord, R. S., Peterson, G. J., Young, P. I., & Ellerson, N. M. (2011). *The American school superintendent: 2010 decennial study*. Rowan & Littlefield Education.

Koziol, N. A., Arthur, A. M., Hawley, L. R., Bovaird, J. A., Bash, K. L., McCormick, C., & Welch, G. W. (2015). Identifying, analyzing, and communicating rural: A quantitative perspective. *Journal of Research in Rural Education*, *30*(4), 1–14. https://jrre.psu.edu/sites/default/files/2019-08/30-4.pdf

Krause, M. (2013). The ruralization of the world. *Public Culture*, *25*(2), 233–48.

Krumm, B. L., & Curry, K. (2017). Traversing school–community partnerships utilizing cross-boundary leadership. *School Community Journal*, *27*(2), 99–120.

Kubiak, P. M. (1985). An annotated bibliography of the literature dealing with the question of whether teachers as professionals are justified in striking to achieve their goals. (Report No. 263-063). Exit Project, Indiana University at South Bend.

Kučerová, S. R., Meyer, P., & Trahorsch, P. (2020). Factors influencing elementary education systems in selected European countries. In C. Gristy, L. Hargreaves, & S. R. Kučerová (Eds.), *Educational research and schooling in rural Europe: An engagement with changing patterns of education, space, and place* (pp. 21–48). Information Age Publishing.

Kučerová, S. R., & Trnková, K. (2020). A consideration of Czech rural schools from different scales: From centrally directed to autonomous educational policies. In C. Gristy, L. Hargreaves, & S. R. Kučerová (Eds.), *Educational research and schooling in rural Europe: An engagement with changing patterns of education, space, and place* (pp. 103–24). Information Age Publishing.

Kuehl, R. (2020). *Fourth-grade narrative fiction writing: Using content analysis to examine the intersection of place, high ability, and creativity* [Doctoral dissertation, Virginia Tech]. VtechWorks. http://hdl.handle.net/10919/97918

Kuehl, R. (2021). Rural families through the eyes of fourth-grade fiction writers. In A. P. Azano & C. M. Callahan (Eds.), *Gifted education in rural schools: Developing place-based interventions* (pp. 176–85). Routledge.

Kuehl, R., Azano, A. P., & Callahan, C. M. (2020). Gifted rural writers explore place in narrative fiction stories. *Theory & Practice in Rural Education, 10*(2), 26–45. https://doi.org/10.3776/tpre.2020.v10n2p26-45

Kurtzleben, D. (2016). Rural voters played a big part in helping Trump defeat Clinton. *NPR.* https://www.npr.org/2016/11/14/501737150/rural-voters-played-a-big-part-in-helping-trump-defeat-clinton

Kuzemko, C., Bradshaw, M., Bridge, G., Goldthau, A., Jewell, J., Overland, I., Scholten, D., Van de Graaf, T., & Westphal, K. (2020). Covid-19 and the politics of sustainable energy transitions. *Energy Research & Social Science, 68*, 1–7. https://doi.org/10.1016/j.erss.2020.101685

Kuziemko, I. (2006). Using shocks to school enrollment to estimate the effect of school size on student achievement. *Economics of Education Review, 25*(1), 63–75. https://doi.org/10.1016/j.econedurev.2004.10.003

Kvalsund, R. (2020). Rural schools in an iron cage? Words for the reader. In C. Gristy, L. Hargreaves, & S. R. Kučerová (Eds.), *Educational research and schooling in rural Europe: An engagement with changing patterns of education, space, and place* (pp. xi–xxiii). Information Age Publishing.

Kvalsund R., & Hargreaves, L. (2009). Reviews of research on rural schools and their communities: Analytical perspectives and a new agenda. *International Journal of Educational Research, 48*(2), 140–9. https://doi.org/10.1016/j.ijer.2009.02.002

Ladd, H. F., Clotfelder, C. T., & Holbein, J. B. (2017). The growing segmentation of the charter school sector in North Carolina. *Education Finance and Policy, 12*(4), 536–63.

Ladson-Billings, G. (2003). *Critical race theory perspectives on the social studies: The profession, policies, and curriculum.* Information Age Publishing.

Lambert, D., Gale, J., & Hartley, D. (2008). Substance abuse by youth and young adults in rural America. *The Journal of Rural Health, 24*(3), 221–8.

Lambert, D. M., Clark, C. D., Wilcox, M. D., & Park, W. M. (2009). Public education financing trends and the grey peril hypothesis. *Growth and Change, 40*(4), 619–48. https://doi.org/10.1111/j.1468-2257.2009.00503.x

Landry, S. H., Smith, K. E., & Swank, P. R. (2003). The importance of parenting during early childhood for school-age development. *Developmental Neuropsychology, 24*, 559–91. https://doi.org/10.1080/87565641.2003.9651911

Lane, K. L., Carter, E. W., Jenkins, A., Dwiggins, L., & Germer, K. (2015). Supporting comprehensive, integrated, three-tiered models of prevention in schools: Administrators' perspectives. *Journal of Positive Behavior Interventions, 17*, 209–22. https://doi.org/10.1177/1098300715578916

Lapayese, Y., Aldana, U., & Lara, E. (2014). A racio-economic analysis of Teach for America: Counterstories of TFA teachers of color. *Perspectives on Urban Education, 11*(1), 11–25.

Larkin, H., Shields, J. J., & Anda, R. F. (2012). The health and social consequences of Adverse Childhood Experiences (ACE) across the lifespan: An introduction to prevention and intervention in the community. *Journal of Prevention & Intervention in the Community, 40*(4), 263–70.

Larsen, S. C., & Johnson, J. T. (2017). *Being together in place: Indigenous coexistence in a more than human world.* University of Minnesota Press. http://www.jstor.org/stable/10.5749/j.ctt1pwt81r

References

Larson, D. (2018, January 25). Racist chants reported at Storm Lake, Spencer high school basketball games. *Globe gazette*. https://globegazette.com/news/iowa/racist-chants-reported-at-storm-lake-spencer-high-school-basketball/article_2a173cf5-c2af-5323-b5d8-5ca5bf979d8f.html

Larson, N. C., & Dearmont, M. (2002). Strengths of farming communities in fostering resilience in children. *Child Welfare League of America, 81*, 821–35.

Latterman, K., & Steffes, S. (2017). Tackling teacher and principal shortages in rural areas. *Legis Brief, 25*(40). https://www.ncsl.org/research/education/tackling-teacher-and-principal-shortages-in-rural-areas.aspx

Lau v. Nichols, 414 U.S. 563 (1974).

Lavalley, M. (2018, January). *Out of the loop: Rural schools are largely left out of research and policy discussions, exacerbating poverty, inequity, and isolation.* Center for Public Education. https://education.wsu.edu/documents/2018/12/center-public-education-rural-schools-report.pdf/

Lawrence, B. K. (2009). Rural gifted education: A comprehensive literature review. *Journal for the Education of the Gifted, 32*(4), 461–94. https://doi.org/10.1177/016235320903200402

Lawrence, B. K., Bingler, S., Diamond, B., Hill, B., Hoffman, J., Howley, C., Mitchell, S., Rudolph, E., & Washor, D. (2002). *Dollars and sense: The cost effectiveness of small schools.* Knowledge Works & The Rural School and Community Trust.

Lawson, H. A. (2004). The logic of collaboration in education and the human services. *Journal of Interprofessional Care, 18*(3), 225–37.

Lawson, H. A. (2013). Third-generation partnerships for P-16 pipelines and cradle-through-career education systems. *Peabody Journal of Education, 88*(5), 637–56. https://doi.org/10.1080/01619 56x.2013.835187

Lawson, H. A., Alameda-Lawson, T., Lawson, M., Briar-Lawson, K., & Wilcox, K. (2014). Three parent and family interventions for rural schools and communities. *Journal of Education and Human Development, 3*(3), 59–78. https://doi.org/10.15640/jehd.v3n3a5

Lawson, V., Jarosz, L., & Bonds, A. (2008). Building economies from the bottom up: (Mis)representations of poverty in the rural American Northwest. *Social and Cultural Geography, 9*(7), 737–53. https://doi.org/10.1080/14649360802382354

Leavitt, P. A., Covarrubias, R., Perez, Y. A., & Fryberg, S. A. (2015). "Frozen in time": The impact of Native American media representations on identity and self-understanding. *Journal of Social Issues, 71*(1), 39–53. https://doi.org/10.1111/josi.12095

LeChasseur, K. (2014). Critical race theory and the meaning of "community" in district partnerships. *Equity & Excellence in Education, 47*(3), 305–20. https://doi.org/10.1080/10665684.2014.933069

Lee, A. (2018). *U.S. poverty thresholds and poverty guidelines: What's the difference?* Population Reference Bureau. https://www.prb.org/insight/u-s-poverty-thresholds-and-poverty-guidelines-whats-the-difference/

Lee, R., & Ahtone, T. (2020, March 30). Land-grab universities. *High Country News*. https://www.hcn.org/issues/52.4/indigenous-affairs-education-land-grab-universities

Lee, S. W., Lohmeier, J. H., Niileksela, C., & Oeth, J. (2009). Rural schools' mental health needs: Educators' perceptions of mental health needs and services in rural schools. *Rural Mental Health, 33*(1), 26–31.

Lee, T. S., & McCarty, T. L. (2017). Upholding Indigenous education sovereignty through critical culturally sustaining/revitalizing pedagogy. In D. Paris & H. S. Alim (Eds.), *Culturally sustaining pedagogies: Teaching and learning for justice in a changing world* (pp. 61–82). Teachers College Press.

Lefebvre, H. (1970). *The production of space.* Blackwell.

Lefebvre, H. (2003). *The urban revolution.* University of Minnesota Press.

Leithwood, K., Patten, S., & Jantzi, D. (2010). Testing a conception of how school leadership influences student learning. *Educational Administration Quarterly, 46*(5), 671–706. https://doi.org/10.1177/0013161X10377347

Leonardo, Z. (2009). *Race, Whiteness, and education.* Routledge.

References

Leonardo, Z., & Porter, R. K. (2010). Pedagogy of fear: Toward a Fanonian theory of "safety" in race dialogues. *Race, Ethnicity, and Education, 13*(2), 139–57.

Leopold, A. (1949). *A Sand County almanac.* Oxford University Press.

Lesnick, J., Goerge, R., Smithgall, C., & Gwynne J. (2010). *Reading on grade level in third grade: How is it related to high school performance and college enrollment?* Chapin Hall at the University of Chicago.

Levin, J., Manship, K., Chambers, J., Johnson, J., & Blankenship, C. (2011). *Do schools in rural and nonrural districts allocate resources differently? An analysis of spending and staffing patterns in the West Region states.* (Issues & Answers Report, REL 2011–No. 099). U.S. Department of Education, Institute of Education Sciences, National Center for Education Evaluation and Regional Assistance, Regional Educational Laboratory West. https://files.eric.ed.gov/fulltext/ED515211.pdf

Levin, S., & Bradley, K. (2019). *Understanding and addressing principal turnover: A review of the research.* National Association of Secondary School Principals.

Lewis, D. R. (1994). *Neither wolf nor dog: American Indians, environment, and agrarian change.* Oxford University Press.

Lewis, L., & Gray, L. (2016). *Programs and services for high school English Learners in public school districts: 2015–16.* U.S. Department of Education. National Center for Education Statistics. https://nces.ed.gov/pubs2016/2016150.pdf

Ley, J., Nelson, S., & Beltyukova, S. (1996). Congruence of aspirations of rural youth with expectations held by parents and school staff. *Journal of Research in Rural Education, 12*(3), 133–41. https://jrre.psu.edu/sites/default/files/2019-08/12-3_3.pdf

Li, X. (2019). Challenging both rural advantage and disadvantage narratives: The effects of family factors on American student college expectations in the early 2010s. *Journal of Research in Rural Education, 35*(5), 1–16. https://jrre.psu.edu/sites/default/files/2019-07/35-5_0.pdf

Lichter, D. T. (2012). Immigration and the new racial diversity in rural America. *Rural Sociology, 77*(1), 3–35. https://doi.org/10.1111/j.1549-0831.2012.00070.x

Lichter, D. T., & Brown, D. L. (2011). Rural America in an urban society: Changing spatial and social boundaries. *Annual Review of Sociology, 37,* 565–92. https://doi.org/10.1146/annurev-soc-081309-150208

Lichter, D. T., & Graefe, D. R. (2011). Rural economic restructuring: Implications for children, youth, and families. In K. E. Smith & A. R. Tickamyer (Eds.), *Economic restructuring and family well-being in rural America* (pp. 25–39). The Pennsylvania State University Press.

Lichter, D. T., & Parisi, D. (2008). Concentrated rural poverty and the geography of exclusion [Policy brief]. Carsey Institute. https://doi.org/10.34051/p/2020.55

Lichter, D. T., Parisi, D., & Taquino, M. C. (2012). The geography of exclusion: Race, segregation, and concentrated poverty. *Social Problems, 59*(3), 364–88. https://doi.org/10.1111/cico.12314

Lichter, D. T., Parisi, D., & Taquino, M. C. (2016). Emerging patterns of Hispanic residential segregation: Lessons from rural and small-town America. *Rural Sociology, 81*(4), 483–518. https://doi.org/10.1111/ruso.12108

Lichter, D. T., Parisi, D., & Taquino, M. C. (2018). White integration or segregation? The racial and ethnic transformation of rural and small town America. *City & Community, 17*(3), 702–19. https://doi.org/10.1111/cico.12314

Lichter, D. T., & Schafft, K. A. (2016). People and places left behind: Rural poverty in the new century. In D. Brady & L. M. Burton (Eds.), *The Oxford handbook of the social science of poverty* (pp. 317–40). Oxford University Press. https://doi.org/10.1093/oxfordhb/9780199914050.013.15

Lingard, B. (2010). Policy borrowing, policy learning: Testing times in Australian schooling. *Critical studies in education, 51*(2), 129–47. https:doi.org/10.1080/17508481003731026

Lipman, P. (2011). *The new political economy of urban education: Neoliberalism, race, and the right to the city.* Routledge.

Lipscomb, A. A., & Bergh, A. E. (Eds.). (1903). *The writings of Thomas Jefferson* (Vol. 15). Washington, DC.

Logan, J. R., & Burdick-Will, J. (2016). School segregation, charter schools, and access to quality education. *Journal of Urban Affairs, 38*(3), 323–42. https://doi.org/10.1111/juaf.12246

References

Logan, J. R., & Burdick-Will, J. (2017). School segregation and disparities in urban, suburban, and rural areas. *The ANNALS of the American Academy of Political and Social Science, 674*(1), 199–216. https://doi.org/10.1177/0002716217733936

Lohman, D. F. (2013). Identifying gifted students: Nontraditional uses of traditional measures. In C. M. Callahan & H. L. Hertberg-Davis (Eds.), *Fundamentals of gifted education: Considering multiple perspectives* (pp. 112–27). Routledge.

Lomawaima, K. T. (1995). Educating Native Americans. In J. A. Banks & C. A. McGee Banks (Eds.), *Handbook of research on multicultural education* (pp. 331–47). Palgrave Macmillan.

Lomawaima, K. T. (1999). The unnatural history of American Indian education. In K. G. Swisher & J. W. Tippeconnic (Eds.), *Next steps: Research and practice to advance Indian education* (pp. 3–31). ERIC Clearinghouse on Rural Education and Small Schools.

Lomawaima, K. T., & McCarty, T. L. (2002). When tribal sovereignty challenges democracy: American Indian education and the democratic ideal. *American Educational Research Journal, 39*(2), 279–305. https://doi.org/10.3102/00028312039002279

Love, B. L. (2019). *We want to do more than survive: Abolitionist teaching and the pursuit of educational freedom*. Beacon Press.

Lovenheim, M. F. (2009). The effect of teachers' unions on education production: Evidence from union election certifications in three midwestern states. *Journal of Labor Economics, 27*(4), 525–87. https://doi.org/10.1086/605653

Luallen, J. (2006). School's out . . . forever: A study of juvenile crime, at-risk youths and teacher strikes. *Journal of Urban Economics, 59*(1), 75–103. https://www.journals.elsevier.com/journal-of-urban-economics.

Lubienski, C. A., & Lubienski, S. T. (2014). *The public school advantage: Why public schools outperform private schools*. The University of Chicago Press.

Luby, J., Belden, A., Botteron, K., Marrus, N., Harms, M. P., Babb, C., Nishino, T., & Barch, D. (2013). The effects of poverty on childhood brain development: The mediating effect of caregiving and stressful life events. *JAMA Pediatrics, 167*, 1135–42. https://doi.org/10.1001/jamapediatrics.2013.3139

Lucas, T. (2010). *Teacher preparation for linguistically diverse classrooms: Resources for teacher educators*. Routledge.

Luo, M., & Williams, J. E. (2013). Geographic characteristics and first-year retention: An examination of the linkages. *Journal of the First-Year Experience & Students in Transition, 25*(2), 77–94.

Lyons, S. R. (2000). Rhetorical sovereignty: What do American Indians want from writing? *College Composition and Communication, 51*(3), 447–68. https://doi.org/10.2307/358744

Lyson, T. A. (2002). What does a school mean to a community? Assessing the social and economic benefits of schools to rural villages in New York. *Journal of Research in Rural Education, 17*(3), 131–7. https://jrre.psu.edu/sites/default/files/2019-08/17-3_1.pdf

Lyson, T. A., & Falk, W. W. (Eds.). (1993). *Forgotten places: Uneven development in rural America*. University Press of Kansas.

Mackellar, D. (2010). *My Country*. Scholastic .

MacKinnon, C. T. (2001). Viewing school facilities as community development projects: The case of Hinesburg, Vermont. *Small Town, 30*(2), 28–31.

Macrine, S. L. (2016). Pedagogies of neoliberalism. In S. Springer, K. Birch, & J. MacLeavy (Eds.), *The handbook of neoliberalism* (pp. 308–19). Routledge.

MacSwan, J., Thompson, M. S., Rolstad, K., McAlister, K., & Lobo, G. (2017). Three theories of the effects of language education programs: An empirical evaluation of bilingual and English-only policies. *Annual Review of Applied Linguistics, 37*, 218–40.

Mader, J. (2018). *Rural children often go without critical mental health treatment*. The Hechinger Report. https://hechingerreport.org/rural-children-often-without-critical-mental-health-treatment/

Madison, J., Hamilton, A., & Jay, J. (1961). *The Federalist*. Penguin Books.

Magnuson, K., & Duncan, G. J. (2016). Early childhood interventions decrease inequality of economic opportunity. *The Russell Sage Foundation Journal of the Social Sciences, 2*(2), 123–41. https://doi.org/10.7758/rsf.2016.2.2.05

References

Magnusson, D., & Cairns, R. B. (1996). Developmental science: Principles and illustrations. In R. B. Cairns, G. H. Elder, Jr., & J. Costello (Eds.), *Developmental science* (pp. 7–30). Cambridge University Press.

Malatzky, C., Mitchell, O., & Bourke, L. (2018). Improving inclusion in rural health services for marginalised community members: Developing a process for change. *Journal of Social Inclusion, 9*(1), 21–36.

Malik, R., Hamm, K., Adamu, M., & Morrissey, T. (2016, October 27). *Child care deserts: An analysis of child care centers by ZIP codes in eight states.* Center for American Progress. https://www.americanprogress.org/issues/early-childhood/reports/2016/10/27/225703/child-care-deserts/

Malik, R., Hamm, K., Schochet, L., Novoa, C., Workman, S., & Jessen-Howard, S. (2018). *America's child care deserts in 2018.* Center for American Progress. https://www.americanprogress.org/issues/early-childhood/reports/2018/12/06/461643/americas-child-care-deserts-2018/

Maltzan, T. L. (2006). *Rurality and higher education: Implications for identity and persistence* [Unpublished doctoral dissertation]. The Ohio State University.

Mandeel, E. W. (2014). The Bracero program 1942–1964. *American International Journal of Contemporary Research, 4*(1), 171–84. https://doi.org/10.1093/acrefore/9780199366439.013.590

Mann, B., Kotok, S., Frankenberg, E., Fuller, E., & Schafft, K. A. (2016). Choice, charter schools, and the educational marketplace for rural schools in Pennsylvania. *The Rural Educator, 37*(3), 17–29. https://doi.org/10.35608/ruraled.v37i3.248

Mann, C. (2014). The role of philanthropy in collective impact. *The Philanthropist, 26*(1), 55–64.

Maranto, R., & Shuls, J. V. (2011). Lessons from KIPP Delta. *The Phi Delta Kappan, 93*(3), 52–6. https://doi.org/10.1177/003172171109300313

Maranto, R., & Shuls, J. V. (2013). How do we get them on the farm? Efforts to improve rural teacher recruitment and retention in Arkansas. *The Rural Educator, 34*(1). https://doi.org/10.35608/ruraled.v34i1.406

Marema, T., & Bishop, B. (2020, June 26). Rural counties set record for new cases of covid-19. *The Daily Yonder.* https://dailyyonder.com/rural-counties-set-record-for-new-cases-of-covid-19/2020/06/26/

Marré, A. (2017). *Rural education at a glance* (No. 1476-2017-3899). United States Department of Agriculture.

Marré, A., & Rupasingha, A. (2020). School quality and rural in-migration: Can better rural schools attract new residents? Journal of Regional Science, *60,* 156–73. https://doi.org/10.1111/jors.12437

Martin, J. C. (1980). Amazing and inevitable: Observations on a teacher strike. *Kappa Delta Pi Record, 17*(2), 51–4. https://doi.org/10.1080/00228958.1980.10518270

Marvin, C. A., Moen, A. L., Knoche, L. L., & Sheridan, S. M. (2020). Getting Ready strategies for promoting parent–professional relationships and parent–child interactions. *Young Exceptional Children, 23*(1), 36–51. https://doi.org/10.1177/1096250619829744

Massey, D. S. (Ed.). (2008). *New faces in new places: The changing geography of American immigration.* Russell Sage Foundation.

Massey, D. S. (2020). Creating the exclusionist society: From the war on poverty to the war on immigrants. *Ethnic and Racial Studies, 43*(1), 18–37. https://doi.org/10.1080/01419870.2019.1667504

Massey, D. S., & Denton, N. A. (1993). *American apartheid: Segregation and the making of the underclass.* Harvard University Press.

Massey, D. S., Durand, J., & Pren, K. A. (2015). Border enforcement and return migration by undocumented Mexicans. *Journal of Ethnic and Migration Studies, 41*(7), 1015–40. https://doi.org/10.1080/1369183x.2014.986079

Masta, S. (2018). What the grandfathers taught me: Lessons for an Indian country researcher. *The Qualitative Report, 23*(4), 841–52.

Masumoto, M., & Brown-Welty, S. (2009). Case study of leadership practices and school-community interrelationships in high-performing, high-poverty, rural California high schools. *Journal of Research in Rural Education, 24*(1), 1–18. https://jrre.psu.edu/sites/default/files/2019-08/24-1.pdf

Mathema, S., Svajlenka, N. P., & Hermann, A. (2018). *Revival and opportunity: Immigrants in rural America.* Center for American Progress. https://www.americanprogress.org/issues/immigration/reports/2018/09/02/455269/ revival-and-opportunity/

References

Mattingly, P. H., & Stevens, E. W. (1987). *Schools and the means of education shall forever be encouraged: A history of education in the Old Northwest, 1787–1880.* Ohio University Libraries.

Matz, J., & Renfrew, D. (2015). Selling "fracking": Energy in depth and the Marcellus Shale. *Environmental Communication, 9*(3), 288–306. https://doi.org/10.1080/17524032.2014.929157

Maxwell, G. M., Locke, L. A., & Scheurich, J. J. (2014). The rural social justice leader: An exploratory profile in resilience. *Journal of School Leadership, 24*(3), 482–508. https://doi.org/10.1177/105268461402400304

Mayer, A., Malin, S. A., & Olson-Hazboun, S. K. (2018). Unhollowing rural America? Rural human capital flight and the demographic consequences of the oil and gas boom. *Population and Environment, 39*, 219–38. https://doi.org/10.1007/s11111-017-0288-9

Mayer, D. (2014). Forty years of teacher education in Australia: 1974–2014. *Journal of Education for Teaching, 40*(5), 461–73.

McCabe, L. A., & Sipple, J. W. (2011). Colliding worlds: Practical and political tensions of prekindergarten implementation in public schools. *Educational Policy, 25*(1), e1–e26.

McCarroll, M. (2019). On and on: Appalachian accent and academic power. In A. Harkins & M. McCarroll (Eds.), *Appalachian reckoning: A region responds to* Hillbilly Elegy (pp. 249–53). West Virginia University Press.

McCauley, L. (2018, November 19). Residents, native leaders ask Skowhegan school board to finally retire racist mascot. *Maine Beacon.* https://mainebeacon.com/residents-native-leaders-ask-skowhegan-school-board-to-finally-retire-racist-mascot/

McCollow, J. (2017). Teacher Unions. *Oxford Research Encyclopedia of Education.* https://doi.org/10.1093/acrefore/9780190264093.013.201

McCollum, J. A., & Yates, T. J. (1994). Dyad as focus, triad as means: A family-centered approach to supporting parent–child interactions. *Infants and Young Children, 6*, 54–63. https://doi.org/10.1097/00001163-199404000-00008

McCoy, M. L. (2005). *The evolution of tribal sovereignty over education in federal law since 1965* (Indian Education Legal Support Project: Tribalizing Indian Education). Native American Rights Fund. http://www.narf.org/wordpress/wp-content/uploads/2015/01/gold.pdf

McDermott, K. A. (2003). What causes variation in states' accountability policies? *Peabody Journal of Education, 78*(4), 153–76. https://doi.org/10.1207/s15327930pje7804_08

McDermott, K. A., & Jensen, L. S. (2005). Dubious sovereignty: Federal conditions of aid and the No Child Left Behind Act. *Peabody Journal of Education, 80*(2), 39–56. https://doi.org/10.1207/S15327930pje8002_3

McDonald, J., & Klein, E. (2003). Networking for teacher learning: Toward a theory of effective design. *Teachers College Record, 105*(8), 1606–21. https://www.montclair.edu/profilepages/media/1411/user/Networking_for_Teacher_Learning.pdf

McDonald, T. (2018). School closure and loss: Guiding a district through the change process. *Journal of Cases in Educational Leadership, 21*(2), 15–27. https://doi.org/10.1177/1555458917728757

McDonough, P. M., Gildersleeve, R. E., & Jarsky, K. M. (2010). The golden cage of rural college access: How higher education can respond to the rural life. In K. Schafft & A. Y. Jackson (Eds.), *Rural education for the twenty-first century: Identity, place and community in a globalizing world* (pp. 191–209). The Pennsylvania State University Press.

McFarland, J., Hussar, B., Zhang, J., Wang, X., Wang, K., Hein, S., Diliberti, M., Forrest Cataldi, E., Bullock Mann, F., & Barmer, A. (2019). *The condition of education.* National Center for Education Statistics. https://nces.ed.gov/programs/coe/

McGranahan, D., Cromartie, J., & Wojan, T. (2010). *Nonmetropolitan outmigration counties: Some are poor, many are prosperous.* Economic Research Report No. (ERR-107). U.S. Department of Agriculture Economic Research Service. https://doi.org/10.2139/ssrn.1711309

McHenry-Sorber, E. (2014). The power of competing narratives: A new interpretation of rural school–community relations. *Peabody Journal of Education, 89*(5), 580–92. https://doi.org/10.1080/0161956X.2014.956520

McHenry-Sorber, E. (2018, March 6). The West Virginia teachers have launched a movement. *CNN*. https://www.cnn.com/2018/03/06/opinions/west-virginia-teachers-oklahoma-strike-rural-education-mchenry-sorber-opinion/index.html

McHenry-Sorber, E. (2019, January 15). 3 Reasons to pay attention to the L.A. teacher strike. *The Conversation*. http://theconversation.com/3-reasons-to-payattention-to-the-la-teacher-strike-109766

McHenry-Sorber, E., & Budge, K. (2018). Revisiting the rural superintendency: Rethinking guiding theories for contemporary practice. *Journal of Research in Rural Education, 33*(3), 1–15. https://jrre.psu.edu/sites/default/files/2019-08/33-3.pdf

McHenry-Sorber, E., & Provinzano, K. (2017). Confronting rapid change: Exploring the practices of educational leaders in a rural boomtown. *Leadership and Policy in Schools, 16*(4), 602–28. http://dx.doi.org/10.1080/15700763.2016.1232833

McHenry-Sorber, E., & Schafft, K. A. (2015). "Make My Day, Shoot a Teacher": Tactics of inclusion and exclusion, and the contestation of community in a rural school–community conflict. *International Journal of Inclusive Education, 19*(7), 733–47. https://doi.org/10.1080/13603116.2014.964571

McHenry-Sorber, E., & Sutherland, D. H. (2020). Metaphors of place-conscious leadership in the multidistrict superintendency: Negotiating tensions of place-consciousness and district-wide goal attainment. *Journal of School Leadership, 30*(2), 105–26. https://doi.org/10.1177/1052684619852693

McInerney, P., Smyth, J., & Down, B. (2011). "Coming to a place near you?" The politics and possibilities of a critical pedagogy of place-based education. *Asia-Pacific Journal of Teacher Education, 39*(1), 3–16. https://doi.org/10.1080/1359866x.2010.540894

McKeough, A., & Genereux, R. (2003). Transformation in narrative thought during adolescence: The structure and content of story compositions. *Journal of Educational Psychology, 95*(3), 537–52. https://doi.org/10.1037/0022-0663.95.3.537

McLean, B. (2018). *Saudi America: The truth about fracking and how it is changing the world*. Columbia Global Reports.

McShane, M. Q., & Smarick, A. (Eds.). (2018). *No longer forgotten*. Rowman & Littlefield.

Meaney, M. J. (2010). Epigenetics and the biological definition of gene x environment interactions. *Child Development, 81*(1), 41–79. https://doi.org/10.1111/j.1467-8624.2009.01381.x

Means, A. J. (2013). *Schooling in the age of austerity*. Palgrave Macmillan.

Means, D. R. (2018). *Supporting the pathways to postsecondary education for rural students: Challenges, opportunities, and strategies for moving forward*. National Association for College Admission Counseling. https://www.nacacnet.org/news--publications/Research/supporting-the-pathways-to-postsecondary-education-for-rural-students/

Means, D. R. (2019). Crucial support, vital aspirations: The college and career aspirations of rural Black and Latinx middle school students in a community- and youth-based leadership program. *Journal of Research in Rural Education, 35*(1), 1–14. https://jrre.psu.edu/sites/default/files/2019-06/35-1.pdf

Means, D. R., Clayton, A. B., Conzelmann, J. G., Baynes, P., & Umbach, P. D. (2016). Bounded aspirations: Rural, African American high school students and college access. *The Review of Higher Education, 39*(4), 543–69. https://doi.org/10.1353/rhe.2016.0035

Meece, J. L., Askew, K. S., Agger, C. A., Hutchins, B. C., & Byun, S. (2014). Familial and economic influences on the gender-related educational and occupational aspirations of rural adolescents. *Journal of Educational and Developmental Psychology, 4*(1), 238–57. https://doi.org/10.5539/jedp.v4n1p238.

Meece, J. L., Hutchins, B. C., Byun, S., Farmer, T. W., Irvin, M. J., & Weiss, M. (2013). Preparing for adulthood: A recent examination of the alignment of rural youth's future educational and vocational aspirations. *Journal of Educational and Developmental Psychology, 3*(2), 175–92. https://doi.org/10.5539/jedp.v3n2p175

Mendelson, T., Tandon, S. D., O'Brennan, L., Leaf, P. J., & Ialongo, N. S. (2015). Moving prevention into schools: The impact of a trauma-informed school-based intervention. *Journal of Adolescence, 43*, 142–7.

Mendiola, B., & Sun, J. (2018). Preparing bold, visionary leaders for school turnaround. In E. H. Reames (Ed.), *Rural turnaround leadership development: The power of partnerships* (pp. 45–65). Information Age Publishing.

References

Menzies, K. (2019). Understanding the Australian Aboriginal experience of collective, historical and intergenerational trauma. *International Social Work*, *62*(6), 1522–34.

Mersky, J. P., Topitzes, J., & Reynolds, A. J. (2013). Impacts of adverse childhood experiences on health, mental health, and substance use in early adulthood: A cohort study of an urban, minority sample in the U.S. *Child Abuse & Neglect*, *37*(11), 917–25.

Michael, K. D., Albright, A., Jameson, J. P., Sale, R., Kirk, A., Massey, C., & Egan, T. (2013). Does cognitive-behavioral therapy in the context of a rural school mental health program have an impact on academic outcomes? *Advances in School Mental Health Promotion*, *6*(4), 247–62. https://doi.org/10.10 80/1754730X.2013.832006

Michael, K. D., Renkert, L. E., Wandler, J., & Stamey, T. (2009). Cultivating a new harvest: Rationale and preliminary results from a growing interdisciplinary rural school mental health program. *Advances in School Mental Health Promotion*, *2*(2), 40–50.

Miller, A. (2013). Consider Native American students in rural school consolidation. *Great Plains Research*, *23*(2), 137–9.

Miller, K. (2010). *Why definitions matter: Rural definitions and state poverty rankings*. Rural Policy Research Institute: Data Brief. http://www.rupri.org/Forms/Poverty%20and%20Definition%20of%20 Rural.pdf

Miller, L. C. (2012). Understanding rural teacher retention and the role of community amenities. Center on Education Policy and Workforce competitiveness. https://curry.virginia.edu/sites/default/files/files/ EdPolicyWorks_files/1_Miller_CEPWC%20WP%20Rural%20Retention.pdf

Miller, P. (2012). Mapping educational opportunity zones: A geospatial analysis of neighborhood block groups. *Urban Review*, *44*(2), 189–218. https://doi.org/10.1007/s11256-011-0189-7

Miller, P., Brown, T., & Hopson, R. (2011). Centering love, hope, and trust in the community: Transformative urban leadership informed by Paulo Freire. *Urban Education*, *46*(5), 1078–99. https:// doi.org/10.1177/0042085910395951

Miller, P., Scanlan, M. K., & Phillippo, K. (2017). Rural cross-sector collaboration: A social frontier analysis. *American Educational Research Journal*, *54*, 193S–215S. https://doi. org/10.3102/0002831216665188

Mills, M. (2020, May 15). Will distance learning be the new normal when schools reopen? Here's what experts predict after COVID-19. *Parents*. https://www.parents.com/news/distance-learning-could-be-the-new-normal-when-schools-reopen-after-covid-19-according-to-experts/

Milner, R. (2006). The promise of Black teachers' success with Black students. *Educational Foundations*, *20*(3–4), 89–104. https://eric.ed.gov/?id=EJ794734

Milner, R. (2013). Analyzing poverty, learning, and teaching through a critical race lens. *Review of Research in Education*, *37*(1), 1–53. https://doi.org/10.3102/0091732x12459720

Minner, D. D., & Hiles, E. (2005). Rural school-community partnerships: The case of science education. *Issues in Teacher Education*, *14*(1), 81–94. https://files.eric.ed.gov/fulltext/EJ796423.pdf

Mitra, D., Serriere, S., & Kirshner, B. (2014). Youth participation in US contexts: Student voice without a national mandate. *Children & Society*, *28*(4), 292–304.

Mitra, D. L. (2004). The significance of students: Can increasing "student voice" in schools lead to gains in youth development? *Teachers College Record*, *106*, 651–88.

Mitra, D. L. (2018). *Educational change and the political process*. Routledge.

Mochaidean, M. (2018, April 9). The other West Virginia teacher strike. *Jacobin*. https://www.jacobinmag. com/2018/04/west-virginia-teachers-strike-1990-unions

Modeste, M. E., Pavlakis, A. E., & Nguyen, C. (2020). Theory amid policy and practice: A typology of theory use in educational leadership scholarship. *Journal of Research on Leadership Education*. https://doi.org/10.1177/1942775120941904

Moll, L. C., Amanti, C., Neff, D., & Gonzalez, N. (1992). Funds of knowledge for teaching: Using a qualitative approach to connect homes and classrooms. *Theory Into Practice*, *31*(2), 132–41.

Monk, D. H. (2007). Recruiting and retaining high-quality teachers in rural areas. *The Future of Children*, *17*(1), 155–74. https://doi.org/10.1353/foc.2007.0009

Monnat, S. (2020, March 24). Why coronavirus could hit rural areas harder. *Lerner Center Issue Brief Number 16*. https://lernercenter.syr.edu/2020/03/24/why-coronavirus-could-hit-rural-areas-harder/

Montana Office of Public Instruction. (n.d.). *Indian Education for all*. Montana Office of Public Instruction. https://opi.mt.gov/Educators/Teaching-Learning/Indian-Education-for-All

Montero, M. K., Newman, S., & Ledger, S. (2014). Exploring early reading instructional strategies to advance the print literacy development of adolescent SLIFE. *Journal of Adolescent and Adult Literacy, 58*(1), 59–69. https://doi.org/10.1002/jaal.318

Moon, T. R. (2018). Uses and misuses of matrices in identifying gifted students: Considerations for better practice. In C. M. Callahan & H. L. Hertberg-Davis (Eds.), *Fundamentals of gifted education: Considering multiple perspectives* (2nd ed., pp. 116–24). Routledge.

Morrison, D., Annamma, S. A., & Jackson, D. D. (Eds.). (2017). *Critical race spatial analysis: Mapping to understand and address educational inequity*. Stylus.

Morrissette, P. J. (2000). The experiences of the rural school counselor. *Professional School Counseling, 3*(3), 197–207.

Mortensen, P. (1994). Representations of literacy and region: Narrating 'Another America'. In P. Sullivan & D. Qualley (Eds.), *Pedagogy in the age of politics: Writing and reading (in) the academy* (pp. 100–20). National Council of Teachers of English.

Morton, B. M., & Berardi, A. (2018). Creating a trauma-informed rural community. In R. M. Reardon & J. Leonard (Eds.), *Making a positive impact in rural places: Change agency in school-university-community collaboration in education* (pp. 193–215). Information Age Publishing.

Morton, T. R., Ramirez, N. A., Meece, J. L., Demetriou, C., & Panter, A. T. (2018). Perceived barriers, anxieties, and fears in prospective college students from rural high schools. *The High School Journal, 101*(3), 155–76. https://doi.org/10.1353/hsj.2018.0008

Mountford, M. (2004). Motives and power of school board members: Implications for school board–superintendent relationships. *Educational Administration Quarterly, 40*(5), 704–41. https://doi.org/10.1177/0013161x04268843

Moustakas, C. (1994). *Phenomenological research methods*. Sage. https://doi.org/10.4135/9781412995658

Mukhopadhyay, A. (2020, May 6). The rise of online learning raises questions about the price we put on education. *Quartz India*. https://qz.com/india/1852436/e-learning-amid-covid-19-raises-questions-about-cost-of-education/

Murdock, S., Cline, M., & Zey, M. (2012). Challenges in the analysis of rural populations in the United States. In L. J. Kulcsár & K. J. Curtis (Eds.), *International handbook of rural demography* (pp. 7–15). Springer.

Murphy, M. A., & Ruble, L. A. (2012). A comparative study of rurality and urbanicity on access to and satisfaction with services for children with autism spectrum disorders. *Rural Special Education Quarterly, 31*(3), 3–11. https://doi.org/10.1177/875687051203100302

Muskett, C. (2014). Trauma-informed care in inpatient mental health settings: A review of the literature. *International Journal of Mental Health Nursing, 23*(1), 51–9.

Nadel, W., & Sagawa, S. (2002). *America's forgotten children: Child poverty in rural America*. Save the Children. https://files.eric.ed.gov/fulltext/ED467475.pdf

Namit, C. (1986). The union has a communications strategy—and your board should, too. *American School Board Journal, 173*(10), 30–1.

Nancy, J.-L. (1991). *Inoperative community*. University of Minnesota Press.

Nancy, J.-L. (2016). *The disavowed community* (P. Armstrong, Trans.). Fordham University Press.

Nash, M. A. (2019). Entangled pasts: Land-grant colleges and American Indian dispossession. *History of Education Quarterly, 59*(4), 437–67. https://www.cambridge.org/core/services/aop-cambridge-core/content/view/79E42113A0A51B21903DFB1229F7DE88/S0018268019000311a.pdf/entangled_pasts_landgrant_colleges_and_american_indian_dispossession.pdf

Nasir, N. S. (2018). When development is not universal: Understanding the unique developmental tasks that race, gender, and social class impose: Commentary on Rogers and Way. *Human Development, 61*(6), 332–6. https://doi.org/10.1159/000494302

References

National Association for Gifted Children. (n.d.-a). *Frequently asked questions about gifted education.* Author. https://www.nagc.org/resources-publications/resources/frequently-asked-questions-about-gifted-education

National Association for Gifted Children. (n.d.-b). *Myths about gifted students.* Author. https://www.nagc.org/myths-about-gifted-students

National Association for Gifted Children. (2010a). *NAGC position statement and white papers* [White Paper]. https://www.nagc.org/about-nagc/nagc-position-statements-white-papers

National Association for Gifted Children. (2010b). *Pre-k–Grade 12 gifted programming standards.* Author.

National Association for Gifted Children & Council of State Directors of Programs for the Gifted. (2013). *State of the states in gifted education, 2012–2013.* Author.

National Center for Education Statistics (NCES). (n.d.). *Rural education in America: Prior urban/rural classification systems.* https://nces.ed.gov/surveys/ruraled/priorclassification.asp

National Center for Education Statistics (NCES). (2000). U.S. Census Bureau: Census 2000 School District Tabulation (STP2) Data Download. https://nces.ed.gov/programs/edge/Demographic/Census

National Center for Education Statistics (NCES). (2006). *School local definitions. Rural Education in America.* https://nces.ed.gov/surveys/ruraled/definitions.asp

National Center for Education Statistics (NCES). (2007). *Parent and family involvement in education, 2006–07 school year, from the National Household Education Surveys Program.* Author. https://files.eric.ed.gov/fulltext/ED502237.pdf

National Center for Education Statistics (NCES). (2012). *Number and percentage of public school students who were identified as limited-English proficient (LEP), by locale and region: 2011–12.* https://nces.ed.gov/surveys/ruraled/tables/B.1.d.-1.asp

National Center for Education Statistics (NCES). (2013). *The status of rural education.* http://nces.ed.gov/programs/coe/pdf/coe_tla.pdf

National Center for Education Statistics (NCES). (2014). *Rural education in America: Data on schools and school districts.* https://nces.ed.gov/surveys/ruraled/tables/a.1.a.-1.asp

National Center for Education Statistics (NCES). (2015a). *Rural education in America.* https://nces.ed.gov/surveys/ruraled/tables/b.3.b.-1.asp

National Center for Education Statistics (NCES). (2015b). *Search for public school districts.* http://nces.ed.gov/ccd/districtsearch/

National Center for Education Statistics (NCES). (2016a). *Programs and services for high school English Learners in public school districts: 2015–16.* https://nces.ed.gov/pubs2016/2016150.pdf

National Center for Education Statistics (NCES). (2016b). *Status and trends in the education of racial and ethnic groups 2016.* https://nces.ed.gov/pubs2016/2016007.pdf

National Center for Education Statistics (NCES). (2018a). *English Language Learner (ELL) students enrolled in public elementary and secondary schools by state: Selected years, fall 2000 through fall 2016.* https://nces.ed.gov/programs/digest/d18/tables/dt18_204.20.asp?current=yes

National Center for Education Statistics (NCES). (2018b). U.S. Census Bureau: American Community Survey 2014–2018. https://nces.ed.gov/programs/edge/Demographic/ACS

National Center for Education Statistics (NCES). (2019a). *Fast facts: Title I.* https://nces.ed.gov/fastfacts/display.asp?id=158

National Center for Education Statistics (NCES). (2019b). Young adult educational and employment outcomes by family socioeconomic status. *The condition of education.* https://nces.ed.gov/programs/coe/indicator_tbe.asp

National Center for Education Statistics (NCES). (2019c). School search. https://nces.ed.gov/ccd/schoolsearch/school_detail.asp?ID=370096000237

National Center for Education Statistics (NCES). (2019d). School search. https://nces.ed.gov/ccd/schoolsearch/school_detail.asp?ID=450333000904

National Center for Education Statistics (NCES). (2019e). *Digest of Education Statistics, 2018* (NCES 2020–009). U.S. Department of Education. https://nces.ed.gov/programs/digest/d18/

National Center for Education Statistics (NCES). (2020a). *Characteristics of traditional public schools and public charter schools.* U.S. Department of Education. https://nces.ed.gov/programs/coe/indicator_cla.asp

National Center for Education Statistics (NCES). (2020b). *Charter schools: Reimagining education.* National Center for Education Statistics.

National Center for Education Statistics (NCES). (2020c). Locale lookup [Map]. U.S. Department of Education. Institute of Education Sciences, National Center for Education Statistics. https://nces.ed.gov/programs/maped/LocaleLookup/

National Commission on Excellence in Education. (1983). *A nation at risk: The imperative for educational reform: A report to the Nation and the Secretary of Education, United States Department of Education.* University of Michigan Press.

National Congress of American Indians. (2020). *Tribal nations and the United States: An introduction.* http://www.ncai.org/about-tribes

National Council of Teachers of English. (2013). *NCTE definition of literacy in a digital age.* https://ncte.org/statement/nctes-definition-literacy-digital-age/print/

National Education Association. (2020). *Issues and actions.* https://educationvotes.nea.org/issues-and-actions/

National Indian Education Association. (n.d.). *Native nations and American schools: The history of Natives in the American education system.* Author. https://www.niea.org/native-education-101-1

National Indian Education Association. (2016). *Building relationships with tribes: A Native process for ESSA consultation.* https://tedna.org/wp-content/uploads/2016/12/niea-building-relationships.pdf

National Indian Education Association. (2017). *Building relationships with tribes: A Native process for local consultation under ESSA.* https://www.issuelab.org/resources/33992/33992.pdf

National Policy Board for Educational Administration. (2015). Professional Standards for Educational Leaders 2015. Author. https://ccsso.org/resource-library/professional-standards-educational-leaders

National Rural Education Association (NREA). (2016). *Research agenda 2016–2021. Ten research priorities.* https://drive.google.com/file/d/0B6jy-_ymJ6lPcEhlbmxPZU5XLTg/view

National Rural Health Association (NRHA). (2008). *Recruitment and retention of quality health workforce in rural areas: A series of policy papers on the rural health careers pipeline,* Paper No. 5 [Policy brief]. https://www.ruralhealthweb.org/getattachment/Advocate/Policy-Documents/WorkforceRuralBehavHealth.pdf.aspx?lang=en-US

National Rural Health Association (NRHA). (2015). *The future of rural behavioral health* [Policy brief]. https://www.ruralhealthweb.org/NRHA/media/Emerge_NRHA/Advocacy/Policy%20documents/The-Future-of-Rural-Behavioral-Health_Feb-2015.pdf

National Student Clearinghouse. (2018). *High school benchmarks 2018: National college progression rates.* https://nscresearchcenter.org/wp-content/uploads/2018_HSBenchmarksReport_FIN_22OCT18.pdf

Nelson, L. (1955). *Rural sociology* (2nd ed.). American Book Company.

Nguyen-Hoang, P., & Yinger, J. (2011). The capitalization of school quality into house values: A review. *Journal of Housing Economics, 20*(1), 30–48.

Ni, Y. (2017). Teacher working conditions, teacher commitment, and charter schools. *Teachers College Record, 119*(6), 1–38.

Ni, Y., Yan, R., Rorrer, A. K., & Nicholson, A. (2017). *Teacher turnover in Utah between 2013–14 and 2014–15.* Utah Education Policy Center.

NICHD Early Child Care Research Network. (2002). Early child care and children's development prior to school entry: Results from the NICHD Study of early child care. *American Education Research Journal, 39,* 133–64. https://doi.org/10.3102/00028312039001133

NICHD Early Child Care Research Network. (2006). Child-care effect sizes for the NICHD study of early child care and youth development. *American Psychologist, 61*(2), 99–116. https://doi.org/10.1037/0003-066X.61.2.99

Nieto, D. (2009). A brief history of bilingual education in the United States. *Perspectives on Urban Education, 6*(1), 61–72. http://citeseerx.ist.psu.edu/viewdoc/download?doi=10.1.1.224.1008&rep=rep1&type=pdf#page=61

Nilson, S. R. (2007). Poverty in America: Consequences for individuals and the economy. In *Testimony before the Chairman, Committee on Ways and Means, House of Representatives*. U.S. Government Accountability Office.

Nitta, K. A., Holley, M. J., & Wrobel, S. L. (2010). A phenomenological study of rural school consolidation. *Journal of Research in Rural Education, 25*(2), 1–19. https://jrre.psu.edu/sites/default/files/2019-08/25-2.pdf

No Child Left Behind (NCLB) Act of 2001, Pub. L. 107–110, § 101, Stat. 1425 (2002).

Noguera, P., & Wells, L. (2011). The politics of school reform: A broader and bolder approach for Newark. *Berkeley Review of Education, 2*(1), 5–25. https://doi.org/10.5070/b82110065

Nora, A., & Crisp, G. (2009). Hispanics and higher education: An overview of research, theory, and practice. In J. C. Smart (Ed.), *Higher education: Handbook of theory and research* (Vol. 24, pp. 321–58). Springer.

Northern Territory Government Department of Education. (2016). *Guidelines and procedures: Gifted education*. https://education.nt.gov.au/__data/assets/pdf_file/0011/439148/Gifted-and-Talented-Education-Guidelines.pdf

Núñez, A.-M. (2014). Advancing an intersectionality framework in higher education: Power and Latino postsecondary opportunity. In M. B. Paulsen (Ed.), *Higher education: Handbook of theory and research* (Vol. 29, pp. 33–92). Springer.

Obama, B. (2009). Remarks of President Barack Obama. Presented for delivery address to Joint Session of Congress. Retrieved from http://www.whitehouse.gov/the-press-office/remarks-president-barack-obama-address-joint-session-congress

O'Connor, M. T., & Daniello, F. (2019). From implication to naming: Reconceptualizing school–community partnership literature using a framework nested in social justice. *School Community Journal, 29*(1), 297–316. https://files.eric.ed.gov/fulltext/EJ1219896.pdf

O'Connor, N., Hammack, F. M., & Scott, M. A. (2010). Social capital, financial knowledge, and Hispanic student college choices. *Research in Higher Education, 51*(3), 195–219. https://doi.org/10.1007/s11162-009-9153-8

Office of Management and Budget. (2000). Standards for defining metropolitan and micropolitan statistical areas; Notice. *Federal Register, 65*(249), 82227–38. https://www.govinfo.gov/content/pkg/FR-2000-12-27/pdf/00-32997.pdf

Olinghouse, N. G. (2008). Student-and instruction-level predictors of narrative writing in third-grade students. *Reading and Writing, 21*(1–2), 3–26. https://doi.org/10.1007/s11145-007-9062-1

Oncescu, J. (2014). Creating constraints to community resiliency: The event of a rural school's closure. *The Online Journal of Rural Research and Policy, 9*(2), 1–30.

Oncescu, J., & Giles, A. (2014). Rebuilding a sense of community through reconnection: The impact of a rural school's closure on individuals without school-aged children. *The Journal of Rural and Community Development, 9*(3), 295–318.

O'Neal, D., Ringler, M., & Lys, D. (2009). Skeptics to partners. *Journal of Staff Development, 30*(4), 52–5, 71.

Organisation for Economic Co-Operation and Development (OECD). (2011). *Regional typology: Directorate for public governance and territorial development*. OECD Publishing.

Organisation for Economic Co-Operation and Development (OECD). (2013). *What makes urban schools different?* (Report No. 28). PISA in Focus. https://www.oecd.org/pisa/pisaproducts/pisainfocus/pisa%20in%20focus%20n28%20%28eng%29--FINAL.pdf

Organisation for Economic Co-Operation and Development (OECD). (2020). *The territorial impact of Covid19 on managing the crisis across levels of government*. http://www.oecd.org/coronavirus/policy-responses/the-territorial-impact-of-covid-19-managing-the-crisis-across-levels-of-government-d3e314e1/

Orgera, K., McDermott, D., Rae, M., Claxton, G., Koma, W., & Cox, C. (2020, April 22). *Urban and rural differences in coronavirus pandemic preparedness*. Peterson-KFF. https://www.healthsystemtracker.org/brief/urban-and-rural-differences-in-coronavirus-pandemic-preparedness/

Orlowski, J. (2020). *The Social Dilemma*. Exposure Labs.

Osborne, D. (2020). Reinventing the New Orleans public education system. *New England Journal of Public Policy, 32*(1), 1–10. https://scholarworks.umb.edu/nejpp/vol32/iss1/10

Osher, D., Cantor, P., Berg, J., Steyer, L., & Rose, T. (2018). Drivers of human development: How relationships and context shape learning and development. *Applied Developmental Science, 24*(1), 6–36. https://doi.org/10.1080/10888691.2017.1398650.

Østby, G. (2015). Rural-urban migration, inequality and urban social disorder: Evidence from African and Asian cities. *Conflict Management and Peace Science, 33*(5), 491–515. https://doi.org/10.1177/0738894215581315

Overstreet, S., & Chafouleas, S. M. (2016). Trauma-informed schools: Introduction to the special issue. *School Mental Health, 8*(1), 1–6.

Owens, J. S., Murphy, C. E., Richerson, L., Girio, E. L., & Himawan, L. K. (2008). Science to practice in underserved communities: The effectiveness of school mental health programming. *Journal of Clinical Child and Adolescent Psychology, 37*(2), 434–47. https://doi.org/10.1080/15374410801955912

Owens, J. S., Watabe, Y., & Michael, K. D. (2013). Culturally responsive school mental health in rural communities. In C. S. Clauss-Ehlers, Z. N. Serpell, & M. D. West (Eds.), *Handbook of culturally responsive school mental health: Advancing research training, practice, and policy* (pp. 31–42). Springer.

Pace, N. J. (2004). Gay, rural, and coming out: A case study of one school's experience. *The Rural Educator, 25*(3), 14–18.

Paciotto, C., & Delany-Barmann, G. (2011). Planning micro-level language education reform in new diaspora sites: Two-way immersion education in the rural Midwest. *Language Policy, 10*, 221–43.

Padron, Y. N., & Waxman, H. C. (2016). Investigating principals' knowledge and perceptions of programs for English Language Learners. *International Journal of Educational Leadership and Management, 4*(2), 127–46. https://doi.org/10.17583/ijelm.2016.1706

Paisley, P. O., Bailey, D. F., Hayes, R. L., McMahon, G. H., & Grimmet, M. (2010). Using a cohort model for school counselor preparation to enhance commitment to social justice. *Journal for Specialists in Group Work, 35*(3), 262–70.

Paraskeva, J. M. (2016). Conclusion: Itinerant curriculum theory: A reiteration. In J. M. Paraskeva (Ed.), *The curriculum: Whose internationalization?* (pp. 203–16). Peter Lang.

Park, M., Zong, J., & Batalova, J. (2018, February). *Growing superdiversity among young U.S. dual language learners and its implications*. Migration Policy Institute. https://www.migrationpolicy.org/research/growing-superdiversity-among-young-us-dual-language-learners-and-its-implications

Parker, F. (1968). Why teachers strike? *Kappa Delta Pi Record, 5*(2), 36–7. https://doi.org/10.1080/00228958.1968.10516820

Parker, K., Horowitz, J., Brown, A., Fry, R., Cohn, D., & Igielnik, R. (2018). *What unites and divides urban, suburban, and rural communities*. Pew Research Center. https://www.pewsocialtrends.org/2018/05/22/what-unites-and-divides-urban-suburban-and-rural-communities/

Parson, L., Hunter, C. A., & Kallio, B. (2016). Exploring educational leadership in rural schools. *Planning and Changing, 47*(1/2), 63–81.

Patton, L. D. (2010). *Culture centers in higher education: Perspectives on identity, theory, and practice*. Stylus Publishing.

Patton, M. Q. (2010). *Developmental evaluation: Applying complexity concepts to enhance innovation and use*. Guilford Press.

Paulgaard, G. (2019, September). Refugee integration and rural resilience? [Paper presentation]. ECER Network 4, Hamburg, Germany.

Pearson, R. E., & Sutton, J. M. (1999). Rural and small town school counselors. *Journal of Research in Rural Education, 15*(2), 90–100. https://jrre.psu.edu/sites/default/files/2019-08/15-2_6.pdf

Peine, E. K., & Schafft, K. A. (2018). [Review of the book *Hillbilly elegy: A memoir of a family and culture in crisis*, by J. D. Vance]. *Rural Sociology, 83*(3), 707–14. https://doi.org/10.1111/ruso.12249.

Penchansky, R., & Thomas, J. W. (1981). The concept of access: Definition and relationship to consumer satisfaction. *Medical Care, 19*, 127–40.

References

Pender, J., Hertz, T., Cromartie, J., & Farrigan, T. (2019). *Rural America at a glance, 2019 Edition*. U.S. Department of Agriculture. http://www.ers.usda.gov/publications/pub-details/?pubid=95340

Pendola, A., & Fuller, E. J. (2018). Principal stability and the rural divide. *Journal of Research in Rural Education, 34*(1), 1–20.

Peralta, C. (2013). Fractured memories, mended lives: The schooling experiences of Latinas/os in rural areas. *Bilingual Research Journal, 36*(2), 228–43. https://doi.org/10.1080/15235882.2013.818594

Pérez Huber, L. (2010). Using Latina/o critical race theory (LatCrit) and racist nativism to explore intersectionality in the educational experiences of undocumented Chicana college students. *Educational Foundations, 24*(1–2), 77– 96.

Perry, D., & Daniels, M. (2016). Implementing trauma-informed practices in the school setting: A pilot study. *School Mental Health, 8*(1), 177–88.

Peshkin, A. (1978). *Growing up American: Schooling and the survival of community*. Waveland Press.

Peshkin, A. (1982). *The imperfect union: School consolidation and community conflict*. The University of Chicago Press.

Pešikan, A., Antić, S., & Ivić, I. (2020). Rural education in Serbia: Conflict between rhetoric and reality. In C. Gristy, L. Hargreaves, & S. R. Kučerová (Eds.), *Educational research and schooling in rural Europe: An engagement with changing patterns of education, space, and place* (pp. 147–74). Information Age Publishing.

Peters, D. J. (2020, June 18). Rural America is more vulnerable to COVID-19 than cities are, and it's starting to show. *The Conversation*. https://theconversation.com/rural-america-is-more-vulnerable-to-covid-19-than-cities-are-and-its-starting-to-show-140532

Peters, S. J., & Gentry, M. (2010). Multigroup construct validity evidence of the *HOPE Scale*: Instrumentation to identify low-income elementary students for gifted programs. *Gifted Child Quarterly, 54*(4), 298–313. https://doi.org/10.1177/0016986210378332

Petrin, R. A., Farmer, T. W., Meece, J. L., & Byun, S. (2011). Interpersonal competence configurations, attachment to community, and residential aspirations of rural adolescents. *Journal of Youth and Adolescence, 40*, 1091–105. https://doi.org/10.1007/s10964-011-9690-2

Petrin, R. A., Schafft, K. A., & Meece, J. (2014). Educational sorting and residential aspirations among rural high school students: What are the contributions of schools and educators to the rural brain drain? *American Educational Research Journal, 51*(2), 294–326. https://doi.org/10.3102/0002831214527493

Petti, J. (2017, October 18). Riggering elections: A spatial statistics analysis of political and unintentional gerrymandering. *Cornell Policy Review*. http://www.cornellpolicyreview.com/rigging-elections-spatial-statistics-analysis-political-unintentional-gerrymandering/

Petts, R. J. (2012). Single mothers' religious participation and early childhood behavior. *Journal of Marriage and Family, 74*, 251–68. https://doi.org/10.1111/j.1741-3737.2011.00953.x

Peurach, D. J., Yurkofsky, M. M., & Sutherland, D. H. (2019). Organizing and managing for excellence and equity: The work and dilemmas of instructionally focused education systems. *Educational Policy, 33*(6), 812–45. https://doi.org/10.1177/0895904819867267

Pew Trusts. (2014). *Changing patterns in US immigration and population*. Issue Brief. https://www.pewtrusts.org/en/research-and-analysis/issue-briefs/2014/12/changing-patterns-in-us-immigration-and-population

Pewewardy, C. (2015). Indigenous leadership. In R. S. Minthorn and A. F. Chavez (Eds.), *Indigenous leadership in higher education* (pp. 70–9). Routledge.

Pewewardy, C. D., Lees, A., & Clark-Shim, H. (2018). The transformational Indigenous praxis model: Stages for developing critical consciousness in Indigenous education. *Wicazo Sa Review, 33*(1), 38–69. https://doi.org/10.5749/wicazosareview.33.1.0038

Phillips, D. A., Lipsey, M. W., Dodge, K. A., Haskins, R., Bassok, D., Burchinal, M. R., Duncan, G. J., Dynarski, M., Magnuson, K. A., & Weiland, C. (2017). *The current state of scientific knowledge on pre-kindergarten effects: A consensus statement from the pre-kindergarten task force*. Brookings and Duke University. https://www.brookings.edu/wp-content/uploads/2017/04/duke_prekstudy_final_4-4-17_hires.pdf

Pierson, A., & Hanson, H. (2015). *Comparing postsecondary enrollment and persistence among rural and nonrural students in Oregon* (REL 2015–076). U.S. Department of Education, Institute of Education Sciences, National Center for Education Evaluation and Regional Assistance, Regional Educational Laboratory Northwest. http://ies.ed.gov/ncee/edlabs/projects/project.asp?ProjectID=341

Pijanowski, J. C., Hewitt, P. M., & Brady, K. P. (2009). Superintendents' perceptions of the principal shortage. *NASSP Bulletin, 93*(2), 85–95. https://doi.org/10.1177/0192636509343963

Pinar, W. F. (2012). *What is curriculum theory?* (2nd ed.). Routledge.

Pinnegar, S., & Daynes, J. G. (2007). Locating narrative inquiry historically. In D. J. Clandinin (Ed.), *Handbook of narrative inquiry: Mapping a methodology* (pp. 3–34). Sage.

Pittman, R. B., McGinty, D. L., & Johnson-Busbin, J. (2014). The rural influence on the relationship between social class and educational outcomes. In C. B. Howley, A. Howley, & J. D. Johnson (Eds.), *Dynamics of social class, race, and place in rural education* (pp. 109–37). Information Age Publishing.

Plucker, J. A., & Callahan, C. M. (2014). Research on giftedness and gifted education: Status of the field and considerations for the future. *Exceptional Children, 80*(4), 390–406. https://doi.org/10.1177/0014402914527244

Polaha, J., Williams, S. L., Heflinger, C. A., & Studts, C. R. (2015). The perceived stigma of mental health services among rural parents of children with psychosocial concerns. *Journal of Pediatric Psychology, 40*(10), 1095–104.

Polkinghorne, D. E. (1995). Narrative configuration in qualitative analysis. In J. A. Hatch & R. Wisniewski (Eds.), *Life history and narrative* (pp. 25–36). The Falmer Press.

Post, D., & Stambach, A. (1999). District consolidation and rural school closure: E Pluribus Unum? *Journal of Research in Rural Education, 15*(2), 106–17. https://jrre.psu.edu/sites/default/files/2019-08/15-2_2.pdf

powell, j. (2008, September 21). Race, place, and opportunity. *The American Prospect, 19*(10). http://prospect.org/article/race-place-and-opportunity

powell, j. (2010). Regionalism and race. *Race, Poverty & the Environment, 17*(1), 45–8.

Powell, j., Reece, J., & Gambhir, S. (2007). *The geography of opportunity: Austin region.* Kirwan Institute for The Study of Race and Ethnicity.

Prater, D. L., Bermudez, A. B., & Owens, E. (1997). Examining parental involvement in rural, urban, and suburban schools. *Journal of Research in Rural Education, 13*(1), 72–5. https://jrre.psu.edu/sites/default/files/2019-08/13-1_8.pdf

Preskill, S. (1989). Educating for democracy: Charles W. Eliot and the differentiated curriculum. *Educational Theory, 39*(4), 351–8. https://doi-org.ezproxy.lib.vt.edu/10.1111/j.1741-5446.1989.00351.x

Preston, J. P., & Barnes, K. E. (2017). Successful leadership in rural schools: Cultivating collaboration. *The Rural Educator, 38*(1), 1–10.

Preston, J. P., Jakubiec, B. A., & Kooymans, R. (2013). Common challenges faced by rural principals: A review of the literature. *The Rural Educator, 35*(1). https://doi.org/10.35608/ruraled.v35i1.355

Prins, E., & Kassab, C. (2017). Rural/non-rural differences among Pennsylvania FAFSA applicants pursuing the same type of postsecondary degree. *Journal of Research in Rural Education, 32*(7), 1–16. https://jrre.psu.edu/sites/default/files/2019-08/32-7.pdf

Provasnik, S., KewalRamani, A., Coleman, M. M., Gilbertson, L., Herring, W., & Xie, Q. (2007). *Status of education in rural America.* NCES No. 2007-040. U.S. Department of Education. http://nces.ed.gov/pubs2007/2007040.pdf

Prunty, J. J. (1985). Signposts for a critical educational policy analysis. *Australian Journal of Education, 29*(2), 133–40. https://doi.org/10.1177/000494418502900205

Public Knowledge. (2019). *Rural broadband access.* https://www.publicknowledge.org/issues/rural-broadband-access/

Puryear, J. S., & Kettler, T. (2017). Rural gifted education and the effect of proximity. *Gifted Child Quarterly, 61*(2), 143–52. https://doi.org/10.1177/0016986217690229

Putnam, R. D. (2001). *Bowling alone: The collapse and revival of American community* (1. touchstone ed). Simon & Schuster.

References

Pyles, D. G. (2016). Rural media literacy: Youth documentary videomaking as a rural literacy practice. *Journal of Research in Rural Education, 31*(7), 1–15. https://jrre.psu.edu/sites/default/files/2019-08/31-7.pdf

Raggl, A. (2020). Small rural primary schools in Austria: Places of innovation? In C. Gristy, L. Hargreaves, & S. R. Kučerová (Eds.), *Educational research and schooling in rural Europe: An engagement with changing patterns of education, space, and place* (pp. 196–216). Information Age Publishing.

Raimundo, R., Marques-Pinto, A., & Lima, M. L. (2013). The effects of a social-emotional learning program on elementary school children: The role of pupils' characteristics. *Psychology in the Schools, 50*(2), 165–80. https://doi.org/10.1002/pits.21667

Raja, S., Hasnain, M., Hoersch, M., Gove-Yin, S., & Rajagopalan, C. (2015). Trauma informed care in medicine. *Family & Community Health, 38*(3), 216–26.

Rasheed, M. (2019). Context and content in rural gifted education: A literature review. *Journal of Advanced Academics, 31*(1), 61–84. https://doi.org/10.1177/1932202x19879174

Ratledge, N., & Zachary, L. (2017). *Impacts of unconventional oil and gas booms on public school education: A mixed-methods analysis of six high production states.* Resources for the Future. https://media.rff.org/documents/RFF20Rpt-Shale20Community20Impacts20Schools.pdf

Rautio, P. (2010a). Beauty in the context of particular lives. *The Journal of Aesthetic Education, 44*(4), 38–59. https://doi.org/10.5406/jaesteduc.44.4.0038

Rautio, P. (2010b). *Writing about everyday beauty in a nothern village: An argument for diversity of habitable places.* University of Oulu.

Ravitch, D. (2010). *The death and life of the great American school system: How testing and choice are undermining education.* Basic Books.

Raymond, M. E., Cremata, E., Davis, D., Dickey, K., Lawyer, K., Negassi, Y., & Woodworth, J. L. (2013). National charter school study. In *Center for research on education outcomes.* Stanford University. https://credo.stanford.edu/sites/g/files/sbiybj6481/f/ncss_2013_final_draft.pdf

Reardon, S. F. (2016). *School district socioeconomic status, race, and academic achievement.* https://cepa.stanford.edu/sites/default/files/reardon%20district%20ses%20and%20achievement%20discussion%20draft%20april2016.pdf

Reardon, S. F., & Owens, A. (2014). 60 years after Brown: Trends and consequences of school segregation. *Annual Review of Sociology, 40,* 199–218. https://doi.org/10.1146/annurev-soc-071913-043152

Reardon, S. F., Weathers, E. S., Fahle, E. M., Jang, H., & Kalogrides, D. (2019). *Is separate still unequal? New evidence on school segregation and racial academic achievement gaps* (CEPA Working Paper No.19-06). Stanford Center for Education Policy Analysis. http://cepa.stanford.edu/wp19-06

Red Owl, S., Hall, T., Havens, F., Puskarenko, T., Cannon, D., Martin, P., Juneau, C., Taylor, C., Sly, G., & McCoy, M. (2000, June). *State-tribal partnerships: Cooperating to improve Indian education* [Paper Presentation]. National Congress of American Indians, Juneau, AK.

RedCorn, A. (2020). Liberating Sovereign potential: A working education capacity building model for Native nations. *Journal of School Leadership, 30*(6), 493–518. https://doi.org/10.1177/1052684620951724

RedCorn, A., McCoy, M., & Mackey, H. J. (2019). Indian Country. In D. C. Thompson, R. C. Wood, S. C. Neuenswander, J. M. Heim, & R. D. Watson (Eds.), *Funding public schools in the United States and Indian Country* (pp. 211–47). Information Age Publishing.

Redding, S. (1997). *Parents and learning.* Educational practices series—*2.* International Academy of Education; International Bureau of Education. https://files.eric.ed.gov/fulltext/ED463858.pdf

Reece, J., & Gambhir, S. (2008). *The geography of opportunity: Review of opportunity mapping research initiatives.* Kirwan Institute.

Reeder, R. J., & Brown, D. M. (2005). *Recreation, tourism, and rural well-being.* https://www.ers.usda.gov/webdocs/publications/46126/15112_err7_1_.pdf?v=0

Reese, L., Jensen, B., & Ramirez, D. (2014). Emotionally supportive classroom contexts for young Latino children in rural California. *The Elementary School Journal, 114*(4), 501–26. https://doi.org/10.1086/675636

References

Reid, J. (2017). Rural education practice and policy in marginalised communities: Teaching and learning on the edge. *Australian and International Journal of Rural Education, 27*(1), 88–103.

Reid, J. (2021). Preface. In S. White & J. Downey (Eds.), *Rural education across the world: Models of innovative practice and impact.* Springer.

Reid, J., Green, B., Cooper, M., Hastings, W., Lock, G., & White, S. (2010). Regenerating rural social space? Teacher education for rural–regional sustainability. *Australian Journal of Education, 54*(3), 262–76. https://doi.org/10.1177/000494411005400304

Renzulli, J. S. (1977). *The Enrichment Triad Model: A guide for developing defensible programs for the gifted and talented.* Creative Learning Press.

Renzulli, J. S., & Reis, S. M. (1997). *The Schoolwide Enrichment Model: A how-to guide for educational excellence* (2nd ed.). Creative Learning Press.

Renzulli, J. S., Smith, L. S., White, A. J., Callahan, C. M., Harman, R. K., Westberg, K. L., Gavin, M. K., Reis, S. M., Seigle, D., & Systema Reed, R. E. (2010). *Scales for rating the behavioral characteristics of superior students* (3rd ed.). Prufrock Press.

Rey, J. C. (2014). The rural superintendency and the need for a critical leadership of place. *Journal of School Leadership, 24*(3), 509–36. https://doi.org/10.1177/105268461402400305

Reyhner, J., & Eder, J. (2004). *American Indian education: A history.* University of Oklahoma Press.

Reyhner, J., & Eder, J. (2017). *American Indian education: A history* (2nd ed.). University of Oklahoma Press.

Rhoda, E. (2017). What it's really like to be a Maine principal—and why so many don't survive. *Bangor Daily News.* https://bangordailynews.com/2017/12/04/mainefocus/what-its-really-like-to-be-a-maine-principal-and-why-so-many-dont-survive/

Rhubart, D. C., & Engle, E. W. (2017). The environment and health. In A. Tickamyer, J. Sherman, & J. Warlick (Eds.), *Rural poverty in the United States* (pp. 299–312). Columbia University Press.

Rice, J. M. (1912). *Scientific management in education.* Hinds, Noble, & Eldridge.

Richardson, T., Morrissette, M., & Zucker, L. (2012). School-based adolescent mental health programs. *Social Work Today, 12*(6), 24.

Riel, V., Parcel, T. L., Mickelson, R. A., & Smith, S. S. (2018). Do magnet and charter schools exacerbate or ameliorate inequality? *Sociology Compass, 12*(e12617), 1–15.

Riggs, N. R. (2006). After-school program attendance and the social development of rural Latino children of immigrant families. *Journal of Community Psychology, 34*(1), 75–87. https://doi.org/10.1002/jcop.20084

Righi, C. (1993). Scab! Crossing the picket line in a teacher strike. *The Clearing House: A Journal of Educational Strategies, Issues and Ideas, 66*(6), 332–4. https://doi.org/10.1080/00098655.1993.11478596

Riley, T., & Bicknell, B. (2013). Gifted and talented education in New Zealand Schools: A decade later. *APEX: The New Zealand Journal of Gifted Education, 18*(1), 1–16. https://hdl.handle.net/10289/8872

Rimm-Kaufman, S. E., Pianta, R. C., & Cox, M. J. (2000). Teachers' judgments of problems in the transition to kindergarten. *Early Childhood Research Quarterly, 15*, 147–66. https://doi.org/10.1016/S0885-2006(00)00049-1

Ringler, M. C., O'Neal, D., Rawis, J., & Cumiskey, S. (2013). The role of school leaders in teacher leadership development. *The Rural Educator, 35*(1), 34–43. https://eric.ed.gov/?id=EJ1022613

Rios, B. R. D. (1988). "Rural"—a concept beyond definition? *Eric Digest* (ED296820). https://files.eric.ed.gov/fulltext/ED296820.pdf

Robert Wood Johnson Foundation (RWJF). (2018). *Life in Rural America.* https://www.rwjf.org/en/library/research/2018/10/life-in-rural-america.html

Roberts, G. S. (2001). The consolidation of public schools in Randolph County, West Virginia: A case study. (ERIC Document Reproduction Service No. ED 462 211). http://rave.ohiolink.edu/databases/record/eric/ED462211

Roberts, P. (2014). Researching from the standpoint of the rural. In S. White & M. Corbett (Eds.), *Doing educational research in rural settings: Methodological issues, international perspectives and practical solutions* (pp. 135–40). Routledge.

References

Roberts, P. (2018). Looking for the rural. In A. Reid & D. Price (Eds.), *The Australian Curriculum: Promises, problems and possibilities* (pp. 201–10). Australian Curriculum Studies Association.

Roberts, P., Dean, J., & Lommatsch, G. (2019, December 13). *Still winning? Social inequity in the NSW Senior Secondary Curriculum hierarchy (Centre for Sustainable Communities Monograph Series, No.1)*. Rural Education and Communities Research Group. University of Canberra. https://researchprofiles.canberra.edu.au/en/publications/still-winning-social-inequity-in-the-nsw-senior-secondary-curricu

Roberts, P., & Downes, N. (2020, March 23). Online schooling and distance ed? Don't be afraid, we've been doing and improving it for 100 years. *AARE EduResearch Matters*. https://www.aare.edu.au/blog/?p=5305

Roberts, P., & Green, B. (2013). Researching rural places: On social justice and rural education. *Qualitative Inquiry, 19*(10), 765–74. https://doi.org/10.1177/1077800413503795

Robinson, G. (1990). *Conflict and change in the countryside. Rural society, economy and planning in the developed world.* Bellhaven Press. https://www.cabdirect.org/cabdirect/abstract/19901882434

Robinson, J., Cox, G., Malone, A., Williamson, M., Baldwin, G., Fletcher, K., & O'Brien, M. (2013). A systematic review of school-based interventions aimed at preventing, treating, and responding to suicide-related behavior in young people. *Crisis: The Journal of Crisis Intervention and Suicide Prevention, 34*(3), 164–82. https://doi.org/10.1027/0227-5910/a000168

Rodriguez, S. (2016). "We need to grab power where we can": Teacher activists' responses to neoliberal policies during the Chicago teacher's strike of 2012–2013. *Workplace: A Journal for Academic Labor, 26*, 74–90.

Rogers, J. D., Glesner, T. J., & Meyers, H. W. (2014). Early experiences implementing voluntary school district mergers in Vermont. *Journal of Research in Rural Education, 29*(7), 1–14. https://jrre.psu.edu/sites/default/files/2019-08/29-7.pdf

Rogers, L. O., & Way, N. (2018). Reimagining social and emotional development: Accommodation and resistance to dominant ideologies in the identities and friendships of boys of color. *Human Development, 61*(6), 311–31. https://doi.org/10.1159/000493378

Rogers, P. J. (2008). Using program theory to evaluate complicated and complex aspects of interventions. *Evaluation, 14*(1), 29–48.

Roll, N. (2017, June 28). Summer reading, not light reading. *Inside Higher Ed.* https://www.insidehighered.com/news/2017/06/28/books-race-social-justice-issues-dominate-selections-summer-reading-freshmen.

Roscigno, V. J., & Crowley, M. L. (2001). Rurality, institutional disadvantage, and achievement/attainment. *Rural Sociology, 66*(2), 268–92. https://doi.org/10.1111/j.1549-0831.2001.tb00067.x

Roscigno, V. J., Tomaskovic-Devey, D., & Crowley, M. (2006). Education and the inequalities of place. *Social Forces, 84*(4), 2121–45. https://doi.org/10.1353/sof.2006.0108

Rose, C. P., Maranto, R., & Ritter, G. W. (2017). From the Delta banks to the upper ranks: An evaluation of KIPP Charter Schools in rural Arkansas. *Educational Policy, 31*(2), 180–201.

Rosenboom, V., & Blagg, K. (2018). *Disconnected from higher education: How geography and internet speed limit access to higher education.* Urban Institute. www.urban.org/research/publication/disconnected-higher-education.

Ross, E. A. (1916). Folk depletion as a cause of rural decline. *Publications of the American Sociological Society*, XI, 21–30.

Ross, M. R. V., McGlynn, B. L., & Bernhardt, E. S. (2016). Deep impact: Effects of mountaintop mining on surface topography, bedrock structure, and downstream waters. *Environmental Science and Technology, 50*(4), 2064–74. https://doi.org/10.1021/acs.est.5b04532

Rothstein, R. (2017). *The color of law: A forgotten history of how our government segregated America.* Liveright.

Rubisch, J. (1995). Promoting postsecondary education in rural schools. *School Counselor, 42*(5), 405–10.

Rude, H., & Miller, K. J. (2018). Policy challenges and opportunities for rural special education. *Rural Special Education Quarterly, 37*(1), 21–9. https://doi.org/10.1177/8756870517748662

References

Rural School and Community Trust. (2013). *It's complicated . . . Why what's rural matters*. https://www.ruraledu.org/articles.php?id=3127

Rural Services Network. (2020). *Surge in interest for rural properties following Covid 19 pandemic*. https://www.rsnonline.org.uk/surge-in-interest-for-rural-properties-following-covid-19-pandemic

RuraLEARN. (2007). *Rural learning for development: Experiences from Europe*. Report on Rural Learning for Development and Book of Proceedings of the 2007 RuraLEARN Conference and Workshops. http://www.ruralearn.eu/media/RuraLEARN_Book.pdf

Sabzalian, L. (2019). *Indigenous children's survivance in public schools*. Routledge.

Sacks, V., & Murphey, D. (2018). The prevalence of adverse childhood experiences, nationally, by state, and by race or ethnicity. *Childhood Trends*. https://www.childtrends.org/publications/prevalence-adverse-childhood-experiences-nationally-state-race-ethnicity

Saeki, E., Jimerson, J. R., & Earhart, J. (2011). Response to intervention (RTI) in the social, emotional, and behavioral domains: Current challenges and emerging possibilities. *Contemporary School Psychology*, *15*, 43–52.

Sáenz, R. (2008). *A profile of Latinos in rural America*. The Carsey Institute.

Sáenz, R. (2012). Rural race and ethnicity. In L. J. Kulcsár & K. J. Curtis (Eds.), *International handbook of rural demography* (pp. 207–24). Springer.

Sáenz, R., & Torres, C. C. (2003). Latinos in rural America. In D. L. Brown & L. D. Swanson (Eds.), *Challenges for rural America in the twenty-first century* (pp. 57–70). Pennsylvania State University Press.

Sage, R., & Sherman, J. (2014). "There are no jobs here": Opportunity structures, moral judgement, and educational trajectories in the rural Northwest. In C. B. Howley, A. Howley, & J. D. Johnson (Eds.), *Dynamics of social class, race, and place in rural education* (pp. 67–94). Information Age.

Sahlberg, P. (2016). The global educational reform movement and its impact on schooling. *The handbook of global education policy* (pp. 128–44). https://doi.org/10.1002/9781118468005.ch7

Salazar, M. (2016). State recognition of American Indian tribes. *National Conference of State Legislatures LegisBrief*, 24(39).

Sale, R., Michael, K. D., Egan, T., Stevens, A., & Massey, C. (2014). Low base rate, high impact: Responding to teen suicidal threat in rural Appalachia. *Report on Emotional & Behavioral Disorders in Youth*, *14*, 4–8.

Saltman, K. J. (2010). *The gift of education*. Palgrave Macmillan.

Saltman, K. J. (2012). *The failure of corporate school reform*. Paradigm.

Sanchez, A. L., Cornacchio, D., Poznanski B., Golik, A. M., Chou, T., & Comer, J. S. (2018). The effectiveness of school-based mental health services for elementary-aged children: A meta-analysis. *Journal of American Academy of Child & Adolescent Psychiatry*, *57*(3), 153–65.

Sanders, M. G. (2001). The role of "community" in comprehensive school, family, and community partnership programs. *The Elementary School Journal*, *102*(1), 19–34.

Sanders, M. G. (2003). Community involvement in schools: From concept to practice. *Education and Urban Society*, *35*(2), 161–80.

Sanes, M., & Schmitt, J. (2014). *Regulation of public sector collective bargaining in the states*. Center for Economic and Policy Research. https://www.cepr.net/documents/state-public-cb-2014-03.pdf

Sansone, V. A. (2019, October). *Geography need not be destiny: Latinx rural students and the spatial (in) equity gap* [Keynote address]. Teachers College, New York, NY.

Sansone, V. A., Leal, D. R., & Mabrie, P. K. (2020, February). *The spatial experiences of rural Latinx youth: Geography, power, and college choice in the borderlands of south Texas* [Paper presentation]. Annual meeting of the Texas Association for Chicanos in Higher Education, Sugar Land, TX.

Santos, B. d. S. (2014). *Epistemologies of the South: Justice against epistemicide*. Paradigm Publishers. https://doi.org/10.4324/9781315634876

Satullo, S. (2019, August 19). Governor wants to take PA's charter law from among the nation's worst to one of its best. *Lehighvalleylive.com*. https://www.lehighvalleylive.com/news/2019/08/gov-wolf-wants-to-take-pas-charter-school-law-from-1-of-nations-worst-to-1-of-its-best.html

Savage, G., & O'Connor, K. (2019). What's the problem with "policy alignment"? The complexities of national reform in Australia's federal system. *Journal of Education Policy*, *34*(6), 812–35. https://doi.org/10.1080/02680939.2018.1545050

References

Schaefer, A., & Mattingly, M. J. (2016). Demographic and economic characteristics of immigrant and native-born populations in rural and urban places. *Carsey Research National Issue Brief* (Vol. 106). Carsey School of Public Policy: University of New Hampshire.

Schaefer, A., Mattingly, M. J., & Johnson, K. M. (2016). *Child poverty higher and more persistent in rural America* [Policy brief]. Carsey School of Public Policy: University of New Hampshire. https://carsey.unh.edu/publication/rural-child-poverty-higher

Schafft, K. A. (2006). Poverty, residential mobility, and student transiency within a rural New York school district. *Rural Sociology, 71*(2), 212–31. https://doi.org/10.1526/003601106777789710

Schafft, K. A. (2016). Rural education as rural development: Understanding the rural school-community well-being linkage in a 21st century policy context. *Peabody Journal of Education, 91*(2), 137–54. https://doi.org/10.1080/0161956x.2016.1151734

Schafft, K. A. (2017). Case study: Education, economic disadvantage, and homeless students in Pennsylvania's Marcellus Shale gas region. In A. Tickamyer, J. Sherman, & J. Warlick (Eds.), *Rural poverty in the United States* (pp. 339–42). Columbia University Press. https://doi.org/10.7312/tick17222-022

Schafft, K. A., Alter, T. R., & Bridger, J. C. (2006). Bringing the community along: A case study of a school district's information technology rural development initiative. *Journal of Research in Rural Education, 21*(8), 1–10. https://jrre.psu.edu/sites/default/files/2019-08/21-8.pdf

Schafft, K. A., & Biddle, C. (2013). Place and purpose in public education: School district mission statements and educational (dis) embeddedness. *American Journal of Education, 120*(1), 055–076.

Schafft, K. A., & Biddle, C. (2014). School and community impacts of hydraulic fracturing within Pennsylvania's Marcellus Shale Region, and the dilemmas of educational leadership in gasfield Boomtowns. *Peabody Journal of Education, 89*(5), 670–82. https://doi.org/10.1080/0161956X.2014.956567

Schafft, K. A., & Biddle, C. (2015). Opportunity, ambivalence, and youth perspectives on community change in Pennsylvania's Marcellus Shale region. *Human Organization, 74*(1), 74–85. https://doi.org/10.17730/humo.74.1.6543u2613xx23678

Schafft, K. A., Brasier, K. B., & Hesse, A. (2019). Reconceptualizing rapid energy resource development and its impacts: Thinking regionally, spatially and intersectionally. *Journal of Rural Studies, 68*, 296–305. https://doi.org/10.1016/j.jrurstud.2018.12.007

Schafft, K. A., Frankenberg, E., Fuller, E., Harman, W., Kotok, S., & Mann, B. (2014). *Assessing the enrollment trends and financial impacts of charter schools on rural and non-rural school districts in Pennsylvania*. The Center for Rural Pennsylvania. https://www.rural.palegislature.us/documents/reports/Charter_School_2014.pdf

Schafft, K. A., Glenna, L. L., Borlu, Y., & Green, B. (2014). Local impacts of unconventional gas development within Pennsylvania's Marcellus Shale region: Gauging boomtown development through the perspectives of educational administrators. *Society & Natural Resources 27*, 389–404. https://doi.org/10.1080/08941920.2013.861561

Schafft, K. A., & Harmon, H. (2011). The role of education in community development. In J. W. Robinson & G. P. Green (Eds.), *Introduction to community development: Theory, practice, and service-learning* (pp. 245–60). Sage.

Schafft, K. A., & Jackson, A. Y. (2010a). Introduction: Rural education and community in the twenty-first century. In K. A. Schafft & A. Y. Jackson (Eds.), *Rural education for the twenty-first century* (pp. 1–13). The Pennsylvania State University Press.

Schafft, K. A., & Jackson, A. Y. (Eds.). (2010b). *Rural education for the twenty-first century: Identity, place and community in a globalizing world*. The Pennsylvania State University Press.

Schafft, K. A., Killeen, K. M., & Morrissey, J. (2010). The challenges of student transiency for rural schools and communities in the era of No Child Left Behind. In K. A. Schafft & A. Y. Jackson (Eds.), *Rural education for the twenty-first century: Identity, place, and community in a globalizing world* (pp. 95–114). The Pennsylvania State University Press.

Schafft, K. A., McHenry-Sorber, E., Hall, D., & Burfoot-Rochford, I. (2018). Busted amidst the boom: The creation of new insecurities and inequalities within Pennsylvania's shale gas boomtowns. *Rural Sociology, 38*(3), 503–31. https://doi.org/10.1111/ruso.12196

Schafft, K. A., Petrin, R., & Farmer, T. (2011, July). *Achievers, stayers, seekers, and others: Brain drain and the potential for rural return among rural high school students* [Paper presentation]. 73rd annual Rural Sociological Society meetings, Boise, ID.

Schafft, K. A., Stanić, S., Horvatek, R., & Maselli, A. (Eds.). (2021). *Rural youth at the crossroads: Transitional societies in Central Europe and beyond.* Routledge.

Scharf, T., Walsh, K., & O'Shea, E. (2016). Ageing in rural places. In M. Shucksmith & D. L. Brown (Eds.), *Routledge international handbook of rural studies* (pp. 50–61). Routledge.

Schauber, A. C. (2001). Effecting extension organizational change toward cultural diversity: A conceptual framework. *Journal of Extension, 39*(3). https://archives.joe.org/joe/2001june/a1.php

Schell, E. E. (2007). The rhetorics of the farm crisis: Toward alternative agrarian literacies in a globalized world. In K. Donehower, C. Hogg, & E. E. Schell (Eds.), *Rural literacies* (pp. 77–119). Southern Illinois University Press.

Schirmer, E. B. (2017). When solidarity doesn't quite strike: The 1974 Hortonville, Wisconsin teachers' strike and the rise of neoliberalism. *Gender and Education, 29*(1), 8–27. https://doi.org/10.1080/09540 253.2016.1197381

Schlaffer, J. S. (2018). Financing public education facilities: The role of elderly populations and geographic mobility. *Social Science Quarterly, 99*, 118–35. https://doi.org/10.1111/ssqu.12388

Schmitt-Wilson, S. (2013). Social class and expectations of rural adolescents: The role of parental expectations. *The Career Development Quarterly, 61*(3), 226–39.

Schmitt-Wilson, S., Downey, J., & Beck, A. E. (2018). Rural educational attainment: The importance of context. *Journal of Research in Rural Education, 33*(1), 1–14. https://jrre.psu.edu/sites/default/files/2019-08/33-1.pdf

Schwerdtfeger, R. D. (1984). This new management demeanor reduces post-strike rancor in schools. *American School Board Journal, 171*(4), 40–53.

Scribner, C. F. (2016). *The fight for local control: Schools, suburbs, and American democracy.* Cornell University Press.

Seamster, L., & Henricks, K. (2015). A second redemption? Racism, backlash politics, and public education. *Humanity and Society, 39*(4), 363–75.

Seashore Louis, K., Dretzke, B., & Wahlstrom, K. (2010). How does leadership affect student achievement? Results from a national US survey. *School Effectiveness and School Improvement, 21*(3), 315–36. https://doi.org/10.1080/09243453.2010.486586

Seaton, E. E. (2007). "If teachers are good to you": Caring for rural girls in the classroom. *Journal of Research in Rural Education, 22*(6), 1–16.

Secatero, S. (2015). The Leadership Tree: The emergence of Indigenous well-being factors in rural leadership and higher education. In R. S. Minthorn & A. F. Chavez (Eds.), *Indigenous leadership in higher education* (pp. 111–26). Routledge.

Seelig, J. L. (2017a). Battling declining enrolment in the Upper Midwestern United States: Rural schools in a competitive society. *Australian and International Journal of Rural Education, 27*(2), 77–92.

Seelig, J. L. (2017b). *North of Highway 8: An ethnographic study of a school–community relationship in rural Wisconsin* (Publication No. 10599036) [Doctoral dissertation, The University of Wisconsin–Madison]. ProQuest Dissertations and Theses.

Sell, R. S., Leistritz, F., & Thompson, J. M. (1996). *Socio-economic impacts of school consolidation on host and vacated communities.* Agricultural Economic Report No. 347. https://files.eric.ed.gov/fulltext/ED423100.pdf

Shaffer, D., & Gould, M. S. (2000). Suicide prevention in schools. In K. Hawton & K. Van Heeringen (Eds.), *The international handbook of suicide and attempted suicide*, 645–60. Wiley.

Shahjahan, R. A. (2011). Decolonizing the evidence-based education and policy movement: Revealing the colonial vestiges in educational policy, research, and neoliberal reform. *Journal of Education Policy, 26*(2), 181–206. https://doi.org/10.1080/02680939.2010.508176

Shaia, W. E., & Crowder, S. C. (2017). Schools as re-traumatizing environments. In N. Finnigan-Carr (Ed.), *Linking health and education for African American students' success* (pp. 69–82). Routledge.

References

Shamblin, S., Graham, D., & Bianco, J. A. (2016). Creating trauma-informed schools for rural Appalachia: The partnerships program for enhancing resiliency, confidence, and workforce development in early childhood education. *School Mental Health, 8*, 189–200.

Sharp, G., & Lee, B. A. (2017). New faces in rural places: Patterns and sources of nonmetropolitan ethnoracial diversity since 1990. *Rural Sociology, 82*(3), 411–43. https://doi.org/10.1111/ruso.12141

Sharplin, E. (2002). Rural retreat or outback hell: Expectations of rural and remote teaching. *Issues in Educational Research, 12*(1), 49.

Shear, S. B., Knowles, R. T., Soden, G. J., & Castro, A. J. (2015). Manifesting destiny: Re/presentations of Indigenous peoples in K–12 U.S. history standards. *Theory and Research in Social Education, 43*(1), 68–101. https://doi.org/10.1080/00933104.2014.999849

Sheller, M., & Urry, J. (2006). The new mobilities paradigm. *Environment and Planning A: Economy and Space, 38*(2), 207–26. https://doi.org/10.1068/a37268

Shelly, B. (2008). Rebels and their causes: State resistance to no child left behind. *Publius: The Journal of Federalism, 38*(3), 444–68. https://doi.org/10.1093/publius/pjn008

Shelly, B. (2012). Flexible response: Executive federalism and the No Child Left Behind Act of 2001. *Educational Policy, 26*(1), 117–35. https://doi.org/10.1177/0895904811425912

Shelton, J. (2013). Against the public: The Pittsburgh teachers strike of 1975–1976 and the crisis of the labor-liberal coalition. *LABOR: Studies in Working-Class History of the Americas, 10*(2), 55–75. https://doi.org/10.1215/15476715-2071697

Shen, Q. (1998). Location characteristics of inner-city neighborhoods and employment accessibility of low-wage workers. *Environment and Planning B: Urban Analytics and City Science, 25*(3), 345–65. https://doi.org/10.1068/b250345

Shenkar, M., & Shenkar, O. (2011). Labor conflict on the national stage: Metaphoric lenses in Israel's teachers' strike. *Comparative Education Review, 55*(2), 210–30. https://doi.org/10.1086/657973

Sher, J. P. (1995). The battle for the soul of rural school reform. *Phi Delta Kappan, 77*(2), 143–48.

Sheridan, S. M. (2014). *The tough kid: Teachers and parents as partners*. Ancora.

Sheridan, S. M., Knoche, L. L., Boise, C. E., Moen, A. L., Lester, H., Edwards, C. P., Meisinger, R. E., & Cheng, K. (2019). Supporting preschool children with developmental concerns: Effects of the Getting Ready intervention on school-based social competencies and relationships. *Early Childhood Research Quarterly, 48*, 303–16. https://doi.org/10.1016/j.ecresq.2019.03.008

Sheridan, S. M., Knoche, L. L., Edwards, C. P., Bovaird, J. A., & Kupzyk, K. A. (2010). Parent engagement and school readiness: Effects of the Getting Ready intervention on preschool children's social-emotional competencies. *Early Education and Development, 21*, 125–56. https://doi.org/10.1080/10409280902783517

Sheridan, S. M., Knoche, L. L., Edwards, C. P., Kupzyk, K. A., Clarke, B. L., & Kim, E. M. (2014). Efficacy of the Getting Ready intervention and the role of parental depression. *Early Education and Development, 25*, 746–69. https://doi.org/10.1080/10409289.2014.8621246

Sheridan, S. M., Knoche, L. L., Kupzyk, K. A., Edwards, C. P., & Marvin, C. A. (2011). A randomized trial examining the effects of parent engagement on early language and literacy: The Getting Ready intervention. *Journal of School Psychology, 49*, 361–83. https://doi.org/10.1016/j.jsp.2011.03.001

Sheridan, S. M., & Kratochwill, T. R. (1992). Behavioral parent-teacher consultation: Conceptual and research considerations. *Journal of School Psychology, 30*(2), 117–39. https://doi.org/10.1016/0022-4405(92)90025-Z

Sheridan, S. M., & Kratochwill, T. R. (2008). *Conjoint behavioral consultation: Promoting family-school connections and interventions*. Springer.

Sheridan, S. M., Marvin, C. A., Knoche, L. L., & Edwards, C. P. (2008). Getting ready: Promoting school readiness through a relationship-based partnership model. *Early Childhood Services, 2*, 149–72.

Sheridan, S. M., Witte, A. L., Holmes, S. R., Coutts, M., Dent, A., Kunz, G., & Wu, C. (2017). A randomized trial examining the effects of conjoint behavioral consultation in rural schools: Student outcomes and the mediating role of the teacher–parent relationship. *Journal of School Psychology, 61*, 33–53. https://doi.org/10.1016/j.jsp.2016.12.002

References

Sheridan, S. M., Witte, A. L., Holmes, S. R., Wu, C., Bhatia, S. A., & Angell, S. R., (2017). The efficacy of conjoint behavioral consultation in the home setting: Outcomes and mechanisms in rural communities. *Journal of School Psychology, 62*, 81–101. https://doi.org/10.1016/j.jsp.2017.03.005

Sheridan, S. M., Witte, A. L., Kunz, G. M., Wheeler, L. A., Angell, S. R., & Lester, H. F. (2018). Rural teacher practices and partnerships to address behavioral challenges: The efficacy and mechanisms of conjoint behavioral consultation. *The Elementary School Journal, 119*, 99–121.https://doi.org/10.1086/698694

Sherman, J. (2006). Coping with rural poverty: Economic survival and moral capital in rural America. *Social Forces, 85*(2), 891–913. https://doi.org/10.1353/sof.2007.0026

Sherman, J. (2009). *Those who work, those who don't: Poverty, morality, and family in rural America.* University of Minnesota Press.

Sherman, J. (2018). "Not allowed to inherit my kingdom": Amenity development and social inequality in the rural West. *Rural Sociology, 83*(1), 174–207. https://doi.org/10.1111/ruso.12168

Sherman, J. (2021). *Dividing paradise: Rural inequality and the diminishing American dream.* University of California Press.

Shirley, D. (2001). Faith-based organizations, community development, and the reform of public schools. *Peabody Journal of Education, 76*(2), 222–39.

Shonkoff, J. P., & Phillips, D. A. (Eds.). (2000). *From neurons to neighborhoods: The science of early childhood development.* National Academies Press. https://doi.org/10.17226/9824

Shonkoff, J. P., Richter, L., van der Gaag, J., & Bhutta, Z. A. (2012). An integrated scientific framework for child survival and early childhood development. *Pediatrics, 129*, 1–13. https://doi.org/10.1542/peds.2011-0366

Showalter, D., Hartman, S. L., Johnson, J., & Klein, R. (2019). *Why rural matters 2018–2019: The time is now.* Rural School and Community Trust. http://www.ruraledu.org/WhyRuralMatters.pdf

Showalter, D., Klein, R., & Johnson, J. (2017). *Why rural matters 2015–16: Understanding the changing landscape.* Rural School and Community Trust. https://www.ruraledu.org/user_uploads/file/WRM-2015-16.pdf

Shucksmith, M. (2018). Re-imagining the rural: From rural idyll to Good Countryside. *Journal of Rural Studies, 59*, 163–72. https://doi.org/10.1016/j.jrurstud.2016.07.019

Siceloff, E. R., Barnes-Young, C., Massey, C., Yell, M., & Weist, M. D. (2017). Building policy support for school mental health in rural areas. In K. D. Michael & J. P. Jameson (Eds.), *Handbook of rural school mental health* (pp. 17–34). Springer.

Siddle Walker, V. (2000). Valued segregated schools for African American children in the South, 1935–1969: A review of common themes and characteristics. *Review of Education Research, 70*(3), 253–85. https://doi.org/10.3102/00346543070003253

Siegle, D. (2013). *The underachieving gifted child: Recognizing, understanding, and reversing underachievement.* Prufrock Press.

Sierk, J. (2017). Redefining rurality: Cosmopolitanism, Whiteness, and the New Latino Diaspora. *Discourse: Studies in the cultural politics of eEducation, 38*(3), 342–53. https://doi.org/10.1080/01596306.2017.1306980

Sikes, A. (2018). Rural students' experiences at selective four-year colleges: Pathways to persistence and success (Publication No. 1530192623) [Doctoral Dissertation]. College of William & Mary. http://dx.doi.org/10.25774/w4-rjc7-rx48

Silva, J. M. (2013). *Coming up short: Working-class adulthood in the age of uncertainty.* Oxford University Press.

Sindelar, P. T., Pua, D. J., Fisher, T., Peyton, D. J., Brownell, M. T., & Mason-Williams, L. (2018). The demand for special education teachers in rural schools revisited: An update on progress. *Rural Special Education Quarterly, 37*(1), 12–20. https://doi.org/10.1177/8756870517749247

Singh, G. K., Azuine, R. E., Siahpush, M., & Kogan, M. D. (2013). All-cause and cause-specific mortality among US youth: socioeconomic and rural–urban disparities and international patterns. *Journal of Urban Health, 90*(3), 388–405. https://doi.org/10.1007/s11524-012-9744-0.

References

Sipple, J. W., Fiduccia, P., & LeBeau, K. (2019, July). *#RuralReality in NY State in 2019*. New York State Center for Rural Schools. https://www.researchgate.net/publication/335793379_Rural_Reality_in_NY_State_in_2019

Sipple, J. W., Francis, J. D., & Fiduccia, P. C. (2019). Exploring the gradient: The economic benefits of 'nearby' schools on rural communities. *Journal of Rural Studies, 68*, 251–63. https://doi.org/10.1016/j.jrurstud.2019.02.018

Sipple, J. W., McCabe, L. A., & Casto, H. G. (2020). Child care deserts in New York State: Prekindergarten implementation and community factors related to the capacity to care for infants and toddlers. *Early Childhood Research Quarterly, 51*, 167–77.

Slavin, R. E. (2020). How evidence-based reform will transform research and practice in education, *Educational Psychologist, 55*(1), 21–31. https://doi.org/10.1080/00461520.2019.1611432

Slee, R. (2001). Social justice and the changing directions in educational research: The case of inclusive education. *International Journal of Inclusive Education, 5*(2–3), 167–77. https://doi.org/10.1080/13603110010035832

Smarick, A. (2014, January 29). *A new frontier: Utilizing charter schooling to strengthen rural education*. Bellewether Education Partners. https://bellwethereducation.org/publication/new-frontier-utilizing-charter-schooling-strengthen-rural-education

Smart, A., & Russell, B. (2018, August 21). What rural America can teach us about civil society. *Stanford Social Innovation Review*. https://ssir.org/articles/entry/what_rural_america_can_teach_us_about_civil_society

Smink, J., & Reimer, M. (2015). *Rural school dropout issues: Implications for dropout prevention, strategies and programs*. National Dropout Prevention Center/Network. http://dropoutprevention.org/wp-content/uploads/2015/05/13_Rural_School_Dropout_Issues_Report.pdf

Smit, R., Hyry-Beihammer, E. K., & Raggl, A. (2015). Teaching and learning in small, rural schools in four European countries: Introduction and synthesis of mixed-/multi-age approaches. *International Journal of Educational Research, 74*, 97–103. https://doi.org/10.1016/j.ijer.2015.04.007

Smith, G. A. (2002). Place-based education: Learning to be where we are. *The Phi Delta Kappan, 83*(8), 584–94. https://doi.org/10.1177/003172170208300806

Smith, J., Stern, K., & Shatrova, Z. (2008). Factors inhibiting Hispanic parents' school involvement. *The Rural Educator, 29*(2), 8–13. https://doi.org/10.35608/ruraled.v29i2.468

Smith, K. E., & Tickamyer, A. R. (Eds.). (2011). *Economic restructuring and family well-being in rural America*. Penn State University Press.

Smith, L. B., & Thelen, E. (2003). Development as a dynamic system. *Trends in Cognitive Sciences, 7*, 343–8. https://doi.org/10.1016/S1364-6613(03)00156-6

Smith, L. T. (1999). *Decolonizing methodologies: Research and Indigenous peoples*. Zed Books.

Smith, M., Patterson, K., & Doggett, L. (2008). *Meeting the challenge of rural pre-k*. Pre-K Now. https://www.pewtrusts.org/~/media/legacy/uploadedfiles/pcs_assets/2008/meetingthechallengeofruralprekpdf.pdf

Smith, M. H., Beaulieu, L. J., & Seraphine, A. (1995). Social capital, place of residence, and college attendance. *Rural Sociology, 60*(3), 363–80.

Smith, N. (2008). *Uneven development: Nature, capital, and the production of space* (3rd ed.). University of Georgia Press.

Smith, T. (1969). *A discourse of the commonweal of this realm of England* (Mary Dewar, Ed.). University of Virginia Press.

Snodgrass Rangel, V. (2018). A review of the literature on principal turnover. *Review of Educational Research, 88*(1), 87–124. https://doi.org/10.3102%2F0034654317743197

Snow, C. E. (2015). 2014 Wallace Foundation Distinguished Lecture: Rigor and realism— Doing educational science in the real world. *Educational Researcher, 44*, 460–6. https://doi.org/10.3102/0013189x15619166

Snyder, T., & Musu-Gillette, L. (2015). Free or reduced price lunch: A proxy for poverty? *NCES Blog: National Center for Education Statistics*. https://nces.ed.gov/blogs/nces/post/free-or-reduced-price-lunch-a-proxy-for-poverty

Snyder, T. D., de Brey, C., & Dillow, S. A. (2016). *Digest of education statistics 2014* (NCES 2016–006). National Center for Education Statistics, Institute of Education Sciences, U.S. Department of Education.

Snyder, T. D., & Dillow, S. A. (2010). *Digest of education statistics 2009* (NCES 2010–013). National Center for Education Statistics, Institute of Education Sciences, U.S. Department of Education.

Soja, E. (1989). *Postmodern geographies*. Verso.

Soja, E. W. (2010). *Seeking spatial justice: Vol. 16. Globalization and community*. University of Minnesota Press.

Solstad, K. J., & Karlberg-Grandlund, G. (2020). Rural education in a globalised world: The cases of Norway and Finland. In C. Gristy, L. Hargreaves, & S. R. Kučerová (Eds.), *Educational research and schooling in rural Europe: An engagement with changing patterns of education, space, and place* (pp. 49–78). Information Age Publishing.

Somerville, M., & Rennie, J. (2012). Mobilising community? Place, identity formation and new teachers' learning. *Discourse: Studies in the cultural politics of education, 33*(2), 193–206. https://doi.org/10.1080/01596306.2012.666075

South, S. J., Baumer, E. P., & Lutz, A. (2003). Interpreting community effects on youth educational attainment. *Youth and Society, 35*(1), 3–26. https://doi.org/10.1177/0044118x03254560

Soy, A. (2020, October 7). Coronavirus in Africa: Five reasons why Covid-19 has been less deadly than elsewhere. *BBC News*. https://www.bbc.com/news/world-africa-54418613

Sparks, P. J., & Nuñez, A. (2014). The role of postsecondary institutional urbanicity in college persistence. *Journal of Research in Rural Education, 29*(6), 1–19. https://jrre.psu.edu/sites/default/files/2019-08/29-6.pdf

Spencer, H. (1882). *The study of sociology*. D. Appleton.

Spicker, H. H., Southern, W. T., & Davis, B. I. (1987). The rural gifted child. *Gifted Child Quarterly, 31*(4), 155–7.

Sprang, G., Craig, C., & Clark, J. (2011). Secondary traumatic stress and burnout in child welfare workers: A comparative analysis of occupational distress across professional groups. *Child Welfare, 90*, 149–68.

Spring, J. H. (2012). *Deculturalization and the struggle for equality: A brief history of the education of dominated cultures in the United States* (7th ed.). McGraw-Hill.

Squire, C., Andrews, M., & Tamboukou, M. (2008). Introduction: What is narrative research? In M. Andrews, C. Squire, & M. Tamboukou (Eds.), *Doing narrative research* (pp. 1–21). Sage.

Squire, J. (2018). Right place, right time: The potential of rural charter schools. In M. McShane & A. Smarick (Eds.), *No longer forgotten: The triumphs and struggles of rural education in America* (pp. 135–54). Rowman & Littlefield.

Stachowiak, S., & Gase, L. (2018). Does collective impact really make an impact? Eight findings from a recent study of collective impact initiatives, including their effect on systems and population-level outcomes. *Stanford Social Innovation Review*. https://ssir.org/articles/entry/does_collective_impact_really_make_an_impact

Stambaugh, T., & Wood, S. M. (2016, April). *Serving gifted students in rural settings* [Webinar]. National Association for Gifted Children. http://www.nagc.org/sites/default/files/WebinarPowerPoints/Serving%20Gifted%20Students%20in%20Rural%20Settings.pdf

Stanton-Salazar, R. D. (1997). A social capital framework for understanding the socialization of racial minority children and youths. *Harvard Educational Review, 67*(1), 1–40. https://doi.org/10.17763/haer.67.1.140676g74018u73k

Star, J. R., Caronongan, P., Foegen, A., Furgeson, J., Keating, B., Larson, M. R., Lyskawa, J., McCallum, W. G., Porath, J., & Zbiek, R. M. (2015). *Teaching strategies for improving algebra knowledge in middle and high school students* (NCEE 2015-4010). U.S. Department of Education, Institute of Education Sciences, National Center for Education Evaluation and Regional Assistance. https://ies.ed.gov/ncee/wwc/PracticeGuide/20

Starr, K. (2015). Small rural school leadership: Creating opportunity through collaboration. In S. Clarke & T. O'Donoghue (Eds.), *School leadership in diverse contexts*. (pp. 49–62). Routledge.

References

Starr, K., & White, S. (2008). The small rural school principalship: Key challenges and cross-school responses. *Journal of Research in Rural Education, 23*(5), 1–12. https://jrre.psu.edu/sites/default/files/2019-08/23-5.pdf

State of Utah. (2008). SB0041. International Education Initiative (IEI). https://le.utah.gov/~2008/bills/sbillenr/sb0041.htm

State of Washington Office of Superintendent of Public Instruction. (2018). *Since time immemorial: Tribal sovereignty in Washington state.* http://www.k12.wa.us/IndianEd/TribalSovereignty/default.aspx

Steele, C. M., & Aronson, J. (1995). Stereotype threat and the intellectual test performance of African Americans. *Journal of Personality and Social Psychology, 69,* 797–811. https://doi.org/10.1037/0022-3514.69.5.797

Steele, C. M., Spencer, S. J., & Aronson, J. (2002). Contending with group image: The psychology of stereotype and social identity threat. In M. Zanna (Ed.), *Advances in experimental social psychology* (Vol. 34, pp. 379–440). Academic Press. https://doi.org/10.1016/S0065-2601(02)80009-0

Stein, B. D., Jaycox, L. H., Kataoka, S. H., Wong, M., Tu, W., Elliott, M. N., & Fink, A. (2003). A mental health intervention for school children exposed to violence: A randomized controlled trial. *Journal of the American Medical Association, 290*(5), 603–11.

Stein, S. (2017). A colonial history of the higher education present: Rethinking land-grant institutions through processes of accumulation and relations of conquest. *Critical Studies in Education, 61*(2), 212–28. http://www.tandfonline.com/doi/full/10.1080/17508487.2017.1409646

Stephens, E. R. (1992). Mapping the research task for the construction of a federal system for classifying the nation's rural school districts. *Journal of Research in Rural Education, 8*(3), 3–28. https://jrre.psu.edu/sites/default/files/2019-08/8-3_3.pdf

Stepick, A., & Stepick, C. D. (2009). Diverse contexts of reception and feelings of belonging. *Forum Qualitative Sozialforschung/Forum: Qualitative Social Research, 10*(3). http://archives.pdx.edu/ds/psu/15234

Stern, J. D. (Ed.). (1992). Introduction. *Journal of Research in Rural Education, 8*(3), 1–2. https://jrre.psu.edu/sites/default/files/2019-08/8-3_1.pdf

Sternberg, R. J. (2011). The theory of successful intelligence. In R. J. Sternberg & S. B. Kaufman (Eds.), *The Cambridge handbook of intelligence* (pp. 504–27). Cambridge University Press.

Stewart, C., & Matthews, J. (2015). The lone ranger in rural education: The small rural school principal and professional development. *The Rural Educator, 36*(3), 1–13.

Stewart, H., Jameson, J. P., & Curtin, L. (2015). The relationship between stigma and self-reported willingness to use mental health services among rural and urban older adults. *Psychological Services, 12*(2), 141.

Stone, A. N., Serrata, C., & Martinez, K. (2020). Small town values: Exploring the values of Latina college students from rural communities. *Journal of Latinos and Education,* 1–13. https://doi.org/10.1080/15348431.2020.1727745

Stone, C. N., Henig, J. R., Jones, B. D., & Pierannunzi, C. (2001). *Building civic capacity: The politics of reforming urban schools (Studies in Government and Public Policy).* University Press of Kansas.

Strange, M. (2011). Finding fairness for rural students. *Phi Delta Kappan, 92*(6), 8–15. https://doi.org/10.1177/003172171109200603

Strange, M. (2013). The importance of being Emily: Lessons from legislative battles of forced school consolidations. *Great Plains Research, 23*(2), 107–14.

Strange, M., Johnson, J., & Finical, A. (2009). Many children left behind: How Title I weighted granted formulas favor the few at the expense of the many in Pennsylvania. *Rural School and Community Trust.* https://files.eric.ed.gov/fulltext/ED504956.pdf

Strange, M., Johnson, J., Showalter, D., & Klein, R. (2012). *Why rural matters 2011–12: The condition of rural education in the 50 states.* Rural School and Community Trust.

Street, B. (1995). *Social literacies.* Longman.

Street, B. (2003). What's "new" in New Literacy Studies? Critical approaches to literacy in yheory and practice. *Current Issues in Comparative Education, 5*(2), 77–91.

Strunk, K. O., & Grissom, J. A. (2010). Do strong unions shape district policies? Collective bargaining, teacher contract restrictiveness, and the political power of teachers' unions. *Educational Evaluation and Policy Analysis*, *32*(3), 389–406. https://doi.org/10.3102/0162373710376665

Strunk, K. O., & Marianno, B. D. (2019). Negotiating the Great Recession: How teacher collective bargaining outcomes change in times of financial duress. *AERA Open*, *5*(2), 1–18. https://doi.org/10.1177/2332858419855089

Stuit, D., & Doan, S. (2012). *Beyond city limits: Expanding public charter schools in rural America.* National Alliance for Public Charter Schools (NAPCS). https://www.publiccharters.org/publications/city-limits-expanding-public-charter-schools-rural-america

Subotnik, R. F., Olszewski-Kubilius, P., & Worrell, F. C. (2011). Rethinking giftedness and gifted education: A proposed direction forward based on psychological science. *Psychological Science in the Public Interest*, *12*(1), 3–54. https://doi.org/10.1177/1529100611418056

Substance Abuse and Mental Health Administration. (2014, October). *SAMHSA's Trauma and Justice Strategic Initiative.* https://store.samhsa.gov/product/SAMHSA-s-Concept-of-Trauma-and-Guidance-for-a-Trauma-Informed-Approach/SMA14-4884?referer=from_search_result.

Sugarman, J. (2018, June). *A matter of design: English learner program models in K–12 education* [Policy brief]. Migration Policy Institute. https://www.migrationpolicy.org/research/english-learner-program-models-k-12-education

Sullivan, S. (2006). *Revealing Whiteness: The unconscious habits of racial privilege*. Indiana University Press.

Superfine, B., & Woo, D. (2018). Teacher unions, charter schools, and the public/private distinction in education law and policy. *Teachers College Record*, *12*(10), 1–28.

Superville, D. R. (2018, April 30). Where school employees can't afford housing, some districts try to help. *Education Week*. https://www.edweek.org/ew/articles/2018/05/02/where-school-employees-cant-afford-housing-some.html

Superville, D. R. (2020a). Will academia give rural schools the attention they need? *Education Week*, *39*(19), 5. https://www.edweek.org/ew/articles/2020/01/22/will-academia-give-rural-schools-the-attention.html

Superville, D. R. (2020b, June 24). Is it time to reconsider the year-round school schedule? *Education Week*. https://www.edweek.org/ew/articles/2020/06/25/is-it-time-to-reconsider-the-year-round.html

Surface, J., & Theobald, P. (2014). The rural school leadership dilemma. *Peabody Journal of Education*, *89*(5), 570–9. https://www.tandfonline.com/doi/full/10.1080/0161956X.2014.955753

Sutcher, L., Darling-Hammond, L., & Carver-Thomas, D. (2016). *A coming crisis in teaching? Teacher supply, demand, and shortages in the U.S.* Learning Policy Institute. https://learningpolicyinstitute.org/sites/default/files/product-files/A_Coming_Crisis_in_Teaching_REPORT.pdf

Sutcher, L., Darling-Hammond, L., & Carver-Thomas, D. (2019). Understanding teacher shortages: An analysis of teacher supply and demand in the United States. *Education Policy Analysis Archives*, *27*(35). http://dx.doi.org/10.14507/epaa.27.3696

Sutherland, D. H. (2020). School board sense-making of federal and state accountability policies. *Educational Policy*. https://doi.org/10.1177/0895904820925816

Sutton, A., Lichter, D. T., & Sassler, S. (2019). Rural–urban disparities in pregnancy intentions, births, and abortions among US adolescent and young women, 1995–2017. *American Journal of Public Health*, *109*(12), 1762–9. https://doi.org/10.2105/ajph.2019.305318

Sutton, J. M., Jr. (1988). Work environment perspectives of school guidance counselors in isolated settings. *Research in Rural Education*, *5*(1), 17–21.

Sutton, J. M., Jr., & Pearson, R. E. (2002). The practice of school counseling in rural and small town schools. *Professional School Counseling*, *5*(4), 266–76.

Sutton, J. M., Jr., & Southworth, R. S. (1990). The effect of the rural setting on school counselors. *The School Counselor*, *37*(3), 173–8.

Swift, D. (1988). *Preparing rural students for an urban environment*. ERIC Clearinghouse on Rural Education and Small Schools. (Eric Document Reproduction Service No. ED 296 818).

References

Synott, J. P. (2017). *Teacher unions, social movements and the politics of education in Asia: South Korea, Taiwan and the Philippines*. Routledge.

Szasz, M. (1999). *Education and the American Indian: The road to self-determination since 1928* (3rd ed.). University of New Mexico Press.

Taie, S., & Goldring, R. (2020). *Characteristics of public and private elementary and secondary schools in the United States: Results from the 2017–18 national teacher and principal survey first look*. NCES 2020-142rev. National Center for Education Statistics. https://nces.ed.gov/pubsearch/pubsinfo.asp?pubid=2020142rev

Tantarimäki, S., & Törhönen, A. (2020). School network changes in Finland: The challenges for future planning. In C. Gristy, L. Hargreaves, & S. R. Kučerová (Eds.), *Educational research and schooling in rural Europe: An engagement with changing patterns of education, space, and place* (pp. 259–84). Information Age Publishing.

Tate, W. F., IV. (2008). "Geography of opportunity": Poverty, place, and educational outcomes. *Educational Researcher*, *37*(7), 397–411. https://doi.org/10.3102/0013189X08326409

Taylor, C. (1995). *Philosophical arguments*. Harvard University Press.

Taylor, E. (2009). The foundations of critical race theory in education: An introduction. In E. Taylor, D. Gillborn, & G. Ladson-Billings (Eds.), *Foundations of Critical Race Theory in education* (pp. 1–13). Routledge.

Taylor, F. W. (1911). *Principles of scientific management*. The Plimpton Press.

Taylor, S. (1997). Critical policy analysis: Exploring contexts, texts and consequences. *Discourse: Studies in the Cultural Politics of Education*, *18*(1), 23–35. https://doi.org/10.1080/0159630970180102

Telford, T. (2019, September 26). Income inequality in America is the highest it's been since Census Bureau started tracking it, data shows. *The Washington Post*. https://www.washingtonpost.com/business/2019/09/26/income-inequality-america-highest-its-been-since-census-started-tracking-it-data-show/

Terrazas, A. (2011). *Immigrants in new-destination states*. Migration Policy Institute. https://www.migrationpolicy.org/article/immigrants-new-destination-states

Tervalon, M., & Murray-Garcia, J. (1998). Cultural humility versus cultural competence: A critical distinction in definition. *Journal of Health Care for the Poor and Underserved*, *9*(2), 117–26.

The Times Editorial Board. (2020, June 4). Editorial: A very abbreviated history of police officers killing Black people. *Los Angeles Times*. https://www.latimes.com/opinion/story/2020-06-04/police-killings-black-victims

Thelin, J. R. (2019). *A history of American higher education* (3rd ed.). Johns Hopkins University Press.

Theobald, P. (1995). *Call school: Rural education in the midwest to 1918*. Southern Illinois University Press.

Theobald, P. (1997). *Teaching the commons: Place, pride, and the renewal of community*. Westview Press.

Theobald, P., & Campbell C. (2014). The fate of rural communities and schools in a corporation-dominated political economy. In C. B. Howley, A. Howley, & J. D. Johnson (Eds.), *Dynamics of social class, race, and place in rural education* (pp. 193–216). Information Age Press.

Theobald, P., & Wood, K. (2010). Learning to be rural: Identity lessons from history, schooling and the U.S. corporate media. In K. A. Schafft & A. Y. Jackson (Eds.), *Rural education for the twenty-first century: Identity, place, and community in a globalizing world* (pp. 17–33). The Pennsylvania State University Press.

Thiede, B. C., Brown, D. L., Sanders, S. R., Glasgow, N., & Kulcsar, L. J. (2017). A demographic deficit? Local population aging and access to services in rural America, 1990-2010. *Rural Sociology*, *82*(1), 44–74. https://doi.org/10.1111/ruso.12117

Thiede, B. C., Lichter, D. T., & Slack, T. (2016). Working, but poor: The good life in rural America? *Journal of Rural Studies*, *59*, 183–93. Advance online publication. https://doi.org/10.1016/j.jrurstud.2016.02.007

Thier, M., & Beach, P. (2019). Stories we don't tell: Research's limited accounting of rural schools. *School Leadership Review*, *14*(2), 1–14. https://scholarworks.sfasu.edu/slr/vol14/iss2/5

Thier, M., Longhurst, J. M., Grant, P. D., & Hocking, J. E. (2021). Research deserts: A systematic mapping review of U.S. rural education definitions and geographies. *Journal of Research in Rural Education, 31*(2), 1–24. https://jrre.psu.edu/sites/default/files/2021-02/37-2.pdf

Tholkes, R., & Sederberg, C. (1990). Economies of scale and rural schools. *Research in Rural Education, 7*(1), 9–15.

Thomas, A. R., Lowe, B. M., Fulkerson, G. M., & Smith, P. J. (2011). *Critical rural theory*. Lexington.

Thomson, P. (2000). "Like schools," educational "disadvantage" and "thisness." *Australian Educational Researcher, 27*(3), 157–72. https://doi.org/10.1007%2FBF03219737

Tickamyer, A. R., & Duncan, C. M. (1990). Poverty and opportunity structure in rural America. *Annual Review of Sociology, 16*, 67–86. https://doi.org/10.1146/annurev.so.16.080190.000435

Tickamyer, A. R., Sherman, J., & Warlick, J. (Eds.). (2017). *Rural poverty in the United States*. Columbia University Press.

Tickamyer, A. R., Warlick, J., & Sherman, J. (2017). *Rural poverty in the United States*. Columbia University Press.

Tieken, M. C. (2014). *Why rural schools matter*. University of North Carolina Press.

Tieken, M. C. (2017). The spatialization of racial inequity and educational opportunity: Rethinking the rural/urban divide. *Peabody Journal of Education, 92*(3), 385–404. https://doi.org/10.1080/01619 56X.2017.1324662

Tieken, M. C., & Auldridge-Reveles, T. R. (2019). Rethinking the school closure research: School closure as a form of spatial injustice. *Review of Educational Research, 89*(6), 917–53. https://doi. org/10.3102/0034654319877151

Tieken, M. C., & San Antonio, D. M. (2016). Rural aspirations, rural futures: From "problem" to possibility. *Peabody Journal of Education, 91*(2), 131–6. https://doi.org/10.1080/01619 56X.2016.1151733

Tillman, L. (2004). (Un)intended consequences? The impact of the *Brown v. Board of Education* decision on the employment status of Black educators. *Education and Urban Society, 36*(3), 280–303. https:// doi.org/10.1177/0013124504264360

Tinubu Ali, T., & Herrera, M. (2020, April). *Distance learning during COVID-19: Seven equity considerations for schools and districts* [Issue brief.] Southern Education Foundation. https://www. southerneducation.org/publications/covid-19-digital-equity/

Tonsmeire, J. K., Blanc, K., Bertani, A., Garton, S., Whitely, G., Domaradzki, L., & Kane, C. (2012). Alaska principal preparation and support program: A comprehensive approach strengthening school leadership in rural Alaska. In K. Sanzo, S. Myran, & A. H. Normore (Eds.), *Successful school leadership preparation and development* (pp. 183–207). Emerald Publishing.

Toppin, I. N., & Toppin, S. M. (2016). Virtual schools: The changing landscape of K–12 education in the U.S. *Education and Information Technologies, 21*, 1571–81. https://doi.org/10.1007/s10639-015-9402-8

Tuck, E., & McKenzie, M. (2015). *Place in research: Theory, methodology, and methods*. Routledge. https://doi.org/10.4324/9781315764849

Tuck, E., & Yang, W. (2012). Decolonization is not a metaphor |. *Decolonization: Indigeneity, Education & Society, 1*(1), 1–40.

Turley, R. N. L. (2009). College proximity: Mapping access to opportunity. *Sociology of Education, 82*(2), 126–46. https://doi.org/10.1177/003804070908200202

Turner, J. S., Finch, K., & Ximena, U.-Z. (2017). Staff perspectives of the four-day school week: A new analysis of compressed school schedules. *Journal of Education and Training Studies, 6*(1), 52–62. https://doi.org/10.11114/jets.v6i1.2769

Tussey, A. (2017). *"We run a different kind of school within a school": Educator perceptions of Guatemalan-Maya students in a north Georgia public school system* [Unpublished master's thesis]. Kennesaw State University.

Tyack, D. B. (1972). The tribe and the common school: Community control in rural education. *American Quarterly, 24*(1), 1–25. https://doi.org/10.2307/2711912

References

Tyack, D. B. (1974). *The one best system: A history of American urban education*. Harvard University Press.

Ulrich-Schad, J. D. (2015). Recreational amenities, rural migration patterns, and the Great Recession. *Population and Environment, 37*, 157–80. https://doi.org/10.1007/s11111-015-0238-3

Ulrich-Schad, J. D., & Duncan, C. M. (2018). People and places left behind: Work, culture and politics in the rural United States. *The Journal of Peasant Studies, 45*(1), 59–79.

Ungar, R. (2012, December 11). "Right-to-work" laws explained, debunked, and demystified. *Forbes*. https://www.forbes.com/sites/rickungar/2012/12/11/right-to-work-laws-explained-debunked-demystified/#41eef9ea480b

United States. (1965). Elementary and secondary education act of 1965 : H. R. 2362, 89th Cong., 1st sess., Public law 89–10. Reports, bills, debate and act. [Washington] :[U.S. Govt. Print. Off.].

U.S. Bureau of Labor Statistics. (2020, July 2). *The Employment Situation – June 2020*. USDL-20-1310. U.S. Department of Labor, Bureau of Labor Statistics.

U.S. Census Bureau. (n.d.). Rural America: How does the U.S. Census Bureau define rural? [Story map]. https://gis-portal.data.census.gov/arcgis/apps/MapSeries/index.html?appid=7a41374f6b03456e9d138cb014711e01

U.S. Census Bureau. (2012). *Vermont 2010: Population and housing unit counts*. https://www.census.gov/prod/cen2010/cph-2-47.pdf

U.S. Census Bureau. (2016). *Defining rural at the U.S. Census Bureau*. https://www.census.gov/content/dam/Census/library/publications/2016/acs/acsgeo-1.pdf

U.S. Census Bureau. (2017a). *How the U.S. Census Bureau measures poverty*. https://www.census.gov/content/dam/Census/library/visualizations/2017/demo/poverty_measure-how.pdf

U.S. Census Bureau. (2017b). *What is Rural America?* https://www.census.gov/library/stories/2017/08/rural-america.html

U.S. Census Bureau. (2020). Poverty thresholds. https://www.census.gov/data/tables/time-series/demo/income-poverty/historical-poverty-thresholds.html

U.S. Department of Agriculture. (n.d.). *Opioid misuse in rural America*. https://www.usda.gov/topics/opioids

U.S. Department of Agriculture. (2017). *Rural education at a glance, 2017 edition*. https://www.ers.usda.gov/webdocs/publications/83078/eib-171.pdf?v=0

U.S. Department of Agriculture. (2018). *Rural America at a glance 2018 edition*. U.S. Department of Agriculture. https://www.ers.usda.gov/webdocs/publications/90556/eib-200.pdf

U.S. Department of Agriculture. (2019). *Rural America at a glance 2019 edition*. U.S. Department of Agriculture. https://www.ers.usda.gov/webdocs/publications/95341/eib-212.pdf?v=2888.8

U.S. Department of Agriculture Economic Research Service. (2019). *Rural classifications: Overview*. https://www.ers.usda.gov/topics/rural-economy-population/rural-classifications/

U.S. Department of Agriculture Food and Nutrition Service. (2019). *Community Eligibility Provision*. https://www.fns.usda.gov/cn/community-eligibility-provision

U.S. Department of Education. (n. d.). *What is a charter school?* United States Department of Education.

U.S. Department of Education. (1983). *A nation at risk: The imperative for educational reform*. The National Commission on Excellence in Education.

U.S. Department of Education. (2016). *Study of experiences and needs of Rural Education Achievement Program grantees*. Office of Planning, Evaluation and Policy Development, US Department of Education. https://files.eric.ed.gov/fulltext/ED571888.pdf

U.S. Department of Education. (2020a). *Common Core of Data (CCD), Local education agency universe survey, 2000–01 through 2016–17*. National Center for Education Statistics. Office of English Language Acquisition (OELA). https://nces.ed.gov/programs/digest/d18/tables/dt18_204.20.asp?current=yes

U.S. Department of Education. (2020b). *Common Core of Data. Local Education Agency Universe Survey, 2018–19*. National Center for Education Statistics http://nces.ed.gov/ccd/pubagency.asp.

U.S. Department of Education. (2020c). *The condition of education 2020*. National Center for Education Statistics.

References

U.S. Department of Education. (2020d). *Data story of English Learners.* National Center for Education Statistics. Office of English Language Acquisition (OELA). https://www2.ed.gov/datastory/el-characteristics/index.html#three

U.S. Department of Interior. (2018). *Bureau of Indian education strategic direction 2018–2023.* U.S. Department of Interior. https://www.bie.edu/sites/default/files/documents/idc2-086443.pdf

U.S. Federal Reserve System & The Brookings Institution. (2008). *The enduring challenge of concentrated poverty in America: Case studies from communities across the U.S.* https://www.brookings.edu/wp-content/uploads/2016/06/1024_concentrated_poverty.pdf

U.S. Government Accountability Office. (2018, October). Public high schools with more students in poverty and smaller schools provide fewer academic offerings to prepare for college. Report to the Ranking Member, Committee on Education and the Workforce, House of Representatives. https://www.gao.gov/assets/700/694961.pdf

U.S. Office of Management and Budget. (2020). *A budget for America's future.* https://www.whitehouse.gov/wp-content/uploads/2020/02/msar_fy21.pdf

Vance, J. D. (2016). *Hillbilly elegy: A memoir of a family and culture in crisis.* Harper Collins.

Vandell, D. L., Belsky, J., Burchinal, M., Steinberg, L., Vandergrift, N., & NICHD ECCRN. (2010). Do effects of early child care extend to age 15 years? Results from the NICHD study of early child care and youth development. *Child Development, 81*(3), 737–56. https://doi.org/10.1111/j.1467-8624.2010.01431.x

VanTassel-Baska, J., Zuo, L., Avery, L. D., & Little, C. A. (2002). A curriculum study of gifted-student learning in the language arts. *Gifted Child Quarterly, 46*(1), 30–44. https://doi.org/10.1177/001698620204600104

Velott, D., & Sprow Forté, K. (2019). Toward health equity: Mindfulness and cultural humility as adult education. *New Directions for Adult and Continuing Education, 161*, 57–67. https://doi.org/10.1002/ace.20311

Venzant Chambers, T. (2019). ROC'ing brown: Understanding the costs of desegregation using a racial opportunity cost framework. *Peabody Journal of Education, 94*(5), 535–44. https://doi.org/10.1080/0161956X.2019.1668208

Vergari, S. (2012). The limits of federal activism in education policy. *Educational Policy, 26*(1), 15–34. https://doi.org/10.1177/0895904811425910

Vermont Agency of Education. (2017). *Map of Vermont school unions, districts and town boundaries.* State of Vermont. https://education.vermont.gov/documents/map-vermont-school-unions-districts-and-town-boundaries

Vermont State Board of Education. (2001). *The Equal Educational Opportunity Act: Measuring equity.* Vermont State Board of Education.

Vernon-Feagans, L., Gallagher, K., & Kainz, K. (2008). The transition to school in rural America: A focus on literacy. In J. Meece & J. Eccles (Eds.), *Handbook of research on schools, schooling, and human development* (pp. 163–84). Routledge, Taylor, & Associates.

Versland, T. M. (2013). Principal efficacy: Implications for rural "grow your own" leadership programs. *The Rural Educator, 35*(1), 13–22. https://doi.org/10.35608/ruraled.v35i1.361

Villegas, L., & Pompa, D. (2020, February). *The patchy landscape of state English learner policies under ESSA.* Migration Policy Institute. https://www.migrationpolicy.org/research/state-english-learner-policies-essa

Vizenor, G., Tuck, E., & Yang, K. W. (2014). Resistance in the blood. In E. Tuck & K. W. Yang (Eds.), *Youth resistance research and theories of change* (pp. 107–17). Routledge.

Volk, M. J. (2014). Corporate oligarchy white ethnocentrism, and xenophobia. In C. B. Howley, A. Howley, & J. D. Johnson (Eds.), *Dynamics of social class, race, and place in rural education* (pp. 267–96). Information Age Publishing.

von Reichert, C., Cromartie, J., & Arthun, R. O. (2014). Impacts of return migration on rural U.S. communities. *Rural Sociology, 71*(3), 373–93. https://doi.org/10.1111/ruso.12024

Vyse, G. (2019, January 11). Why the L.A. teacher strike is different from last year's protests. *Governing: The Future of States and Localities.* https://www.governing.com/topics/education/gov-lausd-teacher-strike-education-policy.html

References

Vyskocil, J. R., & Goens, G. A. (1979). Collective bargaining and supervision: A matter of climate. *Educational Leadership, 37*(2), 175–7.

Waldorf, B. S. (2006). *A continuous multi-dimensional measure of rurality: Moving beyond threshold measures* [Paper presentation]. American Agricultural Economics Association Annual Meeting. Long Island, California. https://ageconsearch.umn.edu/record/21383

Walkley, M., & Cox, T. L. (2013). Building trauma-informed schools and communities. *Children & Schools, 35*(2), 123–6.

Waller, L. A., & Gotway, C. A. (2004). *Applied spatial statistics for public health data.* Wiley.

Wang, F. (2020). Principals' self- and interpersonal leadership amid work intensification. *Journal of School Leadership.* https://doi.org/10.1177/1052684620935383

Wang, H. L. (2014). Language barriers pose challenges for Mayan migrant children. *National Public Radio, All Things Considered.* https://www.npr.org/sections/codeswitch/2014/07/01/326426927/language-barriers-pose-challenges-for-mayan-migrant-children

Ward, P. (1980). Why our strike failed. *Learning, 8*(8), 30–3.

Warren, M. R. (2005). Communities and schools: A new view of urban education reform. *Harvard Educational Review, 75*(2), 133–73. https://doi.org/10.17763/haer.75.2.m718151032167438

Warren, M. R., Hong, S., Rubin, C. L., & Uy, P. S. (2009). Beyond the bake sale: A community-based relational approach to parent engagement in schools. *Teachers College Record, 111*(9), 2209–54.

Warren, M. R., & Mapp, K. (2011). *A match on dry grass: Community organizing as a catalyst for school reform.* Oxford Press.

Warrior, R. A. (1995). *Tribal secrets: Recovering American Indian intellectual traditions.* University of Minnesota Press.

Wasley, P. A., Fine, M., King, S. P., Powell, L. C., Holland, N. E., & Gladden, R. M. (2000). *Small schools: Great strides, A study of new small schools in Chicago.* The Bank Street College of Education.

Watanabe-Galloway, S., Madison, L., Watkins, K. L., Nguyen, A. T., & Chen, L. W. (2015). Recruitment and retention of mental health care providers in rural Nebraska: Perceptions of providers and administrators. *Rural and Remote Health, 15*, 1–13.

Webber, J. R. (Ed.). (2018). Return of the strike: A forum on the teachers' rebellion in the United States. *Historical Materialism, 26*(4), 119–63. https://doi.org/10.1163/1569206X-00001808

Weber, J. G. (2012). The effects of a natural gas boom on employment and income in Colorado, Texas, and Wyoming. *Energy Economics, 34*(5), 1580–8. https://doi.org/10.1016/j.eneco.2011.11.013

Weber, J. G., & Brown, J. (2013, December 16). Energy development's impacts on rural employment growth. *Amber Waves.* United States Department of Agriculture. https://www.ers.usda.gov/amber-waves/2013/december/energy-development-s-impacts-on-rural-employment-growth/

Weick, K. E. (1995). *Sensemaking in organizations.* Sage.

Weigel, D. J., Martin, S. S., & Bennett, K. K. (2006). Contributions of the home literacy environment to preschool-aged children's emerging literacy and language skills. *Early Child Development and Care, 176*(3–4), 357–78. https://doi.org/10.1080/03004430500063747

Weiner, L. (2007). A lethal threat to U.S. teacher education. *Journal of Teacher Education, 58*(4), 274–86.

Weiner, L. (2012). *The future of our schools.* Haymarket Books.

Weiner, L. (2019). Why the LA teachers strike matters. *Jacobin.* https://www.jacobinmag.com/2019/01/utla-los-angeles-teachers-strike-privatization

Weiss, M. P., Petrin, R. A., & Farmer, T. W. (2014). Responsibilities of special educators in rural schools: A latent class analysis. *Exceptionality, 22*(2), 69–90. https://doi.org/10.1080/09362835.2013.802235

Welch, N. (2005). Living room: Teaching public writing in a post-publicity era. *College Composition and Communication, 56*(3), 470–92.

Wells, N. M., & Evans, G. W. (2003). Nearby nature: A buffer of life stress among rural children. *Environment and Behavior, 35*, 311–330. https://doi.org/10.1177/0013916503035003001

Wells, R. S., Manly, C. A., Kommers, S., & Kimball, E. (2019). Narrowed gaps and persistent challenges: Examining rural-nonrural disparities in postsecondary outcomes over time. *American Journal of Education, 126*(1), 1–31. https://doi.org/10.1086/705498

Wentzel, K. R. (2019). Introduction to the special issue on social and emotional learning. *Educational Psychologist, 54*(3), 127–8. https://doi.org/10.1080/00461520.2019.1637739

Westover, T. (2018). *Educated: A memoir.* Random House.

Wetzel, C. G., & Wright-Buckley, C. (1988). Reciprocity of self-disclosure: Breakdowns of trust in cross-racial dyads. *Basic and Applied Social Psychology, 9*(4), 277–88. https://doi.org/10.1207/s15324834basp0904_3

White, S. (2016). Teacher education research and education policy-makers: An Australian perspective. *Journal of Education for Teaching, 42*(2), 252–64. https://doi.org/10.1080/02607476.2016.1145369

White, S. (2019). Recruiting, retaining and supporting beginning teachers for rural schools. In A. Sullivan (Ed.), *Developing the next generation of teachers: problems and possibilities* (pp. 143–59). Routledge.

White, S., & Corbett, M. (Eds.). (2014). *Doing educational research in rural settings: Methodological issues, international perspectives and practical solutions.* Routledge.

White, S., & Downey, J (Eds.). (2021). *Rural education across the world: Models of innovative practice and impact.* Springer.

White, S., & Reid, J. (2008). Placing teachers? Sustaining rural schooling through place-consciousness in teacher education. *Journal of Research in Rural Education, 23*(7), 1–11. https://jrre.psu.edu/sites/default/files/2019-08/23-7.pdf

Whitlock, R. U. (2017). A memoir of Littleville School: Identity, community, and rural education in a curriculum study of place. In W. M. Reynolds (Ed.), *Forgotten places: Critical studies in rural education* (pp. 169–88). Peter Lang.

WIDA. (2020). *WIDA consortium: Memberships and programs.* https://wida.wisc.edu/memberships/consortium

Wiet, S., & Ferguson, M. B. V. (2017). Birth and development of a community initiative: The trauma-resiliency collaborative. *Journal of Child & Adolescent Trauma, 10*(3), 233–41.

Wildcat, D. R. (2017). Foreword. In S. C. Larsen & J. T. Johnson (Eds.), *Being together in place: Indigenous coexistence in a more than human world* (pp. xi–xii). University of Minnesota Press.

Wilder, C. S. (2014). *Ebony and ivy: Race, slavery, and the troubled history of America's universities.* Bloomsbury Publishing USA.

Will, M. (2019a, March 6). How teacher strikes are changing. *Education Week.* https://www.edweek.org/ew/articles/2019/03/06/how-teacher-strikes-are-changing.html

Will, M. (2019b, June 27). Teachers' unions expected big membership losses. Here's why those haven't panned out. *Education Week.* https://www.edweek.org/ew/articles/2019/06/27/teachers-unions-expected-big-membership-losses-heres.html

Williams, J. E., & Luo, M. (2010). Understanding first-year persistence at a micropolitan university: Do geographic characteristics of students' home city matter? *College Student Journal, 44*(2), 362–76.

Williams, R. (1975). *The country and the city.* Oxford University Press.

Williams, R. (1985). *Keywords: A vocabulary of culture and society.* Oxford University Press.

Williams, S. M. (2013). Micropolitics and rural school consolidation: The quest for equal educational opportunity in Webster Parish. *Peabody Journal of Education, 88*, 127–38. doi:10.1080/01619 56X.2013.752637

Williams, S. M., & Grooms, A. A. (2016). The politics of place. In S. M. Williams & A. A. Grooms (Eds.), *Educational opportunity in rural contexts: The politics of place* (pp. vii–xii). Information Age Publishing.

Wills, G. (2014). The effects of teacher strike activity on student learning in South African primary schools [Working paper 402]. *Economic Research Southern Africa*, 1–42.

Wilson, A. (1995). To strike or not to strike? *Learning, 24*(3), 13–15.

Wilson, W. (1971). Country versus city. Reprinted in M. Curti, W. Thorp, C. Baker, & J. A. Dowling (Eds.), *American issues: The social record* (4th ed.). Lippincott.

Winchester, B. (2012). *Continuing the trend: The brain gain of the newcomers—A generational analysis of rural Minnesota migration, 1990–2010.* University of Minnesota Extension Center for Community Vitality.

Winfield, A. G. (2007). *Eugenics and education in America: Institutionalized racism and the implications of history, ideology, and memory.* Peter Lang.

References

Winkler, A. M., Scull, J., & Zeehandelaar, D. (2012). *How strong are U.S. teacher unions? A state-by-state comparison*. Thomas B. Fordham Institute. https://fordhaminstitute.org/national/research/how-strong-are-us-teacher-unions-state-state-comparison

Winkler, R. L., & Johnson, K. M. (2016). Moving toward integration? Effects of migration on ethnoracial segregation across the rural-urban continuum. *Demography*, *53*(4), 1027–49. https://doi.org/10.1007/s13524-016-0479-5

Wisconsin Department of Public Instruction. (2016). *Advancing rural Wisconsin to support our schools and communities*. https://dpi.wi.gov/rural

Wisconsin Department of Public Instruction. (2018). *American Indian studies program*. https://dpi.wi.gov/amind

Wisconsin Policy Forum. (2018). School referenda on the rise: Ballot questions for K–12 funding at highest levels since 1990s. *The Wisconsin Taxpayer*, *86*(8), 1–8.

Wixom, M. A. (2014). *States moving from accreditation to accountability*. Education Commission of the States. https://files.eric.ed.gov/fulltext/ED560997.pdf

Wolf, K., Kalinich, M. K., & DeJarnatt, S. L. (2016). Charting school discipline. *The Urban Lawyer*, *48*(1), 1–25.

Wolpow, R., Johnson, M. M., Hertel, R., & Kincaid, S. O. (2009). *The heart of learning and teaching: Compassion, resiliency, and academic success*. Washington State Office of Superintendent of Public Instruction (OSPI) Compassionate Schools. https://www.k12.wa.us/sites/default/files/public/compassionateschools/pubdocs/theheartoflearningandteaching.pdf.

Wong, A. (2018, April 3). The larger concerns behind the teachers' strikes. *The Atlantic*. https://www.theatlantic.com/education/archive/2018/04/the-larger-concerns-behind-the-teachers-strikes/557171

Wong-Fillmore, L., & Snow, C. (2000). *What teachers need to know about language*. ERIC Clearinghouse on Languages and Linguistics. http://people.ucsc.edu/~ktellez/wong-fill-snow.html

Wood, J. N., Finch, K., & Mirecki, R. M. (2013). If we get you, how can we keep you? Problems with recruiting and retaining rural administrators. *The Rural Educator*, *34*(2). https://doi.org/10.35608/ruraled.v34i2.399

Woods, M. (2007). Engaging the global countryside: Globalization, hybridity and the reconstitution of rural place. *Progress in Human Geography*, *31*(4), 485–507.

Woodworth, J. L., Raymond, M. E., Chirbas, K., Gonzales, M., Negassi, Y., Snow, W., & Van Donge, C. (2015). *Online Charter School Study*. CREDO. https://credo.stanford.edu/publications/online-charter-school-study

Woolcock, M. (2001). The place of social capital in understanding social and economic outcomes. *Canadian Journal of Policy Research*, *2*(1), 11–17.

Wortham, S., & Rhodes, C. (2015). Heterogeneity in the new Latino Diaspora. In E. T. Hamann, S. Wortham, & E. G. Murillo, Jr. (Eds.), *Revisiting education in the new Latino Diaspora* (pp. 171–81). Information Age Publishing.

Wray, M. (2006). *Not quite White: White trash and the boundaries of Whiteness*. Duke University Press.

Wuthnow, R. (2019). *The left behind: Decline and rage in small-town America*. Princeton University Press.

Yan, W. (2002). Postsecondary enrollment and persistence of students from rural Pennsylvania. *Center for Rural Pennsylvania*. http://www.rural.palegislature.us/Postsecondary_Ed.pdf

Yarrow, A. L. (2011). The history of federal child antipoverty and health policy in the United States since 1900. *Child Development Perspectives*, *5*(1), 66–72. https://doi.org/10.1111/j.1750-8606.2010.00157.x

Yettick, H., Baker, R., Wickersham, M., & Hupfeld, K. (2014). Rural districts left behind? Rural districts and the challenges of administering the Elementary and Secondary Education Act. *Journal of Research in Rural Education*, *29*(13), 1–15. https://pdfs.semanticscholar.org/4f8c/d811b12cb1b06779c72deb621bedd5d92b8d.pdf

Yosso, T. J. (2005). Whose culture has capital? A critical race theory discussion of community cultural wealth. *Race Ethnicity and Education*, *8*(1), 69–91. https://doi.org/10.1080/1361332052000341006

Young, I. M. (1990). *Justice and the politics of difference*. Princeton University Press.

Young, M. D., VanGronigen, B. A., & Reynolds, A. L. (2019). State Boards of Education: Lesser known policy actors. *Educational Policy*, *33*(1), 205–33. https://doi.org/10.1177/0895904818807311

References

Yull, D., Blitz, L. V., Thompson, T., & Murray, C. (2014). Can we talk? Using community-based participatory action research to build family and school partnerships with families of color. *School Community Journal, 24*(2), 9–31.

Zachary, L., & Ratledge, N. (2017, June 23). *Public education impacts of unconventional oil and gas development*. Resources for the Future. https://www.rff.org/publications/reports/public-education-impacts-of-unconventional-oil-and-gas-development/

Zakszeski, B., Ventresco, N., & Jaffe, A. (2017). Promoting resilience through trauma-focused practices: A critical review of school-based implementation. *School Mental Health, 9*(4), 310–21.

Zanoni, W., & Johnson, A. D. (2019). Child care subsidy use and children's outcomes in middle school. *AERA Open*. https://doi.org/10.1177/2332858419884540

Zeluck, S. (1969). The UFT strike: Will it destroy the AFT? *Phi Delta Kappan, 50*(5), 250–4.

Zetlin, A., MacLeod, E., & Kimm, C. (2012). Beginning teacher challenges instructing students who are in foster care. *Remedial and Special Education, 33*, 4–13.

Zong, J., & Batalova, J. (2015). *The limited English proficient population in the United States*. Migration Policy Institute.

Zuckerman, S. J. (2016a). *Organizing for collective impact in a cradle-to-career network* (Publication No. 10107099) [Doctoral Dissertation]. University at Albany, State University of New York. ProQuest Digital Dissertations.

Zuckerman, S. J. (2016b). Mobilization and adaptation of a rural cradle-to-career network. *Education Sciences, 6*(4), 34. https://doi.org/10.3390/educsci6040034

Zuckerman, S. J. (2019). Making sense of place: A case study of a sensemaking in a rural school–community partnership. *Journal of Research in Rural Education, 35*(6), 1–18. https://jrre.psu.edu/sites/default/files/2020-07/35-6_0.pdf

Zuckerman, S. J. (2020a). "Why can't this work here?" Social innovation and collective impact in a micropolitan community. *Community Development*. https://doi.org/10.1080/15575330.2020.1789183

Zuckerman, S. J. (2020b). The role of rural school leaders in a school–community partnership. *Theory and Practice in Rural Education, 10*(1), 73–91. https://doi.org/10.3776/tpre.2020.v10n1p73-91

Zuckerman, S. J., Campbell Wilcox, K., Schiller, K. S., & Durand, F. T. (2018). Absorptive capacity in rural schools: Bending not breaking during disruptive innovation implementation. *Journal of Research in Rural Education, 34*(3), 1–27.

Zuckerman, S. J., & McAtee, J. R. (2018). Youth voice in a rural cradle-to-career network. *Journal of Ethical Educational Leadership*. https://digitalcommons.unl.edu/cehsedadfacpub/97/

Zuniga, K., Olson, J. K., & Winter, M. (2005). Science education for rural Latino/a students: Course placement and success in science. *Journal of Research in Science Teaching, 42*(4), 376–402. https://doi.org/10.1002/tea.20064

Index

achievement 68, 111, 174, 215–24, 228, 253, 270–2, 296, 298
  gaps 220–4
activism 1, 92, 127, 128, 130–2, 134, 136, 166, 167
adverse childhood experiences (ACEs) 196, 197
African American education 232, 256, 257, 259, 261, 263, 265, 267
  African American students 257, 264–6
  case studies 260–3
  data analysis 259–60
  place, race and educational opportunity 257–8
  policy and practice, implications 265–7
  race and poverty 263–5
  in rural South 256–67
  state of education, Mississippi Delta 258–9
  triumphs and challenges, home 263
after-school programming/program 70, 102, 149, 201, 272
Agger, C. 159, 160
Albritton, S. 123
Alutto, J. A. 129
American Indian students 237, 248
American School Counselor Association 211
Anderson, W. L. 26
Andersson, E. K. 307
Angus, R. 192
Ankeny, R. 252
Anthony, K. V. 40
Apple, M. W. 44
Arriero, E. 272
Arum, R. 140
Au, W. 44
Australia 8, 84, 85, 87–9, 165, 169, 225–7, 229, 230
Azano, A. P. 47, 191, 285

Bacharach, S. 129
Bagley, C. 306
Bailey, L. H. 26, 27
Bass, E. L. 303
Bauch, P. A. 138
Bauman, Z. 49, 50
Beach, D. 306
Beale Codes 12
Belasco, J. 129

Bell, M. M. 15, 193
Berardi, F. 51
Biddle, C. 9, 18, 47, 107
bilingual education programs 251, 253
Bishop, H. N. 123
Black Lives Matter movement 41, 89, 167, 284
Black rural education 25, 41, 109, 159, 221, 257
Black students 257, 259, 267, 278
Bonilla-Silva, E. 277
Bosak, J. 10
Brandt, D. 193
Brayboy, B. M. J. 237
Breen, D. 214
Brenner, D. 34, 253
Bronfenbrenner, U. 306
Brooke, R. 191
Brown, D. L. 14
Brown v. Board of Education 257
Budge, K. 124, 125
Bushnell, M. 15
Butler, A. 37, 39
Byun, S. 157–9, 162–3, 274

Cabrera, N. L. 277–8
Cajete, G. 239
Callahan, R. E. 27
Campbell C. 46
Capps, R. 212
Carney, M. 26
Carr, P. J. 190
Carrillo, J. F. 273
Casto, H. G. 73, 123–4
charter policy/schools 92, 109, 114–16
  resistance to school closure and consolidation 114–16
charter school law 115, 116
childhood adversity 196–8, 202, 203
Chisholm, J. S. 295
Christianson, R. I. 252
Cobbett, William 21
Coladarci, T. 9, 18, 305
Coleman, J. S. 229
collective impact 93, 145–56, 168, 170
  developmental phases 151–2

Index

efforts   146, 147, 149–52, 154, 155
   Grand Isle Network   147–8
   mindset shifts, collective impact   153–5
   Northeast Prairie Coalition   148–9
   softer side of collective impact   153
   successful collaboration, preconditions
      149–51
college education   58, 163
colonization   8
common schools   23, 25
communities   180–1
   and families, challenges confronting   180–1
   family engagement   182
   strengths of   180
   supporting child development in   182
community-aware partnering
   early childcare and education ecosystem
      140–1
   healthy kids and opportunities   142–3
   illustrations   140–3
   windmills and budget restoration   141–2
community-aware perspective   138–44
community schools   103, 109, 111, 112, 114, 115,
   137
Compton, M.   131
Connell, R. W.   229
consolidation   27–9, 39, 46–9, 91, 108–12, 115
contemporary education policies   95, 99, 192
Corbett, M.   1, 3, 15, 49, 187, 190, 242, 305, 308
corporate bureaucracy   6
corporate education   50, 51
corporatization   5, 7, 43–7, 66
Covid-19 pandemic   41
Cubberley, E.   26, 27, 118
Cuervo, H.   40, 41
curriculum   25, 28, 38, 49, 165, 173, 175, 194, 210,
   225–9, 283, 296, 300, 302
curriculum, international response   225–30
   context to curriculum   227–30
   national context   226–7

Dean, M.   73
Delany-Barmann, G.   253
Delcourt, M. A.   295
Deloria, V.   239, 241
Dewees, S.   272
distributive analysis   6, 32, 33, 36, 38, 39
Donehower, K.   14, 51, 88, 187
Dovigo, F.   308
Doyen, P.   121
Drew, D.   214
Dunbar-Ortiz, R.   279

early childhood   69, 149, 150, 152, 173, 177–83,
   185, 186, 228
   programs   149, 177, 179, 181–3, 185, 186
early childhood education   70, 100, 140, 141, 150,
   173, 175, 177–86, 228
   early childhood development   177–8
   early childhood program quality   179
   early childhood service delivery models   178–9
   getting ready intervention   183–4
   rural communities   180–2
   support family engagement   183–5
   Teachers and Parents as Partners (TAPP)   184–5
early education   140
early rural education research   1
Economic Research Service   63–6, 287
educational/education. *See also* rural education
   aspirations   159, 160
   equity   53, 59, 70, 101, 103, 231, 274, 275
   funding   7, 127
   governance   93, 95, 96, 103, 107, 166
   leadership   92, 107, 118, 124–6, 166
   opportunities   178, 180, 256–8, 260–2, 265, 267,
      270
   policy   96, 98, 99, 102, 107, 123, 124, 137, 139,
      191, 198
   programs   38, 201, 203, 253
   research   1, 67, 74, 99, 118, 230, 281, 284, 304–6
   services   100, 105, 106, 177
Elementary and Secondary Education Act of 1965
   (ESEA)   34, 69, 100, 102
Eliot, Charles   25
England, W.   39
English as a second language (ESL) services   249
English Learner (EL) education   247–55
   challenges   250–5
   EL students   232, 247–55
   funding   253
   home languages and educational
      backgrounds   250–1
   instructional models and programs   252–3
   rural English Learner students   249–50
   state-level variations, definitions   252
   strengths and opportunities, students and
      families   253–5
   teachers and leaders, preparation   251–2
English learners   55, 101, 249, 251, 253, 255
Eppley, K.   32, 45, 192
ERS Rural-Urban Continuum Codes   12
Etheridge, B.   279
Eurostat   307
Every Child Succeeds Act (ESSA)   38
Every Students Succeed Act   123

385

Index

Faircloth, S. C.   244
federal education policies   91, 104
Felitti, V. J.   196
Fleisch, B.   130
Ford, D. R.   14, 242, 281
free school systems   22, 23
funds of knowledge   254, 270

Galster, G.   257
Gentry, M.   301
Gibbs, R. M.   158, 163
gifted education   232, 233, 294–303
gifted services   299, 300, 302, 303
Giroux, H. A.   50, 51, 85
Gjelten, T.   14
Goedeken, J. A.   272
Goeman, M.   242
Goffman, Erving   187
Goldblatt, E.   188
governance   43, 44, 91, 93, 95–9, 101–3, 107, 165, 166
Grande, S.   238
Green, B.   125, 250
Greenwood, D. A.   235, 241
Griffin, D.   272
Gruenewald, D. A.   86
Gusa, D. L.   278

Habermas, J.   37
Hall, D.   122
Hamann, E. T.   39
Hamilton, Alexander   19
Hanleybrown, F.   151, 153
Hargreaves, L.   305
Harmon, H. L.   124, 138
Harper, S. R.   284
Harris, C. I.   278
Harris, J. C.   276
Harris, William Torrey   25
Harris Poll   60
Harris-Smedberg, K. J.   125
Harvey, D.   43
Hash, K. M.   231
Heath, S. B.   193
high-poverty communities   63, 233
high schools   25, 29, 110, 217, 223, 247, 252–3, 260, 261, 271, 277, 283
   students   272
Hillyard, S.   306
Hollar, J.   44
Holmes, S. R.   185
home communities   159, 161–3, 190, 290, 291, 294, 296

Hondo, C.   270–1
Howley, A.   279, 297
Howley, C. B.   14, 31, 48, 279, 295, 296

identity formation   4
Indigeneity   86, 226, 231
Indigenous education   231, 235–8, 240, 244
individual schools   35, 110, 197
individual students   288, 291, 293, 301
intellectual work   229, 241
international response, curriculum   225–30
international response, peripheral perspective, rural Europe   304–8
international response, rural   84–9
   rurality and place neutrality   84–5
   rural place matters   85–7
   rural standpoint   87–9
international response, rural schools   165–71
intervention works   293
Irvin, M. J.   157, 158, 163, 271

Jefferson, Thomas   19
John, K. D.   14, 242, 281
Johnson, A. D.   83
Johnson, J. D.   31, 35, 55, 243, 279, 284
Johnson, J. T.   241, 246
Johnson, K. M.   53, 54
Jolliffe, D.   188

Kania, J.   154
Kassab, C.   161
Kefalas, M. J.   190
Keis, R.   270
Kelly, M. G.   58
Kettler, T.   297
Killen, S.   257
Koricich, A.   157
Kovács, K.   306
Koziol, N. A.   13
Kryst, E. L.   162
Kučerová, S. R.   307
Kuehl, R.   303
Kvalsund R.   305

labor issues   92, 127–9, 131, 133, 135, 136
Ladson-Billings, G.   242
Larsen, S. C.   241, 246
Latinx education   39, 232, 268–75, 305
   caring schooling environments   271–2
   demographic characteristics   269–70
   educator-student relationships   271–2

386

Index

families, student achievement and school-family engagement 272–3
PK-12 education and achievement of 270–3
positive youth development programs 271–2
postsecondary education access and outcomes 273–4
practice, policy and future research, implications 274–5
rural Latinxs migration, history 269
schooling experiences 270–1
school practices and policies 271
teacher attitudes and behaviors 271
Lawrence, B. K. 296, 297
Lawson, V. 14
leadership 91, 92, 118–20, 122–6, 134, 135, 148, 152, 239, 252, 283
Leavitt, P. A. 243
Lefebvre, H. 46, 49
Leonardo, Z. 277
Leopold, A. 279
Letts, W. 250
Lichter, D. T. 14, 53, 54, 56, 249
Lipman, P. 44
local communities 70–3, 75, 81, 97, 104, 155, 161, 190, 191, 253–4
Lohman, D. F. 298, 301
Lomawaima, K. T. 237, 240
Love, B. L. 283
low-income families 55, 220, 221
low-income students 59, 69, 70, 100, 287
Luo, M. 311 n.1(Ch 14)
Lyons, S. R. 238
Lyson, T. A. 192

McCarroll, M. 295
McCarty, T. L. 237
Mcclellan, R. L. 123
McCollow, J. 129, 130
McGrath, B. 73, 123, 124
McHenry-Sorber, E. 98, 124, 125, 133, 134, 252
Marré, A. 163
Massey, D. S. 248
Maxwell, G. M. 123
Mayer, A. 58
Means, D. R. 159
Meece, J. L. 157, 158, 161, 163
mental health 174, 198, 200, 201, 204–9, 211–14, 229
issues 174, 204, 209, 211, 214
providers 200, 201, 205, 206, 209–11
services 109, 174, 201, 202, 205–9, 214
Metro-Centric Locale Codes 12

Metro Status Codes 12
Morrow, D. F. 231
Morton, B. M. 160
Moustakas, C. 259

National Center for Education Statistics (NCES) 10–11, 157
classification system, prior versions 12
National Congress of American Indians (NCAI) 238, 311 n.1(Ch 20)
National Council of Teachers of English (NCTE) 194
National Indian Education Association 114, 237
National Rural Health Association (NRHA) 205–7, 209
National Student Clearinghouse 158
Nelson, L. 15
No Child Left Behind Act of 2001 (NCLB) 32
nonrural communities 78, 105, 266
nonrural schools 33, 238, 266
nonrural students 158, 160, 217, 219–21, 223, 238

ontological expansiveness 277–81, 284
Orgera, K. 59
Osti, G. 193
out-migration 6
rural out-migration 244
selective out-migration and aging 53–5

Pace, N. J. 231
Paciotto, C. 253
Paraskeva, J. M. 227
partnerships 70, 92, 93, 137–9, 142, 144–7, 151, 168, 183, 266
Paulgaard, G. 308
Peralta, C. 271, 272
Pérez Huber, L. 276
Perlman, B. 10
Peters, S. J. 301
Pewewardy, C. D. 241
PK-12 education 81, 270, 272, 274
place-based education 235, 241–3, 245
place-based interventions 146, 147
place-based pedagogies 102, 144, 302
place-conscious leadership 124, 125
place neutrality 6, 8, 32, 37, 38, 84
assumption of 6, 32, 37
policy. *See individual entries*
policy borrowing processes 8
Pompa, D. 250
populations 7, 52–6, 58–61, 198, 231, 238, 239, 244

Index

postsecondary education   93, 157–64, 270, 273–5
   families   159–60
   individual factors   159
   postsecondary experiences, rural youth   162–3
   postsecondary persistence and completion   162–3
   rural communities and geography   161–2
   rural schools   160–1
postsecondary transitions   157–64
poverty   7, 62–71
   address through rural schools   69–70
   background on   62–4
   causes of   64–6
   effects of   66–7
   isolation, weak infrastructure and environmental
      destruction   66
   population changes   65–6
   racial oppression   64
   resources and achievement   68–9
   rural economies   64–5
   and rural education, relationship   67–70
   trends in rural America   63–4
preschool children   184
Prins, E.   161
privatization   6
Provasnik, S.   159
Provinzano, K.   252
public education systems   128, 132
Puryear, J. S.   297
Putnam, R. D.   189

qualified teachers   32, 101, 194, 262, 265

Ratledge, N.   58
Reese, L.   272
Reid, J.   14, 88
remote education   226, 228, 229
Rennie, J.   86
Rice, Joseph Mayer   25
Roberts, P.   125
Ross, E. A.   26
Rousseau, Jean-Jacque   19
rural, definition   9–18
rural America
   building administrators   99
   Central Office   98–9
   Chief State School Officer (CSSO)   96
   childhood adversity in   198
   compensatory educational services   100–1
   contemporary education policies   99–102
   educational governance and contemporary
      policy   95–107

   local-level educational governance
      organization   96–7
   local school boards   98
   rural-focused vignettes   102–7
   rural school governance, politics   103–7
   standards and accountability   101–2
   State Board of Education   96
   State Department of Education (SDOE)   96
   state educational governance organization   96
   student achievement in   215–24
   superintendents   97–8
rural critical policy analysis   30–42
   and assumption of neutrality   37–8
   and distributive analysis   38–40
   educational change and new policy   30–42
   era of rapid change   41–2
   and rural-focused policy   40–1
rural education   2, 3
   activist sub-discipline   1
   centering land, sovereignty and survivance
      238–41
   choosing, justifying, and contextualizing,
      definitions   12–13
   community economic vitality, schools
      linking   76–8
   complexities and pitfalls, rural researchers   16–18
   critical Indigenous perspectives in   235–46
   diversity and rural cultural adaptation   245
   economic force, schools   74
   education and health care, linking   78–80
   first rural, second rural and rural plural   15–16
   foundations in   5–8
   Indigenous education   236–7
   Indigenous peoples, visibility   236–8
   for mental health professionals   212–14
   National Center for Education Statistics (NCES)
      classification system   10–11
   need for linking data, conceptualizing   73–5
   Office of Management and Budget (OMB)
      definitions   10
   place-based education, culture and
      curriculum   241–3
   preparers of democratic citizens, schools   75
   preparers of workers, schools   75
   research and practice   3, 5, 7, 9–18, 72–83
   research and projects, multifaceted data
      strategy   75–83
   revisiting durable issues in   243–4
   rural community viability and economics   244–5
   rurality and qualitative definitions,
      theorizing   14–15

Index

scholars   4, 8, 39, 107, 227, 295
scholarship   9, 125, 165, 284
social force, schools   74–5
social reproduction and interruption   245
sociological lens   15–16
trauma-informed approaches in   196–203
two state agencies in communities, linking   80–3
US Census Bureau definition   10
whiteness in   276–85
rural educational policy
European prelude   20–1
free school era   22–3
history and shape of   19–29
public education, goals shifting   24–5
rural *versus* urban, early US   21–2
scientific management era, rural schools   25–7
urban industrial worldview, triumph   27–8
rural gifted education   232, 233, 294, 295, 297, 299,
301–3
case study   301–3
challenges, services to rural gifted students   297–
300
challenges and innovative responses   294–303
defensible identification, rural gifted
students   300–1
deficit notions, rural students   295
giftedness definition, constraints   298–9
high-quality gifted programming, barriers
295–7
serving rural gifted students   301
in varying rural contexts   297
rural high schools   252–3, 273, 274
rural identities   159, 173, 187–95
rurality   1–4, 9
Rural Life Orientation   214
rural literacies   51, 173, 174, 187–95, 227
aesthetics as factor in   194–5
and identity   187–9
mobility as factor in   193–4
research   187, 190, 192
and rural schooling   191–2
and social capital   189–90
and social justice   190–1
Rural Mental Health Preparation/Practice Pathway
(RMHP3)   213
rural policy analysis   31
distributive analysis   32–3
place neutrality, assumption   32
rural, defining   34–6
rural salience   33–4
rural population decline   61

Rural Professional Practicum   214
rural school-based mental health (SBMH)   204–14
accessibility, accommodation and affordability,
difficulties   206–7
barriers, mental health services   205–7
intervention   211–12
mental health needs   204
mental health providers, shortage   205–6
PATHS (promoting alternative thinking strategies)
curriculum   210
PEACE (Prevention of Escalating Adolescent
Crisis Events) protocol   212
prevention approaches   209–11
programs and protocols, delivery   209–12
reticence toward seeking services   207
rural school-community partnerships   137–9
rural school governance, politics   103–7
intergovernmental conflict, Accountability
Mandates in Vermont   103–5
student enrollment and school district funding,
declining in Wisconsin   105–7
rural school leadership   92, 117–23, 125
community relationships, public scrutiny and
micropolitics   122–3
leads schools   119
role complexity, instructional leadership, and
opportunities   120–2
rurality and leadership theory   123–5
rural schools and school districts, leadership
practices   120–3
in twenty-first century   118–23
rural schools   108–9
academic outcomes   111
charter schools   112–16
closures   108, 109, 111, 112, 115, 116, 167
and communities   91–4
community and family outcomes   111–12
corporate influences   43–51
corporatization of   47–8
critical rural education, need   50–1
curriculum studies in   173–5
effects on   48–9
English learners in   247–55
financial implications   110–11
identity and equity in   231–3
international response   165–71
Latinx students in   268–75
leaders   92, 118–20, 122–5, 144, 169, 303
population dynamics and implications   52–61
principalship   120, 125
problem   6, 47, 107, 108, 125

389

Index

public school corporatization, consequences 44–5

rural America's growing diversity 55–7

rural Boomtown development and effects 57–8

rural charter schools 114–16

rural communities and population change, post-pandemic world 59–60

rural corporatization 45–7

rural poverty and 62–71

rural students, effects 49–50

school closure and consolidation 109–12

rural teacher labor 92, 128, 131, 134–6

issues 92, 127–9, 131, 133, 135, 136

research agenda 92, 134–6

rural teacher labor issues 127–36

1974 Wisconsin Strike 133

educational leaders, practical advice 130

first-person strike accounts 129–30

historically situated scholarship 128–30

Mountainville case 133–4

rural teacher labor literature and Nationwide Strike Movement 132–4

rural teacher labor research agenda 134–6

statewide case, West Virginia 132

teacher militancy, survey research 129–30

rural tiered systems, adaptive supports 286–93

developmental systems perspective 287–90

diversity, rural schools 286–7

person-centered, place-based perspective 291–2

responsive professional development, consultation and research 292–3

social and emotional learning, TSAS 291–2

special education and TSAS, linking 290–1

Sabzalian, L. (2019). 240

Saltman, K. J. 44

Sanchez, A. L. 208

Sanes, M. 310 n.2(Ch 11)

Santos, B. d. S. 227

Schafft, K. A. 58, 114, 123–4, 133, 134, 138, 305

Schirmer, E. B. 133, 134

Schmitt, J. 310 n.2(Ch 11)

school board members 81, 98, 105, 133

school closures 30, 39, 47, 53, 91, 109–12, 115, 116

school-community partnerships 70, 92, 137, 145, 168, 169

school consolidation 28, 29, 39, 53, 57, 95, 108, 110, 111, 166, 167

school enrollments 55, 58, 60

schooling experiences 245, 257, 264, 270, 271

school system 67, 123, 127, 132, 208, 211, 229

Secatero, S. 239

Shays's Rebellion 20

Shear, S. B. 242

Shenkar, M. 134

Shenkar, O. 134

Sherman, J. 202

Showalter, D. 249

Shucksmith, M. 305, 308

Sinclair, K. A. 37, 39

Smith, J. 272

Smith, N. 46

Smith-Hughes Act 25

Snyder, T. D. 157

Social Darwinism 23, 29

Somerville, M. 86

spatial injustice 7

special education 96, 99, 137, 232

Spencer, Herbert 23

Squire, J. 48

state funding 98, 105, 107, 132, 168

statehood 19, 20, 24

Strange, M. 33, 35

student achievement 138, 143, 145, 215–24, 226, 228, 267, 272

considerations of place 216–17

differences by income 220–1

differences by race/ethnicity 221–2

differences by region 219–20

nation's report card 217

time and locale, achievement trends 218–19

Sullivan, S. 278

Sumner, William Graham 23

Sutherland, D. H. 98

The Taft-Hartley Act 310 n.3(Ch 11)

Taylor, Frederick Winslow 25

teacher activism 92, 127–8, 130–2

teacher education 48, 85, 87, 250, 283

teacher labor protest 92, 129, 130, 136

teacher militancy 129, 134

teacher unionism 129, 131, 166, 167

Terrazas, A. 249

Theobald, P. 45, 46

third space, mapping 1–4

Thomas, A. R. 15, 51

Thomson, P. 16

Tieken, M. C. 35, 39, 281

traditional public schools 112–14, 116

trauma 173–5, 196–201, 203, 228, 229

trauma-informed care 196–203

centering rurality, case study 200–3

390

Index

inequality related to ACEs, reducing   197
    practices connected to   200
    principles   199–200
    systems approach   199–203
Trent, B.   295
Trnková, K.   307
Turner, J. S.   34
Tyack, D. B.   25

US Census Bureau   204
U.S. Office of Management and Budget (OMB)   311
    n.1(Ch 14)

Valázquez, J. A.   272
Vance, J. D.   279
Villegas, L.   250
Vizenor, G.   240
Volk, M. J.   281

Waldorf, B. S.   12
Ward, P.   129
War on Poverty   2
Warrior, R. A.   241
Washington, Booker T.   25

Webber, J. R.   132
Weiner, L.   48, 131
Westover, T.   279, 282
Wetzel, C. G.   259
White, S.   305
Whiteness   231, 232, 276–85, 306
    defining   277–8
    disrupting   282–4
    educators and community members   283
    and high school athletics   281–2
    and native mascots   279–81
    research   284
    in rural education   278–82
Wildcat, D. R.   239, 241
Williams, J. E.   311 n.1(Ch 14)
Williams, R.   168, 169
Wilson, Warren   26
Winfield, A. G.   26
Wood, K.   45
Wright-Buckley, C.   259

Zachary, L.   58
Zanoni, W.   83
Zuniga, K.   271

Printed in the USA
CPSIA information can be obtained
at www.ICGtesting.com
LVHW081442191023
761572LV00007B/471